This catalogue is published on the occasion of the exhibition :

WW2
War Pictures by British Artists

Morley College London,
61 Westminster Bridge Road,
London, SE1 7HT

Friday 28 October - Wednesday 23 November 2016

LEARNING FOR LIFE at Morley

LISS LLEWELLYN FINE ART
ESTABLISHED 1991

First published in 2016 by Liss Llewellyn Fine Art

ISBN: 978-0-9930884-2-1

Photography:
Glynn Clarkson, Pierre Emmanuel Coste,
Prudence Cuming Associates Ltd & Petra van der Wal

Design and Typesetting by David Maes
Printed by Zenith Media, July 2016

WW II

WAR PICTURES BY BRITISH ARTISTS

Edited by Sacha Llewellyn & Paul Liss

LLFA

25th

ANNIVERSARY

ACKNOWLEDGEMENTS

This project has been hugely enhanced by the participation of Dr Brian Foss, a leading authority on the art of WW2. His introductory essay and 400-name check-list of War Artists' Advisory Committee (WAAC) artists (Appendix II) are an invaluable source of reference.

Elaine Andrew's essay (Appendix III) provides an account of Morley College London's history during WW2, setting the historic scene for this exhibition.

Margaret Bear has contributed an essay on the fascinating (if little known) ICI 'Portraits of an Industry', a scheme inspired by the WAAC initiative which likewise benefited from the expertise of Kenneth Clark.

In the creation of this project Liss Llewellyn Fine Art has been fortunate in being able to call on the skills of a huge team of colleagues who have kindly given their expertise.

Andrew Cormack and Ian Jack have been especially generous in helping with the catalogue notes.

Jane Hartwell and Lena Augustinson have provided logistical support in organising the exhibition at Morley Gallery. We would also like to thank Dr Andrew Gower, principal of Morley College London, for allowing this exhibition to take place in such an appropriate setting.

We are also indebted to:

Pierre Auzereau
Michael Barker
Robert Bear
Nicola Beauman
Claudia Black
James Bone
Susan & Quentin Bone
Erika Brandl
Alan Brooks
Ruth Bubb
David Buckman
Elisabeth Bulkeley
Sarah Bull
Louise Burley (Tate Images)
Michael Campbell
Christopher Campbell-Howes
Jonathan Clark (Sotheran's)
Gill Clarke
Daniel Dullaway
Jane England
Nicholas Finney OBE
James Folley
Francois et Laetitia
Adrian Gibbs (Bridgeman Images)
Ron Goodwin
Janet Greaves
Maggi Hambling CBE (Morley Gallery)
Geoff Hassall (artbiogs.co.uk)
Matt Hervey
Neil Jennings
Richard Kay
Simon Lawrence
David Leighton
Blanche Llewellyn
Evelina Llewellyn
Maude Llewellyn
Mrs Emma Mawdsley (National Army Museum)
John Monnington
Harry Moore-Gwyn
Conor Mullan
John Noott
Imogen Paine
Emmanuel Pédeneau
Adrian Pett
Alan Powers
Jeffrey S. Reznick, PhD (University of Birmingham)
Peter Riley
Malcolm Rogers
Sandra, Lady Lean
Jackie Setter
Jayne Shrimpton
Andrew Sim
Peyton Skipwith
Iain & Bunny Smedley
Julia Sorrell & Ian Sanders
Richard Sorrell
The Hon. Georgina Stonor
James Stourton
Robert Upstone
Mike Wain
Grant Waters
Tom Wheare
Stephen Wittle
Micky Wolfson
Yale University Press

For Tom Wheare

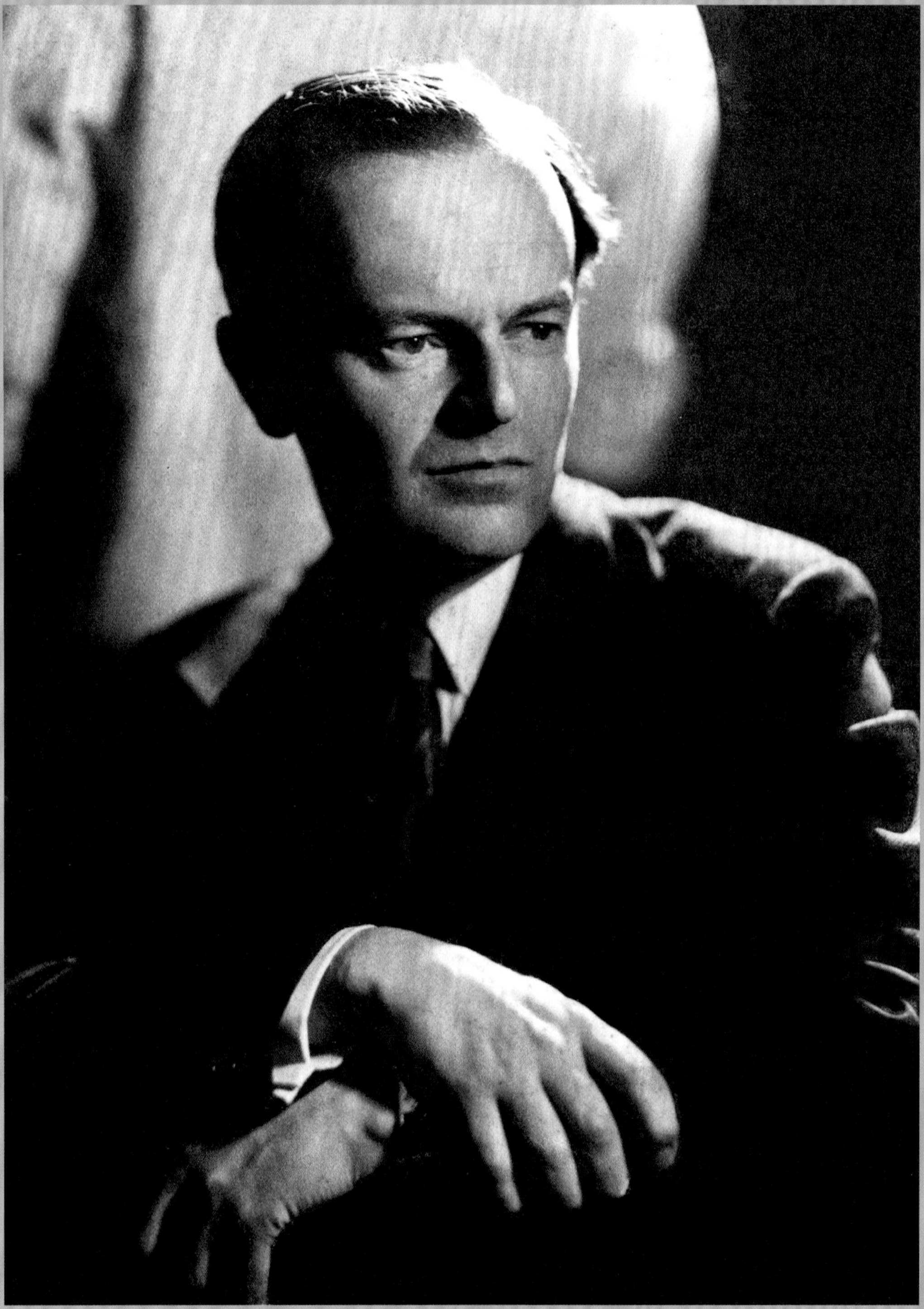

Kenneth Clark, late 1930s, photo by Howard Coster © The National Portrait Gallery.

Contents

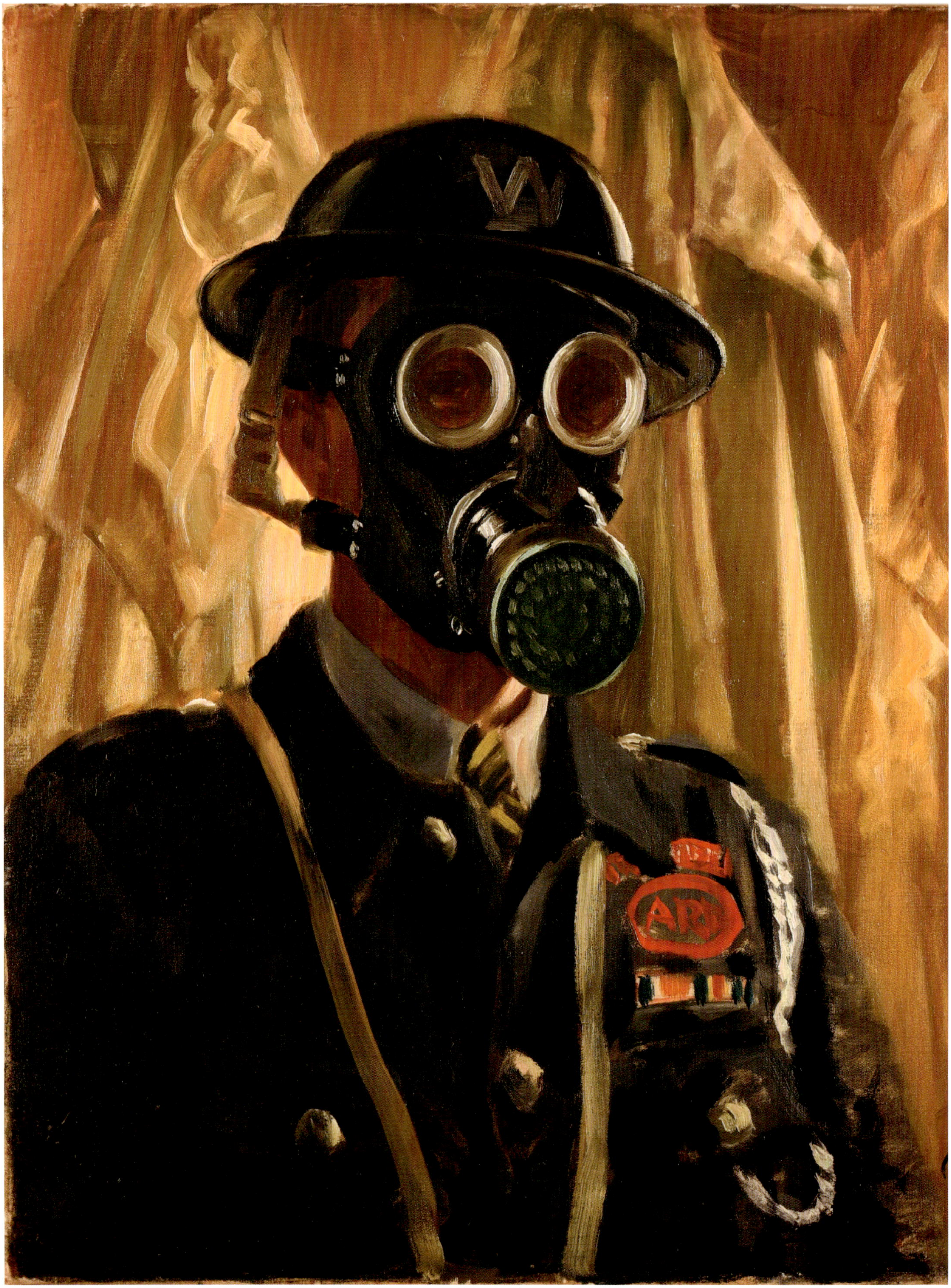
W

Preface

By Paul Liss

'the truth is the most effective form of propaganda'

(J. B. Morton, Introduction to *War Pictures by British Artists, Blitz*, 1942, p 5.)

Instantly recognisable with their distinctive colour-coordinated covers, the eight volumes which make up *War Pictures by British Artists* were published by the Oxford University Press some 75 years ago. Created to achieve wider appreciation of the artworks commissioned by the War Artists' Advisory Committee (WAAC), the eight themed pocket books played an important role in how the war was perceived by those living through it and how it would be remembered by future generations. 'What did it look like? they will ask in 1981, and no amount of description or documentation will answer them' ; so wrote Kenneth Clark in the unsigned text introducing the original series.

Clark, the Director of the National Gallery and driving force behind the establishment of the WAAC, saw its most important role as providing employment for artists during WW2 (what he later paraphrased as '... to keep artists at work on any pretext, and, as far as possible, to prevent them from being killed'). At the point that the WAAC was formed, late in 1939, Clark estimated that up to 9000 artists were already out of work. Over 400 artists took part in the WAAC scheme; 37 of these were salaried, 101 others received one-off contracts and 265 submitted unsolicited work that the WAAC agreed to purchase. While artists on contract were required to give the WAAC right of first refusal of everything they produced, the committee usually returned minor works or examples they deemed not to be of interest.

This new publication is the third in a series of Liss Llewellyn Fine Art projects on war art. *Damn the War*, published in 2008, presented an artistically diverse array of pictures from both world wars bridged by images from the inter-war years. *The Great War As Recorded in the Fine and Popular Arts*, published in 2014, examined imagery of WW1 across a wide range of media. Staged at Morley Gallery, as part of the Imperial War Museum-led WW1 Centenary celebrations, this initiative was described as 'fabulous' in the *Spectator* and

CAT. 27 – **Harold Arthur Riley** (1895-1966), *Me*, 1942. (See page 65.)

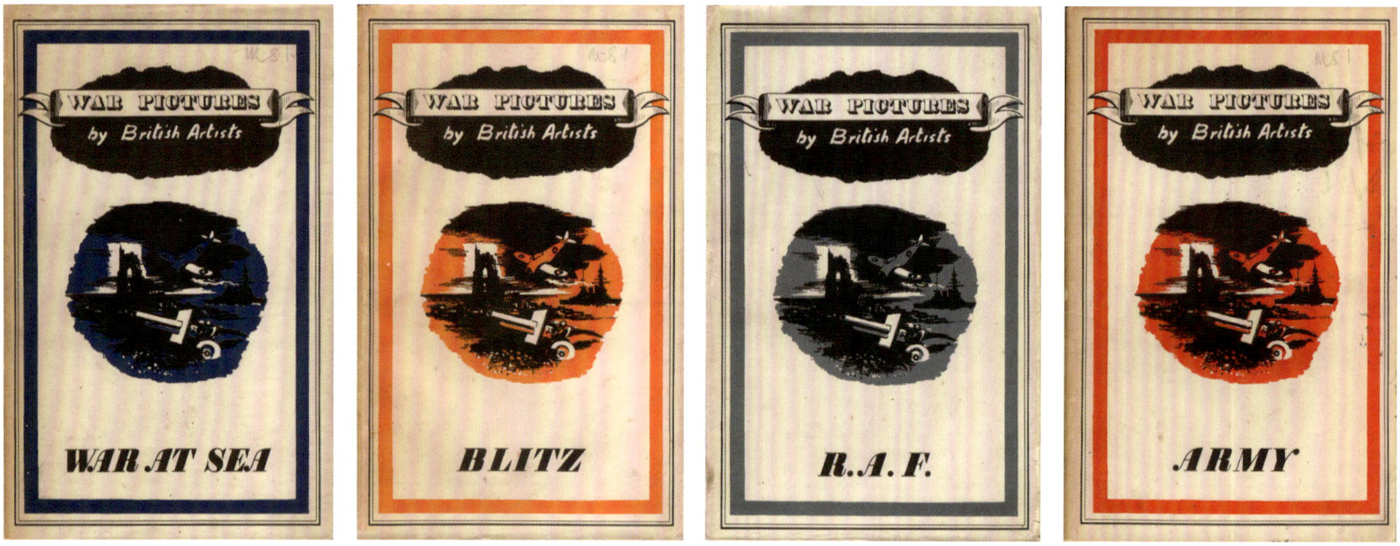

The War Artists' Advisory Committee produced two sets of four paperback booklets during the war, both called *War Pictures by British Artists*. The first set of four, entitled *War at Sea*, *Blitz*, *R.A.F* and *Army*, sold some 24,000 copies and led to a second set, *Women*, *Production*, *Soldiers* and *Air Raids*, being published in 1943.

'spectacular' in the *Daily Mail*. LLFA are delighted to be collaborating once again with Morley Gallery, whose proximity to the Imperial War Museum adds resonance to the venue. Morley College was itself a victim of the Blitz, in 1940, losing as a consequence its celebrated murals by Ravilious, Mahoney and Bawden.

This publication has been arranged in three sections: an introduction to the WAAC by leading expert Dr Brian Foss, (section one) supplemented by a series of appendices, (section three). Section two provides a catalogue to accompany the exhibition at Morley Gallery based on the eight themed subjects of the *War Pictures by British Artists* series: *War At Sea*, *Blitz*, *R.A.F.*, *Army*, *Women*, *Production*, *Soldiers* and *Air Raids*.

When the WAAC was dissolved in 1945 the number of works that had been acquired stood at close to 6,000. Over half of these were retained by the Imperial War Museum with the remaining works distributed to 60 museums and institutions in Britain and abroad. We are fortunate to include in this exhibition a large number of studies for pictures that featured in the *War Pictures by British Artists* series, among them Muirhead Bone's *Winter Mine-laying off Iceland* (CAT. 3-9), Charles Cundall's *Hipper at Kiel* (CAT. 15), Thomas Monnington's *Fortresses* (CAT. 57), Alan Sorrell's *Watch Office* (CAT. 63) and Evelyn Dunbar's *Putting on Anti-gas Protective Clothing* (CAT. 79a-d). Robert Austin's *Spitfire in a Hanger* (CAT. 40) was published

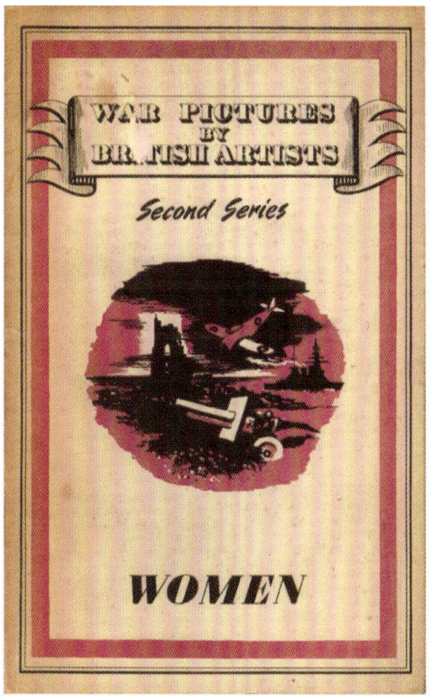

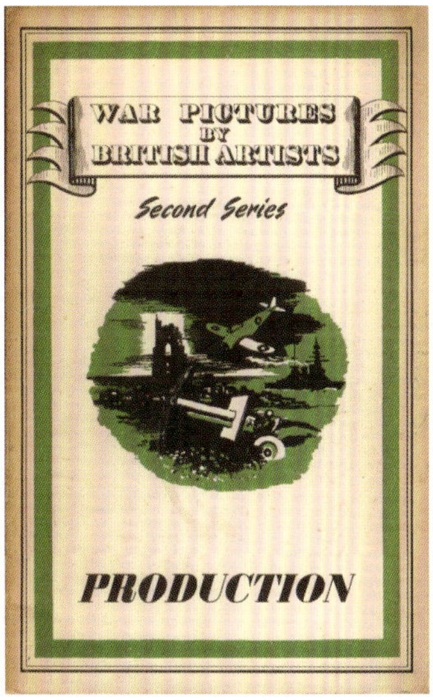

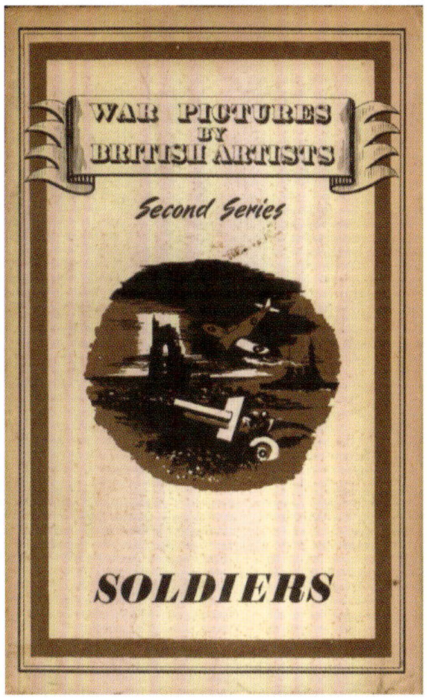

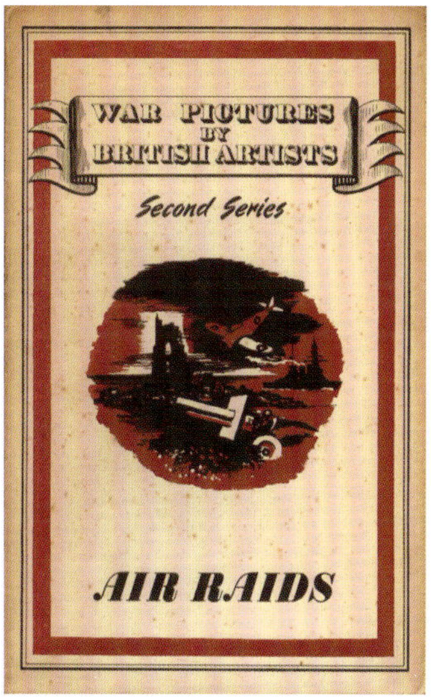

in the original 'R.A.F' volume and Evelyn Dunbar's study for the celebrated *Milking Practice With Artificial Udders* (CAT. 78), is almost identical to the version in the Imperial War Museum.

Clark's hope to save lives no doubt had a positive outcome, though three full-time artists did die during the war (Eric Ravilious, Albert Richards and Thomas Hennell). Certainly the WAAC changed lives for the better. In the case of full-time salaried artists such as Dunbar, Cundall, Monnington and Sorrell, the commissions afforded by the WAAC reinvigorated their careers. Artists outside the scheme seem to have equally been spurred to new heights of creativity. Victor Moody's extraordinary portrait of his mother, *The Day the War Broke Out, Mom* (CAT. 89), Harold Riley's self-portrait *Me* (CAT. 27), Frank Potter's *Fire Watcher* (CAT.38) and Cliff Rowe's *The Call-out*, (CAT. 23) are especially evocative. The strength of such images, from both within and without the WAAC scheme, lay in their power to elevate ordinary men and women – bus conductors, factory workers, nurses, members of the Civil Defence – to the status of heroes. The same process can be observed in the little known initiatives which ran alongside, and were inspired by the WAAC, such as ICI's extraordinary 'Portraits of Industry' (Appendix IV). This was the 'People's War' and as the critic of the *Tatler* noted in May 1941, 'not for many generations can artists have been in closer touch with the general public.'

"The Colour and the Peculiar Feeling of Events": The War Artists' Advisory Committee, 1939-1945

By Brian Foss

'What did it [the Second World War] look like? they will ask in 1981, and no amount of description or documentation will answer them.' Thus declared the first sentence in each of four booklets published in 1942 by the Oxford University Press. The question was answered, at least in part, by the booklets themselves. Titled *War Pictures by British Artists*, they comprised volumes titled *War at Sea*, *R.A.F.*, *Army* and *Blitz*. Each was 63 or 64 pages long and featured a brief introductory essay, followed by four dozen full-page black and white illustrations with summary annotations. The booklets were slim and small enough (19 x 12 cm) to be slipped into a handbag or a coat pocket. The price, too, was attractive: 1s 3d, the equivalent of 15 pence in 1942, or approximately £2.60 in today's currency. The series was printed in an edition of 24,000 and sold out in less than six months.[1] So successful was the experiment that the following year another four booklets were published (*Soldiers*, *Production*, *Air Raids* and *Women*) in an identical physical format but at the slightly increased price of 1s 6d.

All of the many reproductions in the two series came from the collection of the War Artists' Advisory Committee (WAAC). The WAAC was created in November 1939 with a mandate to compile a visual record of all aspects of British participation in the Second World War. It was chaired by the National Gallery's director, Kenneth Clark, whose qualifications for the job included his intelligence and determination, his impeccable social connections, his patrician self-confidence and, above all, his commitment to supporting British artists. Certainly that backing was desperately needed; a survey conducted in September and early October 1939 by the London-based Artists' International Association revealed that 73 per cent of respondents had lost their jobs or had commissions cancelled since the start of the war.[2] In the weeks leading up to September 1939 Clark had been barraged with pleas for help from artists hoping to find employment in wartime camouflage, publicity or propaganda, and he was working with the Ministry of Labour to construct registers of artists and designers appropriate for employment in those and other areas.

However, Clark also intended – based on First World War precedents – to lobby for a project that would hire artists to record war activities. For this, time was of the essence. In October 1939 the Admiralty received Treasury sanction to hire a war artist, and in early November the

War Office requested funding to engage four artists of its own. Clark's hopes for a centralising war art committee were thus at risk of being made redundant by a clutch of smaller projects. By mid-November, though, he had secured the agreement of the armed services to send representatives to a proposed committee that would oversee a large war art scheme and to select their artists based on that committee's recommendations. The committee would be housed within the Ministry of Information (MoI) because artistic documentation was deemed to fall under the heading of wartime publicity, which in turn was within the purview of the MoI. The WAAC convened for the first time on November 23rd, 1939. It would meet almost every week from then until the end of 1945.[3]

Later in life Clark asserted that in founding the WAAC his aim, 'which of course I did not disclose, was simply to keep artists at work on any pretext, and, as far as possible, to prevent them from being killed'.[4] During the war itself, however, he insisted that 'even photographs, which tell us so much, will leave out the colour and the peculiar feeling of events in these extraordinary years. Only the artist, with his heightened powers of perception can recognise which elements in a scene can be pickled for posterity in the magical essence of style.'[5] That said, Clark also seized upon depictions of the war – the omnipresence of which affected and often dominated the lives of just about everyone – as a means to encourage widespread interest in British art. If people recognised their lives in war imagery, he reasoned, they would be more likely to take art seriously.[6]

In recognition that the war radically altered many aspects of society, from technology and production to childcare, employment, the physical urban environment and beyond, the WAAC opted to be as ambitious and to be involved with as many artists as its financial support from the Treasury would allow. The backbone of the undertaking was the thirty-six men and one woman who received renewable full-time contracts, usually of six months' duration at an annual average rate of £650, although by early 1943 this had risen to as much as £800.[7] They were required to give the WAAC right of first refusal of everything they produced while on contract, although the committee usually returned minor or redundant works. Some artists received only one contract, but others were employed for substantial portions of the war.

Those thirty-seven artists made up only nine percent of all the men and women whose art was eventually included in the WAAC's collection. Some 101 others received one-off, short-term contracts to produce one or more works on specific themes and usually in a specified medium: oil paintings, watercolours or drawings, but occasionally prints (Ethel Gabain, A.S. Hartrick, H. Andrew Freeth) and sculptures (more than twenty artists, including Jacob Epstein,

C.W. Dyson-Smith and John Skeaping). Another 265 artists submitted unsolicited work that the WAAC agreed to purchase. For those to whom it issued full-time or short-term contracts, the committee strove to assign subjects that aligned with each artist's geographical location or thematic interests. It also provided, whenever possible in tightly rationed wartime, assistance in obtaining such things as canvas and other restricted art materials, petrol for travel, and access to institutions or sites that would ordinarily be closed to outsiders. The final result of all this activity was an art collection of approximately 6,000 items that did an admirable job of representing the war as it was experienced in England, Scotland, Wales, Northern Ireland and abroad.

A government committee acting as the nation's single biggest patron of living artists required great discretion in order to avoid the appearance of stylistic bias at taxpayers' expense. Kenneth Clark therefore staffed the WAAC with three artist members – Muirhead Bone, Percy Jowett (principal of the Royal College of Art) and Walter Russell (keeper of the Royal Academy Schools) – who, although they tended toward conservatism themselves, were also receptive to more modernist approaches. As a result, the war art collection ran the gamut from academicism (itself a broad category that encompassed artists as diverse as Frank Beresford and Laura Knight) to the work of modernists such as Paul Nash, Stanley Spencer, John Piper, Graham Sutherland and Henry Moore. Indeed, the only artists consistently neglected by the WAAC were those 'pure painters' whose work did not evince an interest 'in facts, drama, human emotions and life generally',[8] and especially Clark's particular bêtes noires – Ben Nicholson, Barbara Hepworth and others – who made 'pictures which represent ... nothing at all but squares and circles'.[9] Aside from being of no interest to the WAAC's members on a personal level, such work would have been difficult to justify to the Ministry of Information and to the Treasury within the context of a project with the raison d'être of compiling a documentary history of the war.

The avoidance of abstraction paralleled the WAAC's inevitable commitment to military subjects. Fully half of the eight *War Pictures by British Artists* booklets were dedicated to military themes: three of the four publications from 1942 (*War at Sea*, *R.A.F.* and *Army*), and one from 1943 (*Soldiers*). The Army, the Royal Navy and the Royal Air Force had widespread geographical fields of operation, the sheer expansiveness of which necessitated the hiring of several full-time artists who then produced more than half of all the artworks ultimately accrued by the WAAC. This, of course, required the cooperation of the armed Services, which were responsible for paying and hosting the full-time artists who were assigned to them and for ensuring that those artists were given the facilities and assistance they required. As per the agreements struck between Clark and the services in mid-November 1939, the War Artists'

Advisory Committee included one representative from each of the War Office, the Admiralty and the Air Ministry. Over the course of the war a total of six artists were attached at various times to the Admiralty (Muirhead Bone, Charles Cundall, Richard Eurich, John Worsley, Roland Pitchforth and James Morris), seven to the Air Ministry (Keith Henderson, Paul Nash, Eric Kennington, Charles Cundall, A.R. Thomson, William Dring and Thomas Hennell), and eleven to the War Office (Barnett Freedman, R.G. Eves, Edward Ardizzone, Edward Bawden, Henry Lamb, Anthony Gross, Henry Carr, William Coldstream, Albert Richards, Carel Weight and Leslie Cole). In addition, a number of the artists who received full-time WAAC commissions to work under the auspices of the Ministry of Information rather than those of the armed services, in fact had contracts requiring them to address military subjects that were not deemed to have received adequate attention from the committee's full-time military artists.[10] Rodrigo Moynihan, for example, was instructed by his MoI commission to produce War Office portraits, and these included records of the Women's Auxiliary Territorial Service (Fig.1).

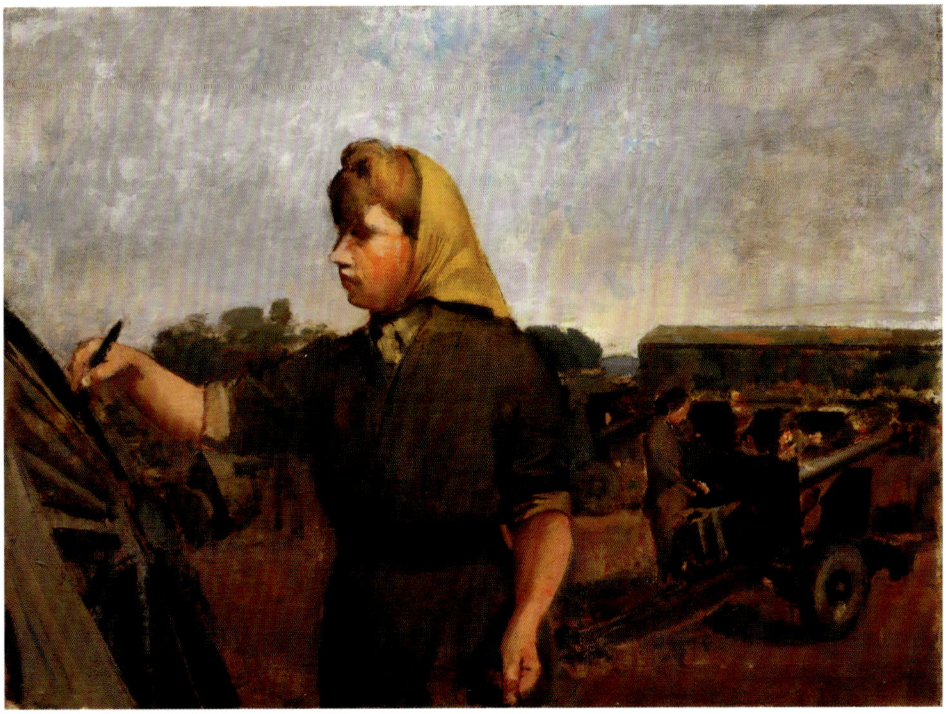

Fig. 1 – **Rodrigo Moynihan** (1910-1990), *Auxiliary Territorial Service at Work*, 1943, oil on canvas, 23 x 30 in. (55.8 x 76.2 cm) © Imperial War Museums (IWM Art LD 3630)

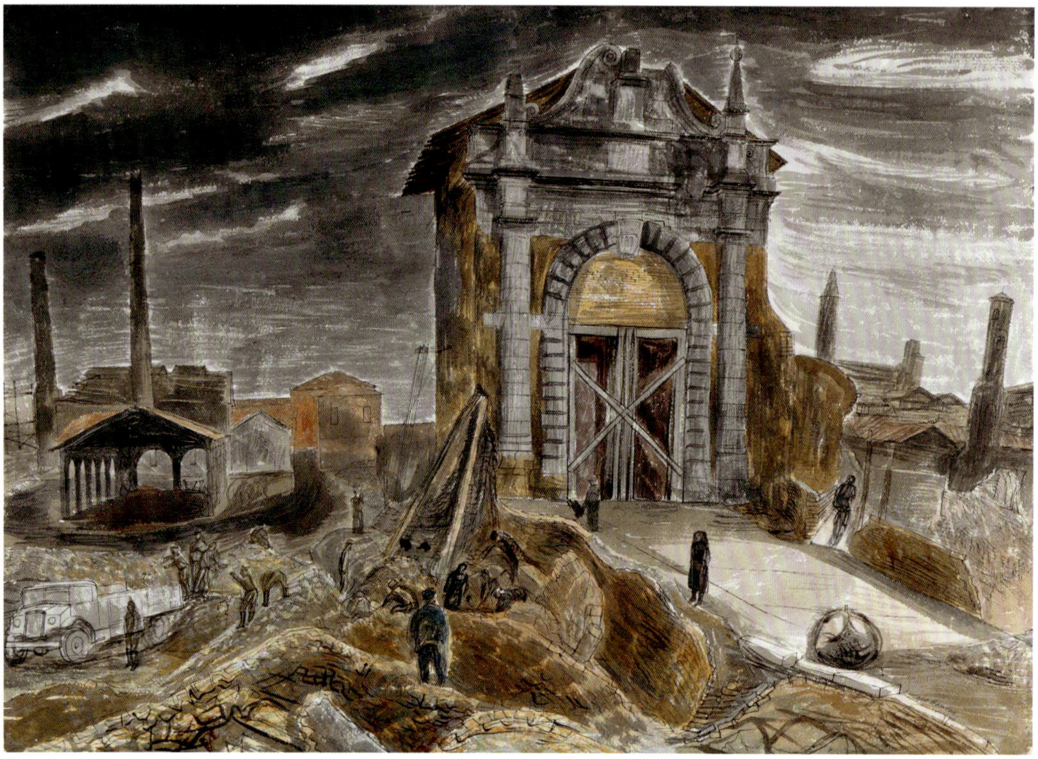

Fig. 2 – **Edward Bawden** (1903-1989) *Ravenna: Royal Engineers' working party collecting material for bridge repairs and road making at the Porta Cybo*, 1945, watercolour on paper, 22 ½ x 31 in. (57.2 x 79 cm)
© Imperial War Museums (IWM Art LD 4967)

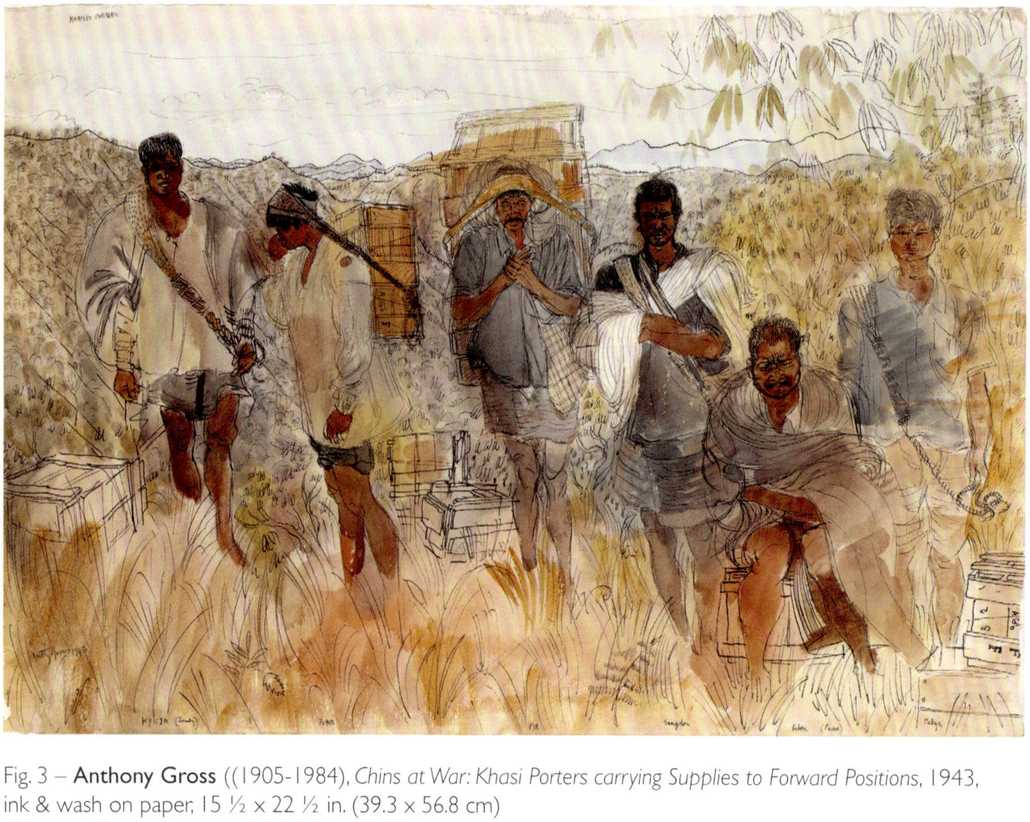

Fig. 3 – **Anthony Gross** ((1905-1984), *Chins at War: Khasi Porters carrying Supplies to Forward Positions*, 1943, ink & wash on paper, 15 ½ x 22 ½ in. (39.3 x 56.8 cm)
© Imperial War Museums (IWM Art LD3337)

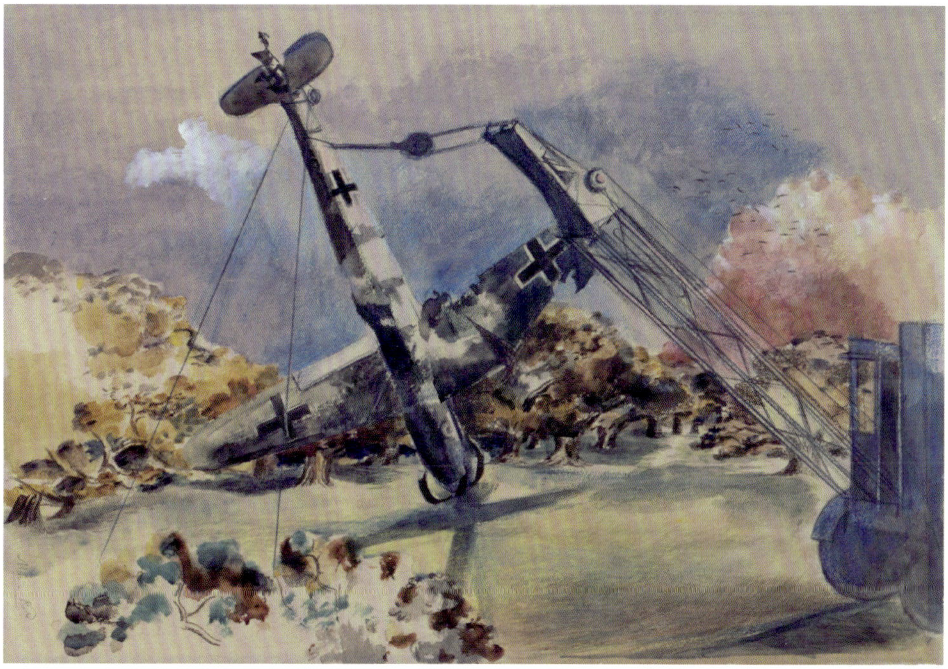

Fig. 4 – **Paul Nash** (1889-1946), *The Messerschmidt in Windsor Great Park*, 1940, pastel, graphite and watercolour on paper, 15 ¾ x 22 ¾ in. (40 x 57.8 cm)
© Tate, London 2016

This large-scale allocation of artists to work with the military, reinforced by short-term contracts and by purchases, meant that the WAAC's art collection would eventually encompass training (and in the case of the RAF, fighting) within Britain, as well as military life and operations in mainland Europe prior to Dunkirk and again after the 1943 and 1944 Allied invasions (Fig. 2), Malta, North Africa and the North Atlantic, as well as substantial coverage of the Middle East, India and Burma (Fig. 3). However, despite the success of its coverage of the military, the WAAC also experienced frustrations. For example, relations between Clark and the committee's armed services representatives were occasionally marred by disputes concerning documentary accuracy versus modernism, or images that were seen to undermine the military's view of itself. Most notably, the Air Ministry's Harald Peake provoked Clark's ire when he refused to renew Paul Nash's contract because he objected, among other things, to Nash's watercolours of crashed German aeroplanes (Fig. 4), deeming them unacceptable to the RAF 'for the same reason that pictures of horses are much more attractive to hunting men than are pictures of the dead fox!'[11] On less quaintly ideological grounds, some military artists experienced bureaucratic hurdles affecting their freedom of movement in the field: a problem partly solved by giving Army artists honorary military ranks shortly after Dunkirk in place of their previous, more militarily ambiguous status as war correspondents.

But perhaps the WAAC's most frequent disappointment was in the general dearth of images of military personnel in action, and the correspondingly large number of views of equipment and of recruits performing routine duties or relaxing (both, admittedly, activities that occupied a disproportionately large amount of time). For artists such as Eric Ravilious (employed as a

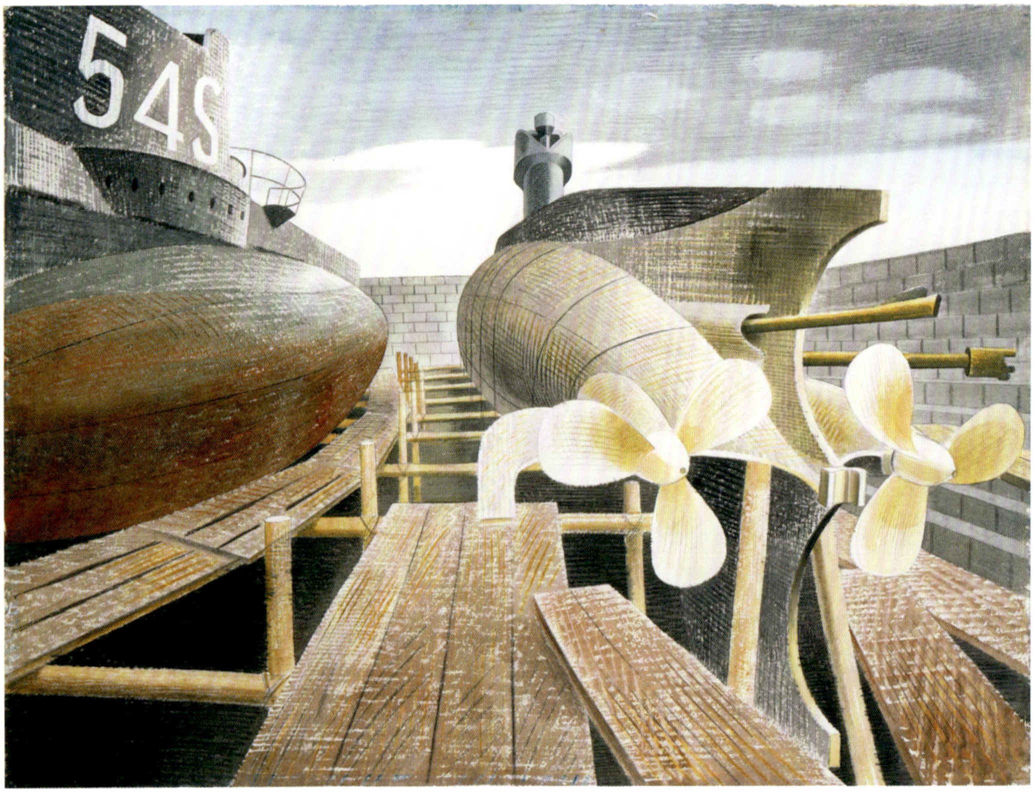

Fig. 5 – **Eric Ravilious** (1903-1942), *Submarines in Dry Dock*, 1940,
graphite, watercolour, crayon and pastel on paper, 17 x 22 ½ in. (43.2 x 57.1 cm)

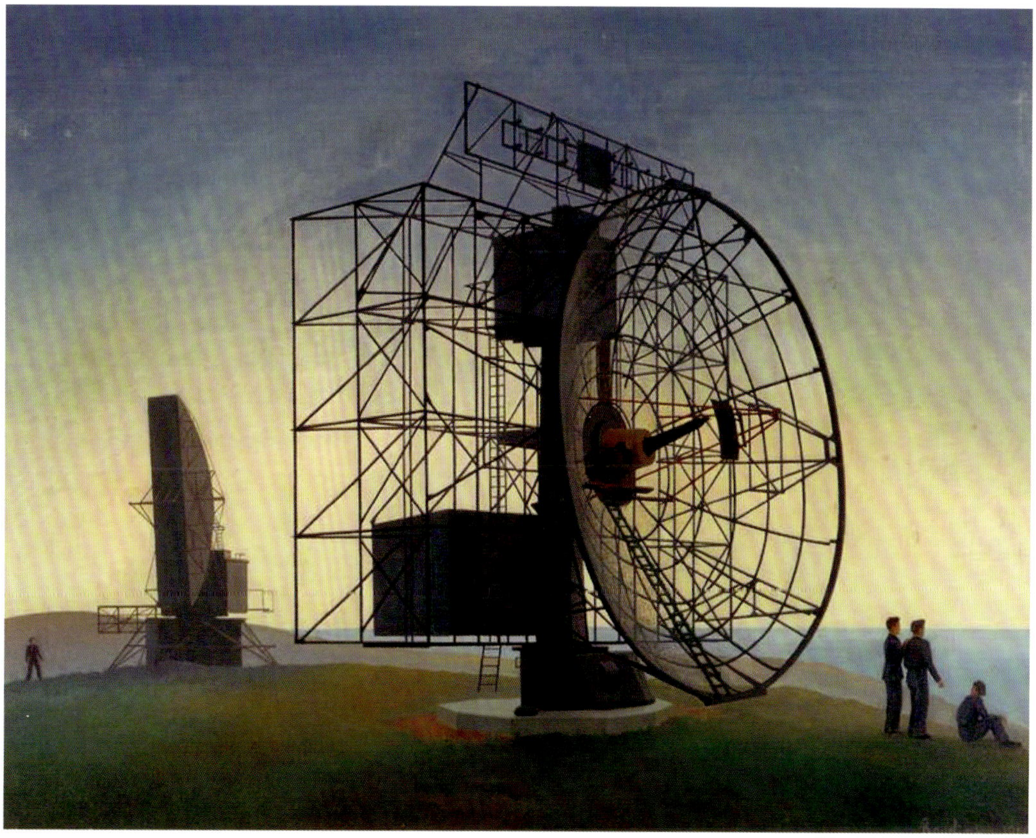

Fig. 6 – **William Thomas Rawlinson** (1912-1993), *A 'Type 16' Fighter Direction Radar Station,* 1946, oil on canvas, 24 x 30 in. (60.9 x 76.2 cm) © Imperial War Museums (IWM Art LD 5833)

Ministry of Information artist specialising in Admiralty topics) and W.T. Rawlinson (who only sold work to the WAAC), the most visually compelling subjects were often those in which the artists could explore the inanimate, intricate geometries and decorative patterns of modern offensive and defensive warfare (Fig. 5 and Fig. 6). Indeed, the three 1942 *War Pictures by British Artists* booklets that zeroed in on armed forces subjects contained a total of only ten views of unmistakable combat. Modern warfare often moved at tremendous speeds, and was thus fundamentally unlike the hand-to-hand battles of the nineteenth century, or even the trench-based combat of the First World War. Moreover, for most artists the scale of modern battle was frequently too epic to be portrayed in art that would be factually accurate but at the same time both visually interesting and narratively meaningful to viewers.

The WAAC was therefore always on the lookout for servicemen who understood military life, who had access to dramatic events, and who were familiar with the difficulties inherent in sketching under pressure. In fact, two men who became full-time Admiralty artists, John Worsley and James Morris, first came to the committee's attention when they submitted active duty images for possible purchase. The similarly young and little-known Albert Richards was made a War Office artist (Fig. 7) after having sold the committee paintings of things he had experienced in the field as a Royal Engineer. (Never one to shy away from danger, Richards was still a War Office artist when he was killed by a landmine in 1945.) In a very few cases the WAAC even issued contracts to record crucial but otherwise undocumented military events that the artists who received the contracts had not actually seen for themselves and

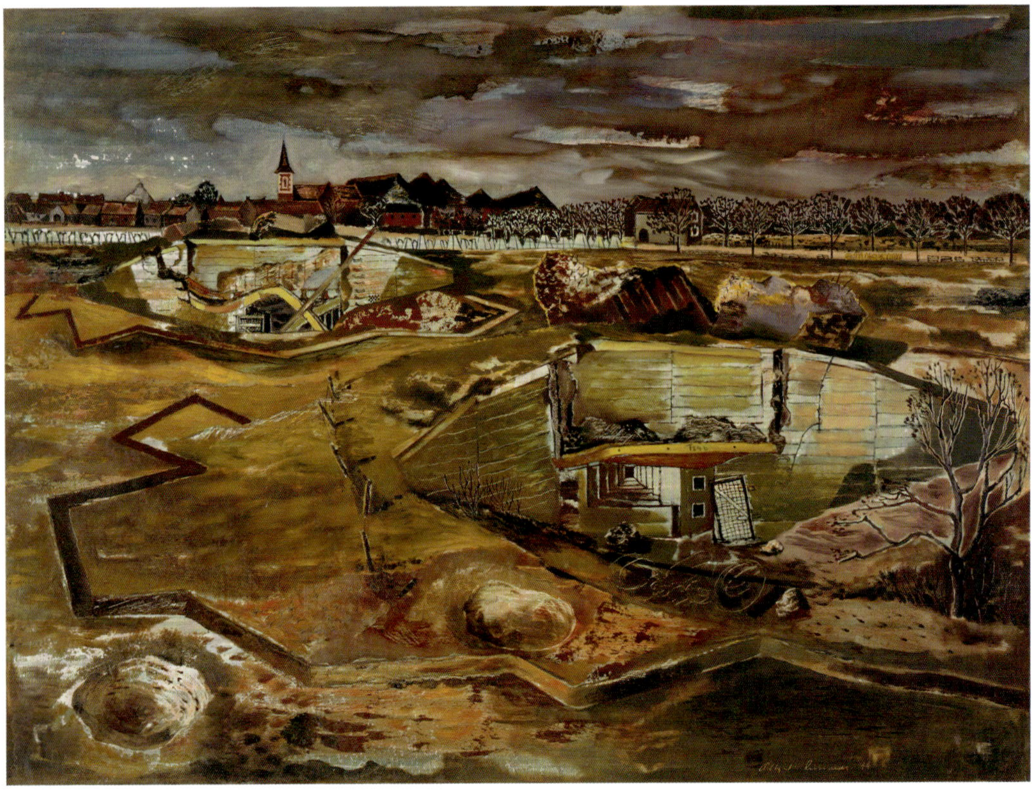

Fig. 7 – **Albert Richards** (1919-1945), *Germany, 1944 : The Siegfried Line between Heerlen and Aachen*, 1944, oil on canvas, 22 ¼ x 30 in. (56.5 x 76.5 cm) © Imperial War Museums (IWM Art LD 4830)

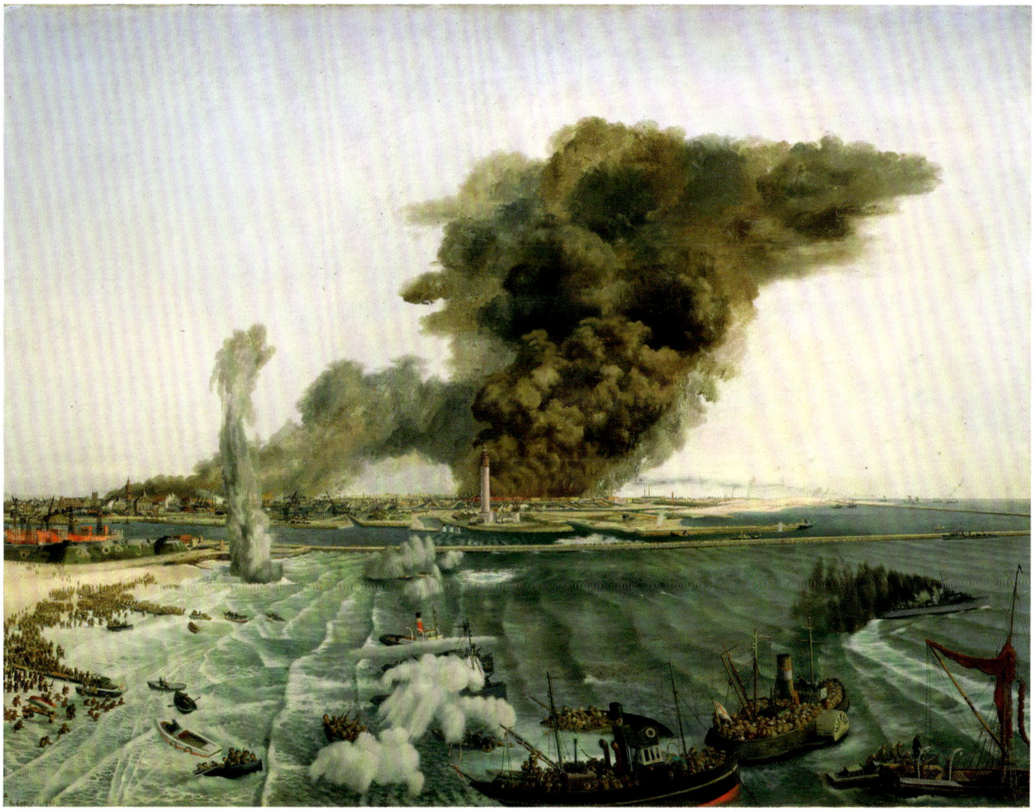

Fig. 8 – **Richard Ernst Eurich** (1903-1992), *Withdrawal from Dunkirk, June 1940*, 1940,
oil on canvas, 30 x 40 in. (76 x 102 cm)
Courtesy of the National Maritime Museum, Greenwich, London

for which they relied instead on photographs and eyewitness accounts. The resulting large oil paintings included reconstructions of such events as an attack on the German battleship *Tirpitz* by British midget submarines in 1943 (portrayed by Charles Pears), the aerial bombing of Berlin as seen from the air (Paul Nash), and two large paintings of the 1940 evacuation from Dunkirk: an event that had enormous psychological implications. One of these was painted by Charles Cundall and the other – much praised for raising the evacuation to the level of Greek tragedy, 'which avoids, wherever possible, the murder and the blood'[12] – was by Richard Eurich (Fig. 8).

Just as the WAAC found itself with fewer action images than it would have liked, so too it experienced serious difficulties in obtaining many representations of the horror, violence and bloodiness of warfare. Many artists had nothing in their training or background that prepared them to deal with gruesome scenes, and most were in any case emotionally unwilling to portray them. 'Little to see and less to draw,' wrote War Office artist Edward Ardizzone when he wandered onto an Italian street strewn with dead bodies.[13] This general lacuna was often noted by journalists and members of the public. Yet although many commentators decried this situation, a great deal of critical and public opinion adopted the opposite view. Hence the popularity of Ardizonne, whose unimposing watercolours chronicled *Army life in Britain, North Africa and Europe*, the latter before Dunkirk and then after the 1943 invasion of Italy and the 1944 Normandy landings. His watercolours attracted much favourable attention for perpetuating his well-established attitude to human subjects: one that combined empathy with gentle humour. Robert Medley, himself a recipient of a short-term WAAC contract, contended that Ardizzone and Anthony Gross were 'the best of the official war artists at rendering what life was actually like with an operational army. … Something about our war made the grand statement impossible; the prevailing mood was honestly anti-heroic, humorously stoic: Ardizzone and Gross caught with perfect authenticity and sympathy this mood of brave irony.'[14] Kenneth Clark held the same opinion, praising Ardizzone as someone 'who would show what military life was really like'.[15] *At a Divisional HQ* of 1940 (Fig. 9) is typical of the mood of Ardizzone's war work. It shows two officers studying a large map with a placidity suggestive of two old friends planning a tour of wineries. Ardizzone carried over his focus on small, personal foibles and dramas from pre-Dunkirk images, into his sketches made during

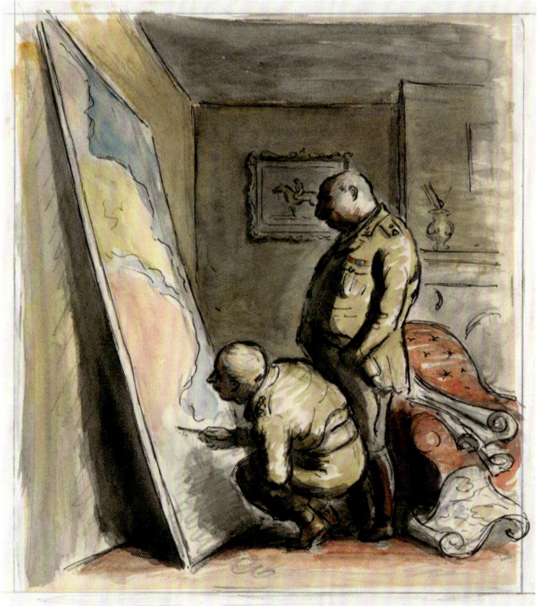

Fig. 9 –
Edward Ardizzone (1900-1979), *At a Divisional HQ*, 1940, watercolour on paper, 11 x 9 ½ in. (27.6 x 24.4 cm)
© Imperial War Museums (IWM Art LD 652)

the evacuation itself: a fact that helps explain why the WAAC commissioned Cundall and Eurich to create large canvases that provided information-filled aerial overviews of the retreat as a whole.

Ultimately, among the very few war artists who showed themselves capable of portraying horror, the most prominent was Leslie Cole. He refused to back away from the dreadful things he witnessed (Fig. 10), and was one of only four artists from whom the WAAC acquired images of the liberation of Nazi concentration camps. Another of the four was Doris Zinkeisen, whose uncompromising view of corpses in Belsen, April 1945 (Fig. 11) is one of the grimmest images of the entire war art collection.

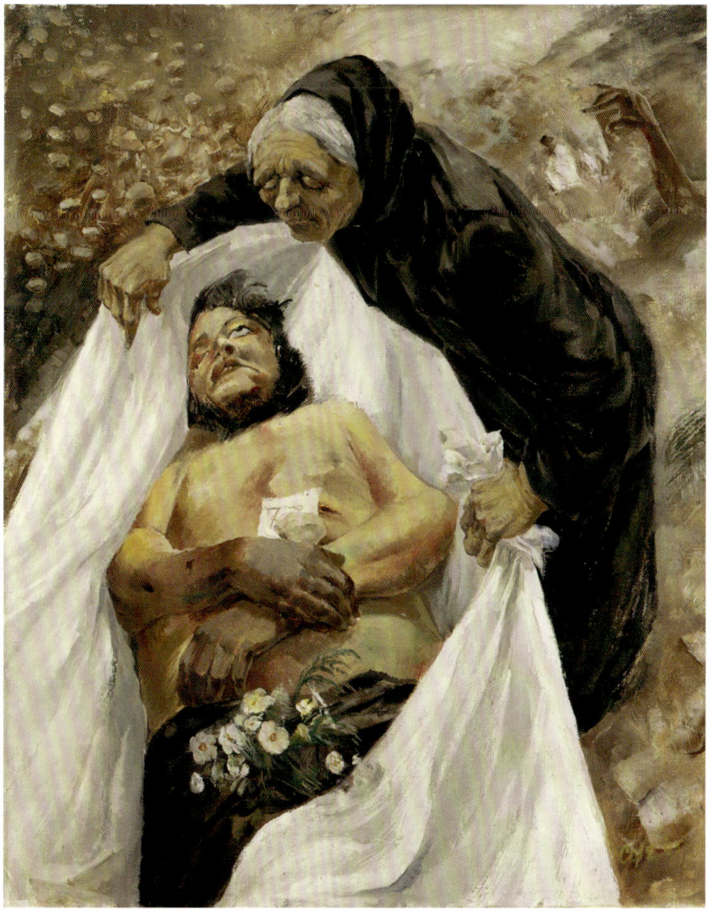

Fig. 10 –
Leslie Cole (1910–1976),
Mother Mourning the Death of a Village Priest, 1945,
oil on canvas,
23 ½ x 19 ¼ in.
(59.6 x 48.8 cm)
© Imperial War Museums
(IWM Art LD 5042)

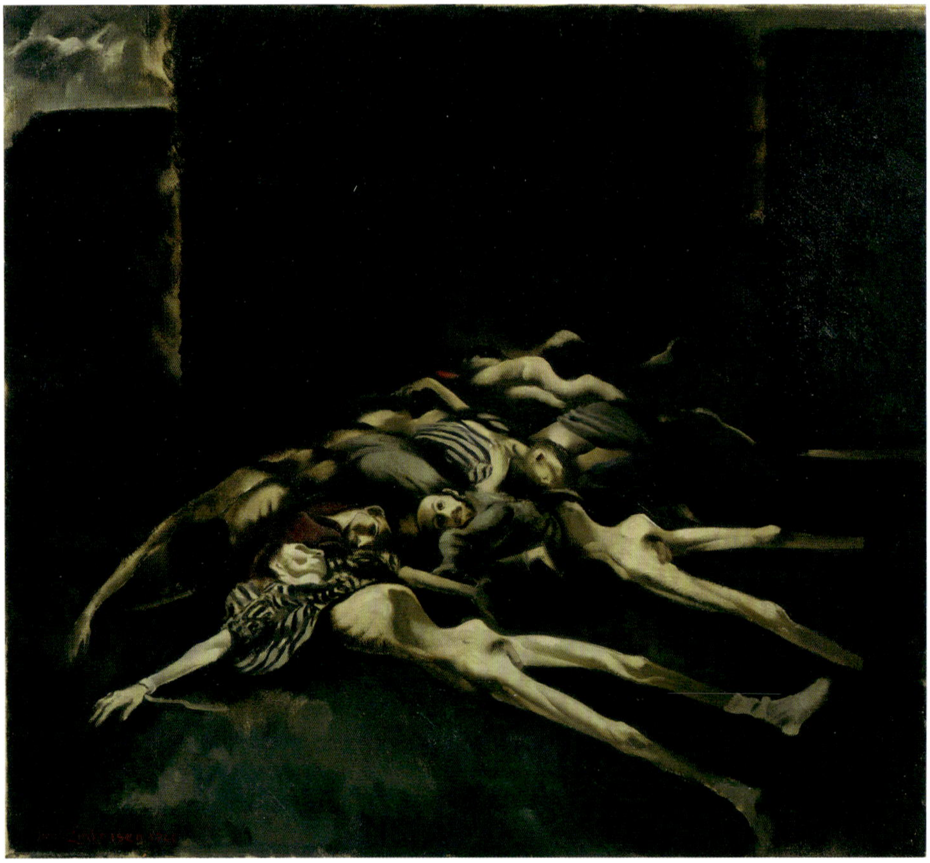

Fig. 11 – **Doris Zinkeisen** (1898–1991), *Belsen: April 1945*, 1945,
oil on canvas, 24 ½ x 27 ½ in. (62.2 x 69.8 cm)

At the opposite extreme from the work of artists such as Cole and Zinkeisen was military portraiture. This was a traditional genre that in the hands of some artists descended into the worst excesses of academic blandness, but that other artists were able to enliven in various ways. Portraiture was especially vital to the RAF, where the cult of the youthful, heroic and doomed Battle of Britain aircrews defined the RAF's public image. It was therefore unsurprising that the Air Ministry insisted on always having a portraitist as one of its full-time artists: first Eric Kennington (1940-42), followed by A.R. Thomson (1942-44) and William Dring (1944-45). The best known of these was Kennington, whose military portraits had both staunch champions and vociferous critics (Fig.12), One sceptic concluded that 'in real life the male only wears that look of clear-eyed hunger for the Good, the True, and the Beautiful when one of his physical appetites is being denied; Kennington probably waits until they want their dinner.'[16] However, the artist and the WAAC, despite their squabbles over the propaganda potential of war art (Kennington adopting the more hawkish stance), agreed that portrait subjects must – in keeping with the popular characterization of the Second World War as 'the People's War' – include everyone from senior officers, to noted heroes, to completely ordinary enlisted personnel.

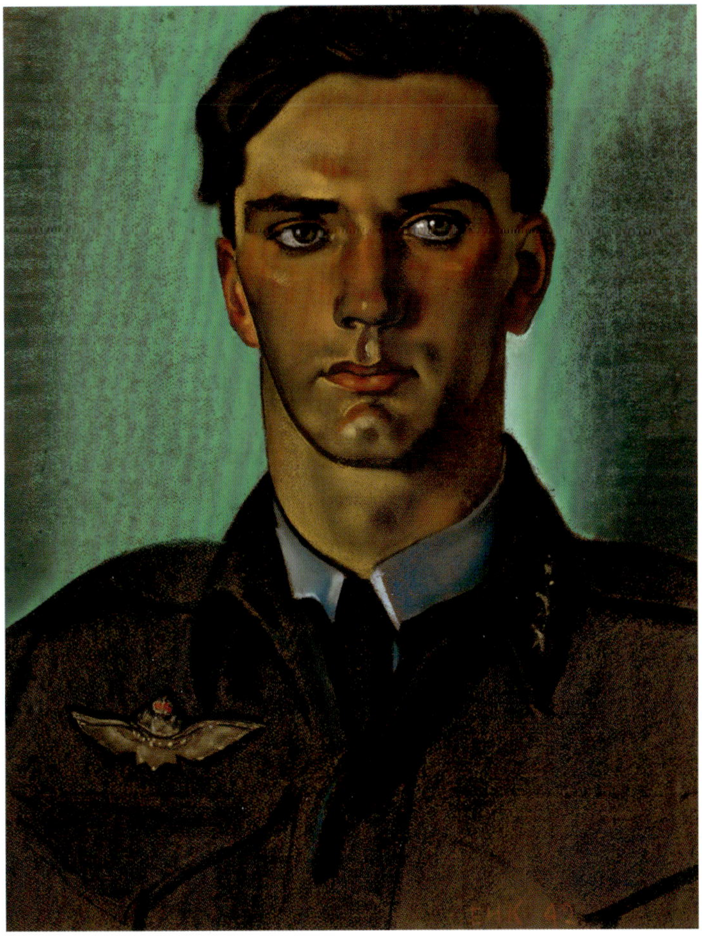

Fig. 12 –
Eric Kennington (1888-1960),
Captain W. Mohr: A Squadron Commander of the Royal Norwegian Air Force Serving with the RAF, 1942,
pastel on paper,
22 ½ x 18 ½ in.
(57.1 x 46.9 cm)
© Imperial War Museums
(IWM Art LD 2322)

A broadly democratic approach to portraiture also marked the WAAC's many home front images. Noted public figures were much in evidence, but so too were many previously unknown people whose valour earned them awards for bravery, along with unheralded sitters whose likenesses were recorded for the committee but who were otherwise anonymous cogs in the national war machine. A striking aspect of this recognition of the importance of often unsung home front work was the inclusion of women as subjects in single or group portraits. Conscription into the women's auxiliary forces, and especially into crucial home front industries such as armaments manufacture and aircraft production, fundamentally altered employment and family patterns, such that by 1943 there were 7.25 million women, including fully eighty percent of those with children older than fourteen years, engaged in war-related employment in agriculture (Evelyn Dunbar's full-time commission with the Ministry of Information was for 'agricultural and women's subjects'), manufacturing, civil defence (Fig. 13) and other activities. Henry Carr, a future war artist, queried the WAAC at the end of 1940 about what was at the time the committee's paucity of portraits of women, describing it as 'a strange omission, considering the position of women in the war'.[17] Just five months later the Ministry of Home Security's representative on the WAAC was urging that '[o]ther things being equal, it was desirable that women's portraits should have priority.'[18]

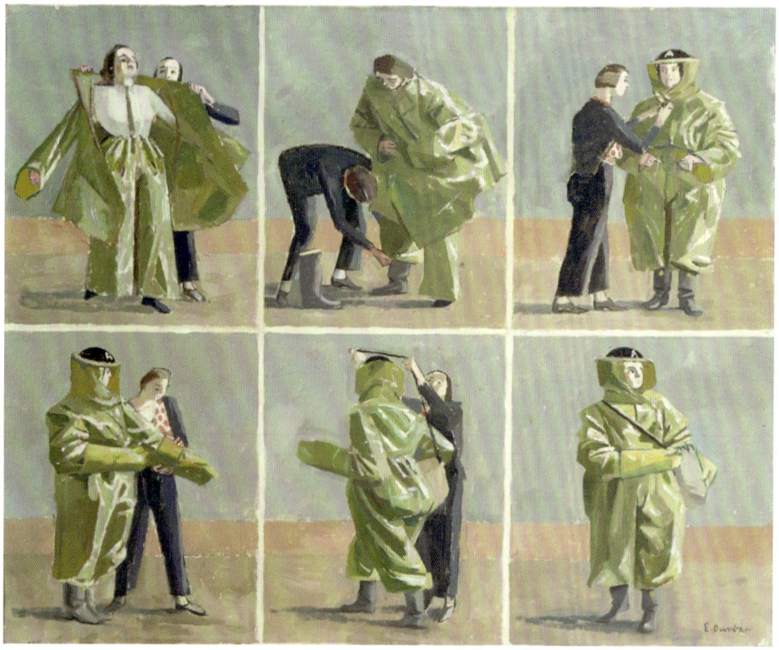

Fig. 13 –
Evelyn Dunbar
(1906-1960),
Putting on Anti-Gas Protective Clothing, 1940,
oil on canvas,
24 x 30 in.
(60.9 x 76.2 cm)
© Imperial War Museums
(Art.IWM ART LD 247)

The War Artists' Advisory Committee made a serious effort to respond to these recommendations: a resolve that was made clear in the *Women* volume of the 1943 *War Pictures by British Artists* booklets. The introductory essay by Dame Laura Knight – who received several contracts to produce large paintings for the WAAC – concluded with the question, 'If she ["Woman"] can do what she has done in war, what may she not do in peace?'[19] That same year Knight exhibited the WAAC's recently acquired *Ruby Loftus Screwing a Breech Ring* (Fig. 14), an image that commanded immediate and enduring popularity. Knight, whose unconventional career had always scorned gender-imposed expectations, here portrayed an equally remarkable woman who had gained national fame by quickly learning a highly technical machining operation restricted in pre-war years to men and for which nothing in her background suggested any particular aptitude. Nonetheless, *Ruby Loftus* and many other paintings and drawings aside, the WAAC's collection of images of women as war workers made significant concessions to tradition, both in numbers and themes. For example, the committee purchased or commissioned fifty percent more named, life-size portraits of nurses – a stereotypically proper and nurturing profession for women – rather than of female armaments and munitions employees, despite the fact that in 1943 the latter outnumbered the former by one hundred to one.

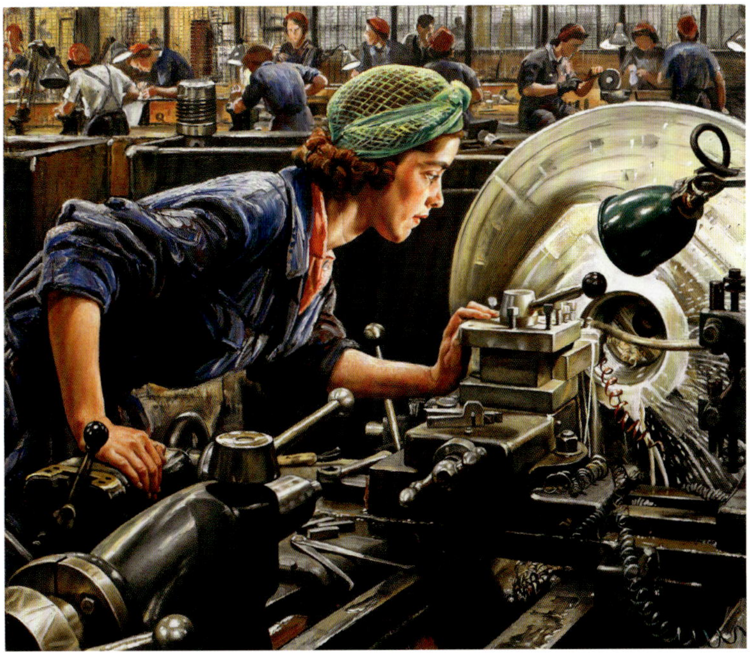

Fig. 14 –
Laura Knight (1877-1970),
Ruby Loftus Screwing a Breech Ring, 1943,
oil on canvas,
34 x 40 in.
(86.3 x 101.9 cm)
© Imperial War Museums
(IWM Art LD 2850)

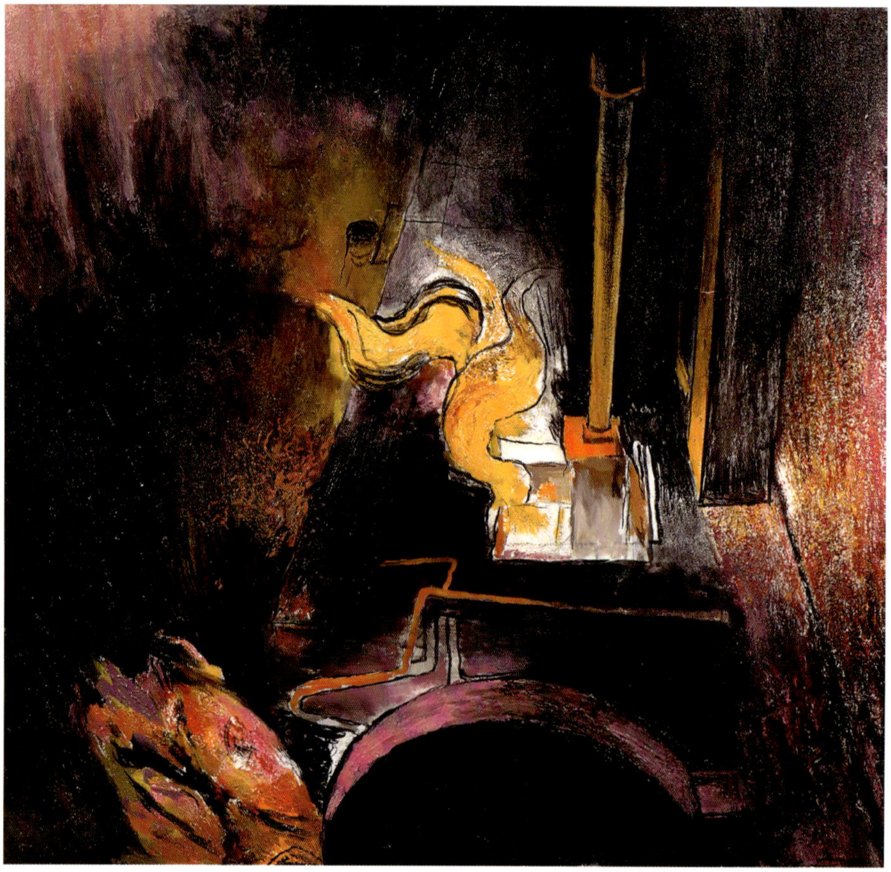

Fig. 15 – **Graham Sutherland** (1903–1980), *Feeding a Steel Furnace*, 1941–2, oil on canvas, 35 ½ x 34 in. (90.2 x 86.4 cm) © Tate, London 2016

Beyond *Ruby Loftus Screwing a Breech Ring*, the WAAC also secured many more manufacturing – and production – themed artworks (although none of them achieved the immediate fame enjoyed by Knight's painting), and also arranged for the publication of the *Production* volume in the 1943 *War Pictures by British Artists* series. At various dates between 1940 and 1945 the committee dispensed full-time commissions to four artists – Bernard Hailstone, Mervyn Peake, Roland Pitchforth and Graham Sutherland – to work with the ministries of Supply, Production and Home Security, focusing primarily or exclusively on production subjects.[20] Among the most successful of the resulting paintings are Sutherland's *Feeding*

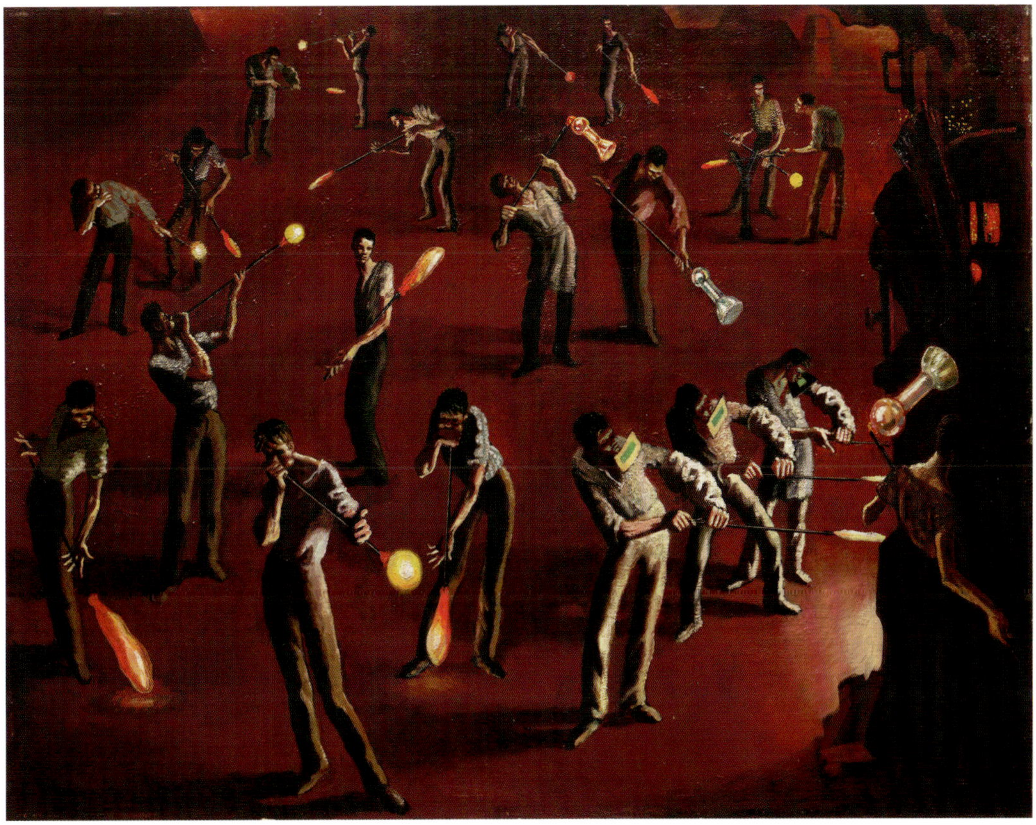

Fig. 16 – **Mervyn Peake** (1911-1968), *The Evolution of the Cathode Ray (Radiolocation) Tube*, 1943, oil on canvas, 33 ½ x 43 ½ in. (85 x 110.4 cm) © Imperial War Museums (IWM Art LD 3685)

a Steel Furnace (Fig. 15), presenting war industry in the guise of the Sublime), and Mervyn Peake's balletic and brilliantly coloured time-lapse painting *The Evolution of the Cathode Ray (Radiolocation) Tube* (Fig. 16). Equally spectacular and hugely more ambitious is Stanley Spencer's multi-panel *Shipbuilding on the Clyde*, painted in fulfilment of various contracts issued by the WAAC over the course of almost the entire war. The idiosyncratic Spencer continued his past practice of imbuing a wealth of human figures and carefully studied details with symbolism that transcended their historical specificity. This led him to describe his shipbuilders as 'more like the angels in "Paradise Lost"; who, though it was not their usual practice and occupation, had to hurl great pieces of rock at Satan's invading army.'[21]

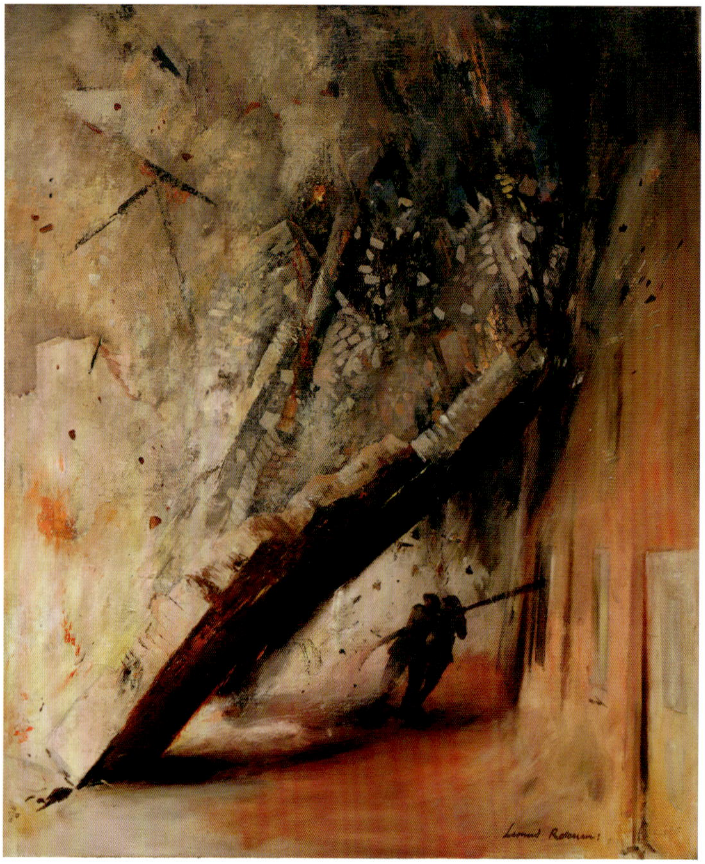

Fig. 17 –
Leonard Rosoman (1913-2012),
A House Collapsing on Two Firemen, Shoe Lane, London, EC4, 1940,
oil on canvas,
36 x 30 ¼ in. (91.8 x 76.8 cm)
© Imperial War Museums
(IWM Art LD 1353)

The civilian home front as portrayed by Knight, Dunbar, Hailstone, Pitchforth, Sutherland, Peake, Spencer and many others loomed almost as large as the military in the WAAC's work, and for good reasons. Aside from the fact that industrial productivity was a *sine qua non* of the war effort, the home front was to a very real degree another version of the military front. Almost 44,000 people had been killed in Britain by the summer of 1941 – a total that was all the more shocking because it was not until September of that year that home front fatalities were exceeded by those of soldiers, sailors and airmen combined, and not until the autumn of 1942 that more soldiers than civilians had died.[22] Threatened, wounded or dead bodies, however, are no more visible in depictions of the home front than they are in military subjects. Even apparently un-'British' behaviour is scarcely visible, the WAAC having expressed concern to artist Carel Weight about depictions of panic in one

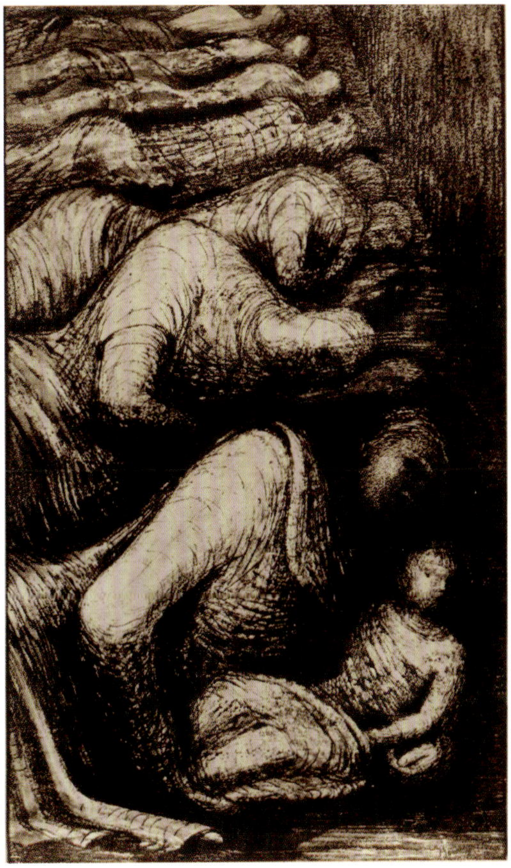

Fig. 18 –
Henry Moore (1898-1986), *Row of Sleepers,* 1941, (illustration from the WAAC book *Air Raids*).

of his 1941 air raid pictures.[23] This squeamishness only heightens the frisson of Leonard Rosoman's comparatively graphic *House Collapsing on Two Firemen, Shoe Lane, London, EC4* (Fig. 17). Even looks of apprehension on the faces of figures in a Frances MacDonald 1940 view of people sheltering from an aerial attack were discouraged by the committee,[24] whereas the less worry-filled shelterers recorded by Edward Ardizzone, Edmund Kapp, Feliks Topolski, Henry Moore and others all passed muster. Of these, Moore's justly famous multi-media drawings of shelterers in the London Underground easily attracted the most critical adulation. Reaction to them was mixed, however, with the figures being unfavourably described as tomb effigies rather than as 'specimens of living, if wearied, humanity'.[25] Typical of this body of work is *Row of Sleepers* (Fig. 18), which manages to be simultaneously physical and ethereal, emotional and detached, timely and timeless: a specific historical event and an abstract, universal comment on endurance.

Aerial attacks were central to the national psyche because they were an essential element in the creation of what Angus Calder later termed 'the myth of the Blitz',[26] with its confirmation of such supposedly archetypal British qualities as maintaining a stiff upper lip and a Cockney grin and bearing disasters uncomplainingly. Small wonder, then, that two of the eight *War Pictures by British Artists* booklets – *Blitz* (1942) and *Air Raids* (1943) – were devoted to the subject. Only the Army (with *Army* (1942) and *Soldiers* (1943)) received a comparable amount of attention. As Stephen Spender remarked in his introductory essay for the *Air Raids* booklet, 'In this war, by "War Pictures" we mean, pre-eminently, paintings of the Blitz. In the last war we would have meant pictures of the Western Front....'[27]

Tellingly, the appalling carnage of the raids was almost always displaced from bodies to architecture. Moreover, much of the WAAC art that deals with bomb damage is obsessed with churches and other heritage buildings (Fig. 19). The concentration in the badly damaged City of London of so many churches by Wren and others, along with historic secular buildings, was amply documented for the committee. But even outside of London, fully one in four of the six dozen pictures of bombed architecture show churches, so tempting was the opportunity to cast Nazi Germany as a barbarian state that had no respect for symbols of peace and civilisation.

Effective though the two *War Pictures by British Artists* series were in publicising WAAC views of the home front and the military, the committee's hopes to promote its collection went well beyond those eight booklets. Unfortunately, though, other publication and reproduction projects were less successful. The marketing of large colour reproductions of selected paintings to military messes, British Restaurants and factory canteens went over well, but attempts to encourage private companies to reproduce WAAC images as postcards, bookmarks, calendars and so on were failures. So was the selling of photographic reproductions to private buyers. A proposal to create a deluxe war art periodical aimed at 'influential people who would appreciate a finely produced publication' was stillborn.[28] *War through Artists' Eyes: Paintings and Drawings by British War Artists*, a follow-up to the *War Pictures by British Artists* booklets, was published by John Murray, but by the time it appeared in 1945 the war was almost over and the demand for war imagery was collapsing.

It was a different story entirely with exhibitions. The WAAC rejected the First World War precedent of putting its art on display only after the fighting had ended. Instead, the committee – capitalising on the National Gallery having evacuated its entire collection to safety outside of London at the beginning of the war – in mid-1940 used some of the building's denuded

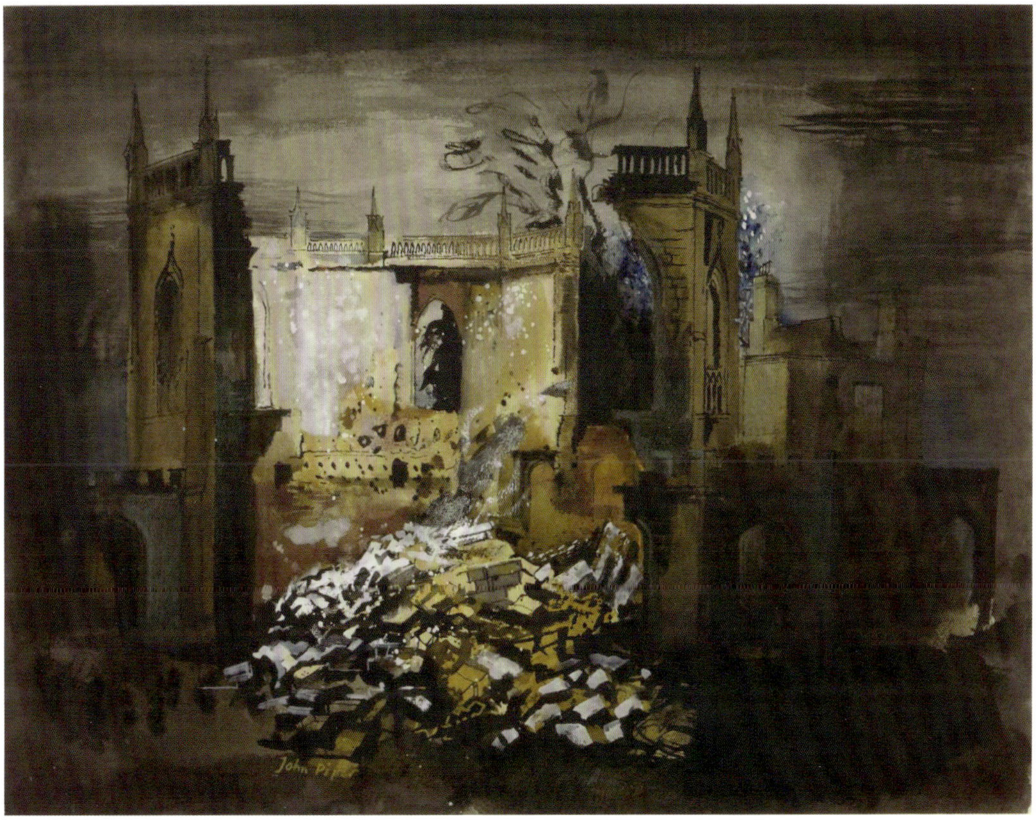

Fig. 19 – **John Piper** (1903–1992), *All Saints Chapel, Bath*, 1942, ink, chalk, gouache and watercolour on paper, 16 ¾ x 22 in. (42.5 x 55.9 cm) © Tate, London 2016

rooms to open a display of war pictures. Over the next five years that exhibition grew and changed, attracting steady audiences and newspaper reviews published not only in London but in other cities and towns as well. Additionally, as early as 1939 Clark had mooted the desirability of touring art to venues other than London. Such a project was one that the fast-growing collection could afford to support and that would be a boon to parts of the kingdom where museums and art galleries had been closed or requisitioned for other wartime purposes.[29] From late 1940 to early 1945, nine large selections of war art toured to well over 100 different cities, towns and villages, five under the auspices of the Museums Association (which tended to favour more sophisticated recipient institutions) and four under the care of the British Institute of Adult Education (which often selected places such as schools, town halls and military barracks in the hope of reaching audiences who did not feel comfortable in more formal settings). In cities, towns and villages alike, attendance figures were impressive, sometimes startlingly so. A 1942 exhibition in a library in the Wiltshire village of Bulford, for example, attracted 1200 people in just six days. Kenneth Clark, determined as he was to build new audiences for contemporary British art, must have been delighted.

Exhibitions were also widely circulated abroad, including a singularly successful display for the United States. Britain at War opened in May 1941 at New York City's Museum of Modern Art, where 3000 people saw it on its opening day alone. The galvanising shock of Pearl Harbor was at that point more than six months in the future, and a sizeable section of American public opinion was still hostile to the idea of being dragged into another European war. The exhibition catalogue text, by Herbert Read, was therefore careful to push the right buttons. 'It must ... be remembered,' Read opined, 'though the English are energetic in action, they are restrained in expression. Our typical poetry is lyrical, not epical or even tragic. Our typical music is the madrigal and the song, not the opera and the symphony. Our typical painting is the landscape. In all these respects war cannot change us, and we are fighting this war precisely because in these respects we refuse to be changed.'[30] Never had the WAAC's lack of flag-waving battle painting, or its reliance on the intimate war zone views of artists such as Ardizzone, Bawden and Gross, or the presence of so many 'ordinary' people in its portraits and home front scenes, been more apropos. In excess of 200 reviews were published during the exhibition's first two weeks. Most of them offered some variation on the sentiments expressed by Read's essay.

The War Artists' Advisory Committee's last major activity was the organisation of a showing of more than 1,000 of its artworks – roughly one-sixth of its total collection – at Burlington House, Piccadilly, in October and November 1945. By then, though, the war was over, and the public appetite for seeing war art was waning. The exhibition lasted for six weeks, during which time it welcomed 19,462 paying customers: [31] a respectable but not a strikingly impressive total. 'It is possible that at no time will these pictures seem less interesting than they do at present,' wrote Kenneth Clark in the exhibition catalogue's preface. 'Their subjects belong to a past which we would gladly forget, but which is not yet remote enough to have become curious, and, as works of art, they are associated in our minds with five years of boredom and privation.'[32]

A few weeks later, at the end of 1945, after six years of work with 400 artists, the WAAC closed down. Another committee, drawing its membership from the Ministry of Information and the Imperial War Museum, assumed responsibility for the massive job of processing some final acquisitions and distributing the collection to sixty interested museums, art galleries, government departments and military establishments throughout Britain and, to a much smaller extent, to galleries in Canada, Australia and South Africa. Rather than enriching the collections only of the Imperial War Museum and a few major art galleries, the goal was to ensure that as many people as possible would have perpetual access to the WAAC's achievement. This was in keeping both with the ideals of the People's War and with Clark's resolve to construct a broad-based commitment to art in general and to contemporary British art in particular. Several months after the end of the war, with the entire collection dispersed to its new homes, the war art project – an undertaking of gigantic ambition and complexity – was finally finished.

Three of the WAAC's full-time artists – Eric Ravilious, Albert Richards and Thomas Hennell – had been killed during the war. Yet for two others, Bernard Hailstone and John Worsley, contact with the committee had launched their careers. (The same was true for Richards.) Other artists, too, praised the opportunities the WAAC had given them. Henry Moore, for example, maintained that his war art 'humanised everything I had been doing'.[33] Many more, among them Anthony Gross and Rosemary Allan (she had done some short-term contract work for the WAAC), were grateful to the committee for giving them the opportunity to come to terms with subjects and conditions that were new and challenging, thereby helping them to grow as artists. 'There is one thing I really enjoy in all this,' Gross wrote to Clark in 1940, 'and that is being told to go somewhere, to do something I have never done before, then the arriving there, finding myself face to face with the subject and at last having to work out how to do it, starting from scratch.'[34]

In the larger picture the WAAC had proved both that the relationship between art and the state could be mutually beneficial, and that contemporary art could reach and be meaningful to a large and diverse public. As a *Tatler and Bystander* journalist had argued as early as 1941, 'the War Paintings at the National Gallery almost justify the war. Not for many generations can artists have been in closer touch with the general public….'[35] Much ink has been spilled about both the degree to which the war years fostered a 'renaissance' of interest in British culture, and the success with which such a phenomenon did or did not navigate the changes that permeated post-war cultural expectations, institutions and infrastructures. To its enduring credit, though, the War Artists' Advisory Committee was a key player in raising those questions in the first place, and in nurturing and sustaining the crucial national conversation to which they gave birth.

ENDNOTES

1 Penelope Curtis, *World War Two: A Display of Pictures from the Collection to Mark the 50th Anniversary of the Outbreak of War in September 1939* (Liverpool: Tate Gallery Liverpool, 1989), p.2.
2 Artists' International Association, *Emergency Bulletin* no.3 (September-October 1939): [1].
3 A more detailed discussion of the origins and creation of the WAAC is given in Brian Foss, *War Paint: Art, War, State and Identity in Britain 1939-1945* (New Haven & London: Yale University Press, 2007), pp.9-23.
4 Kenneth Clark, *The Other Half: A Self-portrait* (London: John Murray, 1977), p.22.
5 Printed on the inside front cover flap in all four 1942 booklets.
6 V.S. Pritchett, Graham Sutherland, Kenneth Clark and Henry Moore, 'Art and Life', *Listener* 26 (13 November 1941): 657; Kenneth Clark, quoted in James Hyman, *The Battle for Realism: Figurative Art in Britain during the Cold War* (New Haven & London: Yale University Press, 2001), p.43.
7 J.A. Barlow (Treasury) to Kenneth Clark, 23 January 1943 (IWM [Imperial War Museum, Department of Art Archive]: WA/72/G(1)).
8 Kenneth Clark, 'War Artists at the National Gallery', *Studio*, 123 (January 1942): 2-3.
9 Kenneth Clark, 'Art for the People', *Listener* (23 November 1939): 1000.
10 These were: Edward Bawden, Stephen Bone, Leslie Cole, William Dring, Bernard Hailstone, Thomas Hennell, W.T. Monnington, John Nash, Roland Pitchforth, Eric Ravilious, Leonard Rosoman and sculptor Charles Wheeler.
11 Harald Peake to Paul Nash, 10 November 1940 (Tate Archive: Paul Nash papers, TGA 7050.47).
12 Eric Newton, 'Paul Nash's War Paintings', *Sunday Times* (1 September 1940).
13 Edward Ardizzone, *Diary of a War Artist* (London: John Murray, 1941), p.36 (entry for 17 September 1943).
14 Robert Medley, *Drawn From Life: A Memoir* (London: Faber and Faber, 1983), p.194.
15 Kenneth Clark, quoted in Denis Hart, 'Life in a Frame, Character in a Line', *Daily Telegraph Magazine* (3 September 1976): 34.
16 'In England Now', *The Lancet* 246 (27 October 1945): 540
17 Henry Carr to WAAC, 30 December 1940 (IWM: WA/55/124).
18 J.T.A. Burke to Mr. Leslie (Ministry of Home Security), 29 May 1941 (National Archives, London: HO 186/1209); WAAC, Minutes of 21 May 1941 meeting (IWM: WA/72/E(1)).
19 Laura Knight, 'Introduction', in *War Pictures by British Artists.* Second Series: *Women* (Oxford: Oxford University Press, 1943), p.8.
20 Later in the war four artists – Bernard Hailstone, John Platt, John Piper and Rupert Shephard – were given full-time commissions with the Ministry of War Transport. Hailstone painted the Merchant Marine in the Mediterranean and in North Africa, but the other three concentrated on home front ship, rail and road transport.
21 Stanley Spencer, quoted in *War Pictures by British Artists,* No.1*: War at Sea* (Oxford: Oxford University Press, 1942), p.60.
22 Richard M. Titmuss, *Problems of Social Policy, History of the Second World War: United Kingdom Civil Series* (London: HMSO, and Longmans, Green, 1950), p.335-36, and Appendix 8.
23 WAAC, Minutes of 30 July 1941 meeting (IWM: WA/72/E(2).
24 E.M.O'R. Dickey (WAAC) to Geoffrey Cunliffe (Ministry of Aircraft Production), 24 September 1940 (IWM: WA/55/56).
25 H. Granville Fell, 'The Connoisseur Divan', *Connoisseur* 109 (February 1942): 78.
26 Angus Calder, *The Myth of the Blitz* (London: Jonathan Cape, 1991).
27 Stephen Spender, 'Introduction', in *War Pictures by British Artists,* Second Series: *Air Raids* (Oxford: Oxford University Press, 1943), p.5.
28 WAAC, Minutes of the 29 November 1939 and 14 February 1940 meetings (IWM: WA/72/A).
29 WAAC, Minutes of the 23 November 1939 meeting (IWM: WA/72/A); Kenneth Clark, "Art for the People": 999-1001.
30 Herbert Read, 'The War as Seen by British Artists', in *Britain at War*, ed. Monroe Wheeler (New York: Museum of Modern Art, 1941), p.12.
31 Royal Academy, Minutes of the 11 December 1945 and 20 June 1946 meetings (RA: 397/RAA/1/28).
32 [Kenneth Clark], 'Preface', in *Exhibition of National War Pictures (And a Few Pieces of Sculpture)* (London: Royal Academy of Arts, 1945), p.4.
33 Henry Moore, quoted in Peter Stansky and William Abrahams, *London's Burning: Life, Death and Art in the Second World War* (London: Constable, 1994), p.48.
34 Anthony Gross to Kenneth Clark, April 1940, quoted in Alan Ross, *Colours of War: War Art 1939-45* (London: Jonathan Cape, 1983), p.150; Rosemary Allan, recorded interview 3820/3 (IWM Sound Archive, 1978).
35 "Seven of the New War Pictures at the National Gallery," *Tatler and Bystander*, 21 May 1941: 282-83.

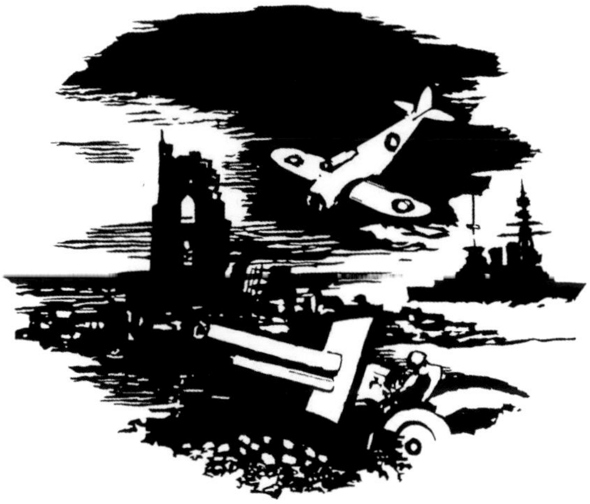

CATALOGUE

Morley Gallery

Morley College,
61 Westminster Bridge Road, London, SE1 7HT

Friday 28 October - Wednesday 23 November 2016

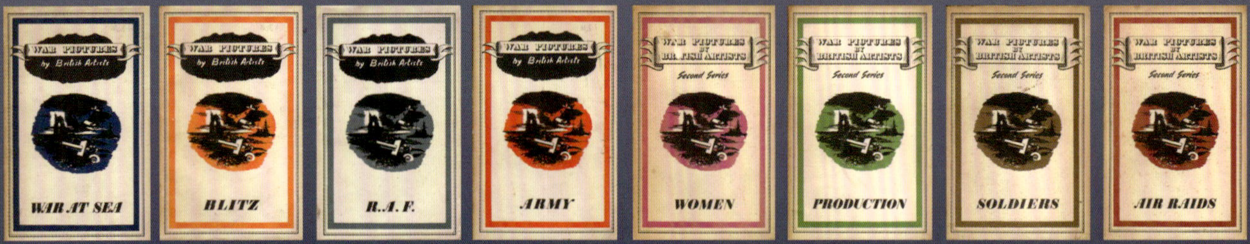

This catalogue follows the four themes set out in the original publication *War Pictures by British Artists* (1942) and the four additional themes set out in the Second Series, (1943). As such the division of work is quite loosely defined: images in *Army* overlap with those of the Second Series *Soldiers*; likewise *Blitz*, repeats much of the theme of the Second Series *Air Raids*.

The original publications were inevitably limited by poor quality war-time paper and with reproductions in black and white only. By definition the WAAC publications were also limited to the work of artists who took part in the scheme. In this new publication we have been at liberty to choose work from both artists who did and who did not submit work to the WAAC. Artists whose work contributed to the original scheme are indicated in the index on the following page in bold.

NB Catalogue numbers marked with an * will not be included in the exhibition at Morley Gallery.
Fuller catalogue entries can be found at www.llfa.gallery.

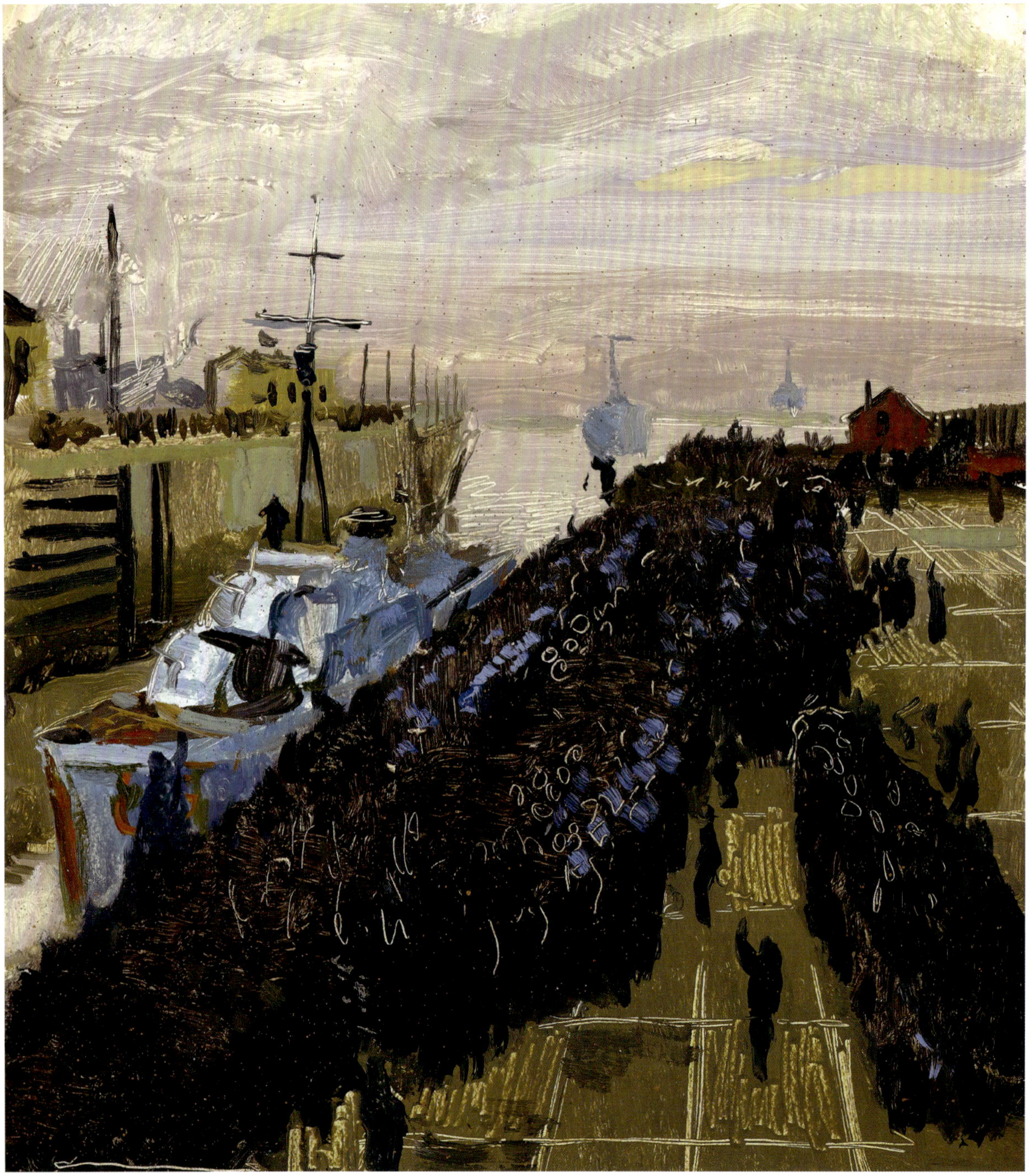

CAT. 1 – **Stephen Bone** (1904-1958), Study for *Arrival of Second Escort Group of Sloops at Liverpool*, 1944, oil on paper with scratching out, 12 ¼ x 11 in. (32 x 28 cm).

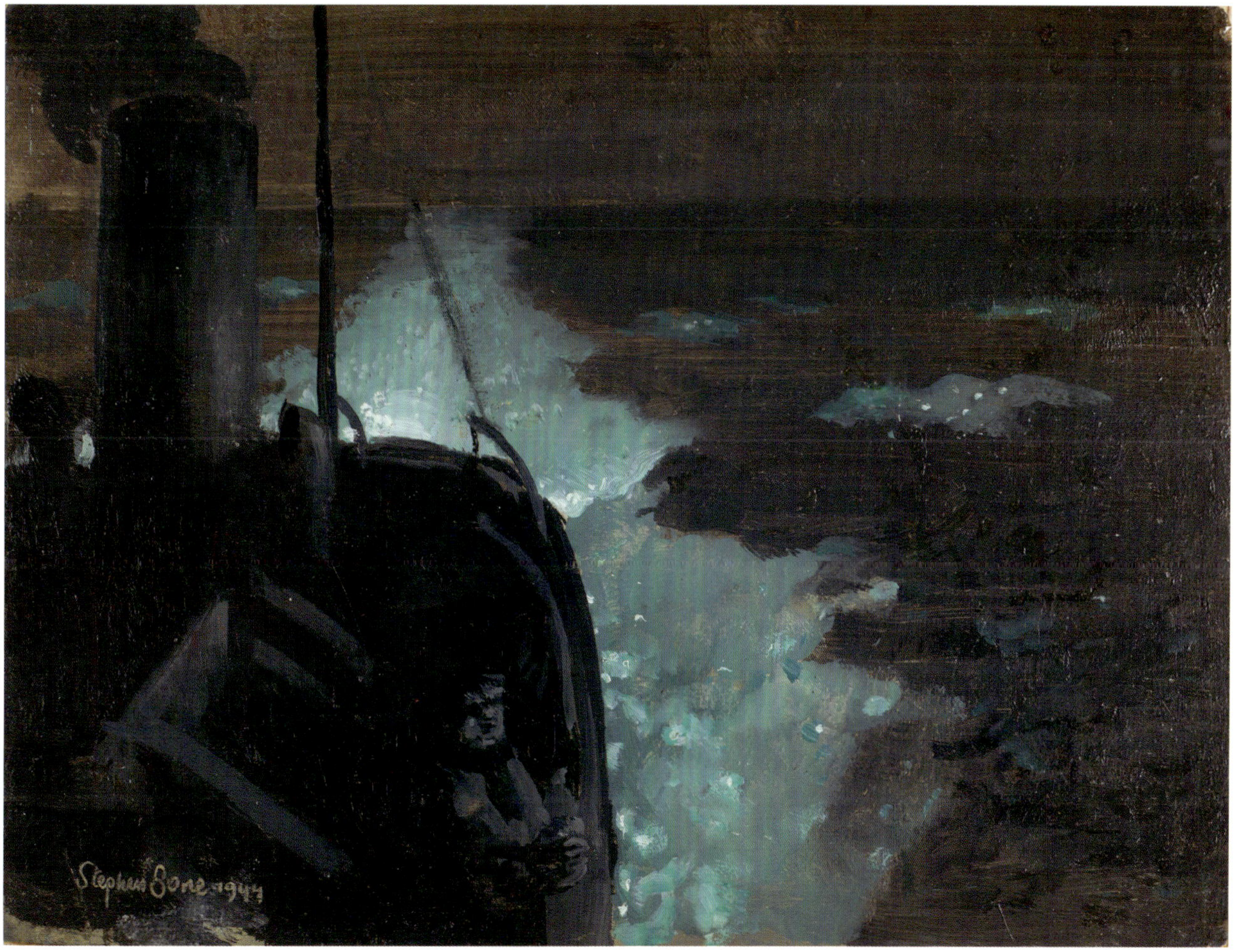

CAT. 2 – **Stephen Bone** (1904-1958), *The night watch, (Normandy landings)*, 1944, signed and dated, oil on board, 10 x 13 ½ in. (25.5 x 34.3 cm).

At the outbreak of WW2, Steven Bone enlisted as an Officer in the Civil Defence Camouflage Establishment based in Leamington Spa. In June 1943 he was appointed by the War Artists' Advisory Committee to be a full-time salaried artist to the Ministry of Information specialising in Admiralty subjects. In 1944 he witnessed the Normandy landings and recorded the event in a number of sketches. This panel, which shows a small ship steaming through the night, is probably one such eye-witness account. The viewpoint is from the bridge looking aft, with ventilators either side of the funnel and the davits for the lifeboats. A seaman, most likely on night-watch, is visible in the foreground. The light blue behind is the ship's phosphorescent wake.

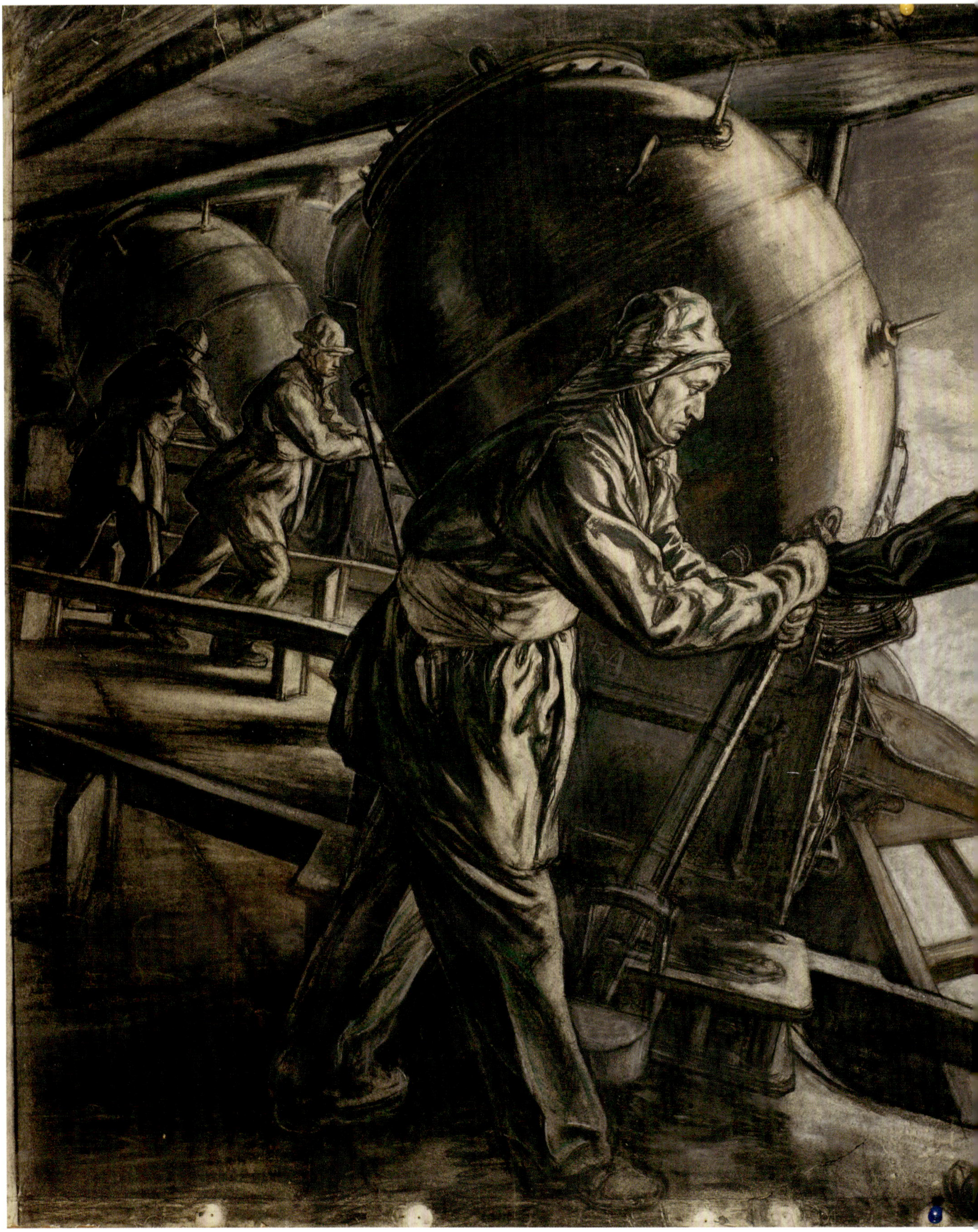

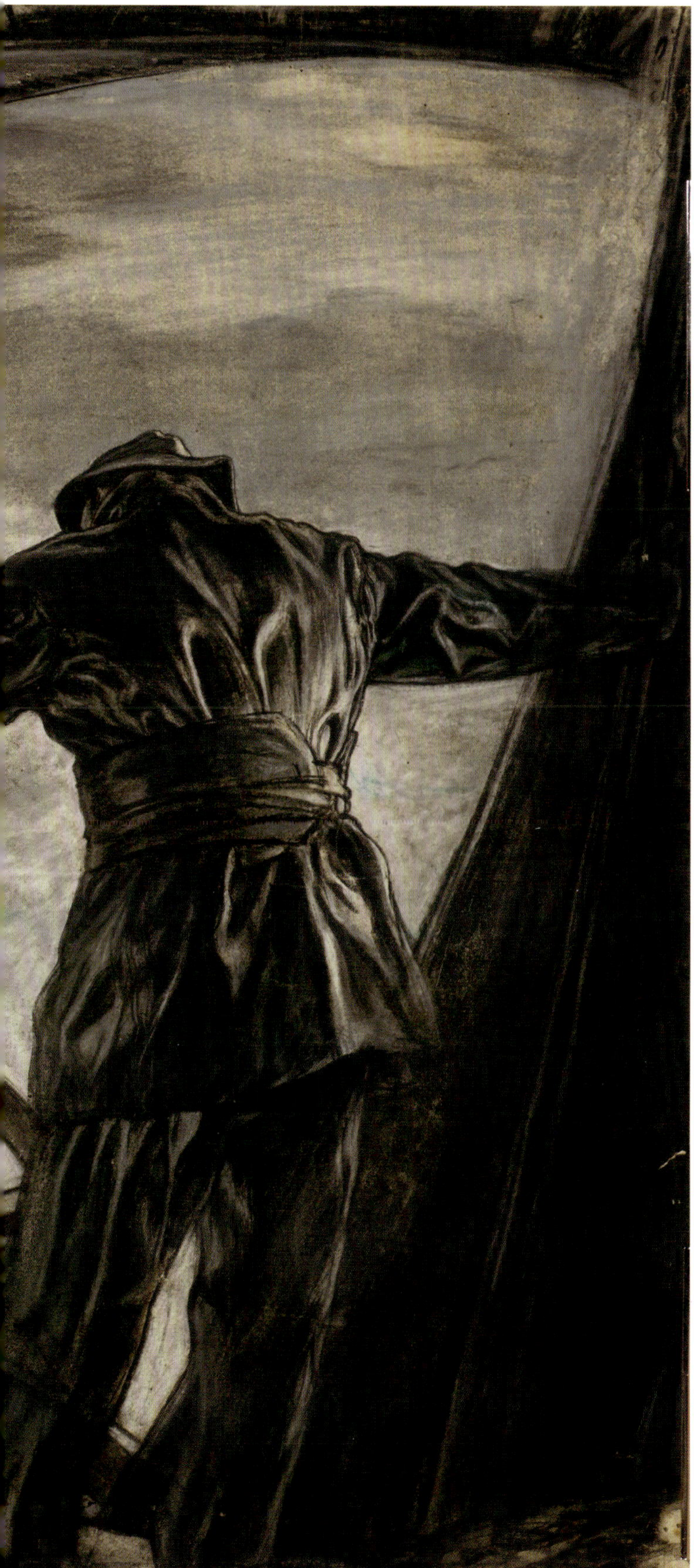

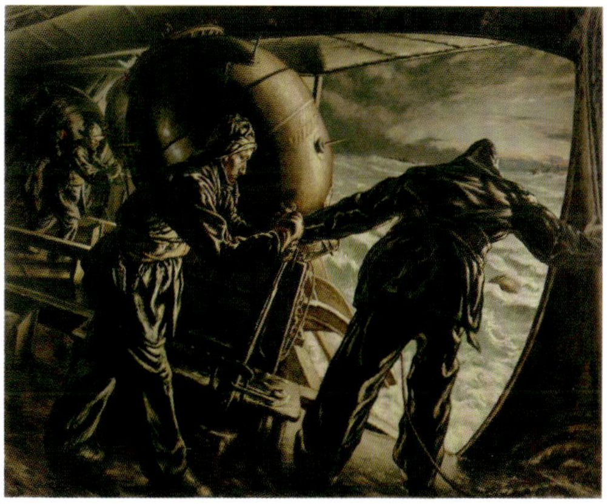

FIG. 1 – **Muirhead Bone** (1876-1953)
Winter Mine-laying off Iceland, 1942,
oil on canvas, 50 ½ x 63 ¼ in. (127.9 x 160.6 cm)
© Imperial War Museums (IWM Art LD 1932)

CAT. 3 – **Muirhead Bone** (1876-1953)
Study for *Winter Mine-Laying off Iceland*, c.1942,
charcoal and coloured chalk on paper,
29 x 39 in. (73.5 x 99 cm).
Provenance: The Artist's Family; thence by desent.

Muirhead Bone was appointed as one of Britain's first official war artists in May 1916. His small black and white drawings were widely reproduced in war-time government-funded publications. In early 1940, at the age of 64 years, Muirhead Bone was again appointed as a war artist, commissioned as a major in the Royal Marines. His pictures of WW2 were on a much larger scale. In London he drew St Paul's Cathedral from the ruined roof of St Bride's Church and the destruction in the East End docks. In Scotland he drew battleships and minesweepers at work in stormy seas. This study for *Winter Mine-Laying off Iceland*, 1942, is almost identical to the finished version, in the Imperial War Museum, though smaller and there is a slight difference in the positioning of the figure to the far right.

OVERLEAF:
CAT 4-9 – **Muirhead Bone** (1876-1953)
6 studies for *Winter Mine-Laying off Iceland*, c.1942.

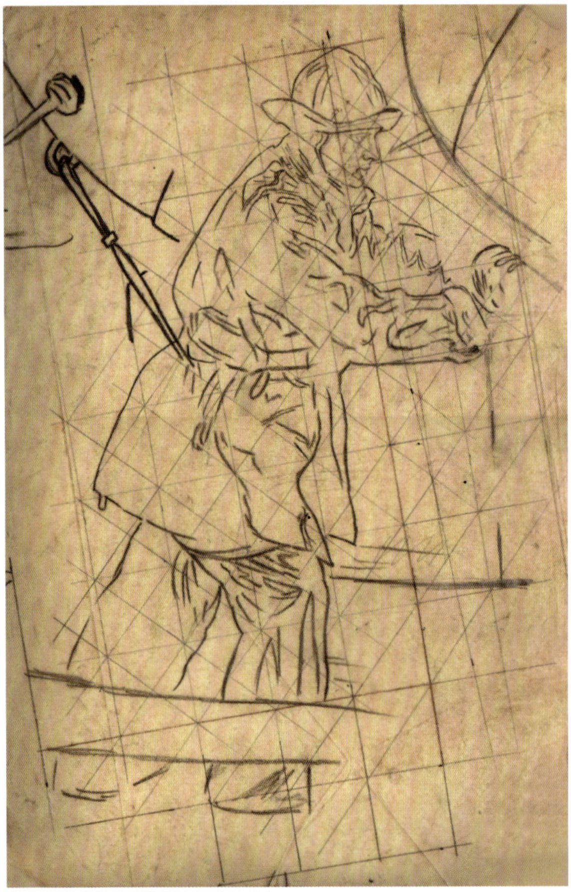

CAT. 4 – *Conté à Paris* carbon pencil on tracing paper, 20 x 13 in. (50.5 x 33.5 cm).

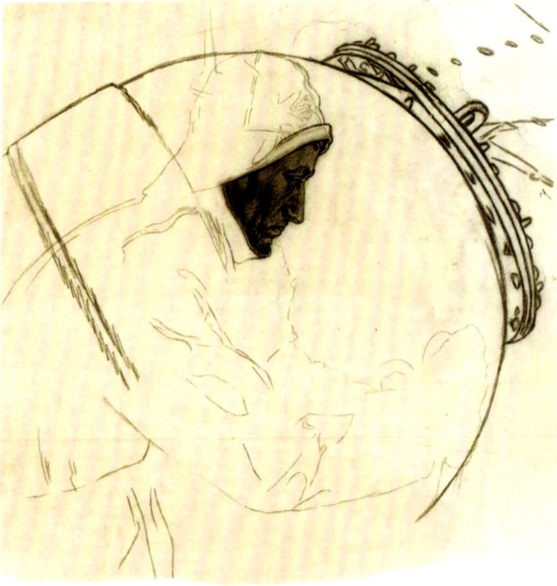

CAT. 5 – *Conté à Paris* carbon pencil on tracing paper, 20 x 20 in. (50.8 x 50.8 cm).

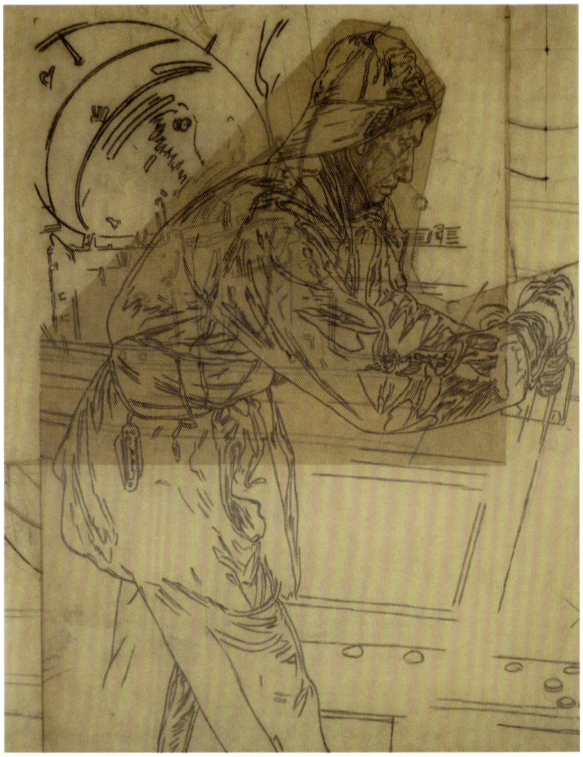

CAT. 6 – *Conté à Paris* carbon pencil on tracing paper, 29 ¼ x 23 ¼ in. (74.3 x 58.6 cm).

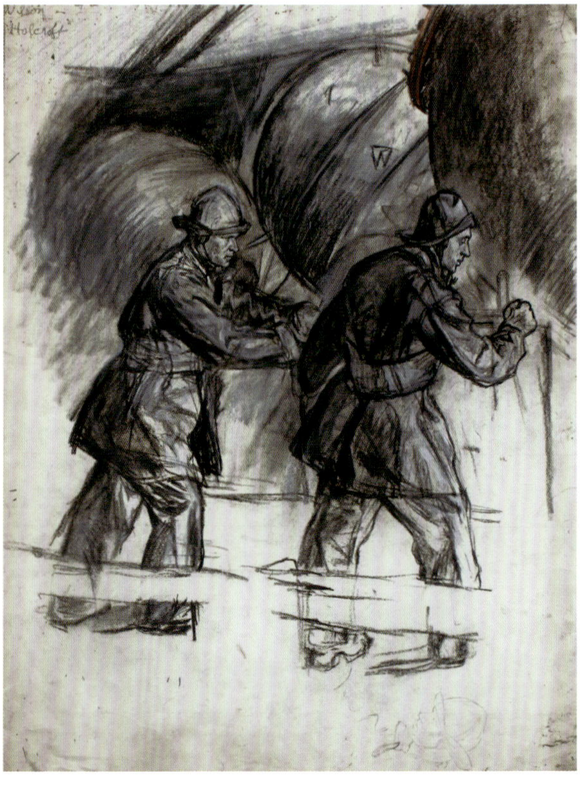

CAT. 7 – *Conté à Paris* carbon pencil, pastel on paper, 30 x 23 in. (76.5 x 58.5 cm).

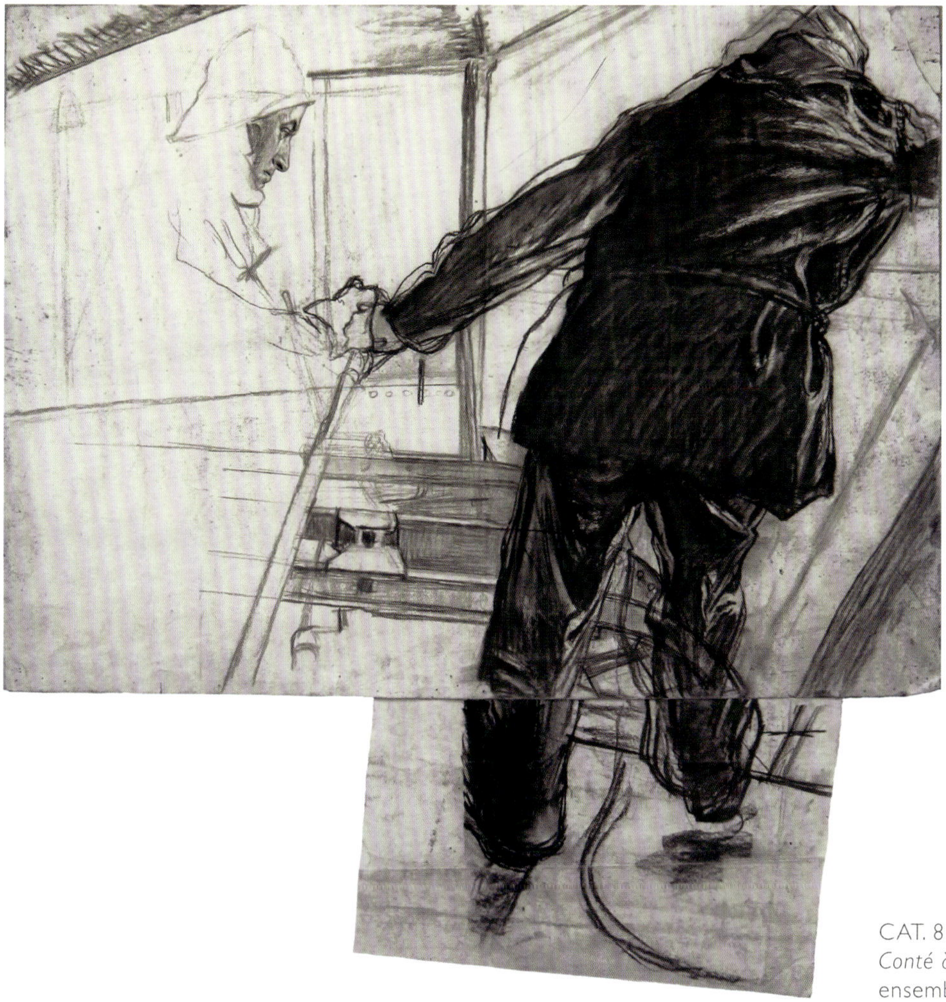

CAT. 8 –
Conté à Paris carbon pencil on paper,
ensemble: 31 x 31 in. (79 x 79 cm).

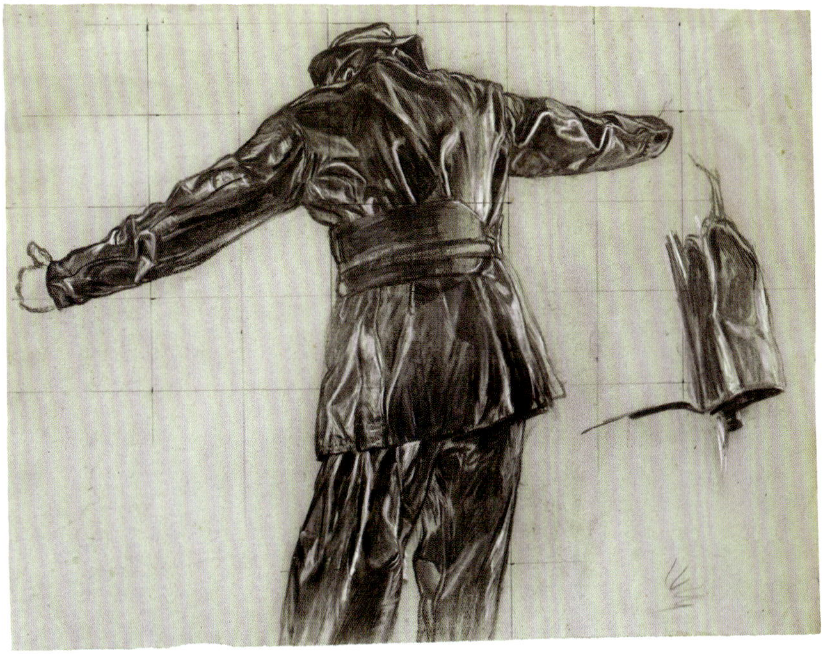

CAT. 9 –
Conté à Paris carbon pencil with
highlights in white chlak on paper,
18 ¾ x 24 ½ in. (47.6 x 62.5 cm).

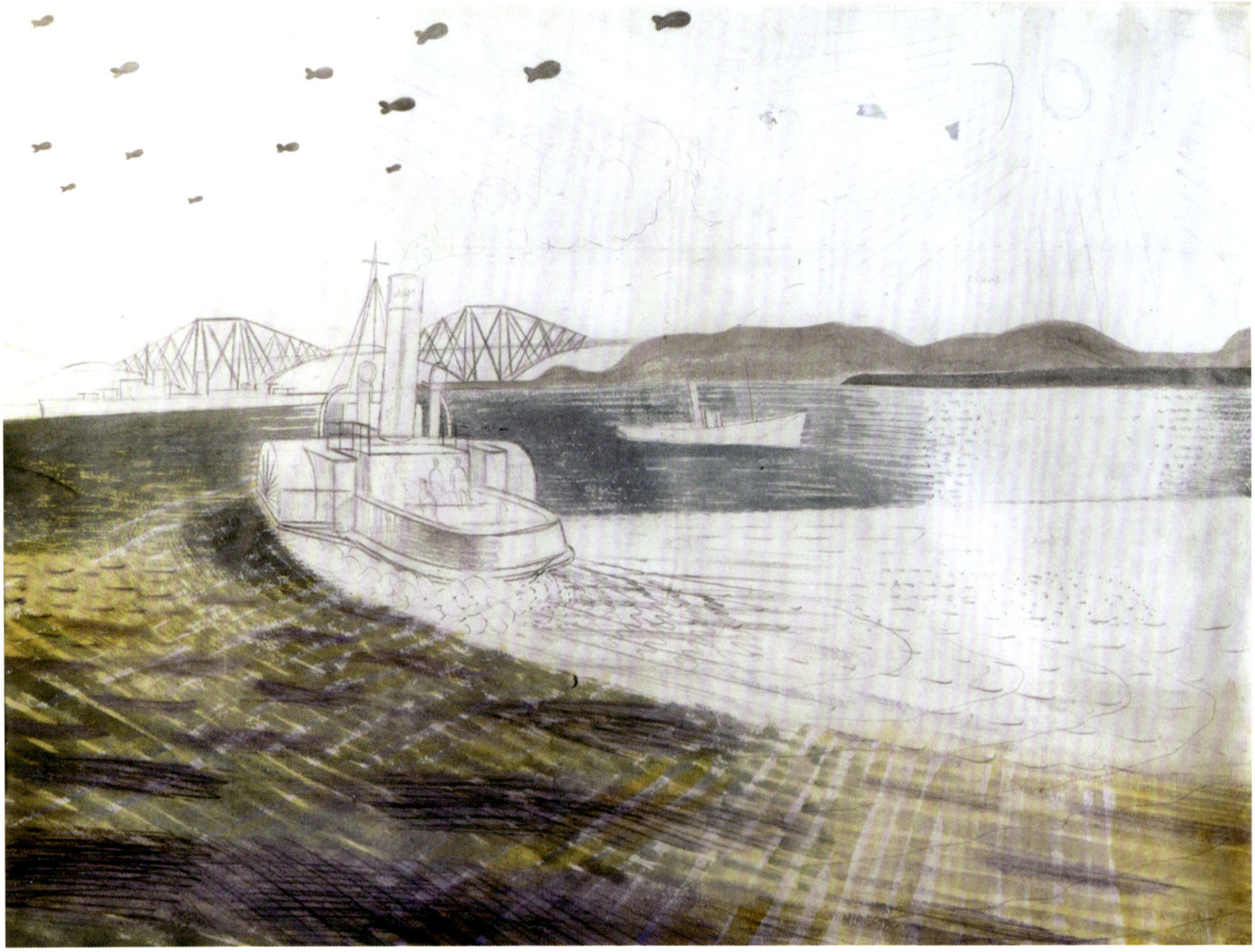

CAT. 10* – **Eric Ravilious** (1903-42), Study for "Leaving Scapa Flow' (recto), c.1940–41, signed, watercolour over pencil, 17 ¼ x 23 in. (43.7 x 58.5 cm).
Provenance: Artist's family until 2005; private collection. Exhibited: Eastbourne Towner Art Gallery, extended loan; The Twentieth Century, The Fine Art Society, London, October 2005 (cat. no. 24).
Literature: Anne Ullmann (ed.), Ravilious at War, The Fleece Press, Upper Denby, Huddersfield, 2002, illus. p. 101, no. 50.

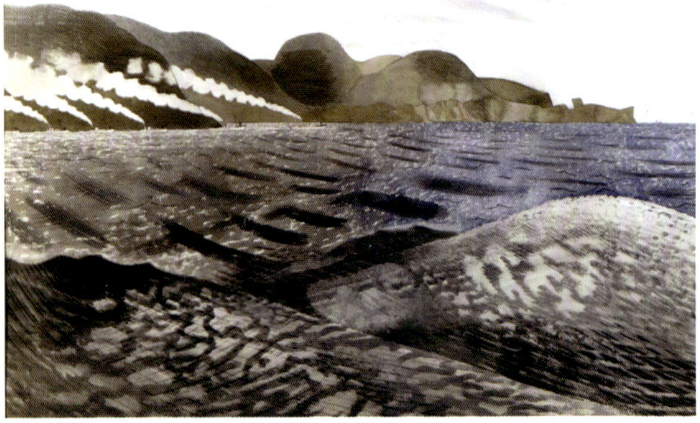

iFIG. 2 – Study for 'Leaving Scapa Flow' (verso)

Scapa Flow is a body of water in the Orkney Islands, Scotland, and was the site of Britain's chief naval base during the Second World War. Churchill ordered the construction of a series of causeways to block the eastern approaches after Scapa Flow was penetrated by German submarine U-47 in October 1939. Ravilious refers to Leaving Scapa Flow in a letter to E.M.O'R. Dickey on 20 June 1940, as one of a series of watercolours intended for exhibition, probably for a war effort show at the National Gallery, London, organised by the Artists' Advisory Committee (see Anne Ullmann [ed.], *Ravilious at War*, Upper Denby 2002, p. 99). The finished watercolour is in the collection of Cartwright Hall, Bradford. In July 1941, again attached to the Admiralty as an Official War Artist, Ravilious painted on the Isle of May, in Scotland, near the Firth of Forth. Weekly east coast convoys formed there to make their hazardous voyages down to Sheerness in Kent. The Forth Bridge here is shown protected by Barrage Balloons. Ravilious was killed on 2 September 1942, accompanying a Royal Air Force air-sea rescue mission off Iceland.

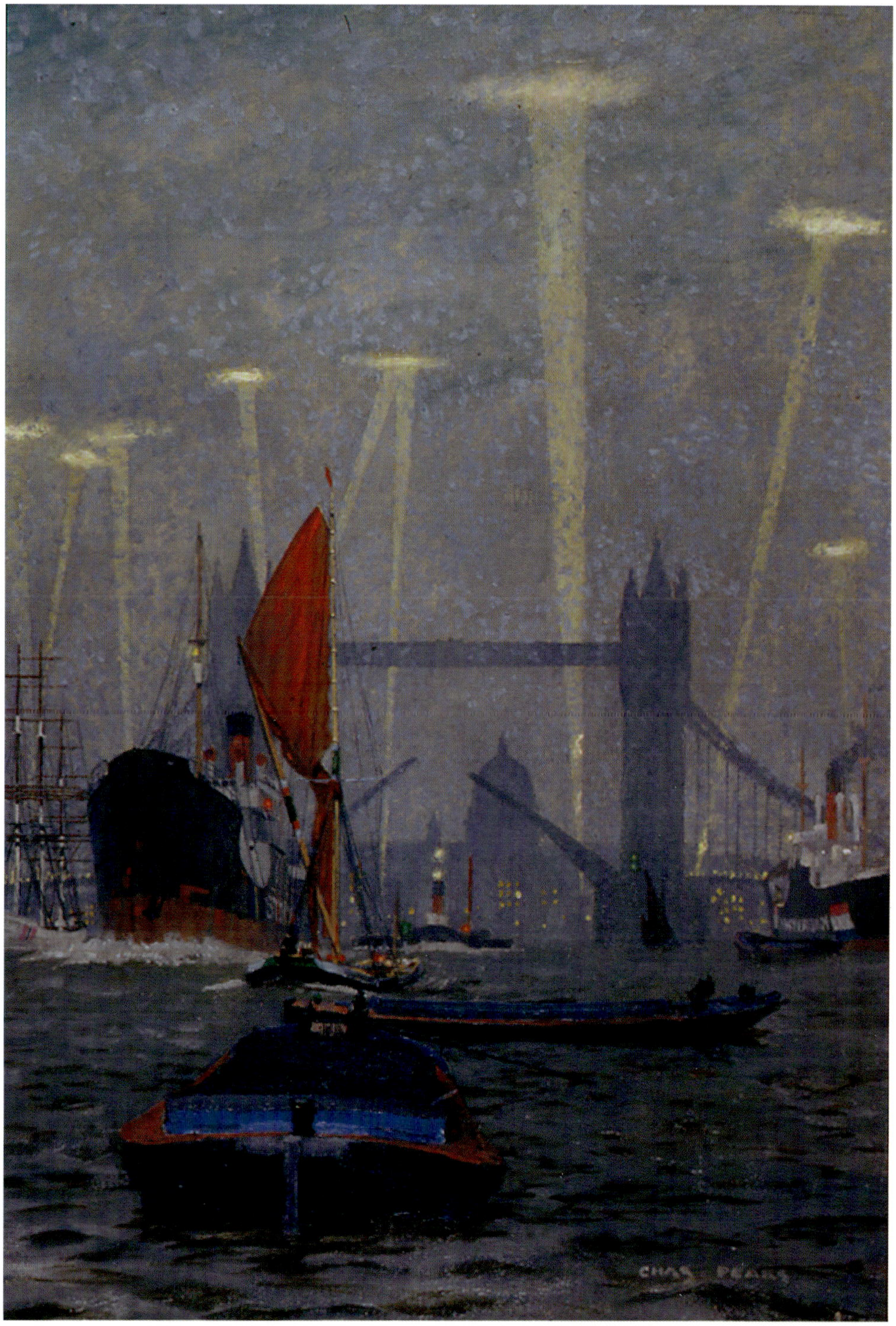

CAT. 11* – **Charles Pears** (1873-1958), *Searchlight Practice*, 1940,
oil on panel, 20 x 14 in. (50.8 x 35.6 cm).
Provenance: Laporte Corporate Collection 2002; Private Collection.

Pears was an Official War Artist for the Admiralty during WWI, a position he repeated during WW2.

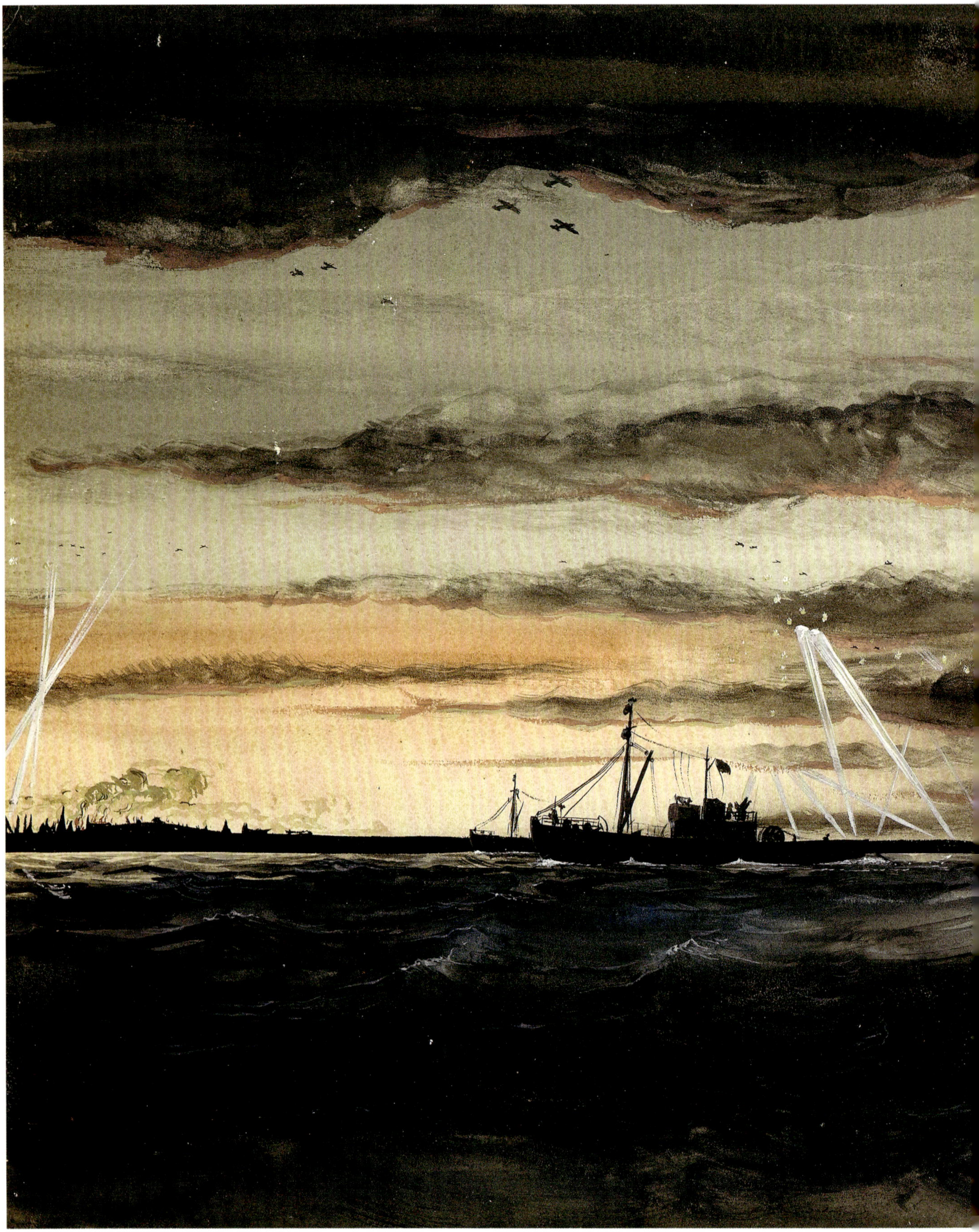

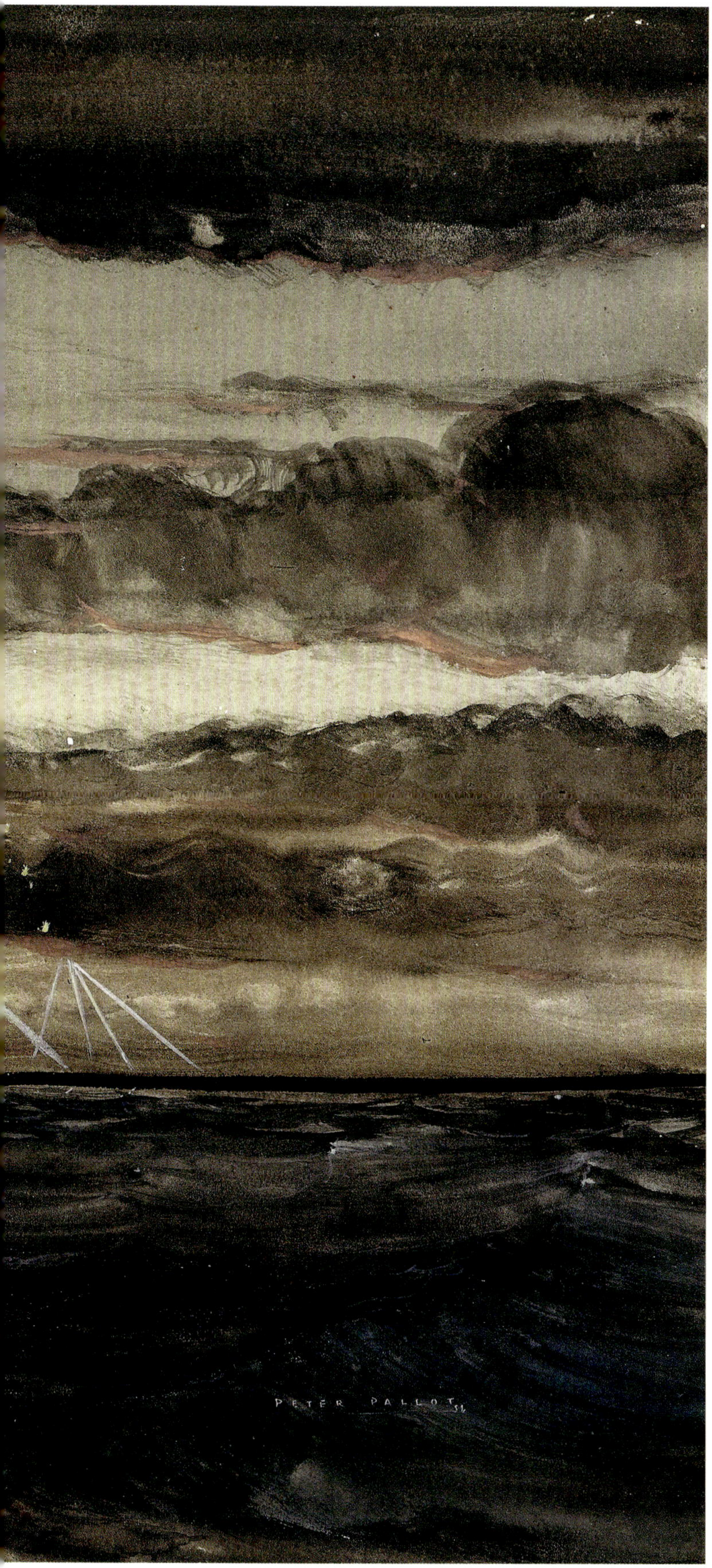

CAT. 12 – **Peter Pallot**
Making for home in an air raid, c.1939, signed and dated, watercolour and gum arabic on board, 13 ¼ × 18 in. (33.7 × 46 cm).

This depicts the approach to a port during an air raid. The boat in silhouette may be an armed trawler. The port's cranes are visible on the horizon to the far left.

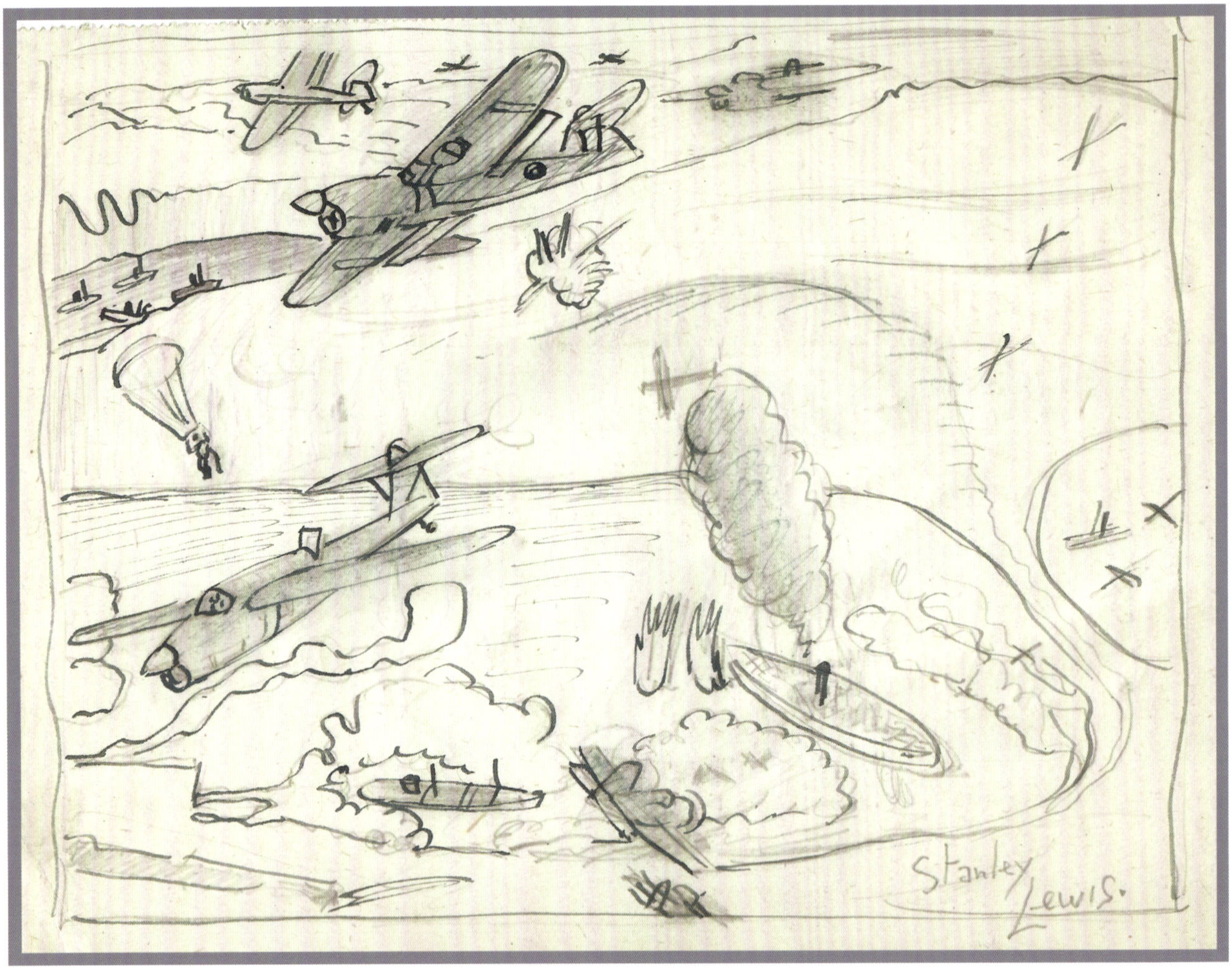

CAT. 13 – **Stanley Lewis** (1905-2009), Study for *The Attack on the Tirpitz by the Fleet Air Arm*, 1944, signed, pen and ink and wash on paper, 6 ¾ x 8 ¼ in. (17 x 21 cm.).
Provenance: The Artist's Family.
Literature: *The Unknown Artist: Stanley Lewis and his contemporaries*, Cecil Higgins Art Gallery & Bedford Museum, 12th June - 5th September 2010. p113.

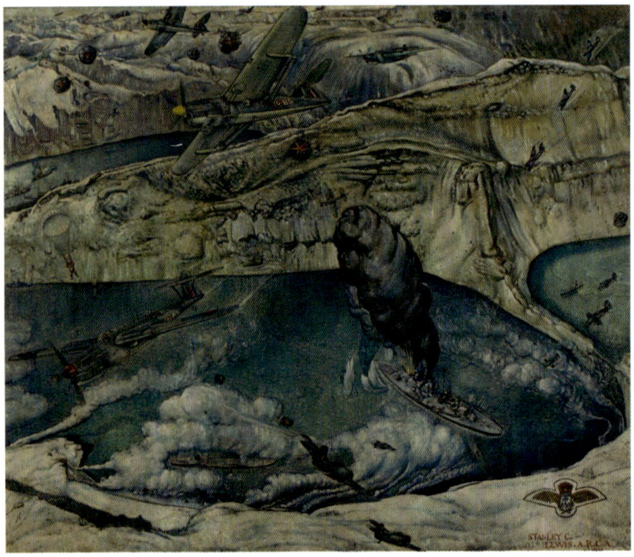

FIG. 3 – **Stanley Lewis** (1905-2009),
Fleet Air Arm Attack on the 'Tirpitz', 1944,
oil on sacking, 29 x 35 ½ in. (74 x 90 cm).
Fleet Air Arm Museum, Accession number E01594.

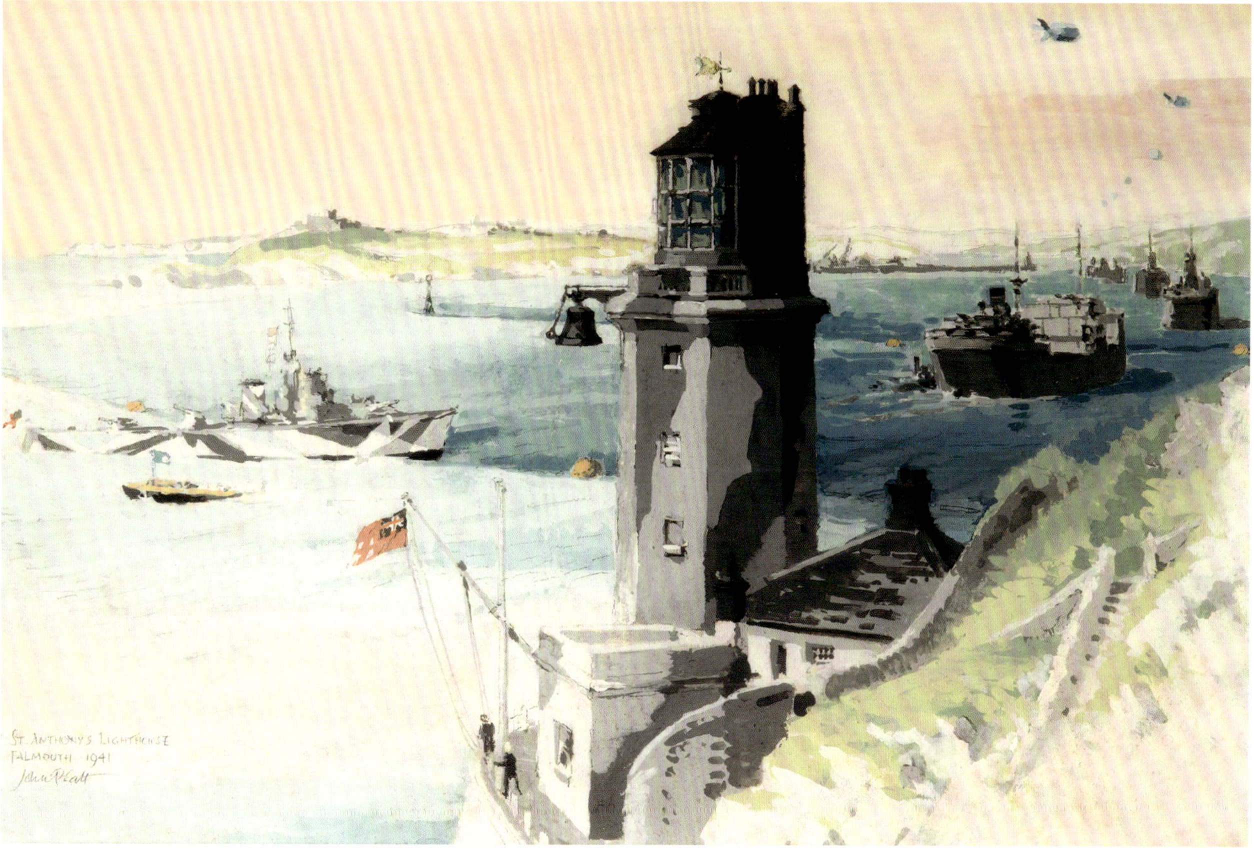

CAT. 14 – **John Edgar Platt** (1886-1967), *St Anthony's Lighthouse, Falmouth*, 1941, signed and dated, watercolour on paper. 8 ½ x 13 ¼ in. (22 x 34 cm).

The convoy system had been introduced during WW1 and proved that ships sailing in organised groups, and escorted by Royal Navy warships, were much less likely to be sunk.

Platt's watercolour shows a convoy arriving safely at Falmouth, passing between St. Anthony's Lighthouse and Pendennis Castle. The convoy is flying kite balloons to discourage attacks by dive-bombers. Bringing up the rear is a Hunt Type 1 Class escort destroyer painted with dazzle camouflage.

This is a study for an oil painting which Platt produced for the WAAC and is now part of the collection of the National Maritime Museum. The WAAC accepted a number of Platt's paintings of convoys and wartime traffic on the Thames.

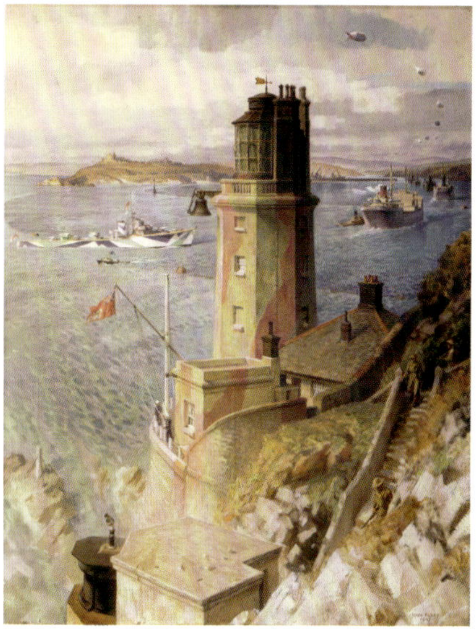

FIG. 4 – *Convoy Arriving off St Anthony's Lighthouse, Falmouth*, 1942, oil on canvas, 36 x 28 in. (91.3 x 71 cm). National Maritime Museum, Greenwich, London. Presented by the War Artists Advisory Committee 1947.

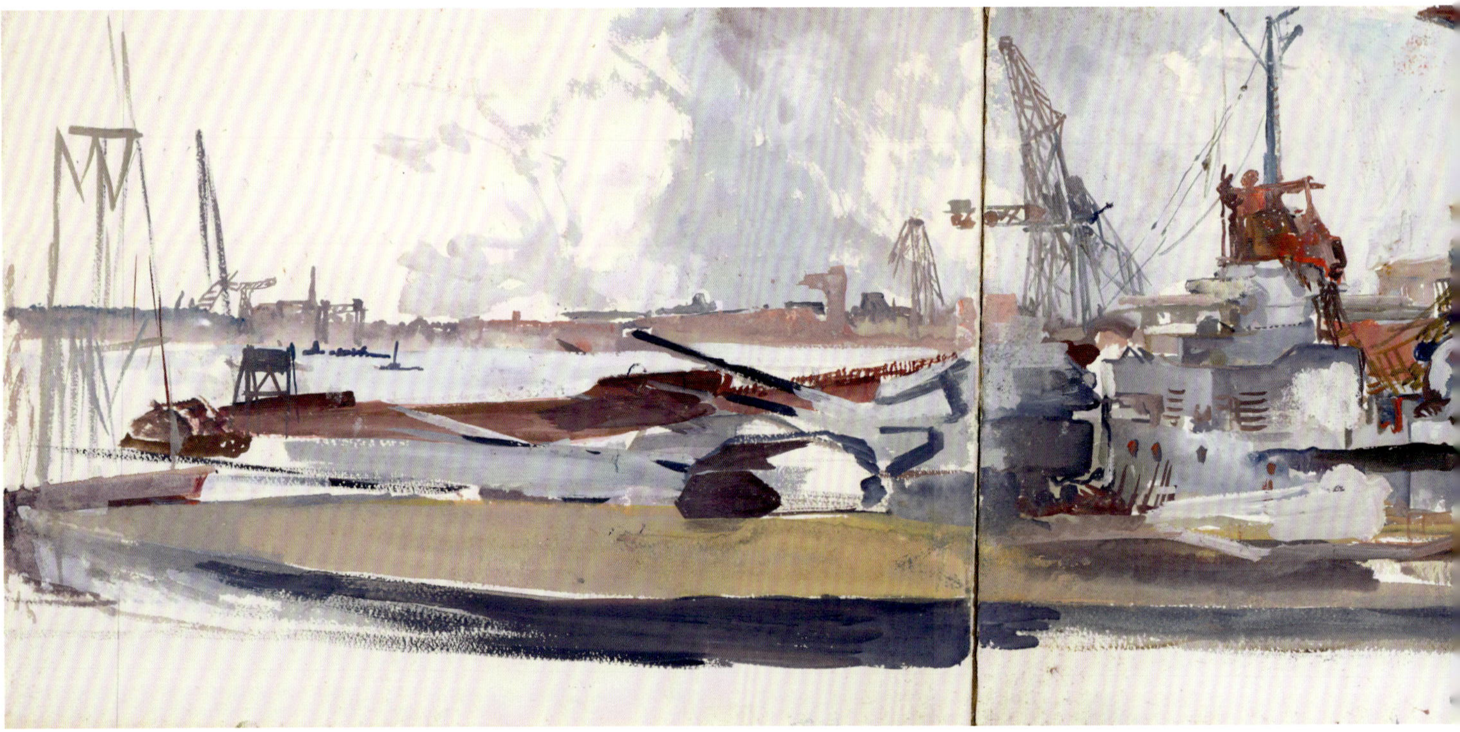

CAT. 15 – **Charles Cundall** (1890-1971), Study for *Hipper at Kiel*, c.1945, incribed with title, oil on thick paper, across three sheets, 14 x 60 ½ in. (36 x 154 cm).

Exhibited: *Charles Cundall – A Working Method*, Young Gallery Salisbury, March- April 2016, Sotheran's, April-May 2016.
Literature: *Charles Cundall – A Working Method*, Edited by Sacha Llewellyn & Paul Liss, published by Liss Llewellyn Fine Art, February 2016.

In July 1940, the WAAC offered Cundall a salaried six-month contract with the Admiralty, focusing on the work of the Merchant Navy: a timely subject that had been urged on the Admiralty by the Chamber of Shipping the previous spring. In 1941, after a brief lull following the end of his Admiralty employment early in the year, he was transferred to the Air Ministry, where he remained until 1945. Muirhead Bone wrote the catalogue Foreward for one of Cundall's exhibitions in 1927 praising him as a "detached observer we feel we can trust".

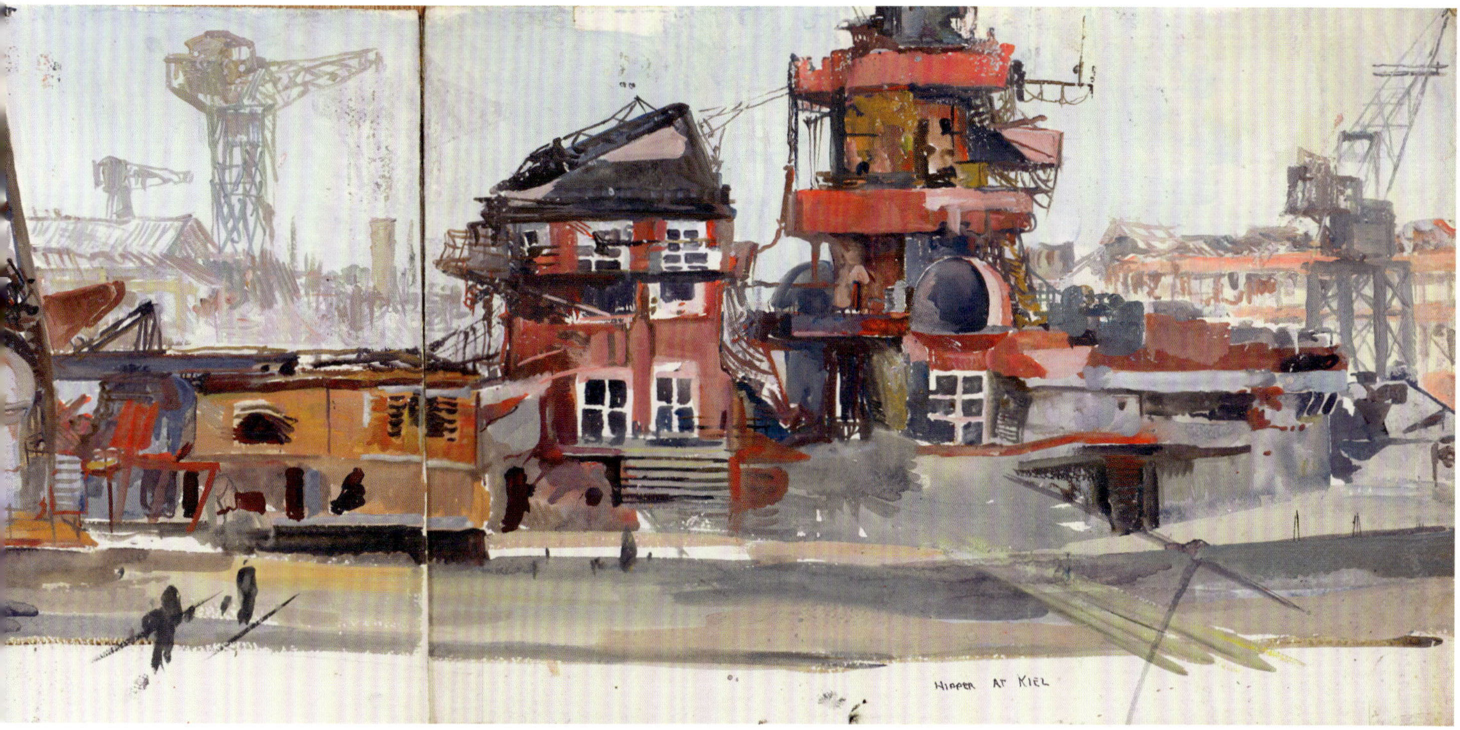

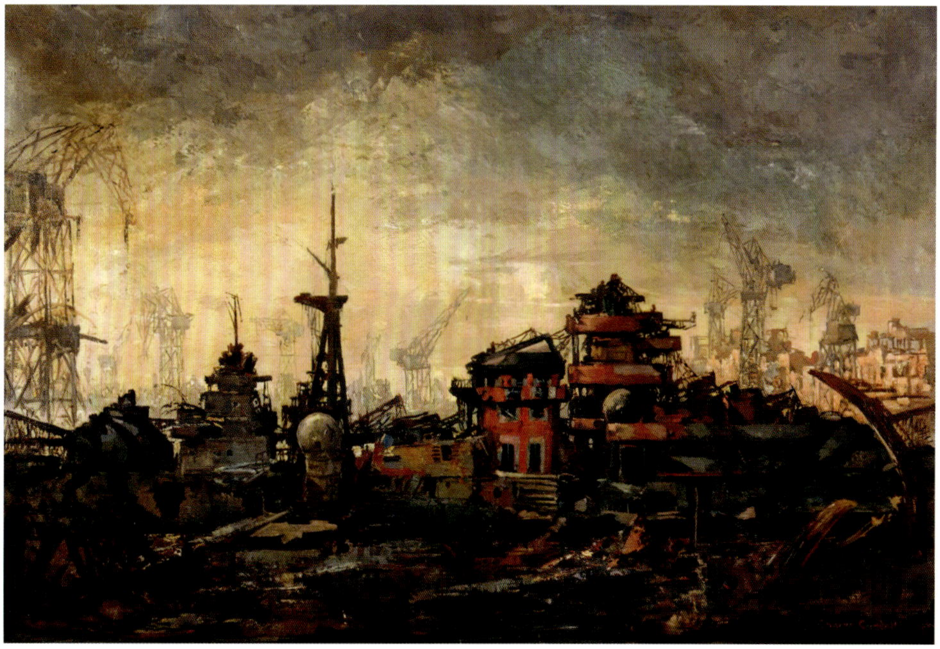

FIG. 5 – **Charles Cundall** (1890-1971), *The Hipper at Kiel*, 1945,
oil on canvas, 32 x 48 in. (81.3 x 121.9 cm) Glasgow Museums Resource Centre (GMRC)
Acquisition method: presented by the War Artists' Advisory Committee through the IWM, 1948.

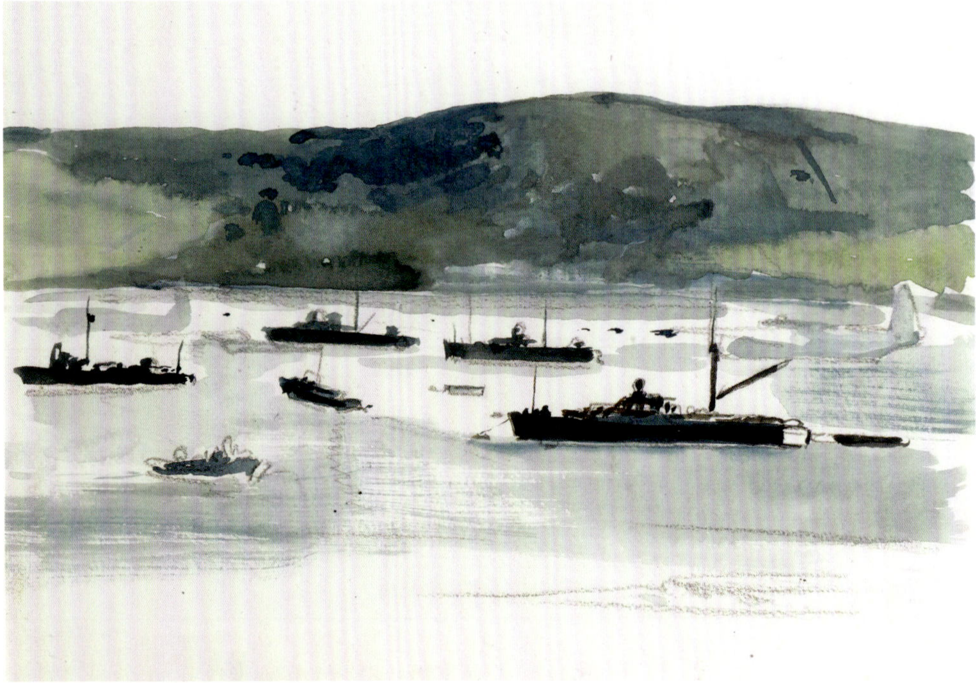

CAT. 16 – **Charles Cundall** (1890-1971), possibly a study for *Tobermory from the Admiral's Flagship*, c.1942, pencil and watercolour on paper, 7 x 9 ½ in. (17.5 x 24.5 cm).
Provenance: acquired directly from the artist's daughter.

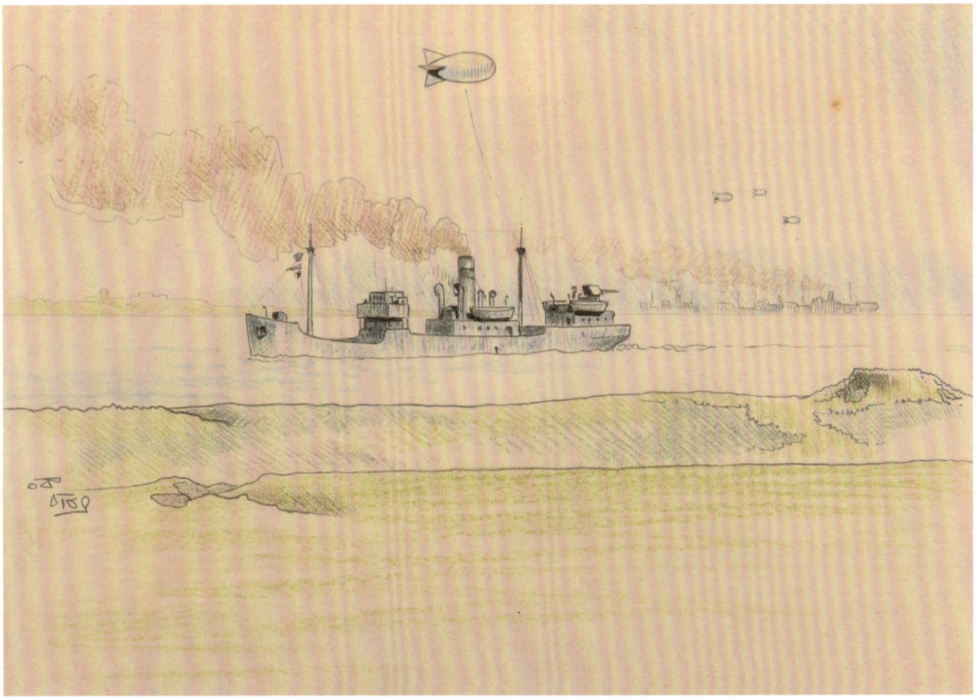

CAT. 17 – **Lt Richard Barrett Talbot Kelly** (1896-1971),
An Armoured merchantman in the Thames Estuary,
pencil and coloured crayons on paper, 6 x 8 ¾ in. (15.5 x 21.7 cm).

Merchant ships were often provided with their own small artillery piece mounted at the stern and served by the crew. Barrage balloons were fitted to both merchant and Royal Navy ships as a means of offering some protection against dive-bombing attacks by Stukas and other Luftwaffe aircraft.

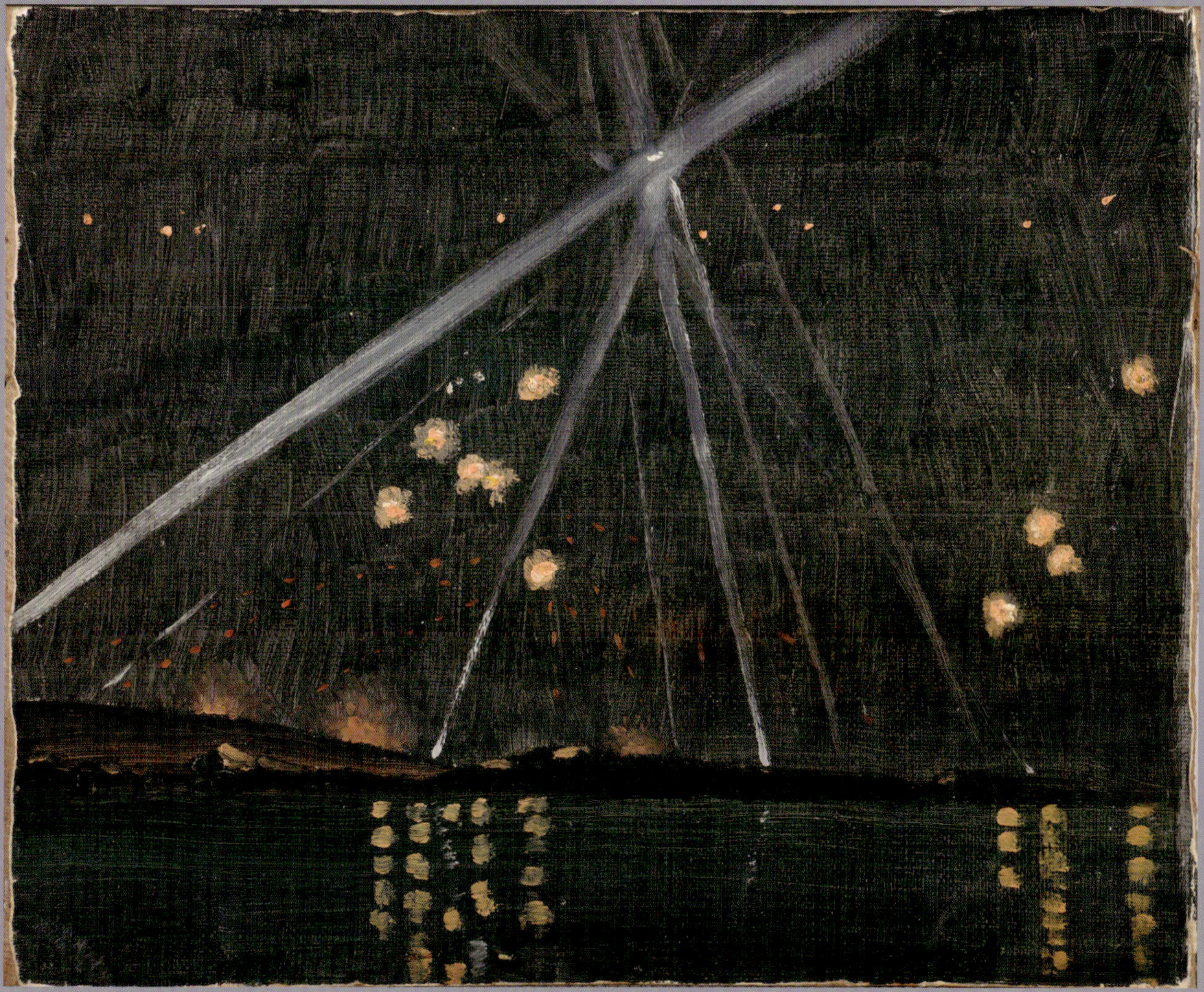

CAT. 18 – **English School**, *Air raid with aircraft caught in intersecting searchlights*,
oil on canvas board, 9 ¼ x 11 ¼ in. (23.5 x 28.5 cm)
Provenance: private collection

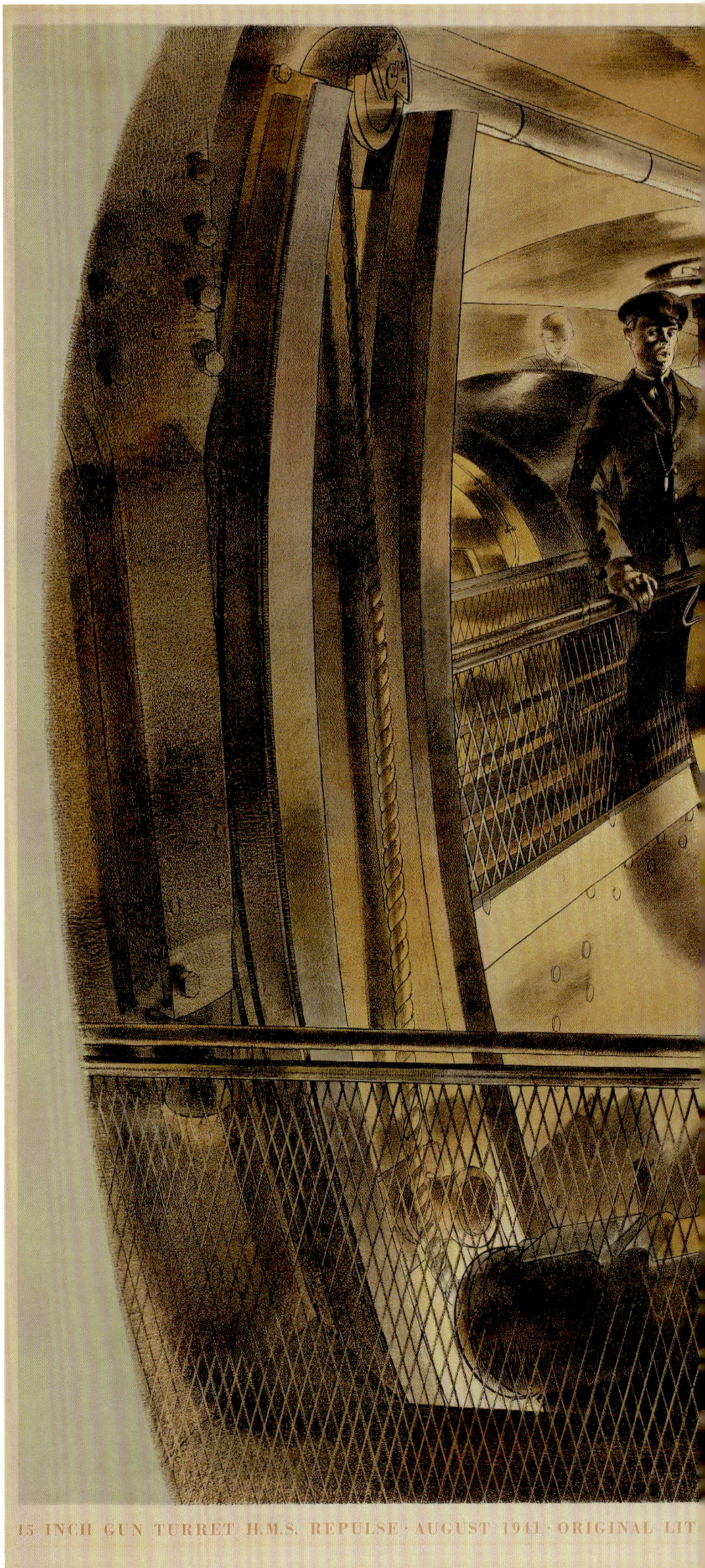

CAT. 19 –
Barnett Freedman (1901-1958), *15-inch Gun Turret,* HMS *Repulse*, 1941,
Lithograph, 30 x 40 in. (76.3 x 101.3 cm),
Original lithographic poster printed for the National Gallery.

Barnett Freedman was one of the first artists to be commissioned by the War Artists Advisory Committee at the start of WW2. He was posted to France staying on as long as possible before being evacuated. He was to return in 1944 to record the setting up of operational harbours in Normandy. In between, his interest was in recording operational methods and he was commissioned to work for the Admiralty, and specifically on HMS *Repulse*, in July 1941. On 10 December the same year Japanese aircraft attacked and sank the *Repulse* and the battleship HMS *Prince of Wales* off the coast of Malaya, with the loss of 840 lives.

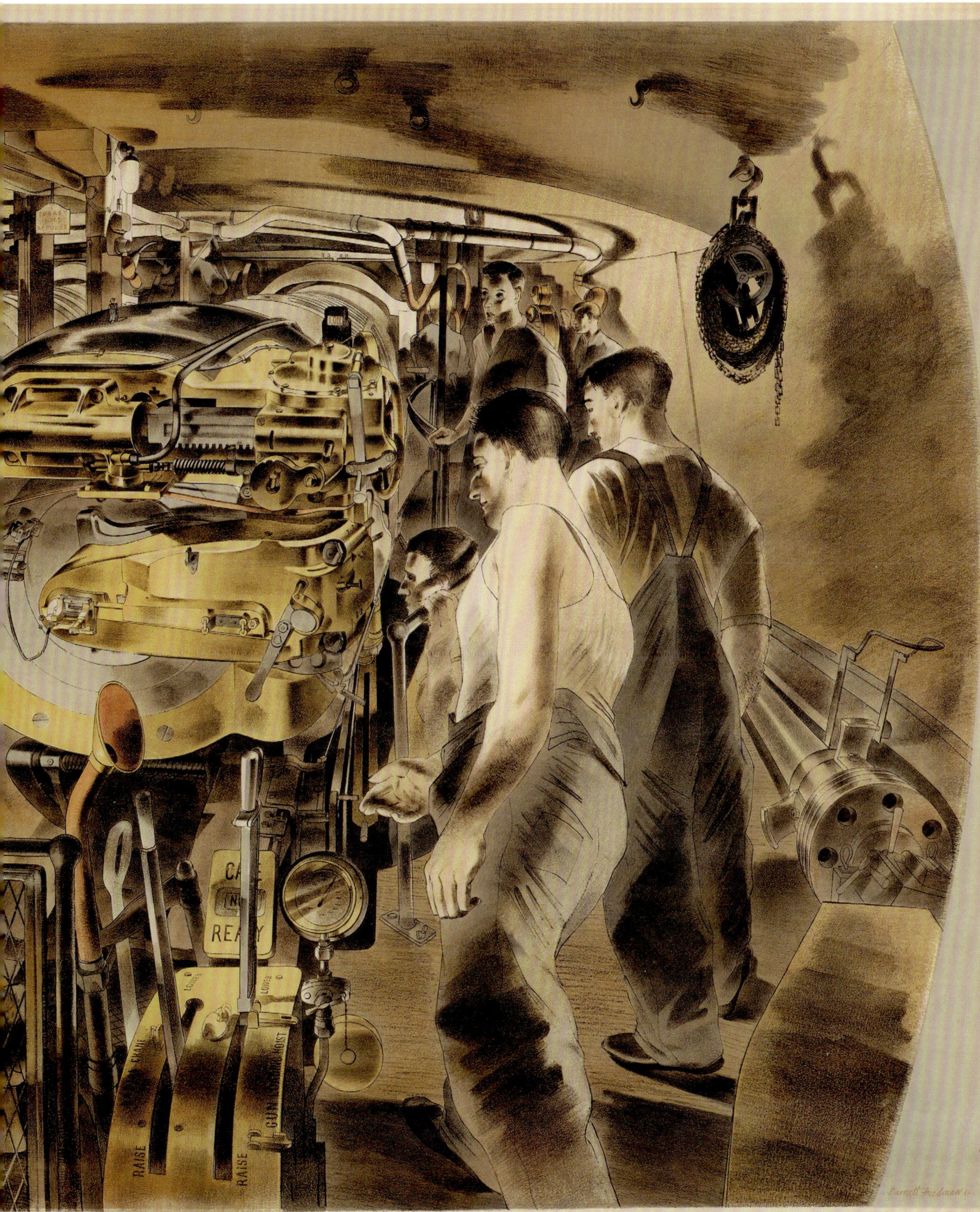

BY BARNETT FREEDMAN

Published by the National Gallery Crown Copyright reserved
The Baynard Press

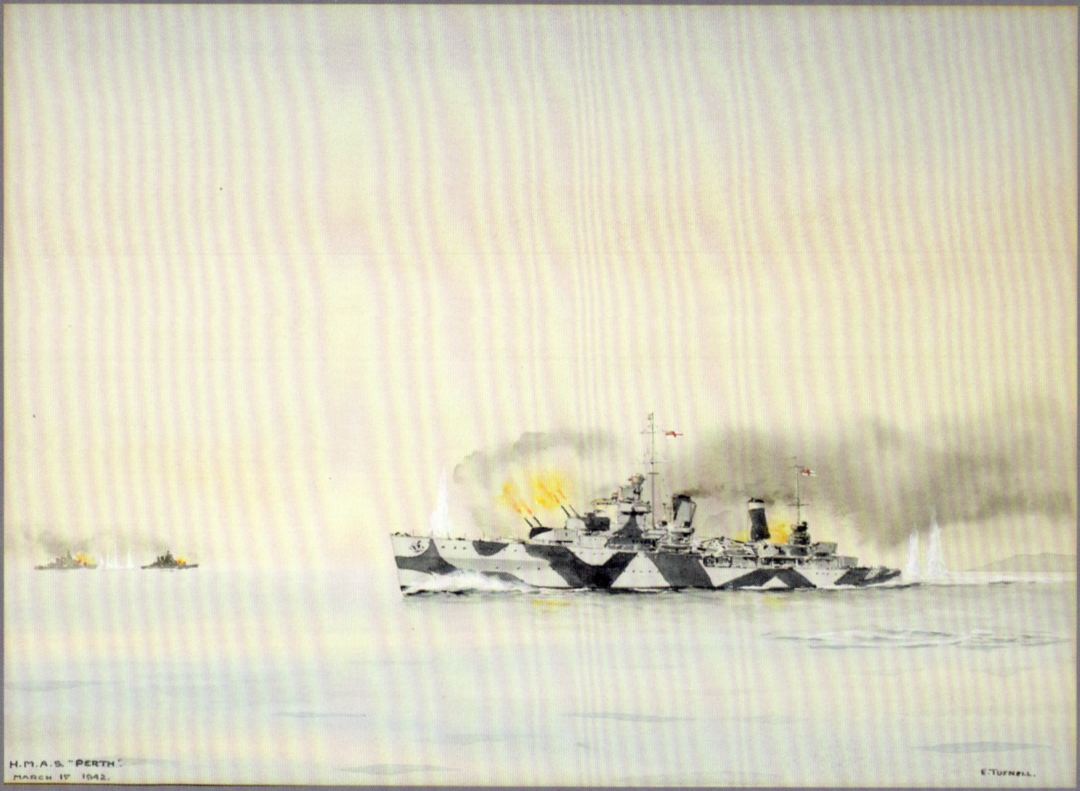

CAT. 20 – **Eric Erskine Campbell Tufnell** (1888-1978), *H.M.A.S.* Perth *March 1st 1942*, 1942, signed and inscribed with title, watercolour on paper, 10 ¼ x 14 ¼ in. (26 x37 cm).

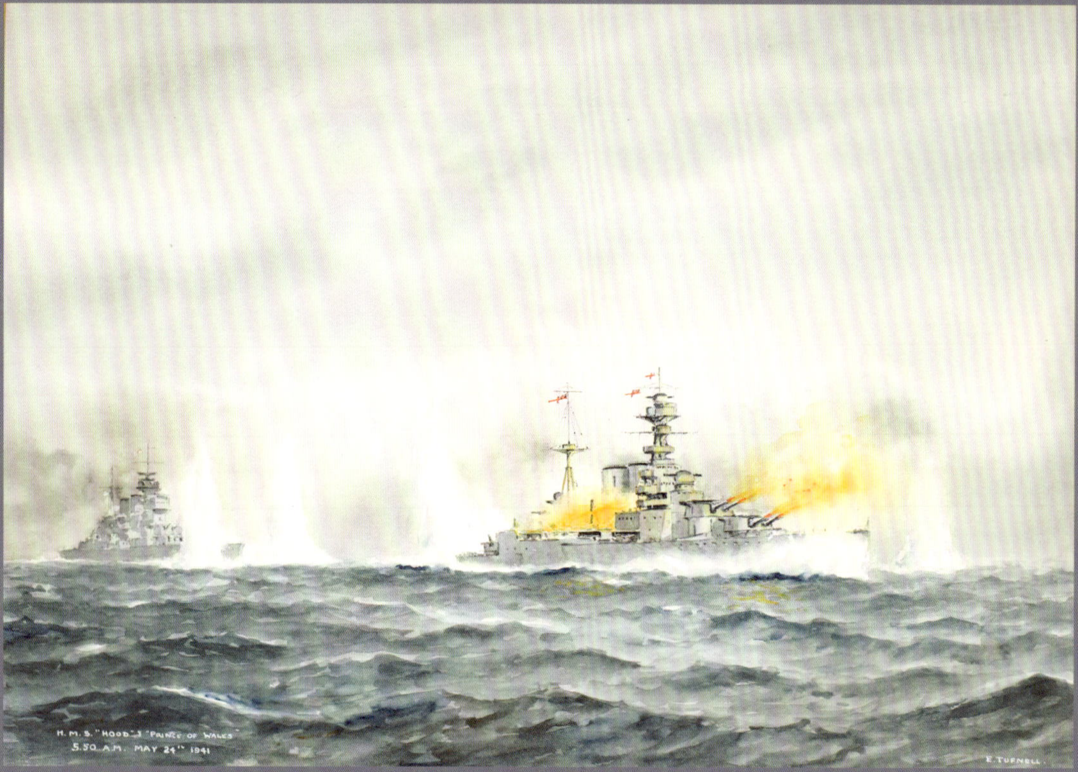

CAT. 21 – **Eric Erskine Campbell Tufnell** (1888-1978), H.M.S. *Hood & Prince of Wales* 5.30 am 24 May1941, signed and inscribed with title, watercolour on paper, 10 ¼ x 14 ¼ in. (26 x37 cm).

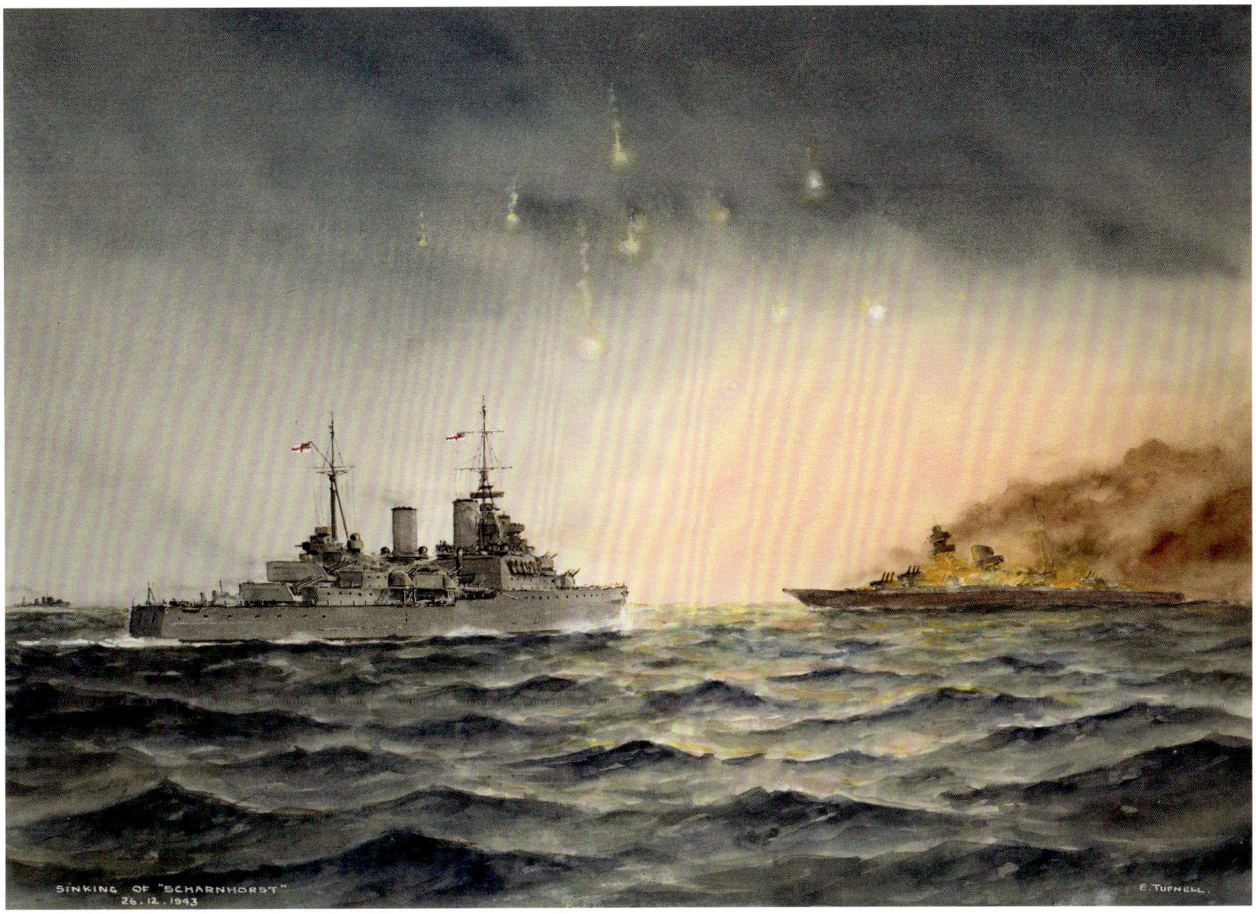

CAT. 22 – **Eric Erskine Campbell Tufnell** (1888-1978), *Sinking of Scharnhorst 26.12.1943* , 1943, signed and inscribed with title, watercolour on paper, 10 ¼ x 14 ¼ in. (26 x37 cm).

The Geman battleship *Scharnhorst* was sailing to attack an Allied convoy which was loaded with supplies for the Soviet Union when a superior British force met her off the North Cape (Norway). Of the 1,968 on board, only 36 men survived. The ship in the foreground is the battleship *Duke of York*. The scene shows the last hours of the action when the British fired star shells to illuminate their target. The cruiser HMS *Belfast*, now moored in the Pool of London, played an important role in the battle.

Starting as a Cadet in 1903 at the age of fifteen Tufnell had a long career in the Navy. During WW1 he served as CO of D4 which had HMS *Vulcan* as its depot ship on the Firth of Forth and was part of the 3rd Submarine Flotilla. He was described by a senior officer as "having an artistic temperament but does not appear to mind discomfort". After WW1 he was posted to the aircraft carrier HMS *Argus* while training under the RAF at Lee-on-Solent as an Observer. In December 1926 he was sent as "acting Observer" to HMS *Furious* with the Atlantic Fleet and in April 1927 to Farnborough for a course at the RAF School of Photography. He retired from the Royal Navy in 1929, in his early 40s, with the intention of taking up painting full time. A prolific artist, many commissions were secured through the of Saville Row naval outfitters, Gieves and Hawkes, whose naval officer customers asked Tufnell to paint meticulously accurate watercolours of the ships on which they served.

BLITZ

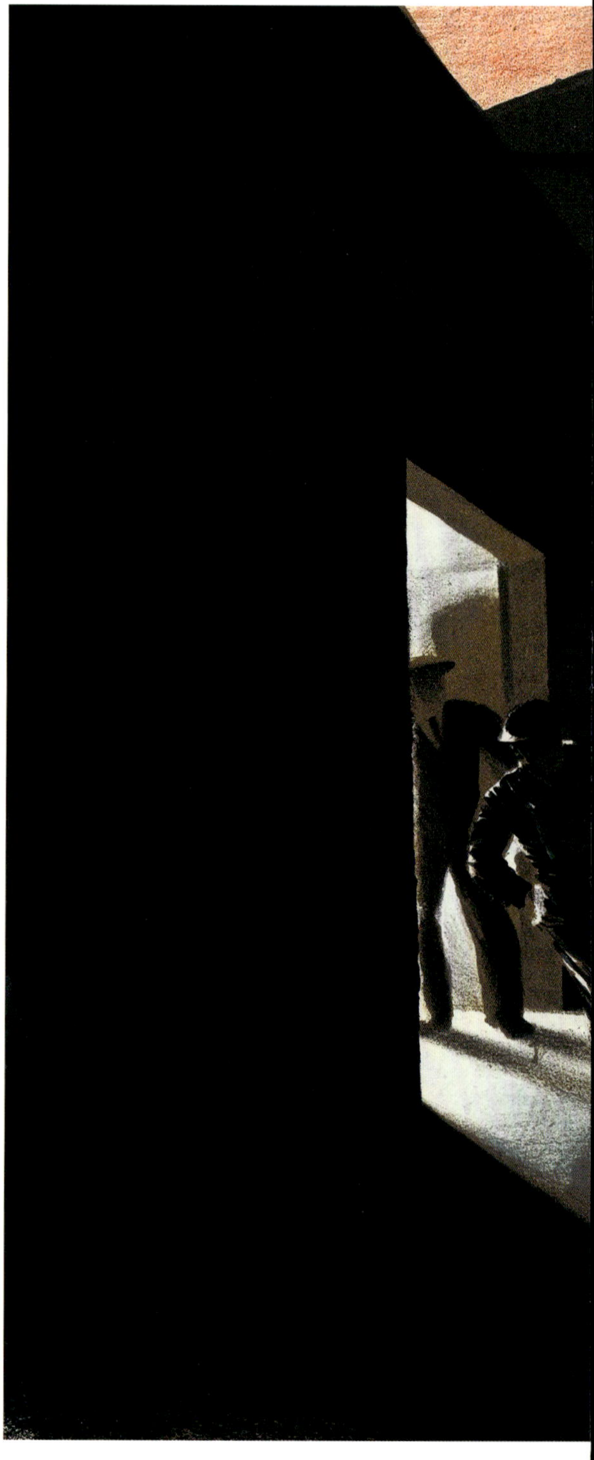

CAT. 23 – **Cliff Rowe** (1904-1989), *The Call-out,* c.1941, signed in the plate, lithograph, 15 x 21 in. (38 x 53.2 cm).

Rowe was a politically active artist – in the early 1930s he made designs for Communist Party publications and spent eighteen months travelling and working in the Soviet Union. In 1934 he helped establish the Artists' International Association whose work included helping refugees from Hitler's Germany and providing medical aid to the British International Brigade during the Spanish Civil War.

In this lithographic poster (produced to aid the war effort) Rowe depicts a National Fire Service crew scramble to their truck in response to an ominous glow on the horizon. With little protective gear other than a steel helmet and a pair of gum boots these volunteers were transported in trucks equipped with extension ladders and a trailer holding baskets to move rubble and trestles to prop up masonry or roof structures that had collapsed.

All of the Municipal Fire and Rescue services suffered casualties during raids, not only from high explosives dropped by the enemy, but from the falling debris from exploded shells fired by British anti-aircraft artillery batteries.

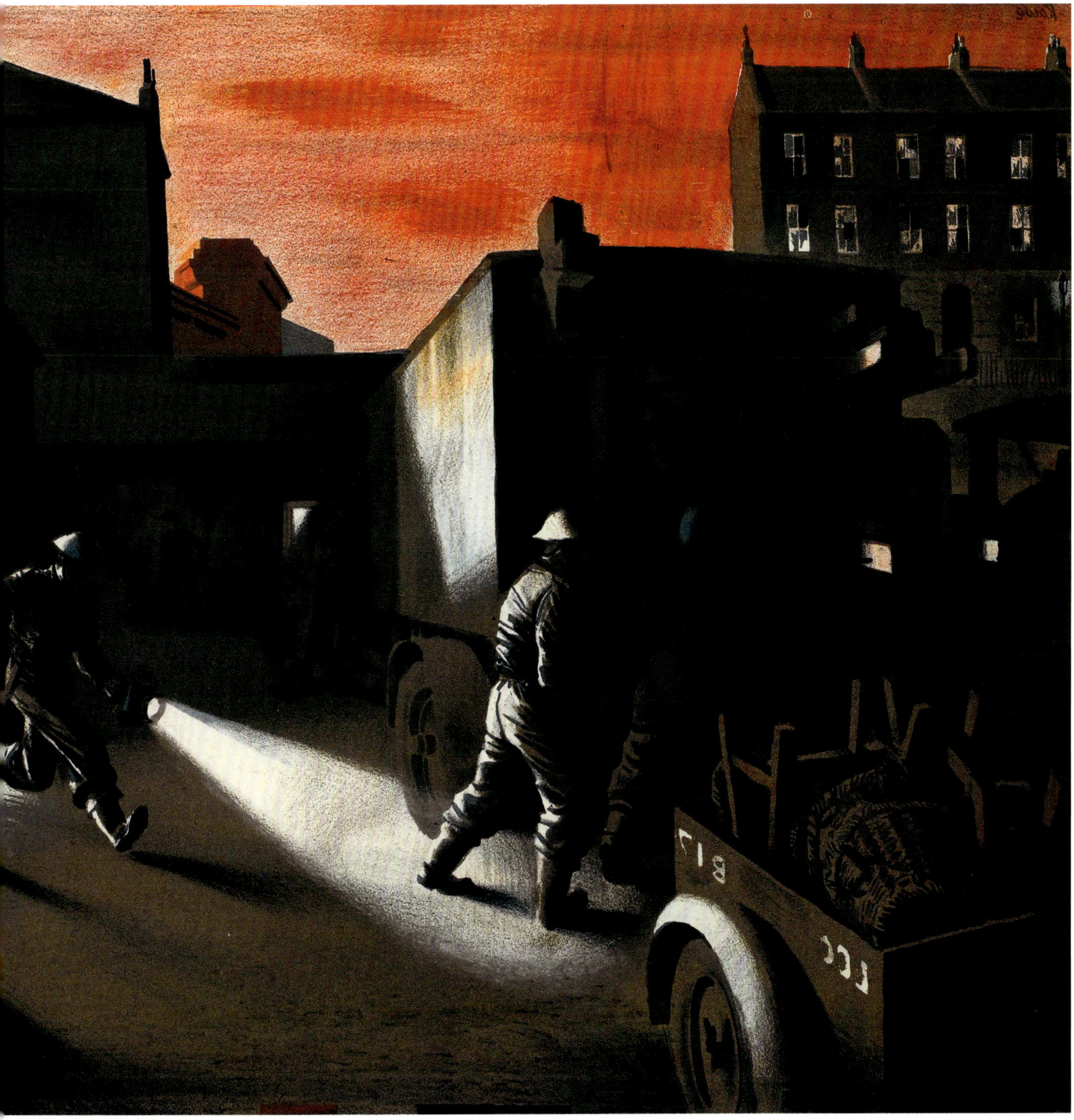

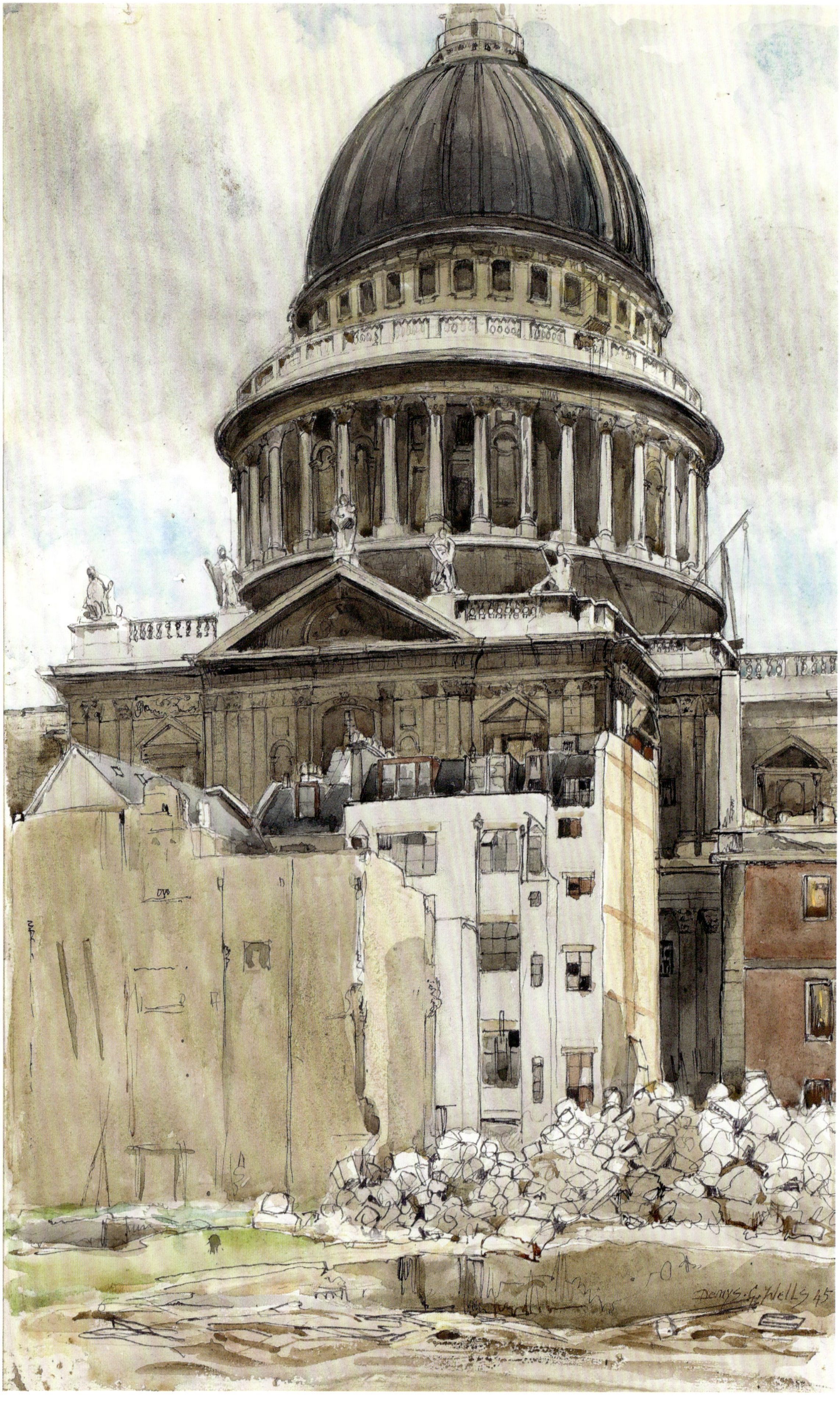
Denys G. Wells 45

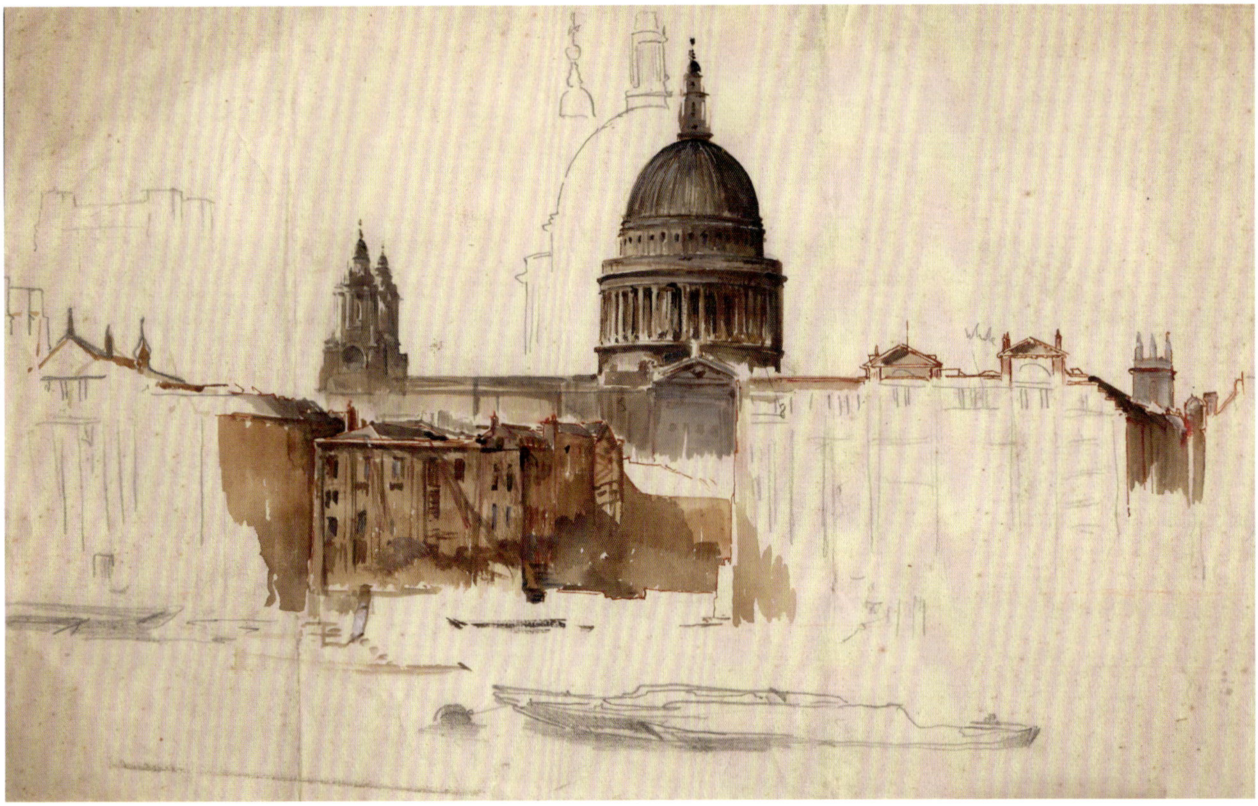

CAT. 25 – **Charles Cundall** (1890-1971), Study for St Paul's Cathedral,
Inscribed verso: "I confirm this sketch of St Paul's to be the work of my husband Charles Cundall RA RWS – Jacqueline C",
pencil and watercolour on paper, 10 ½ x 17 in. (27 x 43.3 cm).
Provenance: Acquired directly from the Artist's daughter.
Exhibited: *Charles Cundall – A Working Method*, Young Gallery Salisbury, March- April 2016, Sotheran's, April-May 2016.
Literature: *Charles Cundall – A Working Method*, Edited by Sacha Llewellyn & Paul Liss, published by Liss Llewellyn Fine Art, February 2016.

St Paul's Cathedral became an inspiration to the British people during WW2. Throughout the Blitz, St Paul's miraculously escaped major bomb damage, whilst buildings in the surrounding areas were reduced to rubble. Images of St Paul's framed by smoke and fire became a symbol of the nation's indomitable spirit. In 1945 services at St Paul's, marking the end of the war in Europe, were attended by 35,000 people.

CAT. 24 – **Denys Wells** (1881-1973), *St Paul's*, 1945, signed and dated,
watercolour, pen and ink on paper, 22 x14 in. (56 x 35.5 cm).

Bomb damaged buildings – especially churches – were a common theme amongst WAAC commissions. For the purpose of propaganda such images had an obvious message about the uncivilised nature of German aggression. There was also a strong visual appeal which linked with the drama afforded by the new shapes and forms of structures blasted open.

Having served as a commissioned officer with the Artists'at Rifles in France during WW1, by the start of WW2 Wells was too old for regular service and instead served as an air raid warden. Perfectly placed to record the destruction of the City that he witnessed first hand, Wells embarked on a series of watercolours often painted *in situ* the morning immediately after an air raid attack. A number of these were exhibited at the Royal Academy of Arts, (such as *Waterloo in War-time*, 1943 no. 596).

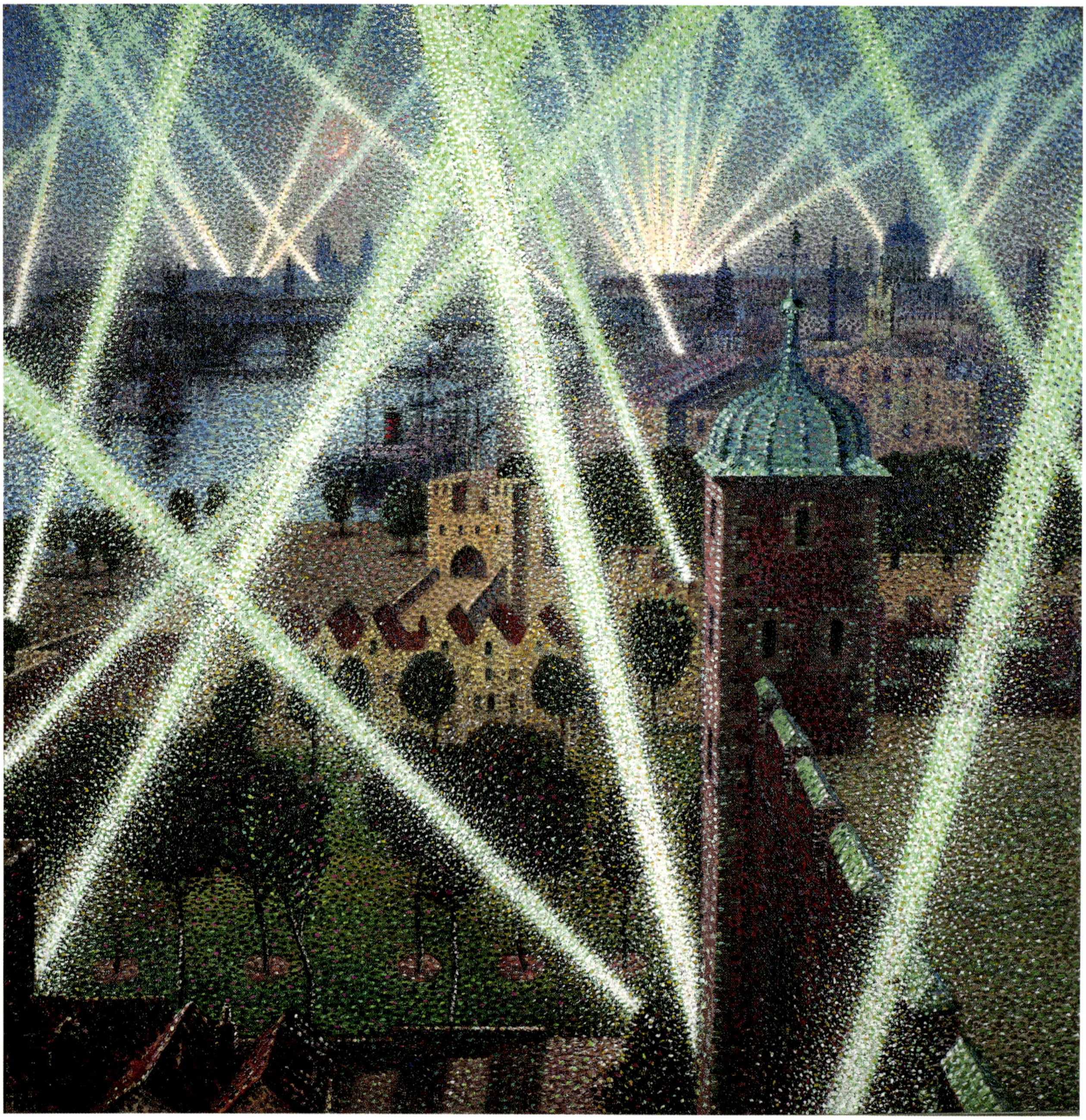

CAT. 26* – **Claude Francis Barry** (1883-1970), *London Blitz*, 1940, signed, inscribed with title and date on the reverse, oil on canvas, 36 x 36 in. (90 x 90 cm).
Provenance: the artist's estate, cat.798; Liss Llewellyn Fine Art, 2008; Private Collection.
Exhibited: The Royal Society of British Artists, 1944.
Literature: Katie Campbell, *Moon Behind Clouds: An Introduction to the Life and Work of Sir Claude Francis Barry*, Jersey 1999, repr. p.79.

Barry's striking image of the Tower of London during the Blitz is closely related to his *Heart of the Empire* in its neo-pointillist treatment and the futuristic use of searchlights to heighten the sense of a state of alert for an aerial attack by the German Luftwaffe. The painting's viewpoint is the eastern of the two riverside towers of the White Tower, William the Conqueror's moated fortress located within the walls of the Tower of London. On the skyline, above the old London Bridge, reading from left to right, are depicted Southwark Cathedral, the Houses of Parliament, the slim tower of Westminster Cathedral, one of the Victorian towers of Cannon Street Station, and Wren's Monument to the Great Fire of 1666. St Paul's Cathedral dominates the scene.

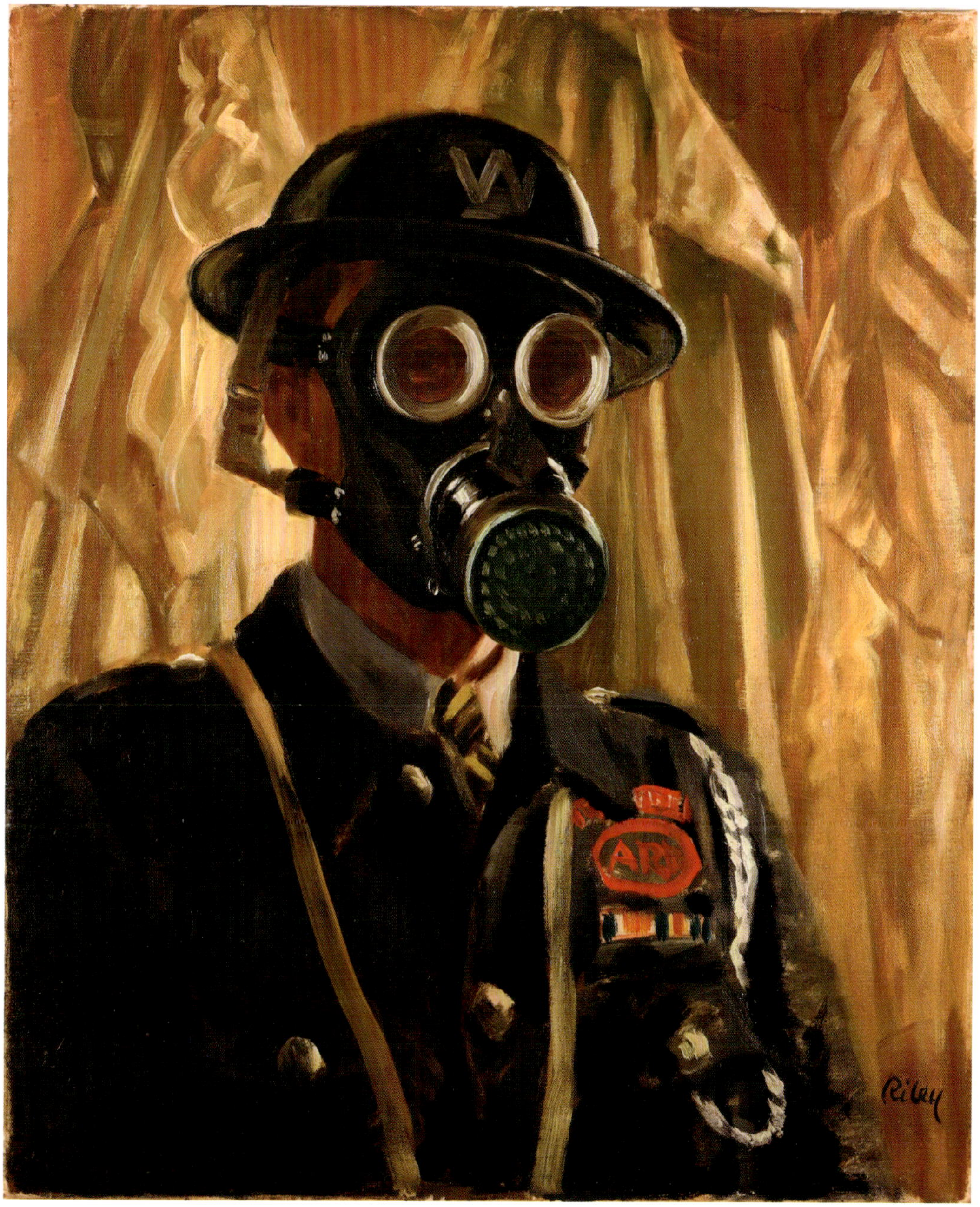

CAT. 27 – **Harold Arthur Riley** (1895-1966), *Me*, 1942, signed and inscribed with title and date on the stretcher, oil on canvas, 24 x 20 in. (61 x 51 cm).
Provenance: With the artist until 1966; thence by descent.

This striking self-portrait shows Riley in his ARP (Air Raid Precautions) uniform. Three anti-gas coats, worn by ARP volunteers, form the backdrop. Although Riley saw active service during WW1, when WW2 broke out he was in his mid-40's and therefore not called up (the National Service-Armed Forces-Act imposed conscription on all men aged 18 to 41). Men and women of all ages, however, could serve in the ARP, a voluntary force dedicated to the protection of civilians from the danger of air raids. During the war, the ARP was responsible for the issuing of gas masks, pre-fabricated air raid-shelters, the upkeep of local public shelters, and the maintenance of the blackout, patrolling the streets to ensure that no light was visible. During and after air raids they neutralised incendiary bombs with sandbags and helped rescue people, administer emergency first aid, search for survivors and help recover bodies. There were around 1.4 million ARP wardens in Britain during the war, almost all unpaid part-time volunteers, who also held day-time jobs. They had a basic uniform consisting of a set of overalls, wellington boots, an armlet, and a black steel helmet and a small silver badge. The steel helmet had W for Warden in bold white writing across it, except for Chief Wardens who wore white helmets with black lettering.

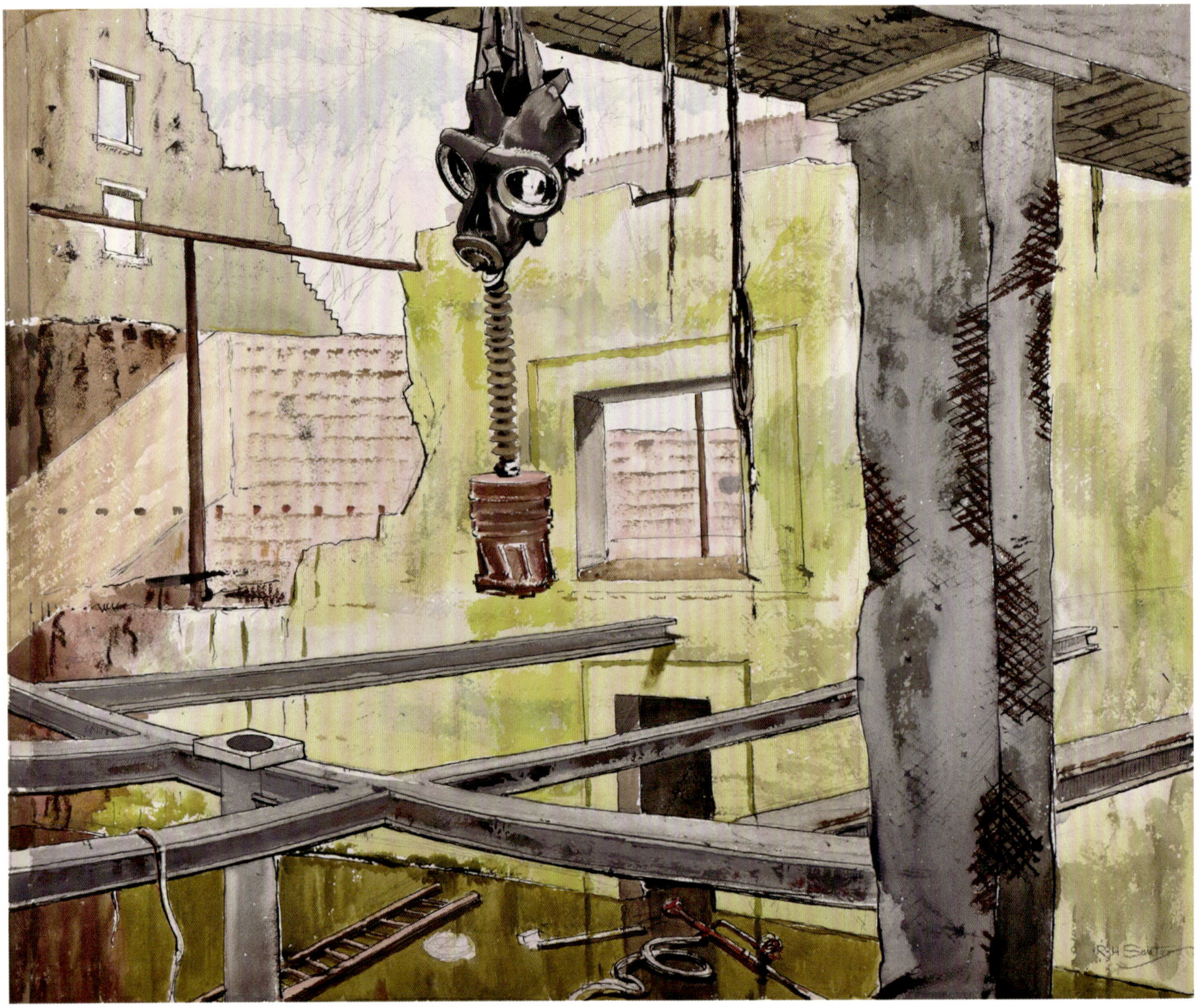

CAT. 28 – **Rudolph Sauter** (1895-1977), *After the raid*,
watercolour on paper, 19 ½ x 23 ½ in. (49.5 x 60 cm).

CAT. 29 – **Rudolph Sauter** (1895-1977), *Soldier holding a gas mask*, (believed to be a self-portrait),
signed and dated 1939,
pencil and watercolour on paper, 31 x 22 ¼ in. (78.5 x 56.5 cm).

During WW2, Rudolf Sauter was an Army Welfare Officer under South Eastern Command. Although he was never an official war artist the events he witnessed informed his work.

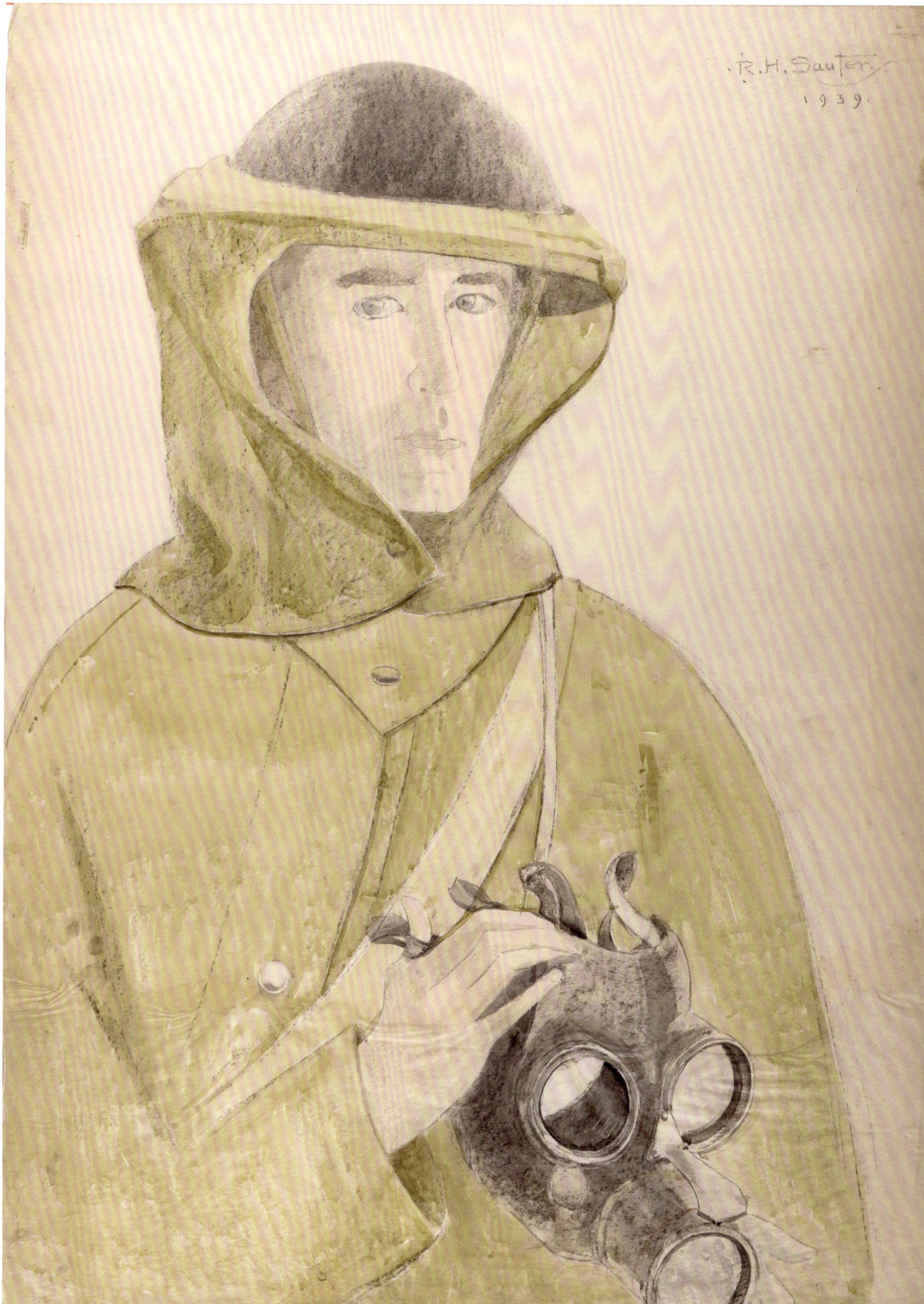
R.H. Sauter
1939.

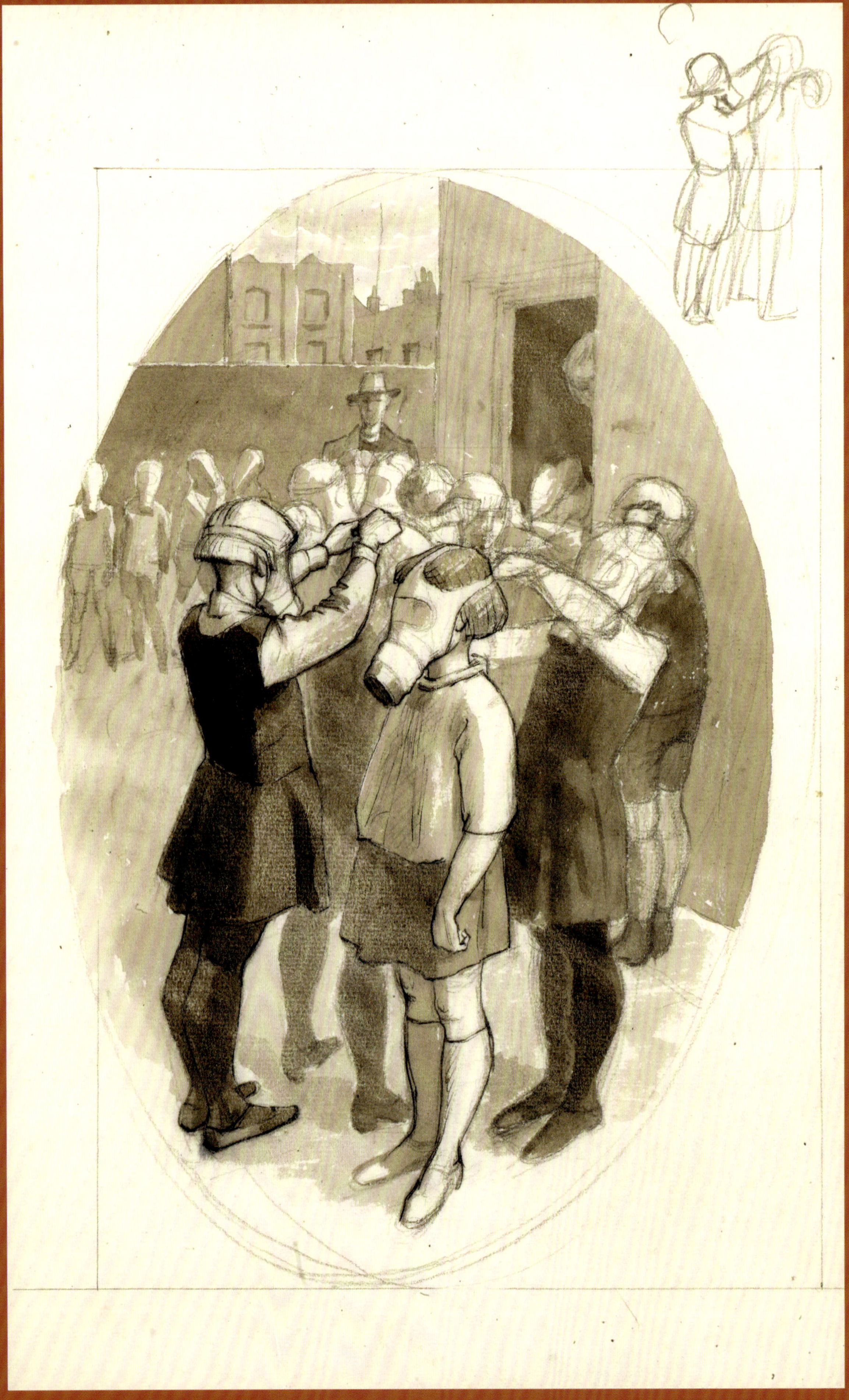

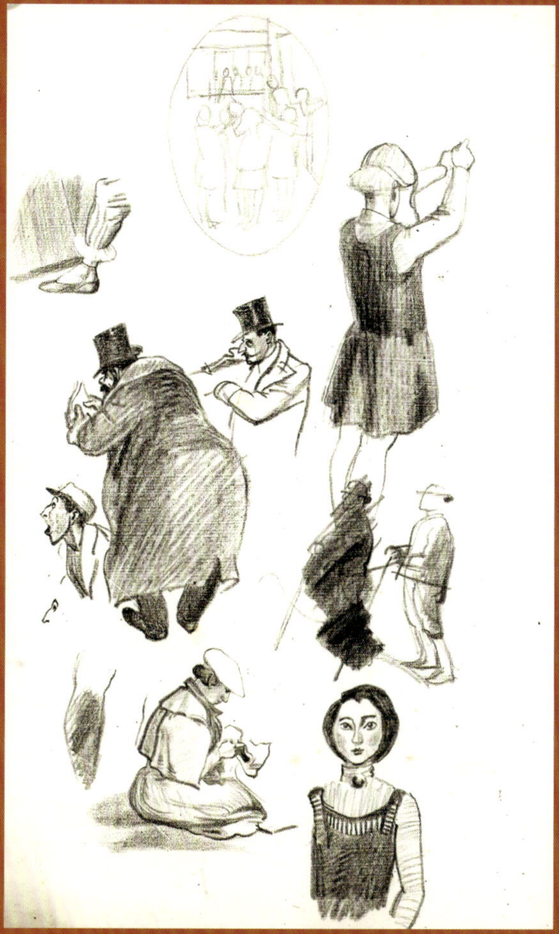

CAT. 31 – **Charles Mahoney** (1903-1968),
Study sheet with figures for *Gas Mask Drill*, 1939,
signed, inscribed with title and dated
Pen and wash over pencil on paper 17 x 11 in. (43 × 23 cm)
Provenance: Artist's estate.
Literature: Paul Liss, *Charles Mahoney*, London 1999, p. 54.

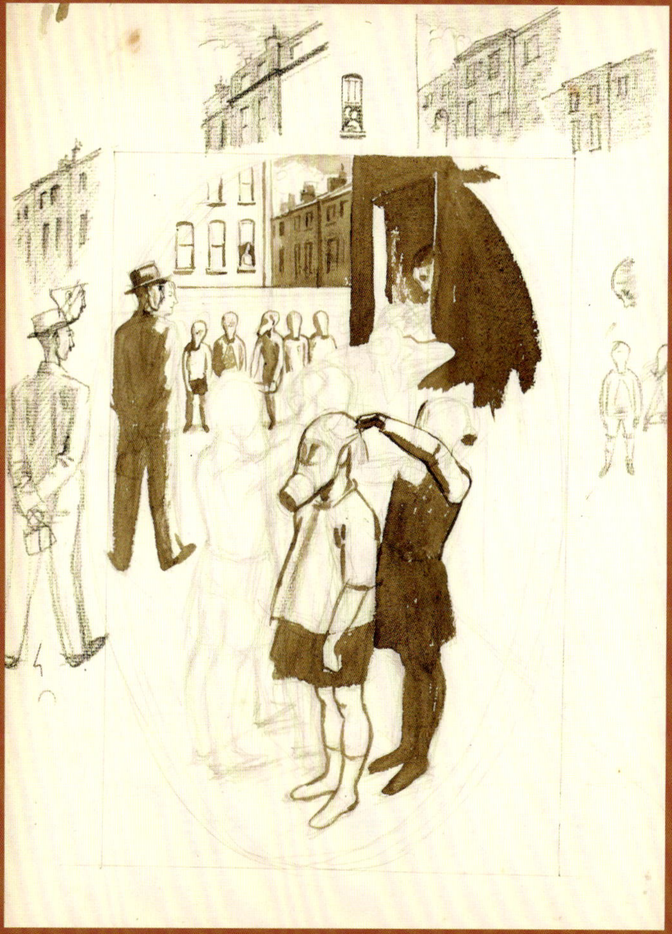

CAT. 32 – **Charles Mahoney** (1903-1968),
Street scene with children wearing gas masks, 1939,
Brown wash and pencil on paper, 16 x 12 ½ in. (40.5 x 32 cm)
Provenance: Artist's estate.
Literature: Paul Liss, *Charles Mahoney*, London 1999, p. 54.

Gas masks were issued to all children as a precaution against attack by gas bombs, and gas-mask drill ('remove mask from box, put mask on face, check mask fits correctly, breathe normally') was a daily feature of school life during WW2. The masks came in cardboard boxes with a string for carrying them on the shoulder. Children were instructed to keep their masks with them at all times.

CAT. 30 – **Charles Mahoney** (1903-1968), *Gas Mask Drill*, (oval with sketch to top right), 1939, signed, inscribed with title and dated, pen and wash over pencil on paper, 17 x 11 in. (43 × 23 cm)
Provenance: Artist's estate.
Literature: Paul Liss, *Charles Mahoney*, London 1999, p. 54.

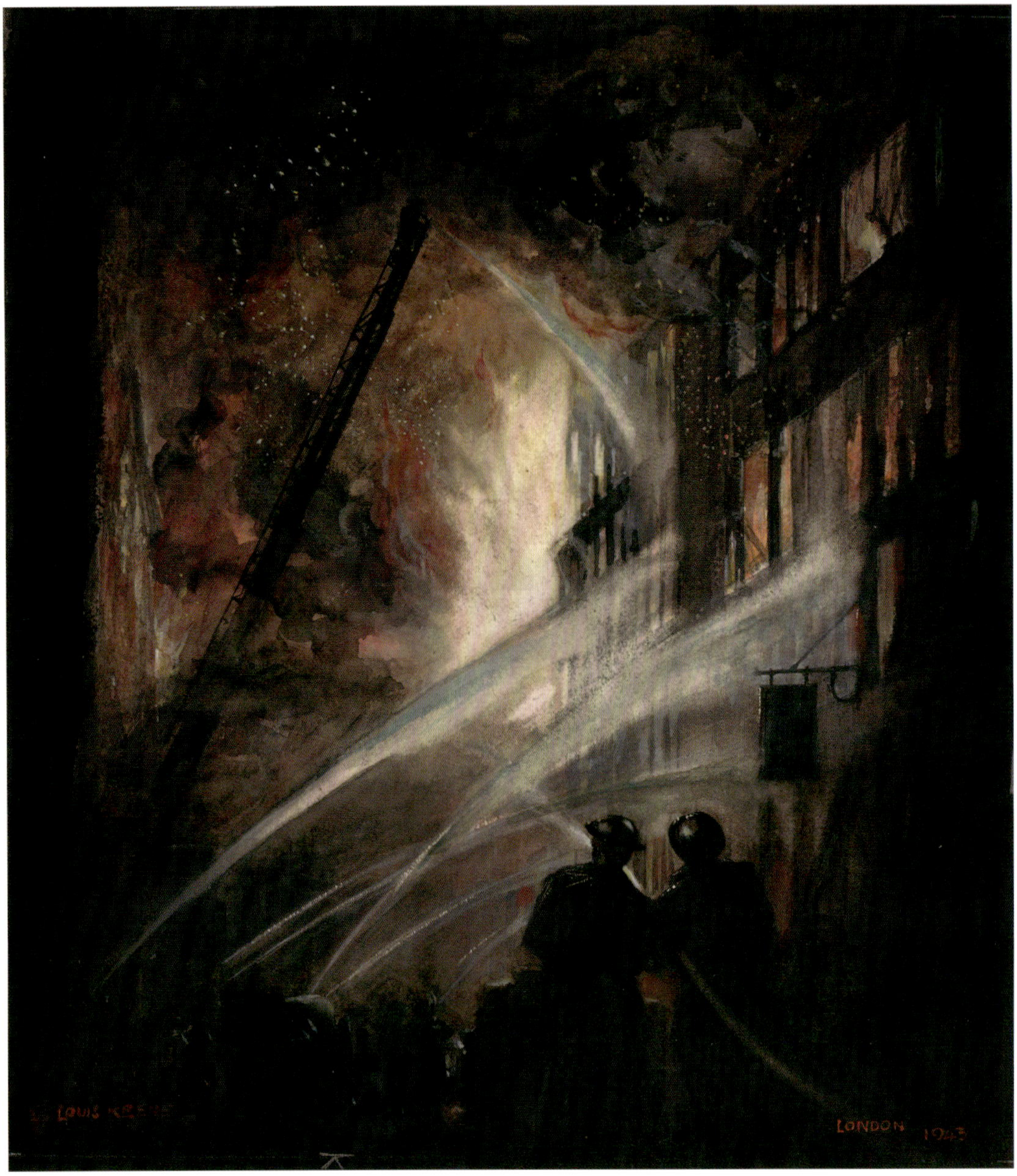

CAT. 33 – **Louis Keene** (1888-1972), *Fire services, London*, 1943, signed and inscribed 'London 1943', watercolour, india ink, pencil, and chalk on paper, 13 ½ x 15 ¼ in. (34.2 x 38.7 cm)
Provenance: The Artist's daughter, Canada.

As Commanding Officer of the Lorne Scots during WW2 Keene witnessed the bombing of Liverpool and London. In a review of the National Gallery exhibition 'War Paintings' (*Evening Standard*, May 29, 1942), a vivid painting of an incendiary bomb by Keene was singled out for praise. Favouring night-time views, illuminated by searchlights, fires and bombs, Keene's pictures are often characterised by a surreal feeling, heightened by the use of shallow perspectives and intense colours.

CAT. 34 – **Louis Keene** (1888-1972), Barrage Balloons and Searchlights, c.1941, signed, watercolour, india ink, pencil, and chalk on paper, 13 ¾ x 15 ½ in. (35 x 39.3 cm)

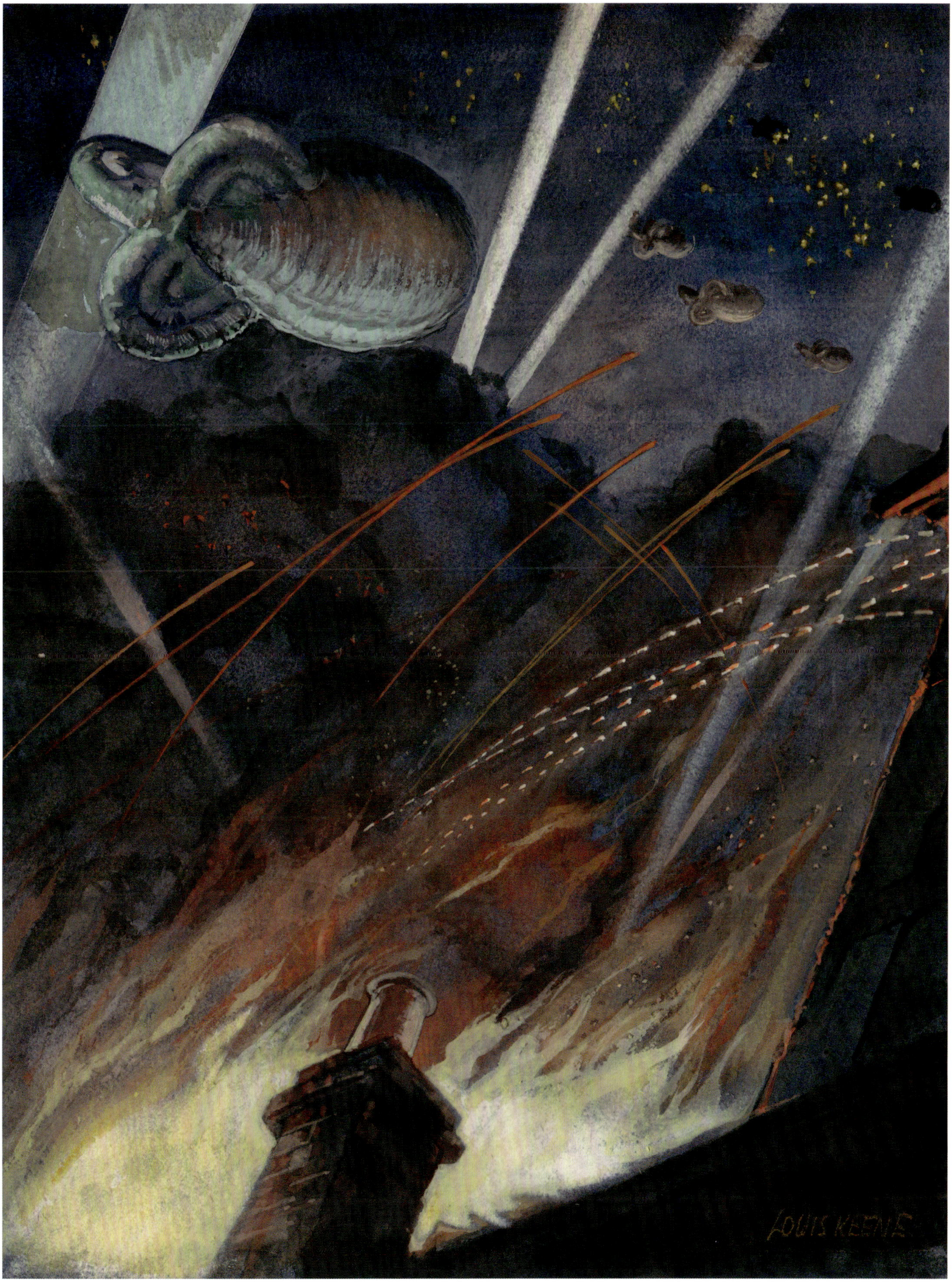
LOUIS KEENE

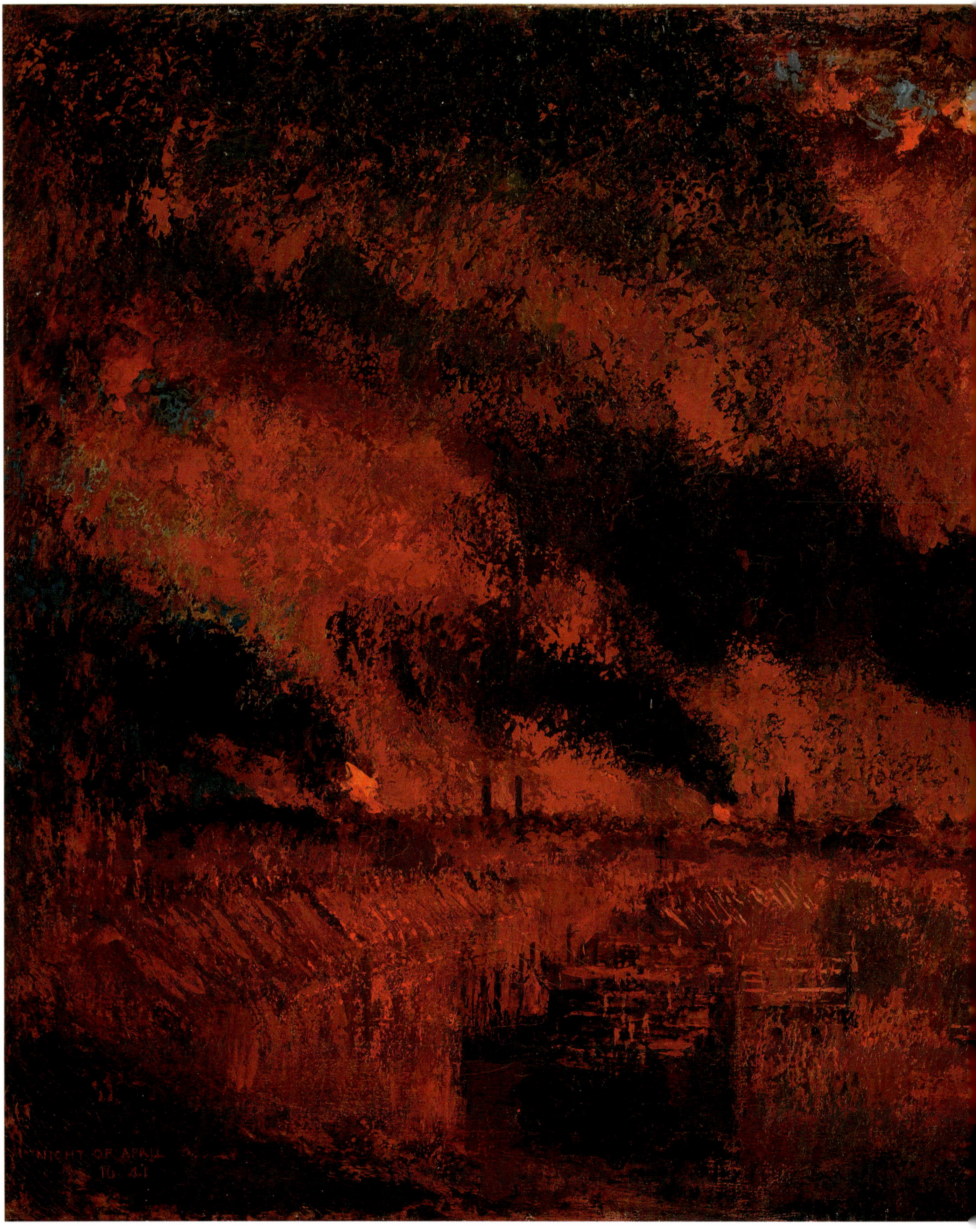
NIGHT OF APRIL
16 41

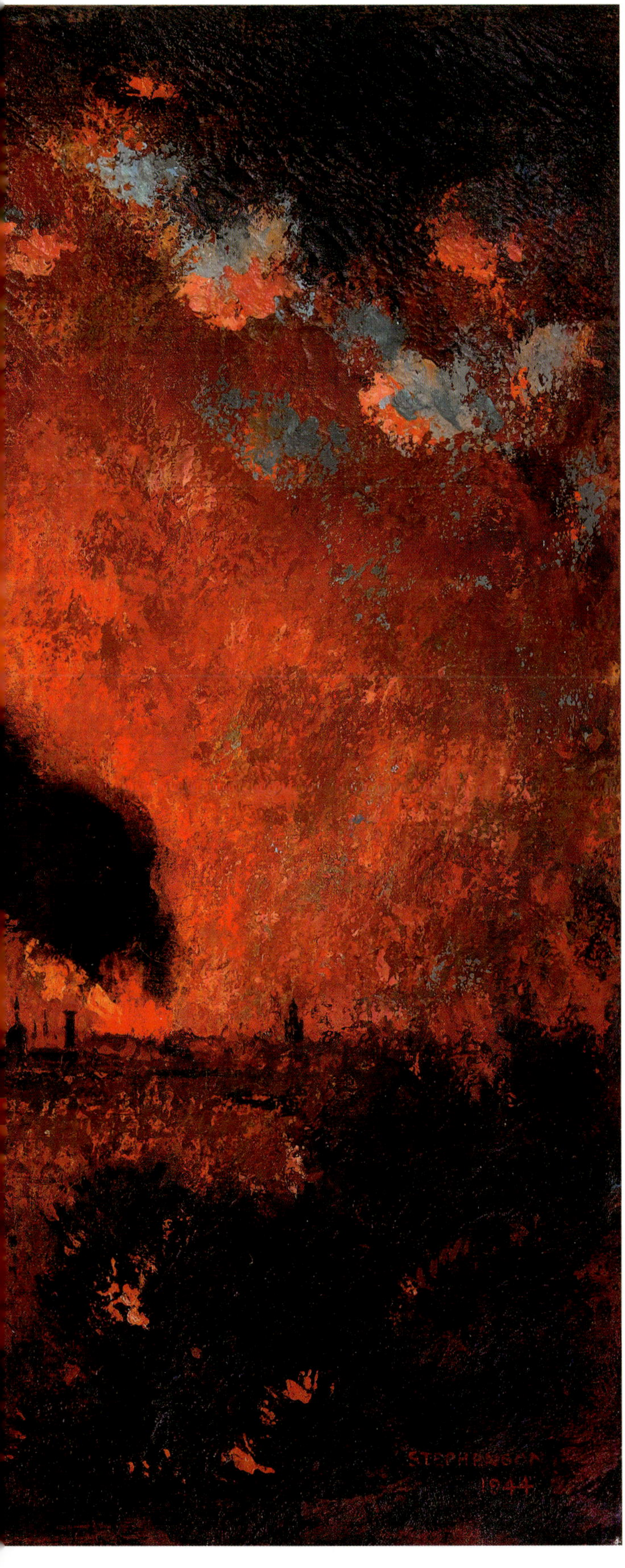

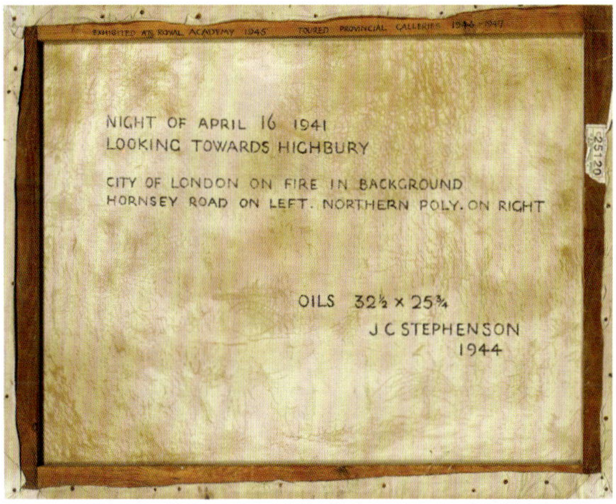

FIG. 6 – Reverse side of John Cecil Stephenson's painting.

CAT. 35 – **John Cecil Stephenson** (1889-1965),
Looking towards Highbury, city of London on fire in background... night of April 16, 1941, 1944,
signed and dated,
inscribed and titled on the reverse,
oil on canvas, 32 ½ x 25 ¾ in. (82.5 x 65.5 cm)
Exhibited at Royal Academy 1945,
Toured Provincial Galleries 1946-1947.

This painting records the massive attack which took place overnight on 16th April 1941 when the Luftwaffe bombed London with 681 aircraft. At the time Stephenson was living at Mall Studios in London, his neighbours Ben Nicholson and Henry Moore having evacuated their studio and left London. This view is – with some artistic licence – taken from eastern Highgate/ Crouch End (possibly Queens Wood). Although Stephenson had been made redundant by Northern Polytechnic in 1940 (he had been director of Art there from 1922) he did continue firewatching at the school throughout the war.

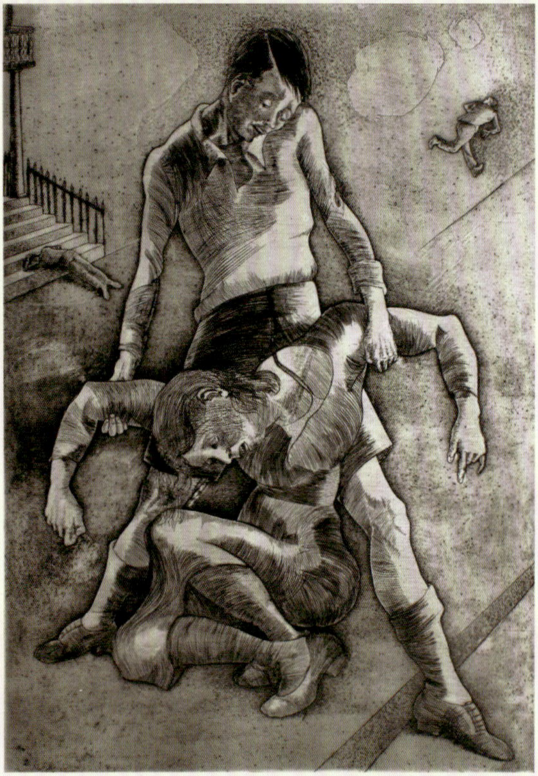

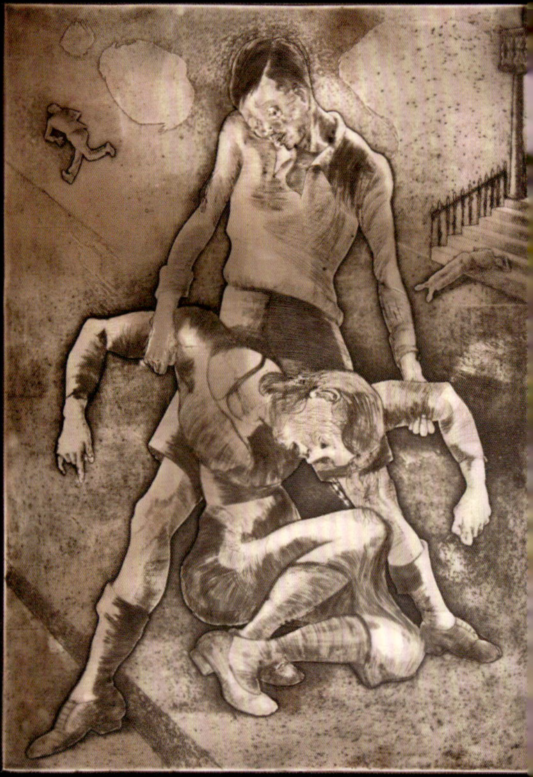

CAT. 36 a & b – **English School,** *Civilians caught in the Blitz,* 1940,
etching, copper plate, 14 x 10 in. (35.5 x 25 cm).

Night after night, from September 1940 until May 1941, German bombers attacked British cities, ports and industrial areas. London alone was bombed every day and night, bar one for 11 weeks, destroying one third of the city. In the first 10 days, almost 6,000 people were killed and twice as many badly injured. The most notorious raid took place on Sunday 29 December.

CAT. 37 – **Eleanor Chilton Price** (1901-1985), *Open for Business as Usual,* 1943, signed and dated
ink and watercolour on gesso primed card, 9 x 7 in. (23 x 18 cm)

Surrounded by the devastation of bombed-out buildings supported by wooden props, this street market nevertheless continue to provide service and enjoys a flourishing trade. The artist was clearly making the point that 'life must go on' and thereby was both supporting and celebrating the morale and resilience of the civilian populatio

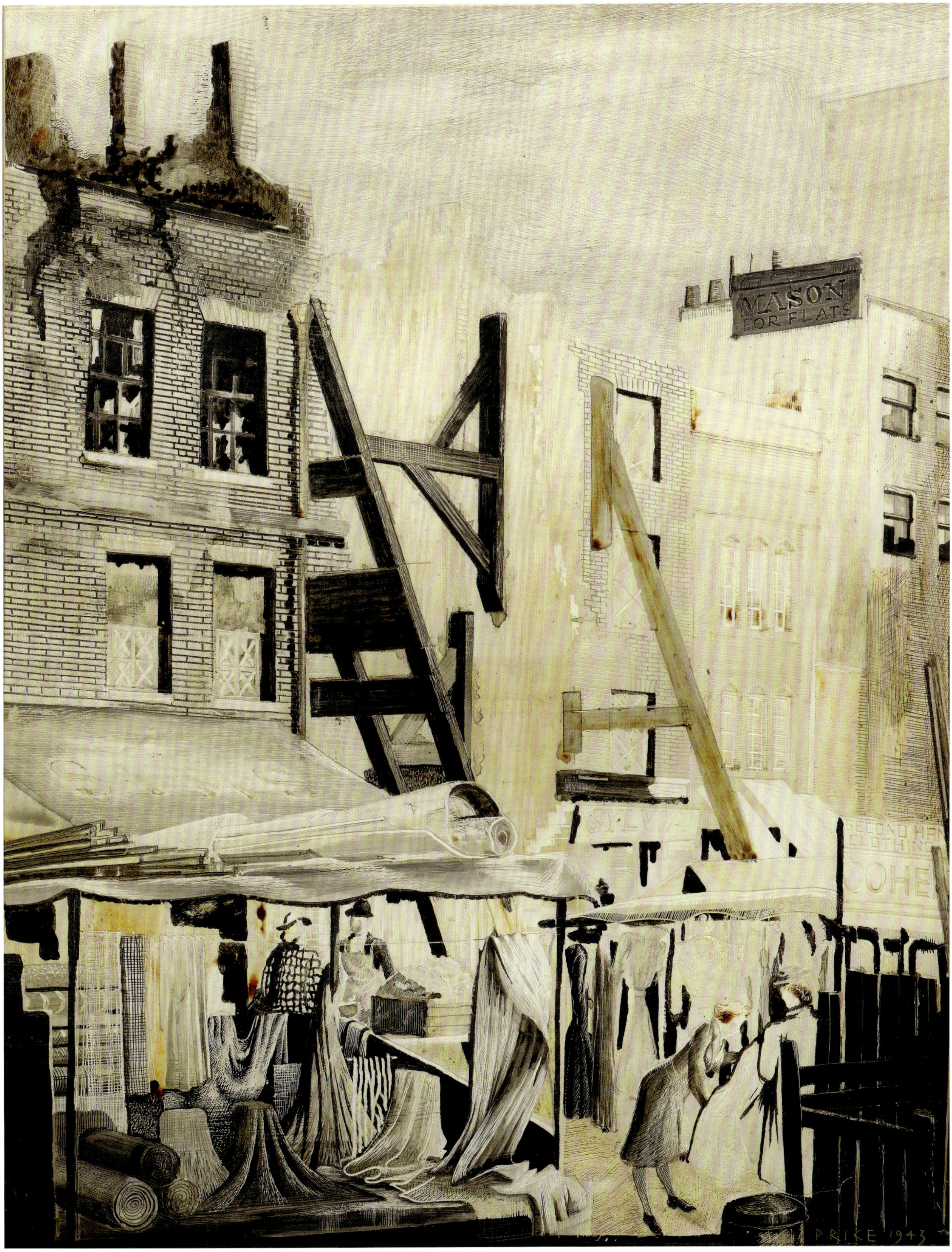
MASON
FOR FLATS
SYLVIA
SECOND HEN
CLOTHIN
COHE
PRICE 1943

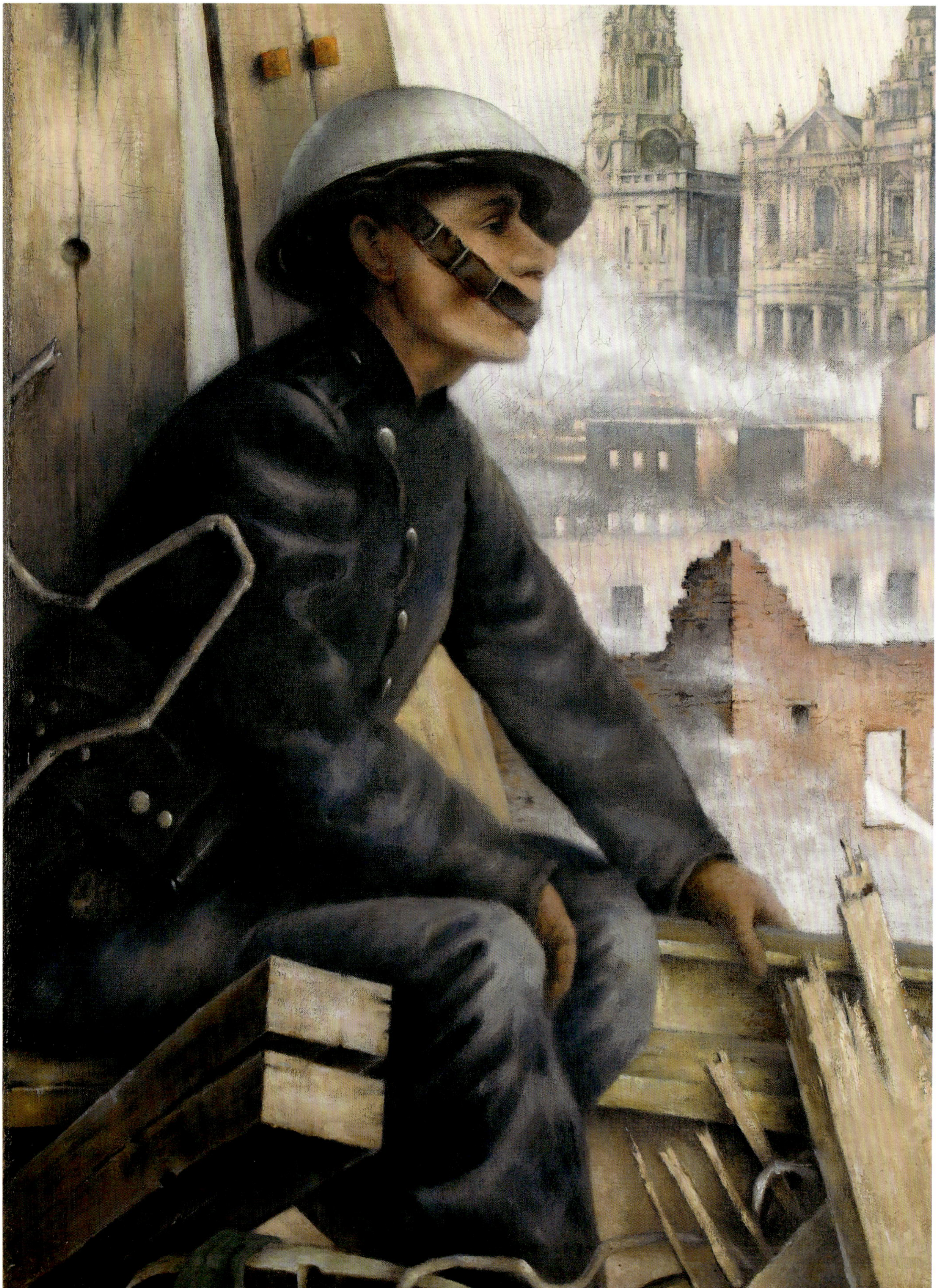

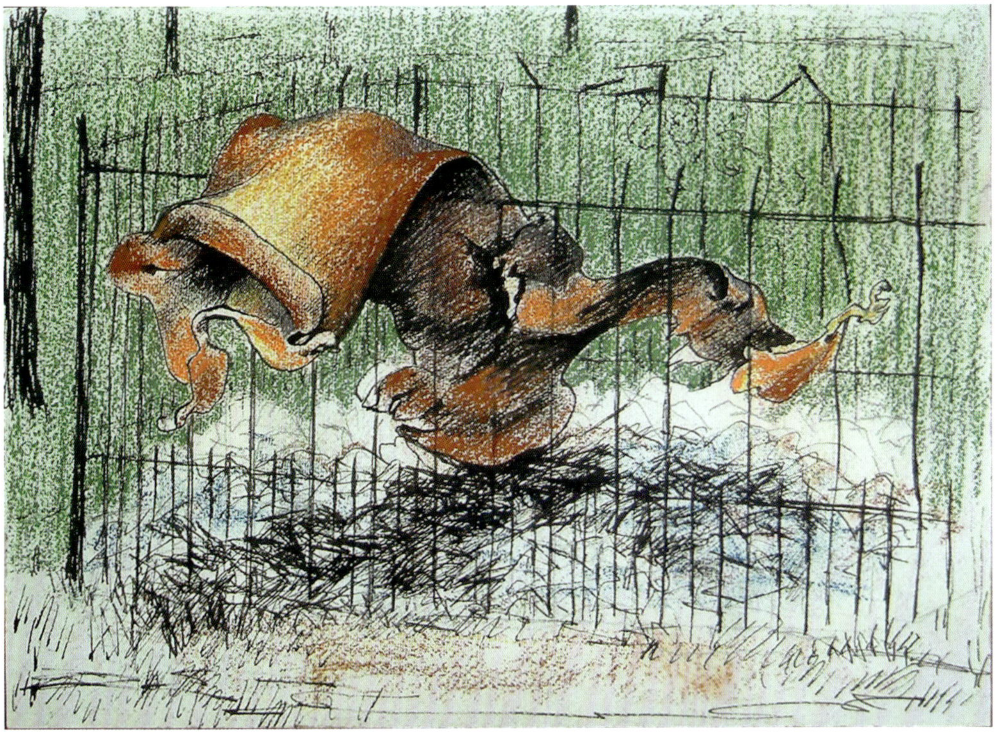

CAT. 39 – **John Cecil Stephenson** (1889-1965) *The End of a Doodlebug, Hampstead Heath,* 1945, signed and dated, chalk and pastel over pencil and pen and ink, 10 x 14 in. (25.5 x 35.5 cm).
Inscribed by the artist on the reverse in pen and ink: 'End of a Doodlebug Hampstead Heath. Oil of this picture shown at Royal Academy 1945 & selected by British Council for exhibition in the provinces.'
Provenance: Artist's family.
Literature: Simon Guthrie, *John Cecil Stephenson*, Cartmel Press Associates, 1997, p. 148.

The V-1, developed by the German Luftwaffe during WW2, was the first guided missile used in war and the forerunner of today's cruise missile. Between June 1944 and March 1945, it was fired at targets in London and Antwerp. The simple pulse-jet engine pulsed fifty times per second, and the characteristic buzzing sound gave rise to the colloquial name of doodle-bug (after an Australian insect). This study depicts the remnants of a doodlebug, which Stephenson (whose Hampstead studio was damaged during the Blitz in 1940) saw on the Heath in 1945. The finished picture was exhibited at the Royal Academy that year (cat. no. 96) and subsequently went on tour with the British Council.

CAT. 38 – **Frank Potter** (1887-1958), *Auxiliary Firemen with St Paul's in the Background*, c.1941, oil on canvas, 62 ¼ x 40 ¼ in. (158 x 102 cm).
Provenance: Andrew Leslie, Leva Gallery, 1974; private collection.
Literature: Grant M.Waters, *Dictionary of British Artists Working 1900–1950*, Eastbourne Fine Art Publications, Eastbourne, 1976, vol. 2, illus. no. 70.

This painting shows an Auxiliary Fireman, with his plastron-fronted tunic buttoning on the right side and his fireman's hatchet in a holder attached to his belt. Potter, who had served in WW1, (enlisting in 1916 at the age of 29), would have been too old to fight in WW2 but is likely to have served on the home front. In this capacity it is possible that Potter himself served as an Auxiliary Fireman – indeed this might even be a self-portrait. Tethered barrage balloons – 1,100 of which were moored at 100-yard intervals around St Paul's – defended the city against dive-bombers, forcing them to fly higher and into the range of concentrated anti-aircraft fire.

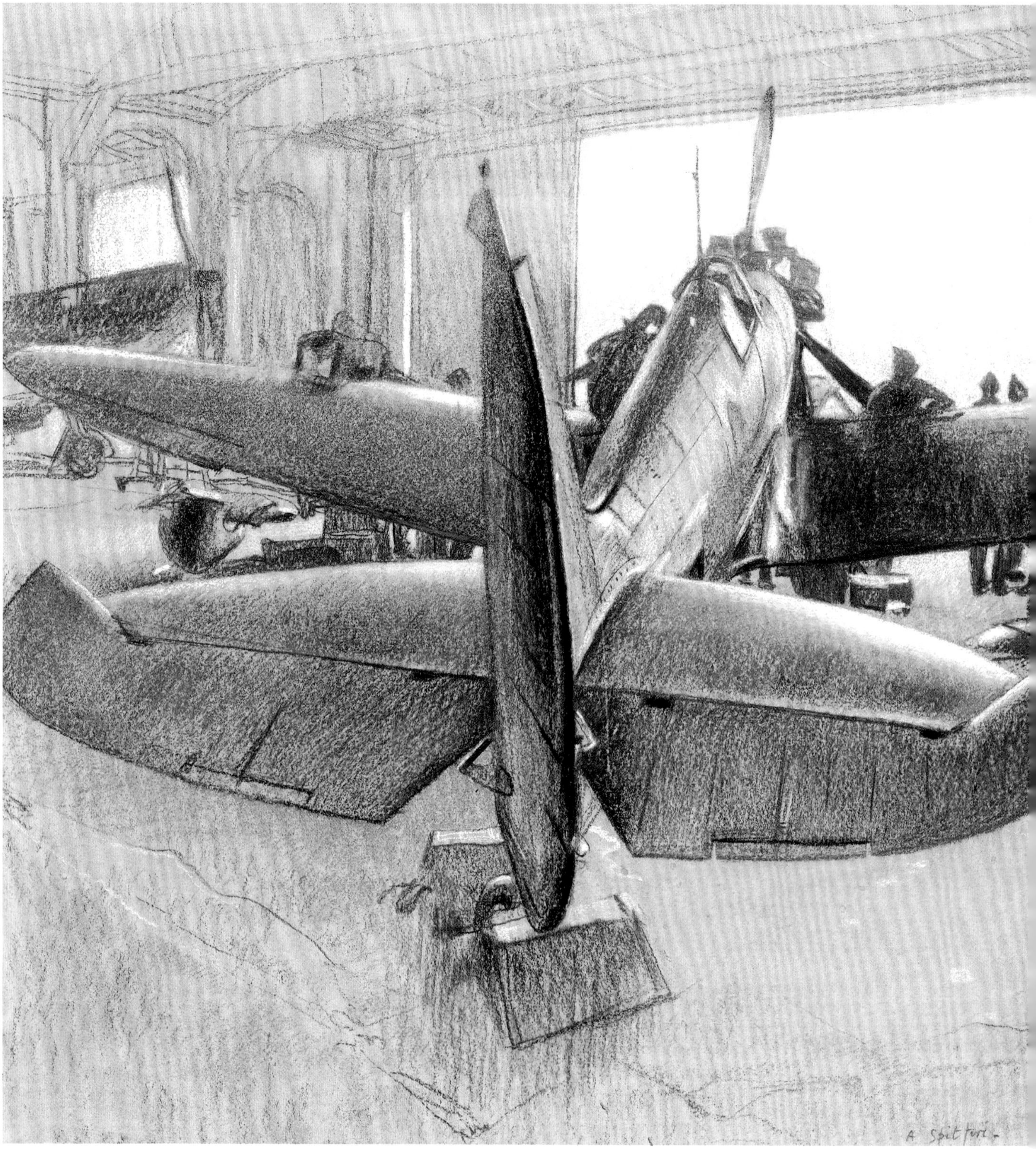
A Spitfire.

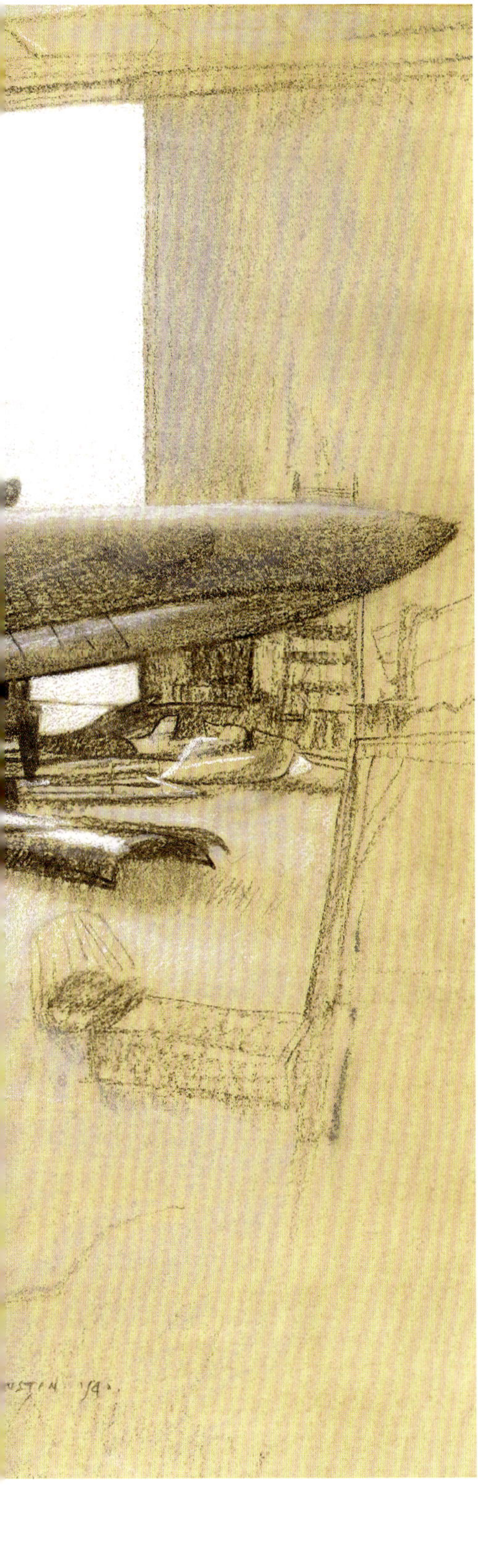

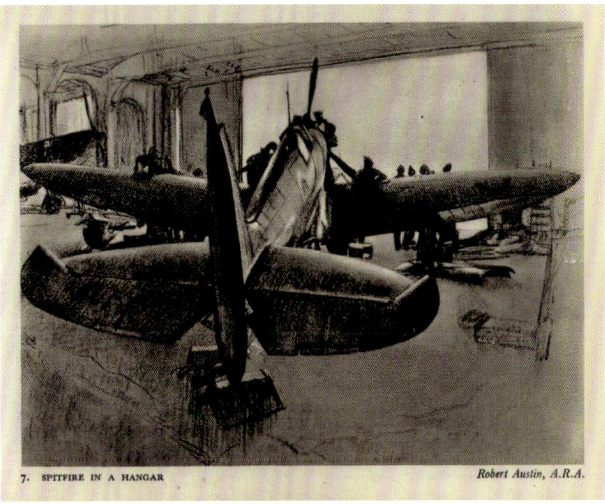

FIG. 7 – The drawing as reproduced in 'War Pictures by British Artist's, N° 3, *R.A.F*, published in 1942.

CAT. 40 – **Robert Austin** (1895-1973), *Spitfire in Hangar*, 1940,
signed, titled and dated 1/40,
charcoal and pastel heightened with white on paper, 16 x 22 in. (41 x 56 cm).

The Supermarine Spitfire was a British single-seat fighter aircraft used by the Royal Air Force and many other Allied countries before, during and after the Second World War. The Spitfire was built in many variants, using several wing configurations, and was produced in greater numbers than any other British aircraft. It was also the only British fighter to be in continuous production throughout the war.

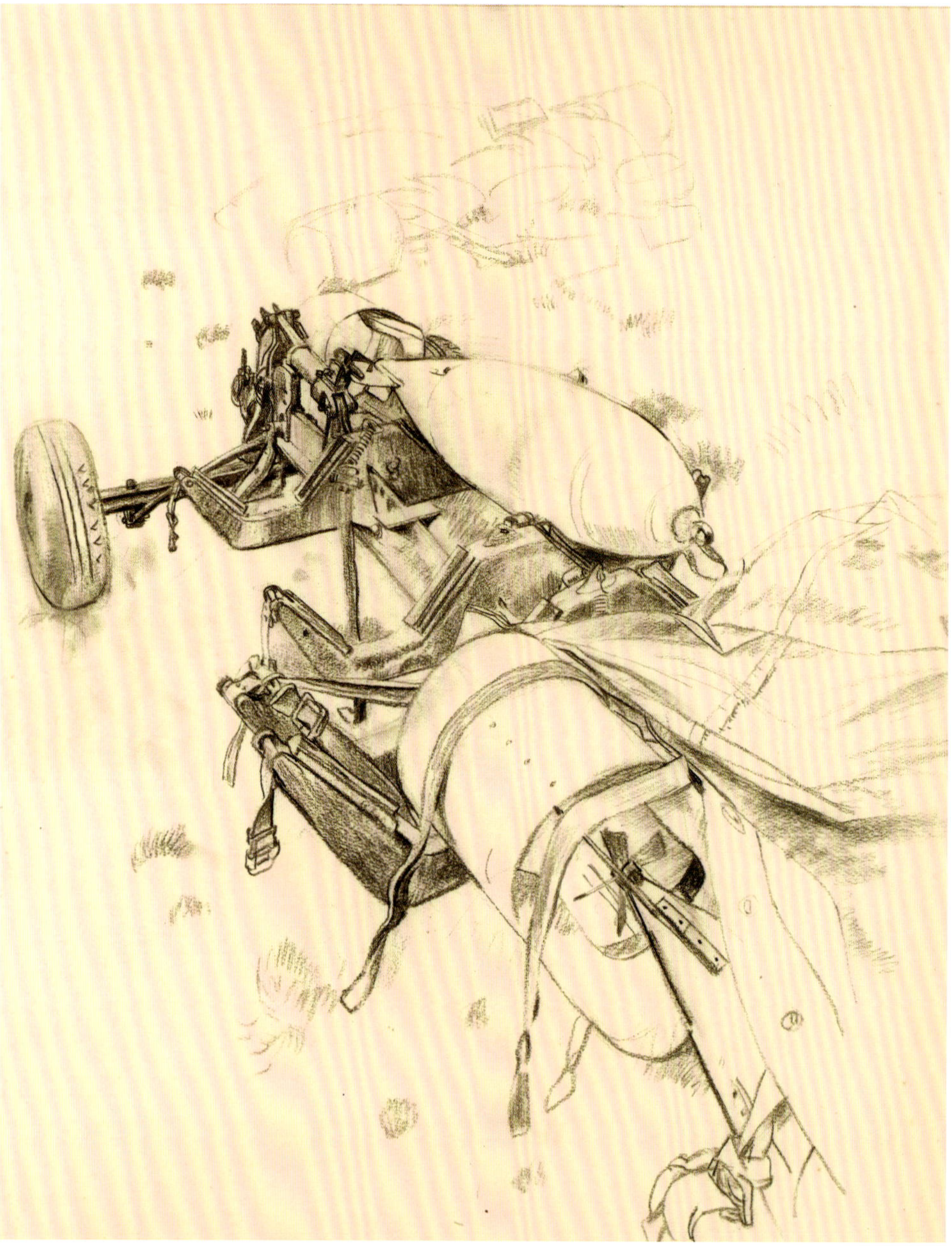

CAT. 41 – **Robert Austin** (1895-1973), *Bomb Trolley*, 1944, signed and dated, pencil on paper, 23 x18 in. (58.3 x 45.6 cm.).
Provenance: Artist's daughters.

This drawing depicts a bomb trolley, which would have been pulled behind a tractor from the bomb dump to the aircraft. The bomb was then loaded into the aircraft's bomb carrier, from which it was eventually dropped.

CAT. 42 – **Anonymous**, *Wings for Victory*,
Lithographic proof, before over-printing, 29 ½ x 19 ½ in. (73.5 x 49.5 cm),
printed by T.G. Porter, issued by The National Saving Committee, London (WFP 268).

Nearly every town had 'Wings for Victory' fund-raising weeks during which people were asked to contribute money for a Spitfire or a Wellington or Lancaster bomber. People were also asked to give aluminum pots and pans for melting down to make aircraft. Events were advertised through a series of posters some of which left space for overprinting so that dates and venues could be added for specific events.

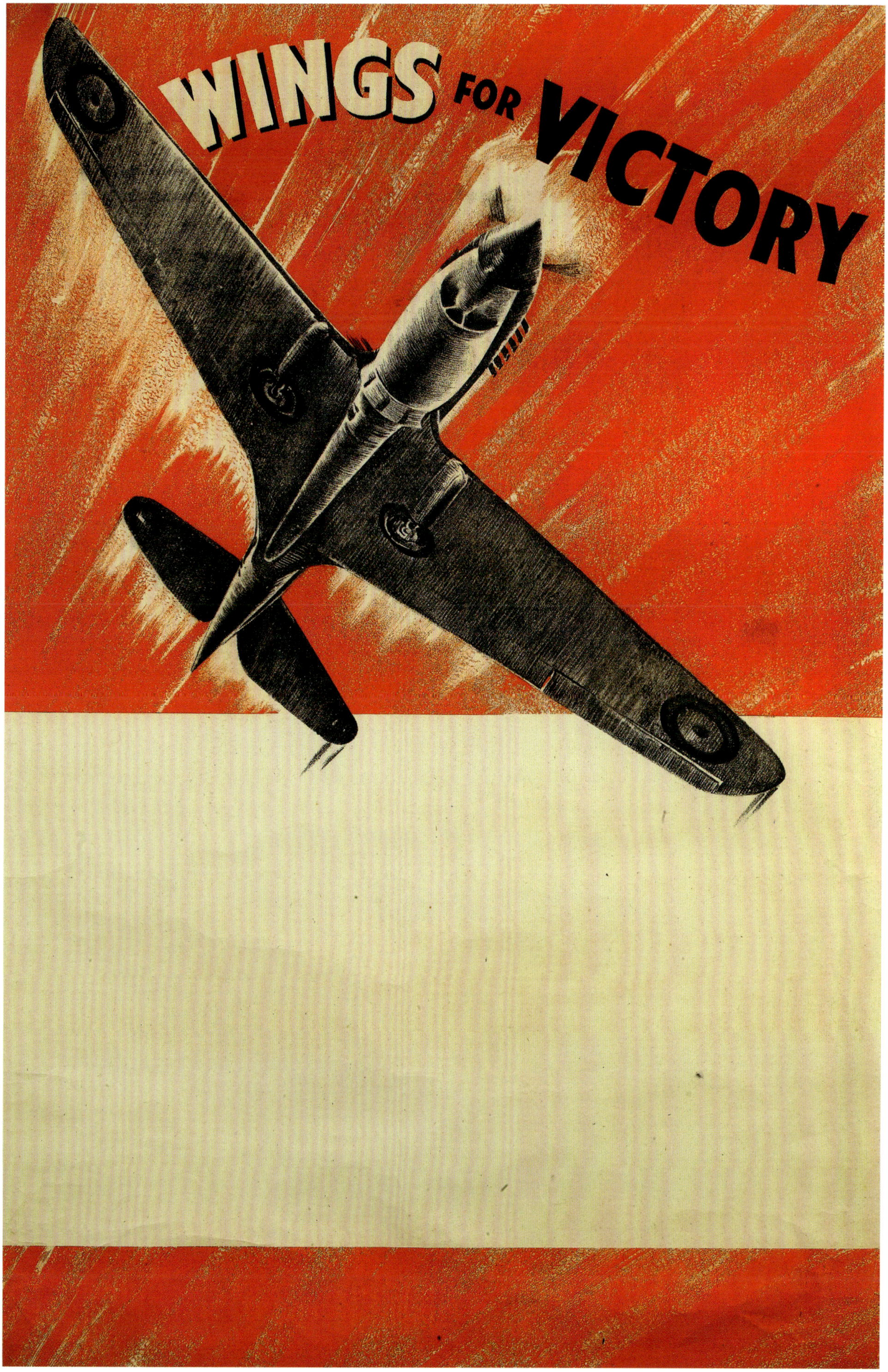
WINGS FOR VICTORY

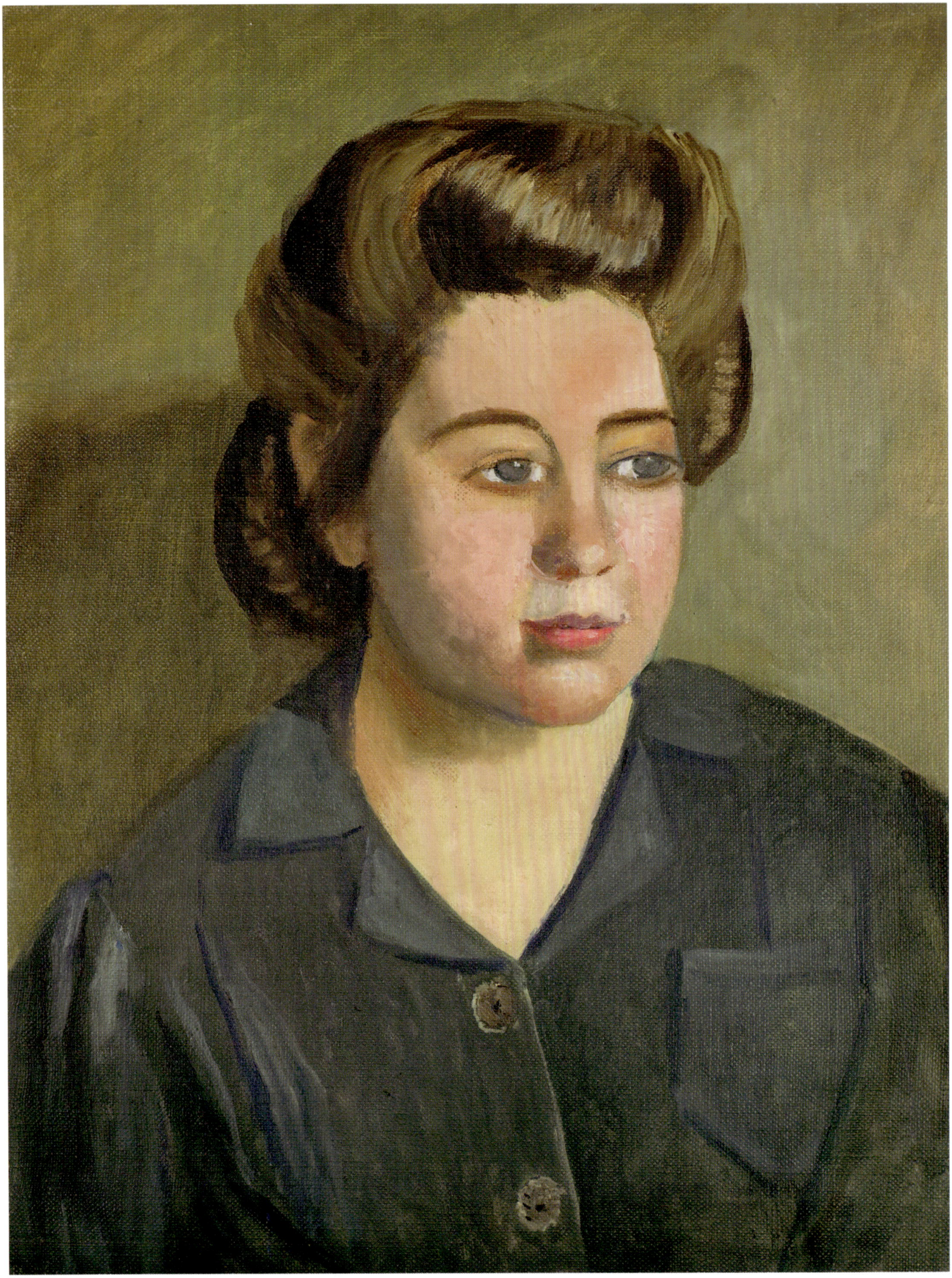

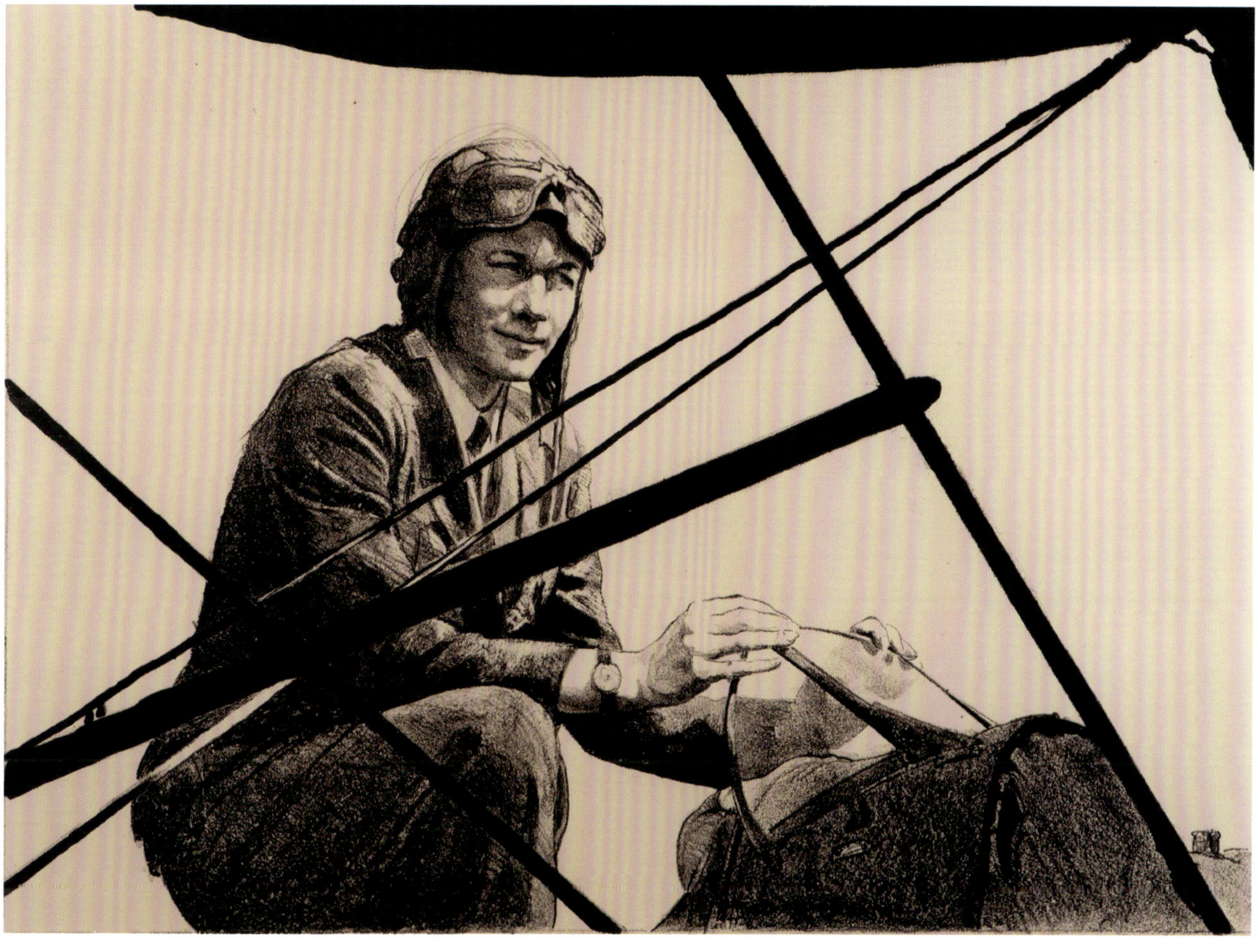

CAT. 44 – **Ethel Gabain** (1883-1950), *Captain Pauline Gower of the Women's Air Transport Auxiliary*, 1941,
Lithographic print from the series *Women's Work in the War (Other than the Services)*, published by The Ministry of Information: His Majesty's Stationery Office, 14 ¾ x 19 ¾ in. (37.8 x 50.2 cm).

Pauline Mary de Peauly Gower, Mrs Fahie (1910–1947), was a British pilot and writer who headed the female branch of the Air Transport Auxiliary during WW2, responsible for ferrying military aircraft from factory or repair facility to storage or operational units. Gower appointed the first eight women pilots for the ATA on 1 January 1940. Gabain was appointed an Official War Artist in the same year and produced two sets of prints published by the Ministry of Information, Children in Wartime and Women's Work in the War (Other than the Services), 1941. The latter contained six lithographs and a commentary on each: 'Women made a fine contribution to victory in the last great war, but on the present occasion they have indeed excelled themselves. In no sphere have they shown greater courage and skill than in the air. The women of the Air Transport Auxiliary, of which Pauline Gower is the leader, have the highly responsible task of flying between the factories and the Royal Air Force Stations.'

Prints were commissioned from three artists as part of the WAAC scheme: Ethel Gabain, A.S. Hartrick and H. Andrew Freeth.

CAT. 43 – **Evelyn Dunbar** (1906-1960),
Study for an unidentified WAAF (Women's Auxiliary Air Force) member,
painted at RAF South Cerney, Gloucestershire, in July 1944,
oil on canvas, 18 x 14 in. (45.7 x 35.6 cm).
Provenance: Roger Folley; Alasdair Dunbar; Hammer Mill Oast Collection.
Exhibited: *Evelyn Dunbar – The Lost Works*, Pallant House Gallery, October 2015 - February 2016. cat 90.
Literature: *Evelyn Dunbar – The Lost Works*, Sacha Llewellyn & Paul Liss, July 2015, cat. 90, page 137.

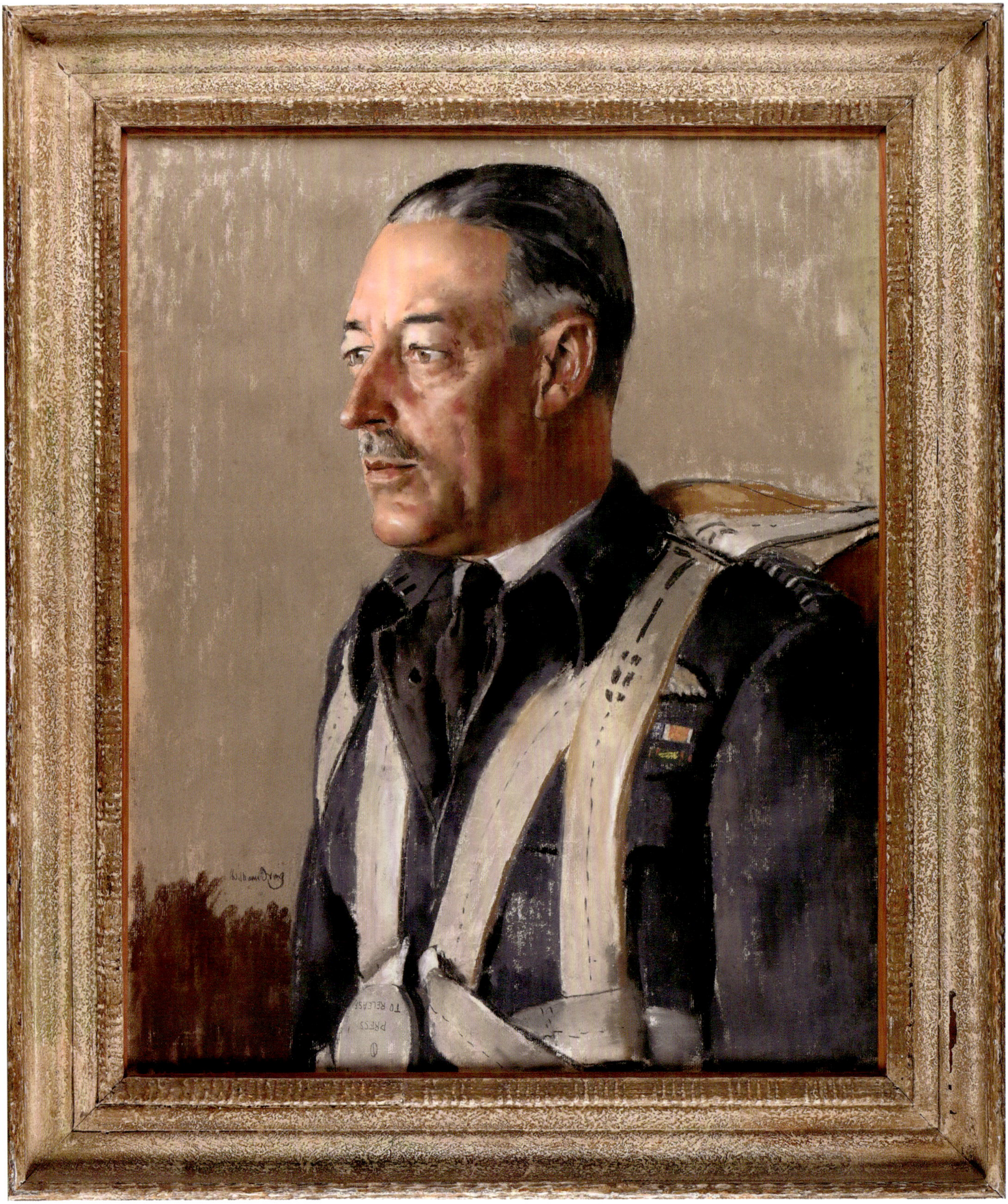
PRESS TO RELEASE

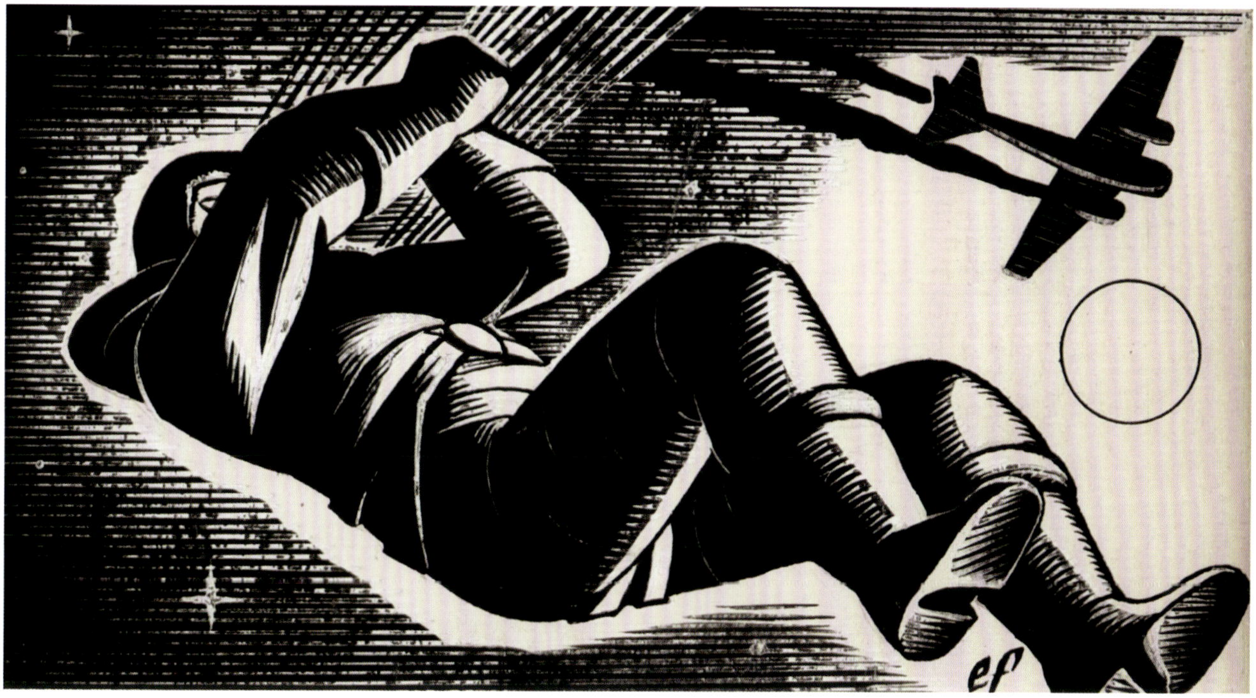

CAT. 46 – **Eric Fraser** (1902-1983), *RAF Pilot Ejecting from his burning plane*, 1942, signed with initials, pen and ink with bodycolour on illustration board, 4 ½ x 7 ½ in. (11.5 x 18.7 cm).

This drawing was an illustration for *Marching On*, a wartime news/propaganda radio programme, edited by Robert Barr, produced by John Glyn-Jones and narrated by James McKechnie.

CAT. 45 – **William Dring** (1904-1990), *Group Captain Maurice Newnham O.B.E. D.F.C.*, signed, pastel on paper, 23 ½ x 19 ½ inches (60 x 49.5 cm), in its original frame.

Maurice Newnham had an eventful and distinguished career. During WW1 he was a fighter pilot and was awarded the D.F.C., a Mention in Despatches, and the French Croix de Guerre avec Palme. His peace-time occupations included the managing directorship of the Triumph Motor Company of Coventry. He was a prominent and successful competitor in motoring events, and was responsible for the design and production of the famous Triumph – Dolomite range of motors.

At the outbreak of WW2 he rejoined the R.A.F. In the autumn of 1940 he was sent to Ringway near Manchester to explore the possibilities of parachute and glider-borne armies. He was then forty-four, and had never made a parachute jump in his life. Accidents were many, but Newnham evolved a parachute flying and landing technique which reduced injuries. In five years more than 60,000 men of nearly all Allied armies and nations passed through his hands for training. In this pastel portrait, a medium Dring excelled in, Newnham is shown wearing his RAF uniform with his parachute strapped to his back.

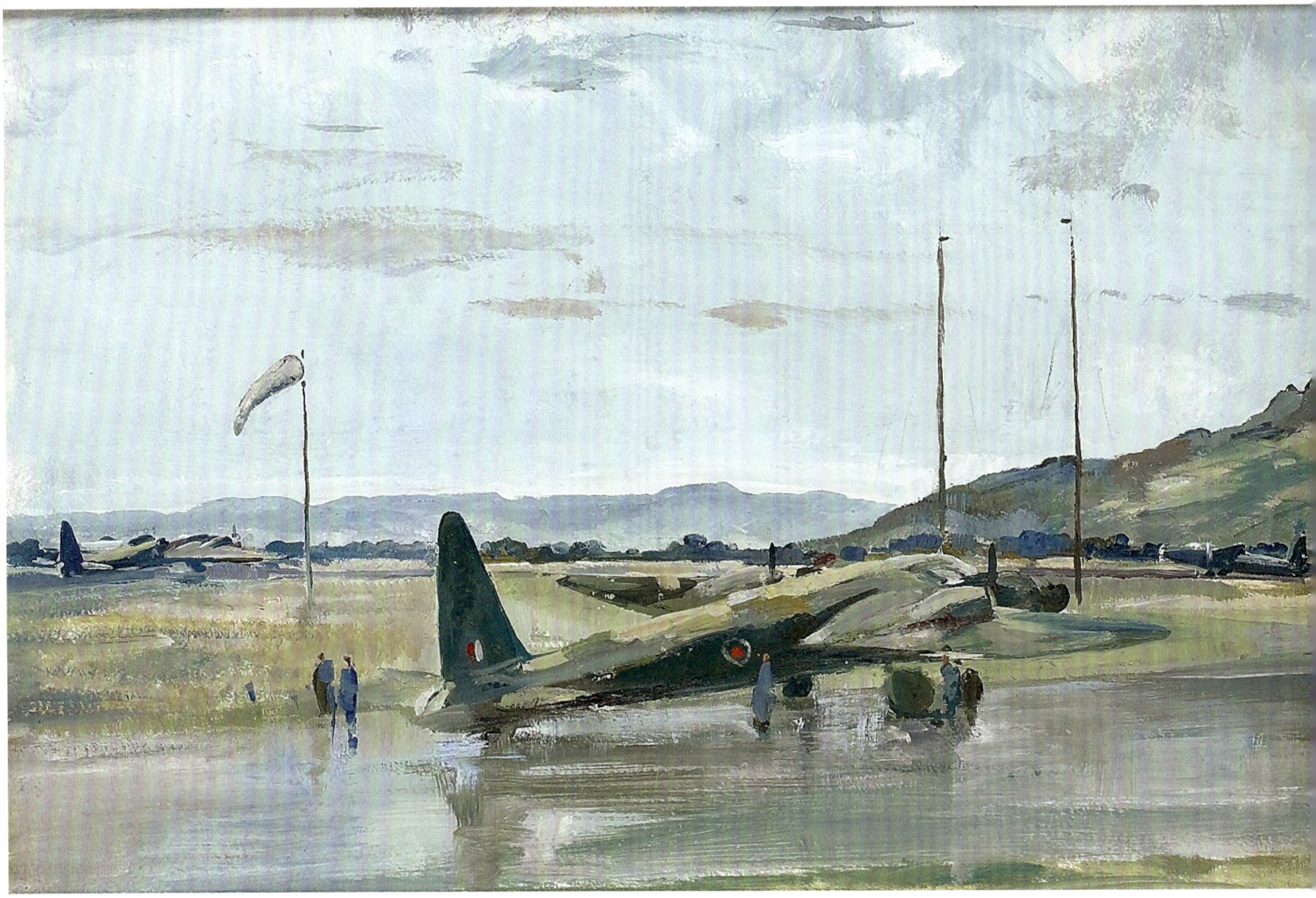

CAT. 47 – **Charles Cundall** (1890-1971), Study for *Coastal Operational Training Unit (Limavady, Northern Ireland)*, c.1942, oil on paper, 14 x 42 in. (35.6 x 106.7 cm).
Provenance: Acquired directly from the Artist's Daughter.
Exhibited: *Charles Cundall – A Working Method*, Young Gallery Salisbury, March- April 2016, Sotheran's, April-May 2016.
Literature: *Charles Cundall (1890-1971)*, Edited by Sacha Llewellyn & Paul Liss, published by Liss Llewellyn Fine Art, February 2016.

This is a sketch for *Coastal Operational Training Unit* (now in the RAF Museum, Hendon). It shows Wellington bombers, the revolutionary (geodetic) aeroplane designed by Barnes Wallis in 1933; the Wellington MK II, introduced into service in 1940, was, according to the RAF Handbook, 'a remarkably fine bomber … used extensively on night bombing raids on enemy targets, including those in Italy' (Eric Sargent, c.1941). When the finished painting was exhibited at the Royal Academy in 1943, it was titled C.O.T.U. Station. Painted for the Nation's War Records, no. 59, the setting (not indicated at the time for security reasons) is Limavady, Northern Ireland.

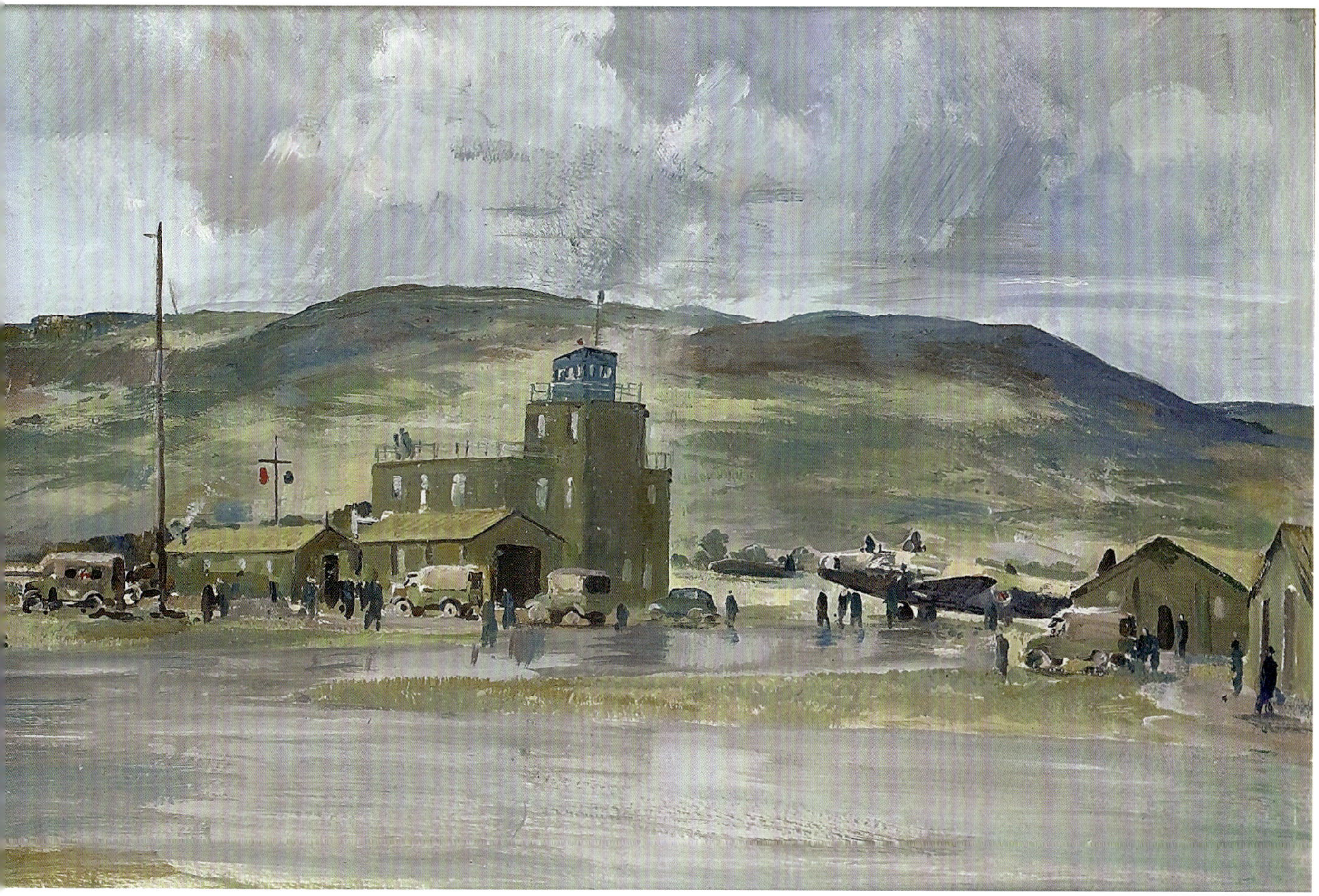

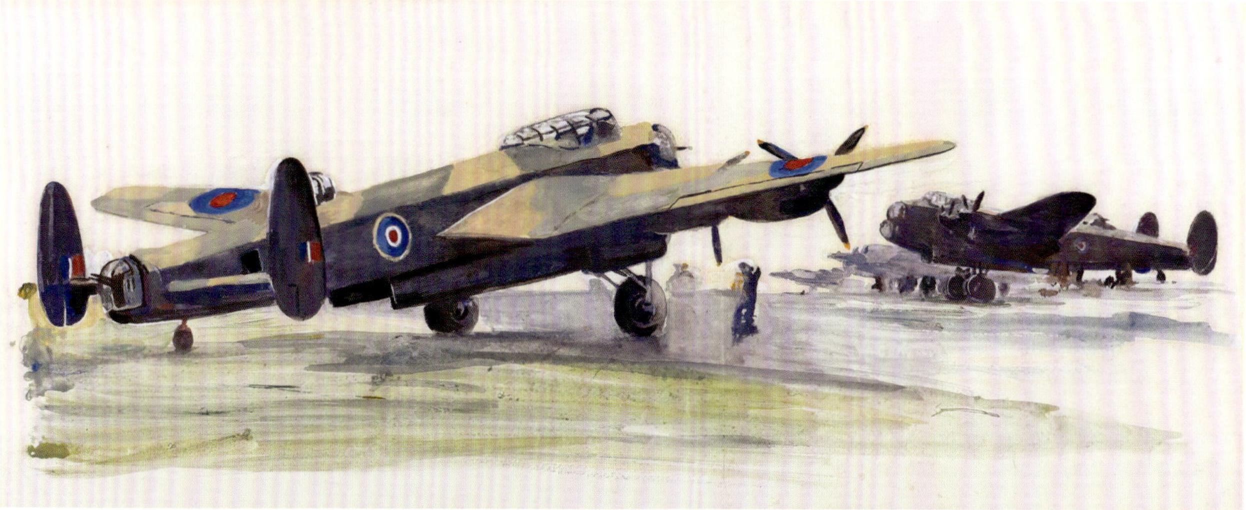

CAT. 48 – **Charles Cundall** (1890-1971), *Lancaster Bombers,*
watercolour on paper, 9 ½ x 24 in. (24 x 61 cm).
Provenance: Acquired directly from the Artist's Daughter.
Exhibited: *Charles Cundall – A Working Method,* Young Gallery Salisbury, March- April 2016, Sotheran's, April-May 2016.
Literature: *Charles Cundall (1890-1971)*, Edited by Sacha Llewellyn & Paul Liss, published by Liss Llewellyn Fine Art, February 2016.

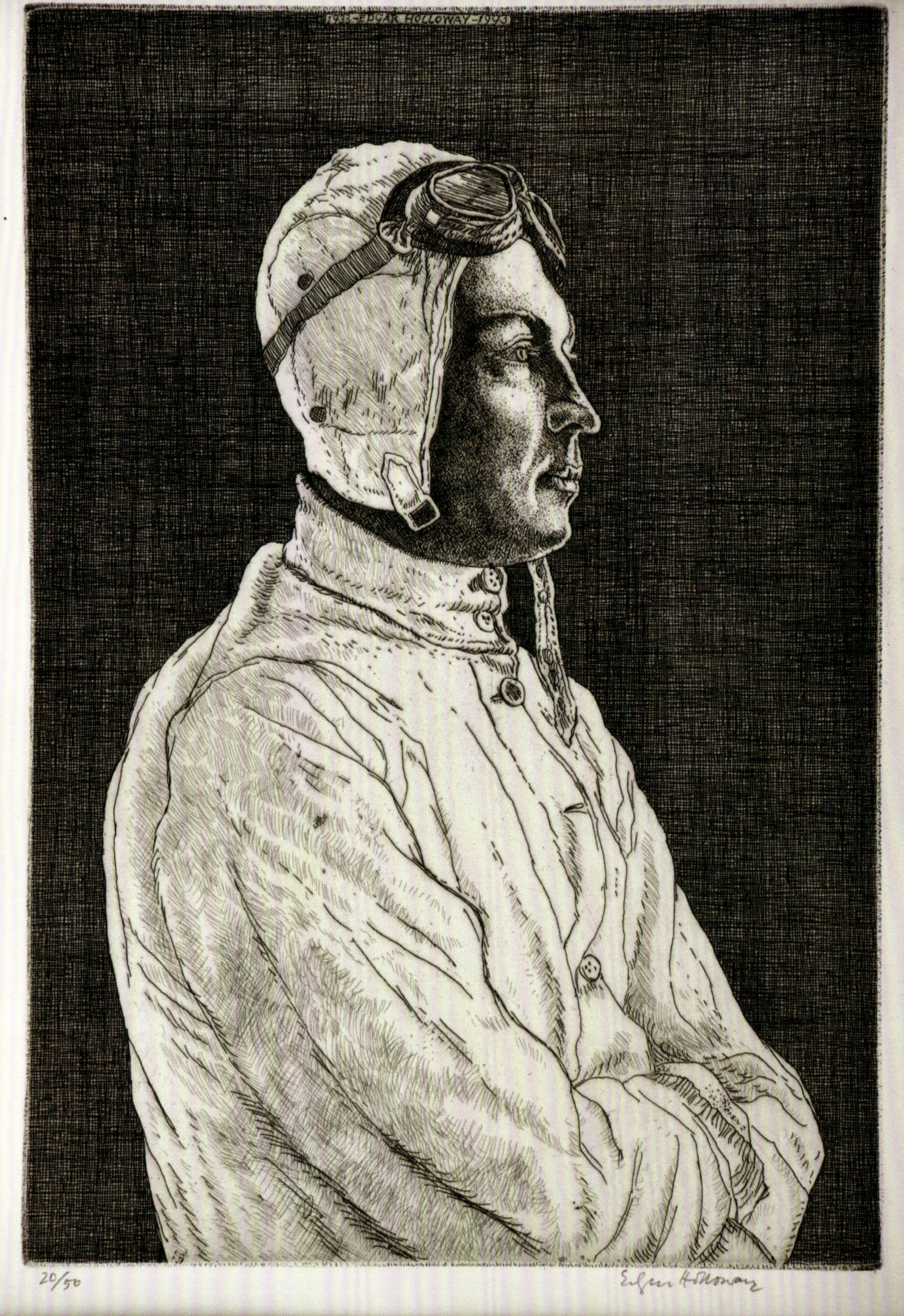

CAT. 49 – **Edgar Holloway** (1914-2008), *The Airman II*, signed and editioned 20/50 in pencil, etching, plate size, 10 x 7 in. (25 x 17.5 cm).

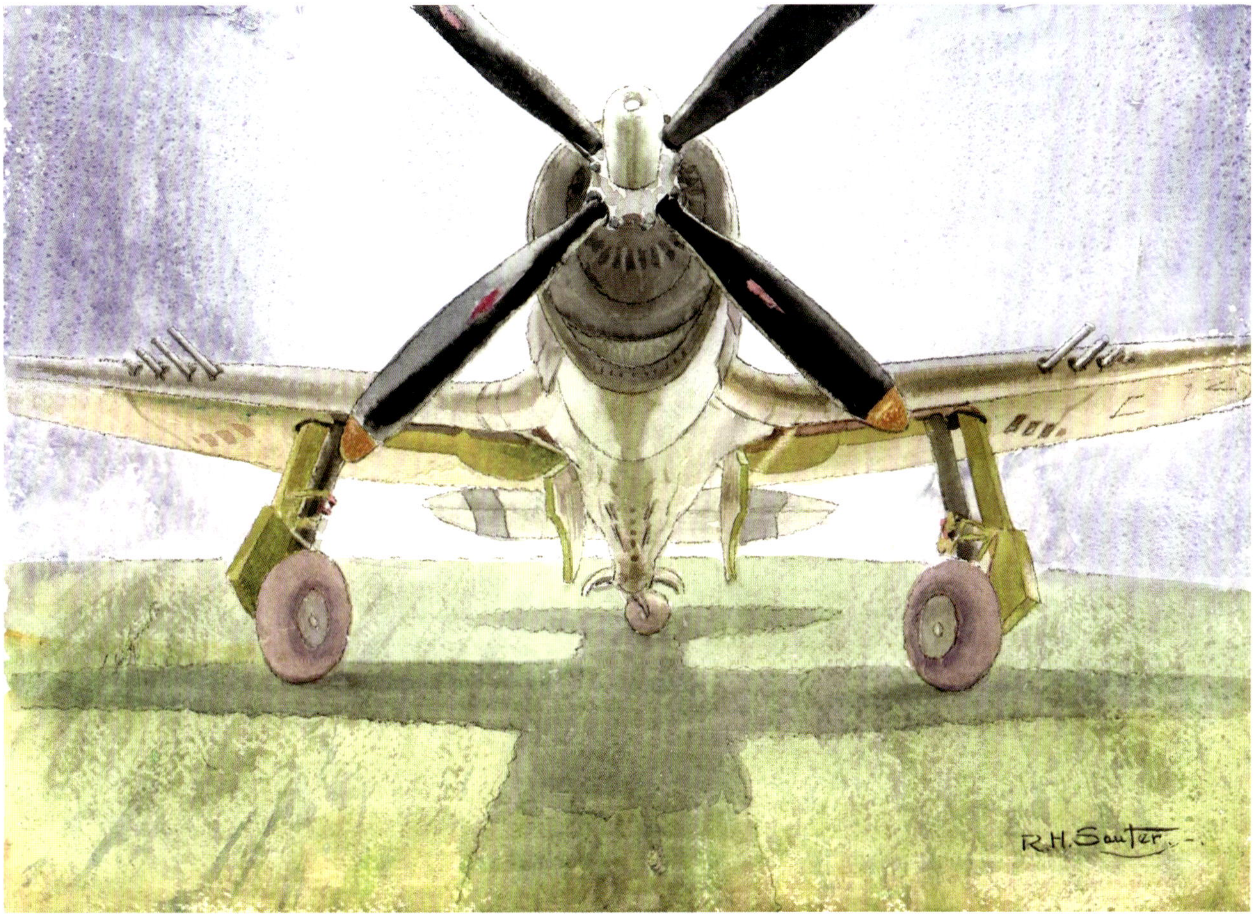

CAT. 50 – **Rudolph Sauter** (1895-1977), *The Sinister Insect: The Dragon Fly,* c.1940, signed, inscribed with title to reverse, watercolour on paper, 11 x 15 ½ in. (27.7 x 39.5 cm)
Provenance: Given by Sauter to the grandmother of the previous owner; private collection South Africa, 2010.

This shows a Republic P-47D Thunderbolt, a tremendously powerful aeroplane capable of lifting a heavy weapons pay-load. The Thunderbolt was used by the RAF as a ground-attack aircraft in the Far East. It had been designed for the United States Army Air Force as a high altitude fighter and was used in that role, but the RAF preferred Spitfires and Mustangs for that work. Sixteen RAF squadrons operated the type in South-East Asia equipping the aircraft with three 500lb bombs or with eight 60lb rocket projectiles below the outer wings. Though showing no American markings, this example appears to be the USAAF fighter version that was used to escort the bombers of the 8th US Air Force on their daylight missions over Germany. This type's eight '50 calibre' 0.5 inch machine guns mounted in the wings gave it significant punch in combatting German fighters.

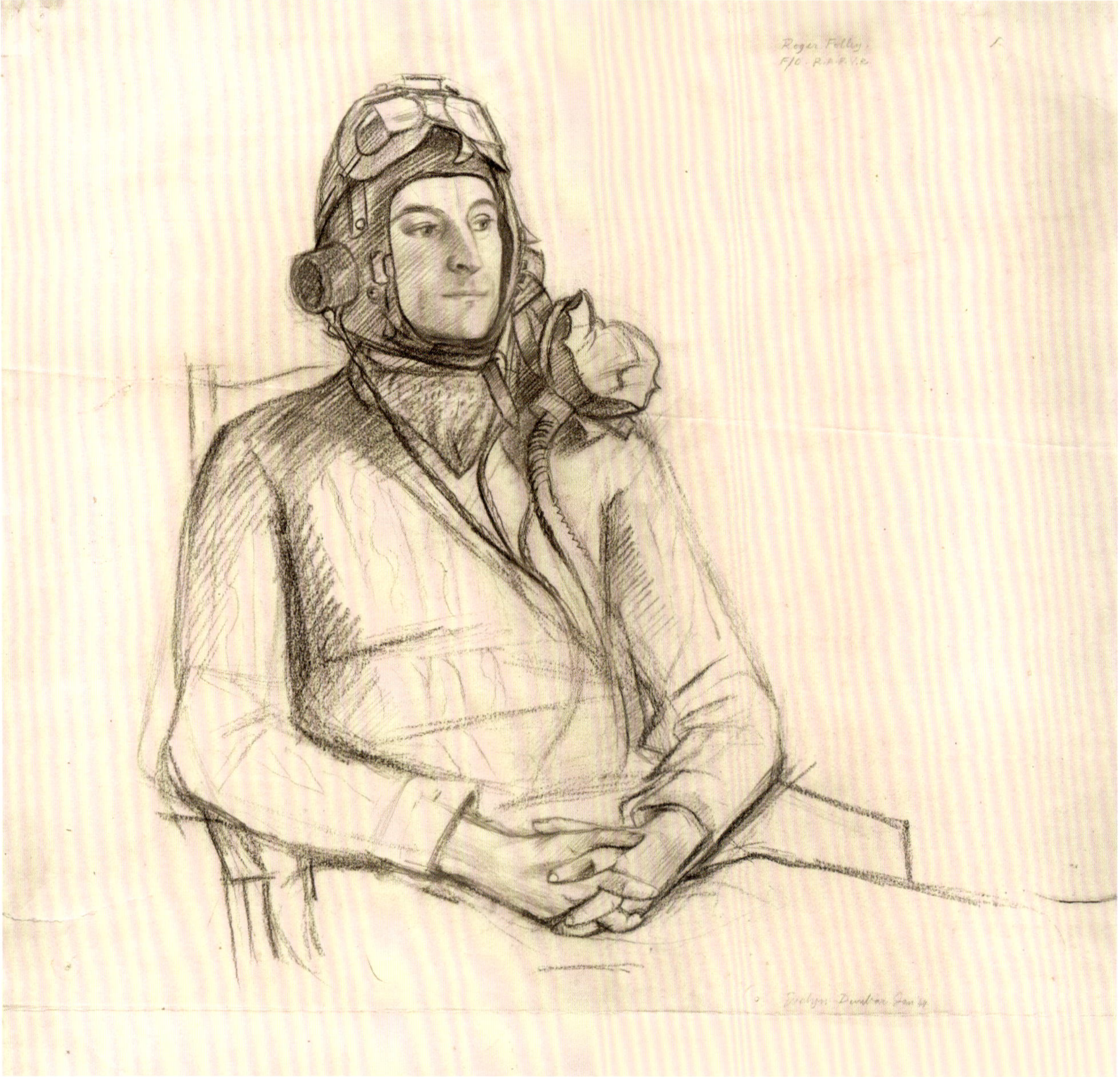

CAT. 51 – **Evelyn Dunbar** (1906-1960), *Portrait of Flying Officer Roger Folley, RAFVR, January 1944*, signed and dated,
pencil and black chalk on paper, 17 ¾ x 17 in. (45 x 43 cm).
Provenance: Roger Folley; Alasdair Dunbar; Hammer Mill Oast.
Exhibited: *Evelyn Dunbar – The Lost Works*, Pallant House Gallery, October 2015 - February 2016 cat 86. Literature: *Evelyn Dunbar – The Lost Works*, Sacha Llewellyn & Paul Liss, July 2015, cat. 86, page 132-133.

Dunbar met Roger Folley, a horticultural economist, at Sparsholt Farm Institute, where he worked before the war. They were married in 1942. Folley, on leave from France when this was drawn, served in the RAF as a Navigator.

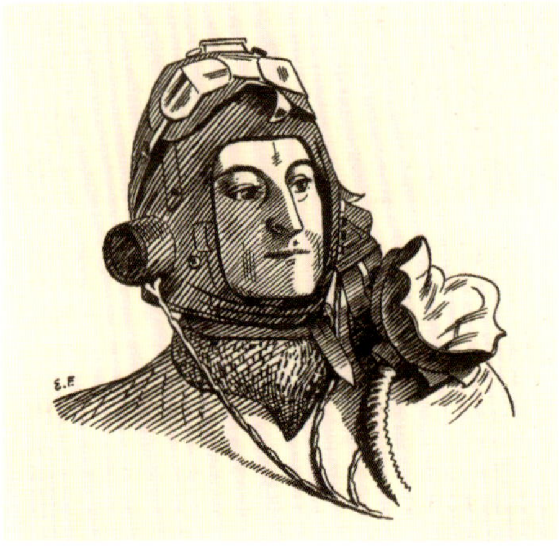

FIG. 8 – Evelyn Dunbar's Christmas card for 1944.

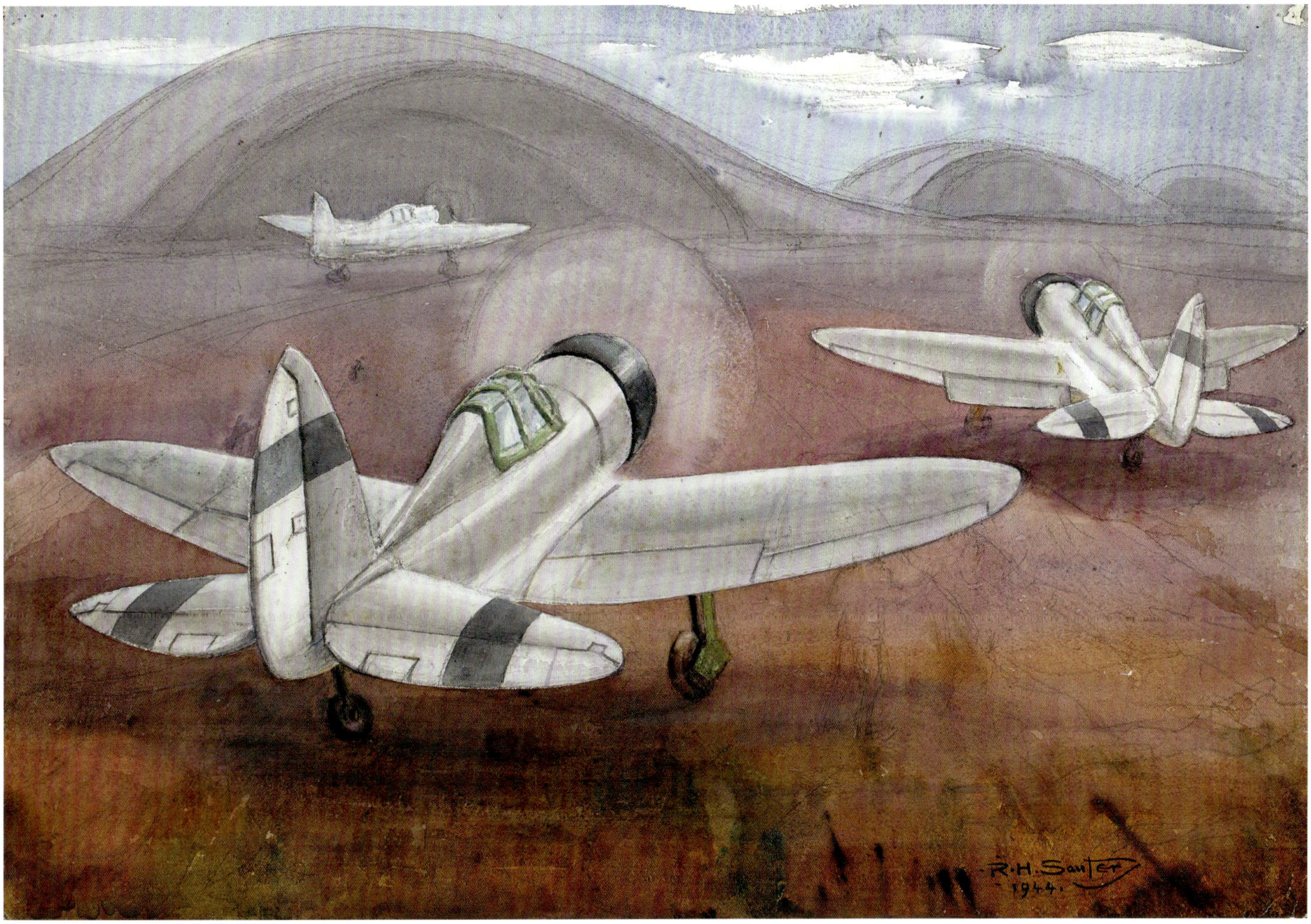

CAT. 52 – **Rudolph Sauter** (1895-1977), *Phantom Eyre*, 1944, signed and dated, label with title to reverse: 'Phantom Eyre – phantasy suggested by a Thunderbolt aerodrome, somewhere in England,' and on a second label, 'Razor Blacks, 256', watercolour on paper, 15 ½ x 22 ½ in. (39.3 x 57.5 cm).

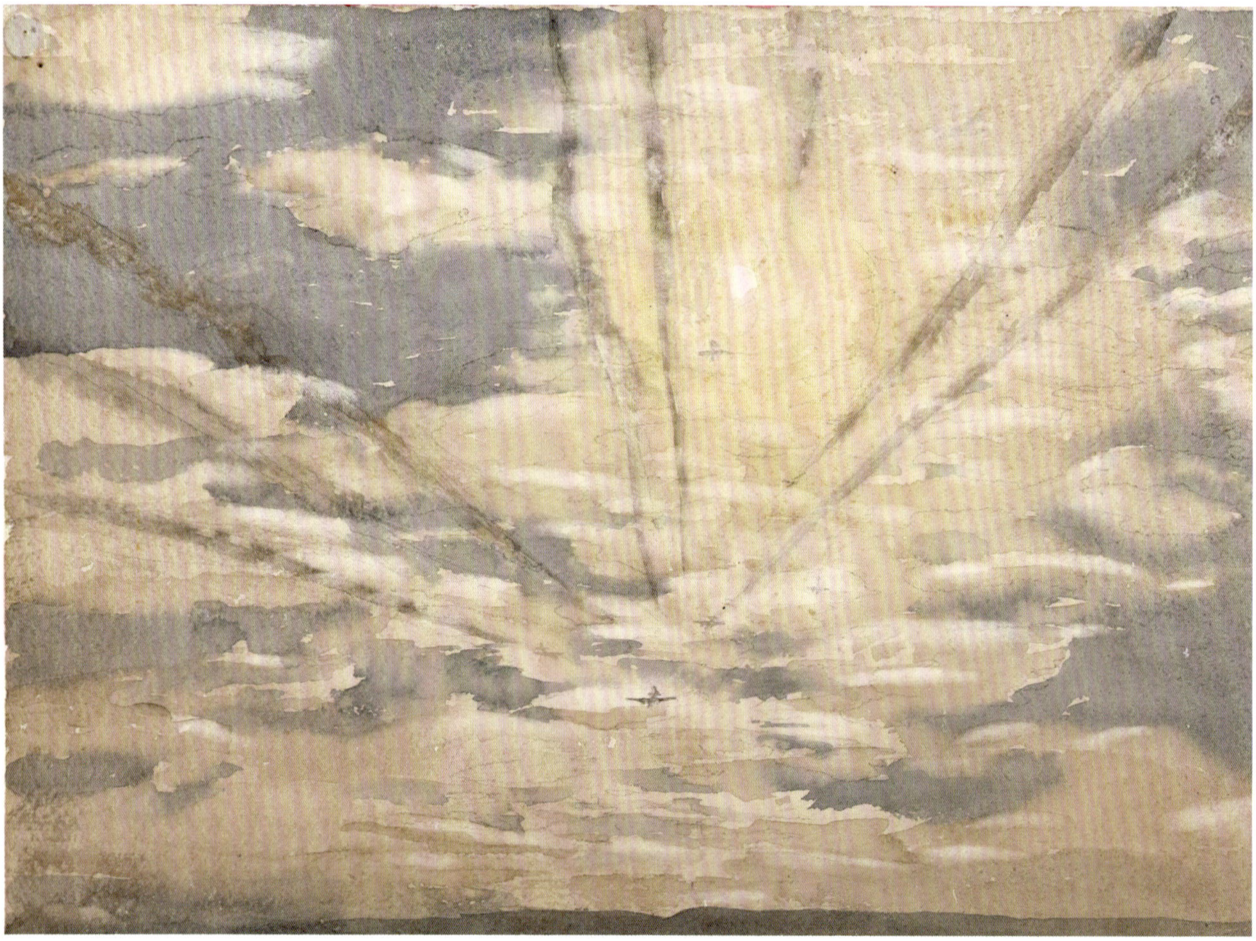

CAT. 53 – **Rudolph Sauter** (1895-1977), *Paths in the moonlight – Bombers going out over the Channel,* signed lower right, 1944, original manuscript label to verso giving title and artist's address, Press & Censorship Bureau inkstamp dated 16 October 1944, watercolour on paper, 11 ½ x 15 ¾ in. (29 x 40 cm).

This composition shows medium bombers on their way to bomb targets in German-occupied France. Bomber Command turned its attention to French transport targets – railway marshalling yards, bridges, rail tunnels etc – from about March 1944. This was done primarily to isolate northern France from the rest of the transport system in order to hamper German troop movements countering the D-Day landings. To conceal the actual point of invasion, transport interdiction had to be widespread, from Caen to the Belgian border and from the northern Loire northwards towards Brest.

Rudolph Sauter (1895-1977),

CAT. 54 – *Doodlebug Alley – The Crooked Cross*, 1944,
signed and dated lower left, titled and additional inscribed to verso, Press & Censorship Bureau approval stamp to verso,
watercolour on paper, 10 x 14 ½ in. (26 x 37cm).

CAT. 55 – *Doodlebug Alley – Death on the Way*, 1944,
signed and dated lower left, Press & Censorship Bureau approval inkstamp to verso,
watercolour over pencil on paper, 10 x 13 ¾ in. (25 x 35 cm).

Sauter produced imaginative compositions with prophetic titles inspired by events he had observed; but he was disinterested in attempting to portray a faithful account. With some considerable liberty here Sauter shows V-1 Flying Bombs under attack from anti-aircraft artillery, indicated by the shell bursts lower right, and/or North American P-51 Mustangs. Flying Bombs were extremely fast and very small so had to be hit directly from behind which made the danger of flying into the debris cloud unavoidable.

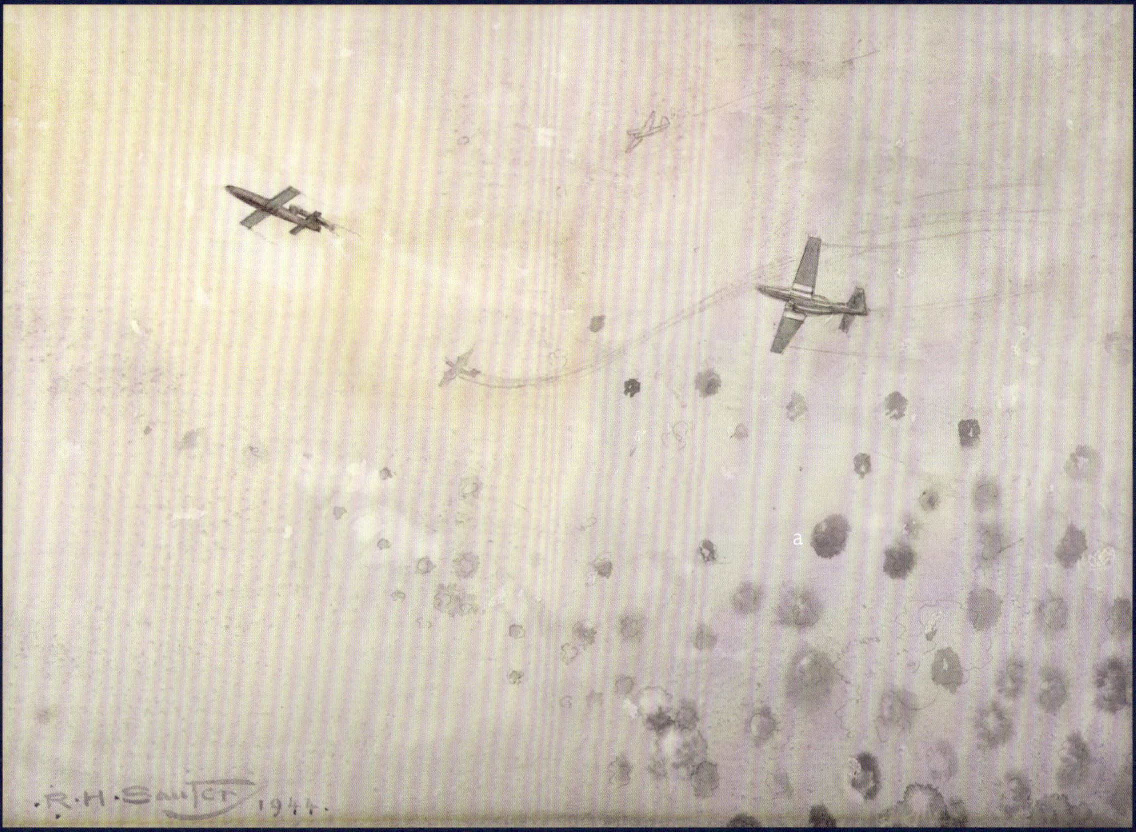

CAT. 54

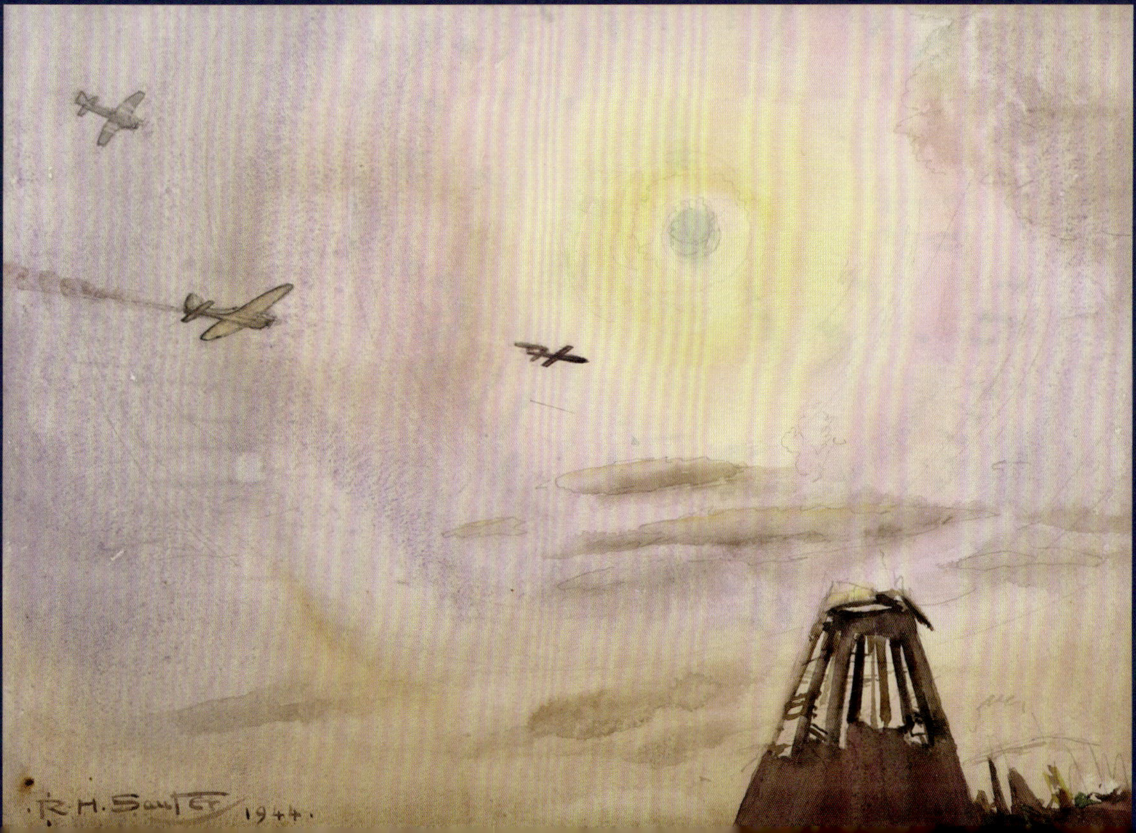

CAT. 55

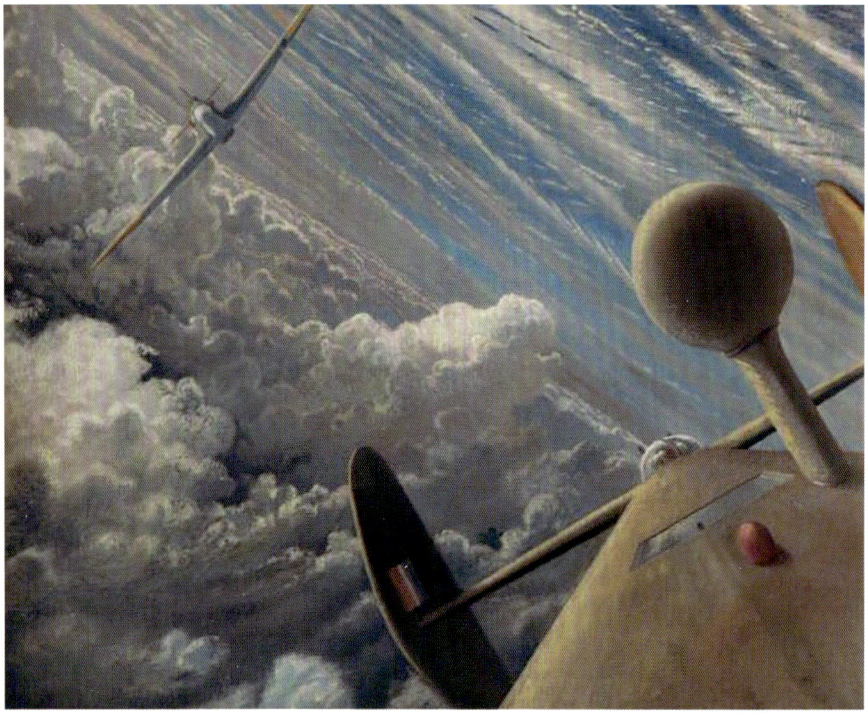

FIG. 9 – **Sir Thomas Monnington** (1902-1976), *Fighter Affiliation : Halifax and Hurricane*, 1943, oil on canvas, 22 ¾ x 28 ½ in. (57.8 x 72.4 cm). Royal Air Force Museum

In 1943 Thomas Monnington, who had taken flying lessons before the war, wrote to the War Artists' Advisory Committee, WAAC, complaining of the lack of an aerial perspective among the works WAAC had so far commissioned. Monnington was passionate about aircraft – by the time he applied to become an official War Artist he had completed over 600 hours of flying time. In November 1943, WAAC issued Monnington with the first of a series of full-time commissions that saw him flying with a training squadron in Yorkshire and with Mitchell bombers to Germany.

Whilst posted at the Brooklands race track during the early part of the war in the Design Team of the Directorate of Camouflage Monnington met Barnes Wallis – designer of the Wellington bomber and the 'bouncing bomb'. Wallis asked Monnington to apply his talent to improving the appearance of a heavy bomber which was being developed at the time, two designs for which are in the collection of the Victoria & Albert Museum.

CAT. 56 – **Sir Thomas Monnington** (1902-1976), *Interception practice over North Sea*, pencil on paper, 8 x 6 ¼ x in. (20 x 16 cm.).

Monnington's wartime paintings have an unusual sense of immediacy – they were based on sketches made *en plein air* – the compositions are seen from the pilot's dynamic point of view.

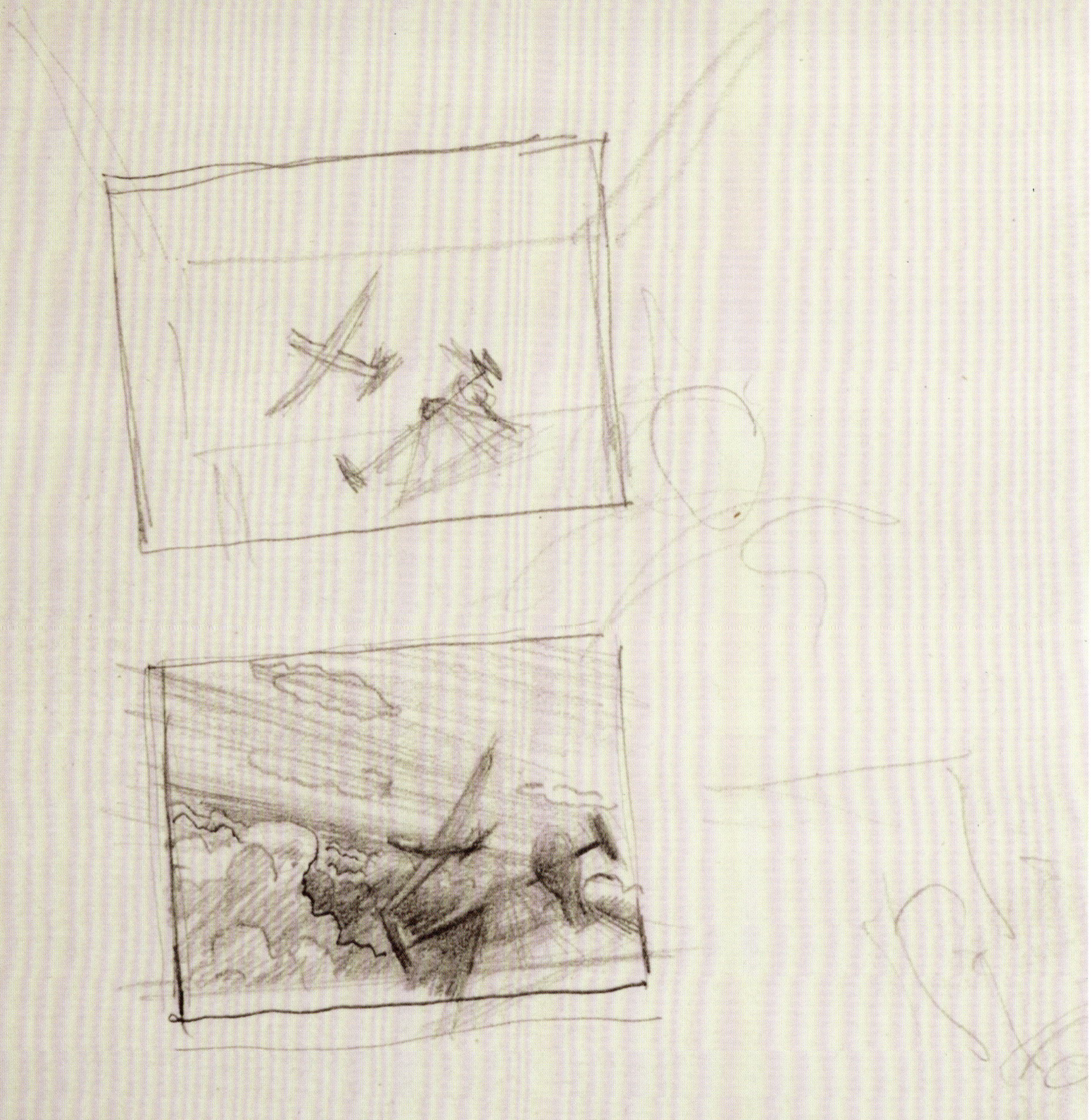

Interception practice over North Sea.

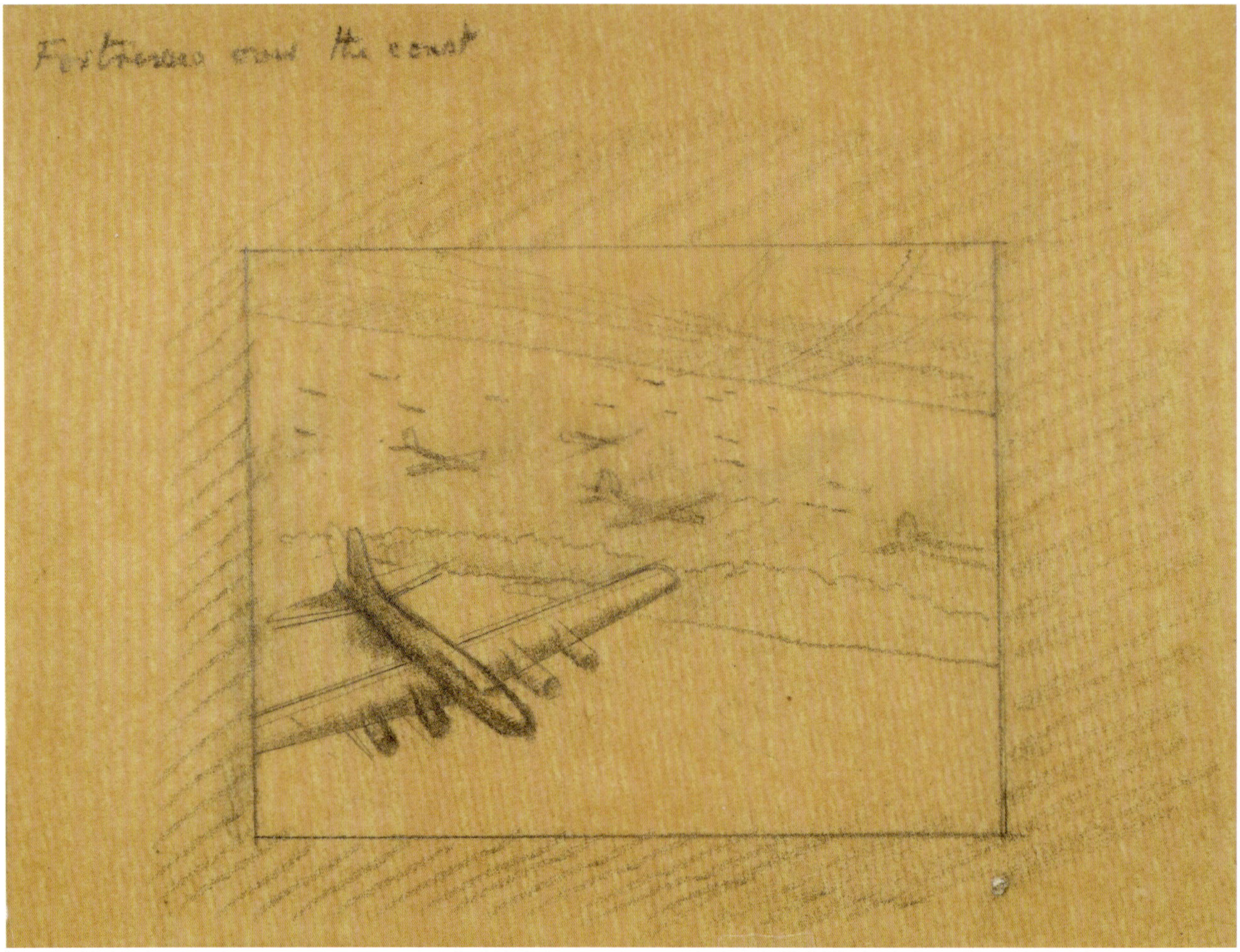

CAT. 57 – **Sir Thomas Monnington** (1902-1976), Study for *Fortresses*, inscribed *Fortresses over the coast,*
pencil on tracing paper, 4 ½ x 6 in. (11 x 15 cm).
Provenance: The Artist's Family

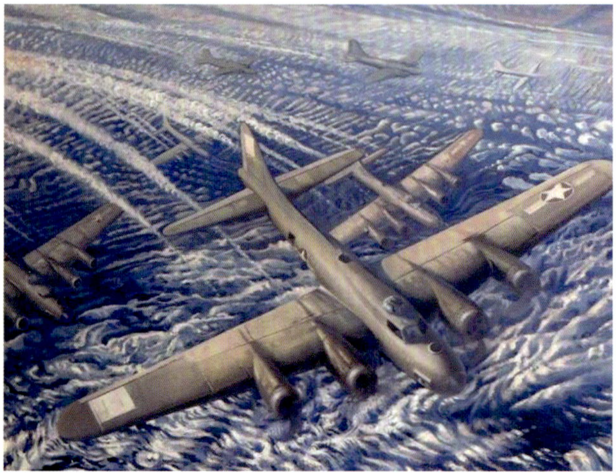

FIG. 10 – **Sir Thomas Monnington** (1902-1976),
Fortresses, 1944,
oil on canvas, 21 ½ x 28 ¼ in. (54.5 x 72 cm).
Russell-Cotes Art Gallery & Museum

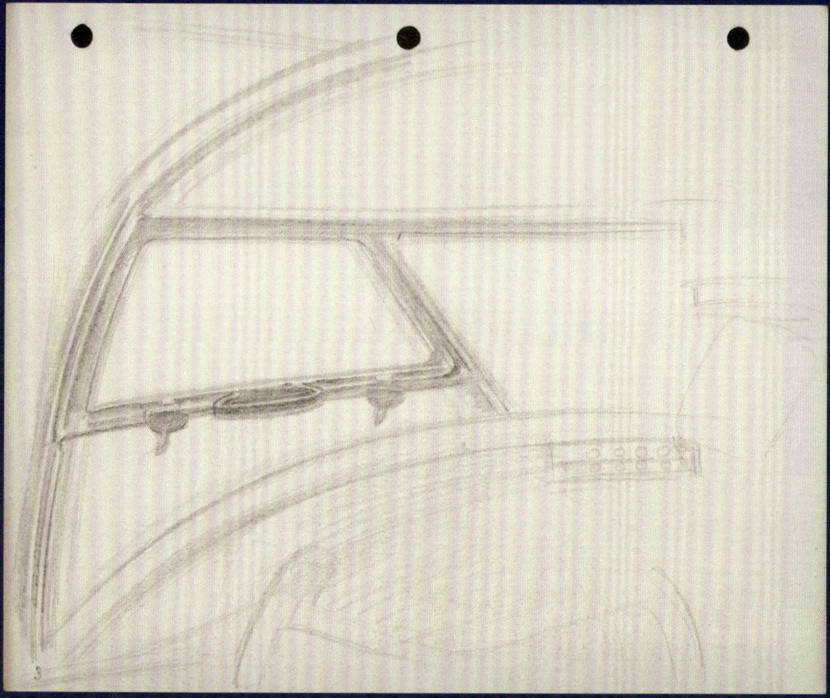

CAT. 58

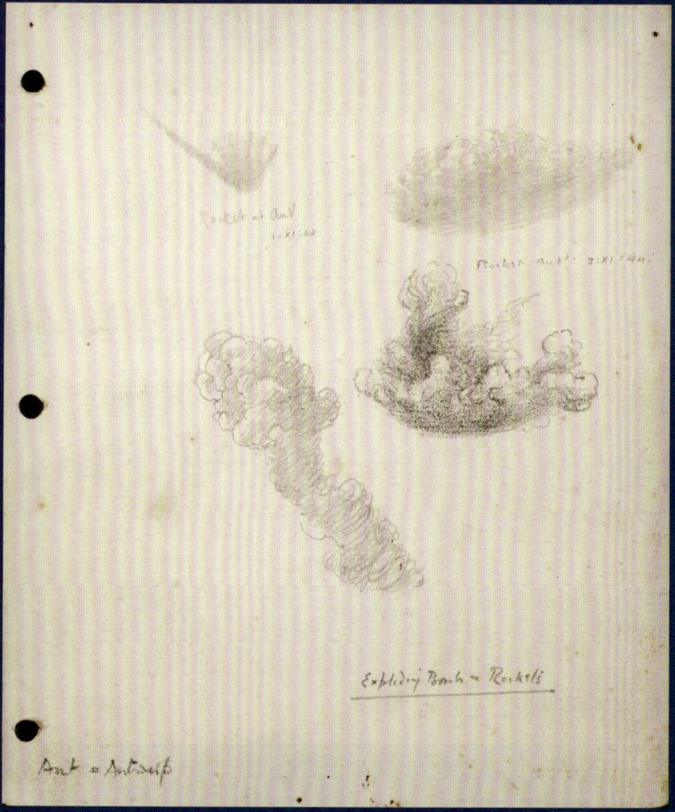

CAT. 59

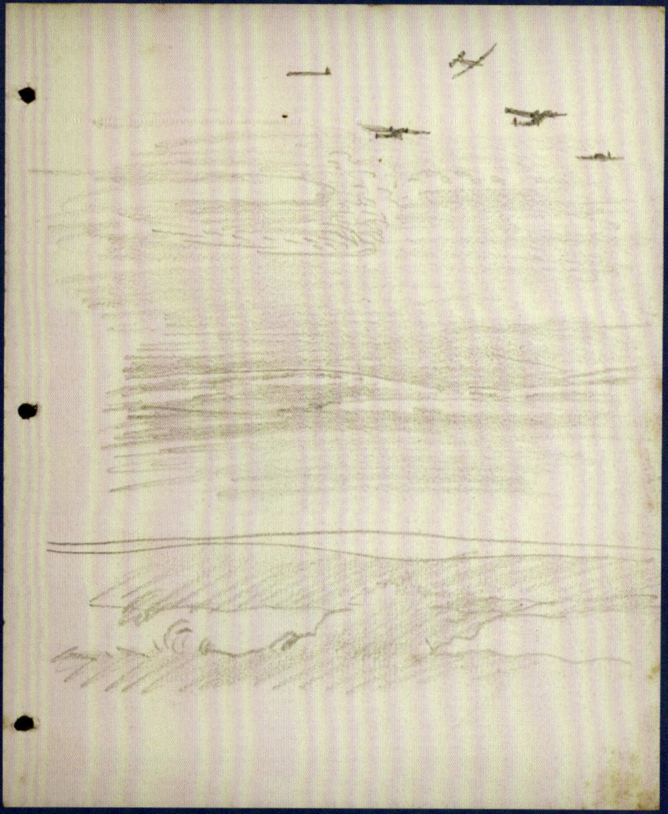

CAT. 60

Sir Thomas Monnington (1902-1976)

CAT. 58 *View from the cockpit*, pencil on paper, 6 ¼ x 8 in. (16 x 20 cm.).
CAT. 59 *Exploding bombs and rockets*, pencil on paper, 8 x 6 ¼ x in. (20 x 16 cm.)
CAT. 60 *Overflying aeroplanes*, 8 x 6 ¼ x in. (20 x 16 cm.)

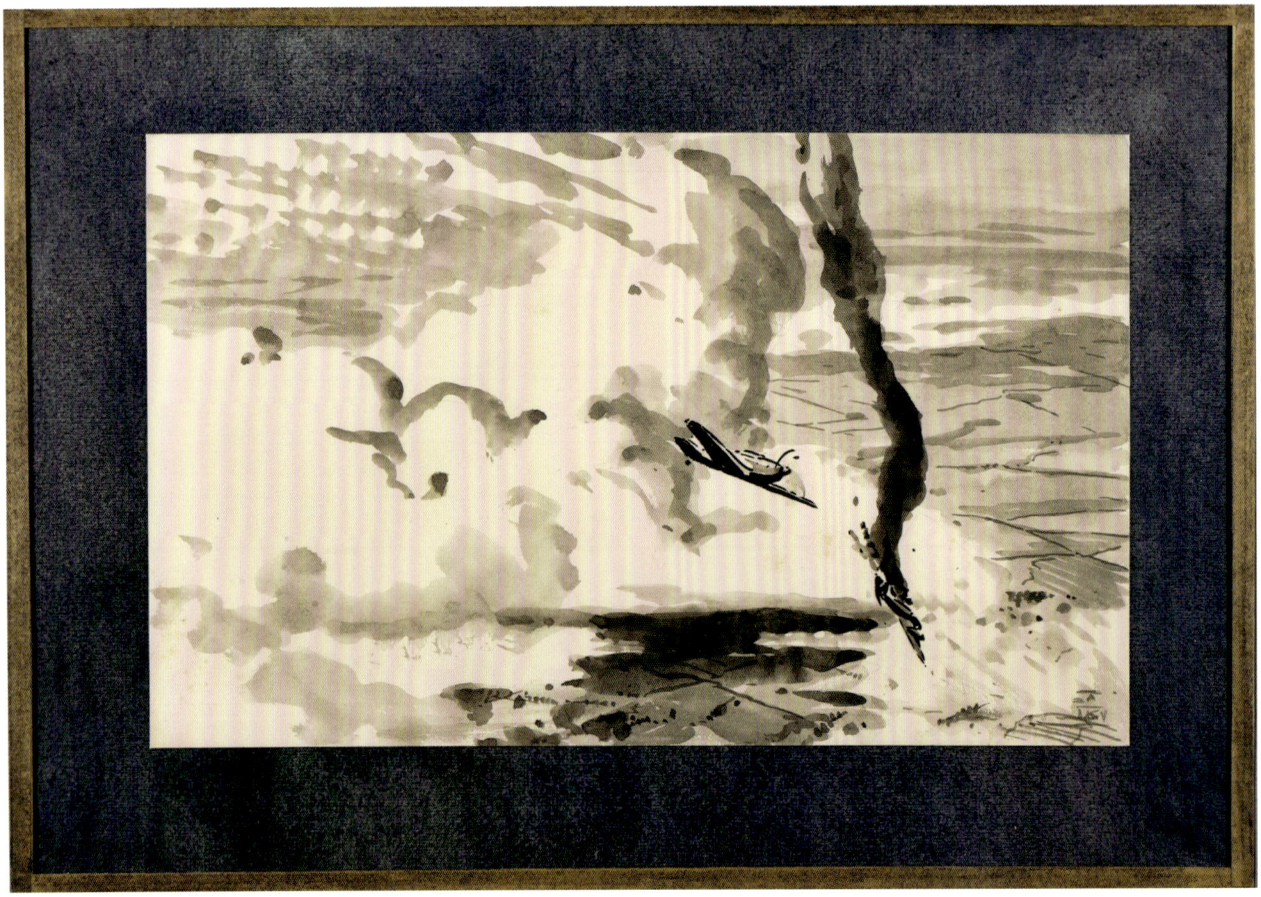

CAT. 61 – **Lt Richard Barrett Talbot Kelly** (1896 -1971), *Battle of Britain – A Hurricane downing a German Heinkel Aircraft*, c 1940, monochrome wash on paper, 8 x 12 ½ in. (19.5 x 32 cm).

Talbot Kelly is considered to be one of the finest aviation artists of his generation. His work is in the collection of the National Army Museum and the Royal Air Force Museum. In 1980 Harper Collins, London, published *A Subaltern's Odyssey: Memoirs of the Great War 1915-1917* based on his diaries.

CAT. 62 – **Barbara Jones** (1912-1978), *The Wind Tunnel – Royal Aircraft Establishment Farnborough*, 1944, signed and dated 1944, titled on the reverse and stamped with a Press Censorship Bureau pass, watercolour on paper, 22 x 14i in. (56 x 35.5 cm.)

This composition is closely related to one of the subject Jones submitted for 'Recording Britain.' There is no record of how Jones, still in her twenties, became involved in 'Recording Britain', but she was one of the first artists to be commissioned and its most prolific contributor. 'Recording Britain' was the brainchild of Sir Kenneth Clark, who saw it as an extension of the Official War Artist scheme. By choosing watercolour painting as the medium of record, Clark hoped that the scheme would also help to preserve this characteristic English art form.

The scheme was intended to boost national morale by celebrating the country's natural beauty and architectural heritage, but it was also a memorial to the war effort itself. The earliest pictures show the landscapes of southern England which were under immediate threat from bomb damage and invasion; in due course the remit was expanded to include those landscapes, buildings and ways of life that were vulnerable to the destructive forces of 'progress' – urban expansion, housing developments, road-building and so on. Recording Britain employed several women, notably Barbara Jones and Enid Marx. Both were fascinated by English popular art – everything from fairgrounds and follies to topiary and inn signs – and both continued to record these 'unsophisticated arts' after the war.

Works for 'Recording Britain', which numbered over 1500 watercolours, were widely exhibited during the war years. In 1949 the Pilgrim Trust gave them to the V&A.

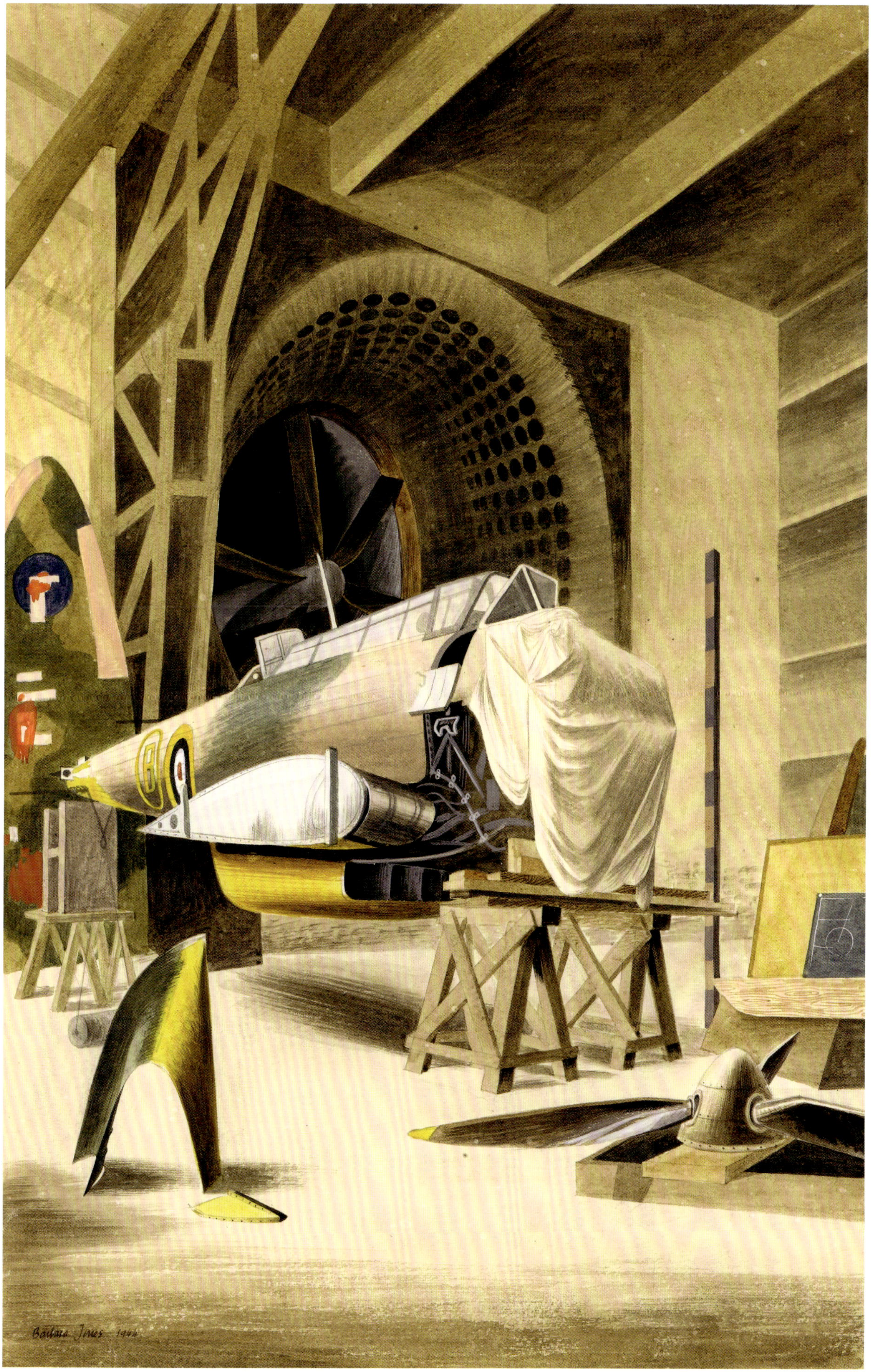

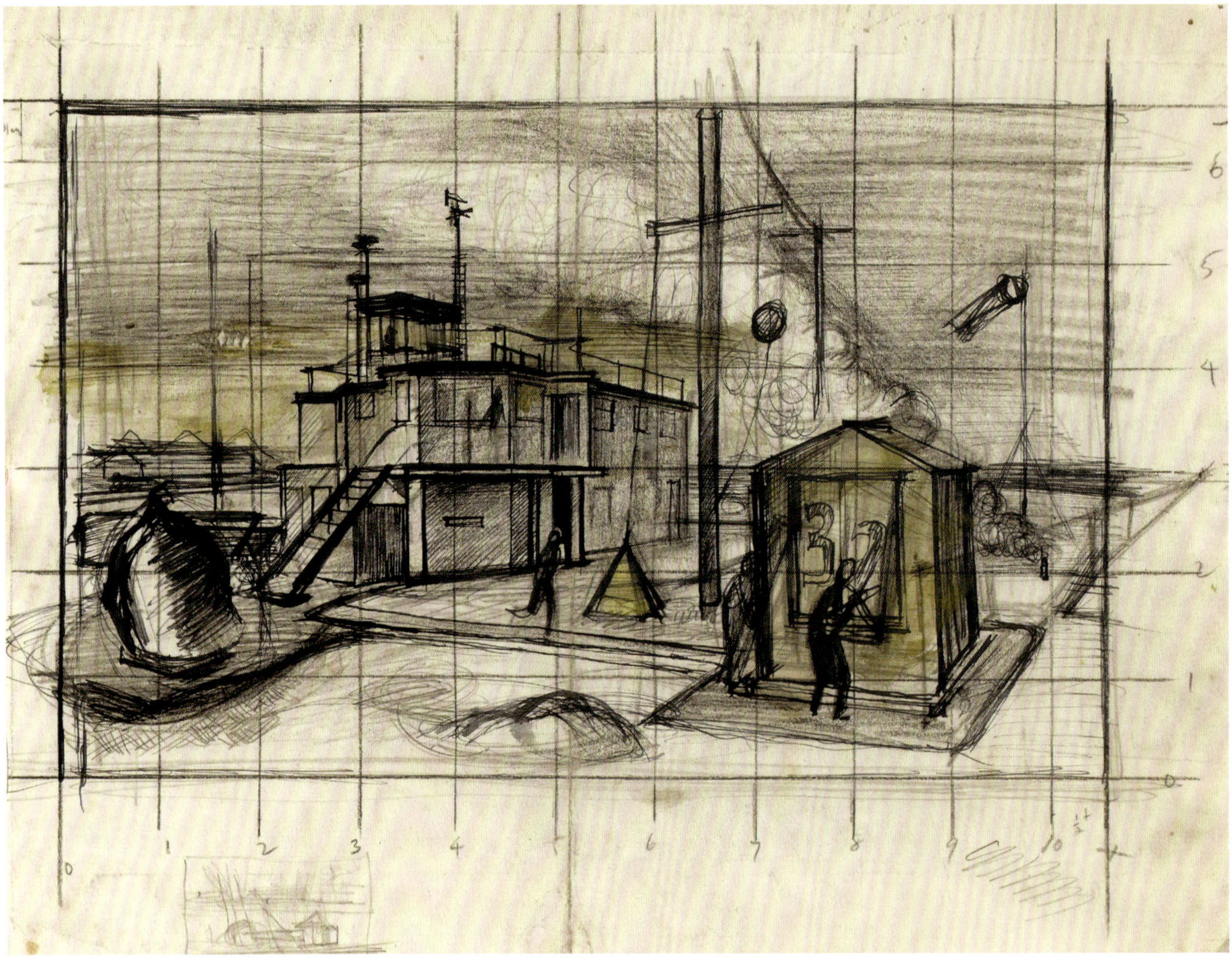

CAT. 63 – **Alan Sorrell** (1904-1974), Study for *Watch Office, RAF Station*, c.1944,
pencil, ink and watercolour on paper. squared and inscribed with measurements, 9 ¾ x 13 ½ in (24.8 x34 cm).
Provenance: The artist's son, Richard Sorrell.
Literature: Sacha Llewellyn & Richard Sorrell (ed), *Alan Sorrell; the Life and Works of an English Neo-Romantic Artist*, (Bristol: Sansom & Co.) 2013, p 108-110.

Sorrell served from 1940 in the RAF, where he was able to make first-hand visual records of daily service life. Twenty-six of these pictures were acquired by the War Artists' Advisory Committee. This is a study for a painting in the Laing Art Gallery, Newcastle-upon-Tyne: a bleak scene with clouds of steam and men rushing about amongst very unattractive buildings in a picture that Sorrell himself described as 'extremely sinister and full of foreboding'.

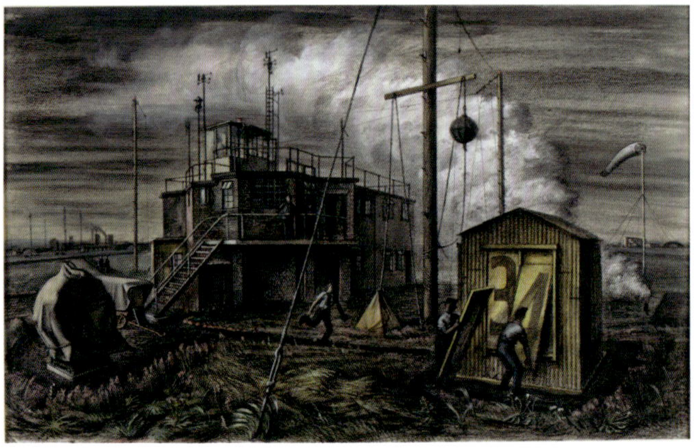

FIG. 11 – **Alan Sorrell** (1904-1974),
Watch Office, RAF Station,
pastel on paper pasted on card,
35 x 54.7 (13 ¾ x 21 ½ in.).
Collection: Laing Art Gallery, Newcastle-upon-Tyne.

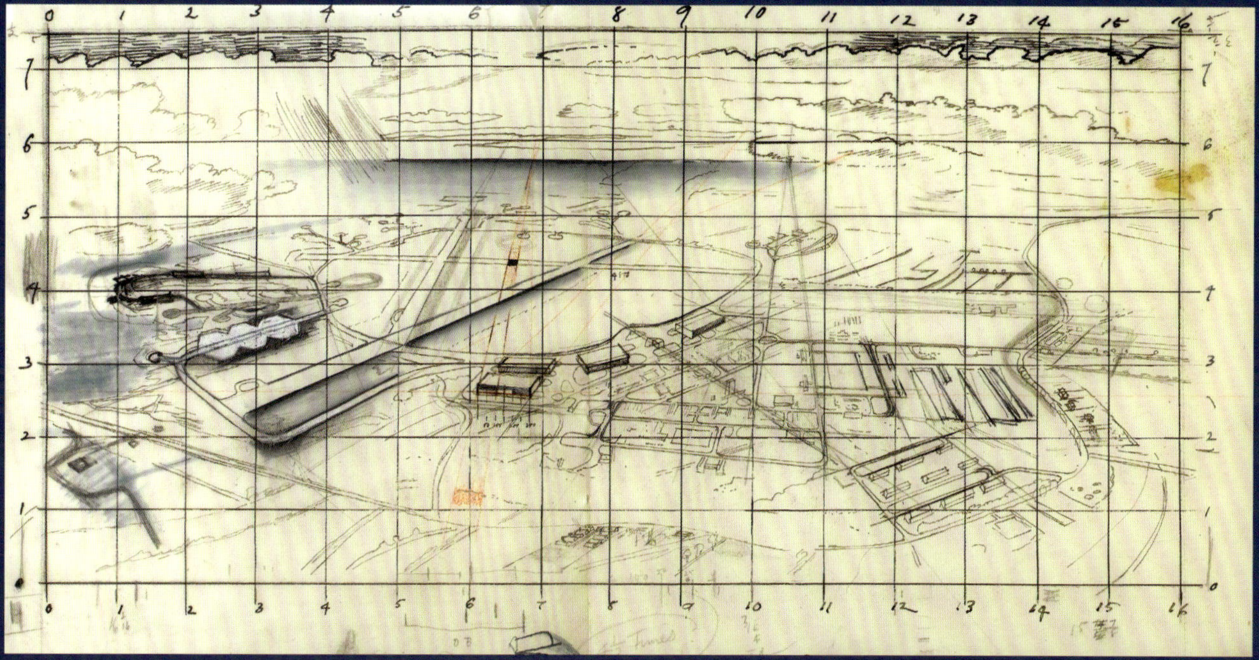

CAT. 64 – **Alan Sorrell** (1904-1974), Sketch for *An Aerial View of a Wartime Airfield*, c.1944,
pencil, ink and gouache on tracing paper, squared, 12 ¼ x 19 ¾ in. (31.2 x 50.5 cm.).
Provenance: The artist's son, Richard Sorrell.
Literature: Sacha Llewellyn & Richard Sorrell (ed), *Alan Sorrell; the Life and Works of an English Neo-Romantic Artist*, (Bristol: Sansom & Co.) 2013, p 98-115.

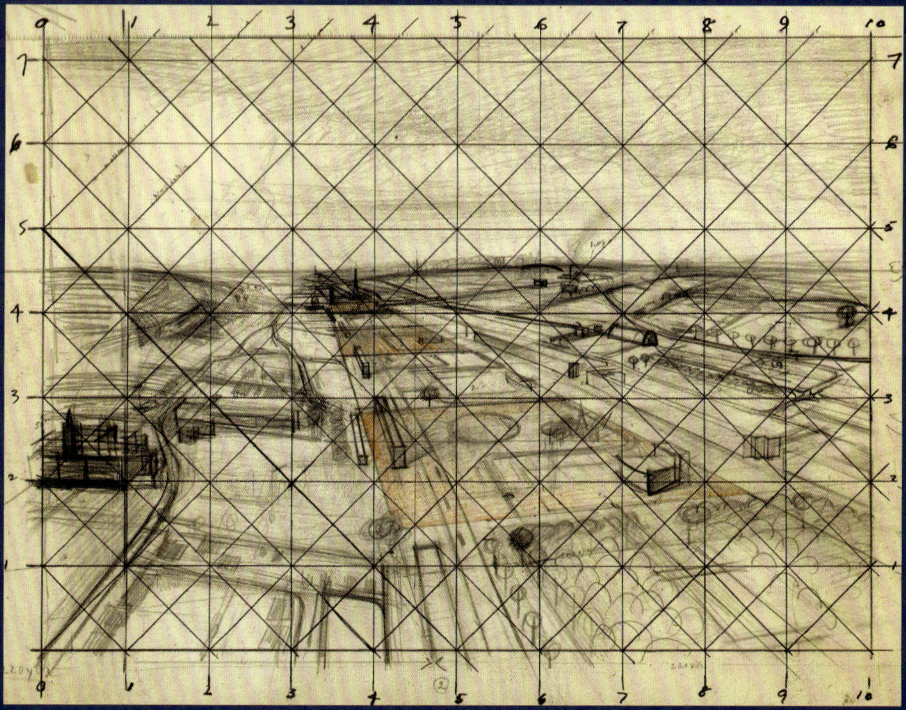

CAT. 65 – **Alan Sorrell** (1904-1974), Sketch for *An Aerial View of a Wartime Airfield*, c.1944,
pencil, red pencil and ink on cardboard, squared, 11 ¾ x 16 in. (24 x 33 cm)
Provenance: The artist's son, Richard Sorrell.
Literature: Sacha Llewellyn & Richard Sorrell (ed), *Alan Sorrell; the Life and Works of an English Neo-Romantic Artist*, (Bristol: Sansom & Co.) 2013, p 98-115.

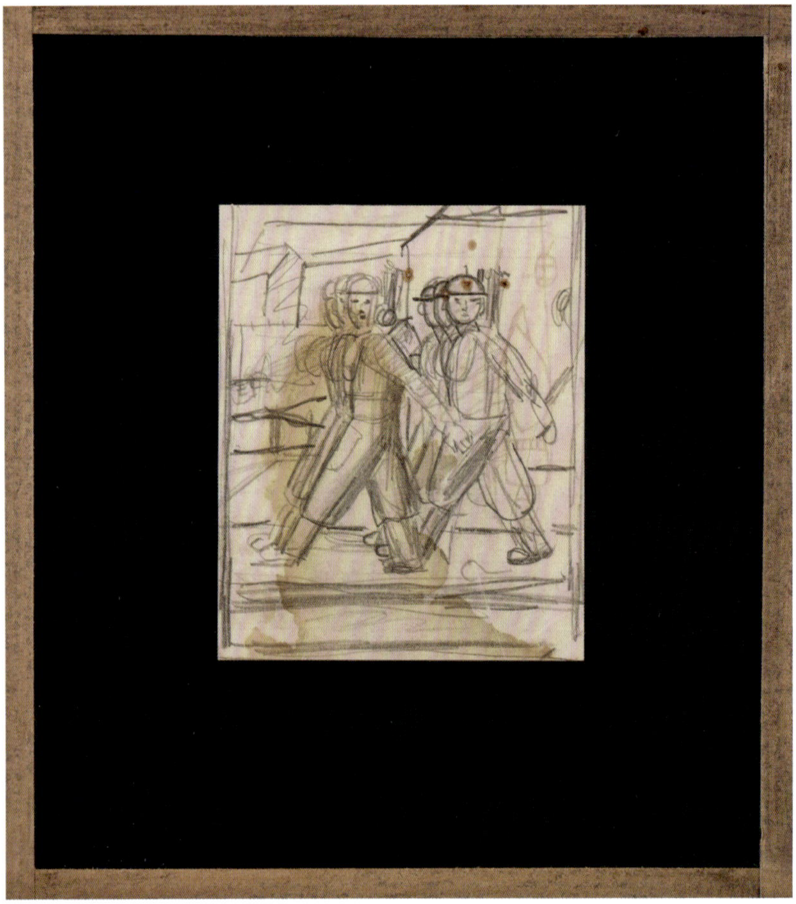

CAT. 66 – **Stanley Lewis** (1905-2009), *Eyes to the Right, Eyes to the Left*, early 1940's
pencil on paper, 4 x 3 in. (10 x 7.5 cm).
Provenance: The Artist's Family.
Exhibited: *The Unknown Artist: Stanley Lewis and his contemporaries*,
Cecil Higgins Art Gallery & Bedford Museum, 12 June - 5 September 2010 (no. 53).

'I enjoyed the war: plenty of exercise, moving from camp to camp. It gave me the opportunity to paint. It kept me going. I remember when I joined I was always sketching - "you better give that stuff up until the war is over", one of my comrades told me: "don't be so bloody silly", I said., "I am an artist." When the war broke out I went on teaching the students. But they all began to disappear. They all went to the forces. It was only the lame and the blind that were left. I didn't know what to do. About a year after the war started Harrison the Principal sent for me. He was sorting out all the A1 men to go into the forces. It was my turn'. After training at Kemmel Park in Prestatyn, North Wales, in the Royal Artillery as a Gunner, and later serving as a Battery Clerk for the 9th Anti-Aircraft Regiment at Ranby, Stanley Lewis was posted to the 66th Searchlight Regiment (Gloucesters) in Somerset. Asked if he would have liked to have been an official war artist Stanley replied: 'yes, but the fact that I was unofficial left me free to do and paint what I chose; and I'll tell you what – many of those Official War Artists were not amongst it – I was a soldier; I was right in the middle of it.' In spite of not being an official war artist Stanley was commissioned to produce three major paintings during WW2: *Wartime Newport, The Home Front* (1940-1941), *Morning Maintenance on a Searchlight Site* (1943) (whereabouts unknown) and *The Attack on the Tirpitz by the Fleet Air Arm* (1944).

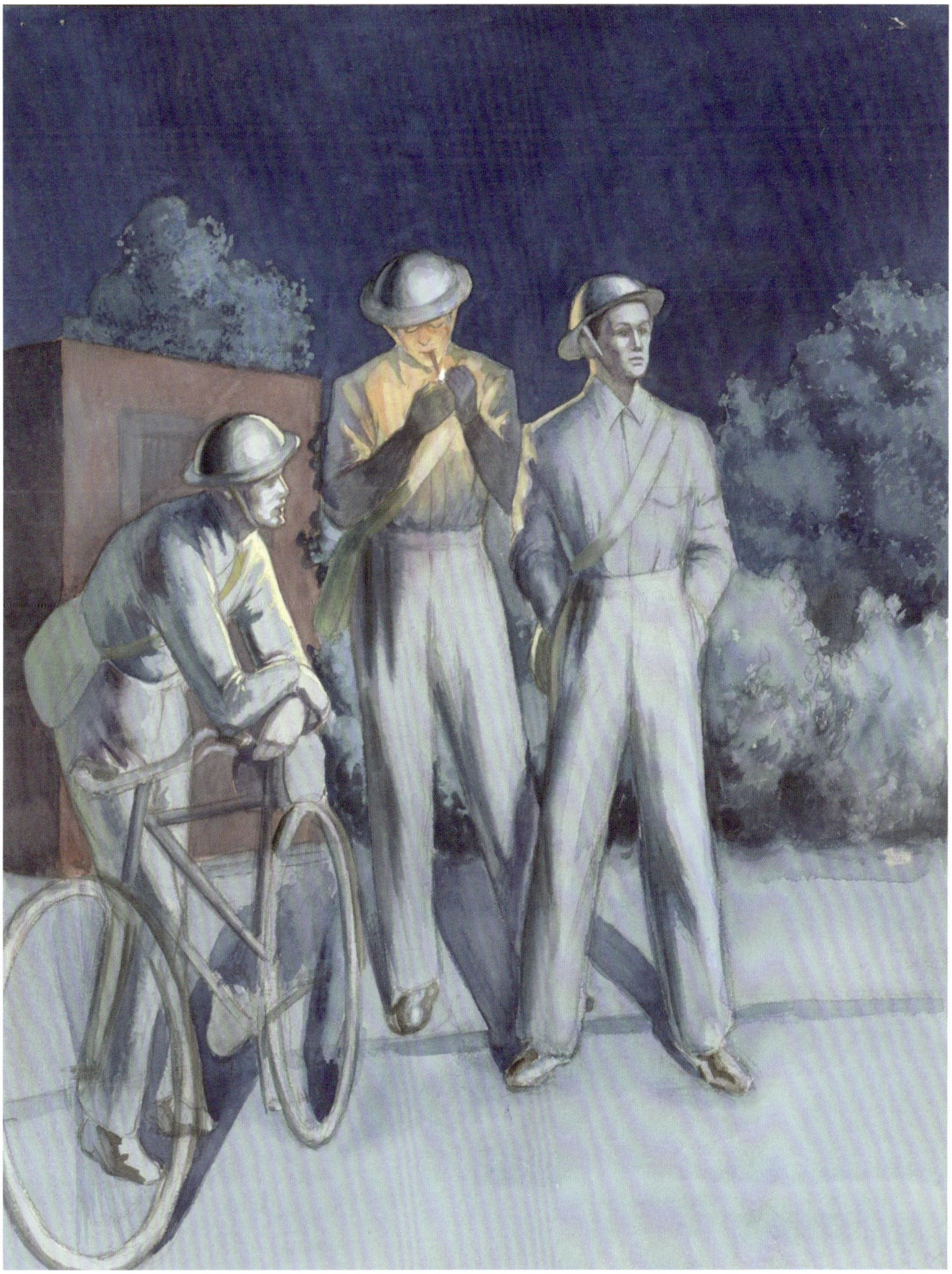

CAT. 67*– **Daphne Rowles** (1922-1967), *Lighting up*, c.1942,
oil on paper, 14¾ x 11 ½ in. (37.5 x 29.5 cm).
Provenance: Private Collection.

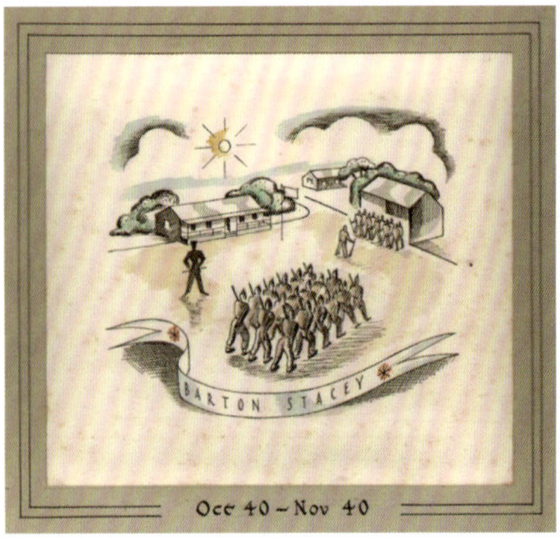

Barton Stacey

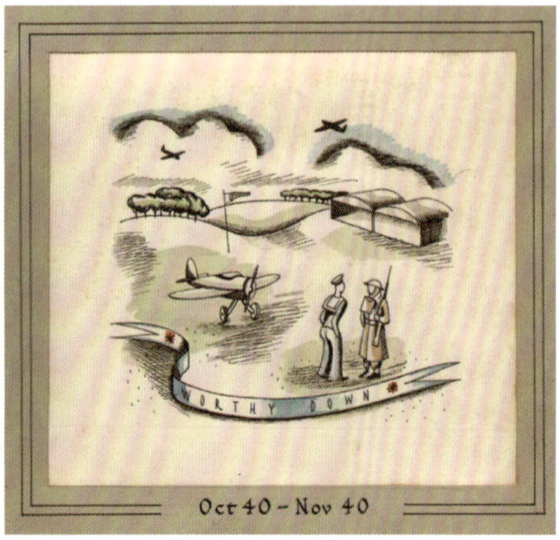

Worthy Down

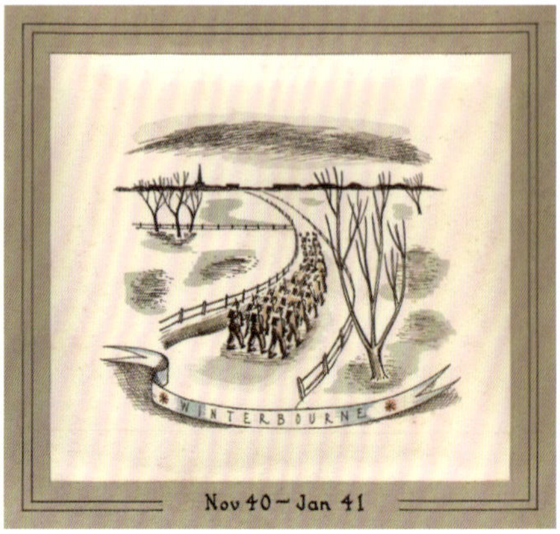

Winterbourne

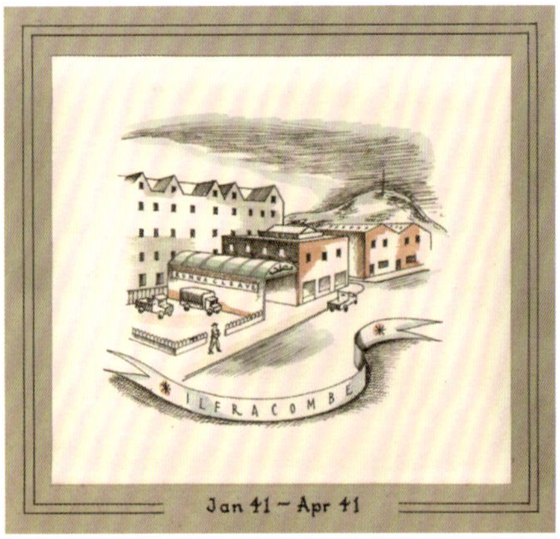

Ilfracombe

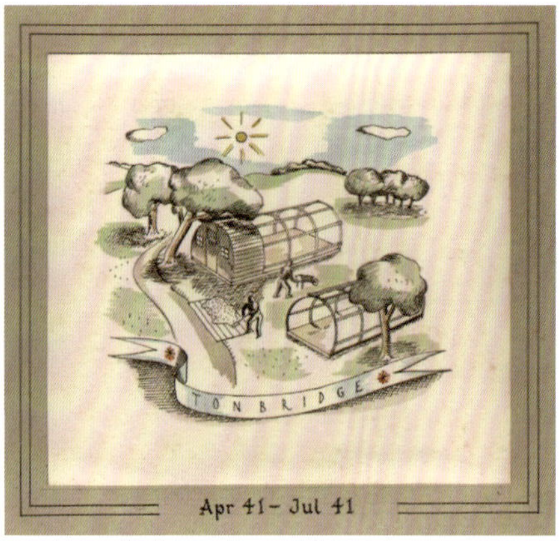

Tonbridge

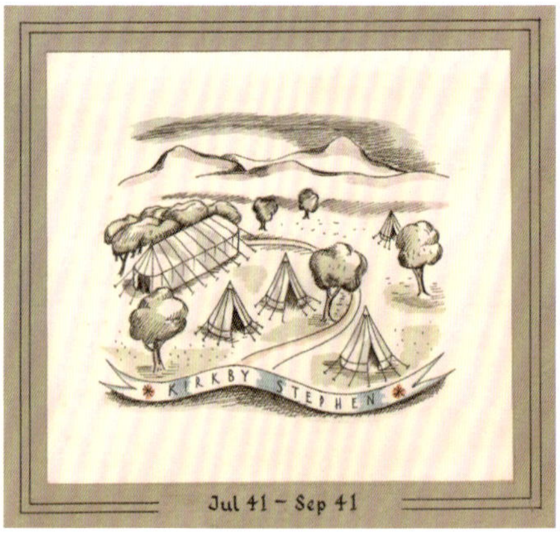

Kirkby Stephen

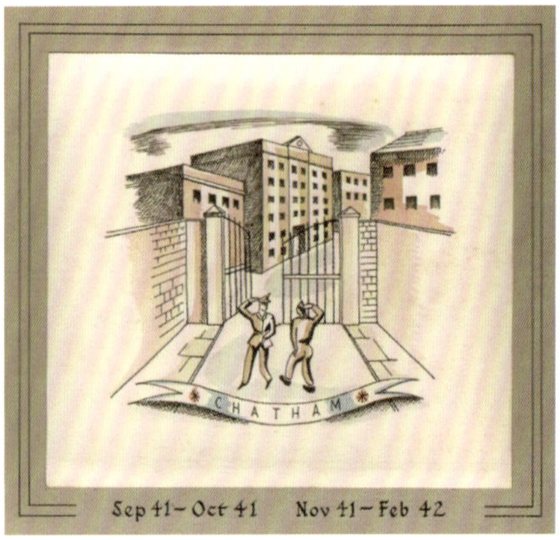

Chatham

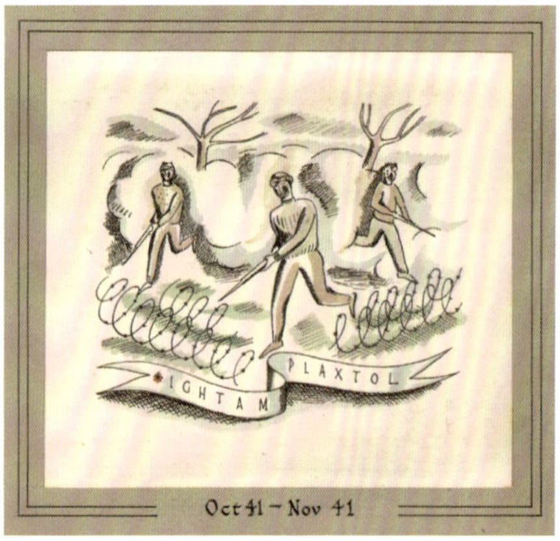

Ightam Plaxtol

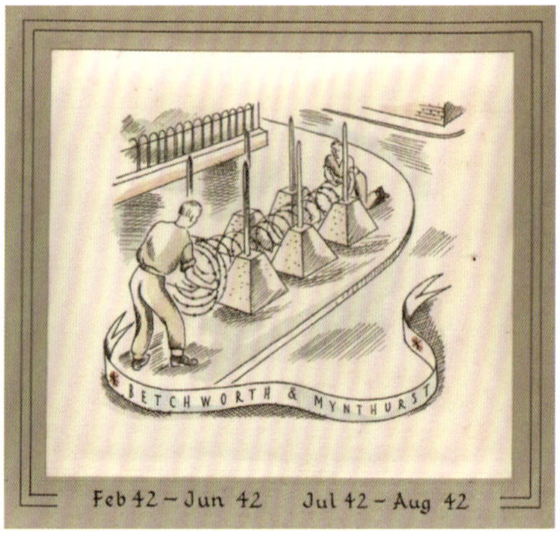

Betchworth & Mynthurst

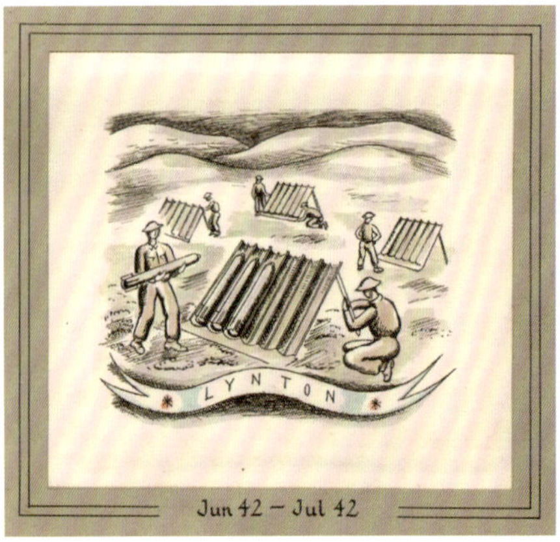

Lynton

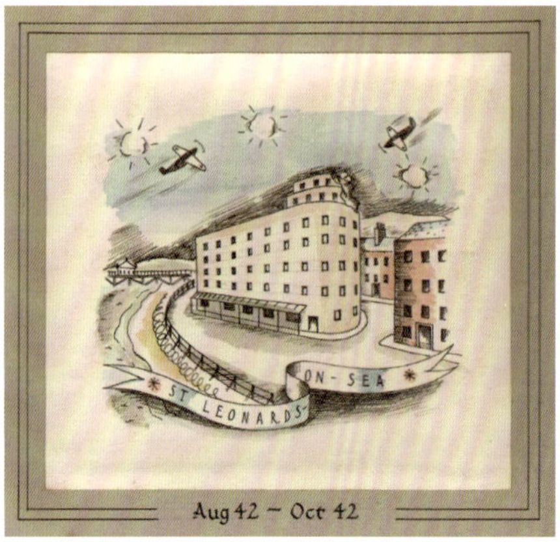

St Leonards-on-Sea

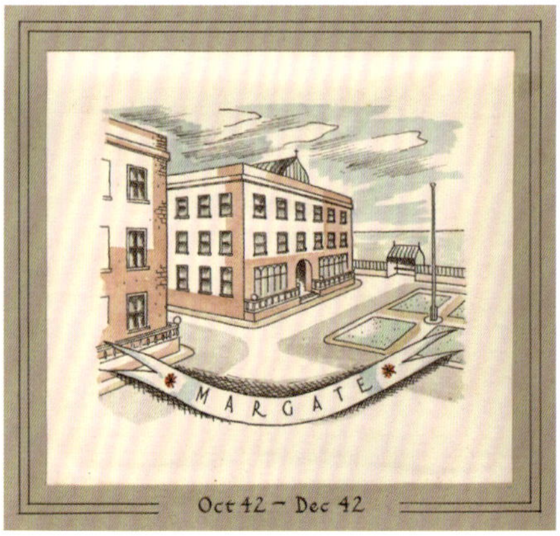

Margate

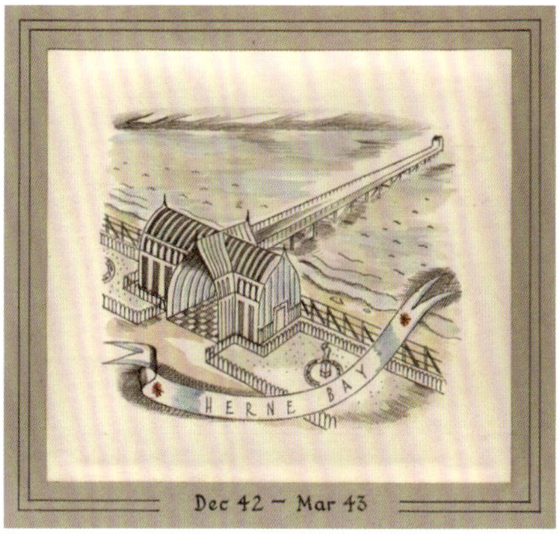

Herne Bay

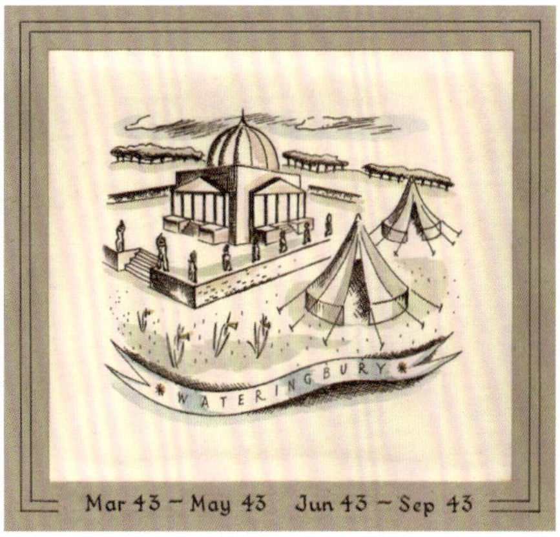

Wateringbury

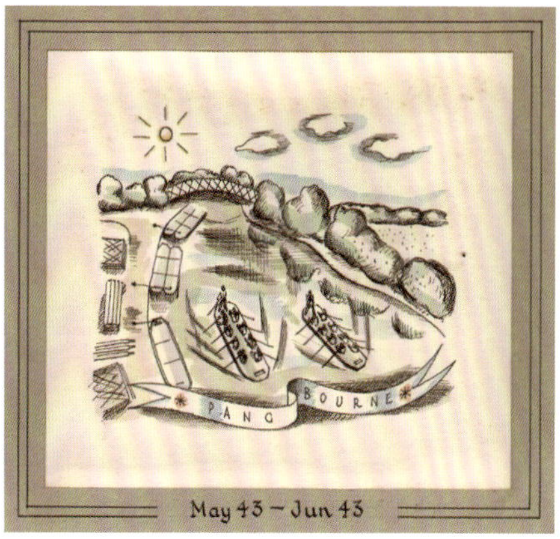

Pangbourne

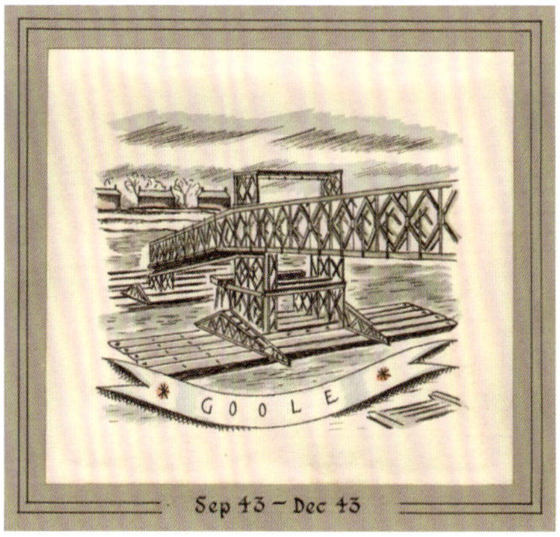

Goole

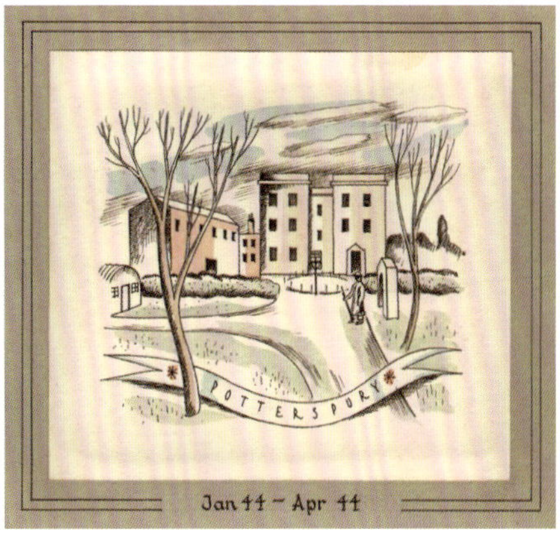

Potterspury

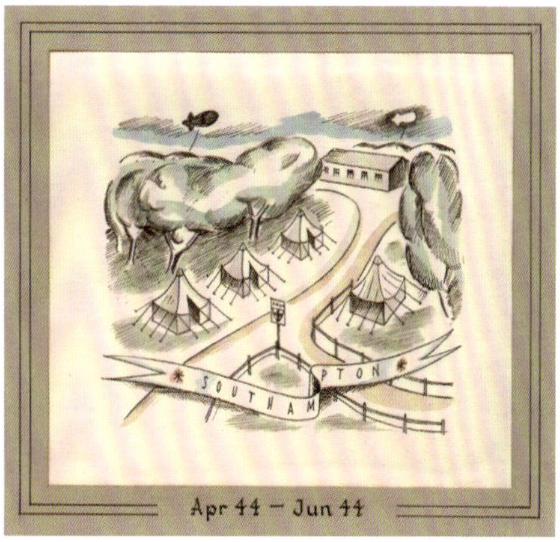

Southampton

73
FIELD COMPANY
ROYAL ENGINEERS

CAT. 68 – **Major Leslie Ernest Wyatt** (1903-1961), *73rd Field Company Royal Engineers*, c.1945, pen and ink and watercolour on paper, each image: 4 ½ x 5 in. (11.5 x 12.5 cm).

Wyatt was born in Portsmouth and worked in his father's radio/gramophone shop. He joined the Royal Engineers at the outbreak of war, was commissioned, and trained in a Beach Clearance Unit. His duties included clearing obstacles, including mines and bombs, putting down wire mesh tracks on the beaches, etc. He was awarded the Military Cross for his gallantry on D-Day. After D-Day his unit became used for forward bridge building. Later Wyatt wrote 'A Short History of the 73rd Field Company, Royal Engineers in the North-West European Campaign'. Stylistically close to Edward Bawden these eighteen watercolours chronicle the training, duties and locations of the Company from October 1940 to June 1944.

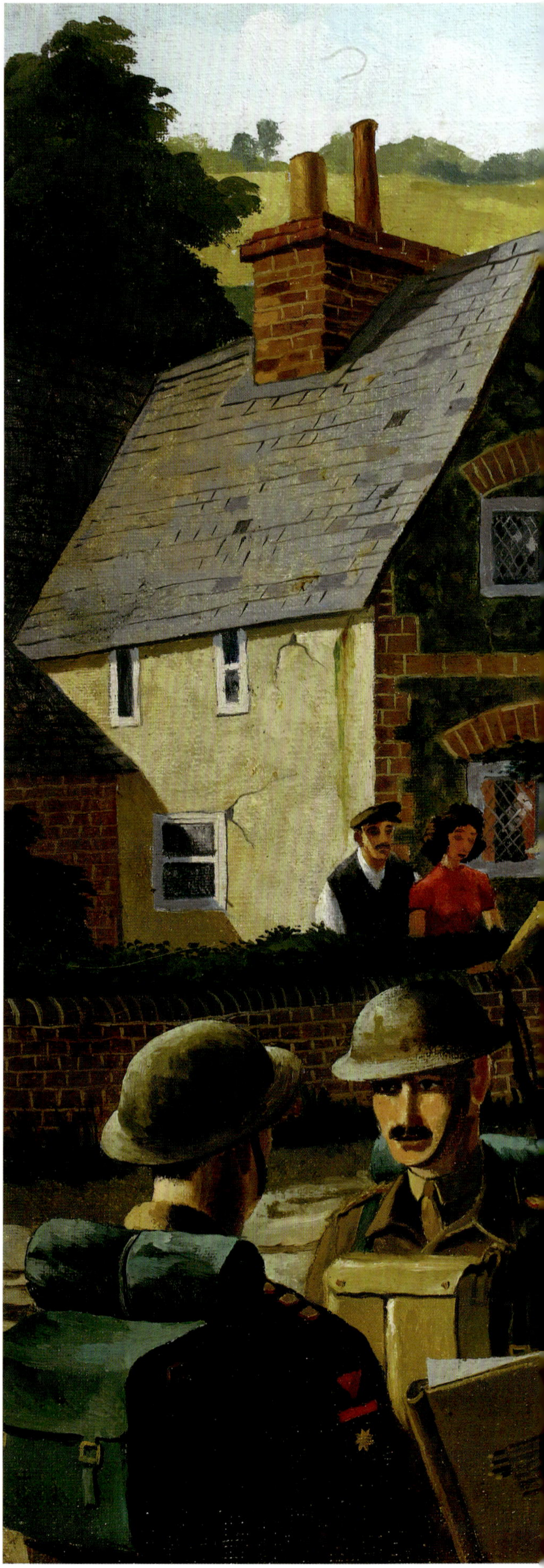

CAT. 69 – **Michael Ford** (1920-2005),
Troops at Middle Assenden near Henley-on-Thames,
oil on canvas, 19 ¾ x 23 ¾ in. (50 x 60 cm).

The scene is set in Middle Assendon – Assendon Farm House is visible behind. The village, in the Stonor valley in the Chiltern Hills (about 2 miles north-west of Henley-on-Thames) was visited by many artists during WW2, including Eric Kennngton, largely on account of Hubert Wellington, Director of Art at the Royal College of Art, who lived in the vicinity.

According to the shoulder badges worn by the soldiers this shows men from the 3rd Infantry Division. This division spent 4 years training in the UK post-Dunkirk which dates the subject to between late in 1940 and mid-1944. The 3rd Infantry was the first GB division to land at Sword Beach on D-Day.

Three of Ford's war-time canvases are in the collection of the Imperial War Museum.

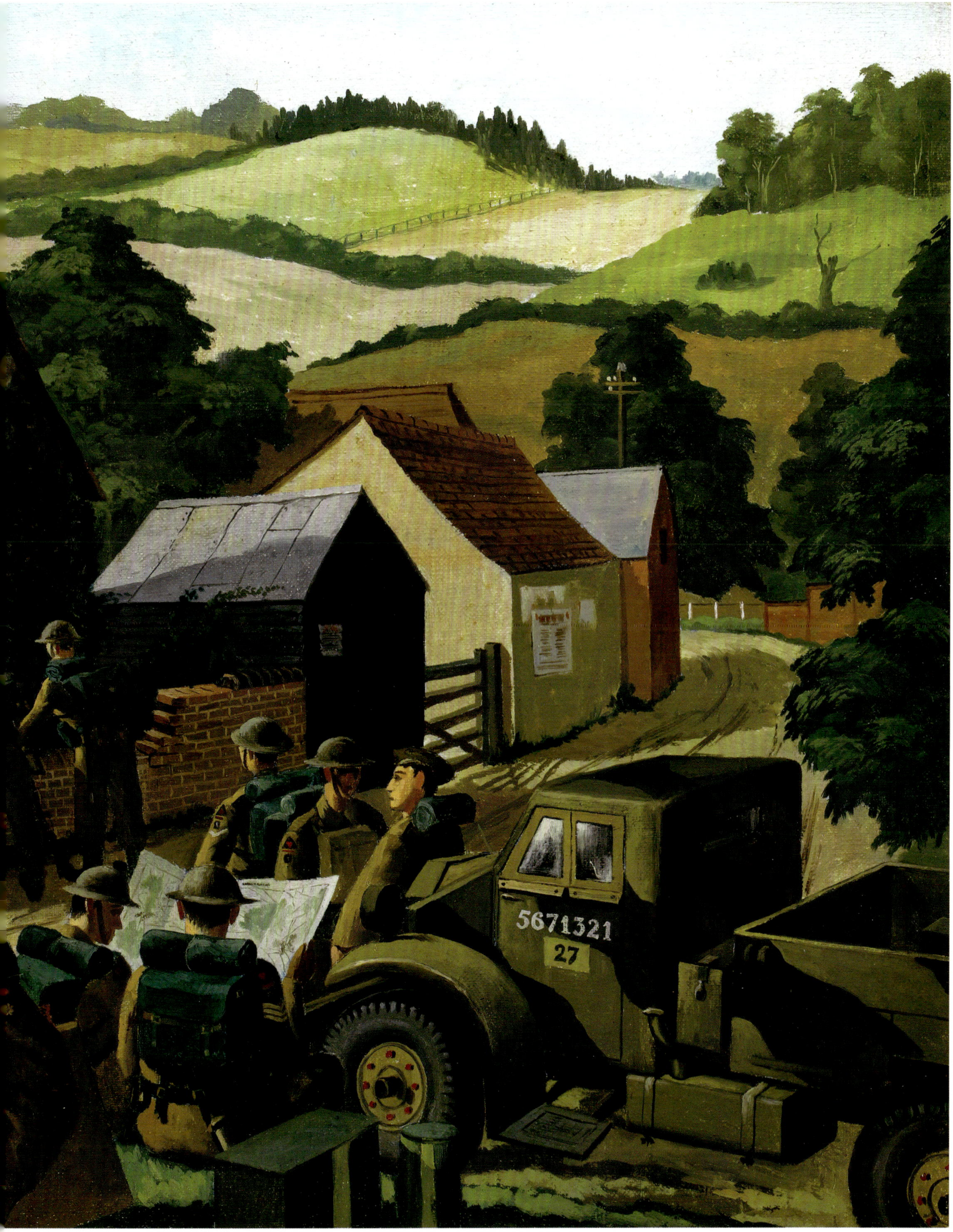
5671321
27

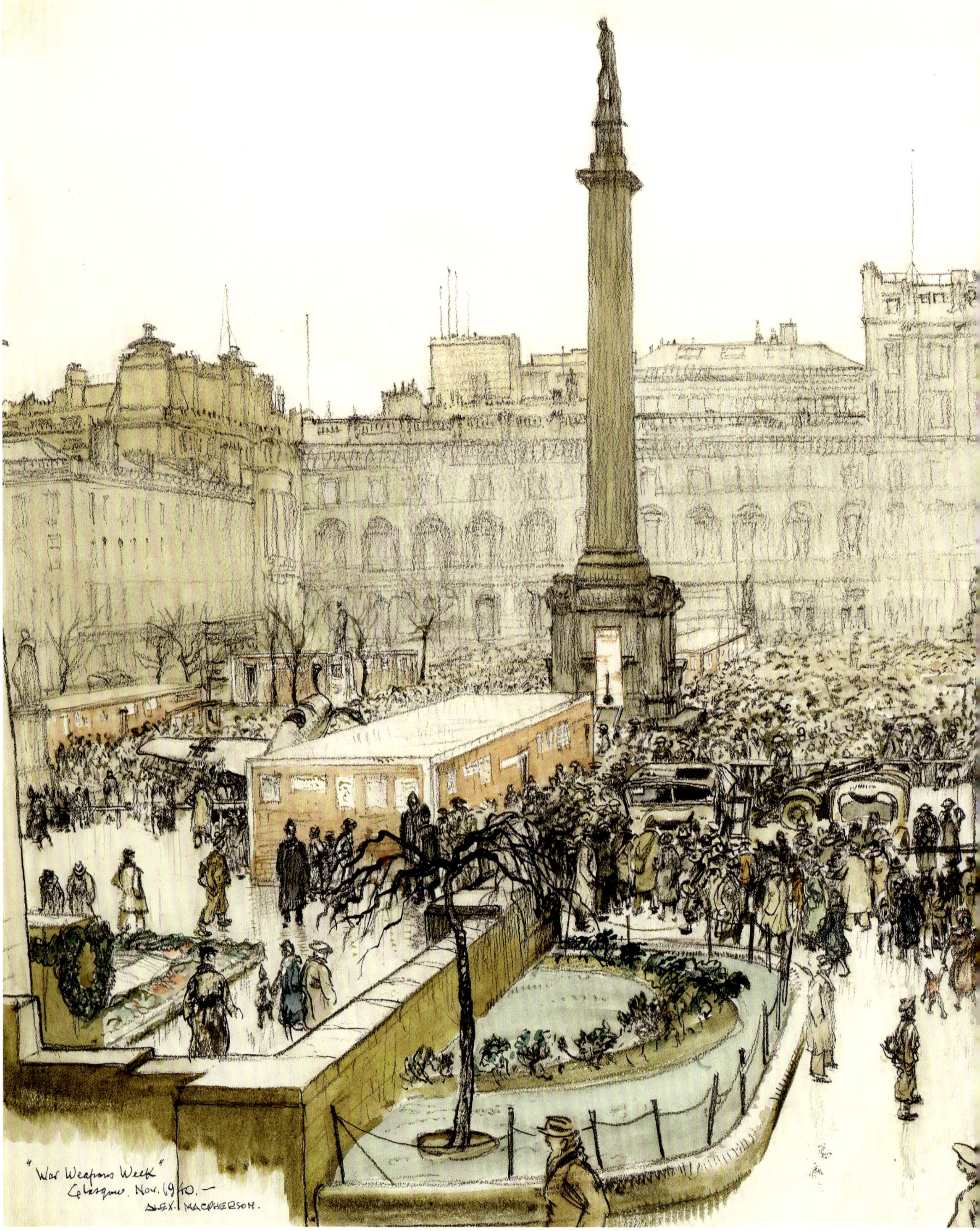
"War Weapons Week"
Glasgow. Nov. 1940. –
ALEX. MACPHERSON.

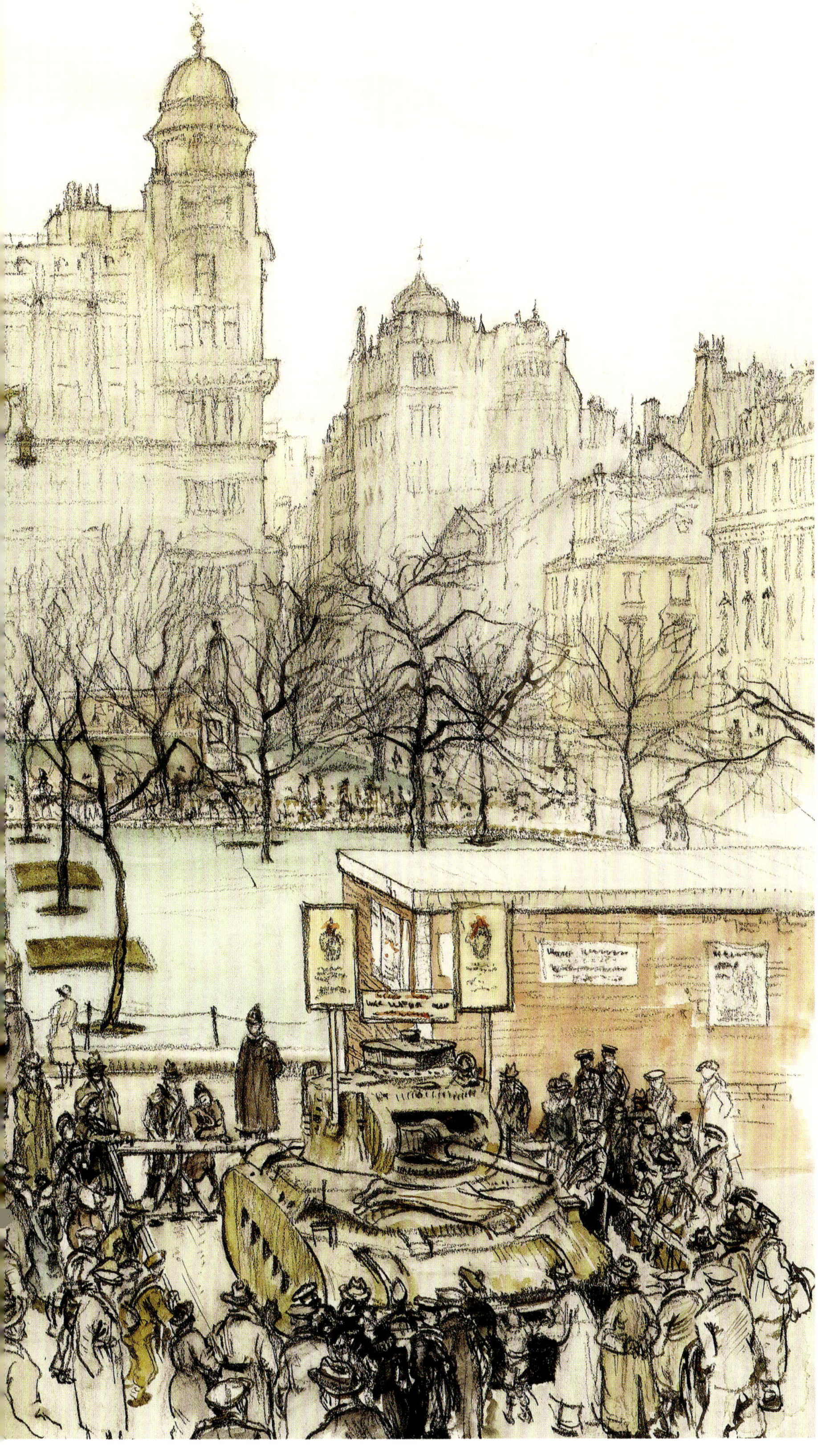

CAT. 70 – **Alexander MacPherson** (1904-1970),
War Weapons Week, (George Square), Glasgow, Nov. 1940,
signed, dated and inscribed with title,
watercolour on paper,
14 ½ x 20 ½ in. (37 x 52 cm).
Provenance: Sotheby's London, 2008.

War Weapons Week took place in several cities at the beginning of the war as a way of raising funds and boosting morale. In Glasgow concerts and parades took place daily as the city sought to raise £10 million in loans for the war effort. An article in the *Glasgow Herald* dated 23rd November 1940 ('Military Parades and Exhibition of Arms and Equipment') recorded that: 'The plan for the outdoor display of war weapons in George Square during the week offers the opportunity to the public of inspecting a large British tank and a German Messerschmitt plane. Other exhibits to be shown in the Square include a gun tractor and trailer and a Bren gun carrier.' In another article in the same edition ('Parade to Quicken Lending: Services Show Needs') 'Many thousands of citizens saw the fighting equipment for which their money is so urgently needed. Bren-gun carriers and other weapons of war were in the parade which passed along some of the principal thoroughfares on the way to the City Chambers. In from of the Cenotaph the Lord Provost ... took the salute as units of the fighting and civil services swung past.' One of the main attractions was 'the yellow-nosed Messerschmitt fighter in George Square' (seen in the middle ground, far left of this watercolour).

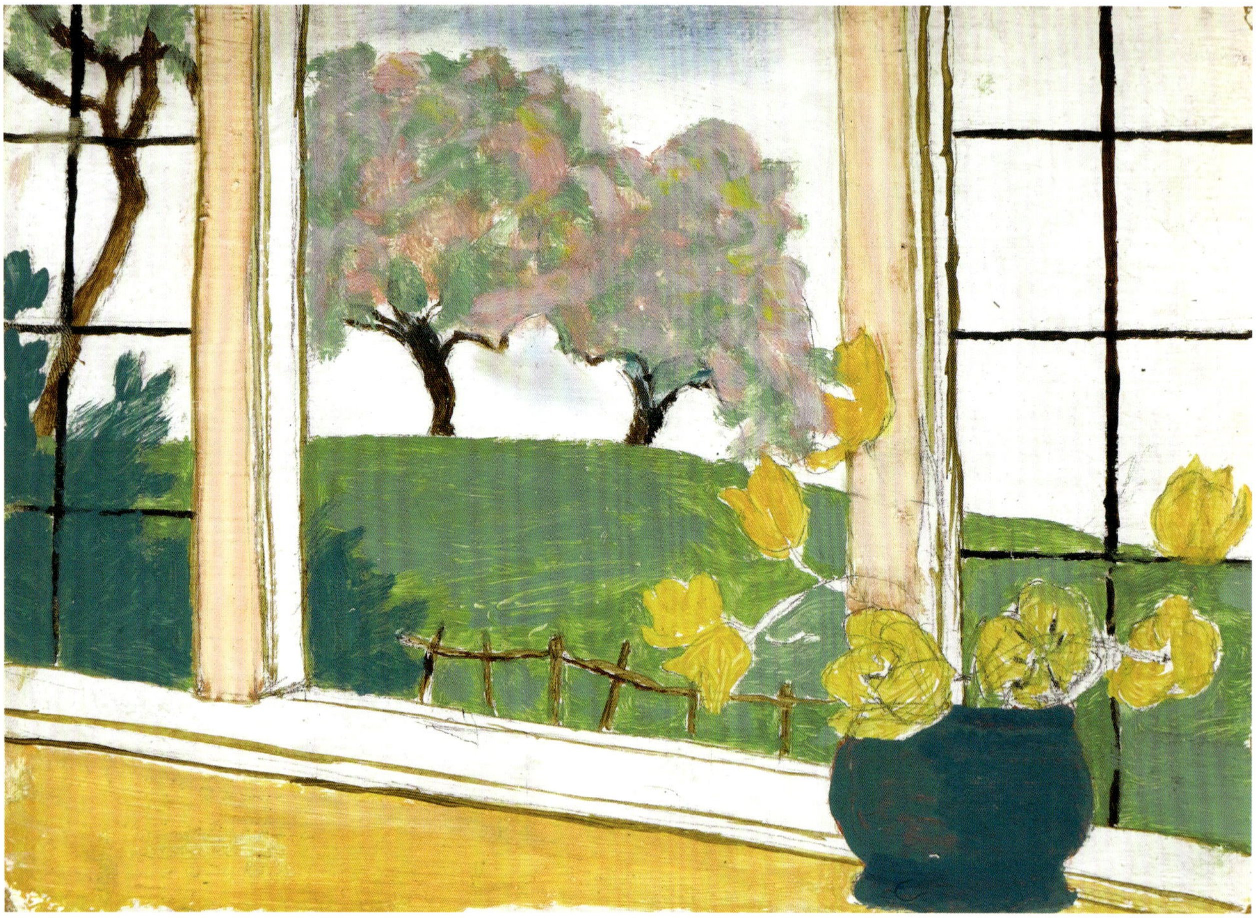

CAT. 71 – **John Moody** (1906-1993), *View from the Window, Great Wolford*, 1941-42, oil on panel, 6 x 8 in. (15.3 x 20.3 cm.).

Born in 1906 Moody had been too young to participate in WW1, but suffered its consequences. His memorable 1928 woodcut, 'War' sums up, poignantly, his sense of the futility of conflict and antagonism towards the 'old order' which had condemned so many to a needless death. As such he was expressing the mood of his generation.

During WW2 Moody served with the Auxiliary Fire Service. He sustained injuries during the Blitz, retiring to Warwickshire to convalesce. His mentor in the theatre, Tyrone Guthrie, retained his services as Director of the evacuated Old Vic Theatre School in Little Wolford. To aid his recovery, Moody continued to paint, though with great difficulty. During this period his style changed as he struggled to redefine his skills in light of his injuries. This particular oil is one of a group he painted looking out of his window in the neighbouring village of Great Wolford.

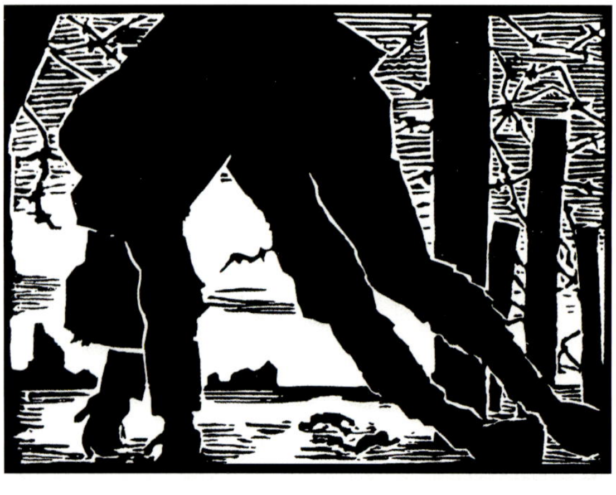

FIG. 12 – **John Moody** (1906-1993), *War*, 1928, wood engraving, 3 x 4 in. (7.6 x 10.2 cm).

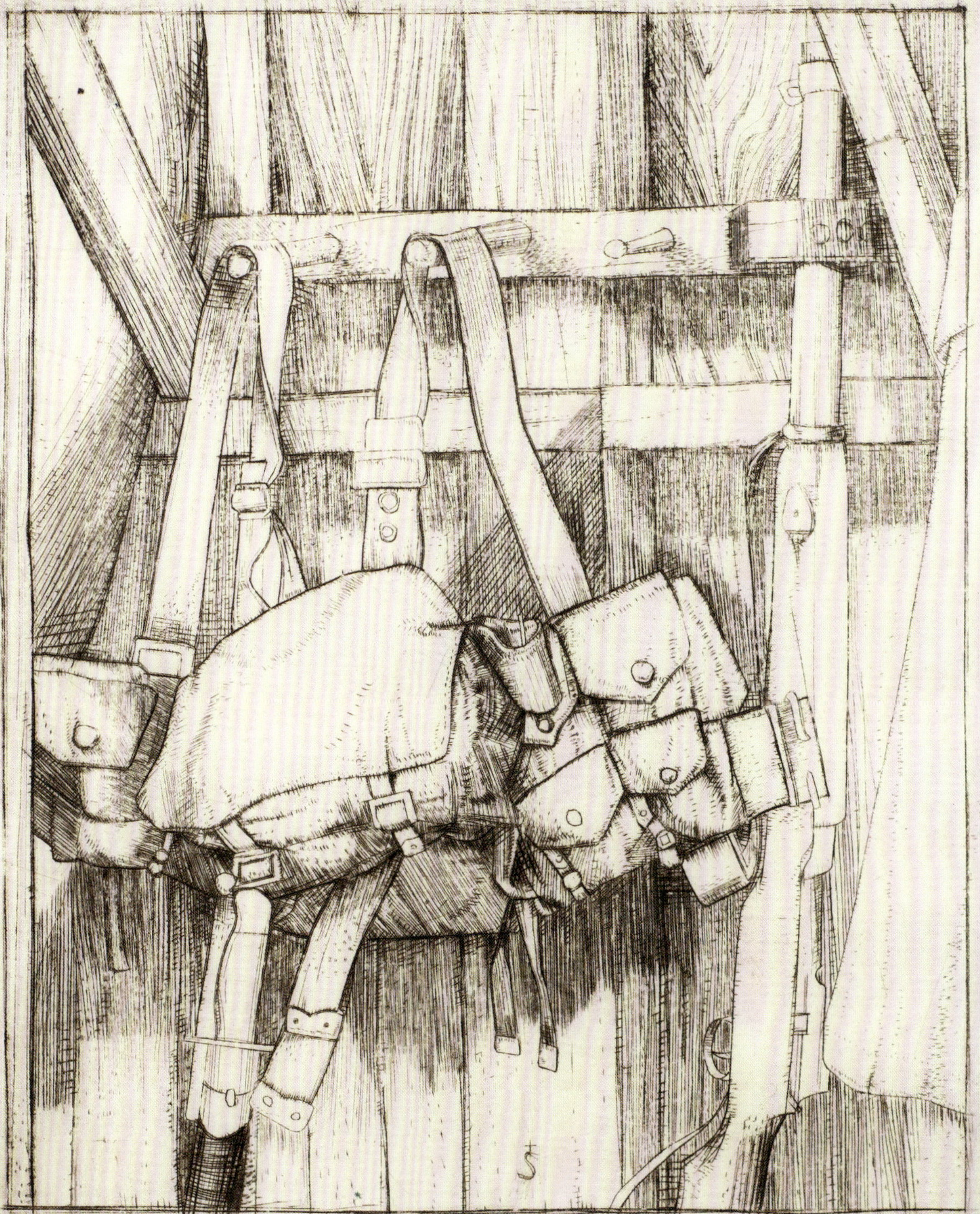

CAT. 72 – **Erik Smith** (1914-1972), *Kit Bag*, c.1940,
etching, artist's proof, 6 ¼ x 5 in. (16 x 12.5 cm).

Smith attended the Royal College of Art 1937-39, until interrupted by the outbreak of WW2. He returned after the war to complete his course, 1945-47.

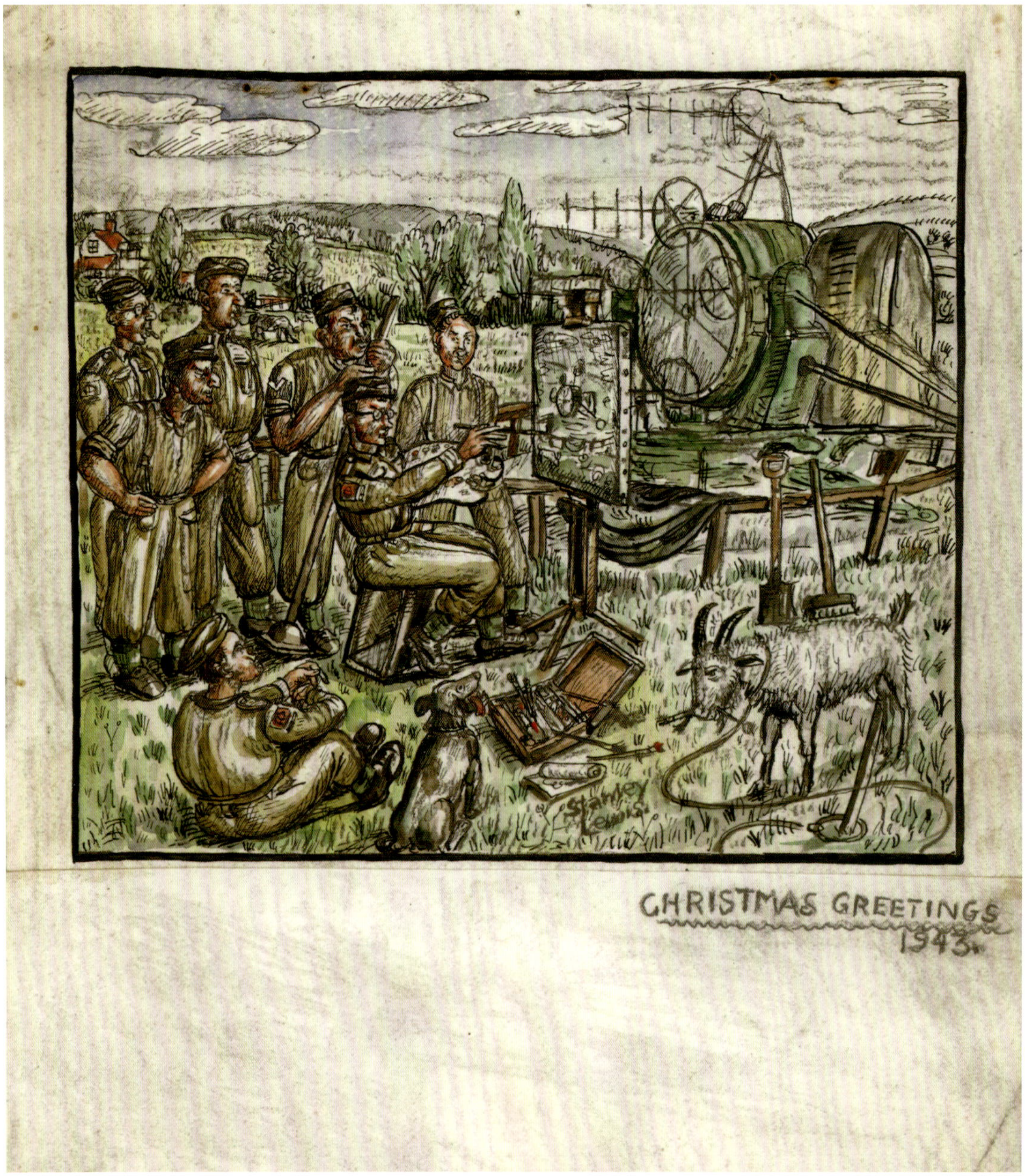

CAT. 73 – **Stanley Lewis** (1905-2009), *Working on The Searchlight*, 1943, signed and dated,
inscribed 'Christmas Greetings 1943',
pen & Ink and watercolour on paper, 10 x 8 ½ in. (25.5 x 21.5 cm).
Literature: *The Unknown Artist: Stanley Lewis and his contemporaries*, Cecil Higgins Art Gallery & Bedford Museum,
12 June - 5 September 2010. p113.

After training at Kinmel Park in Prestatyn, North Wales, in the Royal Artillery and later serving as a Battery Clerk for the 9th Anti-Aircraft Regiment at Ranby, Stanley Lewis was posted to the 66th Searchlight Regiment (Gloucesters). 'Lieut. Colonel MacWaters was in charge and he interviewed me concerning painting a picture commemorating the searchlight service during the war. He gave me a list of fifteen possible subjects for me to choose from and I chose *Morning Maintenance on a Searchlight Site*. He allowed a jeep with a driver to travel to different sites to choose a suitable location for the picture. Eventually I chose a site at Low Ham in Somerset. This site was most suitable as the great searchlight was situated in a Somerset apple orchard and looking North to the hilltop was the famous Glastonbury Tor. I settled there and became one of the searchlight team and in my spare time I worked on the painting.' At one point Colonel MacWaters asked Stanley Lewis to paint the searchlight in a less detailed manner fearing that it might cause a breach of security! Lewis refused to compromise, leading the Colonel to insist the painting was accompanied by one of his officers when the painting was sent to London to be framed.

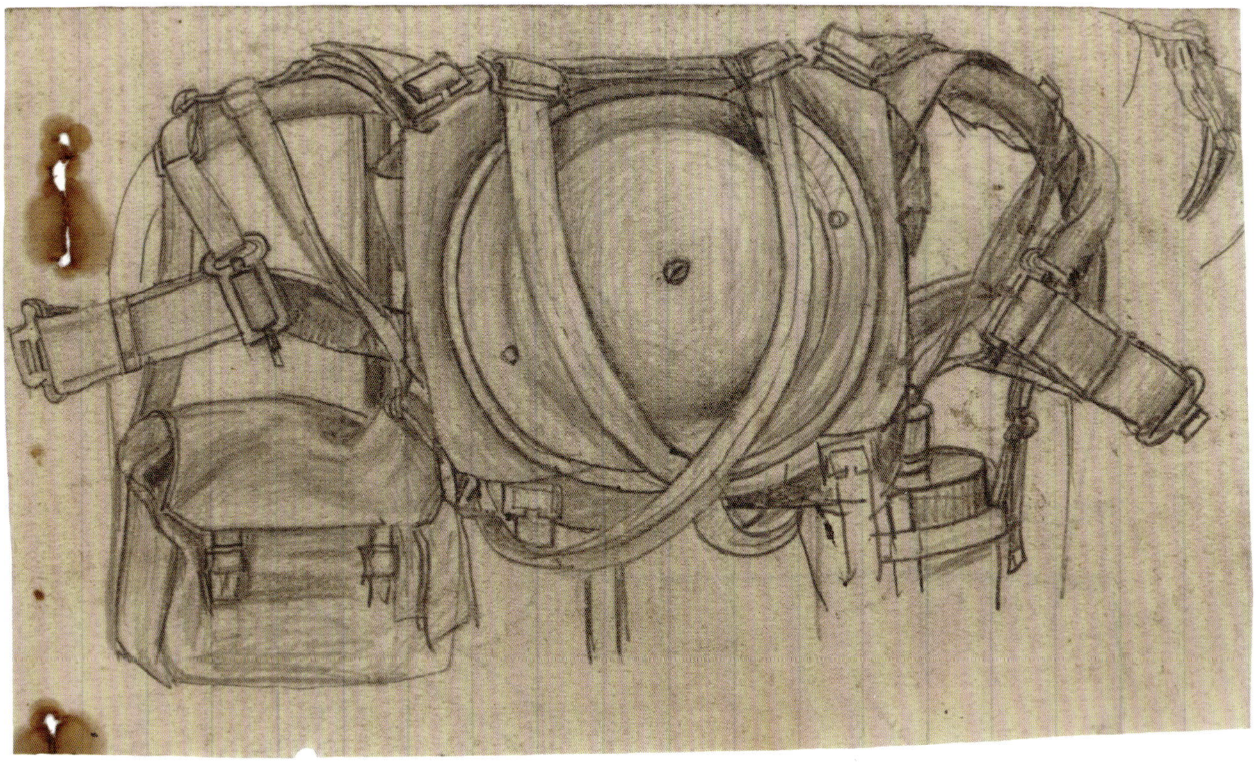

CAT. 74* – **Stanley Lewis** (1905-2009), *Ready for the Off*, early 1940s,
pencil on paper, 3 x 5 ¼ in. (7.5 x 13.5 cm).

Overleaf:
CAT. 75 – **John Powell** (1911-2003), *War Landscape, Britain 1942*, signed,
oil on canvas, 24 x 36 in. (61 x 91.4 cm).

According to Powell, *"the message of 'Corps de Sacks',* (as he sometimes referred to this painting) *by implication presents the grim reality of war, without the explicit violence which is currently fashionable in all the media. Anguish may be felt following from the free-ranging imagination of the observer. In a wider sense the piece is a metaphor for man's inhumanity to man. The word man often equates with evil and wickedness. Men's words are frequently piously utopian, but secretly men seek advantage over their fellows. The 'Corps', therefore, has emblematic content. The 'sacks' with their 'domino like' markings indicating army training, a chance screening, at reserve camp, set me aside to be a technical instructor in radar, while most of my comrades went to Cyprus and were lost. While being privileged to use my intelligence towards the war effort, I never lost awareness that all was concerned with killing."*

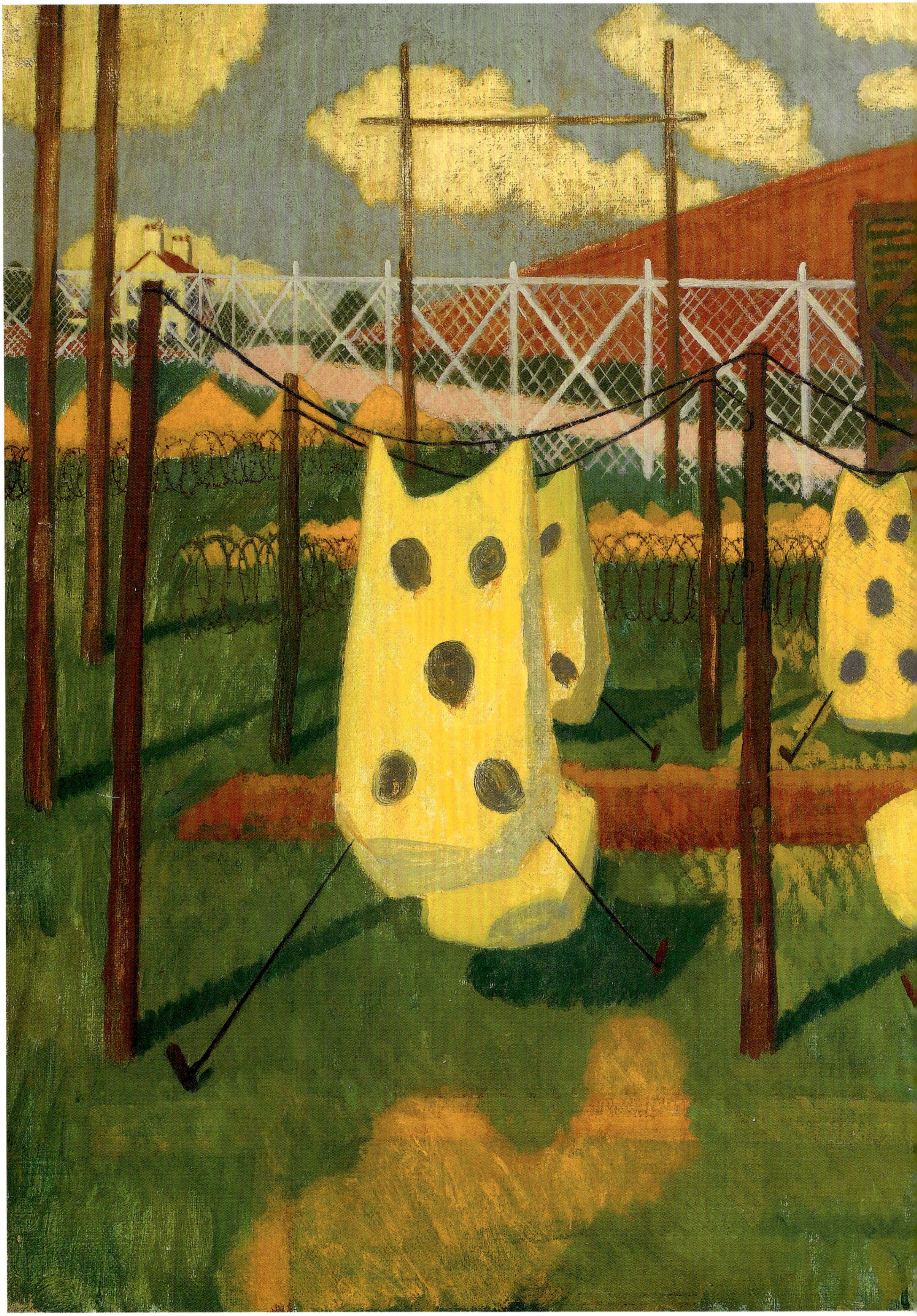

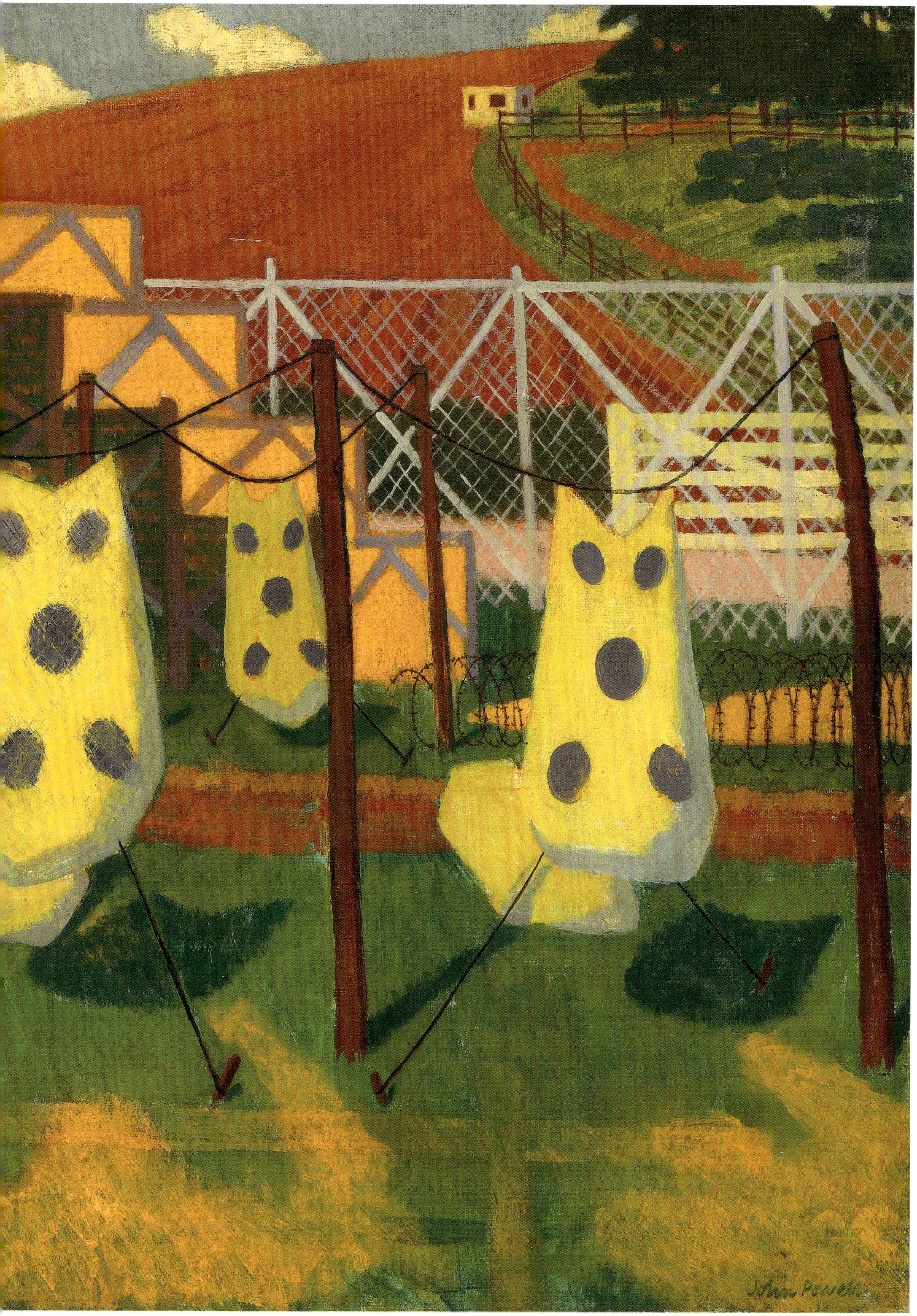
John Powell

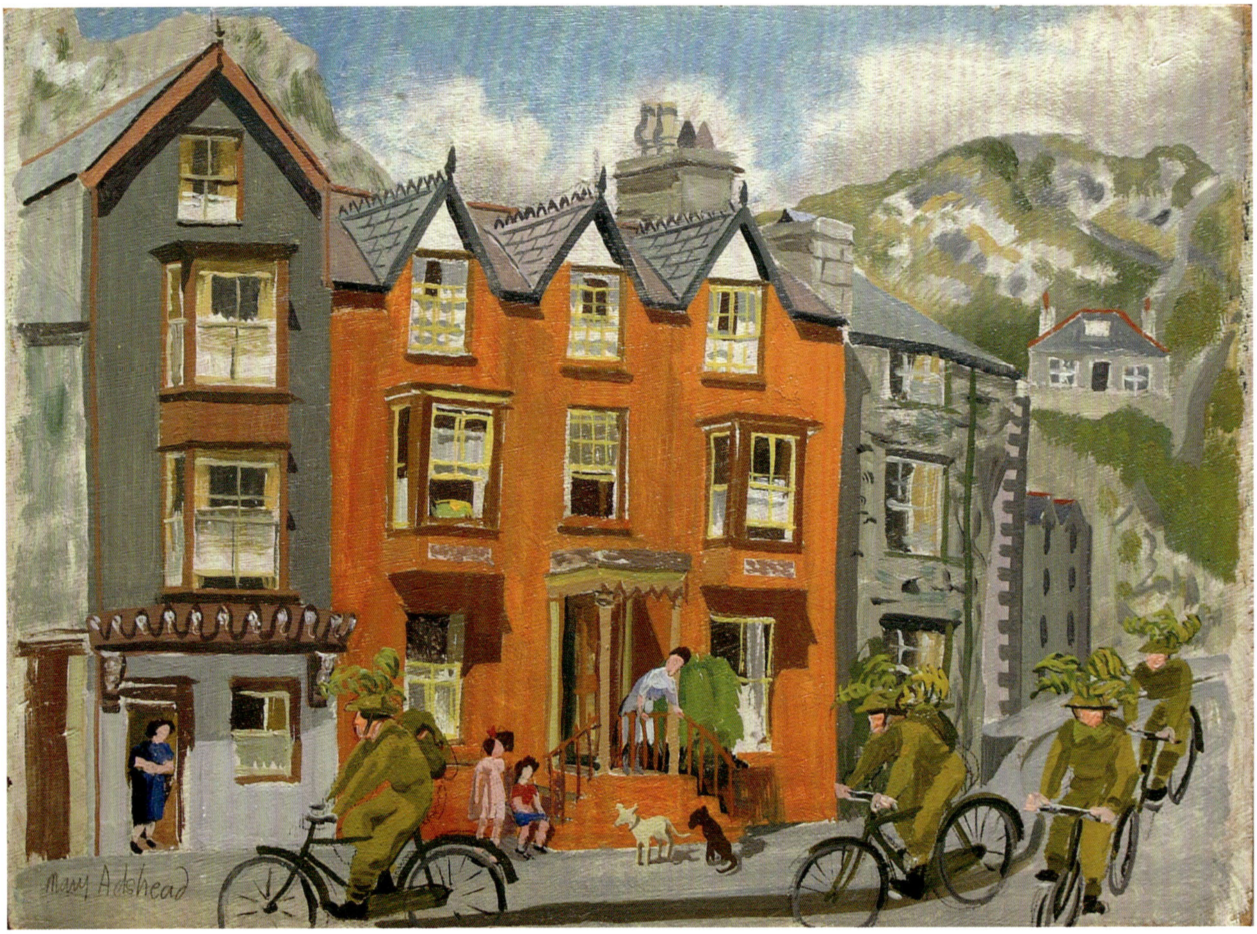

CAT. 76* – **Mary Adshead** (1904-1995), *Riding into Barmouth*, 1944,
oil on panel, 10 x 14 in. (25.4 x 35.5 cm).
Exhibited: New English Art Club.
Sold to the Imperial War Museum by Liss Llewellyn Fine Art in 2000.

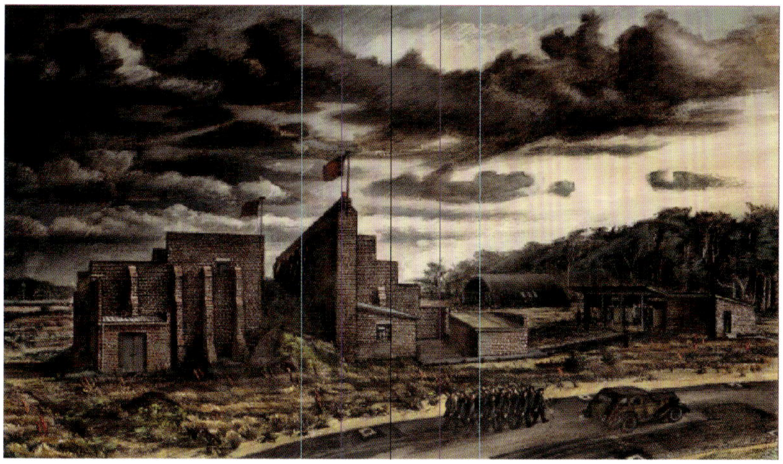

FIG. 13 – **Alan Sorrell** (1904-1974), *Marching Gun Range and Rifle Range, RAF Station*, Museum of Stoke-on-Trent.

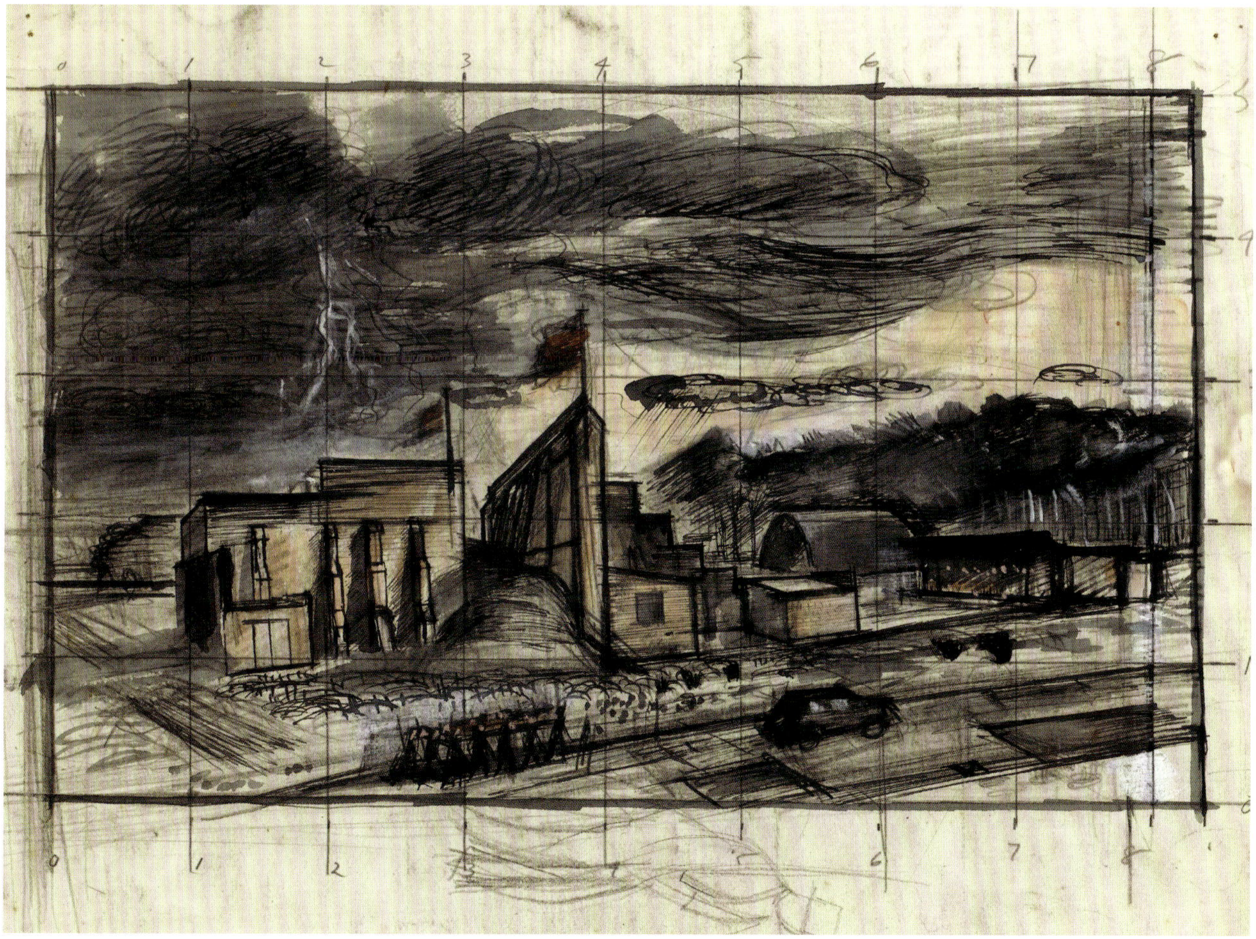

CAT. 77 – **Alan Sorrell** (1904-1974), *Study for Marching Gun Range and Rifle Range, RAF Station*, pencil, ink and gouache on paper, squared and inscribed with measurements, 9 ¾ x 13 ½ in (24.8 x34 cm).
Provenance: The artist's son, Richard Sorrell.
Literature: Sacha Llewellyn & Richard Sorrell (ed), *Alan Sorrell; the Life and Works of an English Neo-Romantic Artist*, (Bristol: Sansom & Co.) 2013, p 104-105.

This is a study for the finished painting in the Museum of Stoke-on-Trent showing a rifle range. During WW2 Sorrell served in the RAF from 1940, where he was able to make first-hand visual records of the daily life in the Air Force. 26 of these pictures were acquired by the War Artists' Advisory Committee. Lightning flickers over this scene of wartime austerity.

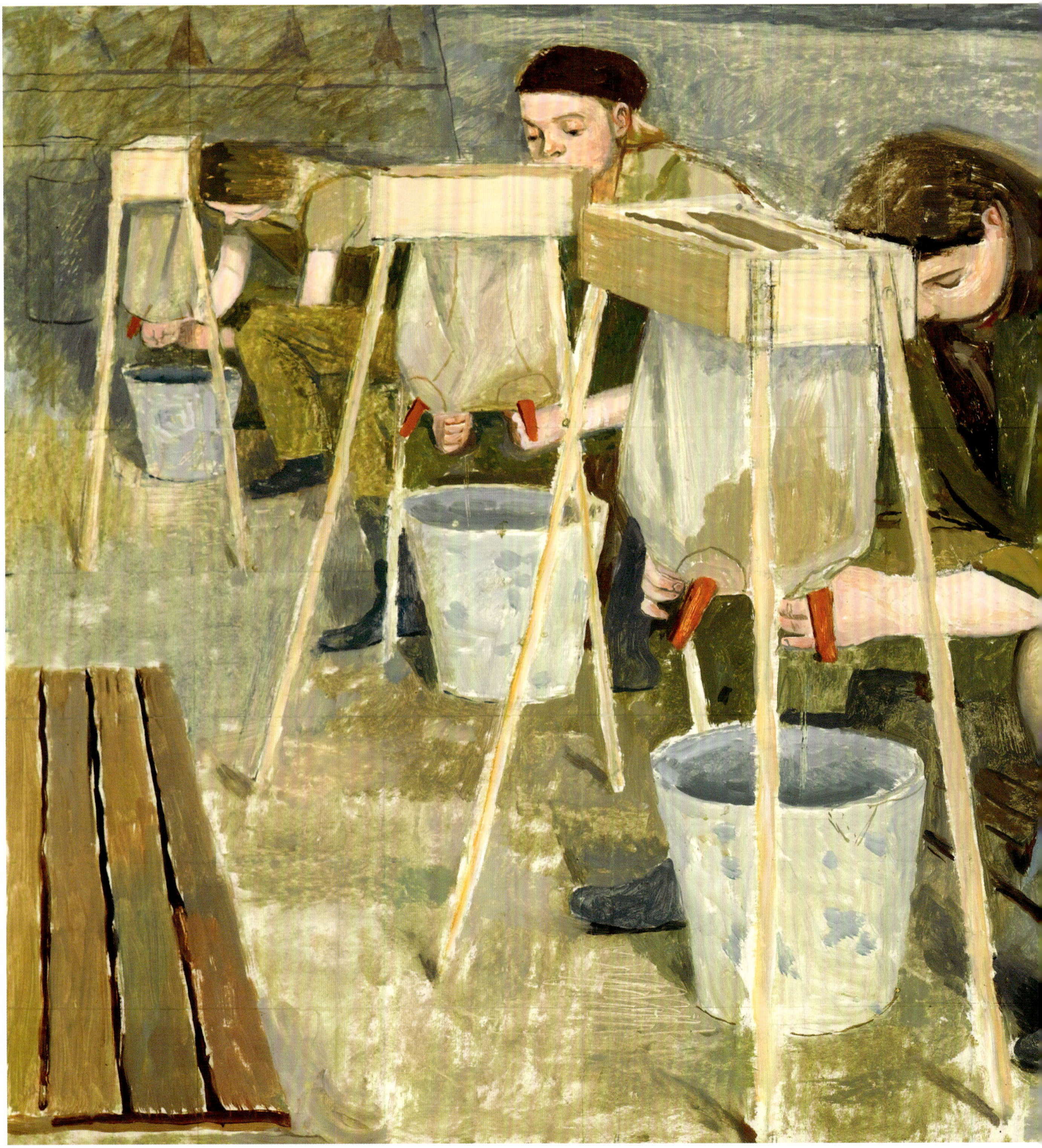

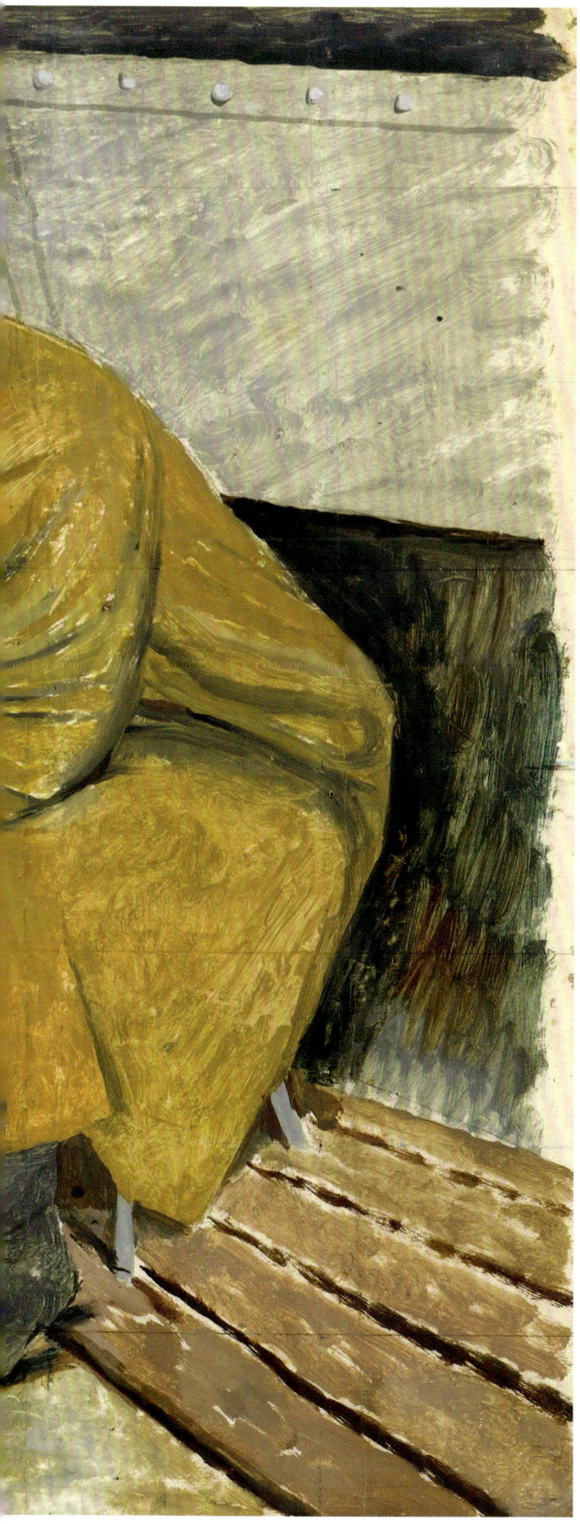

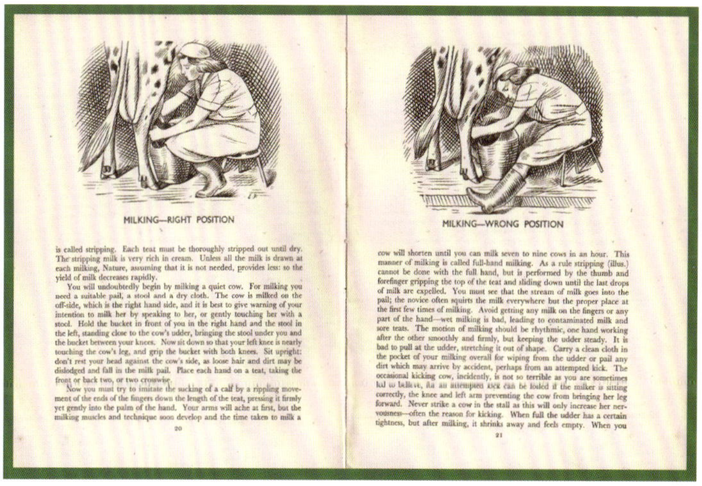

MILKING—RIGHT POSITION

is called stripping. Each teat must be thoroughly stripped out until dry. The stripping milk is very rich in cream. Unless all the milk is drawn at each milking, Nature, assuming that it is not needed, provides less: so the yield of milk decreases rapidly.

You will undoubtedly begin by milking a quiet cow. For milking you need a suitable pail, a stool and a dry cloth. The cow is milked on the off-side, which is the right hand side, and it is best to give warning of your intention to milk her by speaking to her, or gently touching her with a stool. Hold the bucket in front of you in the right hand and the stool in the left, standing close to the cow's udder, bringing the stool under you and the bucket between your knees. Now sit down so that your left knee is nearly touching the cow's leg, and grip the bucket with both knees. Sit upright: don't rest your head against the cow's side, as loose hair and dirt may be dislodged and fall in the milk pail. Place each hand on a teat, taking the front or back two, or two crosswise.

Now you must try to imitate the sucking of a calf by a rippling movement of the ends of the fingers down the length of the teat, pressing it firmly yet gently into the palm of the hand. Your arms will ache at first, but the milking muscles and technique soon develop and the time taken to milk a

20

MILKING—WRONG POSITION

cow will shorten until you can milk seven to nine cows in an hour. This manner of milking is called full-hand milking. As a rule stripping (illus.) cannot be done with the full hand, but is performed by the thumb and forefinger gripping the top of the teat and sliding down until the last drops of milk are expelled. You must see that the stream of milk goes into the pail; the novice often squirts the milk everywhere but the proper place at the first few times of milking. Avoid getting any milk on the fingers or any part of the hand—wet milking is bad, leading to contaminated milk and sore teats. The motion of milking should be rhythmic, one hand working after the other smoothly and firmly, but keeping the udder steady. It is bad to pull at the udder, stretching it out of shape. Carry a clean cloth in the pocket of your milking overall for wiping from the udder or pail any dirt which may arrive by accident, perhaps from an attempted kick. The occasional kicking cow, incidently, is not so terrible as you are sometimes led to believe, for an attempted kick can be foiled if the milker is sitting correctly, the knee and left arm preventing the cow from bringing her leg forward. Never strike a cow in the stall as this will only increase her nervousness—often the reason for kicking. When full the udder has a certain tightness, but after milking, it shrinks away and feels empty. When you

21

FIG. 14 – *A Book of Farmcraft* (Text: Michael Greenhill. Illustrations: Evelyn Dunbar), Longmans, Green & Co., London, was published in 1942. Greenhill was Instructor in Agriculture at Sparsholt Farm Institute, Winchester. *A Book of Farmcraft* was conceived partly as an introductory primer for the Women's Land Army.

CAT. 78 – **Evelyn Dunbar** (1906-1960) *Milking Practice with Artificial Udders*, 1940, oil on paper, laid on board, 22 x 30 in. (55.8 x 76.2 cm).
Provenance: Margaret Goodwin
Exhibited: *Evelyn Dunbar – The Lost Works*, Pallant House Gallery, October 2015 - February 2016, cat 85.
Literature: *Evelyn Dunbar – The Lost Works*, Sacha Llewellyn & Paul Liss, July 2015, cat. 85, page 130.

Evelyn Dunbar, the only woman to receive a full-time salary from the WAAC, was commissioned to produce 'agricultural and woman subjects'. This sketch is a study for, and almost identical to, the finished painting in the IWM.

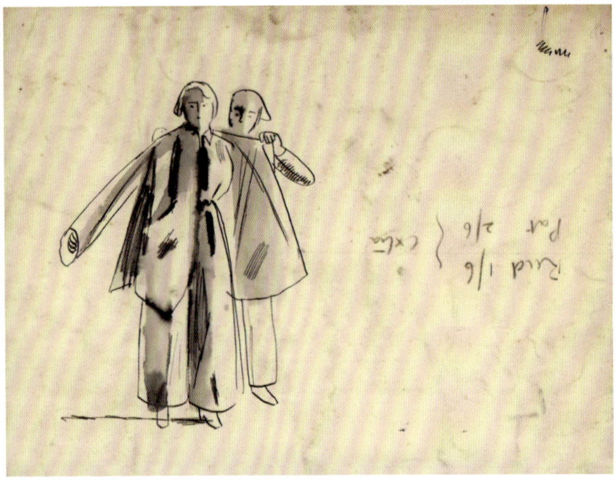

a

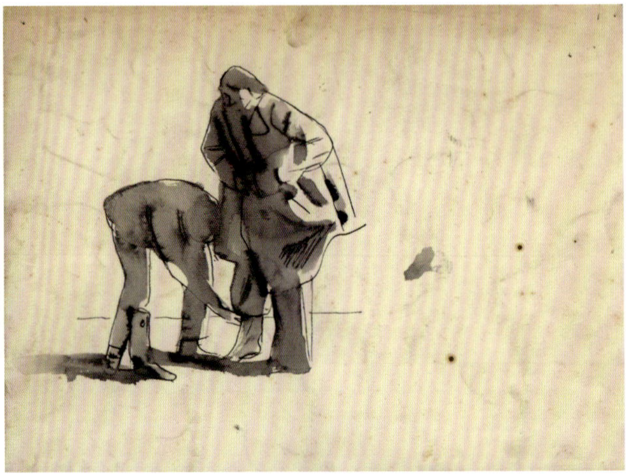

b

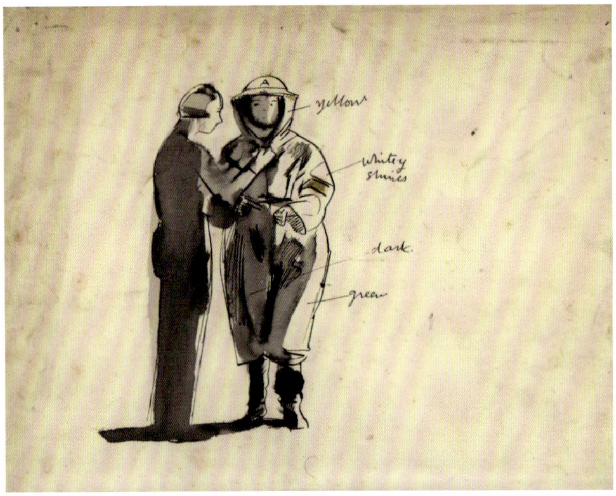

c

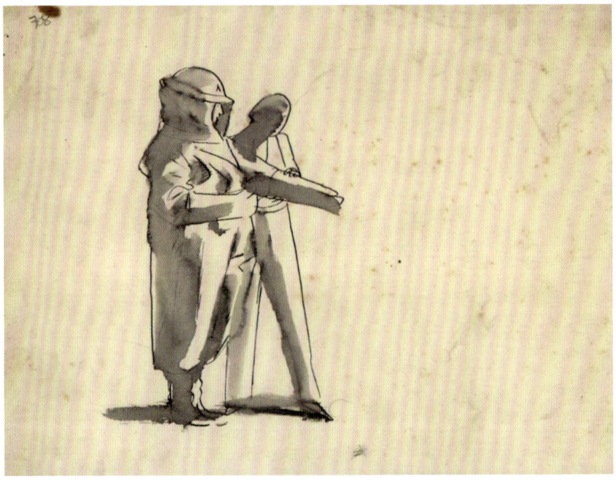

d

CAT. 79 a, b, c, d – **Evelyn Dunbar** (1906-1960), Studies for *Putting on Anti-gas Protective Clothing*, 1940, pen, ink and wash on paper, a and c: 11 ½ x 15 in. (29 x 38.5 cm), b and d: 10 ¾ x 15 in. (27 x 38.5 cm). Provenance: The Artist's Family; thence by descent.

In July 1940 the National Gallery included this compartment painting in an exhibition of wartime art and it was also included in the Britain at War exhibition at the Museum of Modern Art in New York the following year.

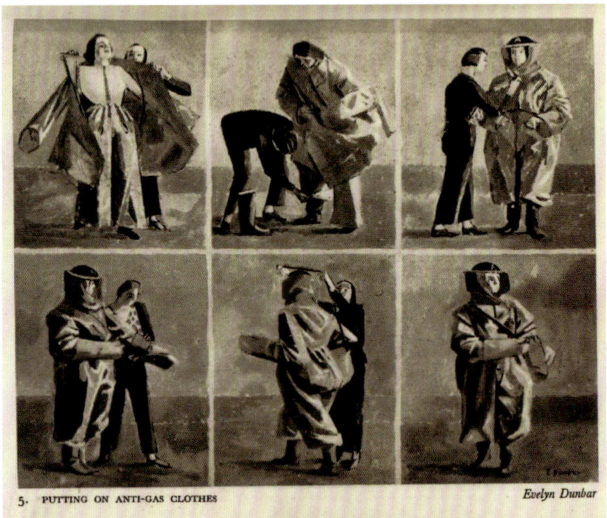

FIG. 15 –
Evelyn Dunbar's *Putting on Anti-Gas Protective Clothing*, 1940, as it appeared in the fifth volume of the *War Pictures by British Artists* series, *Women*.

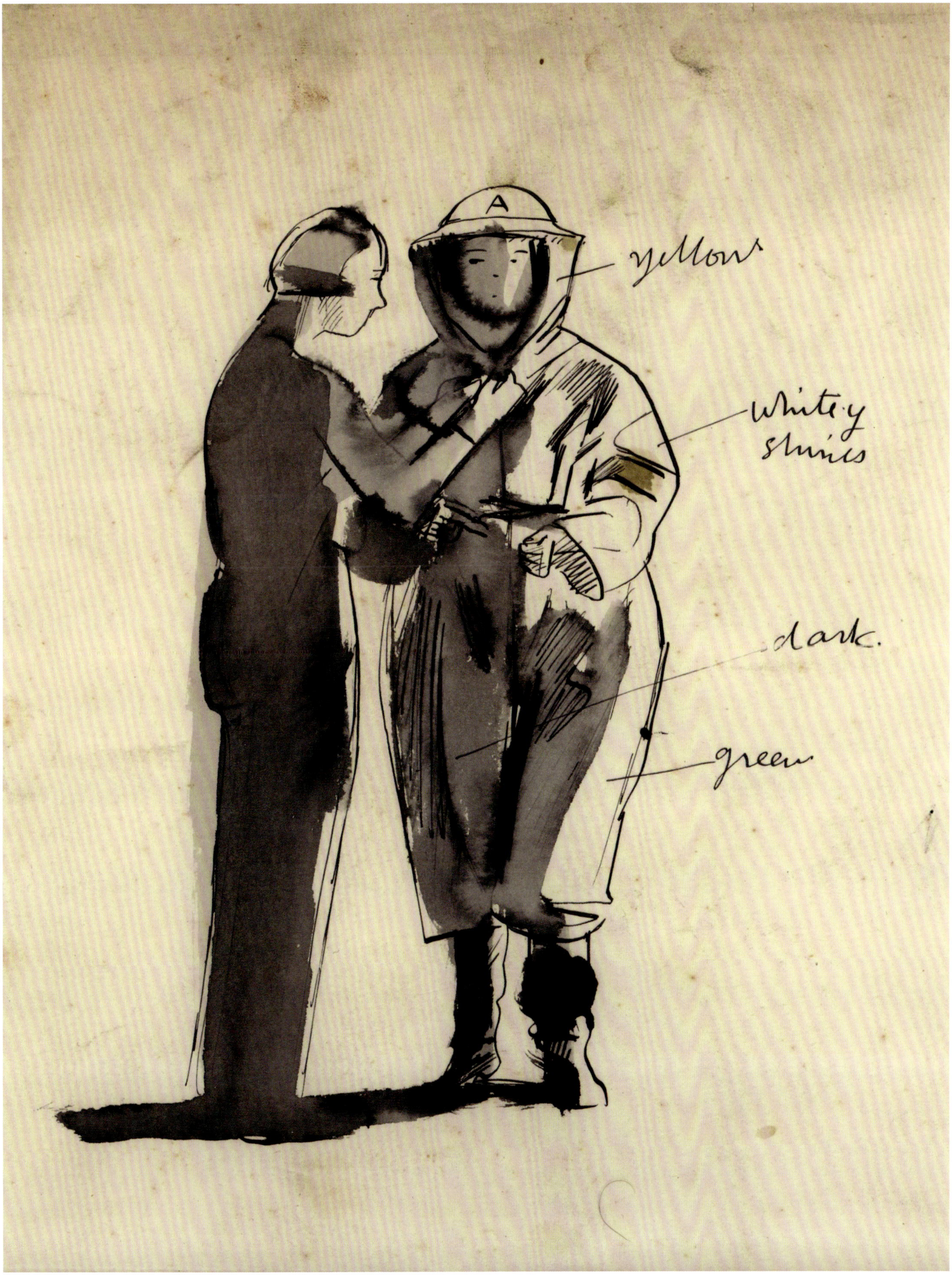
A
yellow
whitey stuins
dark.
green

CAT. 80* –
Evelyn Dunbar (1906-1960),
Men Stooking and Girls Learning to Stook, c. 1943,,
oil on canvas,
29 ½ x 19 in. (75 x 49 cm).
Provenance: Margaret Goodwin; Diss Auction Rooms; Sim Fine Art; Private collection.
Exhibited: *Evelyn Dunbar –The Lost Works*,
Pallant House Gallery, October 2015 - February 2016, cat 100.
Literature: *Evelyn Dunbar –The Lost Works*,
Sacha Llewellyn & Paul Liss, July 2015, cat. 100, pages 146-147.

Painted in the long, hot summer of 1940, when so often the skies of southern England were criss-crossed with vapour trails from RAF Spitfires and Hurricanes defending the homeland from Hitler's Luftwaffe in the Battle of Britain. Dunbar's magnificent canvas is a great reassurance: the harvest is on the way to being in, the wheatfield is limitless, like the Creator's generosity. The Land Girls of the Women's Land Army are marching with the men, so to speak, and have turned the task of stooking into a military operation, mirroring the men on the right. Note the man in the distance with a shotgun, maybe hoping to supplement his meat ration with an unwary rabbit. Note also the way the Land Girl on the left, who appears to be giving the orders, has tucked her left hand behind her back into the crook of her right elbow in a definitely non-military pose, a touch of a gentle feminist subversion often observable in Dunbar's war paintings. Strangely this painting was not accepted by the War Artists' Advisory Committee.

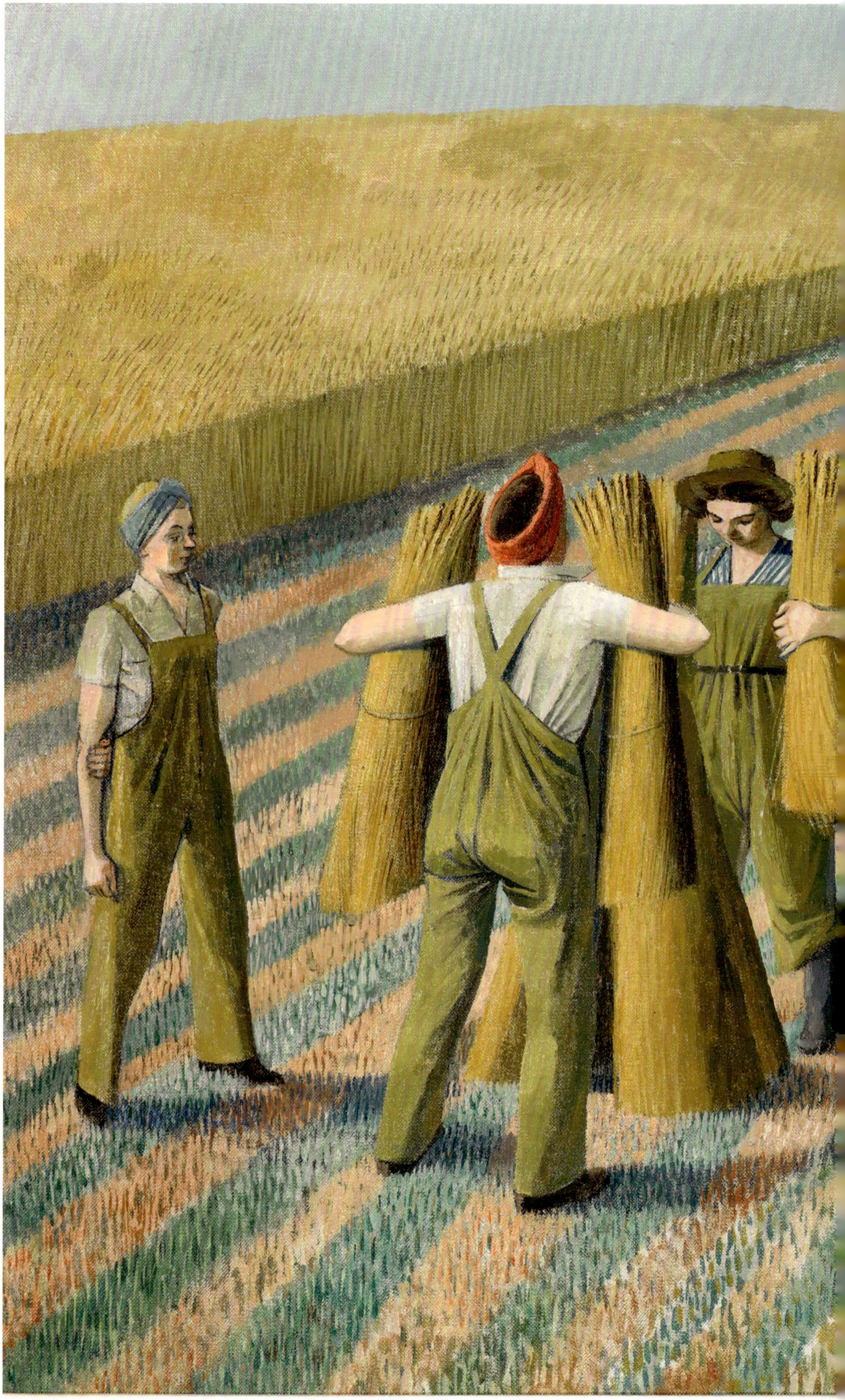

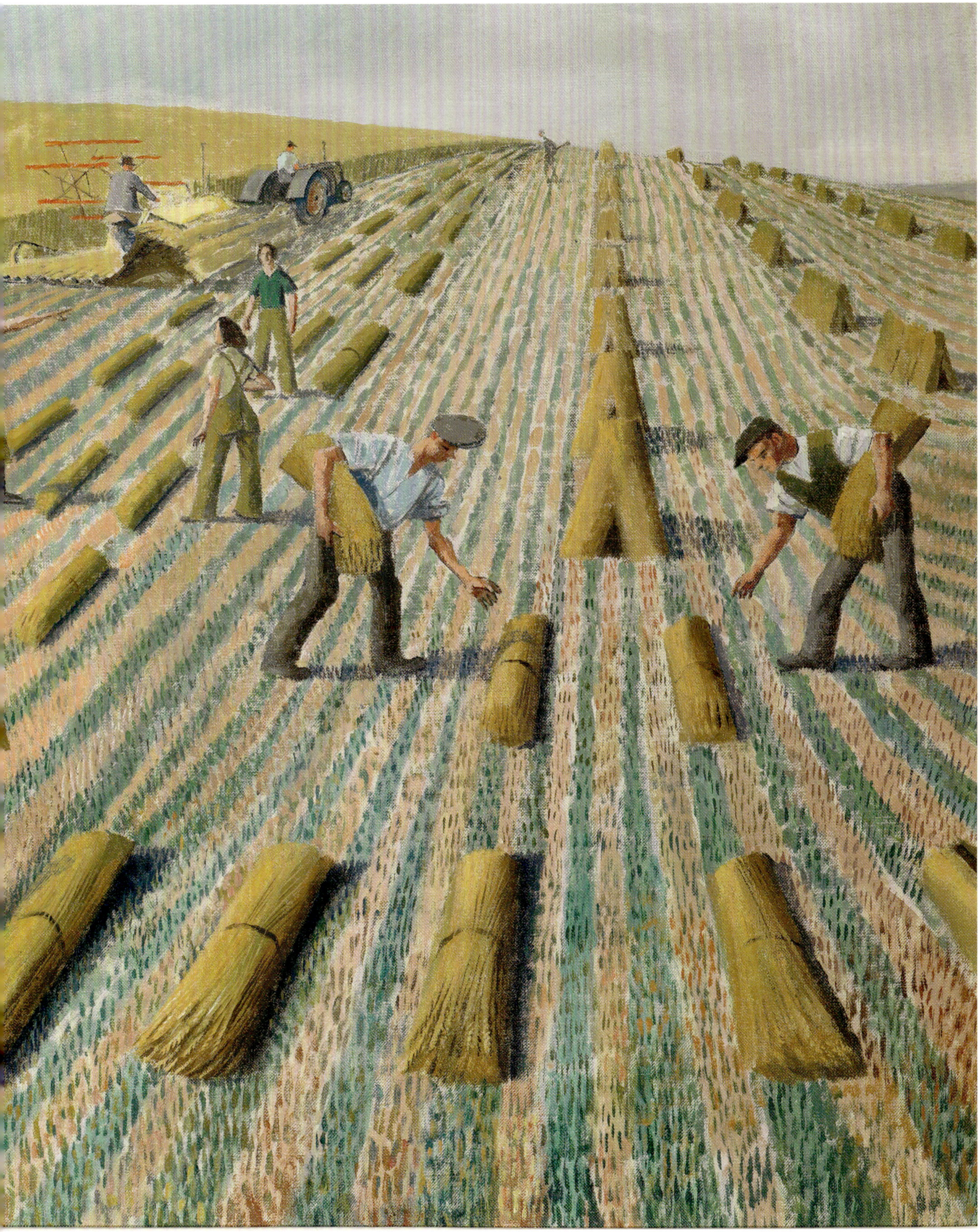

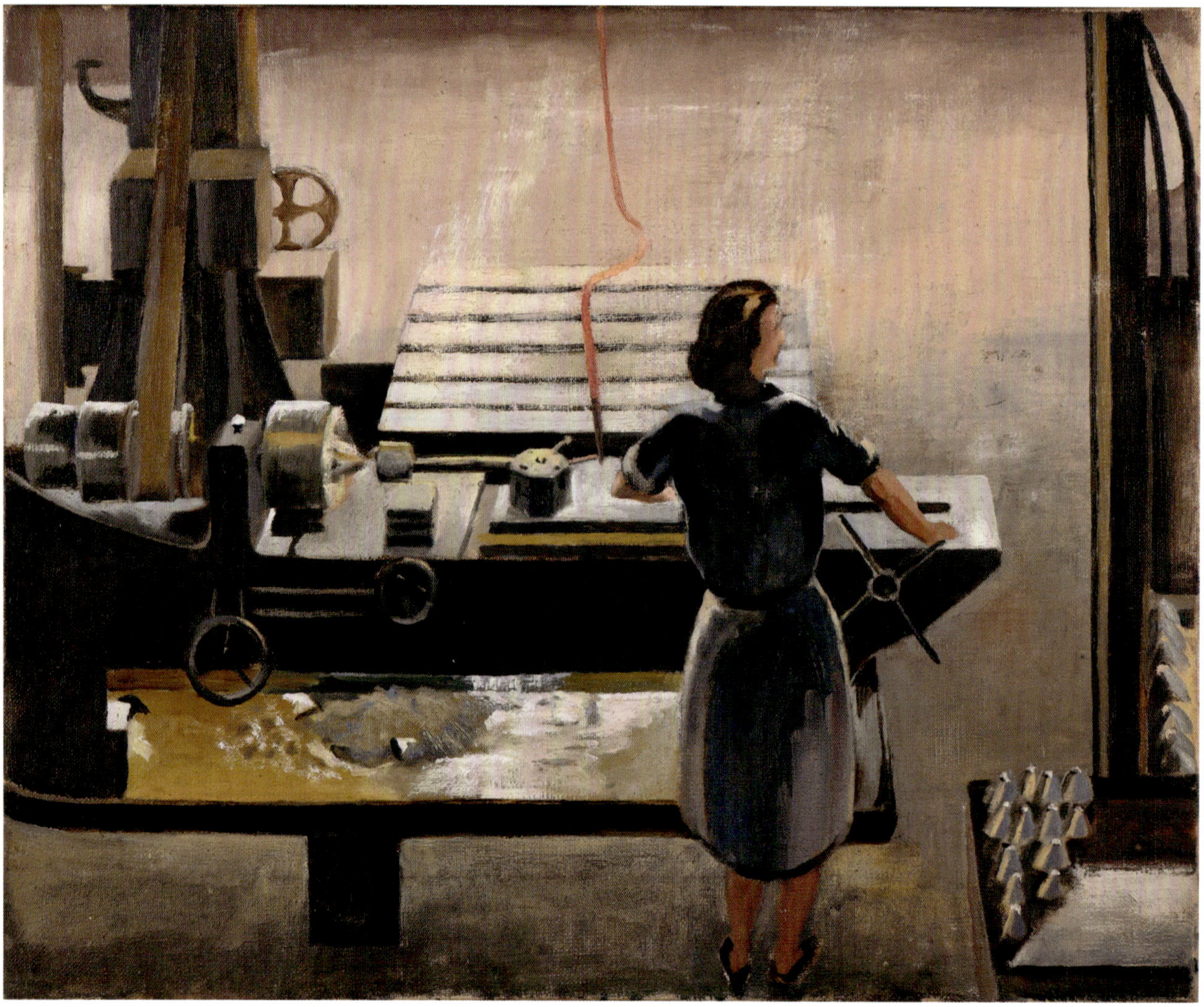

CAT. 81 – **Isobel Atterbury Heath** (1908-1989), *Woman operating a lathe turning the fuse tips of munitions*, c.1944, oil on canvas, 16 ¼ x 20 in. (41.2 x 51 cm).

This painting shows a woman operating a capstan lathe, turning the fuse tips of munitions. The material that is being turned is possibly aluminium because the lathe is flooded with coolant and the swarf appears to be granular and very white.

During WW2 Heath volunteered to work as an artist for Ministry of Information drawing and painting naval subjects and factory workers in Howton's munitions and camouflage factory at St. Ives and the Spitfire fighter station at Perranporth. She married an Italian prisoner of war, Dr Marc Prati – a political correspondent for the Italian newspaper *La Stampa*, who had been interned in Cornwall.

By 1943 there were 7.25 million women engaged in war-related employment, the majority in agriculture, manufacturing and civil defence. Although recording the role of women was one of the stated aims of WAAC, the scheme nevertheless favoured images of women performing conventional roles – for instance the predominance of paintings of women as nurses in spite of the fact that in 1943 munitions workers outnumbered nurses by 100 to 1. Like other female War Artists, Heath delighted in showing women at work in some of the more unusual roles they performed during the war.

CAT. 82 – **Isobel Atterbury Heath** (1908-1989), *Two women arc welding*, signed and inscribed 'War 39-46', oil on canvas, 20 x 16 in. (51 x 40.5 cm).

The two arc-welding women wear protective leather aprons and welders' helmets fitted with a filter shade. They work in separate cubicles to avoid damaging each other's eyes. The bench-height production suggests that the women were making light steel fabrications such as containers for munitions.

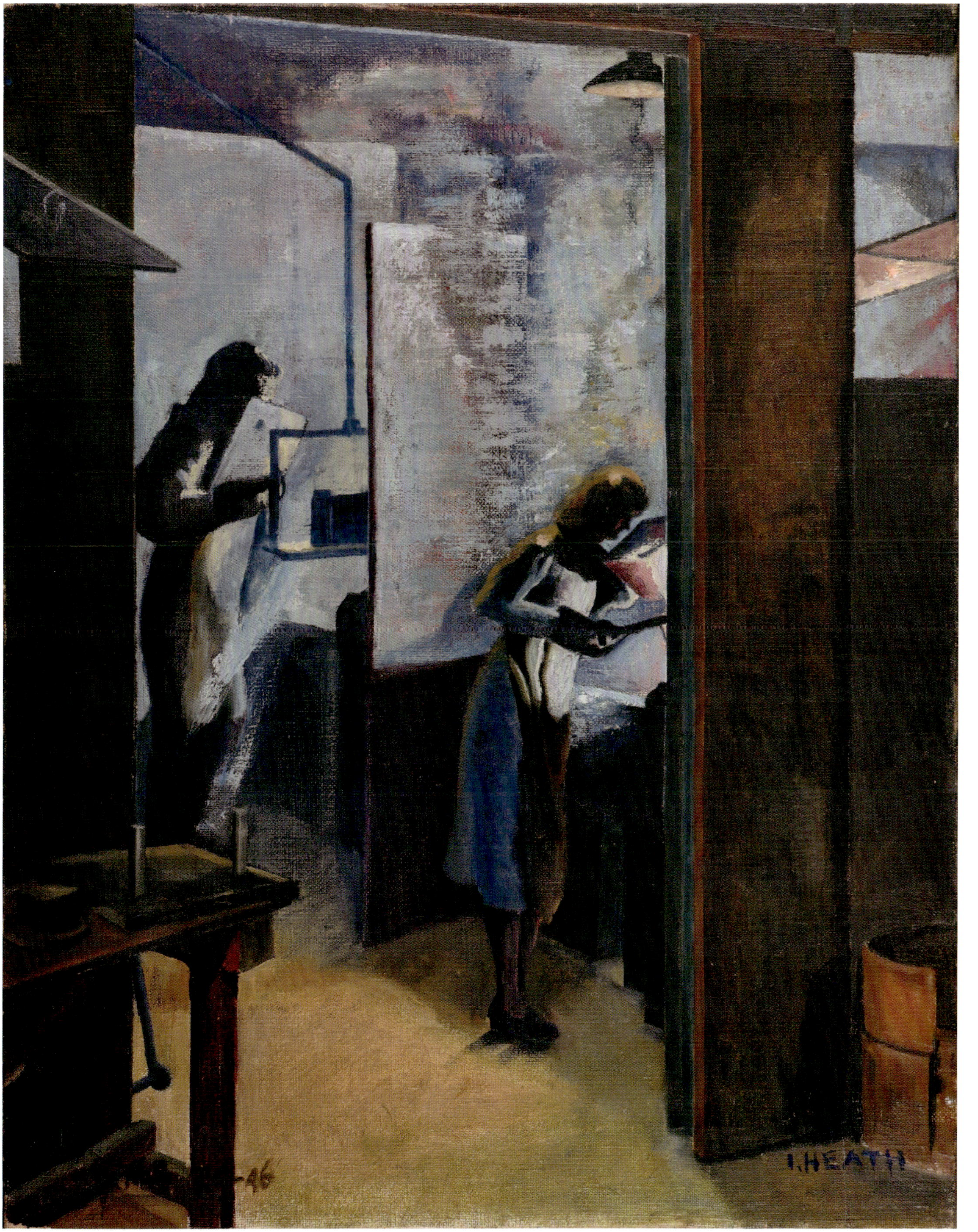
I. HEATH

SEEING IT THROUGH

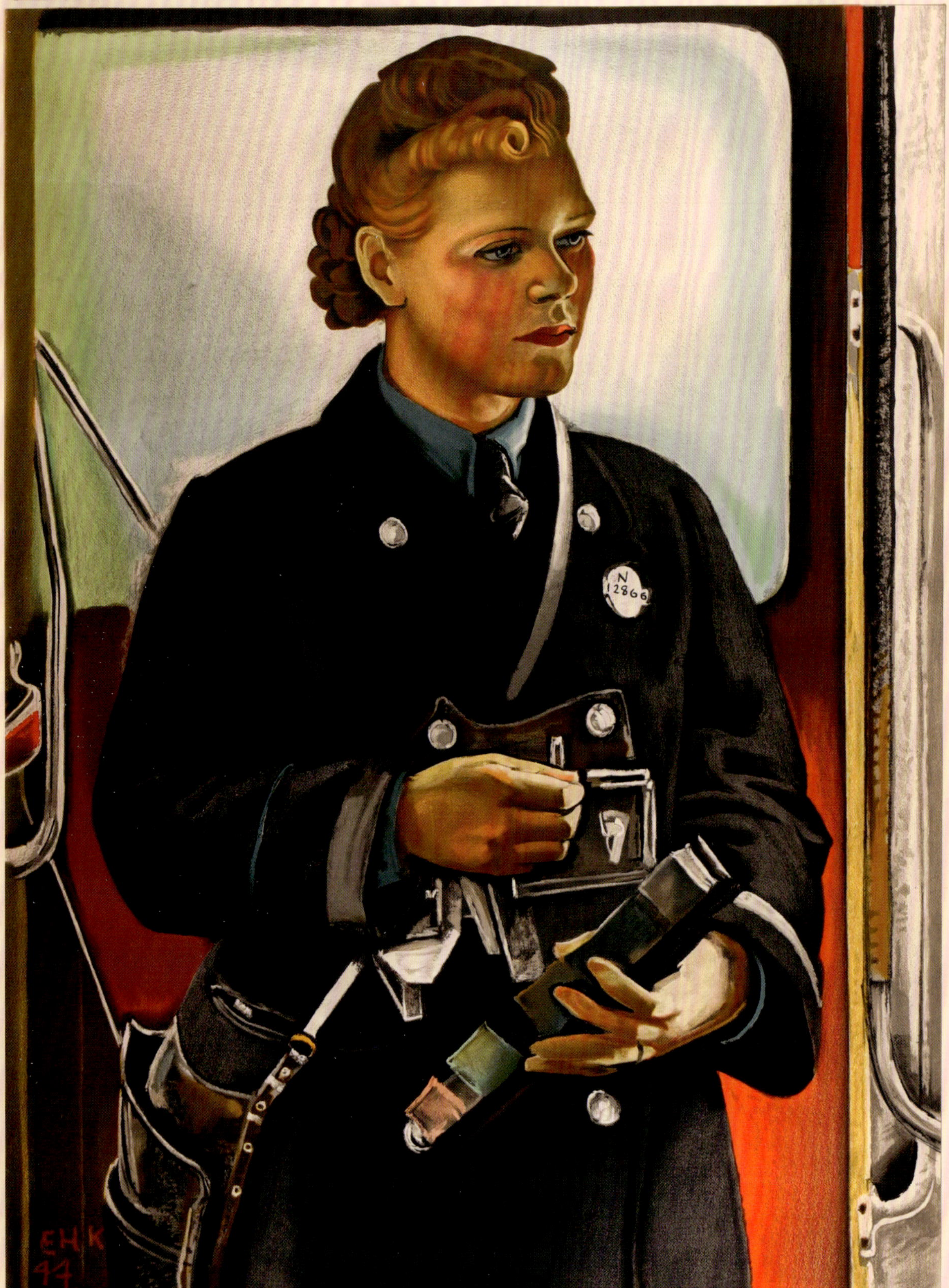

How proud upon your quarterdeck you stand,
Conductor – Captain – of the mighty bus!
Like some Columbus you survey the Strand,
A calm newcomer in a sea of fuss.

You may be tired – how cheerfully you clip,
Clip in the dark, with one eye on the street –
Two decks – one pair of legs – a rolling ship –
Much on your mind – and fat men on your feet!

The sirens blow, and death is in the air:
Still at her post the trusty Captain stands,
And counts her change, and scampers up the stair,
As brave a sailor as the King commands.

A. P. Herbert

CAT. 83* – **Eric Kennington** (1888-1960), *Seeing it through*, 1944, signed with initials, dated and inscribed with title and text lithographic poster, signed in the plate with initials, 31 ¾ x 21 ½ in. (81 x 55 cm).

This poster was produced by Kennington as part of the war posters in the series *Seeing it Through*. The model was a twenty-year-old London bus conductress, Mrs M.J. Morgan. One of the first generation of female bus conductresses employed by London Transport in November 1940, she had only just started her job as a "clippie" when the bus she was assigned to was caught in the blitz. She became an instant heroine when she shielded with her own body two young children, and then helped passengers who'd been injured when the bus was riddled with shrapnel from a bomb exploding nearby. Kennington remembered her well describing her: "…like a Rubens Venus' and she had a complexion that was 'edible as a peach…"

Beneath the portrait of the bus conductor was a short verse by the novelist and humorist, Alan Patrick Herbert:

How proud upon your quarterdeck you stand
Conductor-Captain of the mighty bus!
Like some Columbus you survey the Strand
A calm newcomer in a sea of fuss
You may be tired – how cheerfully you clip
Clip in the dark with one eye on the street –
Two decks – one pair of legs – a rolling ship
Much on your mind and fat men on your feet !
The sirens blow, and death is in the air
Still at her post the trusty Captain stands
And counts her change, and scampers up the stair
As brave a sailor as the King commands.

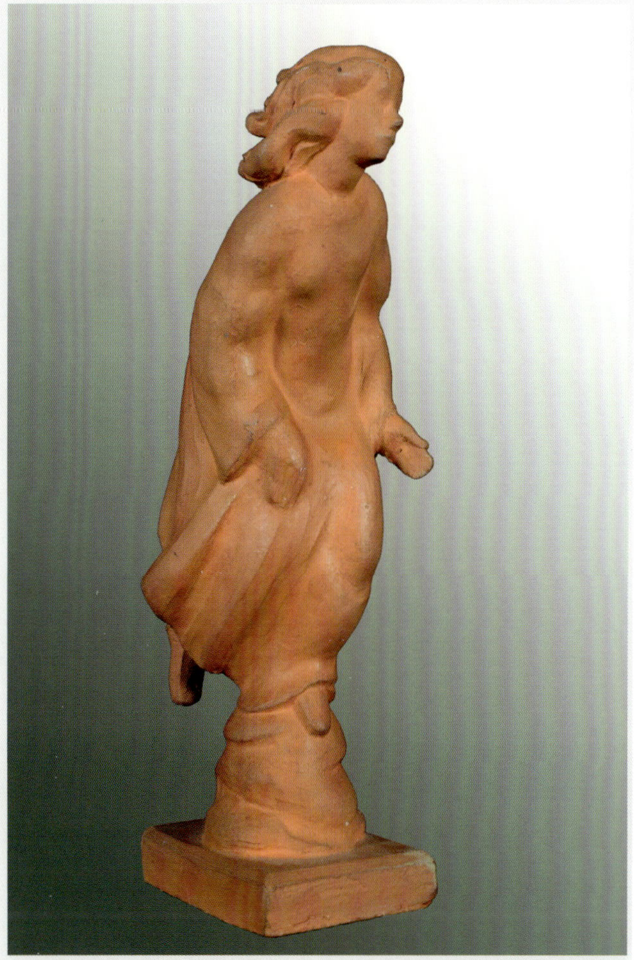

CAT. 84 –
Hermann Nonnenmacher (1892-1988), signed with initials, terracotta sculpture, 9 ¼ x 3 in. (23.5 x 7.6 cm).

Herman Nonnenmacher was born in Germany, but fled to England in 1938 with his wife the sculptor Erna Rosenberg (1889-1980). Before the rise of Nazism, both were well-known sculptors whose works adorned many public buildings in Germany. Hermann and Erna's art was classified as degenerate by the Nazis, and much of their public sculpture was destroyed. During WW2 Hermann and Erna were interned on the Isle of Man. Erna, who was Jewish, was the model for this poignant composition of a fleeing figure

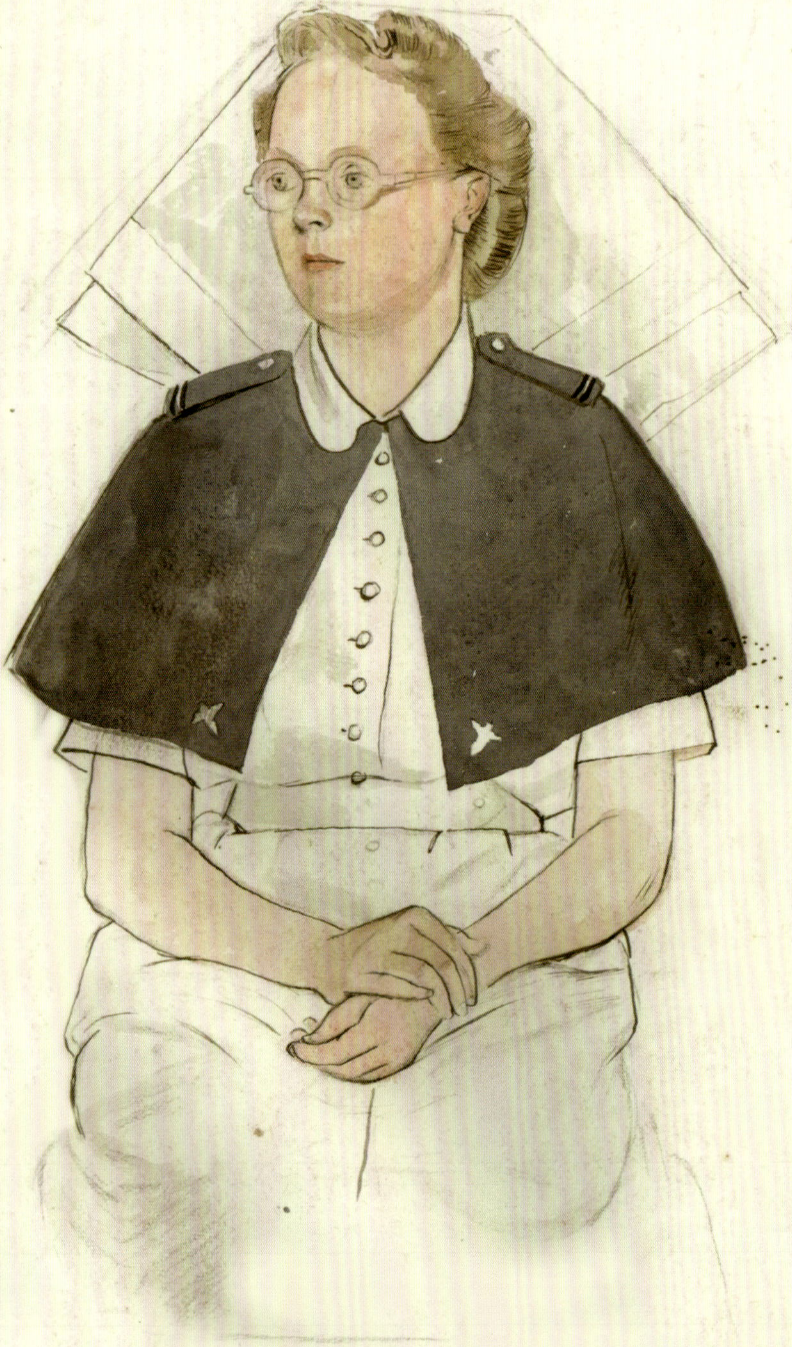

CAT. 85 – **Evelyn Dunbar** (1906-1960), *Senior Sister PMRAF Nursing Service*, 1944,
labelled on verso 'RAF South Cerney 1944' in Roger Folley's handwriting,
pencil and watercolour on paper, 22½ x 15½ in. (58 x 39.5 cm).
Provenance: Roger Folley; Alasdair Dunbar; Hammer Mill Oast Collection
Exhibited: *Evelyn Dunbar – The Lost Works*, Pallant House Gallery, October 2015 - February 2016, cat 100.
Literature: *Evelyn Dunbar – The Lost Works*, Sacha Llewellyn & Paul Liss, July 2015, cat 101, page 148.

Dunbar was directed not to name her subjects. Probably observed at RAF South Cerney, wearing a white ward dress underneath an RAF blue tippet adorned at the points with the Rod of Aesculapius, the shoulder boards identify this sitter as a Senior Sister. This is one of the artist's rare watercolours that she produced for the War Artists' Advisory Committee.

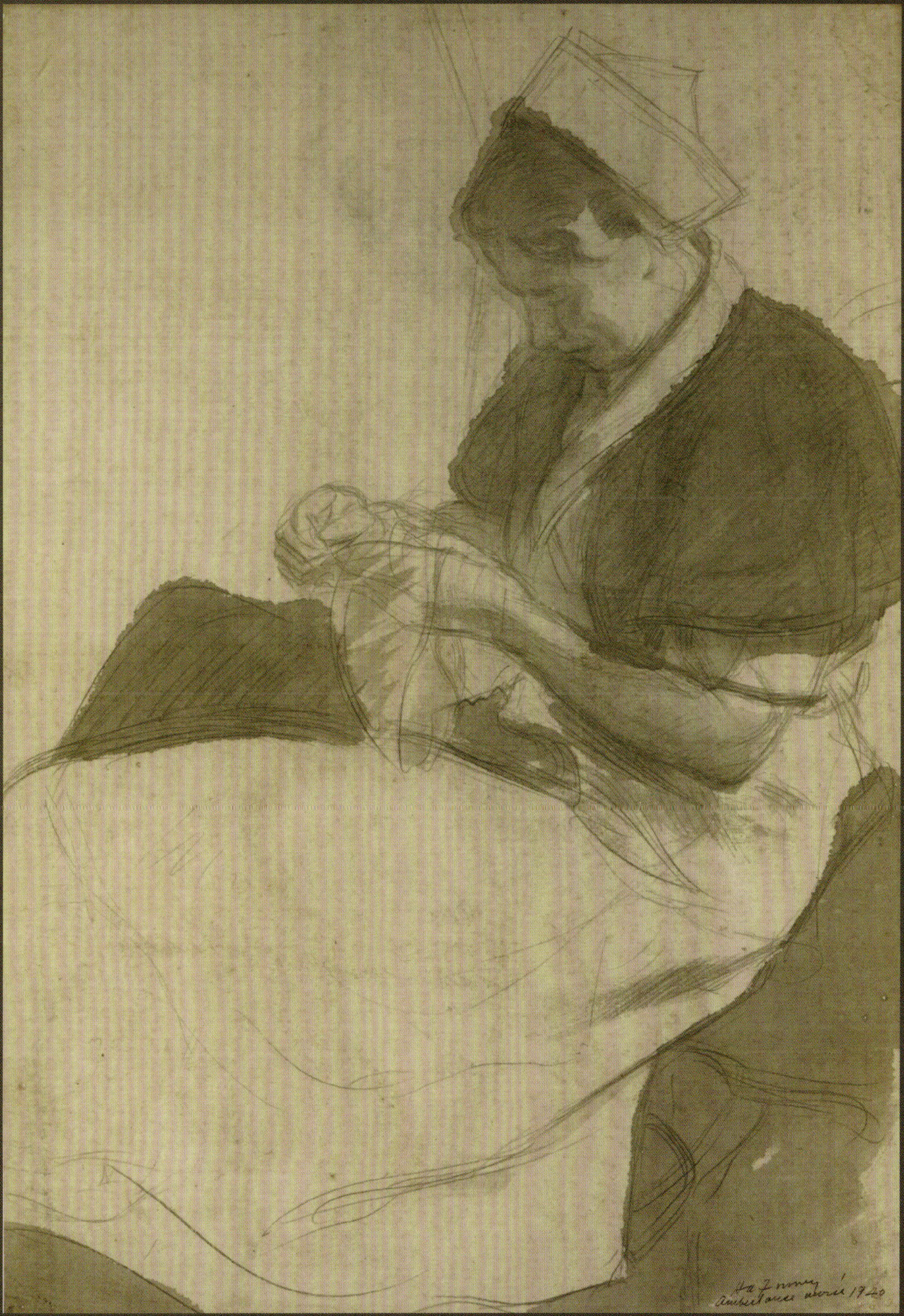

CAT. 86 – **Hubert Arthur Finney** (1905-1991), *Ambulance Nurse*, 1940,
signed, titled and dated with studio stamp and inventory number 455 to reverse,
pencil and wash on paper, 16 x 11 in. (40 x 28 cm).

During the war Finney served in the ambulance crews of the Air Raid Precautions service, later named Civil Defence, for a period of four years until in 1945 he got pleurisy. In his unpublished autobiography he recalled that: 'As we were in contact with the Ambulance Service I made many drawings of the nurses, and I had admiration for many of the Ambulance personnel, who were young girls of good breeding and social standing, for their courage during their work when the night bombing started and we had no defences.'

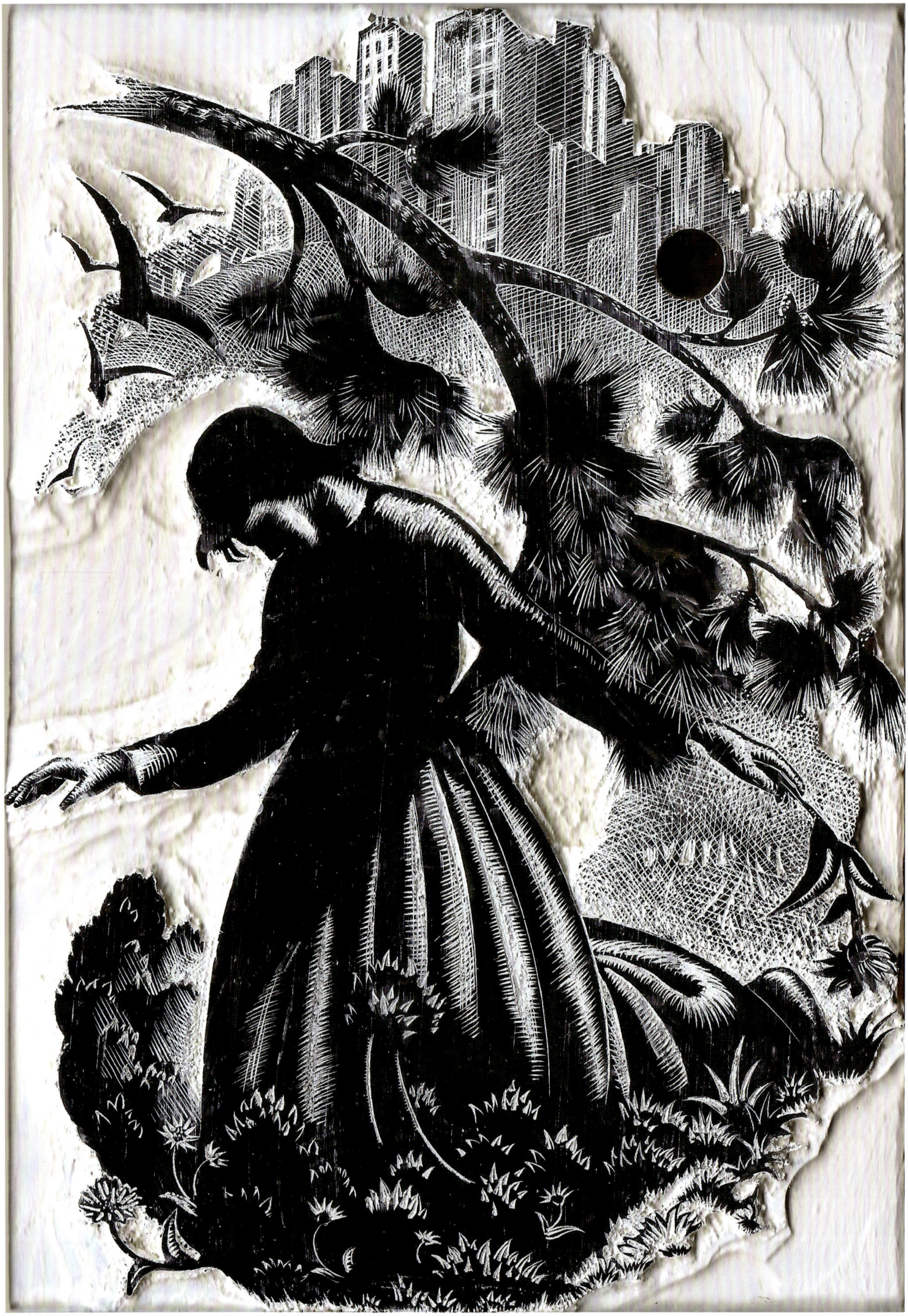

CAT. 87 – **Clare Leighton** (1898-1989), *And Dared to Call the Flowers My Own*, (BPL 489), 1941, original woodblock (cancelled), 5 ¾ x 4 in. (14.5 x 10.3 cm).

The Magic of Handling Earth was published in Elsie Symington's *By Light of Sun*, in 1941, an account of establishing a garden in America by a transplanted Englishwoman. Leighton herself moved to America in 1939 and became a naturalised citizen in 1945.

Clare Leighton had a passionate horror of war ever since burying the stained and tattered uniform of her brother Roland who died of wounds on the Western Front in 1915. Shortly after the end of WW2, in 1946 or 1947, she gave a talk in which she expressed her view of the war:

'An eighty-year-old friend of mine down in North Carolina who is something of a homespun philosopher remarked: "There's a whole heap of things we can begin to see to, when the war done ceases more". He saw the ending of war as a gradual process, not one joyful event. This set me thinking that wars do not necessarily end when the fighting stops; the world that made it possible may still be with us. I realized that the difference between war and peace today is not a matter of black and white, it is a gradualism. And so, when I try to talk to you about the artist's place in the world today, I am talking about a world that is still blurred by war. War does not cease with the end of the killing; the state of war in our minds endures. And it is a more complicated, subtly dangerous state perhaps than the war itself. It is charged with potential danger, more confusion and chaos.
A lot of people were frightened of the end of the war; of its challenge. That is where the artist must come in.
I am not talking of the artist specifically as painter, or engraver, or sculptor; I am talking of the artist in general. The artist is the seismograph, the sensitised plate; the receiving station for life. The artist's sensitivity enables him to see and sense things, if not before they happen, at least before they are recognised by the world at large.
I am talking of the artist and his relationship to life. The artist is above race, creed, class and so on, for visual art, like music, can be understood by the entire world. And the artist has never been more important. I believe that in Buddhist ethics, one of the deadly sins is a lack of awareness. The artist's task is to re-awaken awareness, to re-sensitise it. War produces an emotional deadness: once, a distant massacre or a faraway earthquake moved us to righteous indignation. Now, here in America, the whole of Europe might starve and we would hardly be aware of it. There is a cataract over the eyes of the spirit. The artist must be the quickener of the world; we have seen the death of tenderness. As E.M.Forster put it, "we must not let ourselves be numbed by horrors".
What were we fighting for? For freedom. Freedom to live fully, which means to create our own symbols of freedom and pass them on to others; to allow for a new set of experiences and a new capacity for them.
We are on the edge of a new civilisation and it is up to us to shape it. As the twig is bent, the tree will grow. It is a tender, young civilisation scarcely born, and it can be shaped in materialism or into the things of the mind and spirit. We artists have a strange sense of hurry – hurry before it is too late; hurry before the world has taken hold of its new values based on "things". I have noticed this in many of my fellows. Nylon stockings are not worth our men having died; nor are motor cars. Nor refrigerators, nor limitless gasoline nor vacations in Florida. We owe a debt to our dead. This can only be paid in the slightest degree by creating a new world. This means a really new world, not one with its old values. I can now speak as an American, being a self-elected immigrant and taking out my papers. We run the risk of being a defeated country, for we are putting our faith in things. Apart from our mental values, we must reconstruct the world's symbols which we have had to tear down: Monte Cassino, the Mantegna paintings at Padua; the churches, buildings and libraries. We must slave to rebuild, so that there is as little guilt as possible; so that this age in the eyes of posterity may not be looked on as an age of the ravager and the destroyer. The beneficent influences throughout the world are Mozart, Hans Andersen and the like – not the big bankers and the automobile manufacturers. We must add our weight to the spiritual side of the balance. There is no time to lose, for we are drifting into fear and chaos.
Chaos! We need a sense of order, of benign order as represented by the seasons, the earth, the art of the Bach fugue. The human being needs benign discipline – we may find it in authoritarian, democratic, or religious form, or in awareness of the arts, but always we need something of ordered creativity. We need order in architecture. This state of mind of happy order is the best guard against anarchy and totalitarianism. It is better than armies. Our men are coming home. A friend declared that he had put his soul on ice for the duration of the war. Order is needed to fill their empty hands that have grown accustomed to bombs and planes; we dare not let them stay empty.
In rebuilding our world we need something of the spirit to balance this mechanised age. Mankind is not yet adjusted to wholesale mechanisation. Our spirit is lonely. We are still the mute inactive scared creator. There has been anonymous art from the beginning of mankind; there is a creative urge in us all. It must have an outlet. This is the way to make a world in which peace is a vital, enduring thing, and not a mere negation of the state of war.'

Clare Leighton: The growth and shaping of an artist-writer, p .47-48),
published by The Estate of Clare Leighton, 2009.

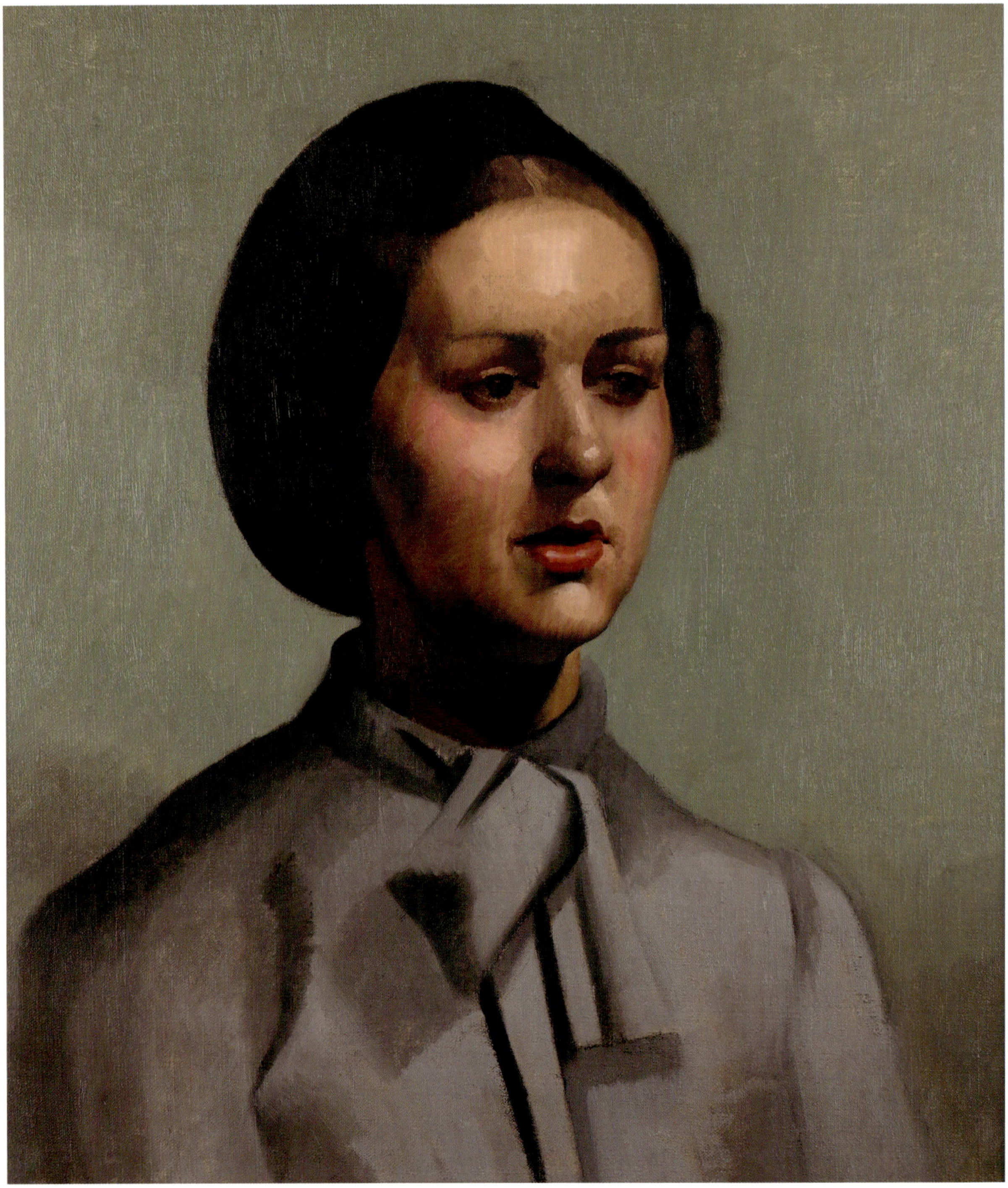

CAT. 88 – **Phoebe Peto Dickinson** (1917-1978), *Young woman in a beret* (possibly a self-portrait), early 1940s,
Inscribed Pheobe Dickinson Tannachie, West Malvern, Worcs, on the canvas return,
oil on canvas, 18 x 16 ½ in. (45.5 x 42 cm).
Provenance: With the artist until 1978; thereafter by descent.

This painting dates to the early 1940s when Dickinson met Alfred Willets, a conscientious objector, and both were in the Land Army. A green felt beret was standard issue headwear for women in the Women's Timber Corps section of the Land Army, but not for regular Land Army girls, who wore a brown felt brimmed hat.
Later in 1957 Pheobe and Alfred were early activists in the Direct Action Committee and the Campaign for Nuclear Disarmament. She served 5 months in prison for civil disobedience. In the 1960s she became ordained as a Deaconess in the Church of England.

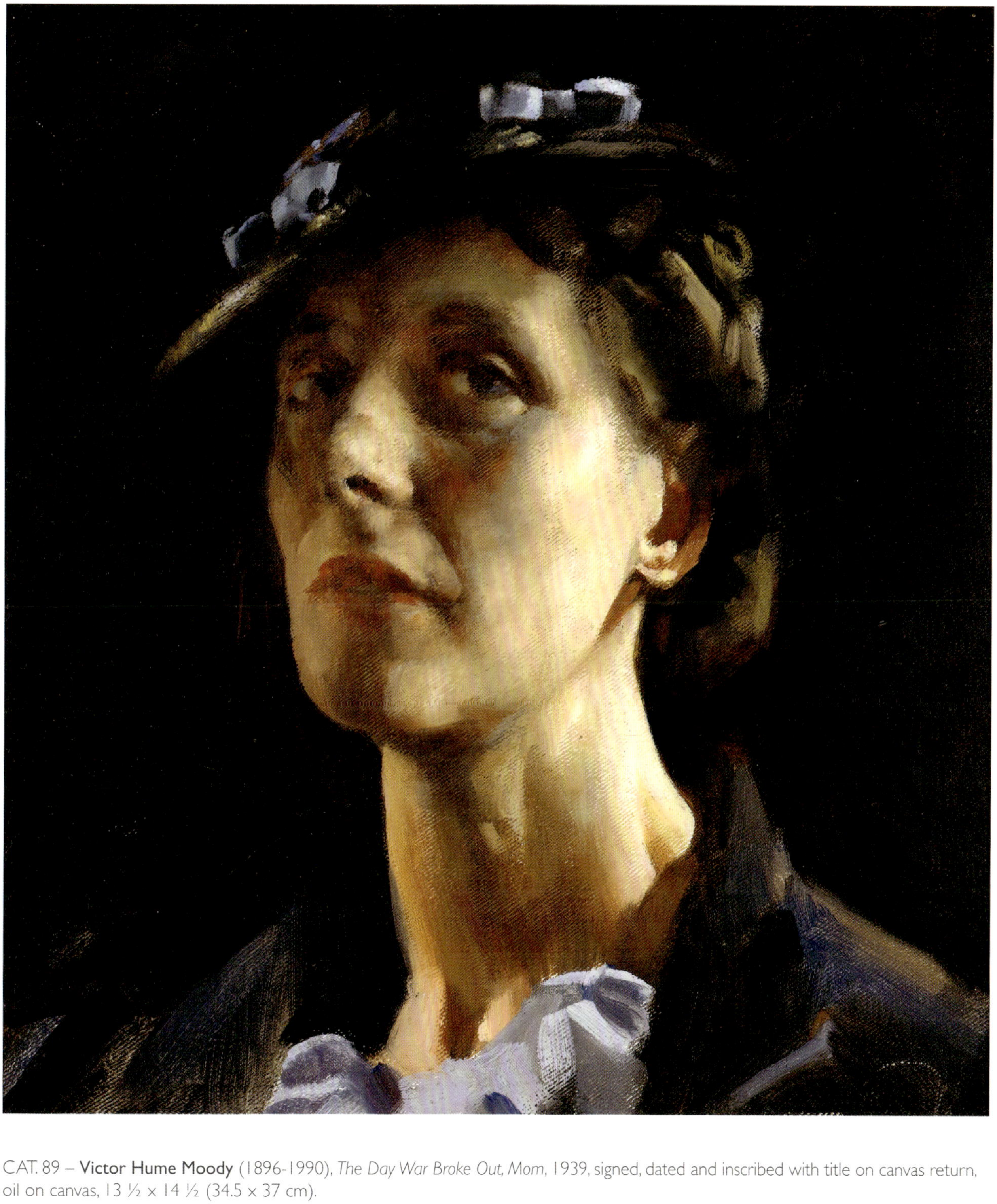

CAT. 89 – **Victor Hume Moody** (1896-1990), *The Day War Broke Out, Mom*, 1939, signed, dated and inscribed with title on canvas return, oil on canvas, 13 ½ x 14 ½ (34.5 x 37 cm).

The war had a measurable effect on Moody's work, prompting him to produce a number of unusually topical subjects. His Royal Academy exhibits from this period, *The End of Summer*, *Europa and the Powers* and *The Return of the Hunting Goddess*, all make veiled reference to conflict and the eventual restoration of peace.

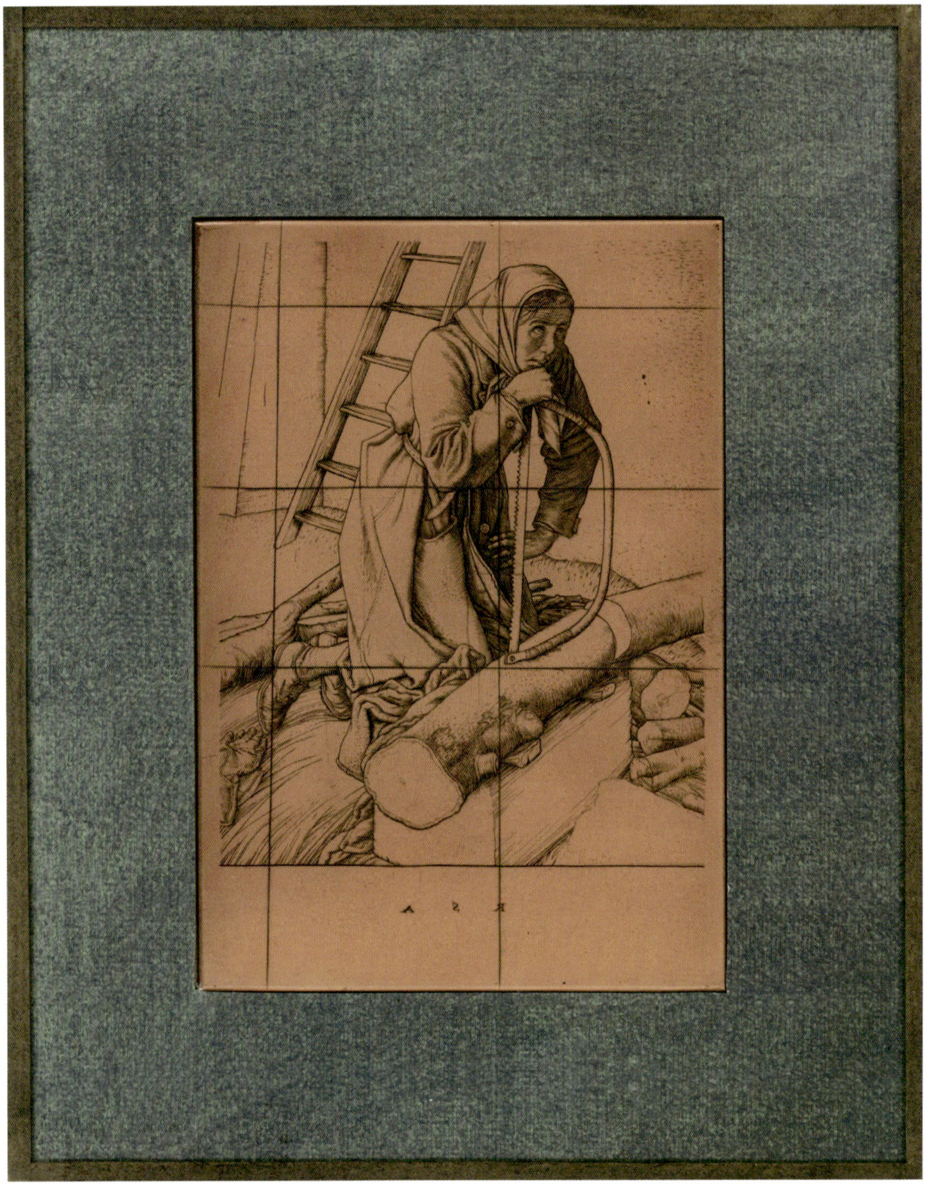

CAT. 90 – **Robert Austin** (1895-1973), *Hero's Widow*, 1944, signed in the plate, original copper plate, cancelled, 9 ¼ x 7 in. (23.5 x 17.5 cm).

The subject of this meticulously handled image is evident in the title – hundreds of thousands of women were widowed during WW2. This engraving was made after the publication of Campbell Dodgson's catalogue on the engraved works of Robert Sargent Austin and has been listed variously under the titles of *Woman with Saw*, *Widow of a Hero* and *Hero's Widow* – it was under this last title that the plate was issued as the presentation plate of the Print Collectors' Club at the end of 1944.

CAT. 91 – **Robert Austin** (1895-1973), *Evening*, 1939, signed in the plate, original etching plate, cancelled, 8 ¾ x 6 ¾ in. (22.5 x 17.2 cm).
Provenance: the artist's family.
Literature: Campbell Dodgson, *Robert Austin*, exh. cat., Twenty-One Gallery, London, 1930; Gordon Cooke, *Drawings and Prints by Robert Austin*, exh. cat., The Fine Art Society, London, 2001.

Evening, a composition created during the early years of the war, is one of Austin's most accomplished engravings. The model praying was Eleanor Hudson, (Austin's student and mistress) a watercolourist, etcher and designer best known for her depictions of women at work during WW2.

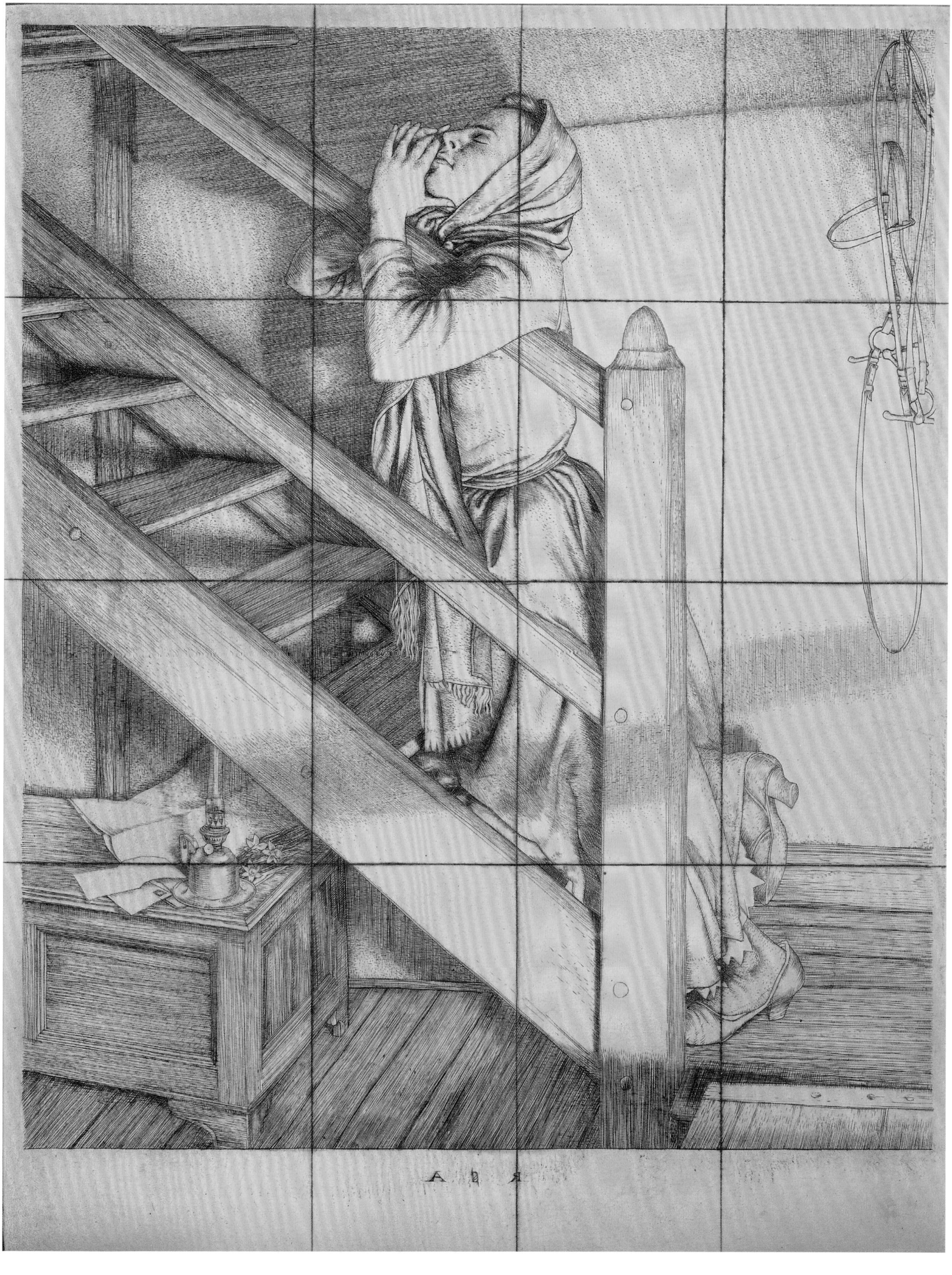

PRODUCTION

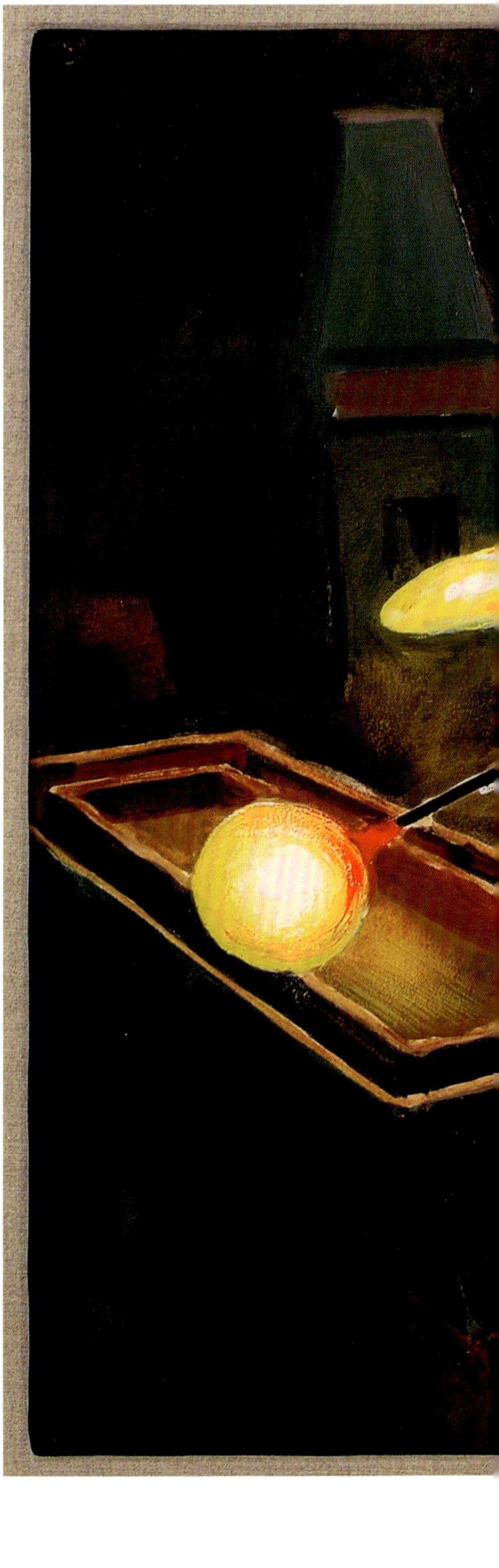

CAT. 92* – **Mervyn Peake** (1911-1968),
Glass-blowers producing cathode-ray tubes for radar use, 1943,
gouache on paper, 20 ¼ x 27 in. (51.5 x 68.5 cm).
Provenance: Chris Gange; Private Collection.

In 1943, the War Artists' Advisory Committee commissioned Peake to paint the glassblowers in the factory of Chance Brothers in Birmingham. The painting shows the glassblowers gathering molten glass as part of the production of cathode-ray oscillation tubes; Chance Brothers was the only company in Britain that had developed the technique of blowing this complex shape, producing 7,000 tubes every week. Peake was fascinated by the manufacturing process and the balletic skills of the work-force. This work is closely related to Peake's drawing *Glass-blowers 'Gathering' from the Furnace*, 1943 (Imperial War Museum, IWM ART LD 2851).

Invalided out of military service, Peake joined the Design, Poster and Visualising Group at the Ministry of Information in 1942, to work on a series of propaganda illustrations, *The Horrors of War.* During the war, his first two volumes of poetry were published and he started writing the first book of the *Gormenghast* trilogy, *Titus Groan*, for which he is best known today.

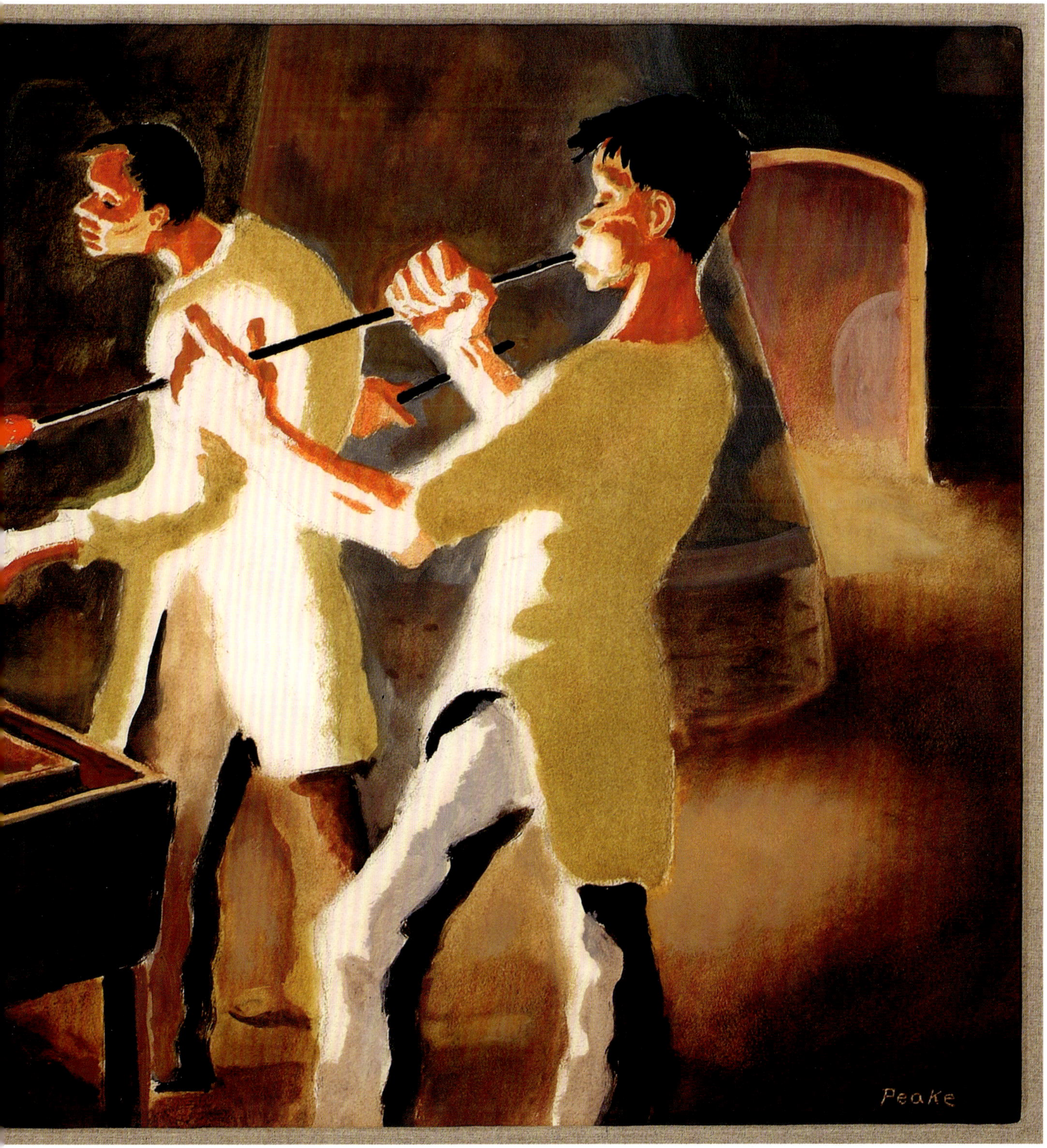
Peake

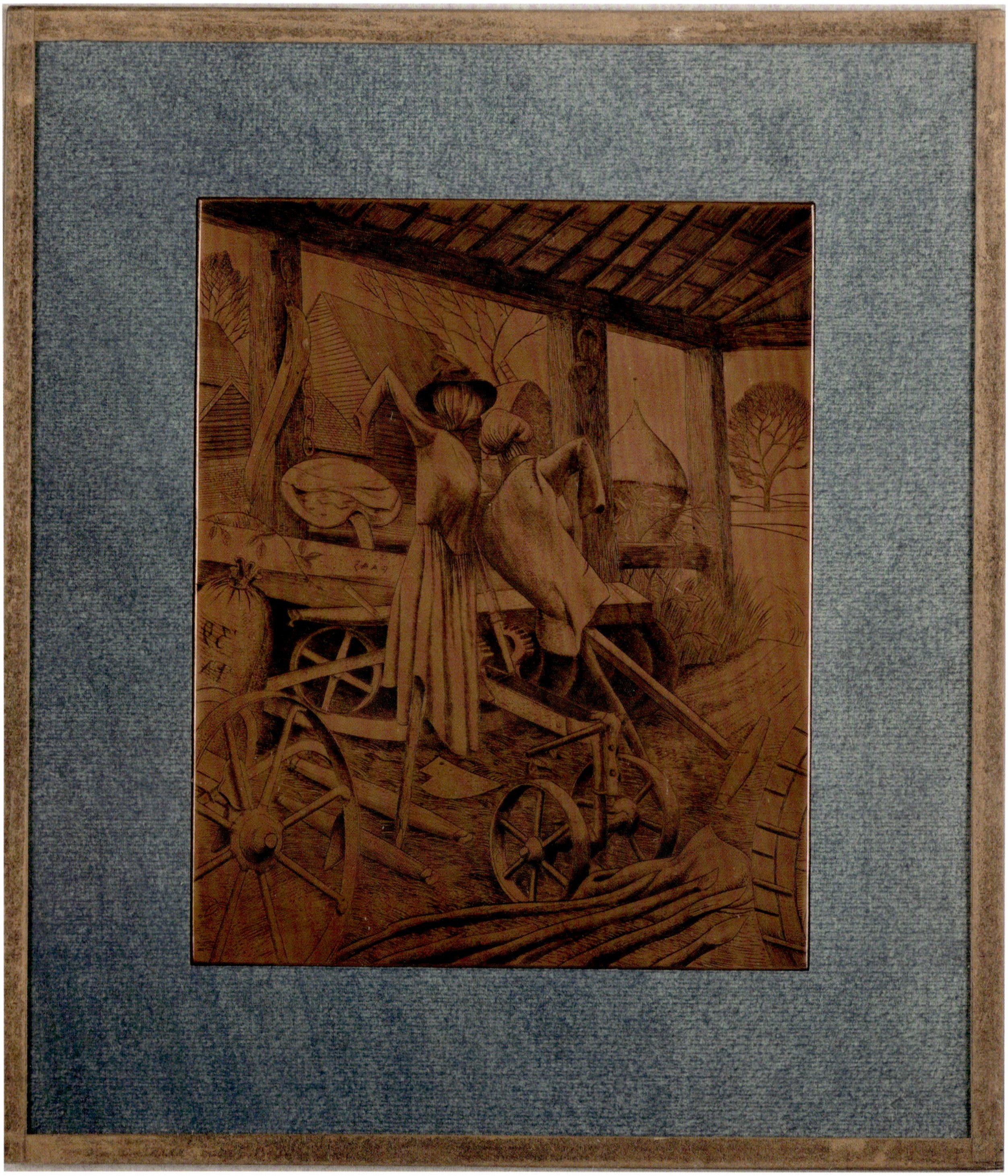

CAT. 93 – **Frederick Austin** (1902-1990), *An Allegory of War*, 1939-1945, signed and dated in the plate
original etching plate, 6 ¾ x 5 ¾ in. (17.5 x 14.5 cm).

This poignant wartime image carries the artist's initials and the dates '39 and '45 within the plate, (on the sack and wooden bar of the threshing machine). As such it clearly has allegorical overtones.

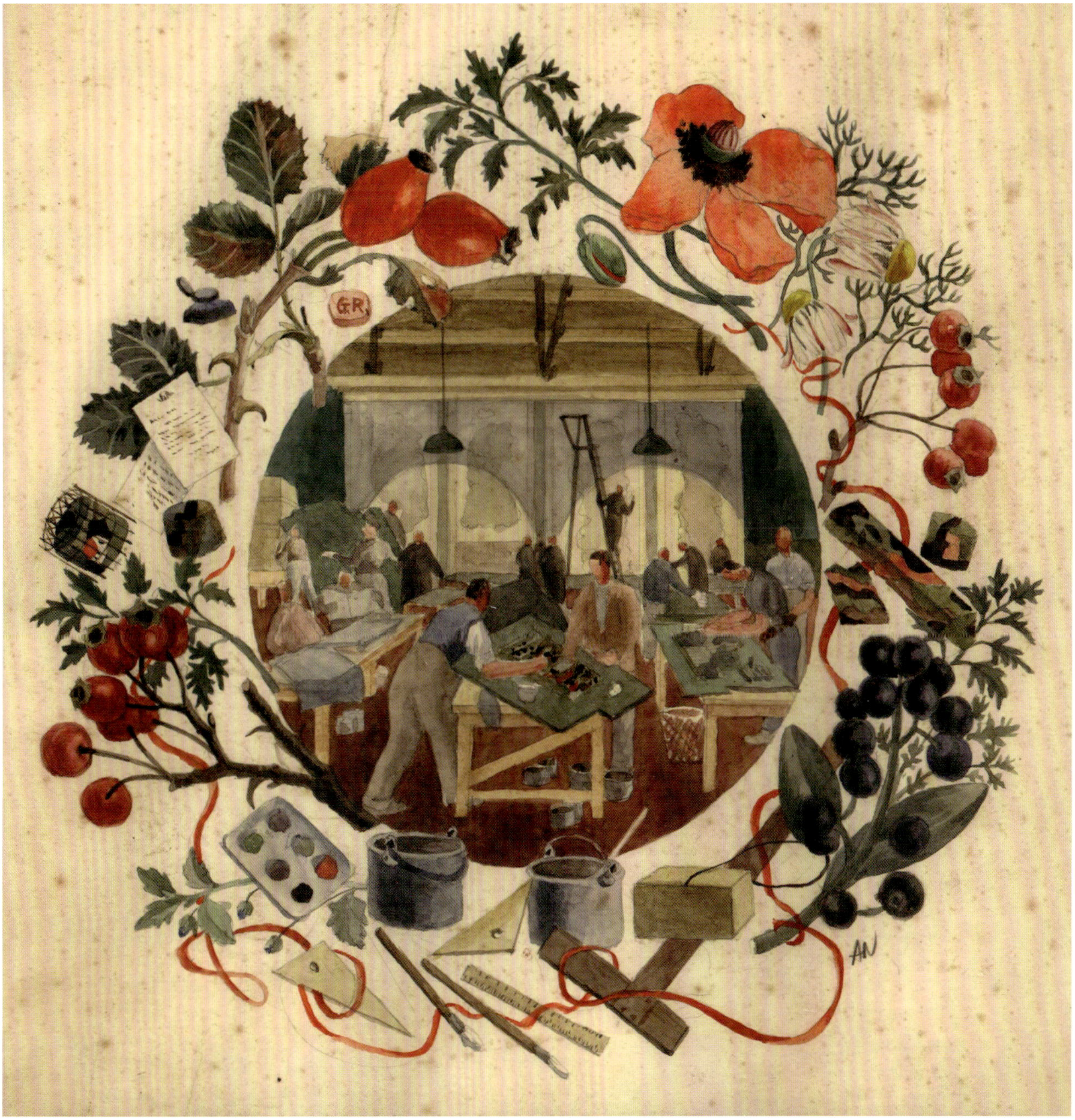

CAT. 94 – **Anne Newland** (1913-1997), *Camouflage workshop*, c.1940, signed with initials ,
watercolor on paper, 9 1/4 x 9 1/4 in. (23.5 x 23.5 cm.),
Literature: *Camouflage and Art: Design for Deception in World War II*, Henrietta Goodden, (Unicorn Press Ltd, 2007).

This is possibly the design for a Christmas or other type of Greetings card produced by the section of the War Office that made accurate to-scale briefing models. The staff was civilian, hence no uniforms, and employed artists, theatrical set designers and architects.

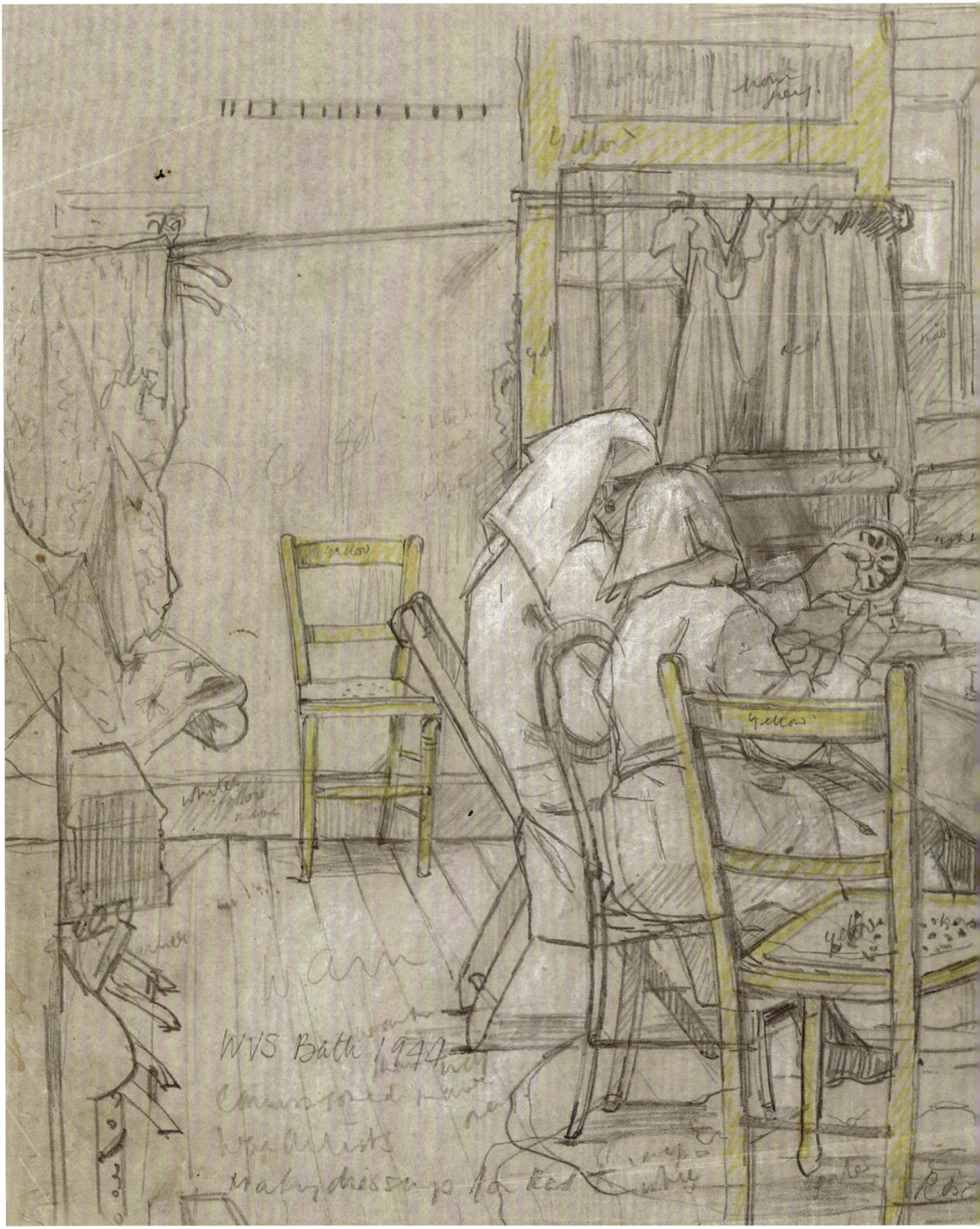
WVS Bath 1944

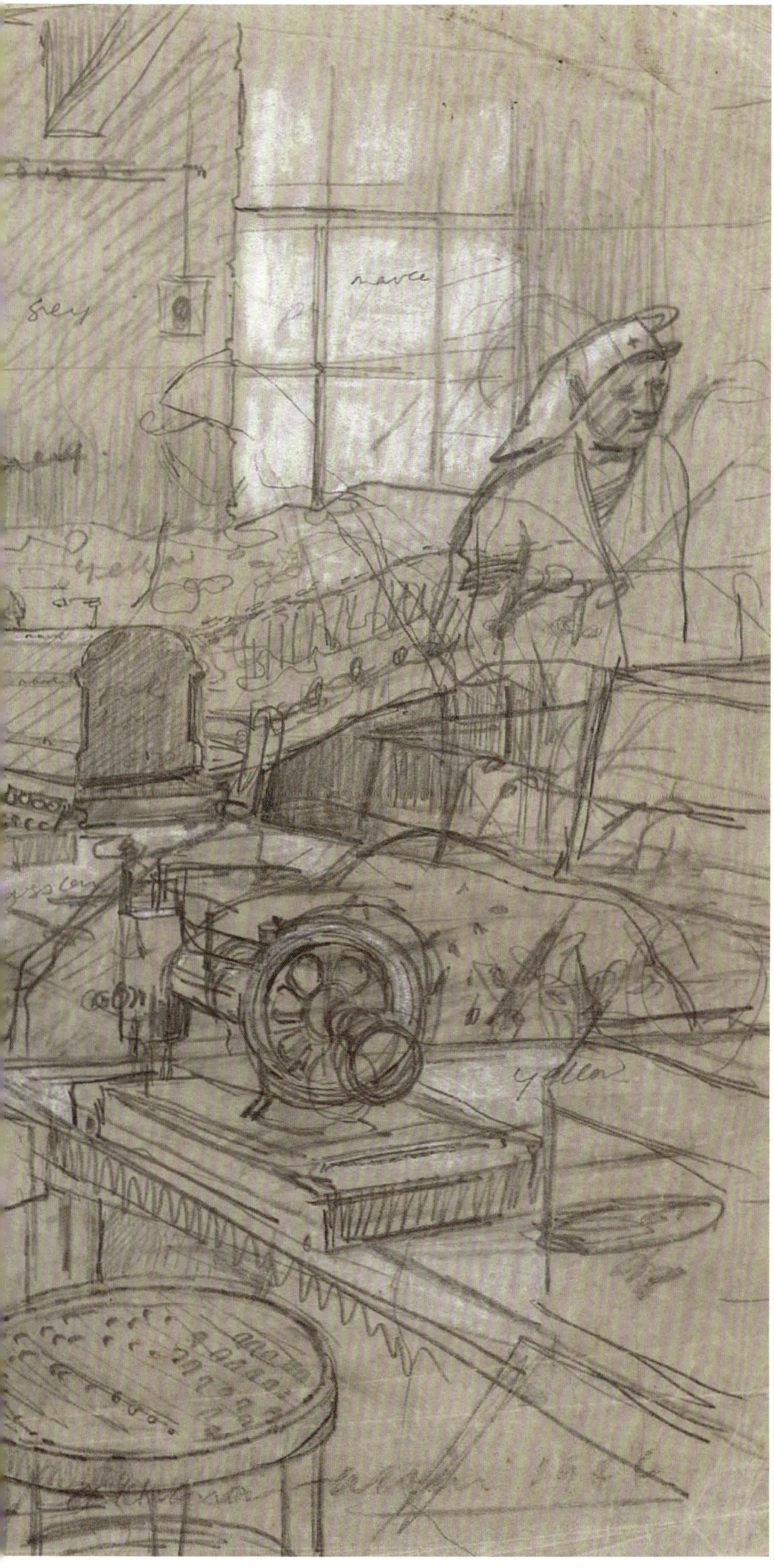

CAT. 95 – **Rosemary Allan** (1911-2009),
Making dresses for the Red Cross, c. 1944,
signed, dated and inscribed with notes,
pencil with yellow highlights in crayon, on tracing paper,
10 ¾ x 14 ¾ in. (27 x 37.3 cm).

Allan undertook short-term contract work for the WAAC. She expressed her gratitude to the committee for giving artists the opportunity to come to terms with subjects and conditions that were new and challenging.

By 1943 there were 7.25 million women engaged in war-related employment, the majority in agriculture, manufacturing and civil defence.

CAT. 96 – **Percy Horton** (1897-1970), *Portrait of J.A. Leach, of Messrs A V Roe of Manchester*, 1943, signed and dated, inscribed 'One of two drawings made for National War Records', (the other is in the Imperial War Museum), red chalk on paper, 16 ¼ x 12 ¾ in. (41x 32.5 cm). Provenance: The Artist's family

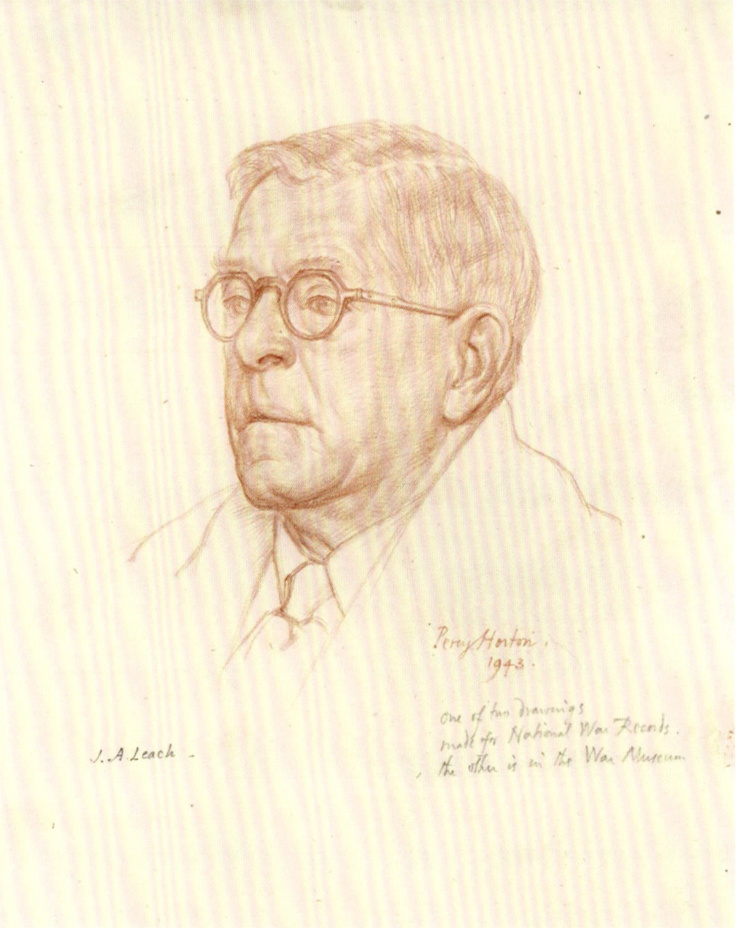

Horton was a member of the teaching staff at the RCA. In 1943 he was given a short-term contract by the War Artists' Advisory Committee to portray ordinary people, including J. A. Leach who worked at the factory of Messrs A V Roe of Manchester (better known as AVRO, makers of planes like the Lancaster bomber). From 1940 the WAAC specifically focused on 'ordinary' people, in keeping with the concept of the 'people's war', but mainly civilians who had made a unique contribution to the war effort, including those honoured for their deeds: for example a few had won the George Cross or the George Medal: ' ... in 1943 the WAAC representative from the Ministry of Production favoured the acquisition of yet more factory scenes and portraits, this time as part of a campaign to mollify production workers whose unhappiness with their working conditions was resulting in a worrisome proliferation of strikes ... Of the factory pictures commissioned by the Committee in that year, Percy Horton's *Blind Workers in a Birmingham Factory* was one in which the subject, by suggesting that even the severely handicapped could make a useful contribution to war production, seemed particularly appropriate to the Ministry of Production's purposes.'

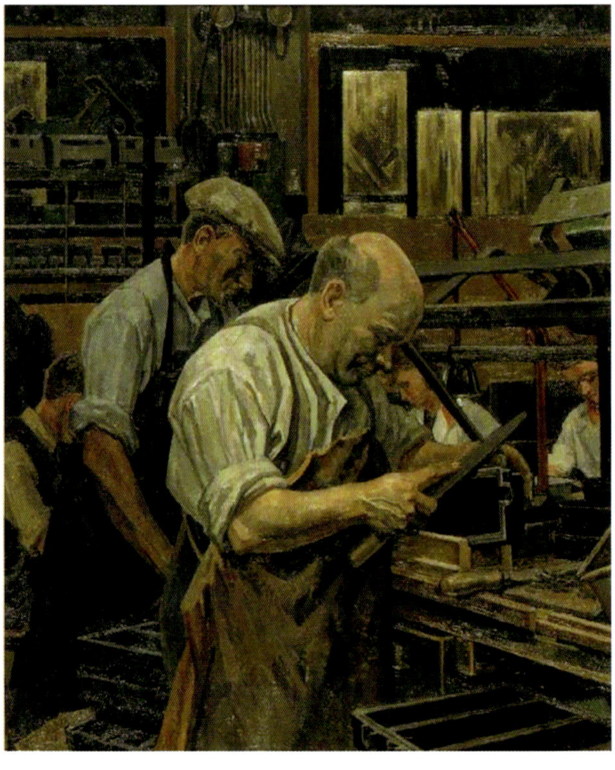

FIG. 16 – **Percy Horton** (1897–1970)
Blind Workers in a Birmingham Factory, c.1942
oil on canvas, 24 x 20 in. (60.9 x 50.8 cm).
© Imperial War Museums (Art.IWM ART LD 3920).
Transferred from the War Artists' Advisory Committee, 1947.

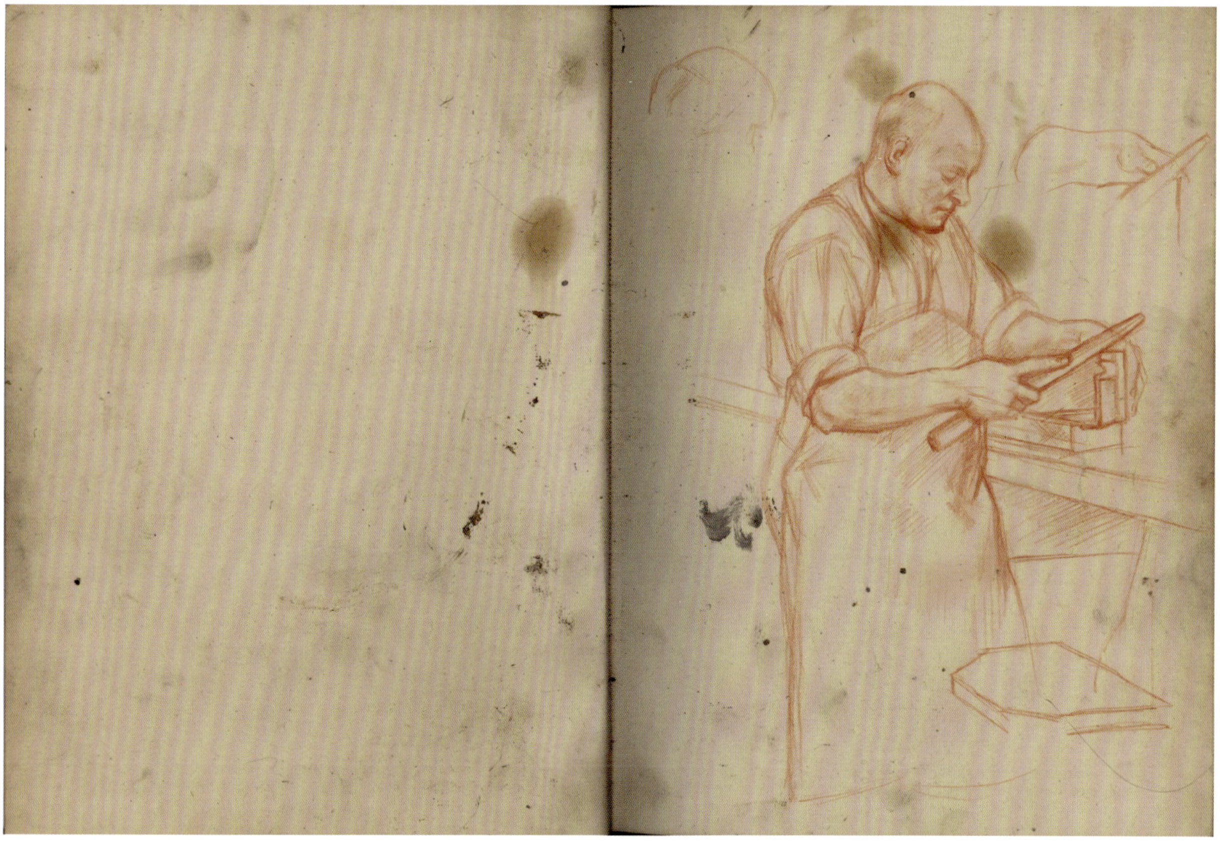

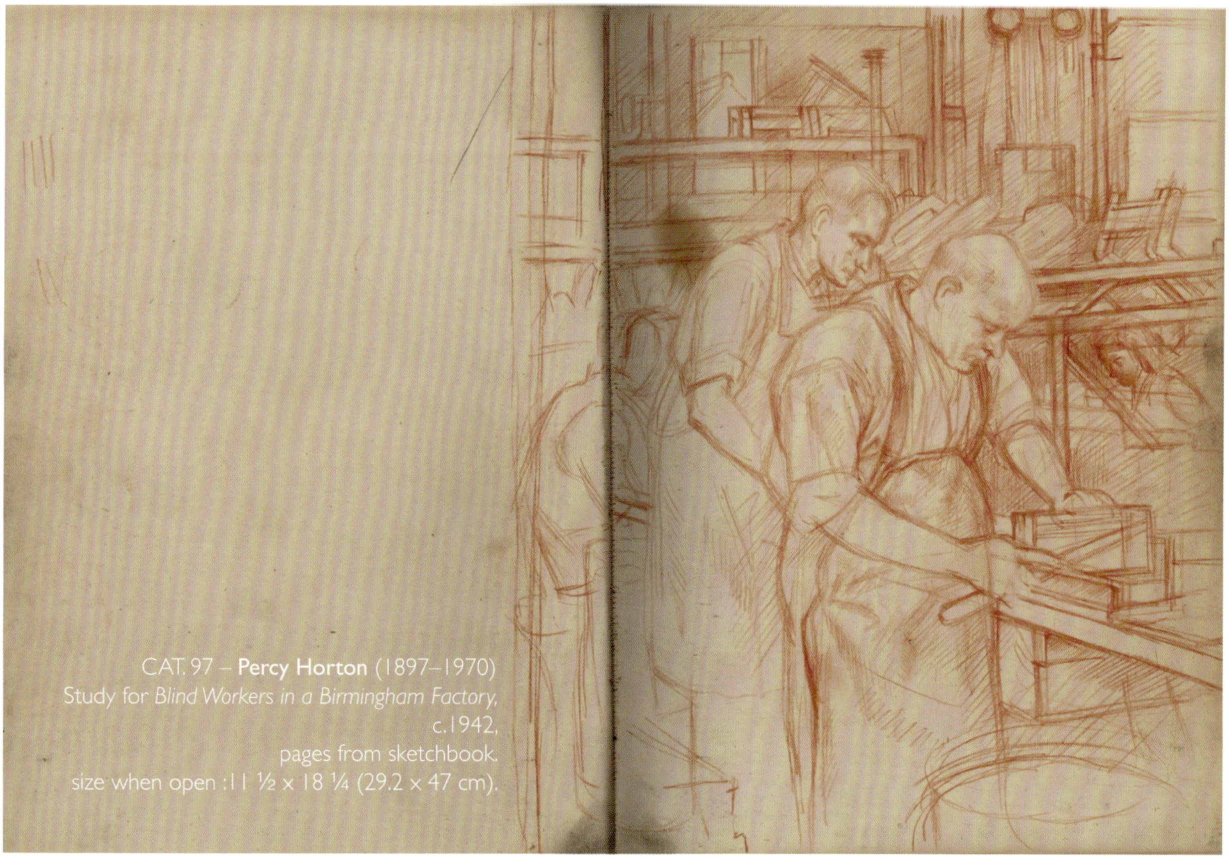

CAT. 97 – **Percy Horton** (1897–1970)
Study for *Blind Workers in a Birmingham Factory*,
c.1942,
pages from sketchbook,
size when open : 11 ½ x 18 ¼ (29.2 x 47 cm).

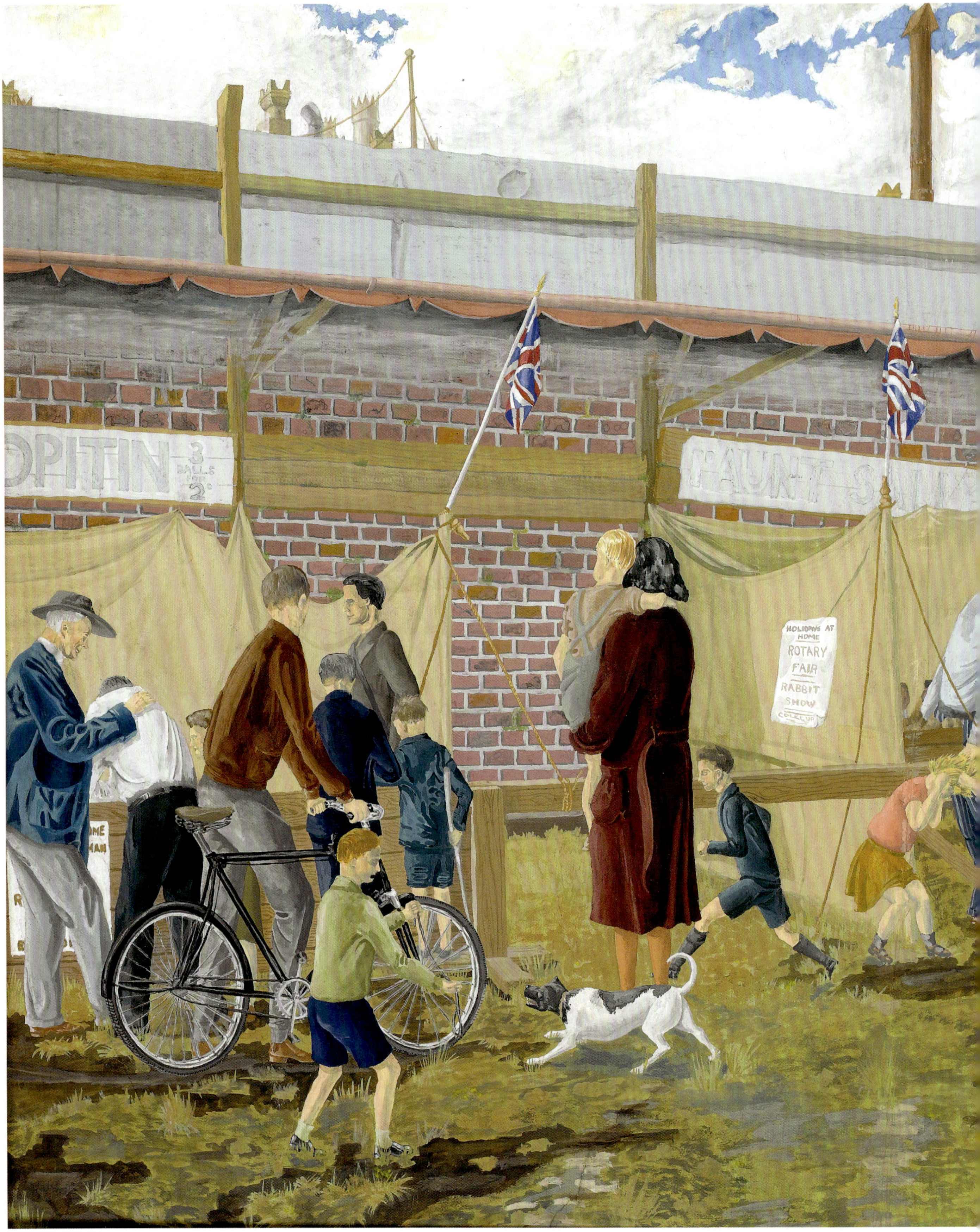
HOLIDAYS AT HOME
ROTARY
FAIR
RABBIT
SHOW

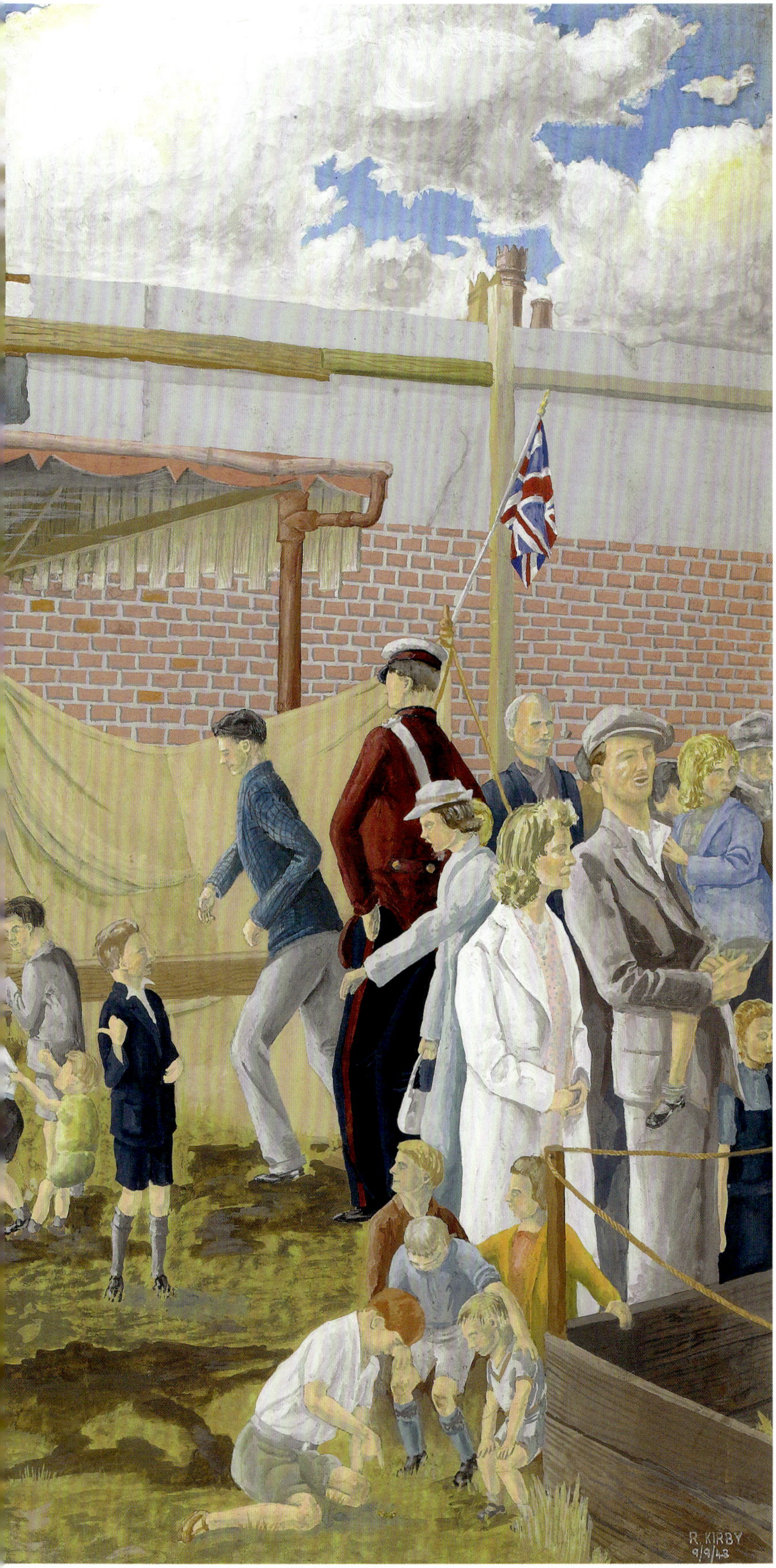

CAT. 98 –
Josh Kirby (1928-2001), *Wartime Fete*, 1943,
signed and dated,
gouache on paper, 20 ¾ x 28 ½ in. (52.7 x 72 cm).

Kirby studied art at the Liverpool City Society of Art in 1943 and in the same year was evacuated to South Wales to avoid the heavy bombing of his native city. Kirby was 15 years old when he painted this remarkable image of a local fete – a scene that almost succeeds in disguising the fact that Britain was at war. There appear, however, to be a few men of service age dressed in 'civvies': some of the youths manning the stalls may have been travelling fairground people, or possibly slightly too young for conscription, while male punters could, for example, be miners or other workers in other reserved occupations. The figure in a blue and scarlet uniform is probably a civilian brass bandsman wearing a quasi-military uniform.

With few exceptions, dress is semi-smart or casual and relatively plain, as was common during wartime when rationing dictated the amount of new clothing that civilians could purchase. Dyes for fabric were restricted to a range of basic colours, which could partly account for the slightly limited colour palette. Lively, down-to-earth and reassuringly ordinary, despite the extraordinary circumstances of the time, this closely-observed scene must have offered a reprieve from the reality of war in 1943, while to the modern viewer it conveys a sense of nostalgia.

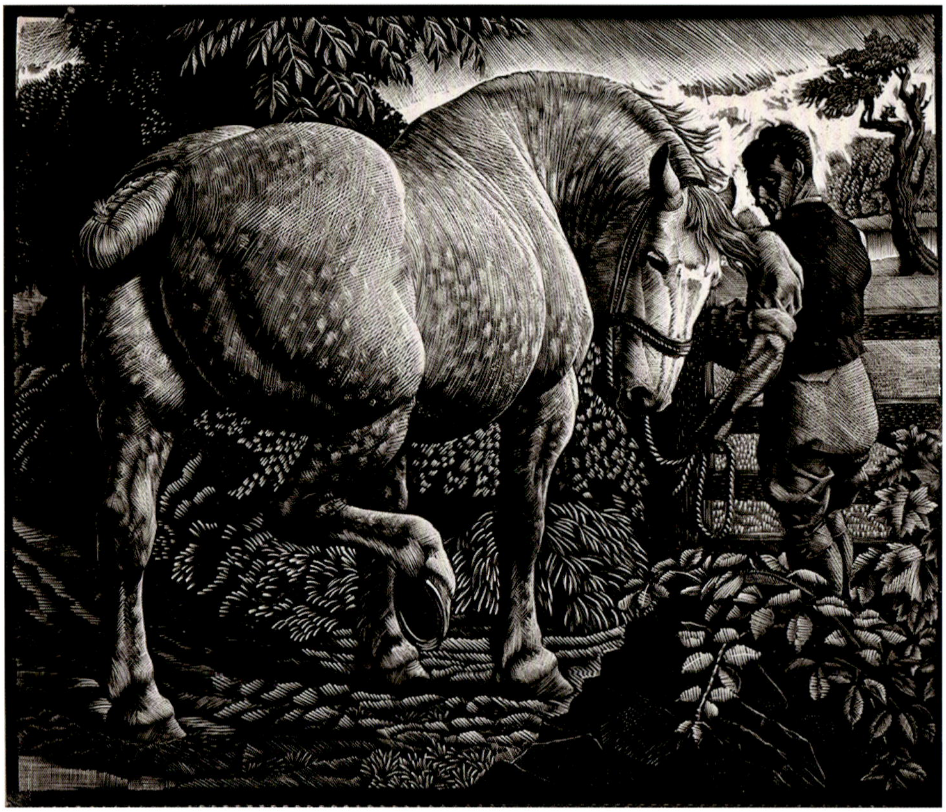

CAT. 99 – **Charles Tunnicliffe** (1901-1979), *The Percheron*, 1940, orignal woodblock, 5 ½ x 7 ½ in. (14 x 19 cm).

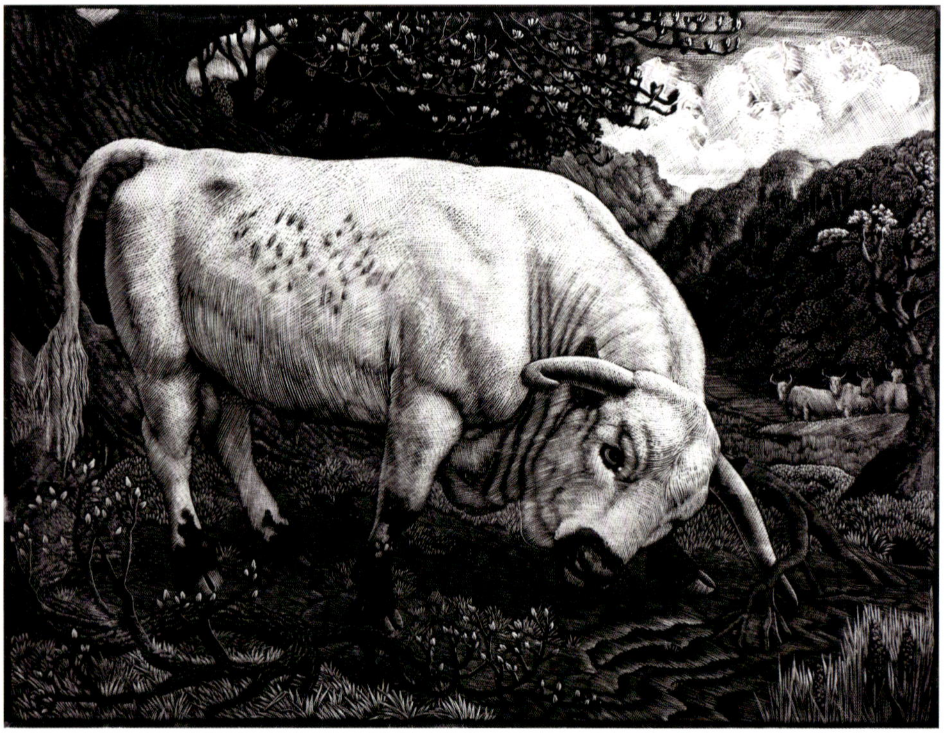

CAT. 100 – **Charles Tunnicliffe** (1901-1979), *The Chartley Bull*, 1939, orignal woodblock, 8 x 10 ¾ in. (20.4 x 27.5 cm).

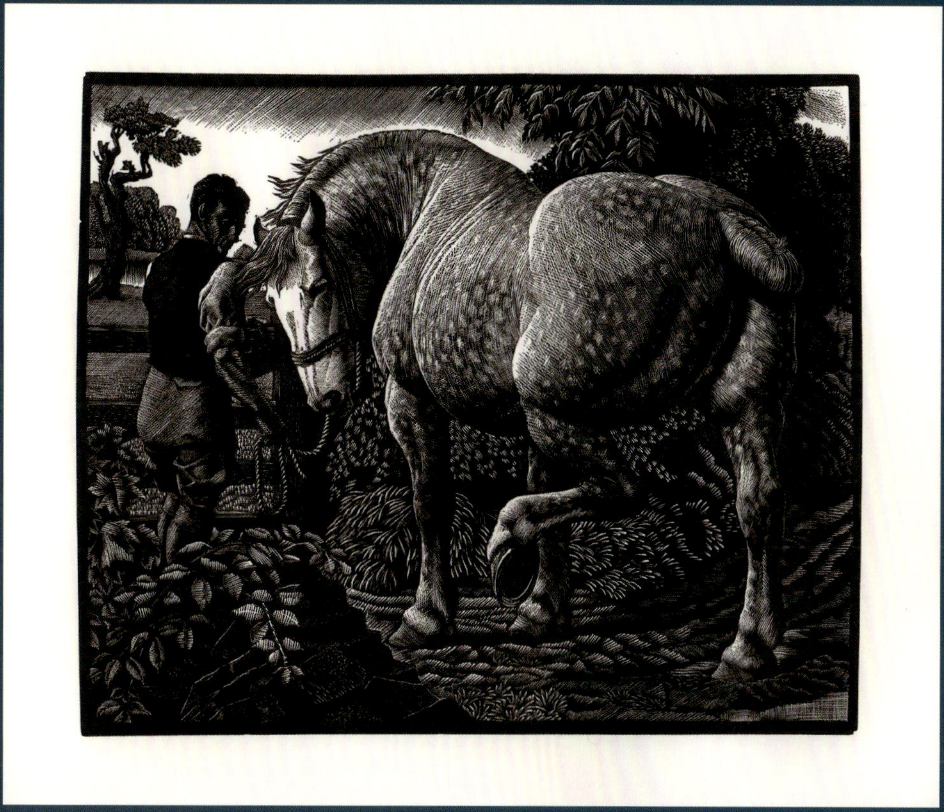

CAT. 101 – **Charles Tunnicliffe** (1901-1979), *The Percheron*, 1940,
wood-engraving, paper size: 7 ½ x 9 in. (19.1 cm x 23 cm).

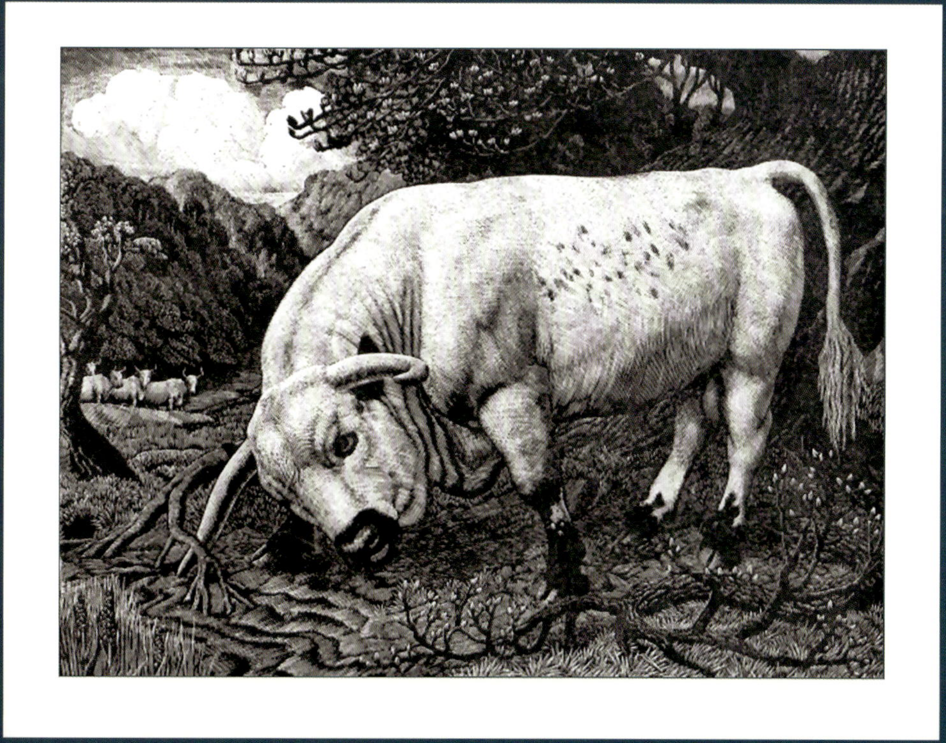

CAT. 102 – **Charles Tunnicliffe** (1901-1979), *The Chartley Bull*, 1939,
wood-engraving, paper size: 10 x 13 in. (25.4 x 32.5 cm).

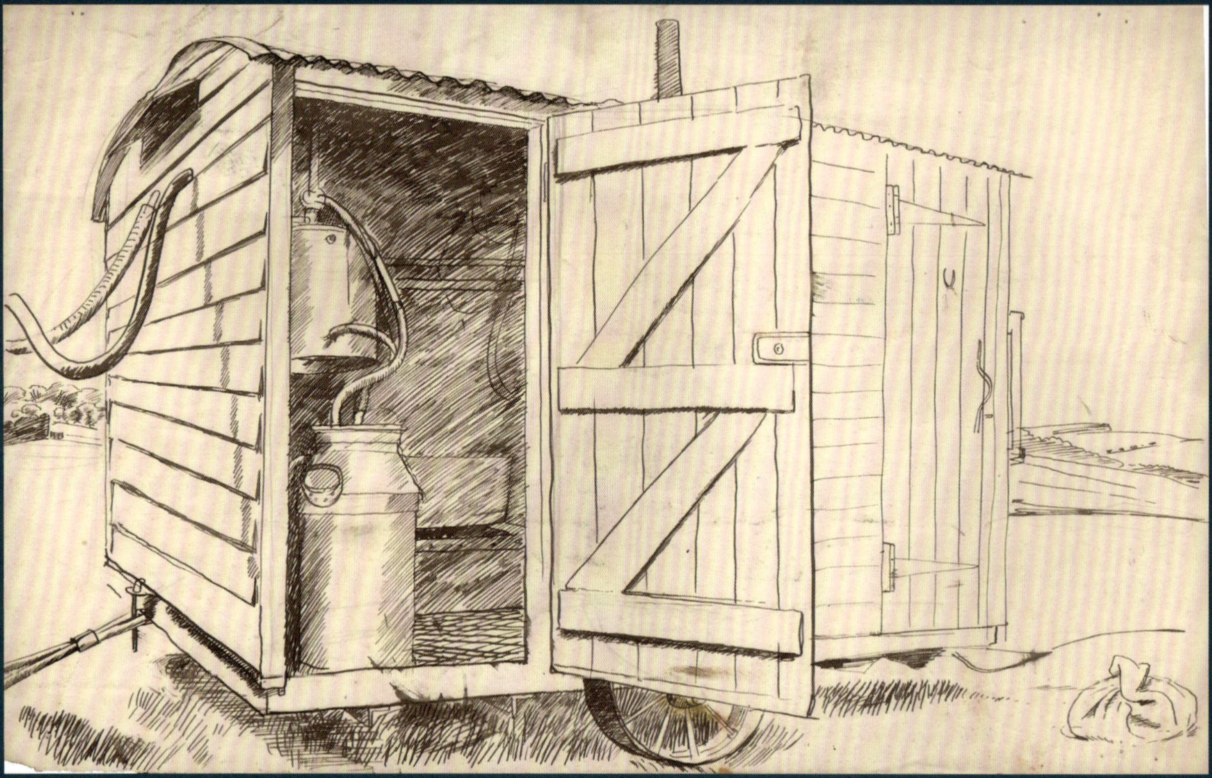

CAT. 103

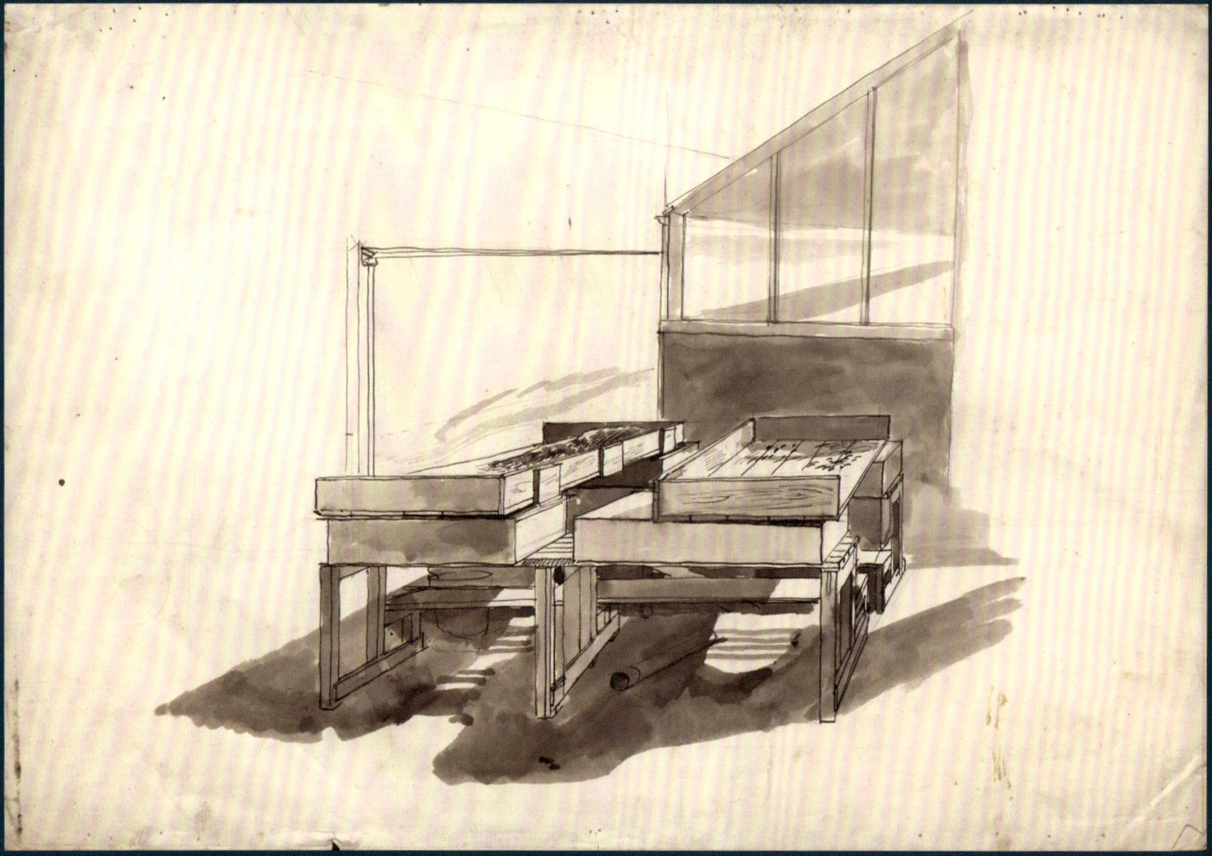

CAT. 104

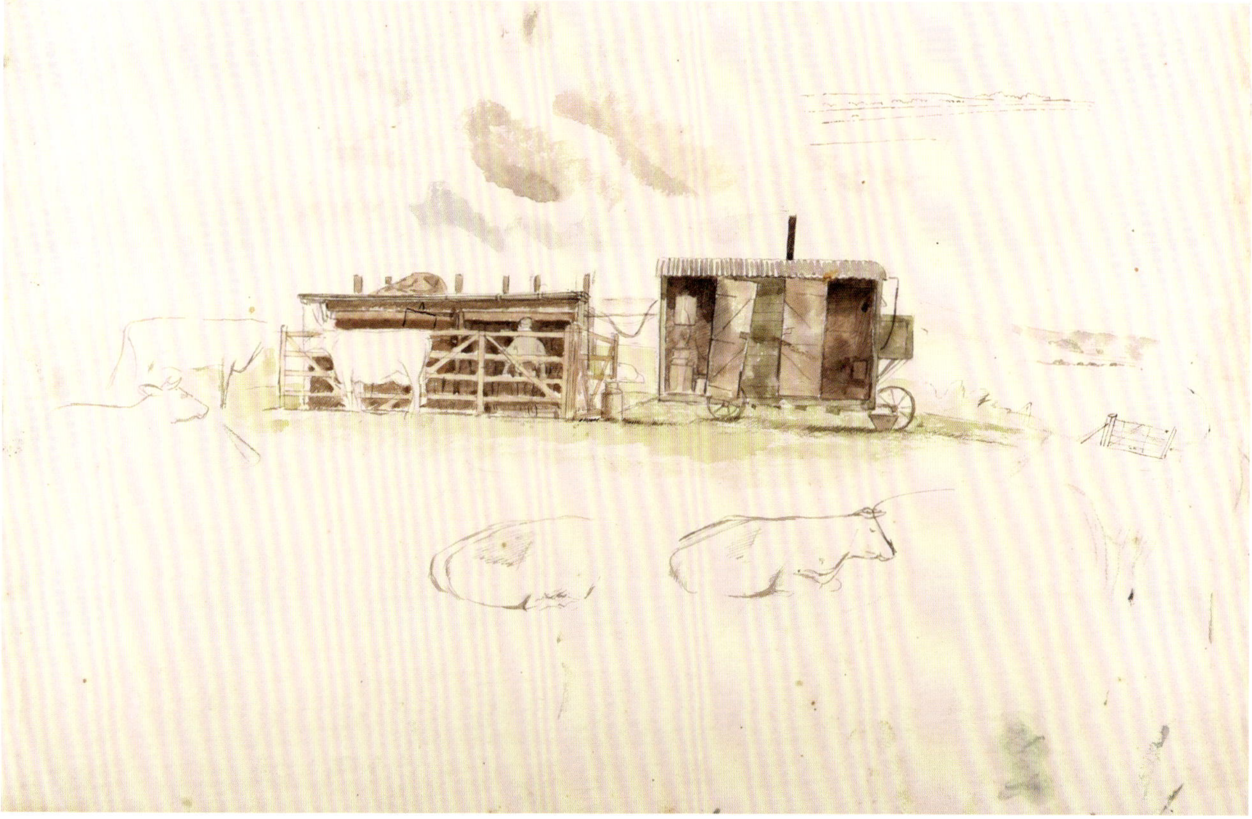

CAT. 105

Evelyn Dunbar (1906-1960)

CAT. 103 – Study at Sparsholt Farm Institute for *A Land Girl and the Bail Bull*, 1944,
pen & ink on paper, 13 x 21 in. (33 x 53 cm).
CAT. 104* – Seed potato trays at Sparsholt Farm Institute, training centre for Women's Land Army recruits, 1940,
pencil, pen & ink and wash on paper, 15 x 22 in. (38 x 56 cm).
CAT. 105 – Study for background of *A Land Girl and the Bail Bull*, 1944,
pencil and watercolour on paper, 13 x 21 in. (33 x 53 cm).

Provenance: Roger Folley; Alasdair Dunbar; Hammer Mill Oast Collection.
Exhibited: *Evelyn Dunbar – The Lost Works*, Pallant House Gallery, October 2015 - February 2016, cat 92.
Literature: *Evelyn Dunbar – The Lost Works*, Sacha Llewellyn & Paul Liss, July 2015, cat. 92, page 138-139.

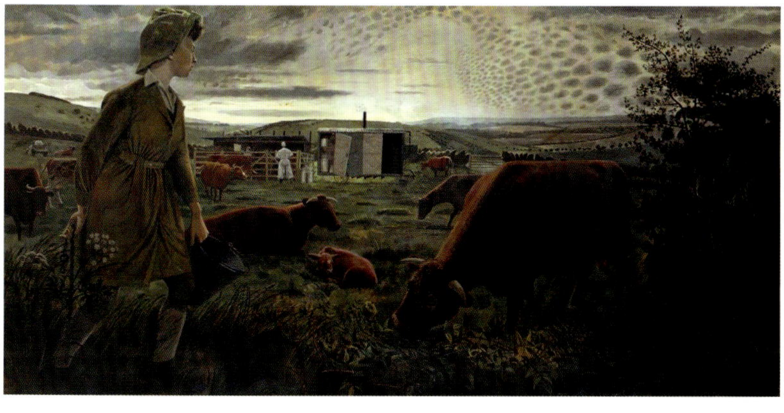

FIG. 17 – *A Land Girl and the Bail Bull*, 1945,
oil on canvas, 36 x 72 in. (91.4 x 182.9 cm)
© Tate, London 2015

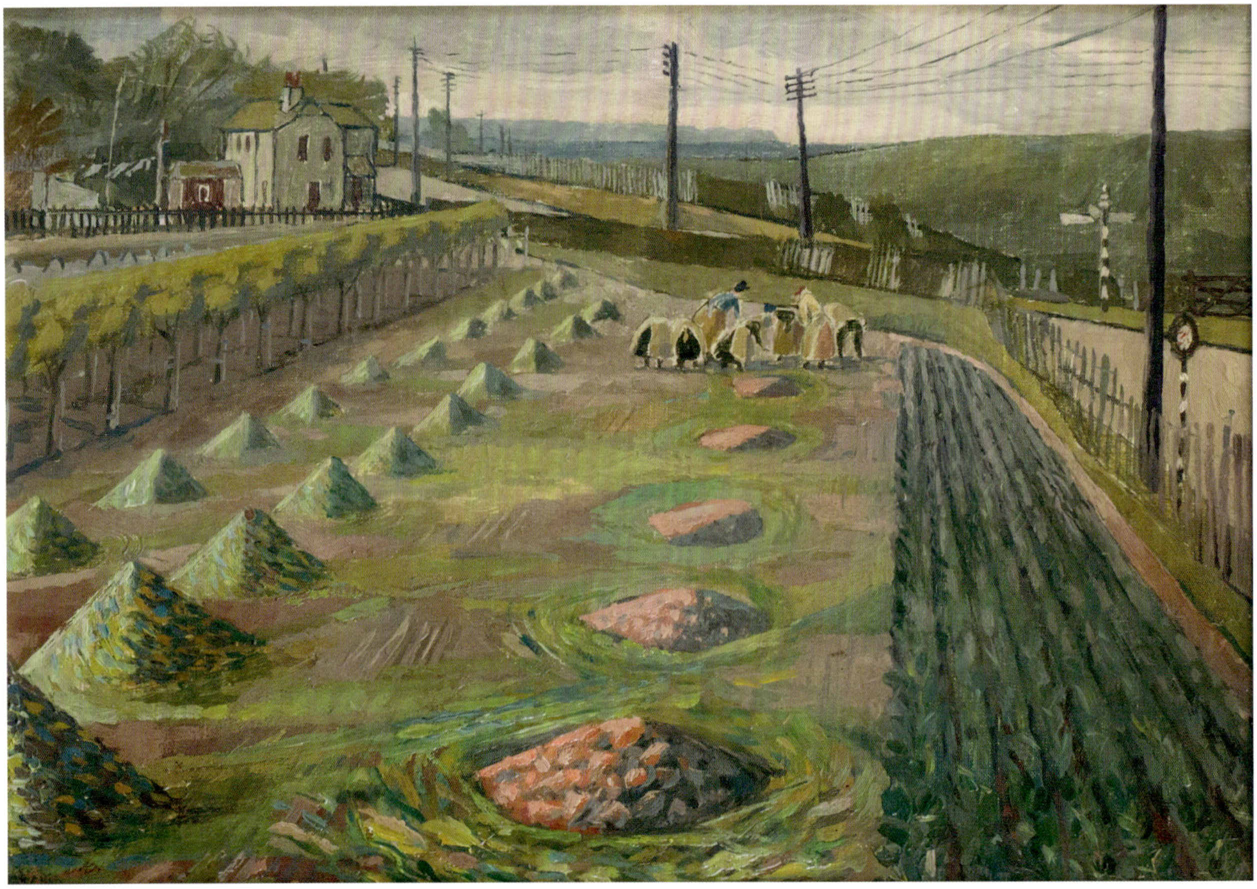

CAT. 106 – **Evelyn Dunbar** (1906-1960), *Land Workers at Strood*, titled on frame. Also known as *Field Workers at Strood*, oil on canvas, 8 ½ x 12 ½ in. (21.6 x 31.7 cm),
Provenance: Roger Folley; Alasdair Dunbar; Hammer Mill Oast Collection.
Exhibited: Wildenstein's, 1938; Royal Academy of Arts, 1943.
Literature: *Evelyn Dunbar – The Lost Works*, Sacha Llewellyn & Paul Liss, July 2015, cat. 92, pages 138-139.

Predating WW2 by some 18 months, this picture is curiously prophetic of some of the artist's wartime painting. 1938,

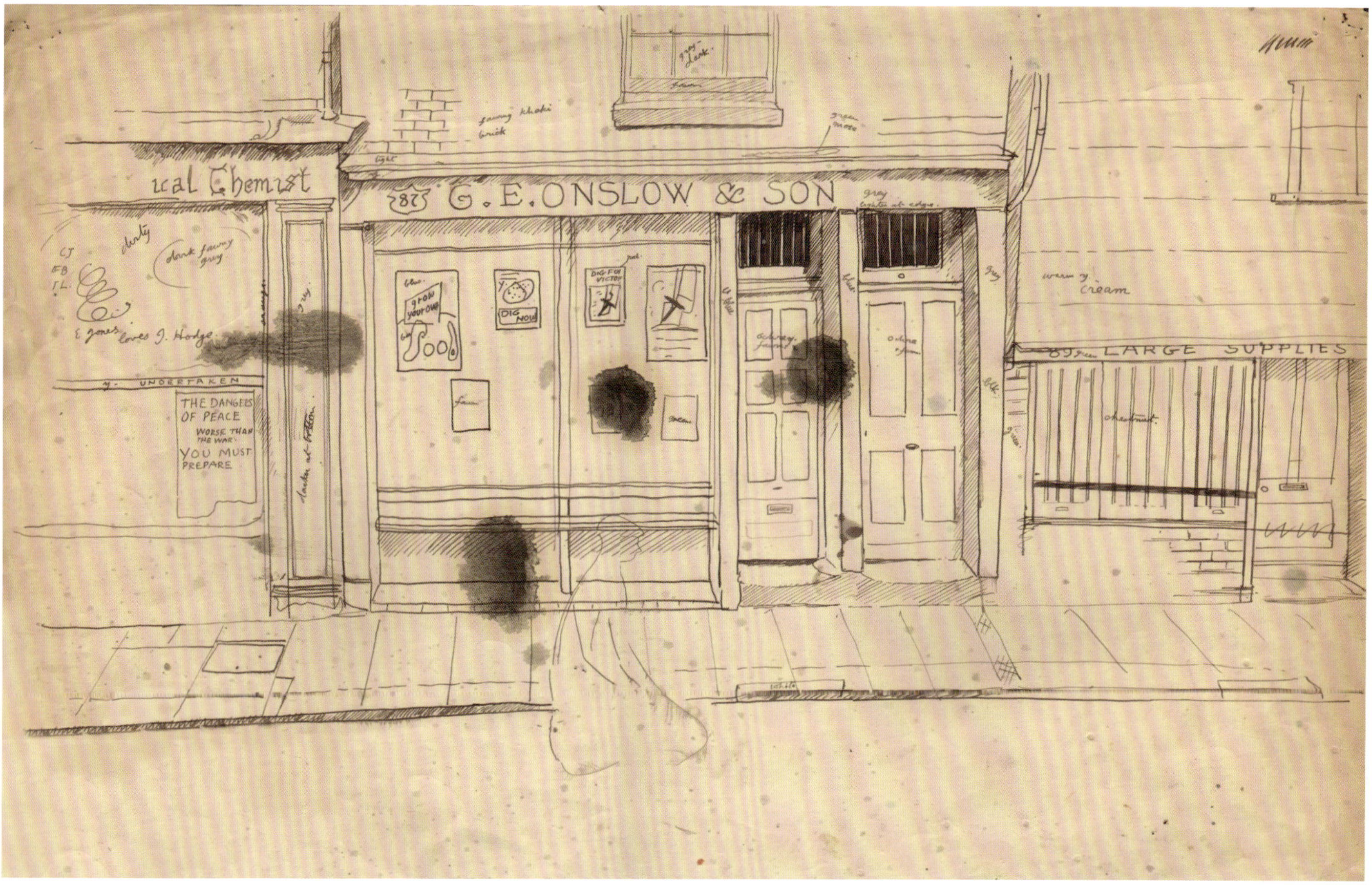

CAT. 107 – **Evelyn Dunbar** (1906-1960), Study for the background to *The Queue at the Fish Shop*, 1942, inscribed with colour notes, pen & ink on paper, 13 x 21 in. (33 x 53 cm).
Provenance: Roger Folley; Alasdair Dunbar; Hammer Mill Oast Collection.

Dunbar's composition shows Hill's fish shop in Strood High Street reduced in height and elongated to accommodate the queue eventually painted in from it.

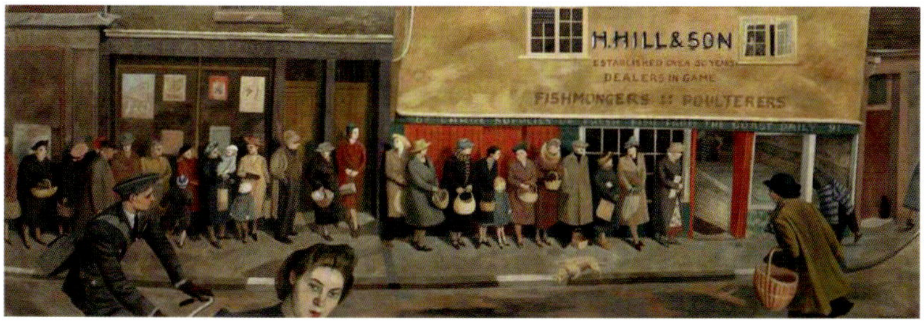

FIG. 18 – *The Queue at the Fish Shop*, 1942,
oil on canvas, 24 ½ x 71 ½ in. (62 x 182 cm).
Collection: © Imperial War Museums (Art.IWM ART LD 3987).

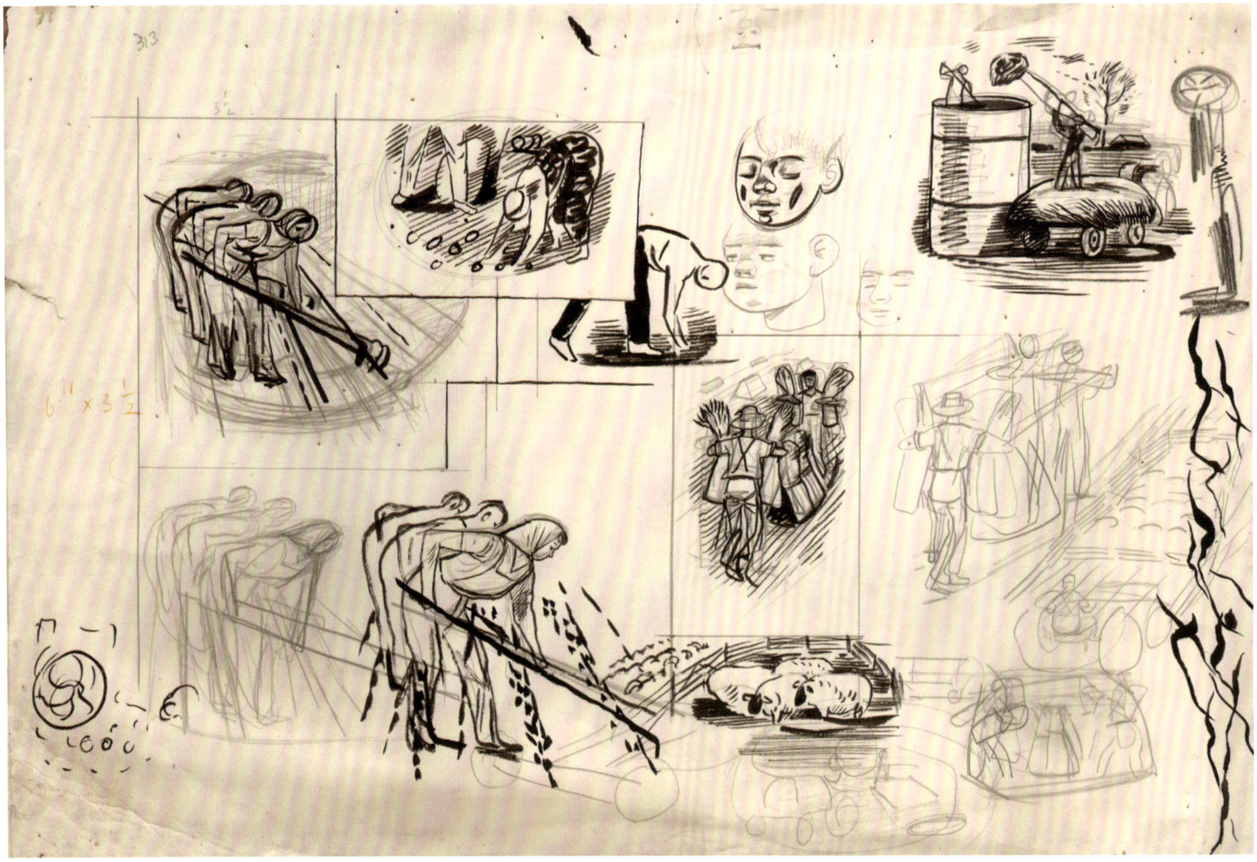

CAT. 108 – **Evelyn Dunbar** (1906-1960), Studies for various Women's Land Army activities, including *Singling Turnips*, 1943, pencil and pen & ink on paper, 15 x 22 in. (38 x 55.5 cm).
Provenance: Roger Folley; Alasdair Dunbar; Hammer Mill Oast Collection.
Exhibited: *Evelyn Dunbar – The Lost Works,* Pallant House Gallery, October 2015 - February 2016, cat 88.
Literature: *Evelyn Dunbar – The Lost Works*, Sacha Llewellyn & Paul Liss, July 2015, cat. 88, page 136.

CAT. 109* – **Evelyn Dunbar** (1906-1960),
Singling Turnips, 1943,
oil on canvas, 20 x 30 in. (50.8 x 76.2 cm).
Private collection courtesy
England & Co Gallery, London.

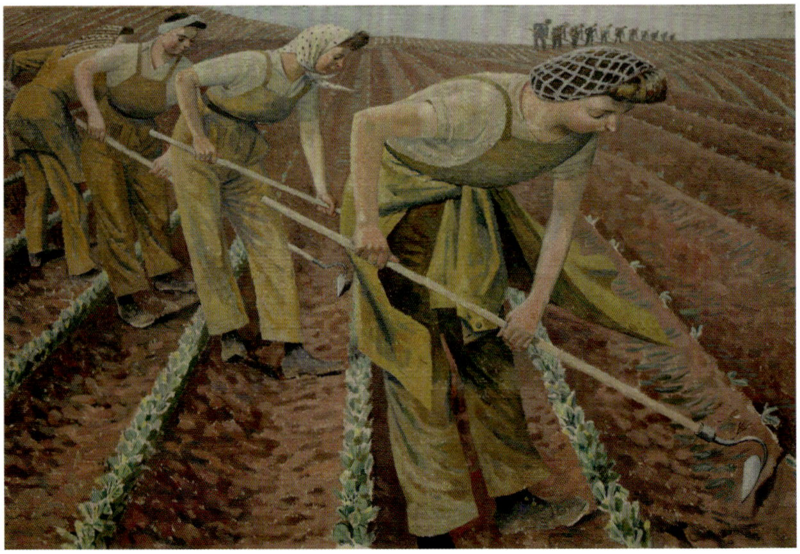

For Dunbar WW2 offered new opportunities to explore the relationship between people and the natural world. Her principal subject, the Women's Land Army, gave rise to compositions such as 'Men Stooking and Girls Learning to Stook' (1940) and 'Milking Practice With Artificial Udders' (1940), closely related to her illustrations for *A Book of Farmcraft.* As well as demonstrating Dunbar's experimentation with new painting techniques, these pictures served a didactic purpose in showing the correct ways of undertaking manual tasks.

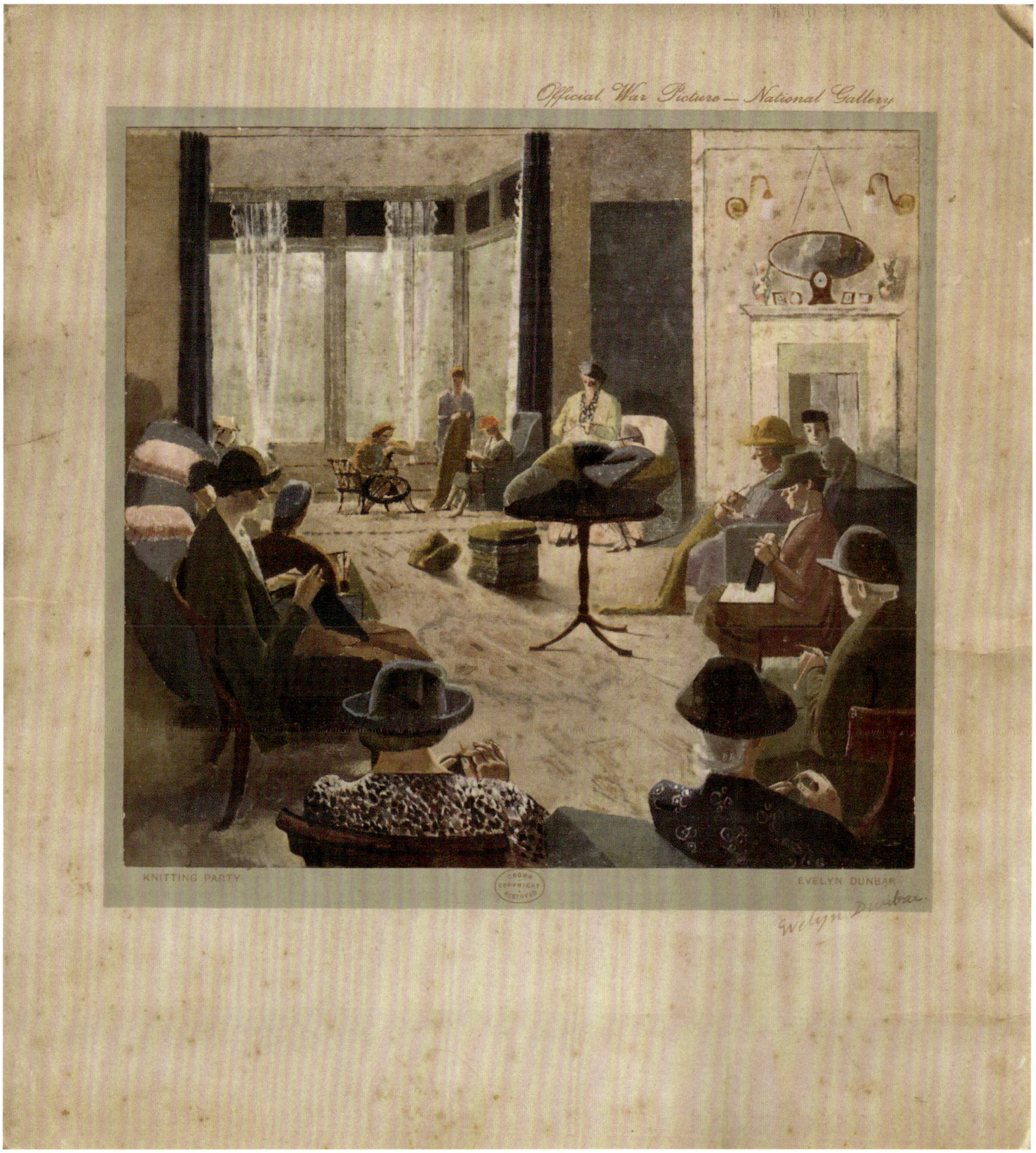

CAT. 110 – **Evelyn Dunbar** (1906-1960), Greeting card, with space for a small calendar, c.1943,
printed on corrugated cardboard, 12 x 11 in. (30.5 x 28 cm).
Provenance: Roger Folley; Alasdair Dunbar; Hammer Mill Oast Collection.
Exhibited: *Evelyn Dunbar – The Lost Works*, Pallant House Gallery, October 2015 - February 2016, cat 126.
Literature: *Evelyn Dunbar – The Lost Works*, Sacha Llewellyn & Paul Liss, July 2015, cat. 126, page 177.

During WW2 private companies were encouraged by the WAAC to reproduce images as postcards, bookmarks, and calendars as a means of raising funds. Such initiatives were unsuccessful partly because with rationing it was impossible to create high-quality prints in colour. Dunbar's *A Knitting Party*, (1940) reproduced here as a greeting card with space for a calendar below, shows sixteen women from the WVS (among them Florence Dunbar, the artist's mother, surreptitiously looking at her watch in the window) knitting balaclavas, socks, etc. for the troops.

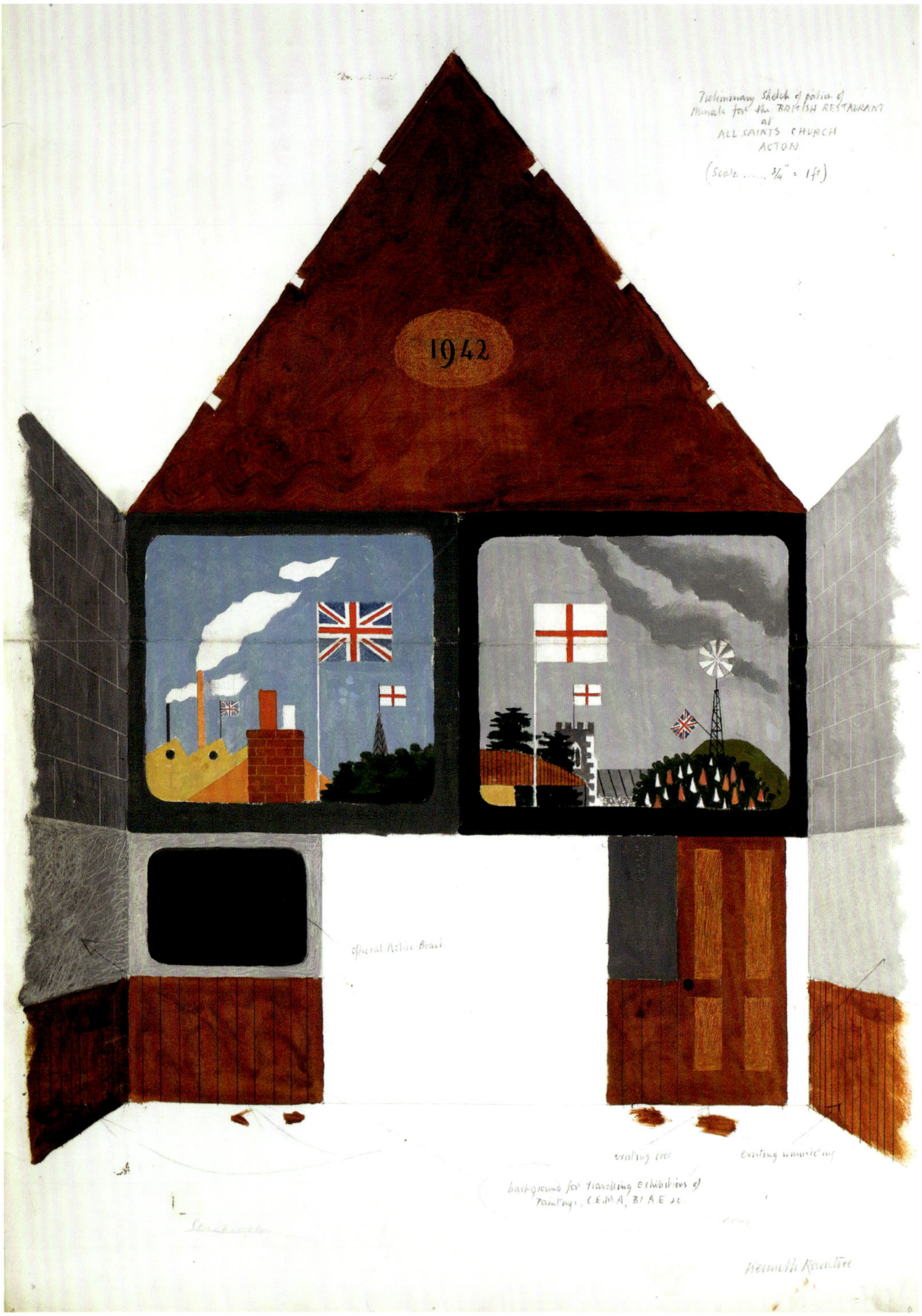

CAT. 111* – **Kenneth Rowntree** (1915-1997), *The British Restaurant at Acton, Middlesex*, 1942, signed and inscribed "Preliminary sketch of portion of murals for the British Restaurant at All Saints Church, Acton. (Scale…3/4" = 1ft)",
watercolour, gouache and pencil on paper, 31 x 22 ¼ in. (78.9 x 56.6 cm).
Provenance: The artist's family; Neil Jennings Fine Art.
Literature: *Art for Everybody – Britain Advances* (British Council publication, 1943, photograph of mural on front cover); John Milner, *Kenneth Rowntree*, Lund Humphries, 2002, pp.28-30; *Kenneth Rowntree, A Centenary Exhibition*, Moore-Gwyn Fine Art and Liss Llewellyn Fine Art, 2015, Cat. 44, p.85.

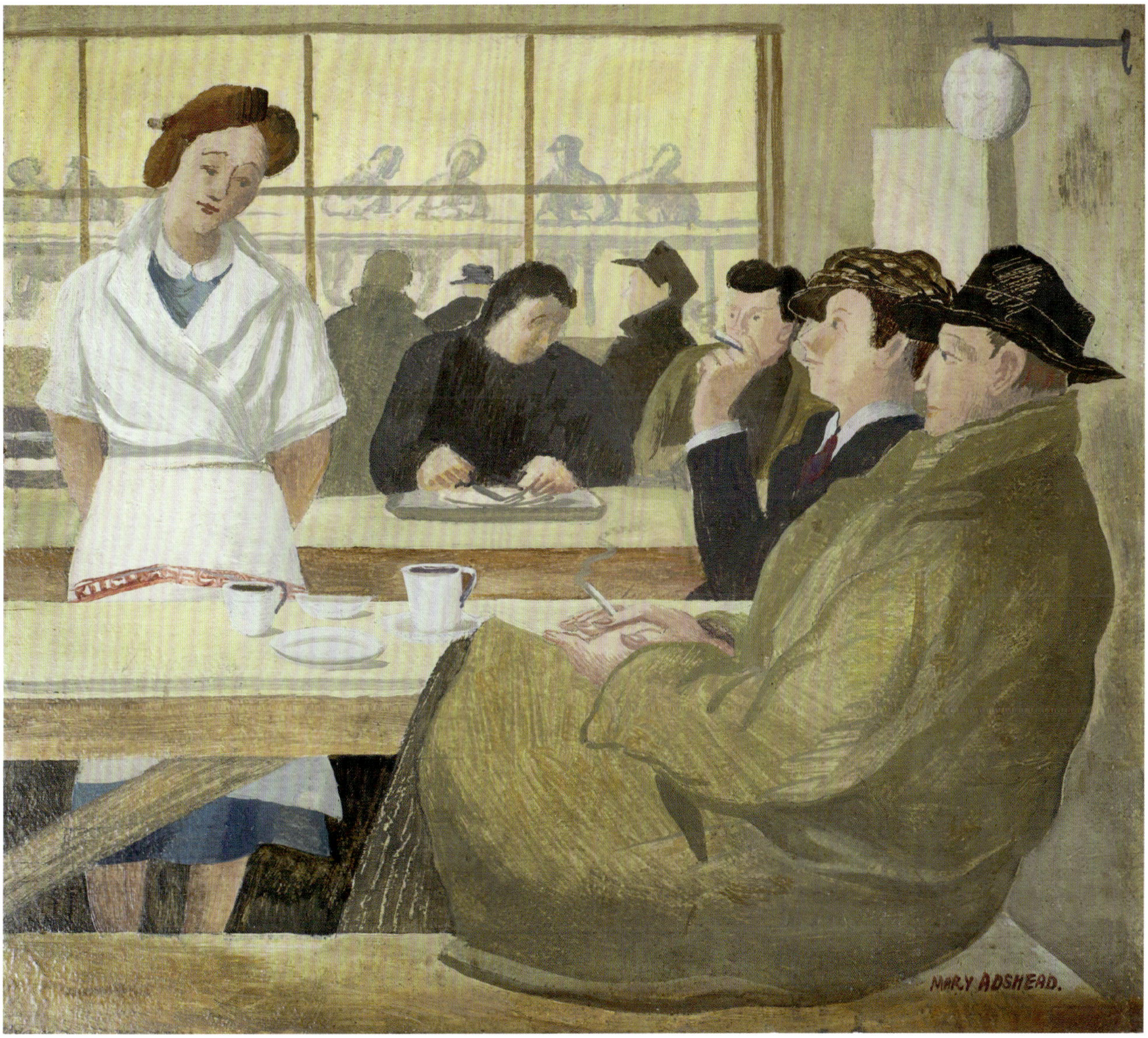

CAT. 112 – **Mary Adshead** (1904-1995), *British Restaurant Coventry After Dinner*, 1941, signed, inscribed with title to reverse, oil on panel, 12 x 13 ¾ in. (30.5 x 35 cm).
Provenance: The Artist's Family; Private Collection.
Exhibited: The New English Art Club, 1941, (no 84?).

British Restaurants were started during the war and served cheap, subsidised meals to feed people who had been bombed out of their homes. Staff wore white overalls and served from behind long, trestle tables. A convoy of mobile canteens would move into bombed areas to feed residents and rescue workers for free, co-ordinated by the Ministry of Food.

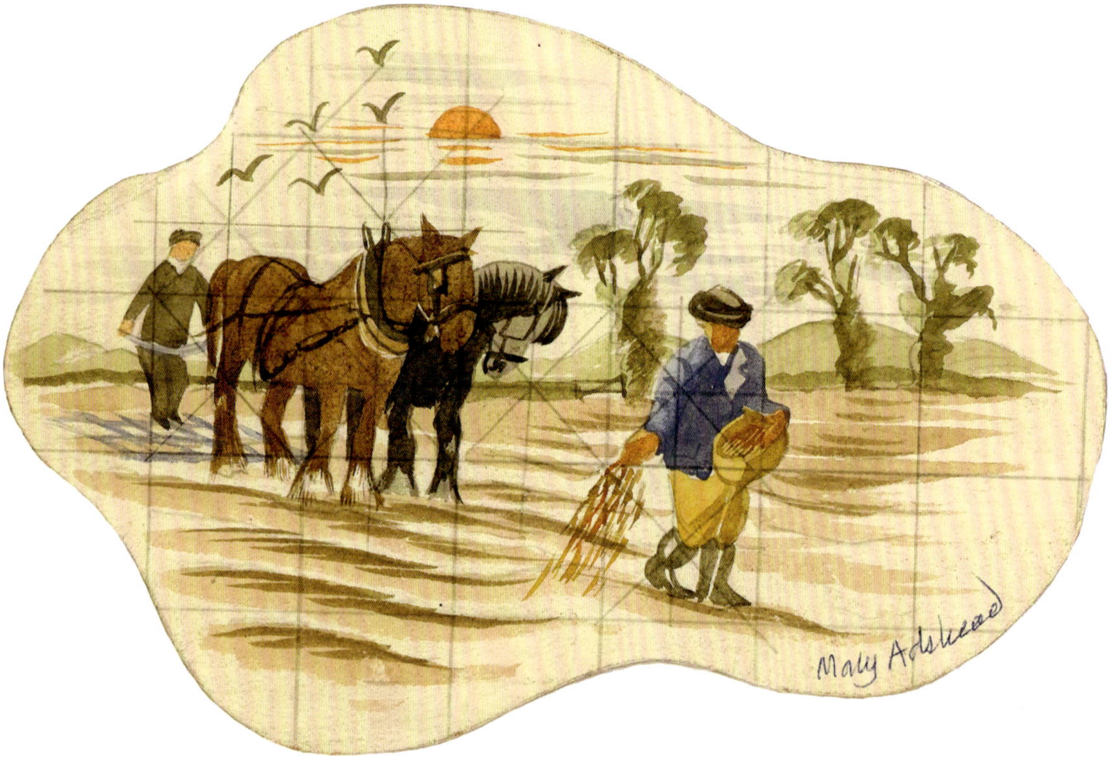

CAT. 113 – **Mary Adshead** (1904-1995), *Farmers ploughing*, Study for *The World's Food* mural, c. 1942, signed, squared in pencil,
watercolour over pencil on paper, 4 ½ x 7 ½ in. (12.2 x 19 cm).
Provenance: The Artist's Estate.

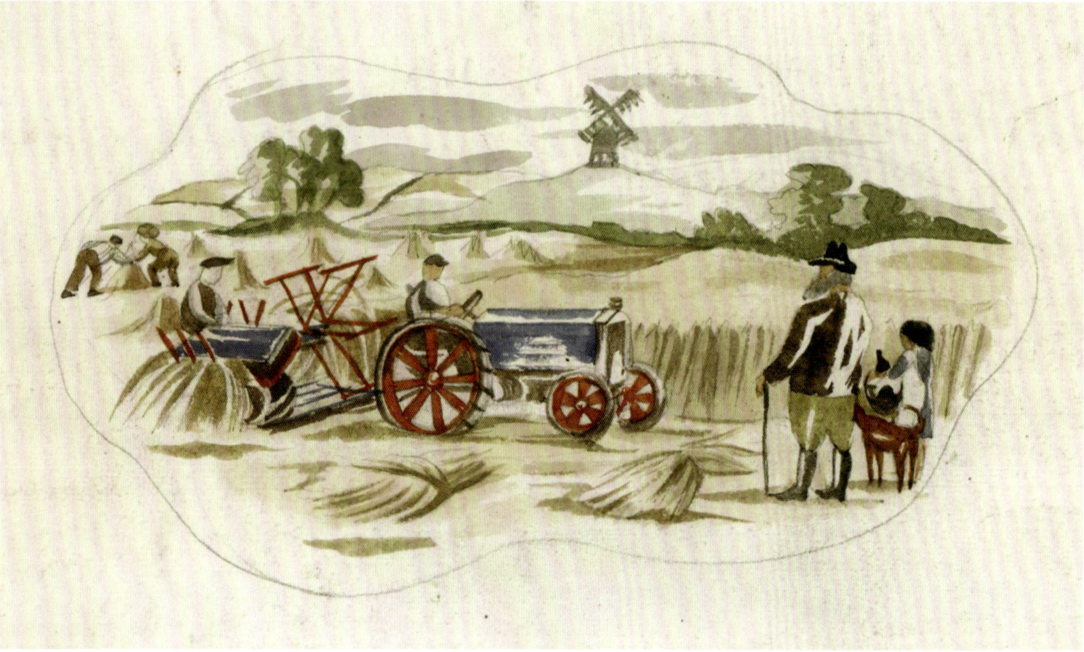

CAT. 114 – *English Harvest*, signed, titled and inscribed 'English Harvest British Restaurant, B.R. Granville St, Birmingham', pencil and watercolour on paper, 10 ½ x 11 in. (26.5 x 28 cm).
Literature: *Modern spaces: Mary Adshead's post-war murals and the promotion of mural painting by the SMP 1939-1965*, by Melanie Unwin. This study and the work above relate to *The World's Food* mural, British Restaurant, Granville Street, Birmingham, 1942.

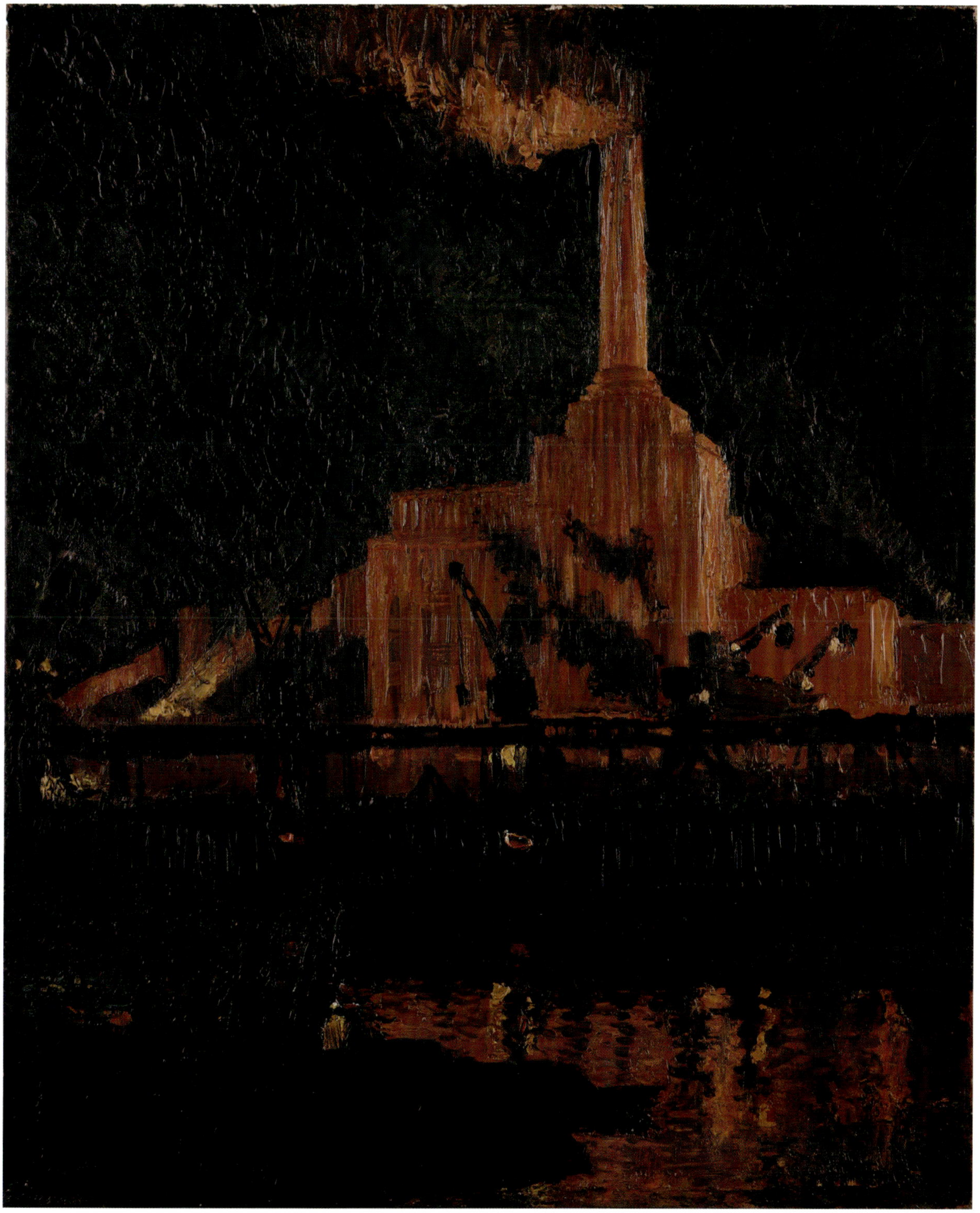

CAT. 115 – **Charles Johnson** (1902-1983), Battersea Power Station, (west half), signed, oil on canvas, 32 x 22 in. (81.2 x 56 cm).
Provenance: The artist Harold Riley; thence by descent.

Battersea Power Station was conceived in two stages. The west half was constructed between 1929 and 1935. The Power Station was a prime target for enemy bombers during WW2 but survived the war relatively unscathed, in spite of some near misses and a serious fire. After the war the east half was added (completed in 1955) giving the Battersea Power Station its distinctive silhouette with four colossal chimney stacks.

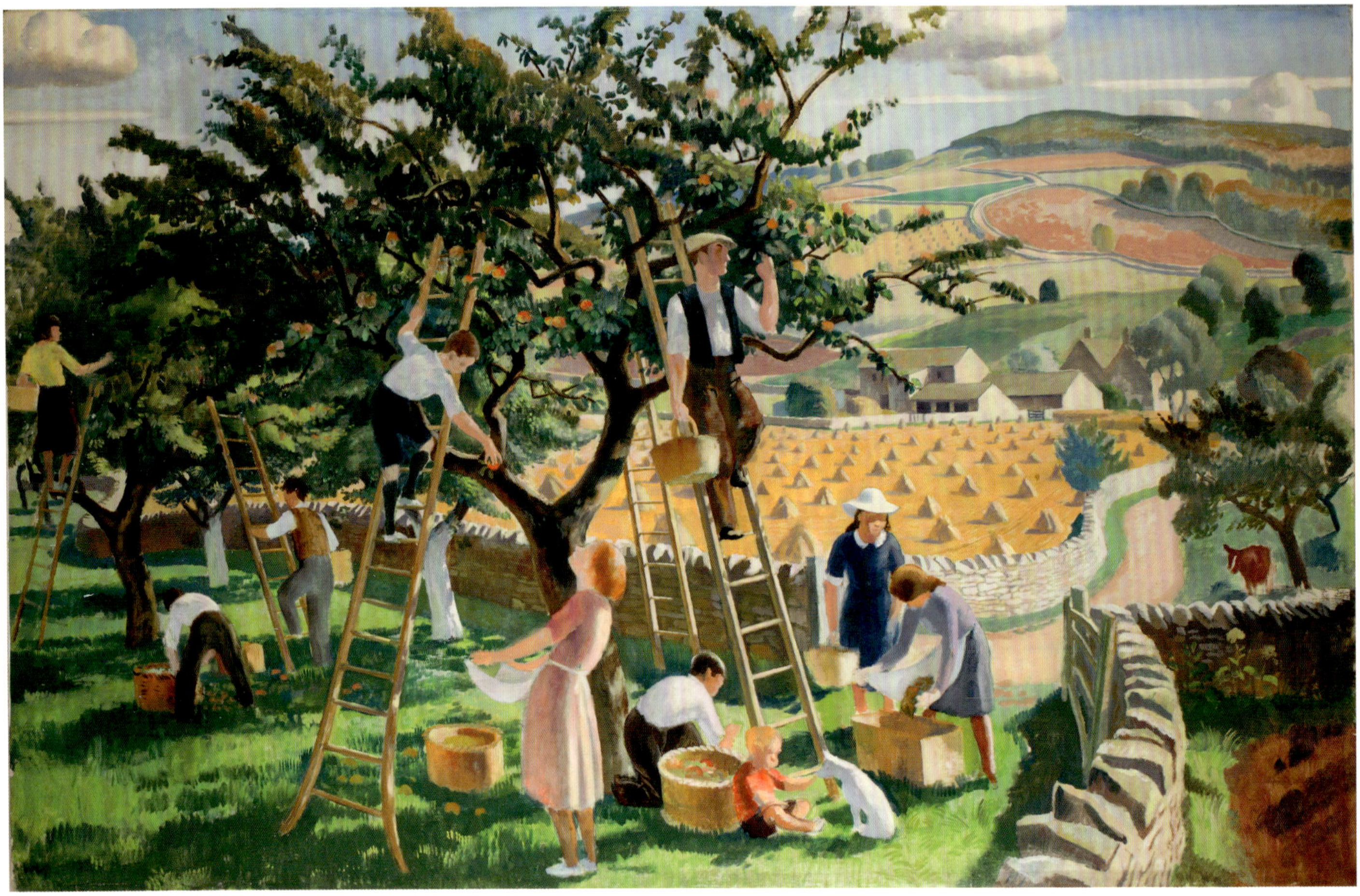

CAT. 116

Adrian Allinson (1890-1959), *The Four Seasons*,
oil on canvas, each appoximately 47 x 74 in. (119.4 x 188 cm).
Provenance: The Fine Art Society; Fortunoff Collection.

CAT. 116 *Autumn in the Cotswolds*
CAT. 117 *Winter in the Alps*
CAT. 118 *Spring in Mallorca*
CAT. 119 *Summer on the South Coast*

In wartime wry humour and nostalgia, particularly in the popular arts – song, film, theatre, and painting – play an important part in combating the enemy and keeping up morale on the home front. Documentary art is for posterity, but for the serviceman or woman on leave something that reminds them of happier times is required. During the dark days of WW2, if you were out for a carefree evening posterity was hardly a priority, especially as you were conscious that there could be no tomorrow. Those on leave and those at home needed relief from the grim realities of the everyday state of affairs. Nostalgia, especially the recall of moments of transient bliss, is often evoked through the senses, sight, sound and smell – the whiff of a particular scent, the half-heard notes of a familiar tune, the sight of a particular image. In times of danger, rose-tinted spectacles have the ability to make the recollection of such transient pleasures more special than they had ever been in reality.

As an artist Allinson was ideally placed to summon up the settings for such idyllic memories; he was not only familiar with the English countryside, but in the 1920s he had spent a considerable time in the Alps and skied for England, before forsaking the frozen north for what he described as 'the quintessential loveliness' of Mallorca. Nothing today is known about the circumstances of the commissioning of this evocative series of canvases depicting the four seasons – *Spring in Mallorca*, *Summer on the South Coast*, *Autumn in the Cotswolds* and *Winter in the Alps* – but their size and broad-brush treatment would suggest that they were painted to decorate a place of relaxation and entertainment. Given the date, the one poignant note is the inclusion of the young Jewish goat boy (who wears a Kippah) looking wistfully at the revellers from the margins of the Alpine fair. A touching note of sympathy and affinity; a reminder of Allinson's own Jewish ancestry, his liberal, freethinking mother, being the granddaughter of a Polish rabbi.

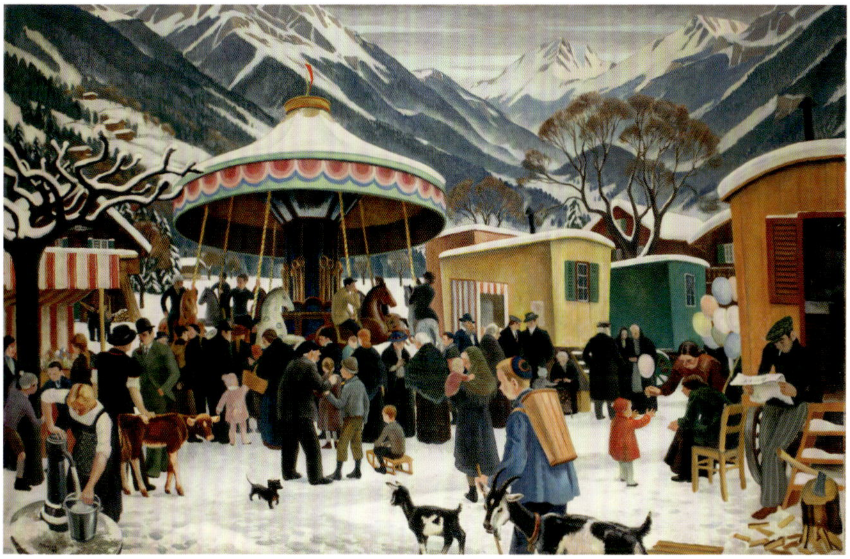

CAT. 117

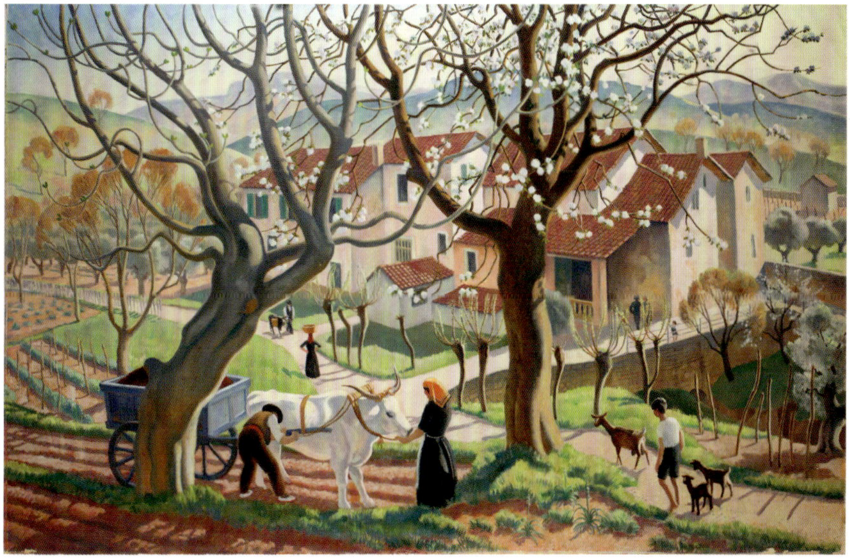

CAT. 118

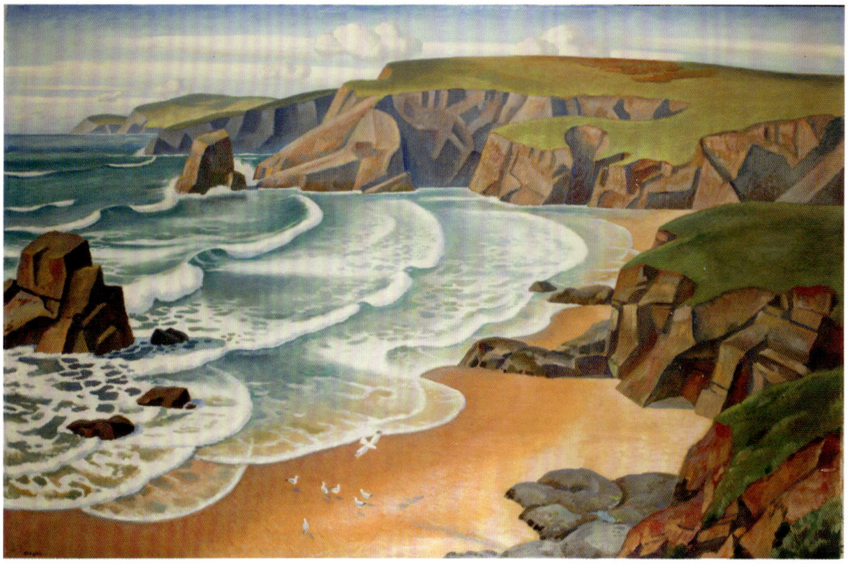

CAT. 119

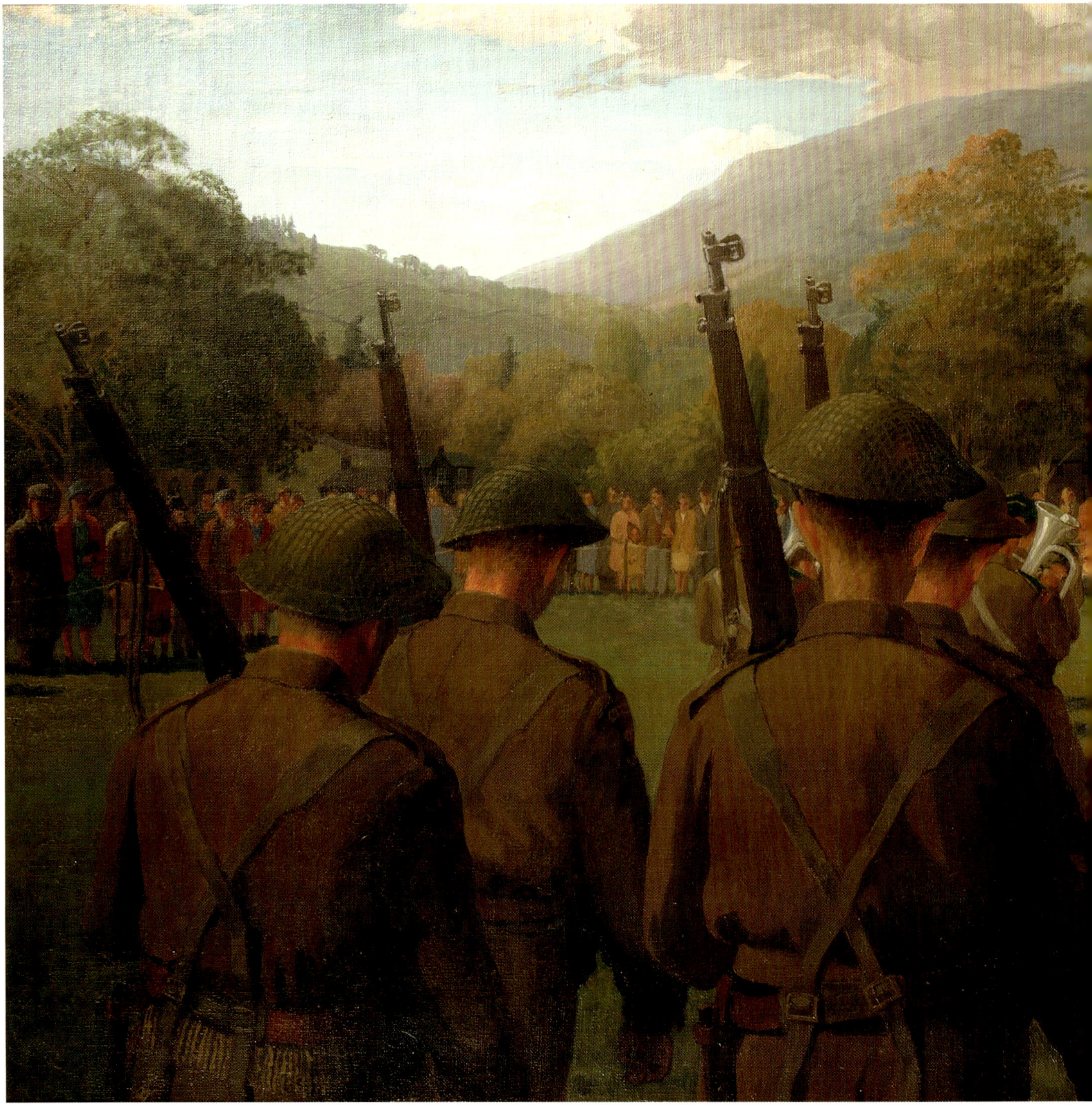

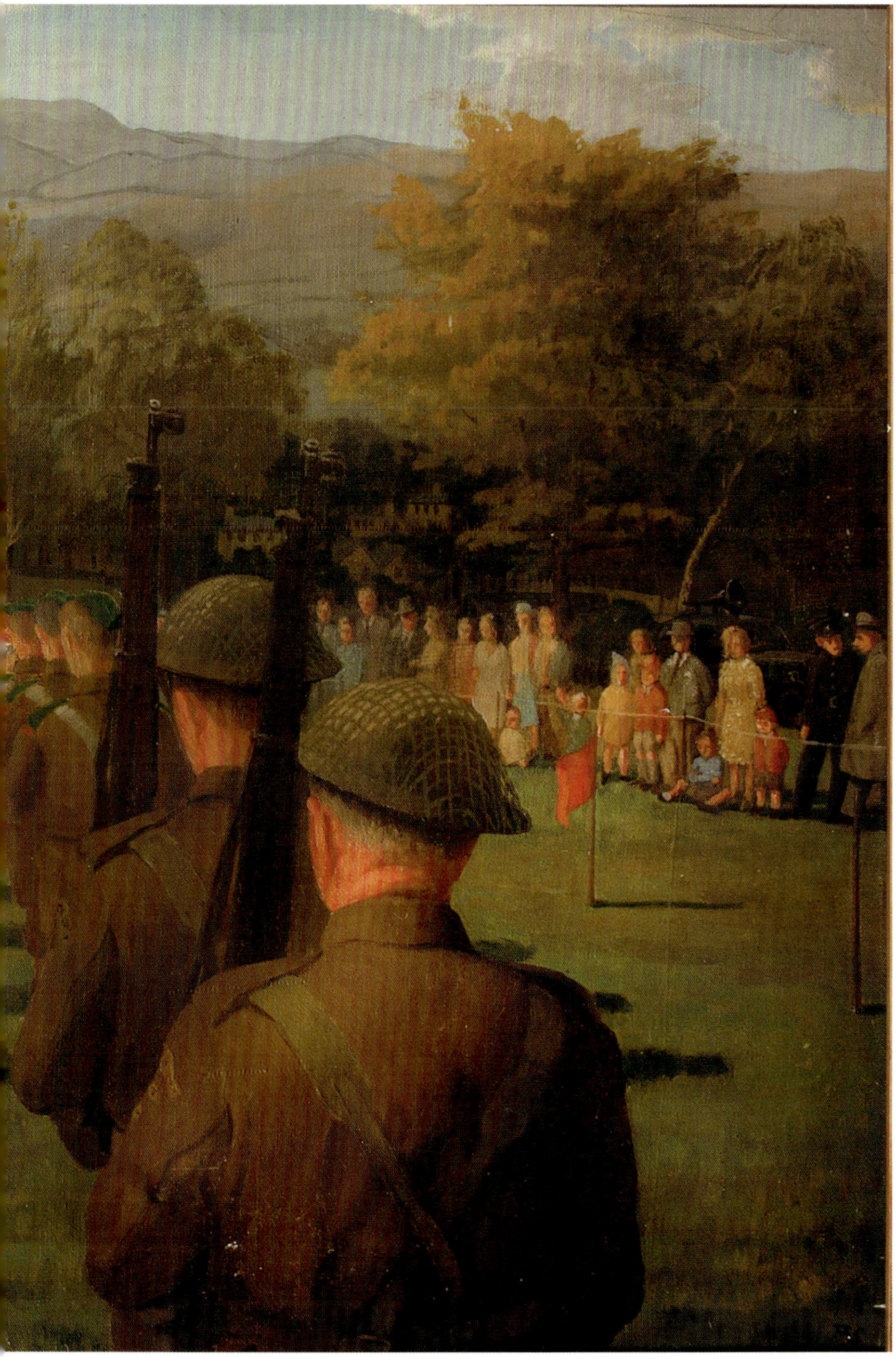

CAT. 120 – **Robert Sawyers** (1923-2002),
Home Guard Parade, Ambleside, c.1944/1945,
signed and dated,
oil on canvas, 21 ½ x 37 ½ in. (55 x 95 cm).

In May 1940 the creation of the Local Defence Volunteers (LDV) was announced by the Secretary of State for War, Anthony Eden. He called for men between the ages of 17 and 65 not in military service to join and help defend their country. Some 250,000 volunteers offered their services in the first week and by July when the LDV was renamed the Home Guard the figure had risen to 1.5 million.

However, equipment uniforms and training were not so quick to appear and until 1943 they were supplied on a somewhat ad hoc basis. The Home Guard quickly gained the nickname 'Dad's Army'. Robert Sawyer's painting made later in the war shows the Home Guard properly kitted out with uniforms and rifles and, if slightly lacking in military bearing, nevertheless putting on a show for the gathered crowd.

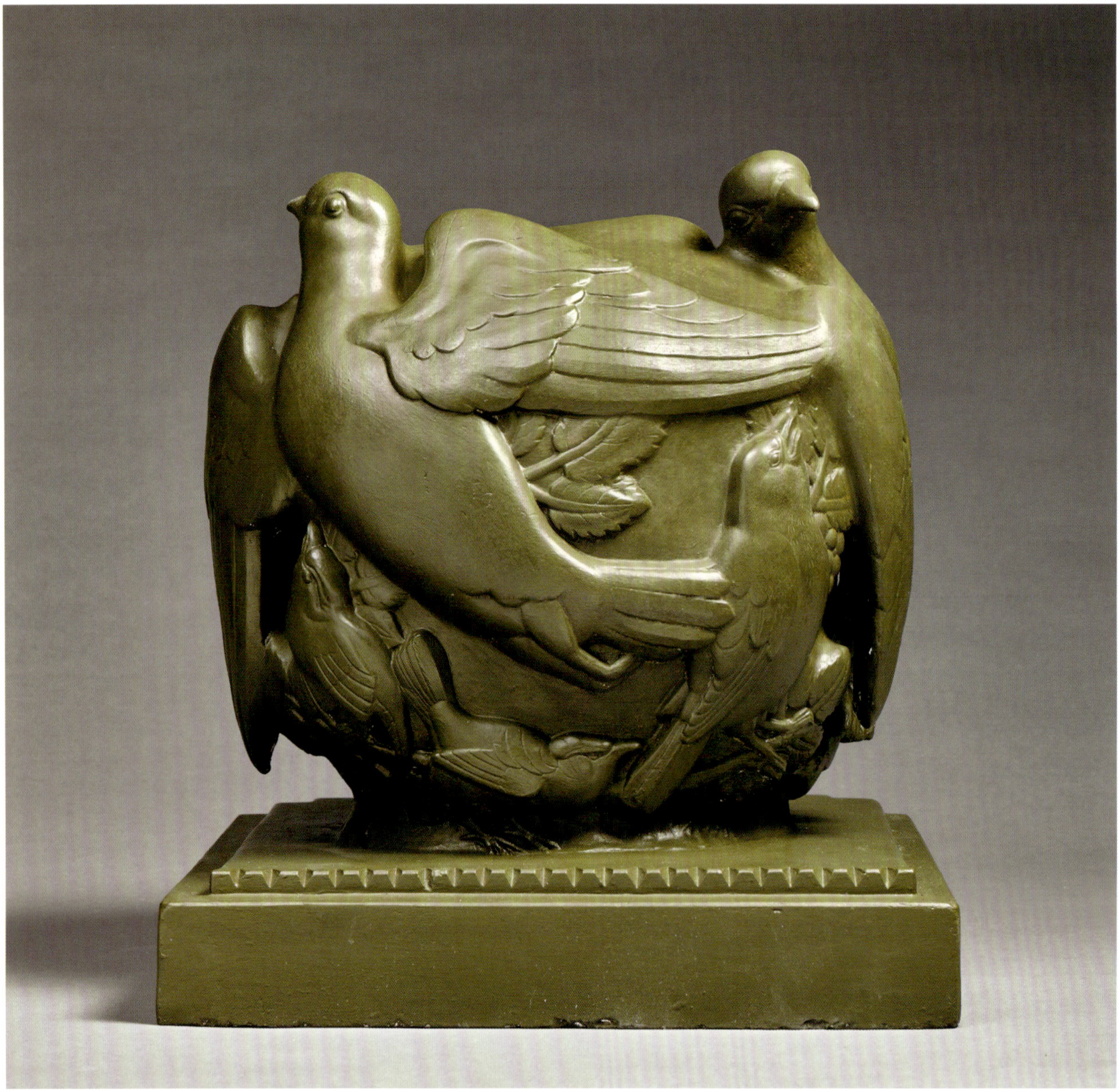

CAT. 121 – **James Woodford** (1893-1976), *Dawn Chorus,* 1946-7, signed, dated and titled (on a label),
Original plaster maquette, with a dark green finish, 17 x 16 in. (43 x 40.5 cm).
Provenance: Private collection.
Exhibited Royal Academy, 1948, (1386), as Bird Group- Dawn Chorus, 1946-7, part of a Memorial to Esmond Carrick Simpson; City of Bradford Art Gallery, 1955 (744).

During WW2 Woodford was a camouflage officer for the Air Ministry. After the war he was responsible for a number of memorials including a Memorial to Esmond Carrick Simpson (1946) and the War Memorial in the Court of Honour of the British Medical Association, Tavistock Square, London (1951). More than twenty artists were commissioned by the WAAC to produce sculptures including Epstein, C.W.Dyson-Smith and Skeaping.

CAT. 122 – **Edward Irvine Halliday** (1902-1984), *Altar (War and Peace)*, 1939,
signed, and dated, inscribed Altar, 1 inch to a 1 foot,
30 x 17 in. (76.2 x 43.2 cm).

During the war Halliday worked as an air traffic controller for the RAF and later was transferred to Intelligence and worked on intercepting German radio signals. *Altar* was conceived in 1939 for an unidentified site, presumably never completed. It offers a deeply personal and kaleidoscopic vision of war and peace.

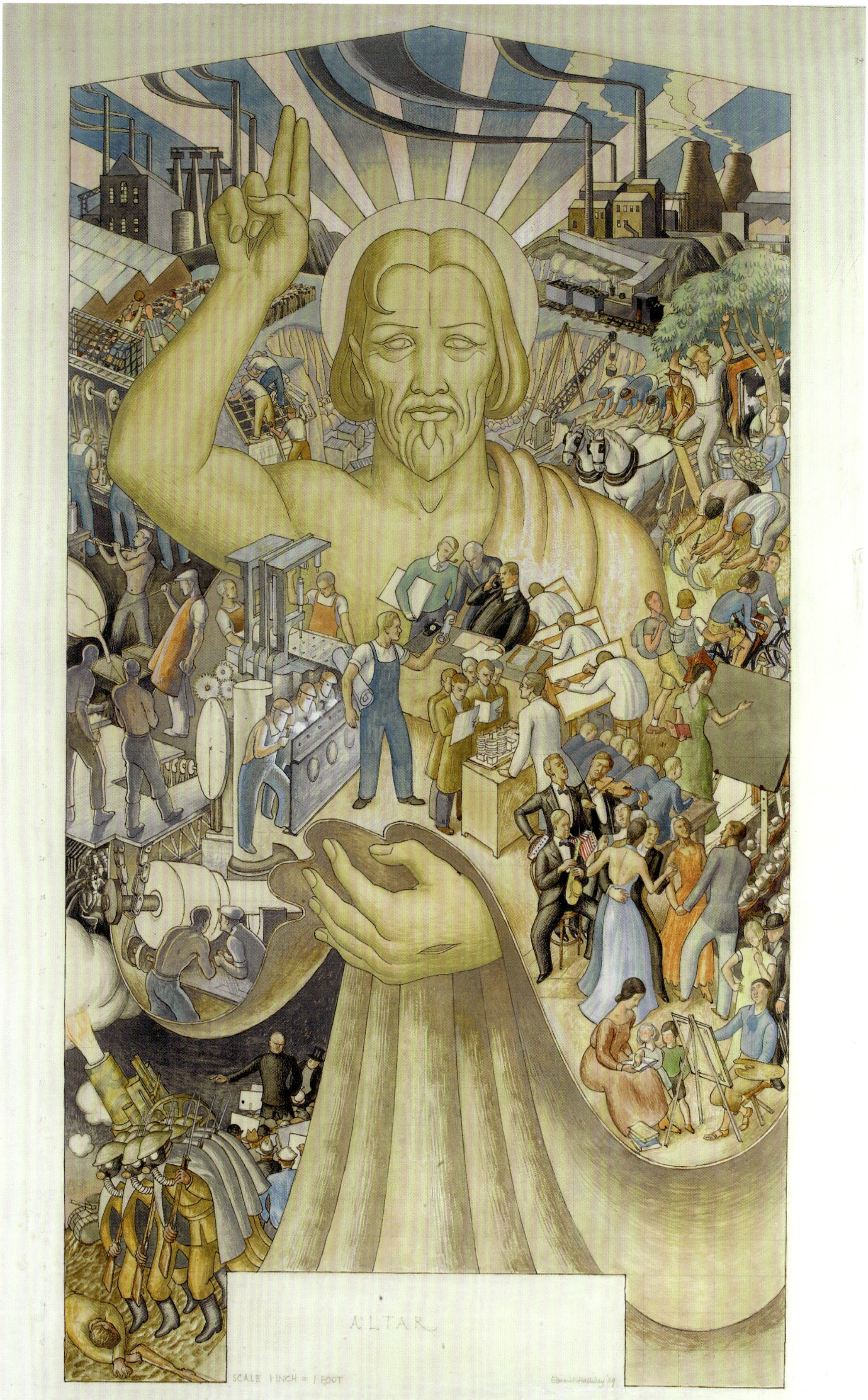
ALTAR
SCALE 1 INCH = 1 FOOT
Edward Halliday '39

OUR HERITAGE

Printed for the passengers and staff of London Transport to recall other occasions of the nation's will and high purpose.

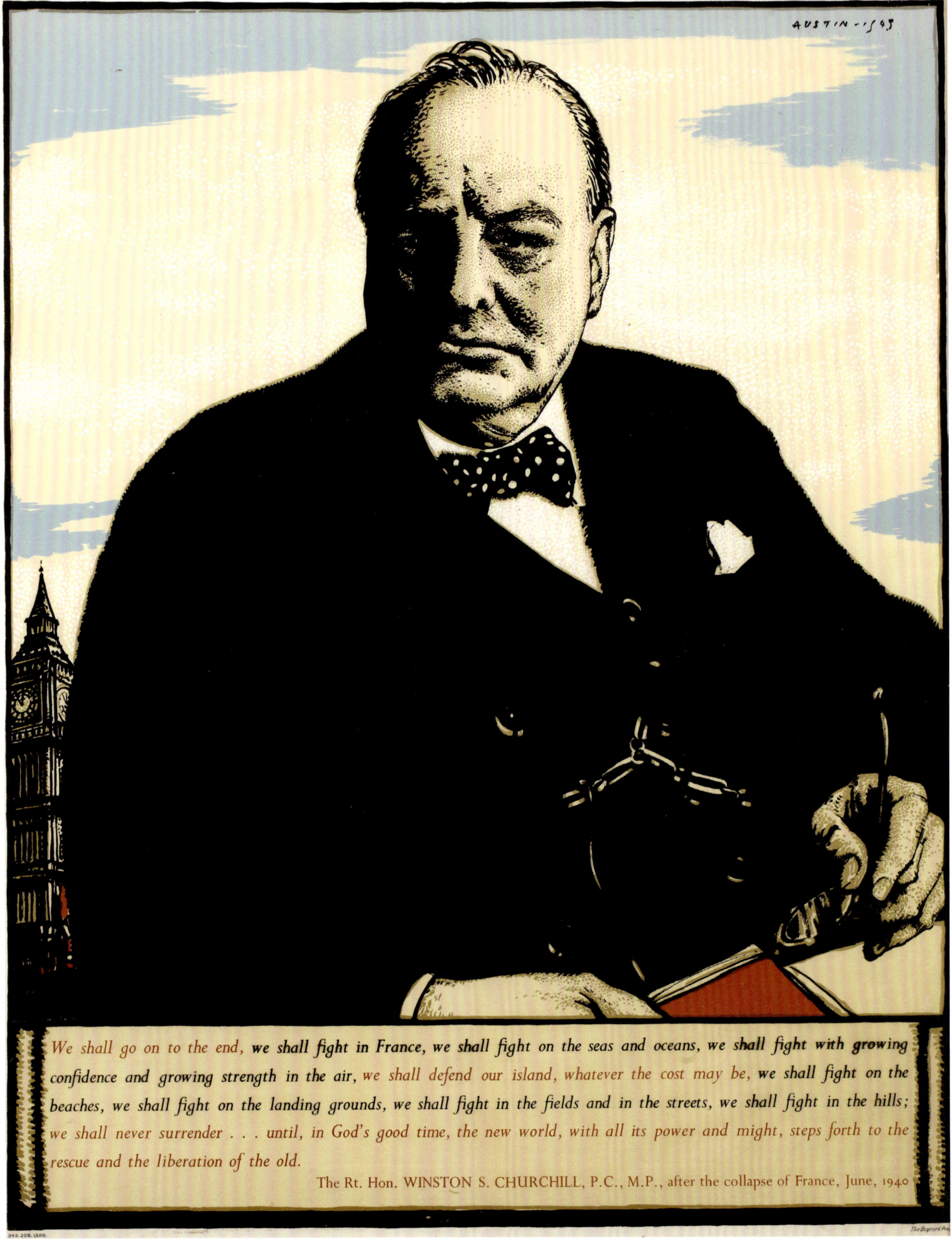

We shall go on to the end, ***we shall fight in France,*** *we shall fight on the seas and oceans, we shall fight with growing confidence and growing strength in the air,* *we shall defend our island, whatever the cost may be,* *we shall fight on the beaches, we shall fight on the landing grounds, we shall fight in the fields and in the streets, we shall fight in the hills;* *we shall never surrender . . . until, in God's good time, the new world, with all its power and might, steps forth to the rescue and the liberation of the old.*

The Rt. Hon. WINSTON S. CHURCHILL, P.C., M.P., after the collapse of France, June, 1940

343.208.1500.

The Baynard Press

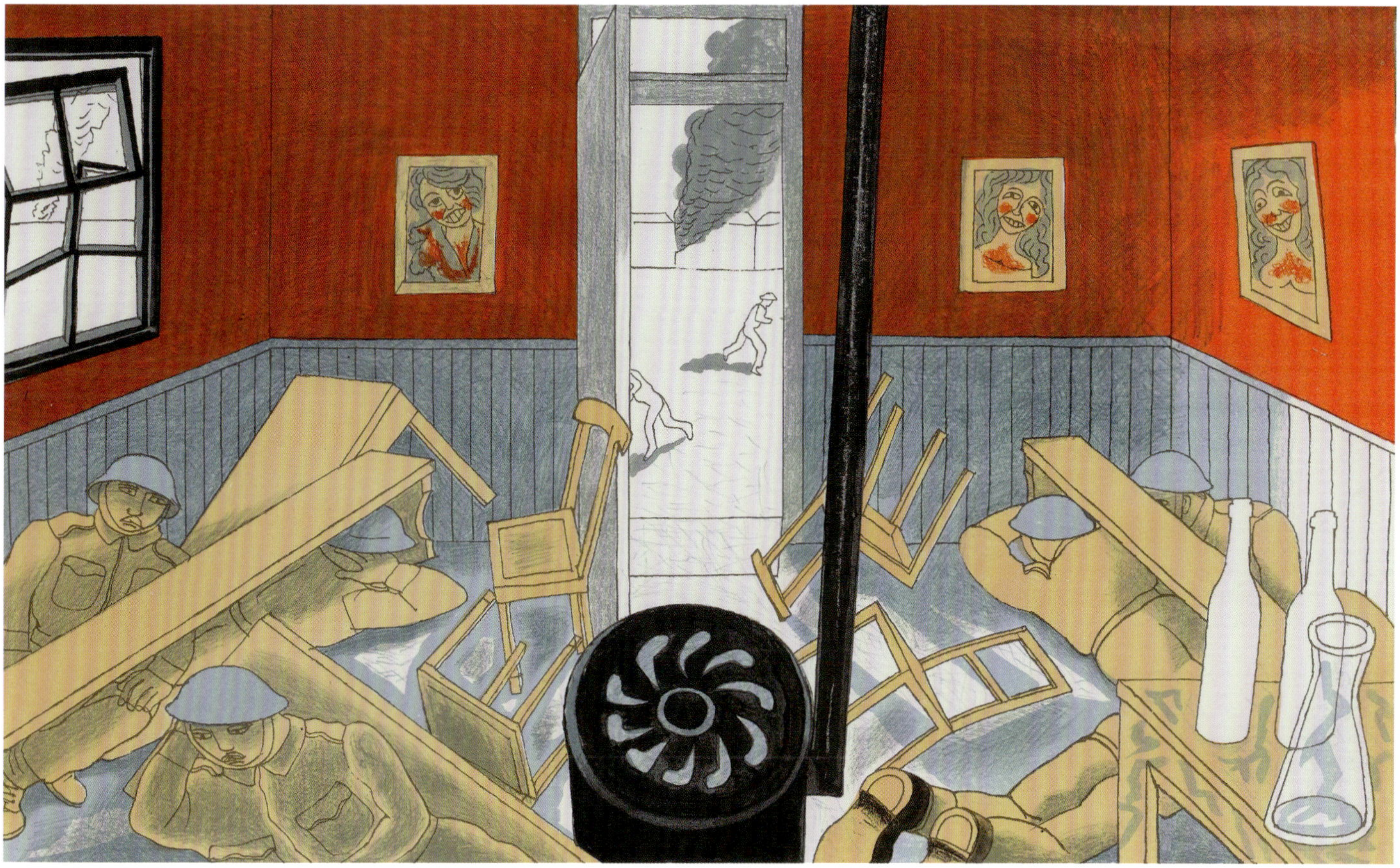

CAT. 124* – **Edward Bawden** (1903-1989) *Dunkirk*, 1940, signed, inscribed and numbered 74/75,
lithograph, 14 x 23 in. (35.5 x 58.5 cm) commissioned by the Hurtwood Press, printed by the Curwen Studio in 1986.
Literature: Jeremy Greenwood, Edward Bawden: Editioned Prints, Wood Lea Press, Woodbridge, 2005, p. 125.

Bawden was made an Official War Artist in 1939. He was initially sent to France, and then evacuated from Dunkirk with the British Expeditionary Force the following year. This scene depicts the chaos in Dunkirk just before the evacuation. Bawden based this lithograph (commissioned by the Hurtwood Press in 1986 and printed by the Curwen Studio) on a watercolour he painted in 1940 (Imperial War Museum, IWM ART LD 173).

CAT. 123* – **Robert Austin** (1895-1973), *Our Heritage: Winston Churchill*, 1943, signed and dated in the plate,
lithograph, 25 ¼ x 20 in. (64. 2 x 50.8 cm),
inscribed 'printed for the passengers and staff of London Transport to recall other occasions of the Nation's will and high purpose', printed by the Baynard Press.
Provenance: Artist's daughter; Private Collection.

The Underground Group (later London Transport) produced a wide variety of posters during WW1 and WW2. There was, however, a marked difference between the propaganda element of the posters in both wars: the posters published during WW1 presented the conflict as an idealised struggle and urged men to enlist, whereas the posters of WW2 stressed the individual's role in helping the war effort at home and also aspired to lift the nation's spirits. Many London Transport posters were issued as a series, for maximum impact. Robert Sargent Austin was commissioned to produce the Our Heritage Series, depicting heroic British leaders, such as Nelson, Drake, Pitt and finally Churchill. The aim of these posters was to boost morale within the travelling public by reminding them what the nation was fighting for.

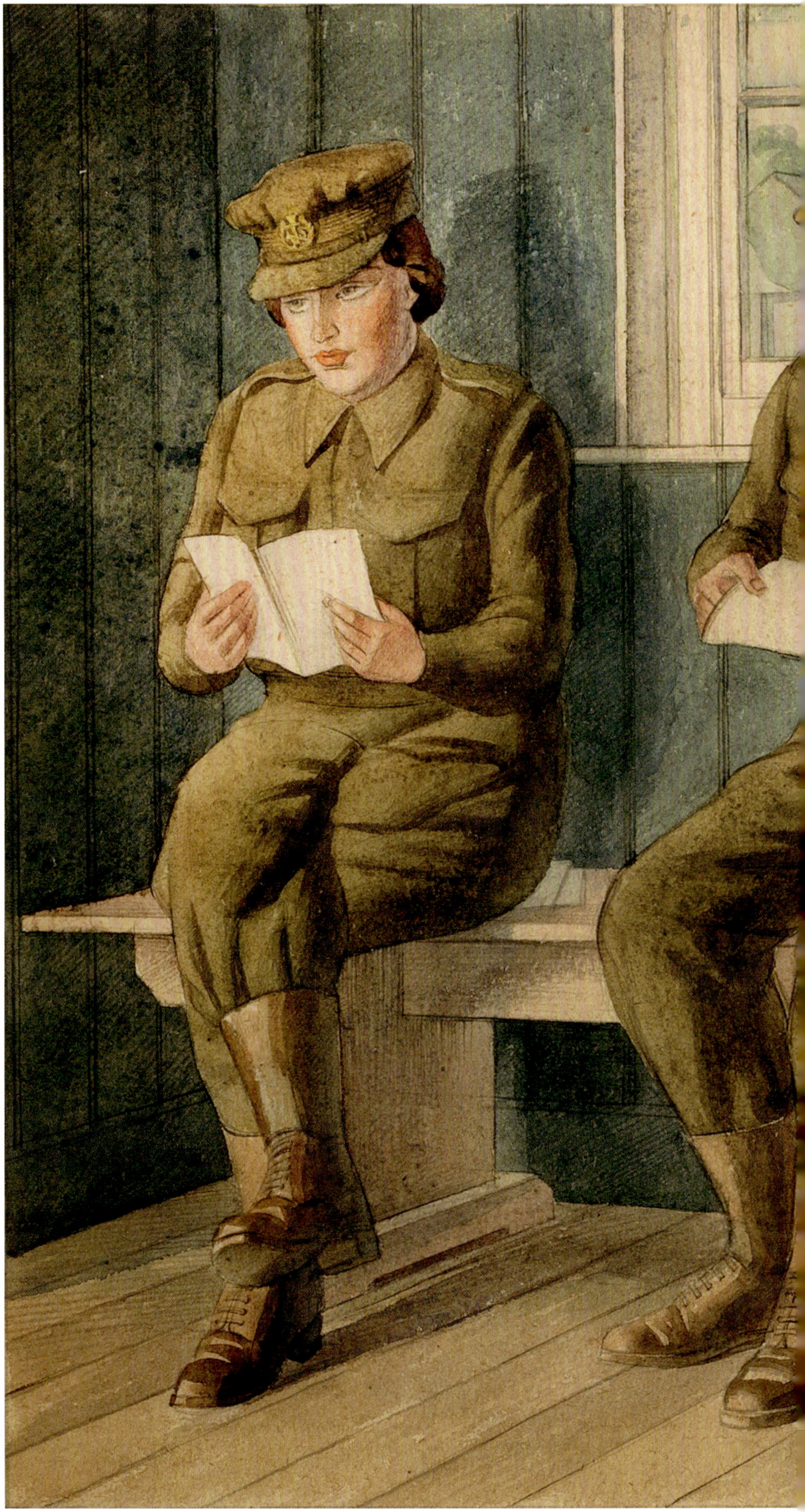

CAT. 125 – **James Walker Tucker** (1898-1972),
Letters from Home, signed
watercolour on paper,
14 ¼ x 20 ½ in. (36 x 52 cm).

Tucker's striking watercolour shows four women of the Auxiliary Territorial Service (ATS) reading letters apparently in a hut at an army camp. The ATS was the women's branch of the British Army, formed in 1938. The National Service Act of 1941 called up unmarried women between 20 and 30 to join one of the forces auxiliary services or take up factory work and by the end of the war there were over 190,000 ATS members. Their duties included working as drivers, radar operators, anti-aircraft and searchlight crew and supporting roles within the Regular Army. Over 700 lost their lives during the war.

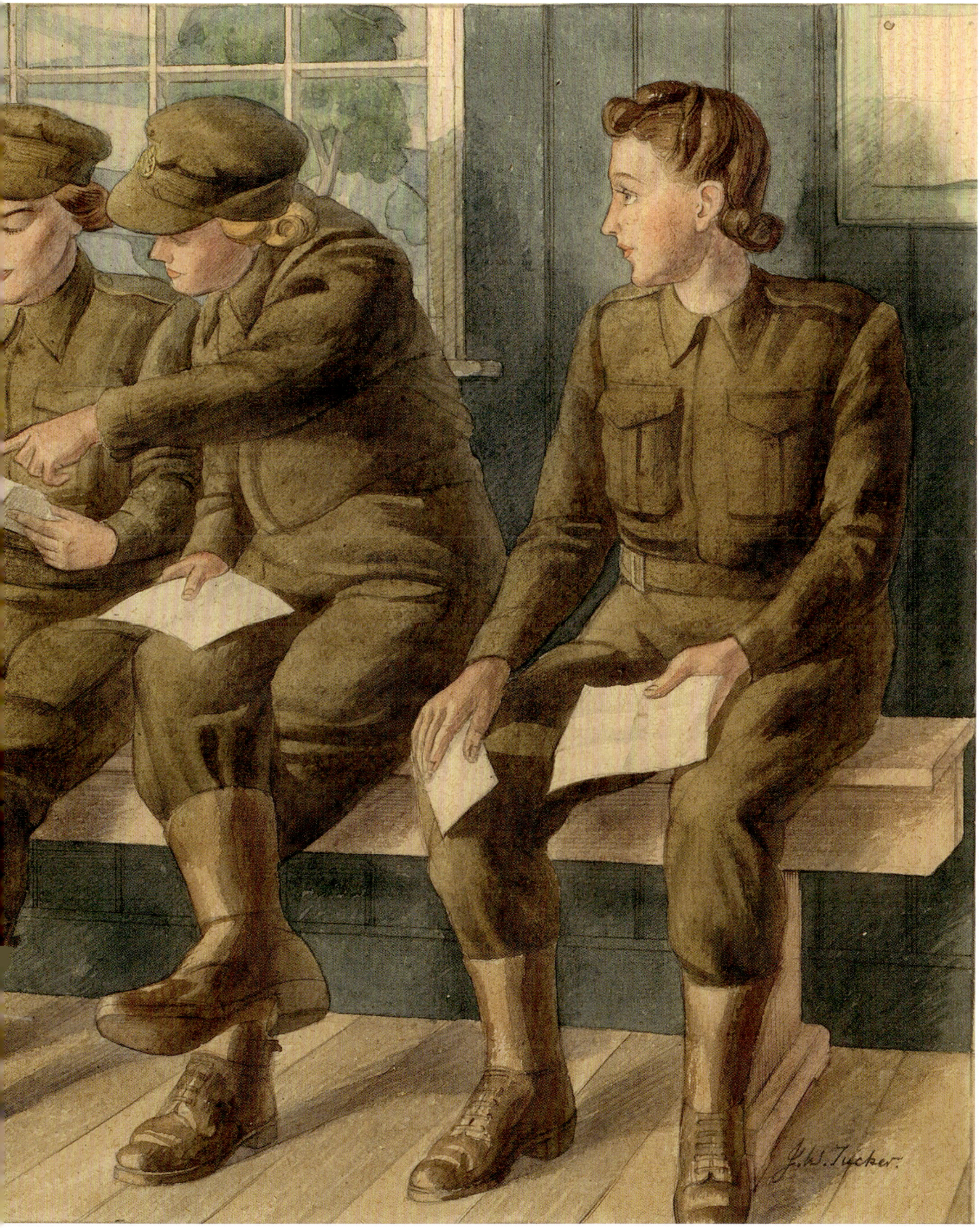
J. W. Tucker.

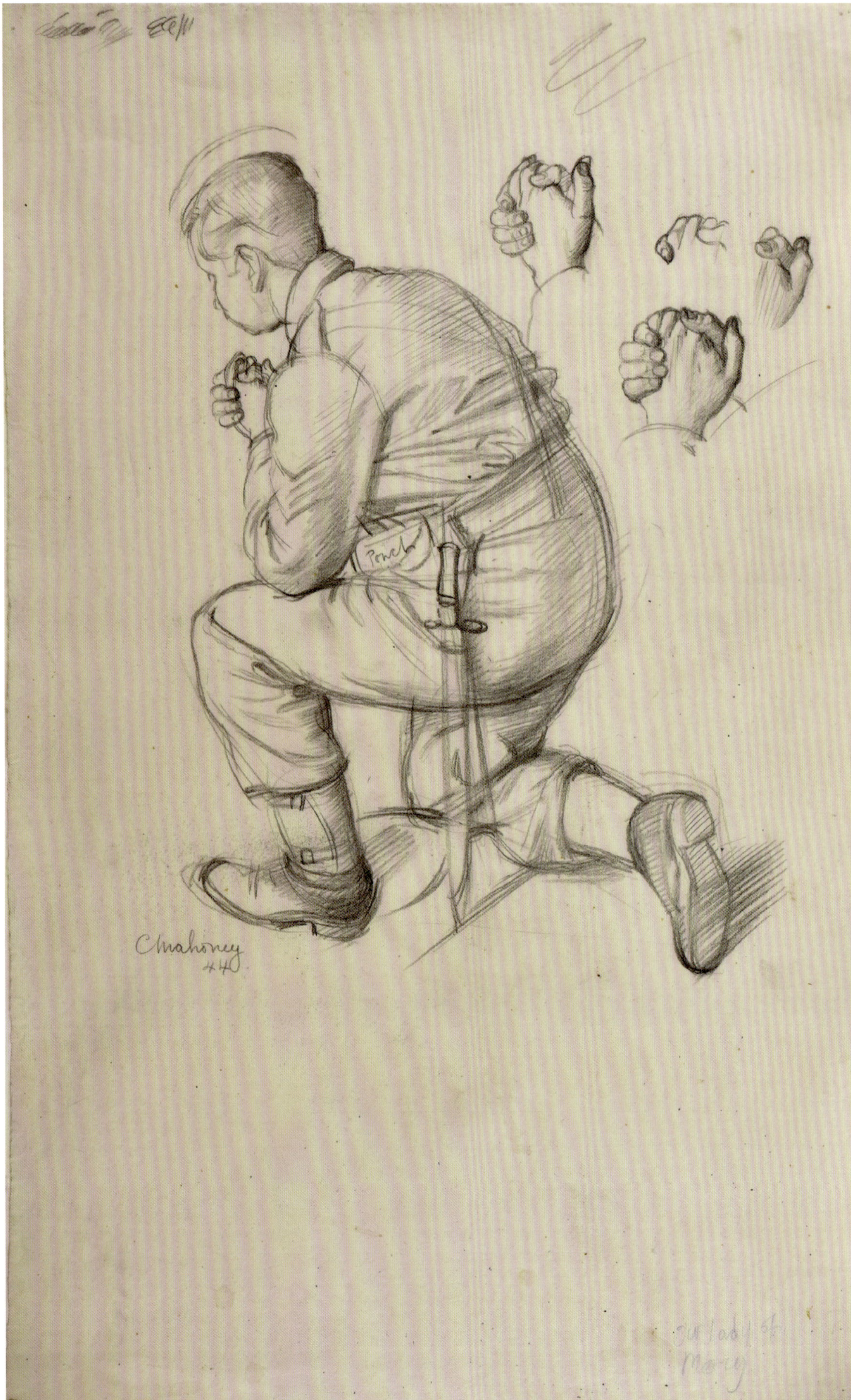
Pouch
CMahoney
44

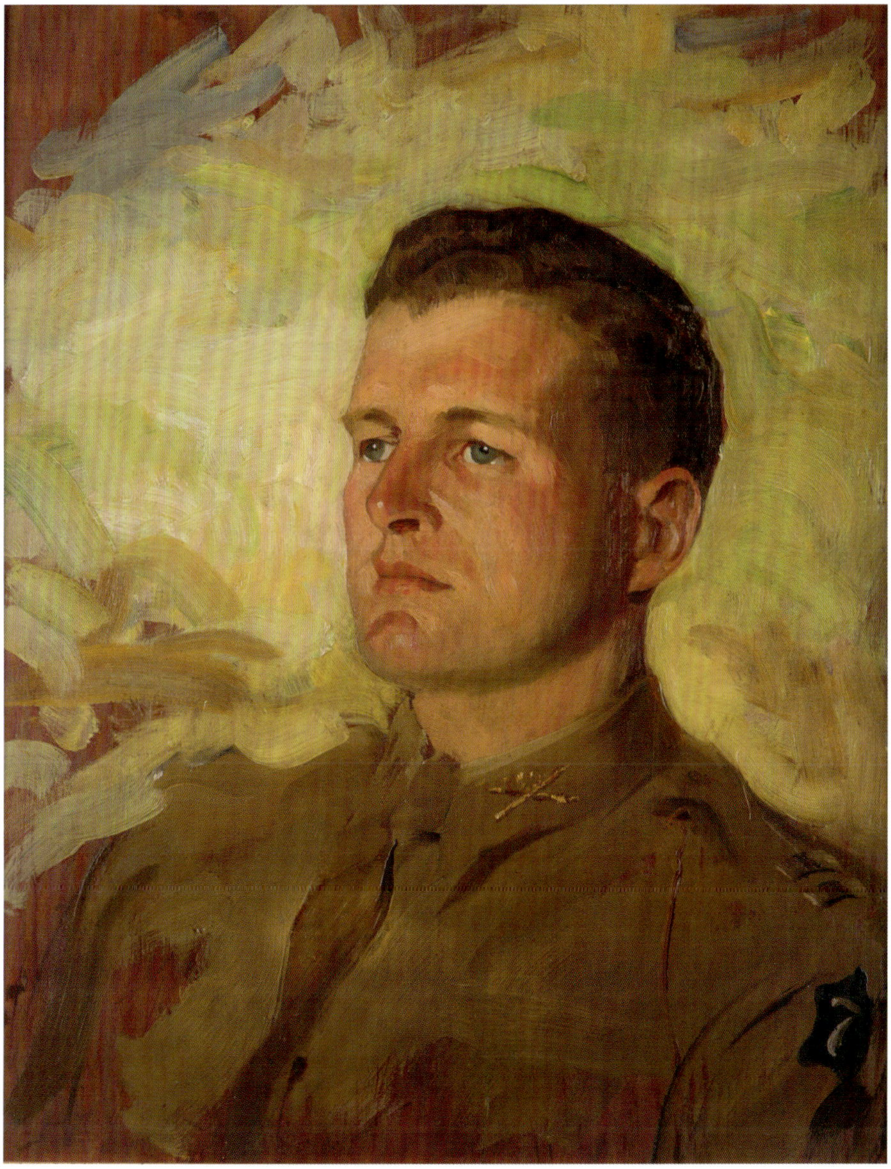

CAT. 127 –
Francis Edwin Hodge (1881-1949), *Portrait of an American Captain, VII Corps*, early 1940s,
oil on panel, 24 ¼ x 19 ¼ in. (62 x 49 cm).

This was probably painted while the soldier was stationed in the UK prior to the reorganisation of regimental badges in April 1944. Hodge who enlisted in the Artists' Rifles saw active service in WW1 as a Captain in the Royal Field Artillery and later published watercolours relating to his battle experiences in France.

CAT. 126 – **Charles Mahoney** (1903-1968), Study of a soldier for *Our Lady of Mercy*, 1942, signed and dated,
pencil on tracing paper, 17 ¾ x 11 ¾ in. (45 x 30 cm.)
Literature: Charles Mahoney, Liss Fine Art, 1999, pp.40-41 and pp.56-57; *British Murals & Decorative Painting 1920-1960*, Sansom & Co, 2013, pp.85-86 and pp.232-243

Mahoney was commissioned to produce a mural scheme for the Lady Chapel at Campion Hall in 1941. The scheme was to be made up primarily of three large panels: the *Nativity and Adoration of the Shepherds*, the *Coronation of the Virgin* and *Our Lady of Mercy*. In detail and composition the paintings owe much to the early Quattrocento. The project continued into the following decade and coincided with a serious decline in the artist's physical health. In spite of these problems, Sir John Rothenstein was moved to describe the scheme as as 'second … only to that by Stanley Spencer at Burghclere'.

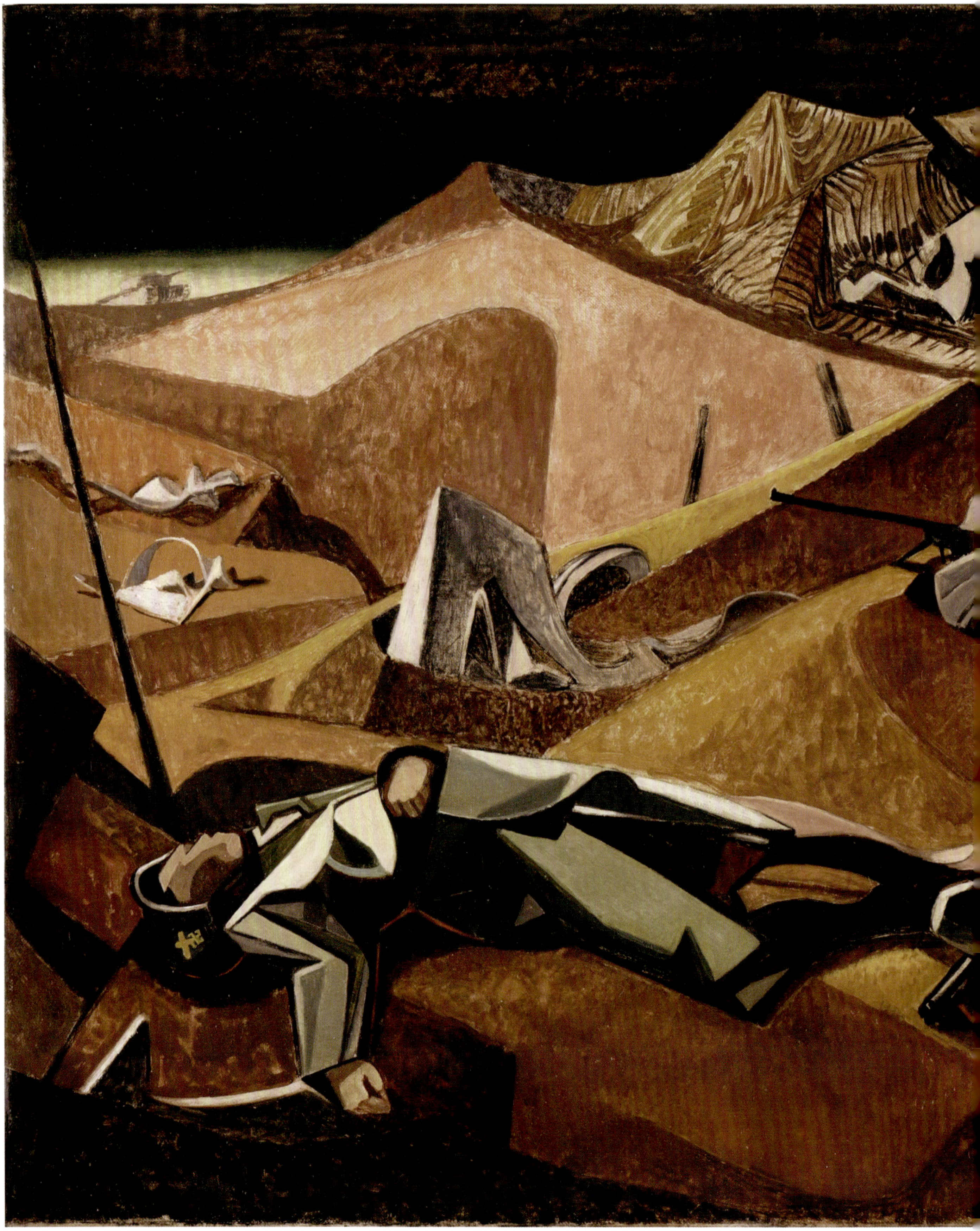

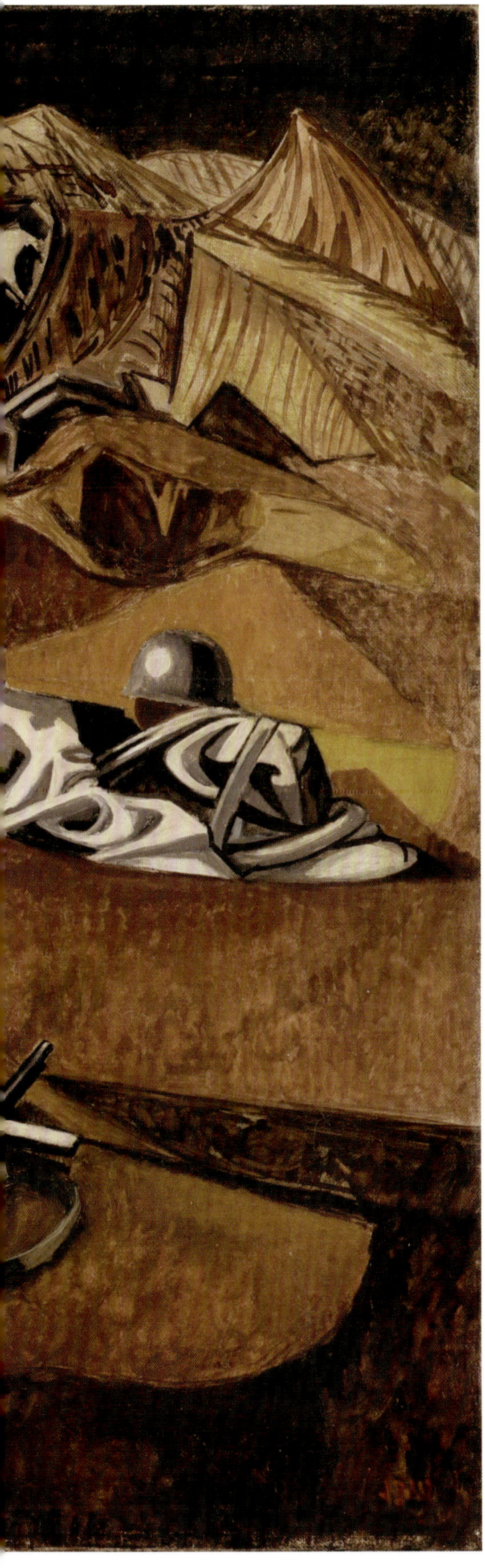

CAT. 128 – **John Buckland Wright** (1897-1954), *Stalingrad*, 1942,
signed, titled and dated on the reverse,
oil on canvas, 20 x 24 in. (50.8 x 61 cm).
Provenance: The Artist (thence by descent).
Exhibited: Adelaide, National Gallery of South Australia, The London Group (one of 34 pictures selected as an overview of the London Group of British artists.

The battle of Stalingrad (August 1942 - February 1943) was a turning point of WW2. The Germans incurred massive losses. The Wehrmacht's gun positions are set within a nightmarish surrealist landscape. On the horizon, emerging from the darkness, looms a Russian T-34 tank. The Germans were strongly outnumbered by the Soviet's 20,000 tanks.

Having joined the Scottish Ambulance Service in WW1, Buckland Wright was seconded to the French Army at Verdun, the sector in which the French suffered the greatest devastation. There he witnessed harrowing scenes of human devastation while rescuing wounded and dying men from the front line trenches.

Although Buckland-Wright was influenced stylistically by Continental art – absorbing at first hand the developments of Cubism and Surrealism during the inter-war years – this composition is close in spirit to Wyndham Lewis' *A Battery Shelled*, 1919, (IWM).

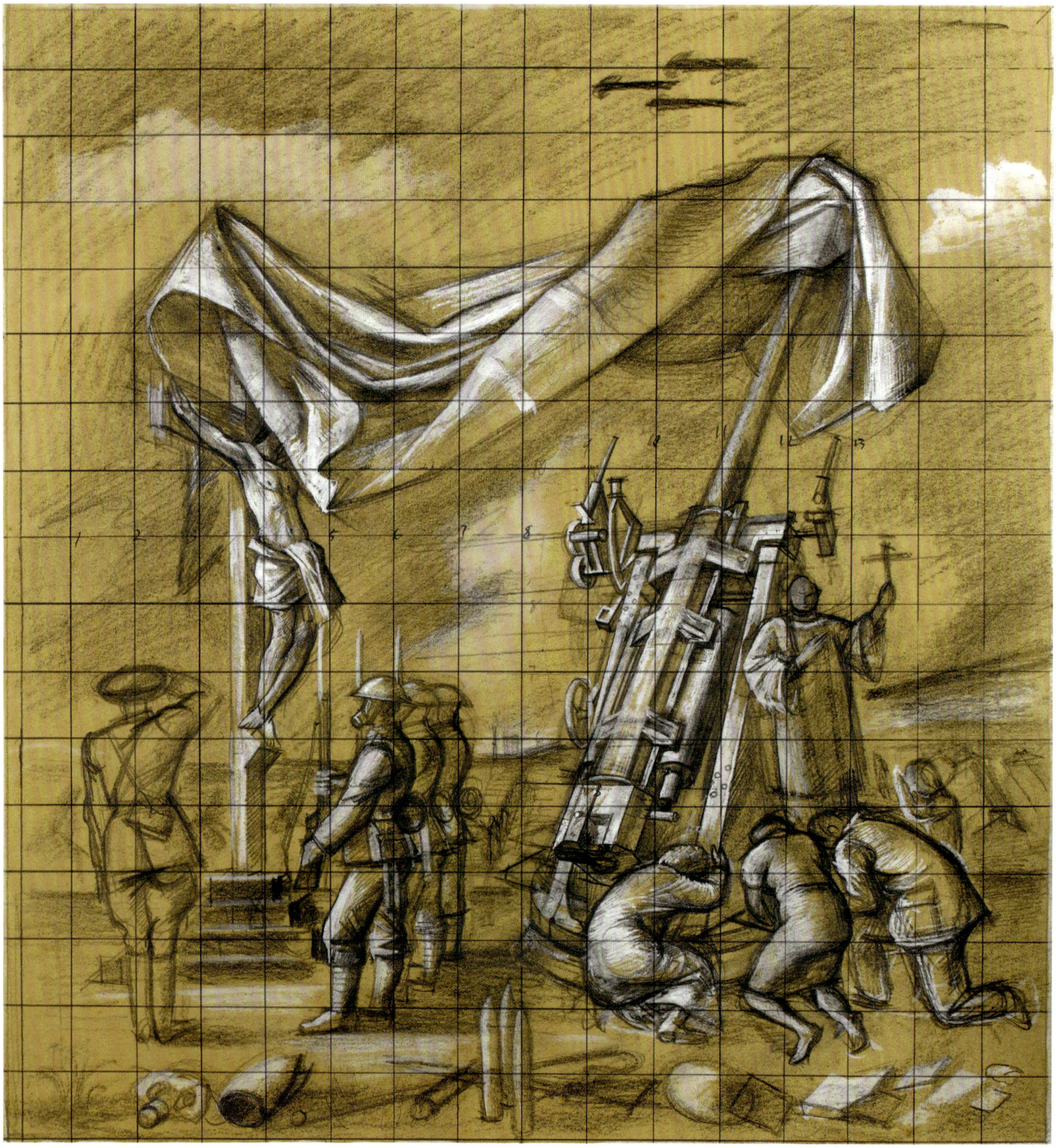

CAT. 129 – **Alan Sorrell** (1904-1974), *A confusion of symbols, June 24, '39,* signed, titled and dated, pencil and gouache on paper, squared, 17 ¾ x 15 in. (45.4 x 38.2 cm).

During WW2 served in the RAF, where he was able to make first-hand visual records of daily life. Although twenty-six of these pictures were acquired by the War Artists' Advisory Committee and Sorrell had canvassed for Rothenstein's support to put his name before the WAAC, he questioned the morality of war. When he enrolled in the RAF he refused to work on terrain models of cities he considered of "irreplaceable artistic importance", what he later referred to as his "one man mutiny". His image, *A Land Fit for Heroes* openly challenged perceptions of the honour and glory that surrounded WW1. Remarkably Sorrell's squared design 'A Confusion of Symbols' (possibly intended as a mural) is dated 24th June 1939 – predating the start of WW2 by well over two months.

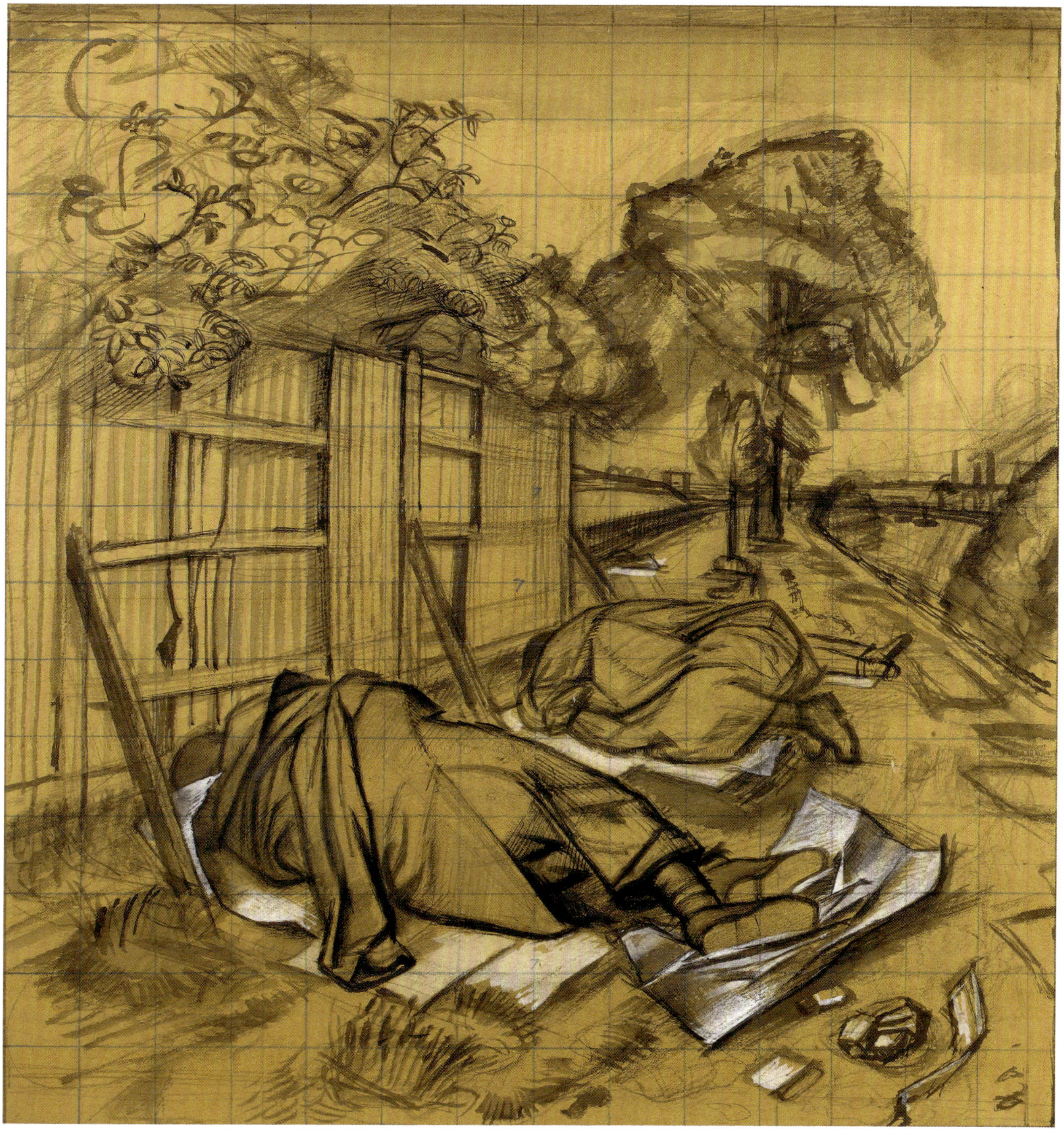

CAT. 130 – **Alan Sorrell** (1904-1974), *May Morning, Putney Embankment, July 6th, 1939*, 1939,
dated and inscribed with title, squared for transfer,
charcoal and wash with white highlights on buff coloured paper, 17 x 15 in. (43 x 38 cm).
Provenance: The Artist's Family.

After WWI promises made to soldiers returning from the trenches, that they would be rewarded with 'A Land Fit for Heroes', evaporated as huge debts, high unemployment, and slow growth wiped out Britain's leadership in the world economy. Many soldiers found themselves unable to reintegrate back into civilian life. This scene of men – probably ex-soldiers – sleeping rough on Putney Embankment, demonstrates that the scars left behind at the end of WW1 were still in evidence as the dawn of WW2 broke.

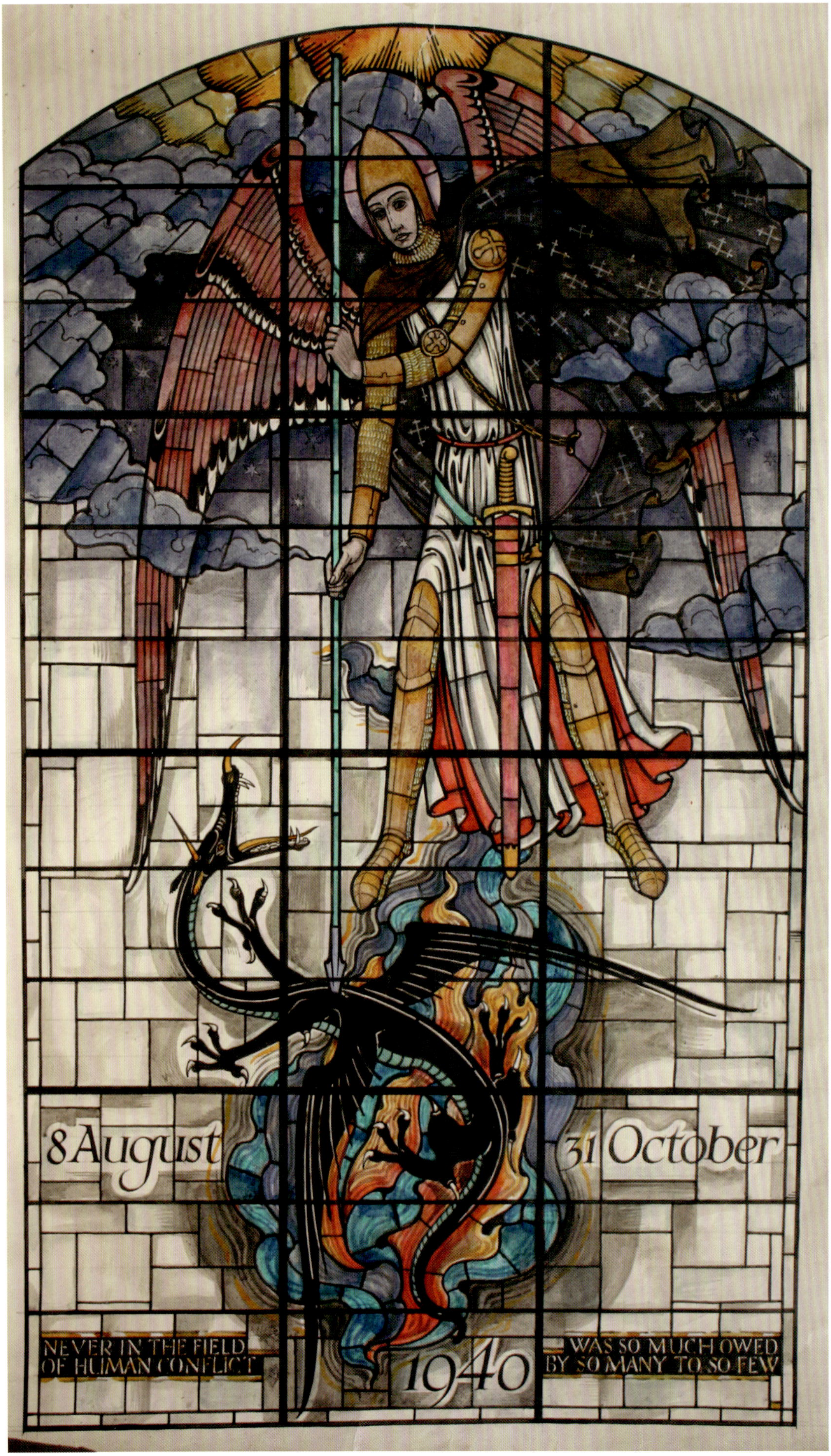
8 August
31 October
NEVER IN THE FIELD
OF HUMAN CONFLICT
1940
WAS SO MUCH OWED
BY SO MANY TO SO FEW

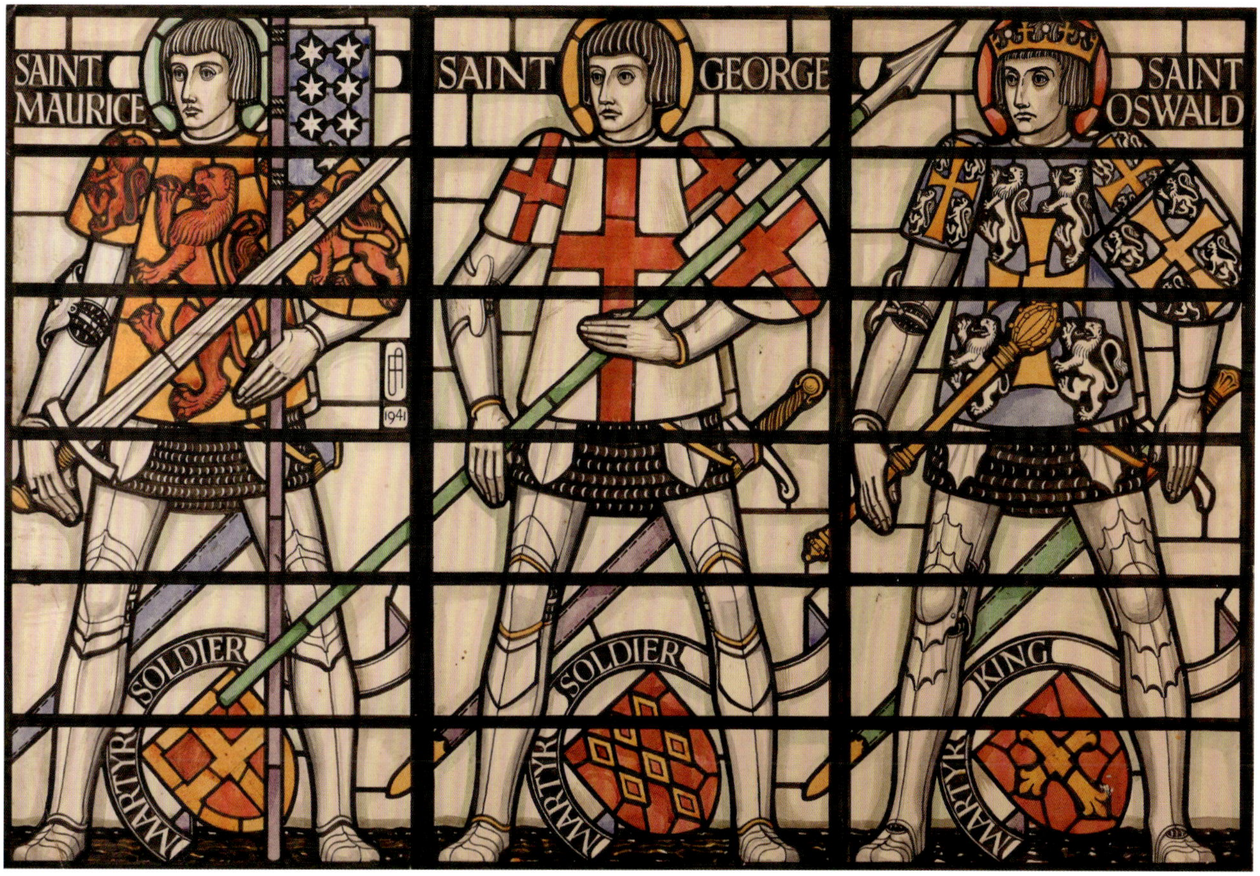

CAT. 132 – **Francis Spear** (1902-1979), *Martyr Soldier*, 1941, signed with monogram and dated, inscribed 'Saint Maurice, Saint George, Saint Oswald, Martyr Soldier, Martyr King', black ink and gouache on paper, 26 ½ x 17 ½ in. (67 x 44.5 cm).

During the war Spear ceased teaching at the RCA (which was evacuated to Ambleside in 1940) and served for three years as a firefighter in Shepherds Bush. This wartime period was not a completely unproductive time for Spear from a professional point of view – he assisted on the removal, for protection, of windows at Canterbury Cathedral. He also experimented with new designs which were more modern in feel, a change that he hoped would 'give the feeling of the subject with the greatest simplicity and with the elimination of all details.' and devised his distinctive monogram of an interlocking S with a sideways F. When the war ended Spear gained so many commissions – to replace stained glass windows destroyed during the Blitz – that by 1947 he was employing four assistants.

During his career, Spear designed windows for over 130 locations; and a short list of notable designs include his earliest window, at Warwick School (1925), St. Olave's in the City (1929), Snaith (1936), Beckenham (1948), Canterbury (1949), Glasgow Cathedral (1951, 1953, 1958), Highbury (1955), Westgate (1960) and Penarth (1962).

CAT. 131 – **Francis Spear** (1902-1979), *Saint Michael Killing Satan*, pen & ink, wash and watercolour on paper, 30 x 15 in. (76 x 38 cm).

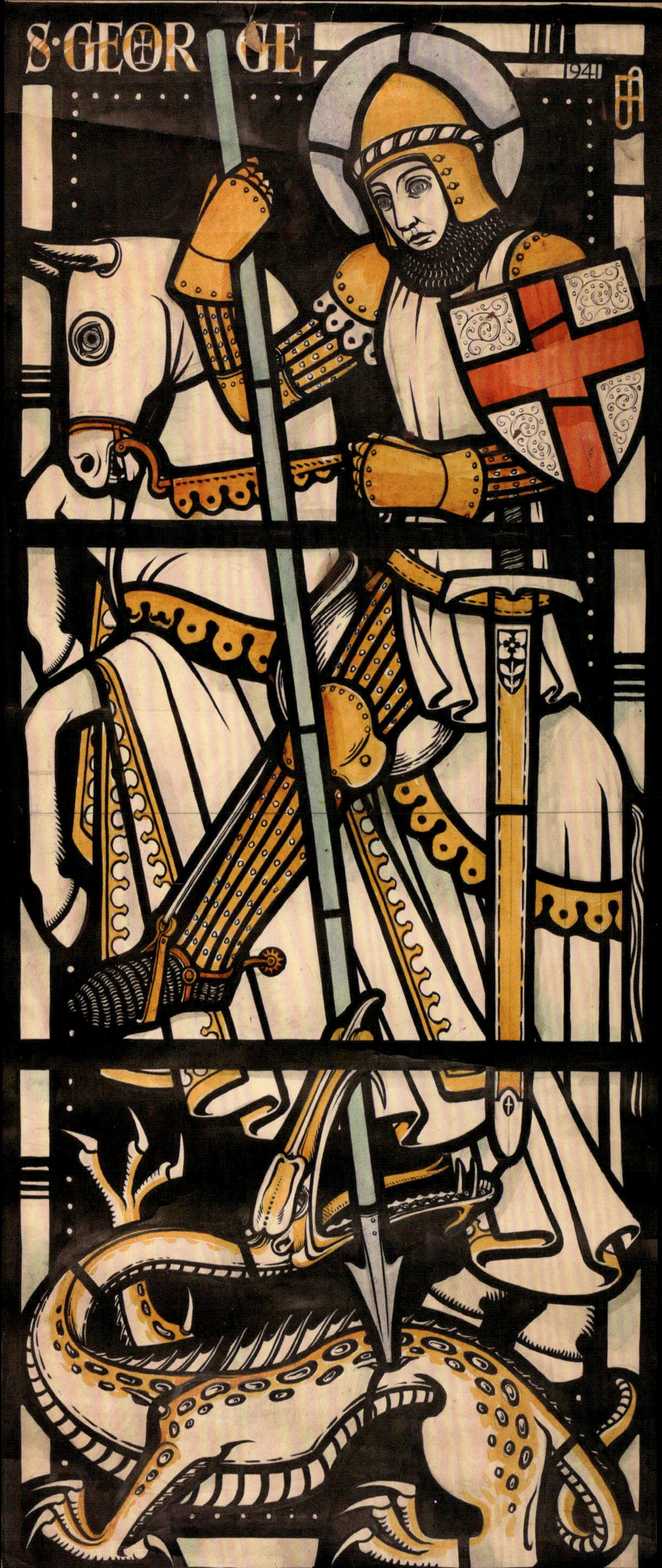
S·GEORGE
1941

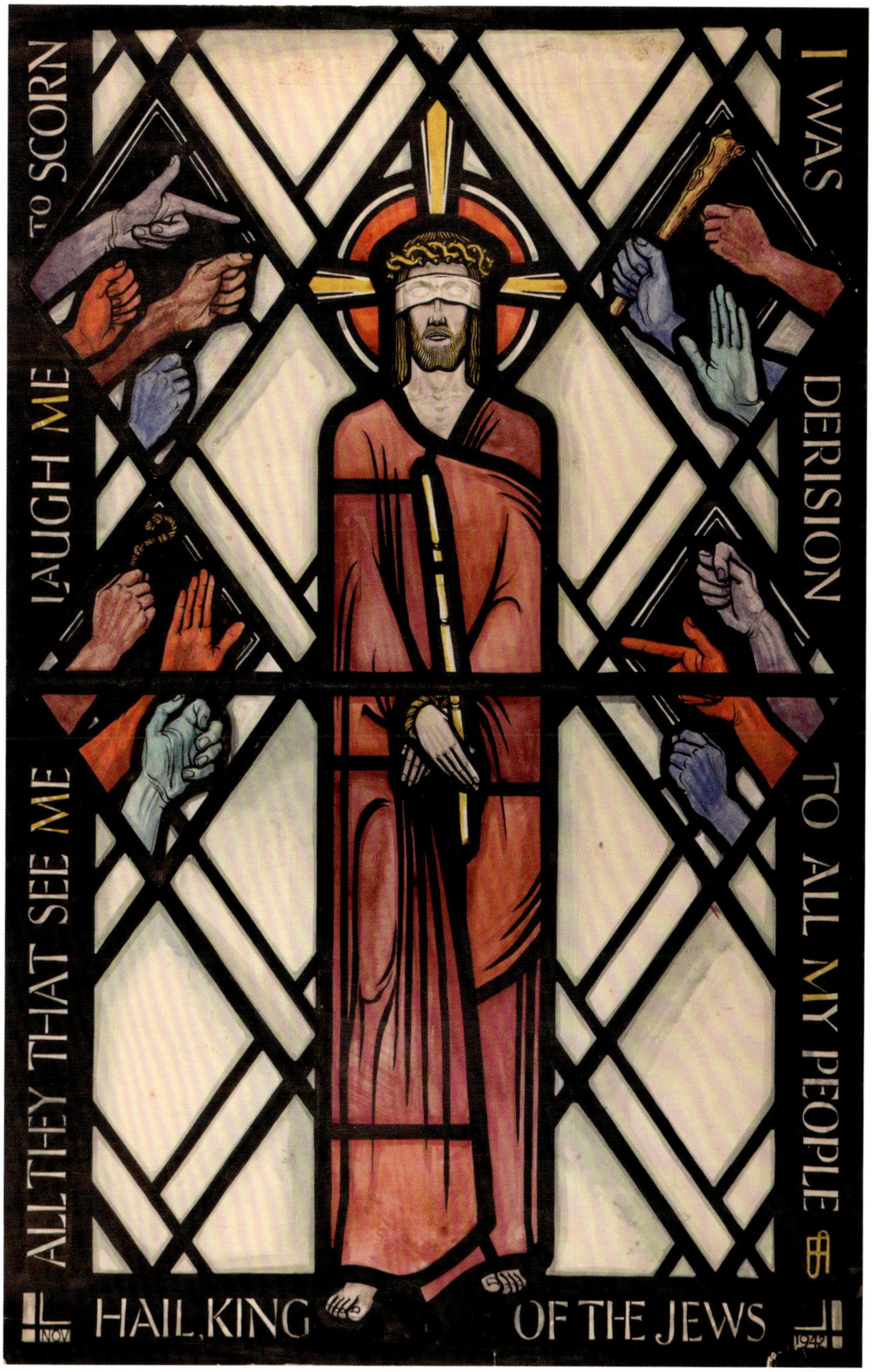

CAT. 134 – **Francis Spear** (1902-1979), *Christ Derided*, Nov 1942,
signed with monogram and dated, inscribed, 'All they that see me laugh me to scorn,
I was derision to all my people, Hail King of the Jews',
black ink, gouache and collage on paper, 28 x 18 ½ in. (71 x 47 cm).

CAT. 133 – **Francis Spear** (1902-1979), *St. George and the Dragon*, 1941,
signed with monogram and dated, inscribed 'S.George',
black ink, and gouache on paper, 42 x 18 ½ in. (104 x 47 cm).

AIR RAIDS

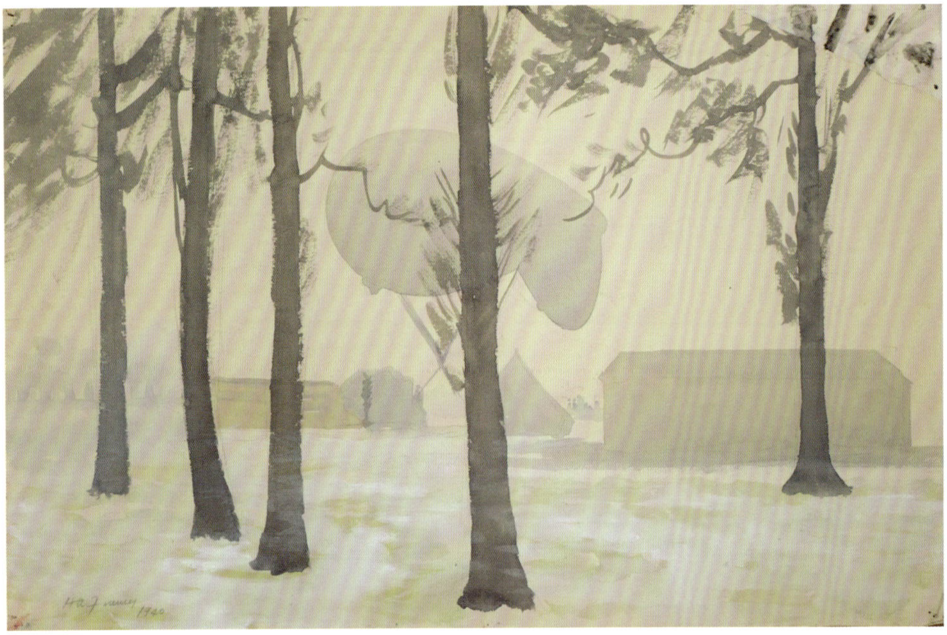

CAT. 135 – **Hubert Arthur Finney** (1905-1991), *Tethered barrage balloon,* 1940, signed and dated, wash on paper, 18 ½ x 12 in. (47 x 30.5 cm).

During the war Finney served in the Ambulance Crews of the Air Raid Precautions Service, later named Civil Defence, for a period of four years until in 1945 he contracted pleurisy.

Barrage balloons were deployed around London towards the end of WW1 and were developed as an effective anti-aircraft defence during the inter-war period. They were operated from winches either from static sites – concrete platforms – or from lorries. The convenience of the latter method was that they could be moved around to protect areas that unexpectedly came under attack, but it also allowed them to be positioned where the attacking force – the Luftwaffe – would not expect them.

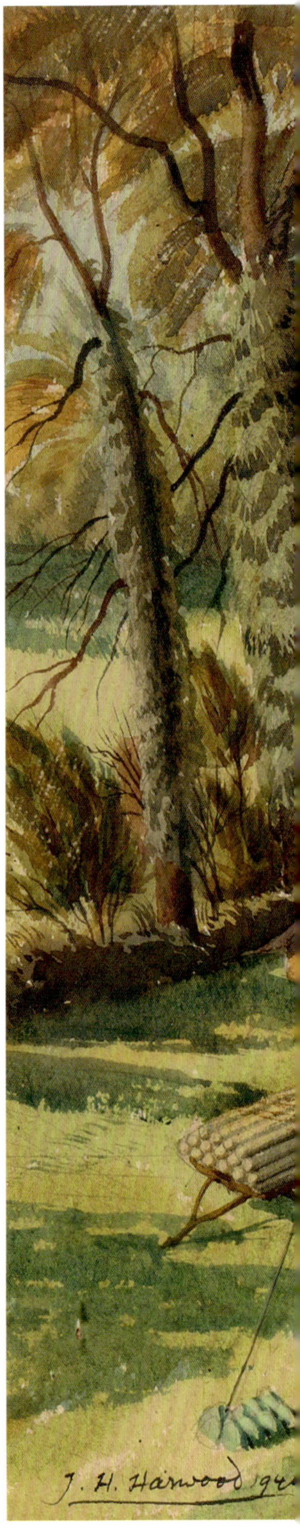

CAT. 136 – **James Hammond Harwood** (1904-1980), *Barrage Balloon,* 1940, signed and dated, watercolour on paper, 14 ¼ x 17 ¼ in. (36 x 44 cm).

Barrage balloons were mainly intended to prevent dive bomber attacks, forcing them to fly higher and into the effective range of anti-aircraft guns. However, they could do little to prevent high-level bombing raids which became the norm for the Luftwaffe. After war broke out the number of balloons multiplied with around 1,500 in place by the middle of 1940, a third of these over London. The RAF operated the balloons on a shift system, using cables and winches to raise and lower them as needed. This watercolour shows two men tethering a balloon with rows of sandbags.

Harwood was born in Lancashire and studied at the Royal College of Art, later teaching at a number of English art schools.

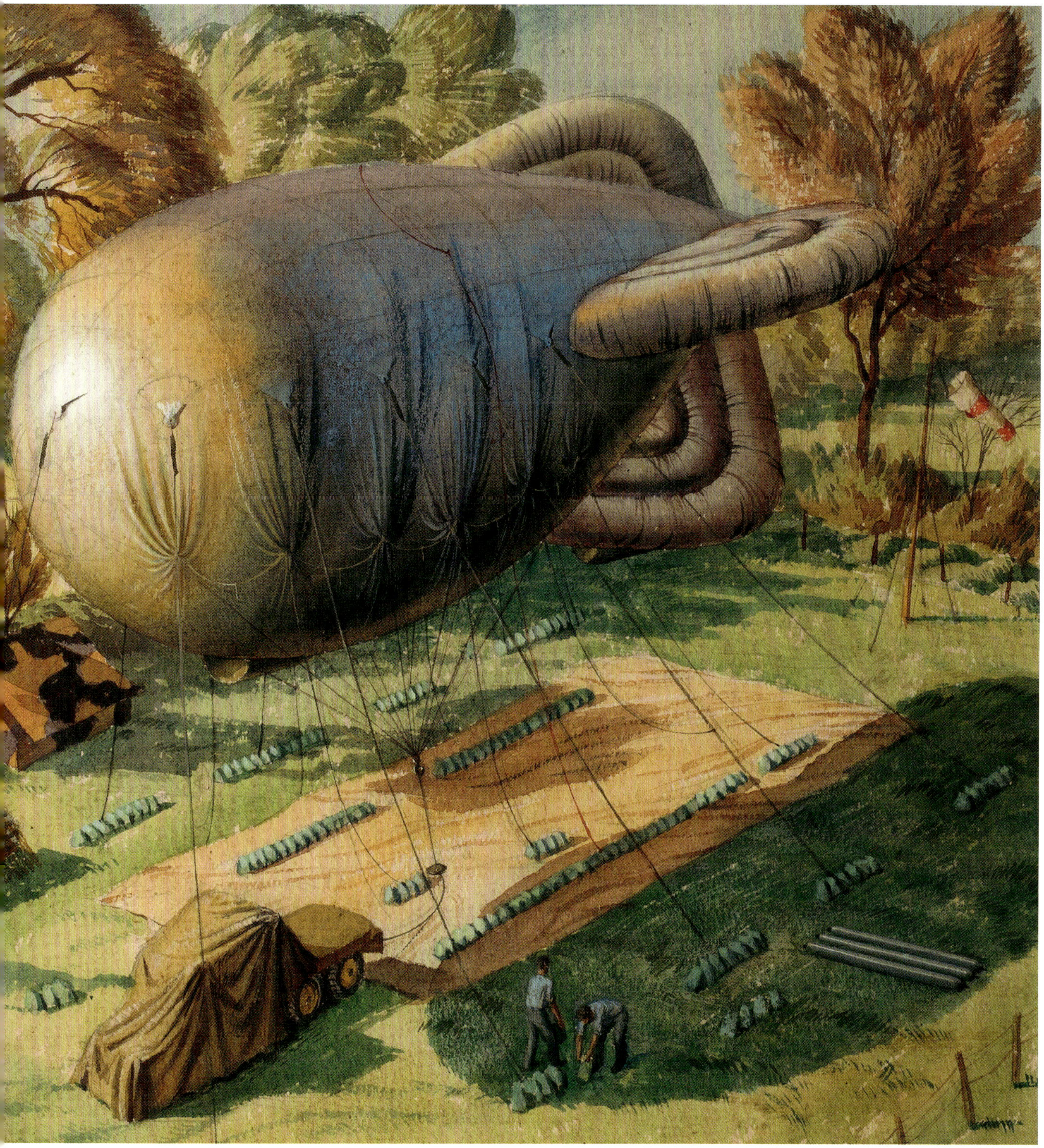

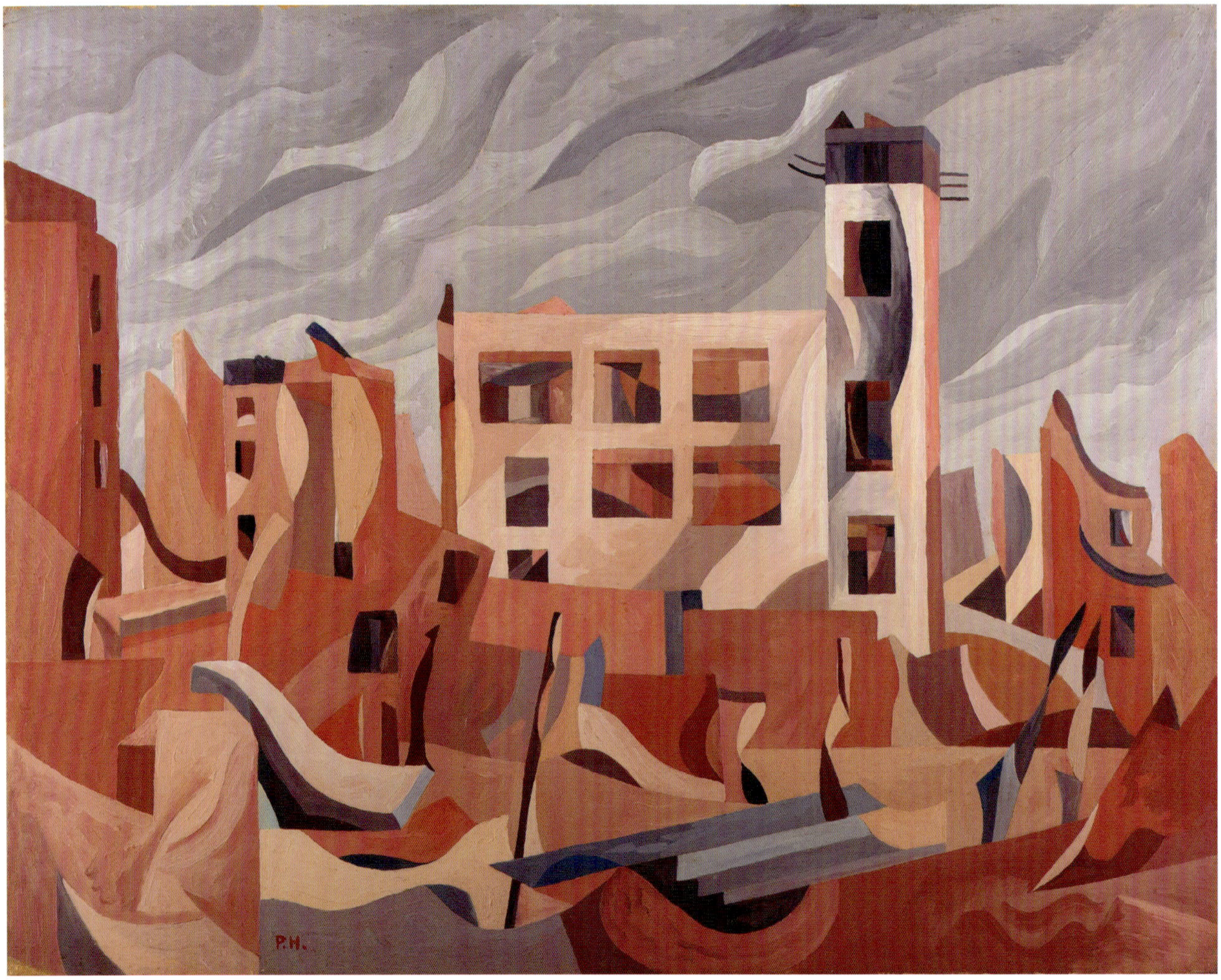

CAT. 137 – **Peter Humphrey** (1913-2001), *Coventry*, 1940,
oil on board, 21 x 27 in. (53.3 x 68.5 cm).

Peter Humphrey was a founding member of the Coventry Art Circle along with Harry Norman. CAC had links with Surrealist painters in Birmingham, and had high-level art critics among their members and developed styles based on cubism, abstraction and other modern movements.

A review in the *Birmingham Post* (7 March 1938) described CAC as follows '…the organisation serves as a rallying point for a number of people…who feel an urge towards some sort of artistic expression… …a prolific contributor, P. Humphries [sic]…the artist has been concerned to minimise the solid appearance of things and insist upon a free interpretation of their rhythmic unity. Art of this kind may tend to become highly mannered, but Mr. Humphries has so much skill and so many styles at his command that monotony is wholly absent from his work.'

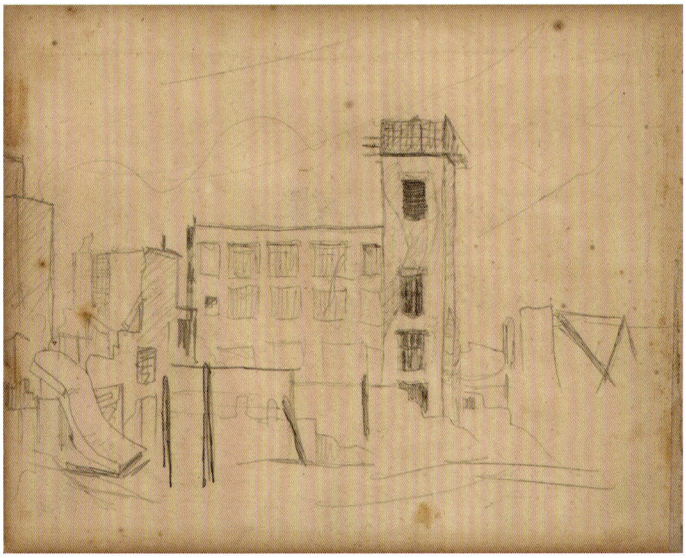

CAT. 138 – Study for *Coventry*, 1940,
pencil on paper, 7 x 8 ¾ in (17.8 x 22.3 cm).

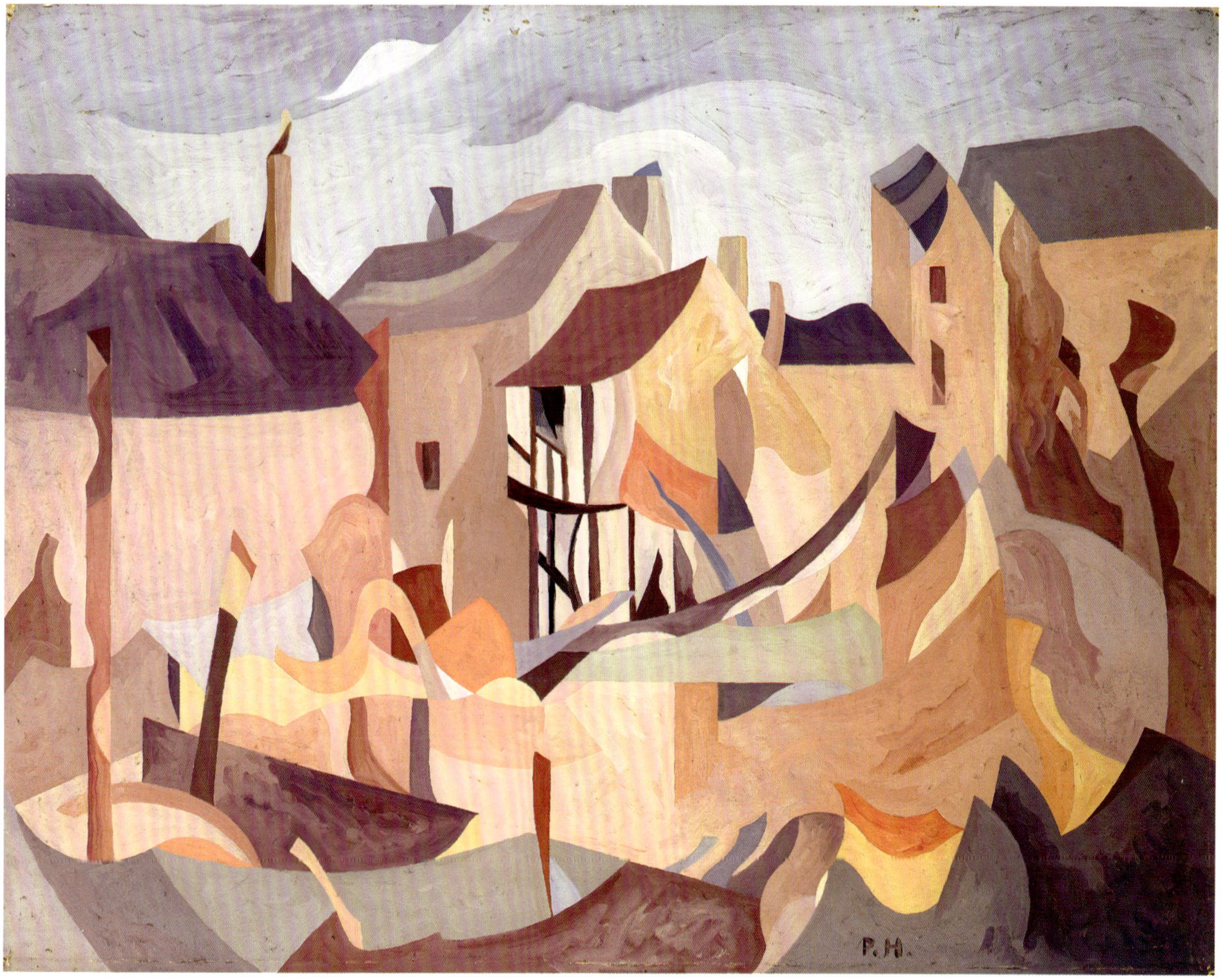

CAT. 139 – **Peter Humphrey** (1913-2001), *Bomb damaged houses, Coventry*, c.1942, signed with initials, oil on board, 21 x 27 in. (53.3 x 68.5 cm).

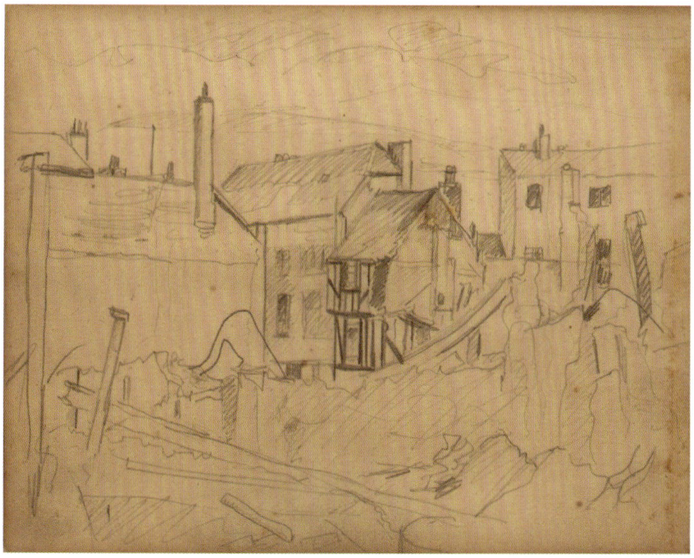

CAT. 140 – Study for *Bomb damaged houses, Coventry*, c.1942, pencil on paper, 7 x 8 ¾ in (17.8 x 22.3 cm).

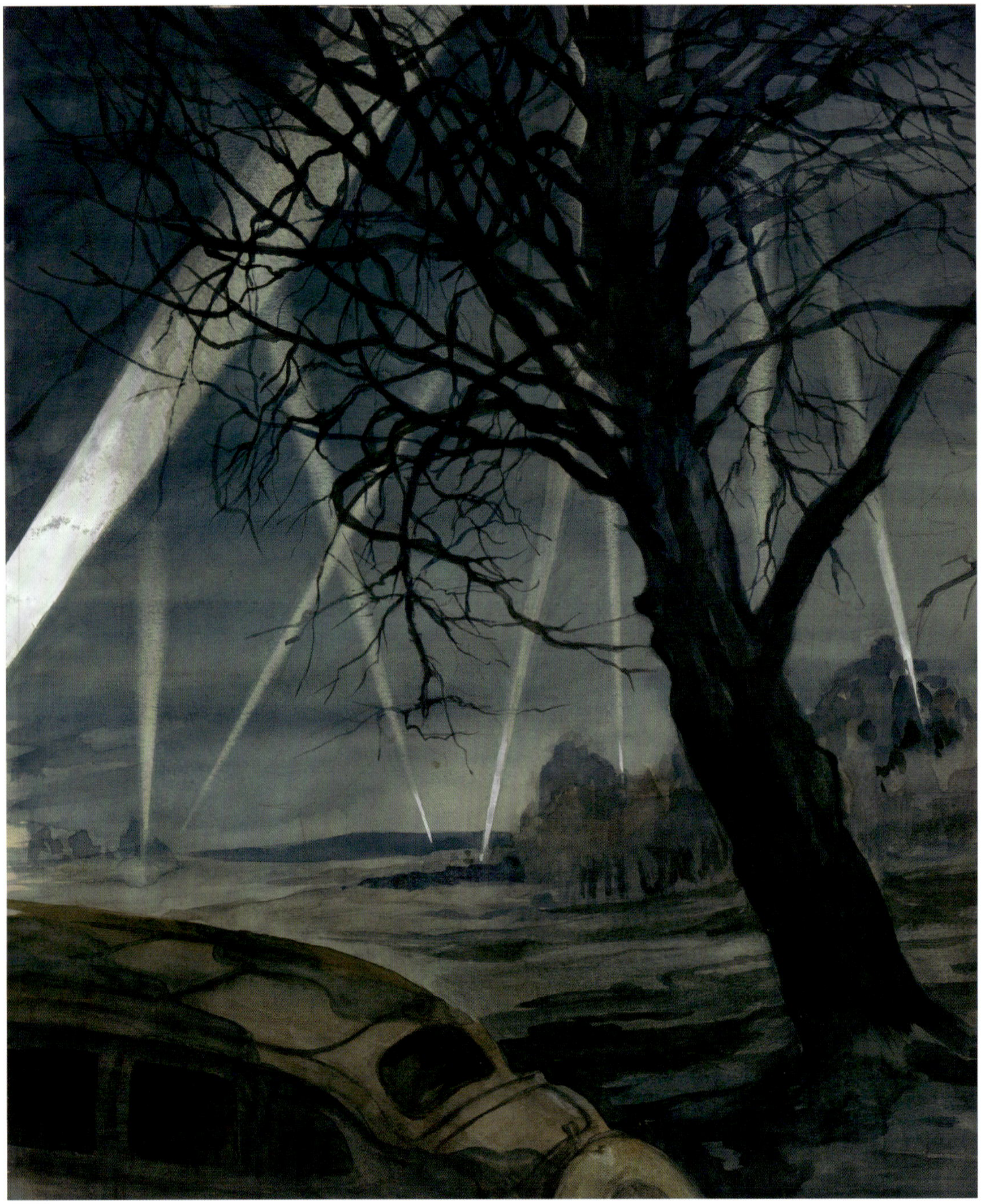

CAT. 141 – **Louis Keene** (1888-1972), *Alert near Aldershot during the Battle of Britain*, 1940, signed and dated, title on the backboard,
watercolour, india ink, pencil, and chalk on paper, 18 x 14 in. (46 x 35.5 cm.).
Provenance: The Artists daughter, Canada.

CAT. 142 – **Cliff Rowe** (1904-1989), *Parachute Flares*, c.1941
oil on canvas, 19 ¾ x 13 in. (50 x 33 cm.)

This composition shows the Luftwaffe returning to bomb a town that has clearly already suffered extensive damage. Parachute flares have been dropped in an effort to illuminate the target for the bombers while anti-aircraft fire from British batteries peppers the sky with red shell bursts.

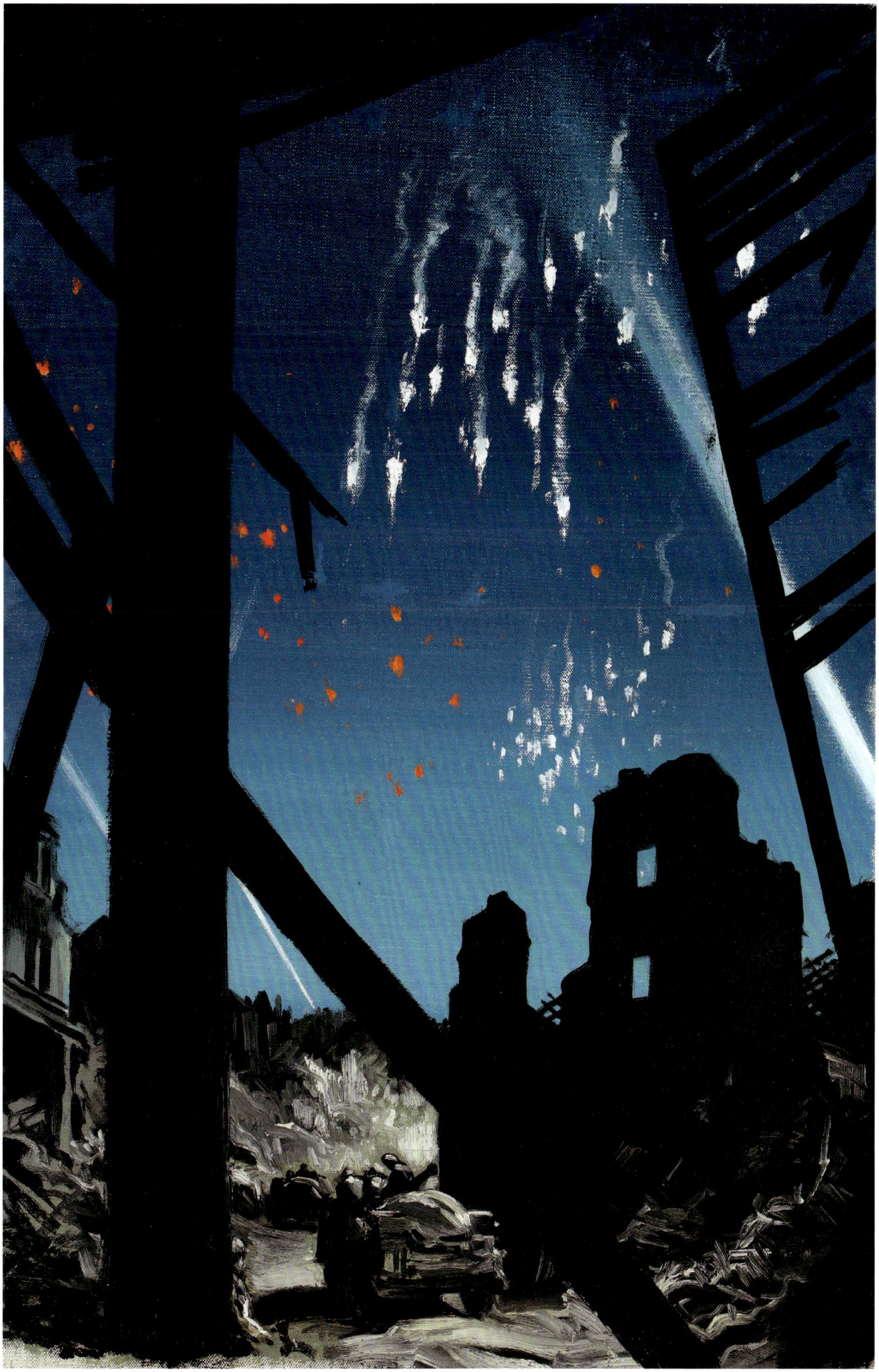

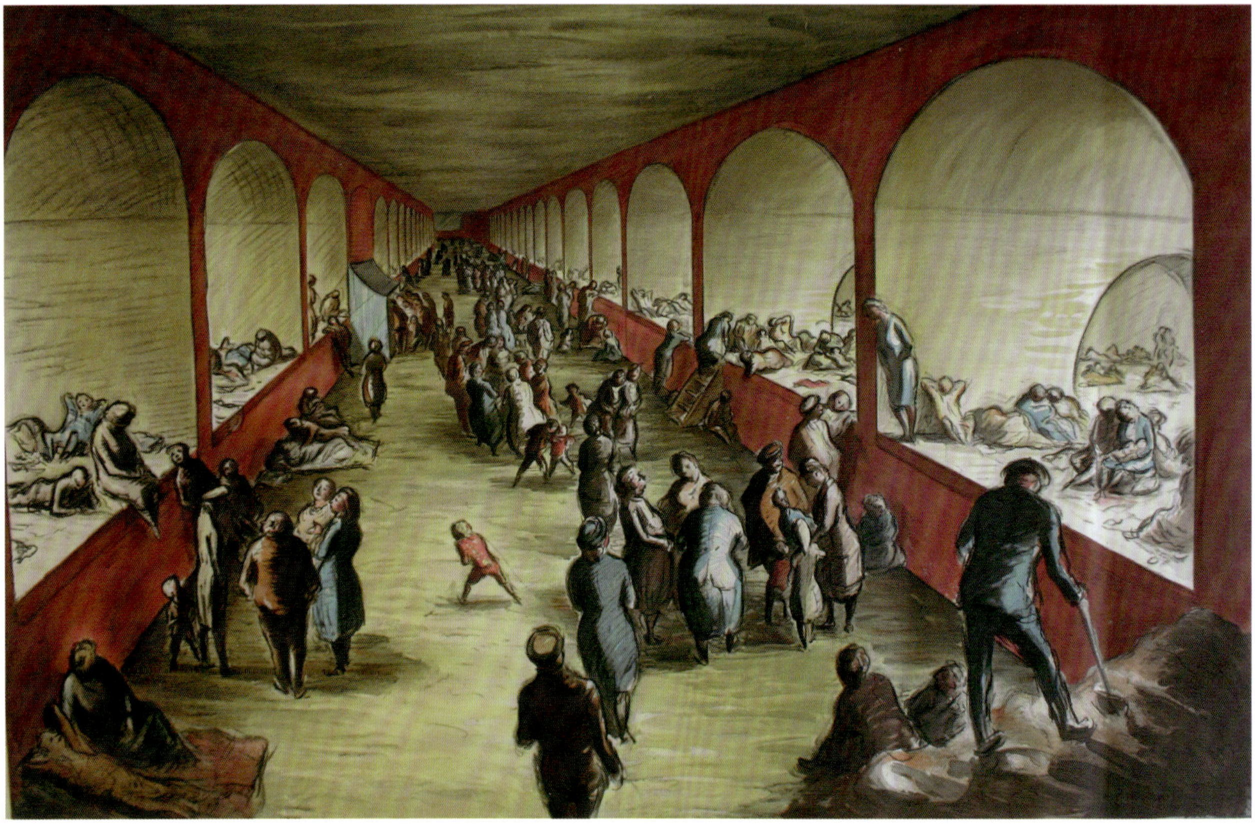

CAT. 143 – **Edward Ardizzone** (1900-1979), *Shelter Scene*, 1941,
colour lithograph, 25 ¾ x 39 in. (65.5 x 99 cm).
Published by the National Gallery, 1941, printed by The Baynard Press on machine glaze wartime paper.

44,000 people had been killed in Britain by the summer of 1941 – more than had at that point been killed in combat on the front line. This shows the Tilbury shelter, (a subject also drawn by Henry Moore) under the railway arches at Stepney, which was estimated to offer protection to as many as 16,000 people on some nights during the Blitz. Ardizonne was appointed as an Official War Artist a year after the start of the war – his commission lasted until September 1945. His work during this period concentrated on the human element of the conflict, depicting soldiers and civilians going about their daily routines with a predominantly cheery air. This contrasts with Henry Moore's altogether grimmer depiction of the same subject. Moore noted in an *aide-mémoire* after visiting Tilbury shelter: 'dramatic, dismal lit, masses of reclining figures fading to a perspective point.... chaotic foreground. Dark wet settings.'

CAT. 144 – **Charles Mahoney** (1903-1968), *Ambleside, View from the Library Roof*, c.1942
oil on canvas, 18 x 14 in. (45.7 x 35.6 cm).
Provenance: The Artist's Daughter; The Fine Art Society; Private collection.
Exhibited: *The Artist as Evacuee, The Royal College of Art in the Lake District, 1940-45*,
Dove Cottage and the Wordsworth Museum, Grasmere 1987, (29)

In 1940 the Royal College of Art was evacuated to Ambleside. Mahoney and Percy Horton were amongst the male staff. The students were housed in two hotels, men at the Queens and women at the Salutation. Mahoney was resident master in charge at the men's hostel. While at Ambleside, Mahoney became engaged to Dorothy Bishop, a calligraphy tutor from the Design School of the RCA. They were married in September 1941. This composition demonstrates Mahoney's fondness for Victorian Gothic buildings.

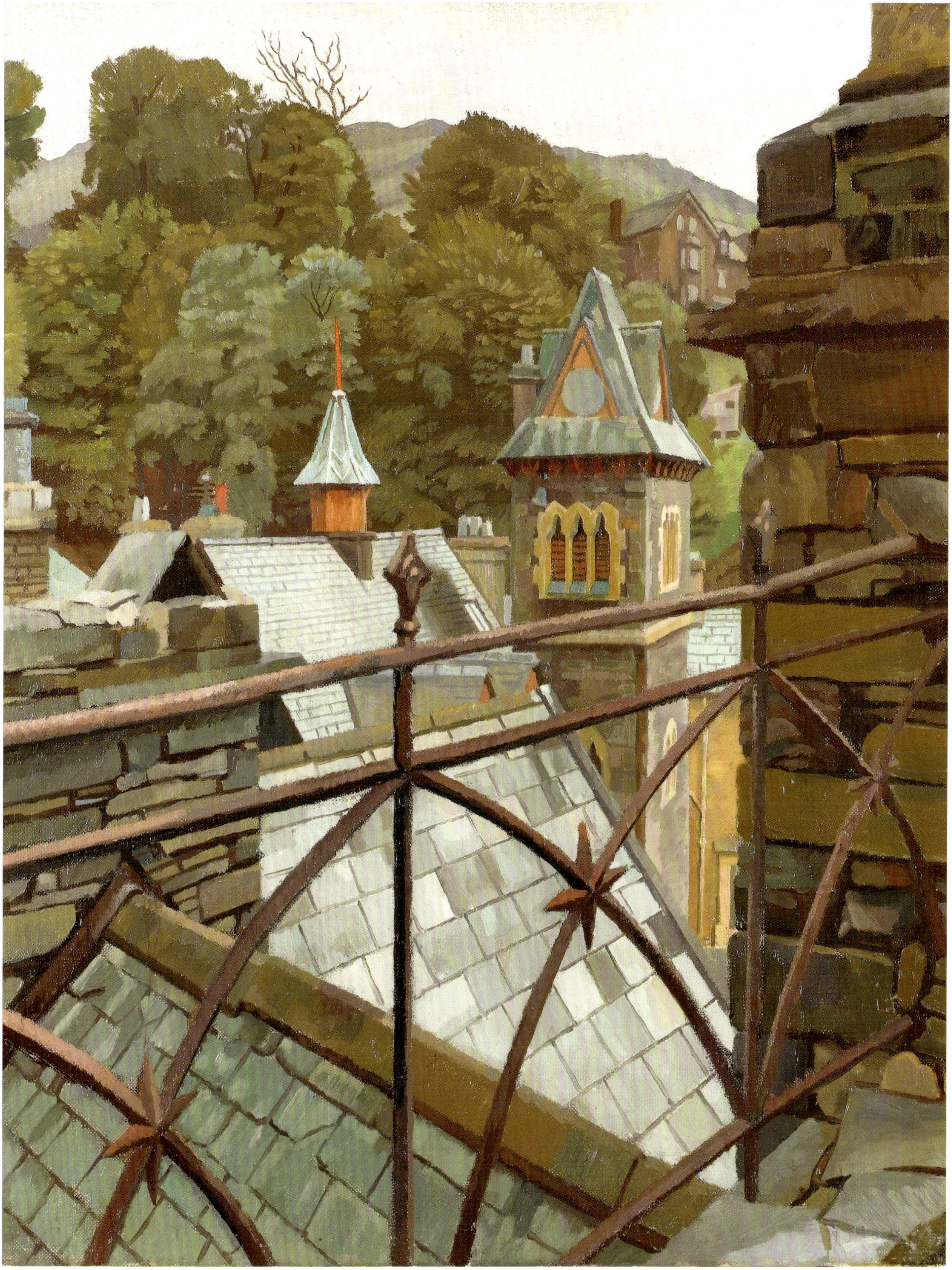

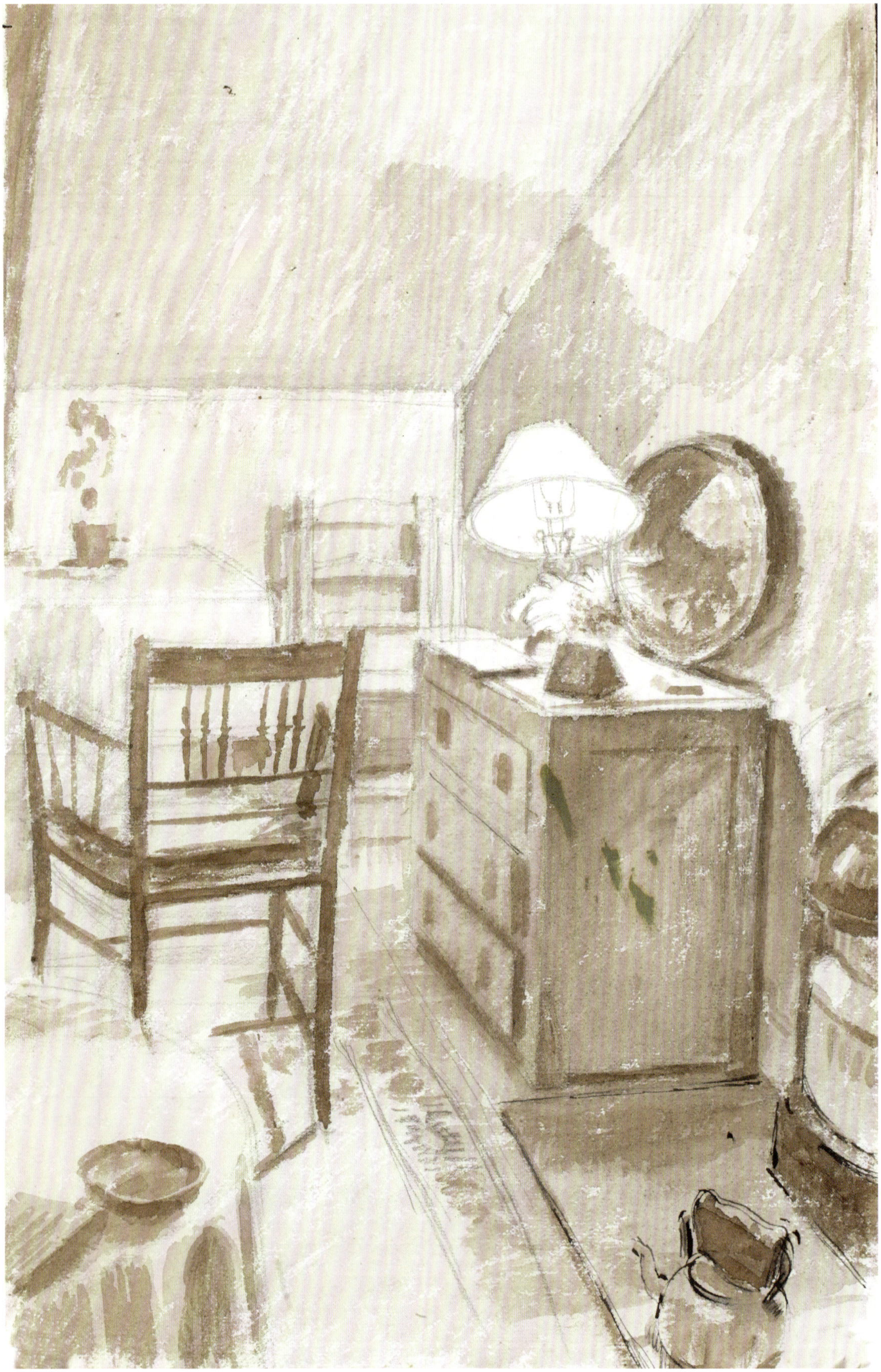

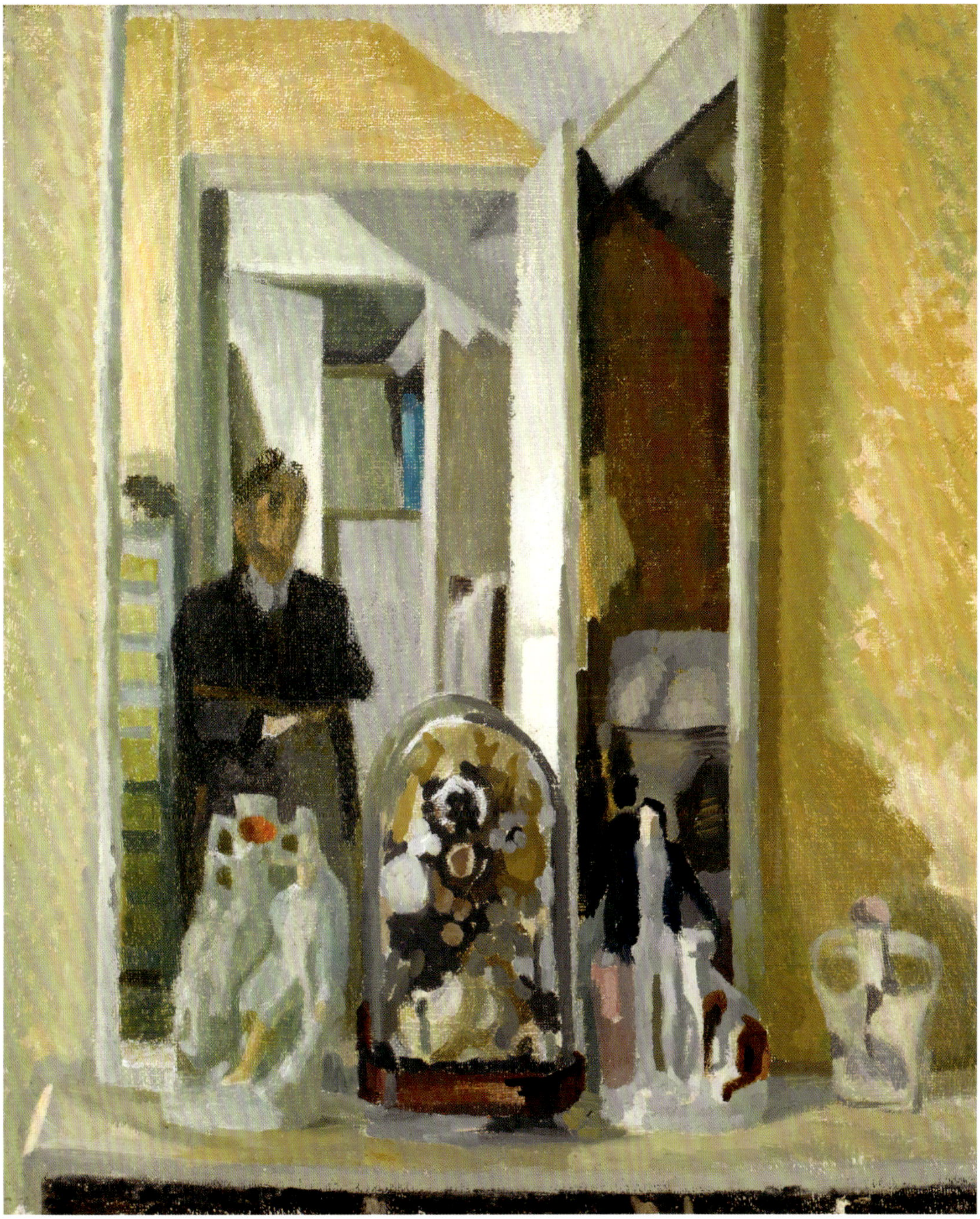

CAT. 146 – **Charles Mahoney** (1903-1968), *Self-portrait, Ambleside,* 1941,
oil on canvas, 24 ¼ x 20 ¼ in. (61.3 X 51.2 cm).
Provenance: the Artist's Estate.

Mahoney married Dorothy Bishop in September 1941. The ornaments on the mantelpiece are souvenirs from the newlyweds' honeymoon in Edinburgh.

CAT. 145 – **Charles Mahoney** (1903-1968), *Digs at Ambleside*, c.1940,
watercolour over pencil with highlights in pen and ink on paper, 18 ½ x 11 ¾ in. (47 x 30 cm).
Provenance: the Artist's Estate.

After their marriage Charles and Dorothy Mahoney moved into lodgings. This drawing is almost certainly of an attic room at Loughrigg Brow where they set up their first home.

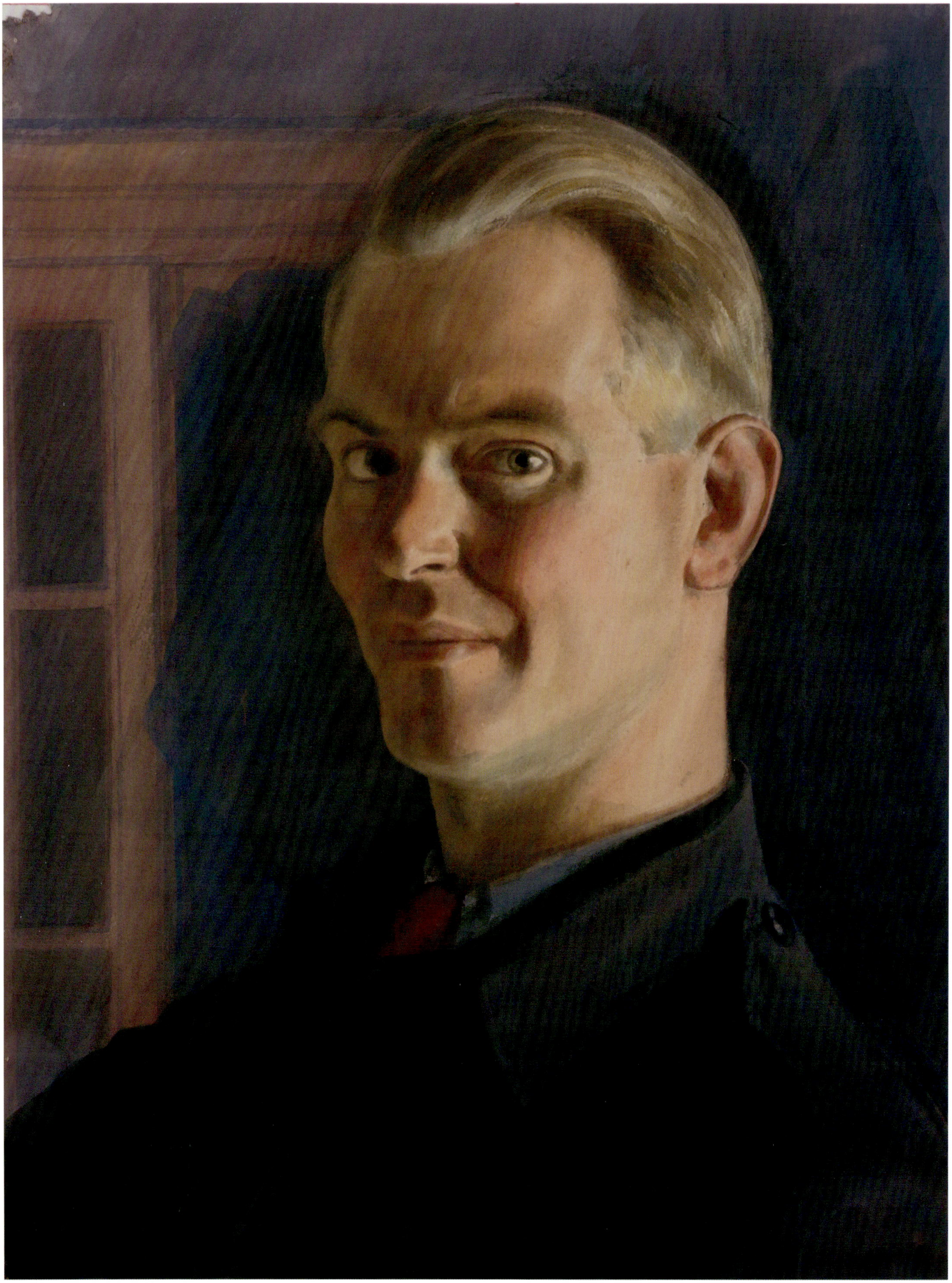

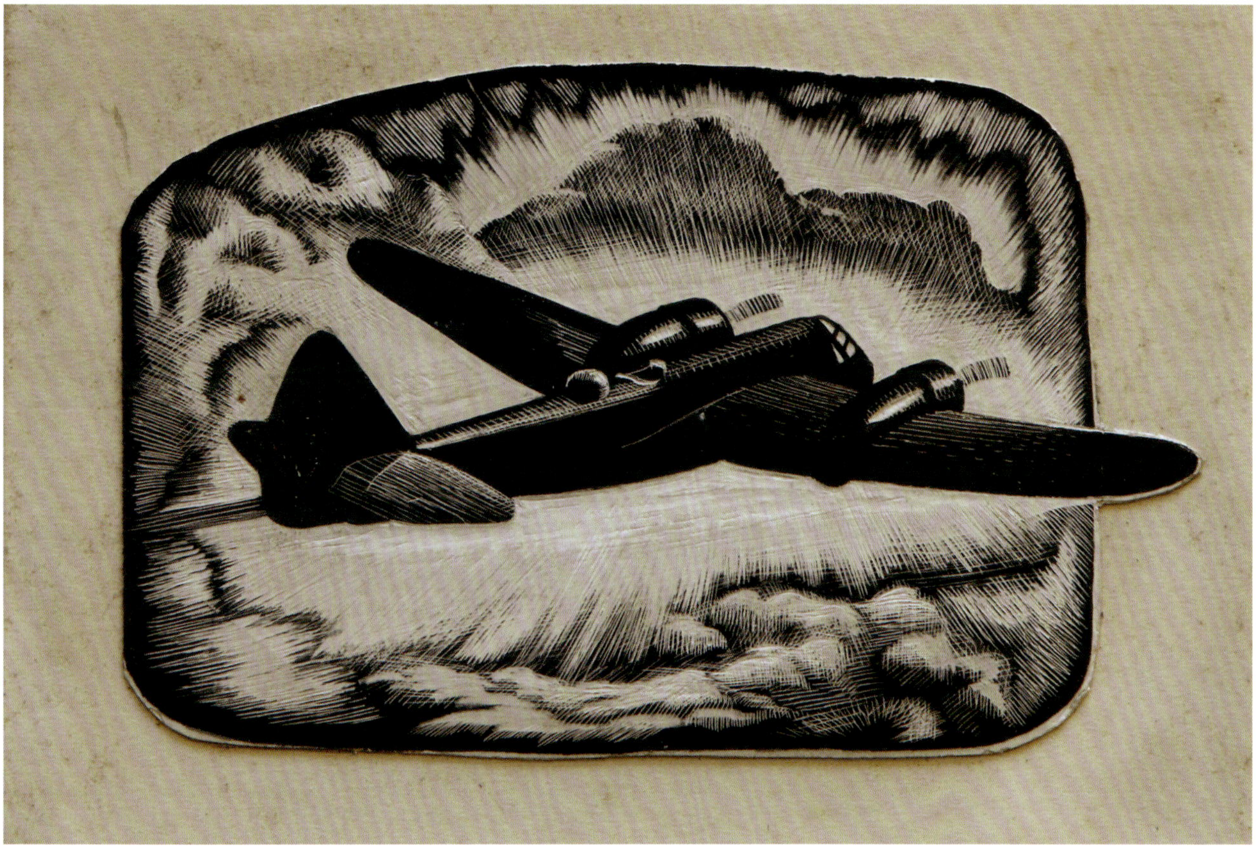

CAT. 148 * – **Keith Henderson** (1883-1982), Bristol Blenheim Mark I: Illustrations for Cecil Lewis's "Sagittarius Rising", c.1940, pen and ink on cut-out gessoed card, each 6 × 3 in. (16.5 × 9 cm.) irregular,
Provenance: Eric Slack; Private Collection.

CAT. 147 – **Hubert Arthur Finney** (1905-1991), *Self portrait*, 1945,
pastel on paper, 17 ½ x 14 ¼ in. (45 x 36 cm).
Provenance: The Artist's Family.

In this self-portrait Finney wears a red tie – suggesting that it dates to 1945 as he was convalescing. (Red ties had been used since WW1 to show that the wearer was ill or wounded and that he was a Serviceman). In his unpublished autobiography Finney records that towards the end of the war: 'My health was beginning to show signs of breaking and I was sent to a Civil Defence Convalescent house after a serious bronchial cold. I never ceased to draw and paint and I presented one painting to the Convalescent Home before I left. I also painted a ceiling in a municipal theatre and the backstage in the depot of Kinston House and held a drawing class one evening a week for the Ambulance and Rescue Service Personnel.' In addition to the red tie hospital clothing consisted of a dark blue serge military type suit, grey or greyish-blue shirt.

Describing his activities in the Civil Defence, Finney wrote: 'My work consisted of 24 hours on duty and 24 hours off and we were eventually organised into squads of five men including a driver to each rescue car. There was a lot of training of first aid and stretcher bearing and for the first year during the so-called phoney war conditions were primitive. This life was a new world to me because I came in contact with every type of human being, from a young lad who had been to Wellington College, Berkshire, to thieves and near-criminal types and men from every walk of life. This new environment made me realise that if there were not millions of people who work at humble occupations what we call civilisation would not function. Among all these different types of human beings I never saw any violence between them and strangely enough after a year or two I felt they had an unspoken regard for someone who possessed my gift because I made many portrait drawings of them on condition that they sat for me twice and I sold the first one which usually was the best for five shillings.'

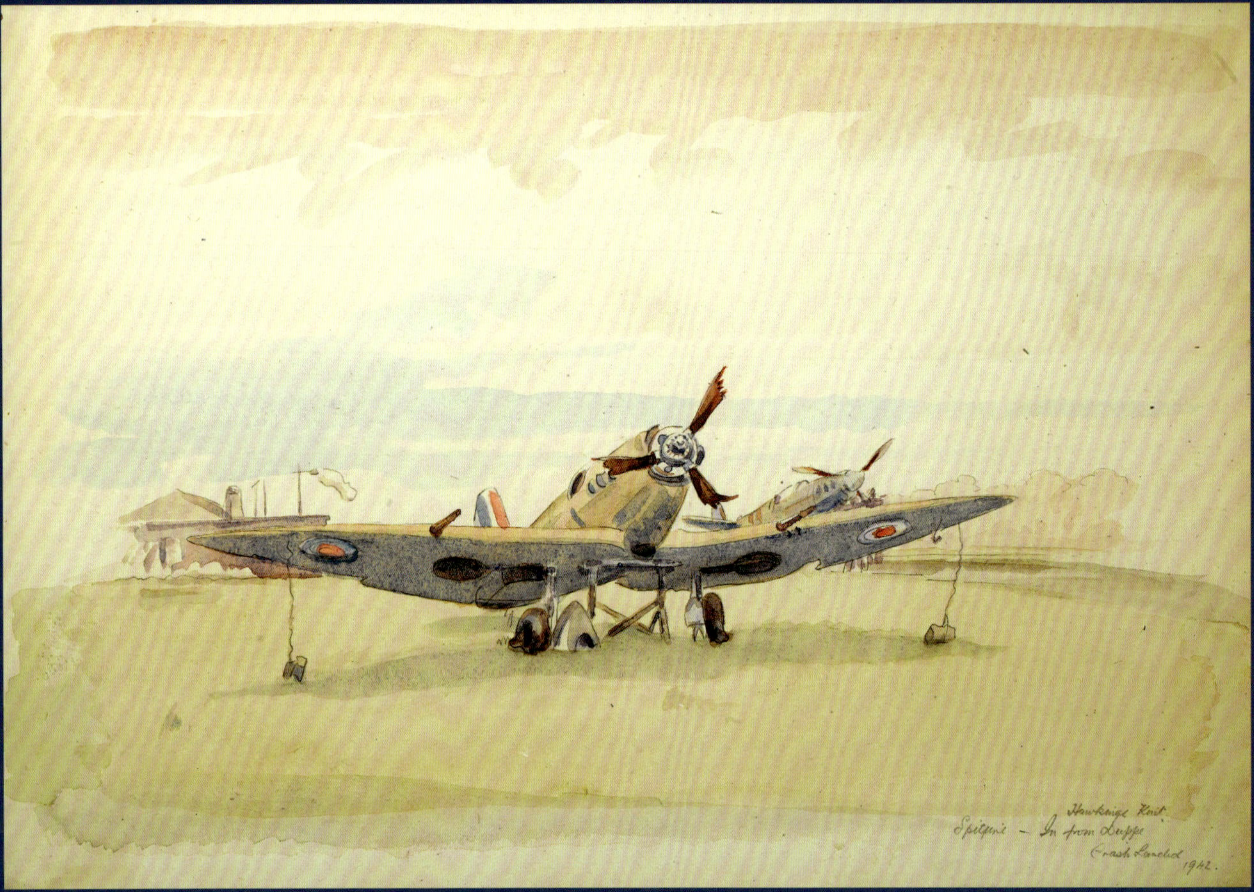

CAT. 149 – **Henry C. O Donnell** (1900-1992), Spitfire, in from Dieppe, Crash Landed 1942, inscribed with 'Hawkinge Kent, Spitfire, in from Dieppe, Crash Landed 1942', watercolour on paper, 13 ¼ x 16 ¾ in. (33 x 42.5 cm).

Looking a little battered but eager to get back to the fight, these Spitfires await the skilled attention of RAF mechanics. Wherever possible aeroplanes were repaired rather than being 'Struck Off'.

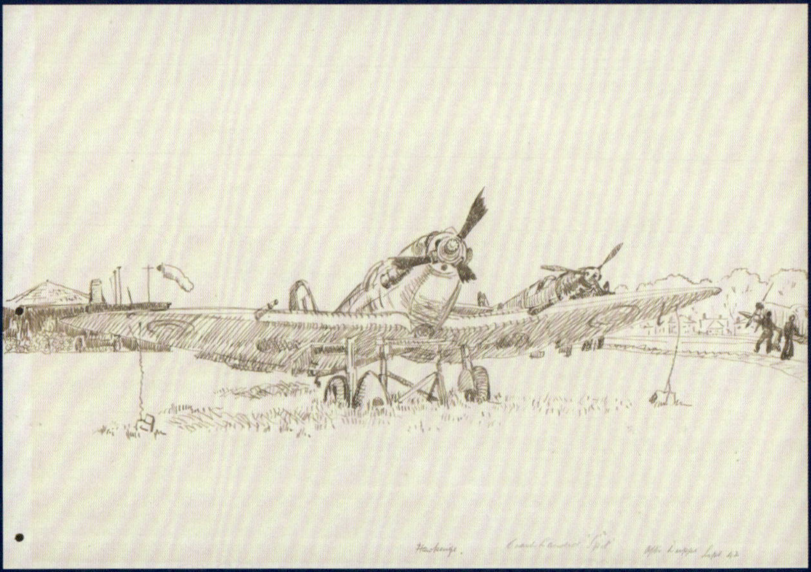

CAT. 150 – Crashed-landed Spit, 1942,
inscribed and dated,
ink on paper,
13 ¼ x 16 ¾ in. (33 x 42.5 cm.)
Exhibited : Retrospective Exhibition Gorry Gallery, Dublin, 22nd April - 5th May 1994.

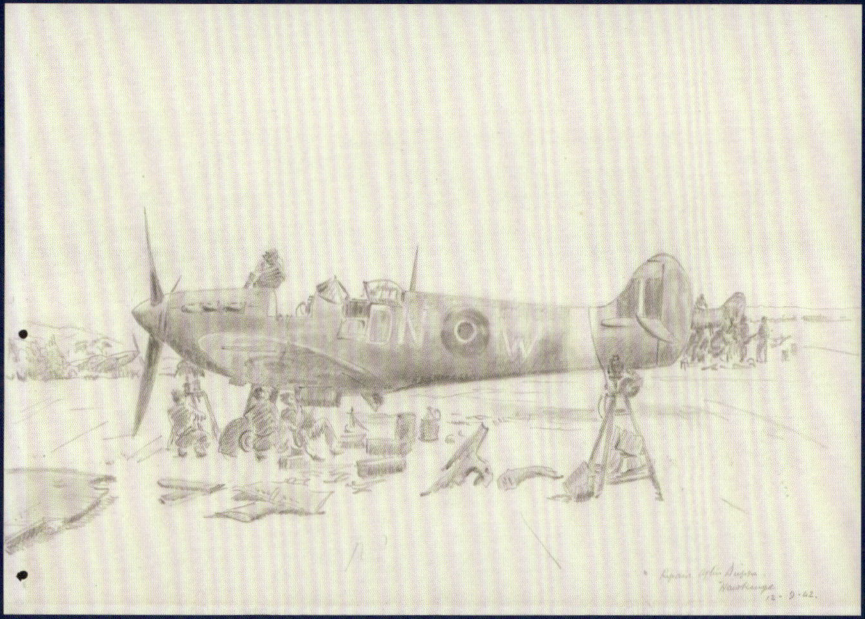

CAT. 151 – *Spitfire being repaired after Dieppe raids,* 1942, inscribed and dated 12-09-42, pencil on paper, 13 ¼ x 16 ¾ in. (33 x 42.5 cm)
Exhibited : Retrospective Exhibition Gorry Gallery, Dublin, 22nd April - 5th May 1994

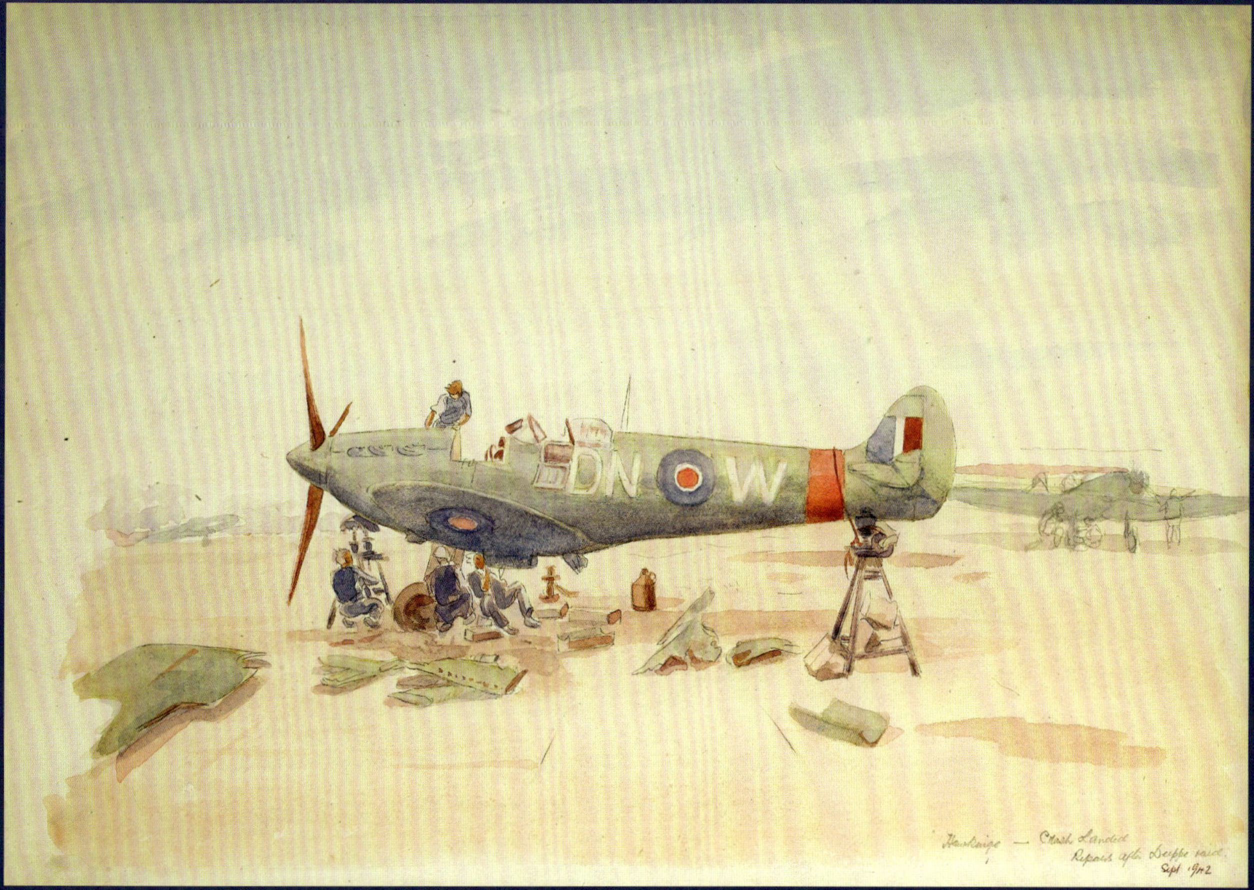

CAT. 152 – **Henry C. O Donnell** (1900-1992), *Crash Landed, repairs after Dieppe Raid,* sept 1942, inscribed with title, watercolour on paper, 13 ¼ x 16 ¾ in. (33 x 42.5 cm).

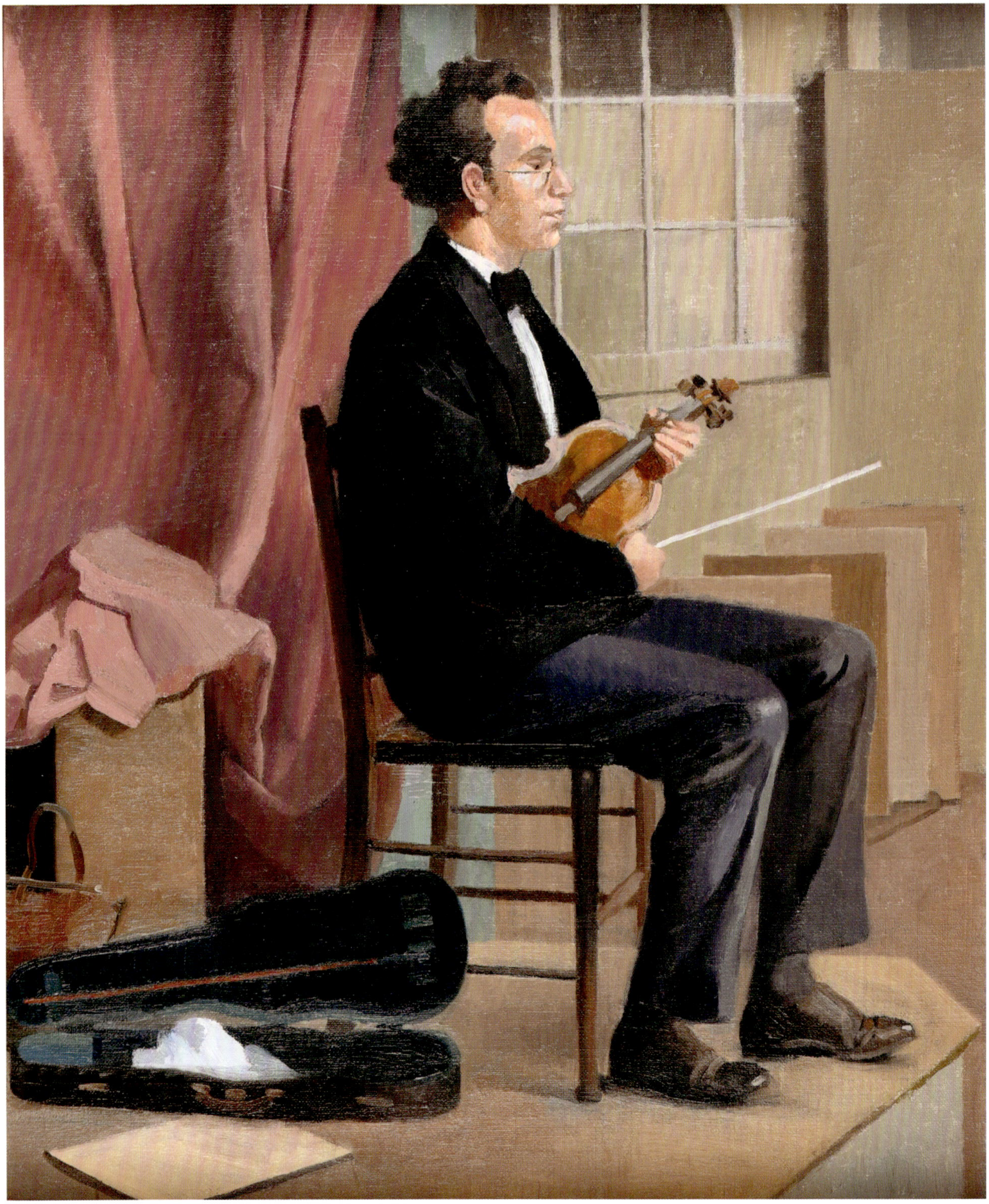

CAT. 153 – **Phoebe Peto Dickinson** (1917-1978), *Portrait of a Jewish refugee*, c.1939, oil on canvas, 24 ¼ x 20 ¼ in. (61.5 x 51.5 cm).

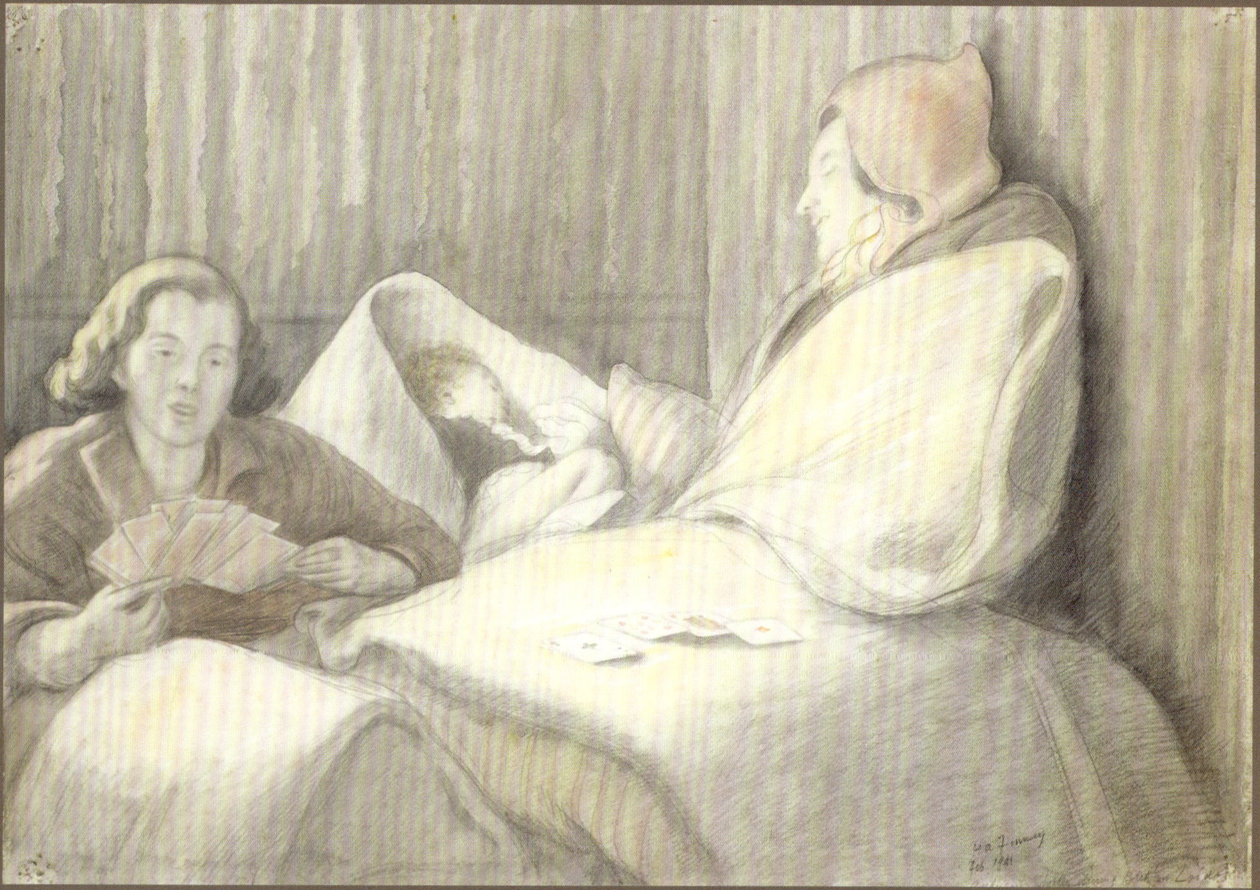

CAT. 154 – **Hubert Arthur Finney** (1905-1991), *Anderson Shelter during Blitz on London at Night, Feb. 1941*,
signed, dated and inscribed with title,
watercolour and pencil on paper, 15 ½ x 22 ½ in. (39.5 x 57 cm).

In his unpublished autobiography Finney wrote:
'During the early part of the Battle of Britain, I would go down to an Anderson Shelter in the garden of the house, in which I rented a room and the tenant above me with two young children also shared the shelter through the long night while the German planes did what they liked in the sky above because except for barrage balloons and a little aircraft fire we had no defences in the beginning of the second world war.'

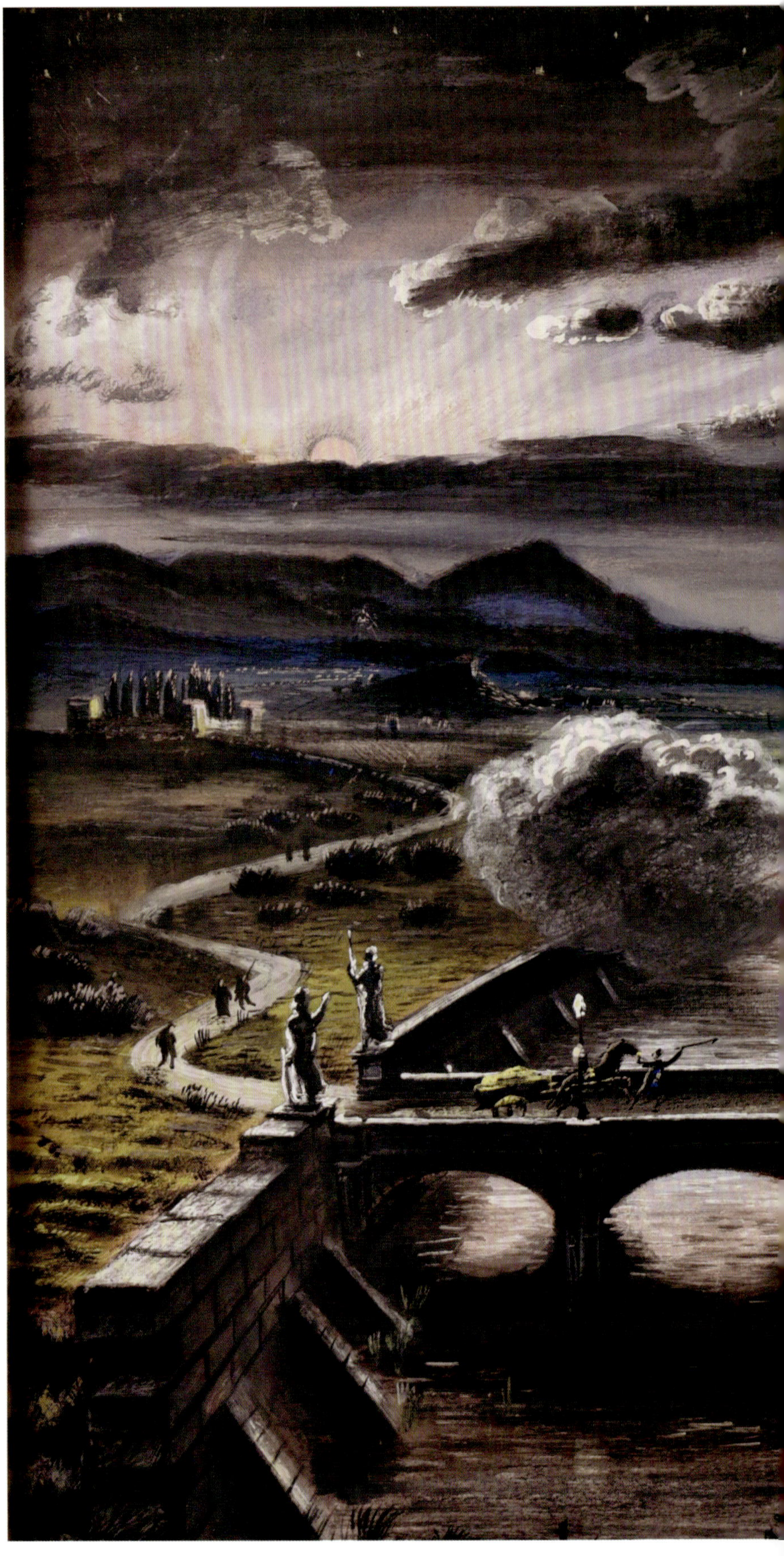

CAT. 155 – **Alan Sorrell** (1904-1974),
The Evening Signal. 1940,
signed and dated,
gouache on paper, 23 ¼ x 24 ¾ in. (59 x 63 cm).
Provenance: Private collection since 2001.

The Signal was painted just before Sorrell joined the R.A.F, following the closure of the Royal College of Art, and an unsuccessful application to be a war artist. The painting conveys a deeply melancholic mood which possibly relates in part to the failure of Sorrell's marriage at this time.

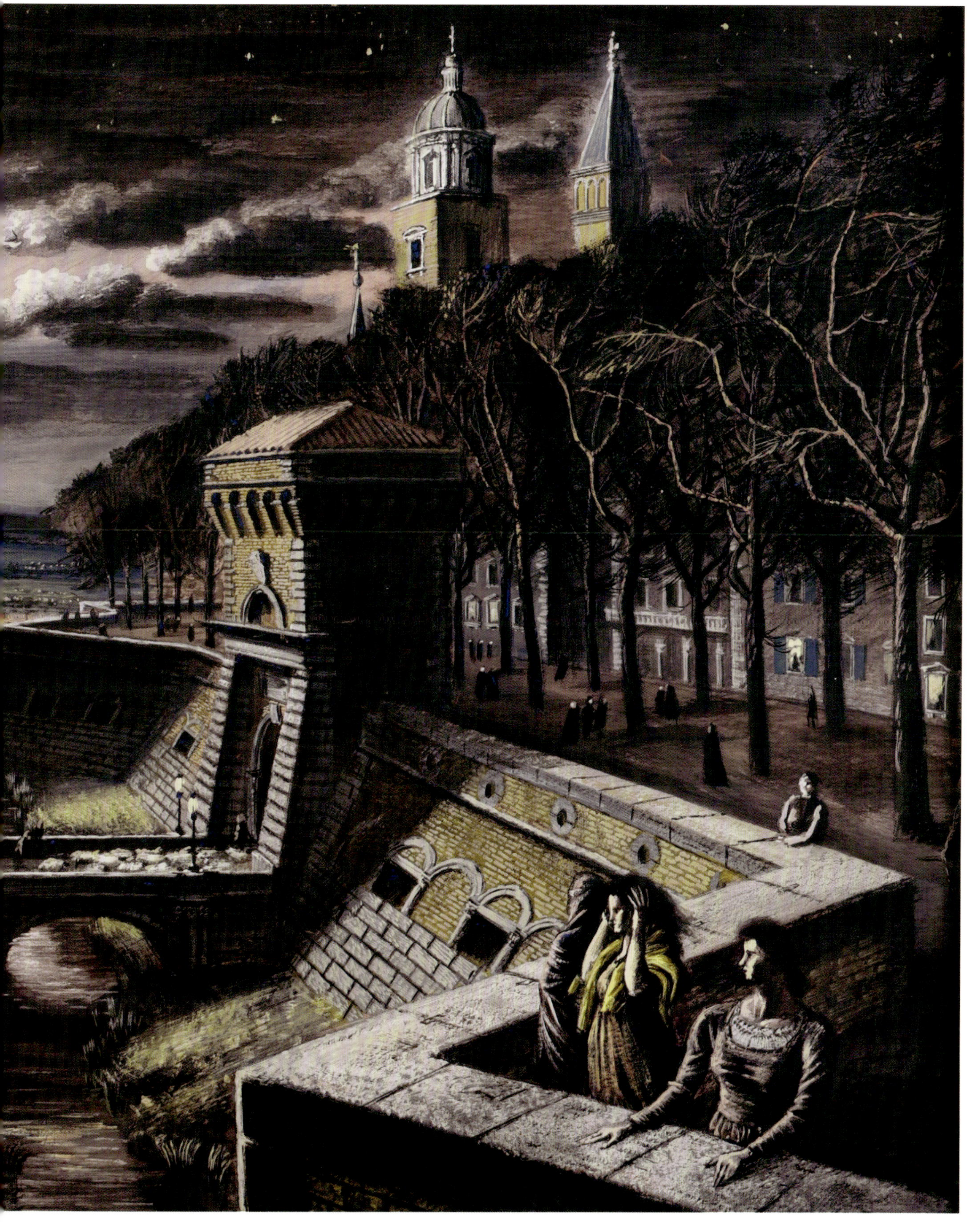

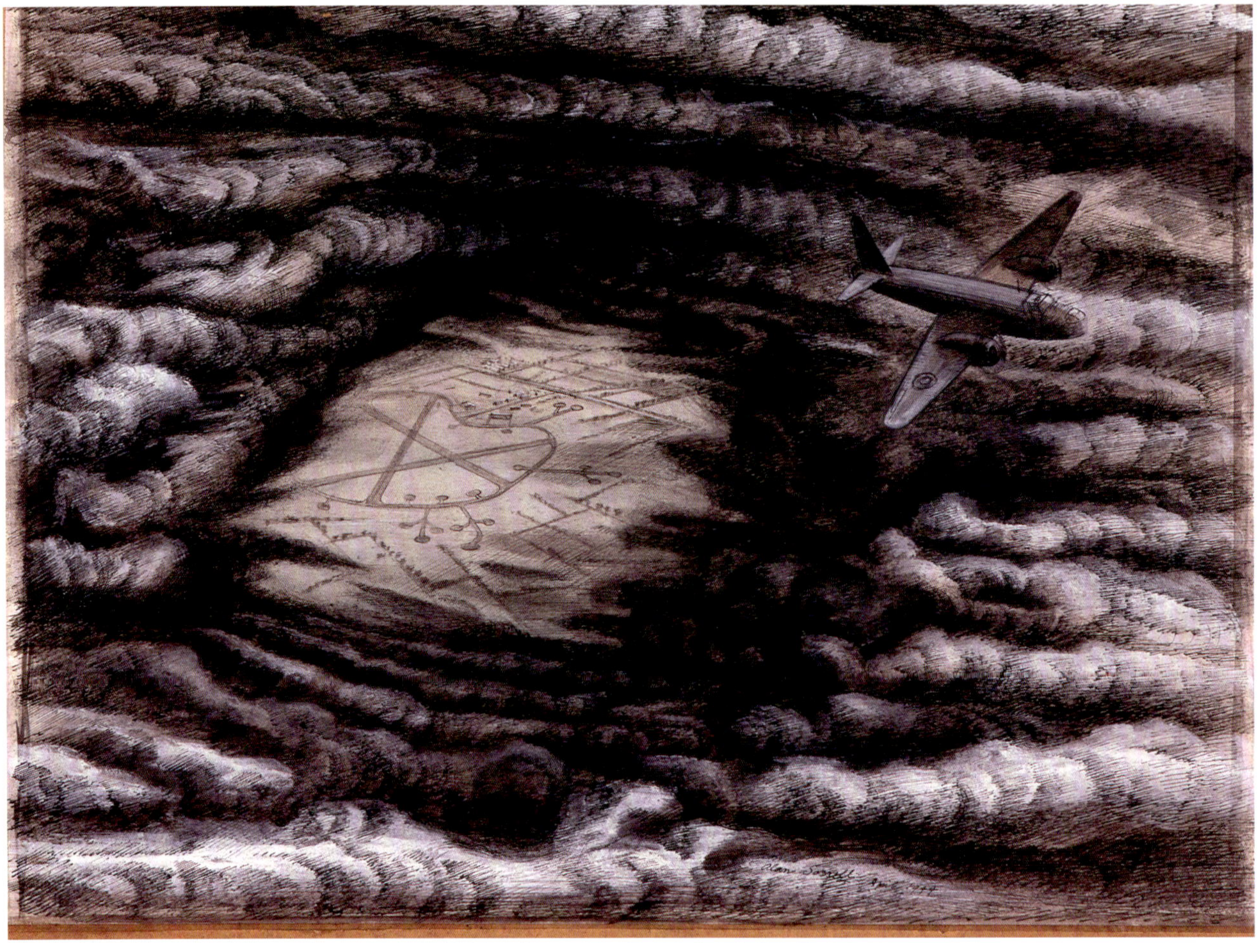

CAT. 156* – **Alan Sorrell** (1904-1974), *A Cavern in the Clouds*, 1944, signed and dated, titled on the reverse, gouache and pen and ink, 11 ½ x 15 ¾ in. (29.4 x 39.8 cm).
Provenance: Richard Sorrell; Private Collection.

The aircraft is a stylised version of a Vickers Wellington, a British twin-engine, medium bomber designed in the mid-1930s at Brooklands in Weybridge, Surrey, by Vickers-Armstrong's Chief Designer, R.K. Pierson. It was widely used as a night-time bomber in the early years of WW2, before being displaced as a bomber by the larger four-engined 'heavies', such as the Avro Lancaster. The Wellington continued to serve throughout the war in other duties, particularly as an anti-submarine aircraft. It was the only British bomber to be produced for the entire duration of the war. The Wellington was popularly known as the 'Wimpy' by service personnel, after J. Wellington Wimpy from the Popeye cartoons, and a Wellington 'B for Bertie' had a starring role in the 1942 propaganda film *One of Our Aircraft Is Missing.*

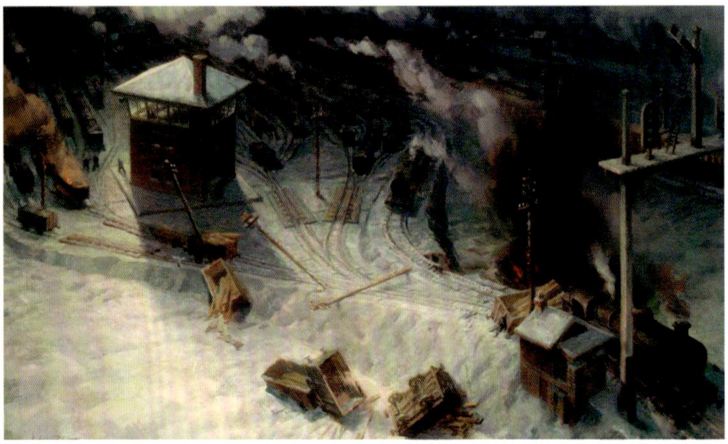

FIG. 19 – **John Edgar Platt** (1886-1967),
A Marshalling Yard in Wartime: 'Bomber's Moon', 1943,
oil on canvas, 24 x 40 in. (60.9 x 101.9 cm).
© Imperial War Museums (IWM Art LD 3530)
Acquisition method: transferred from the War
Artists' Advisory Committee, 1947,

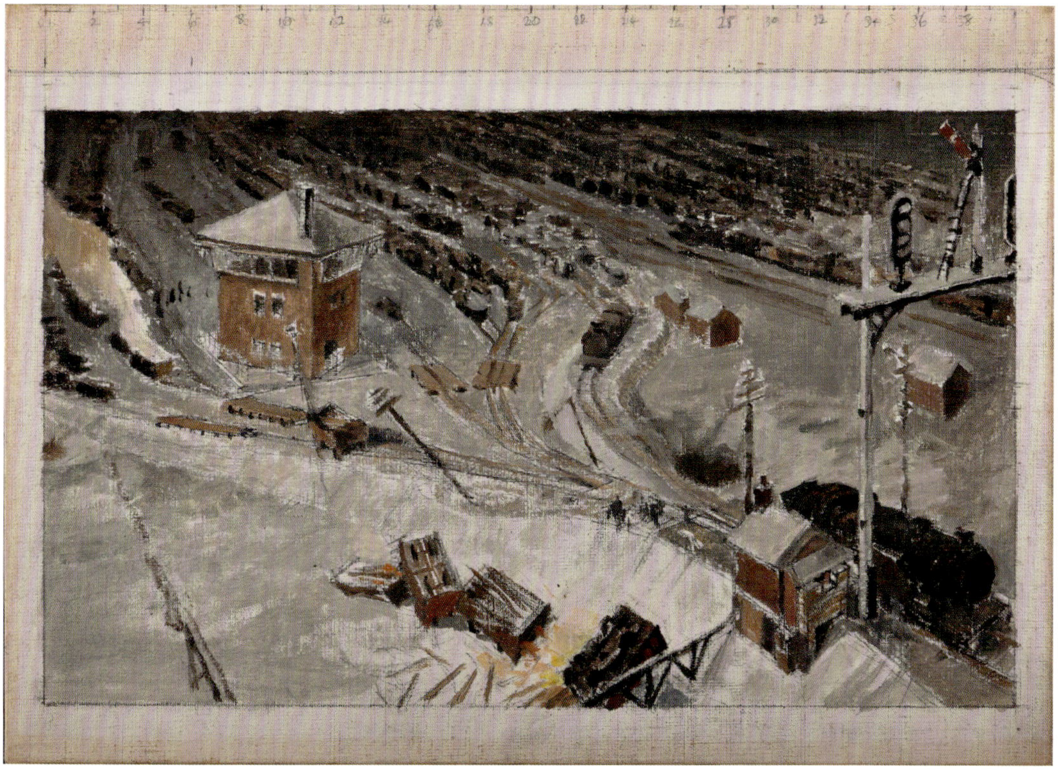

CAT. 157 – **John Edgar Platt** (1886-1967), *A Near Miss*,
oil on board, 6 ½ x 10 in. (16.5 x 25.4 cm).

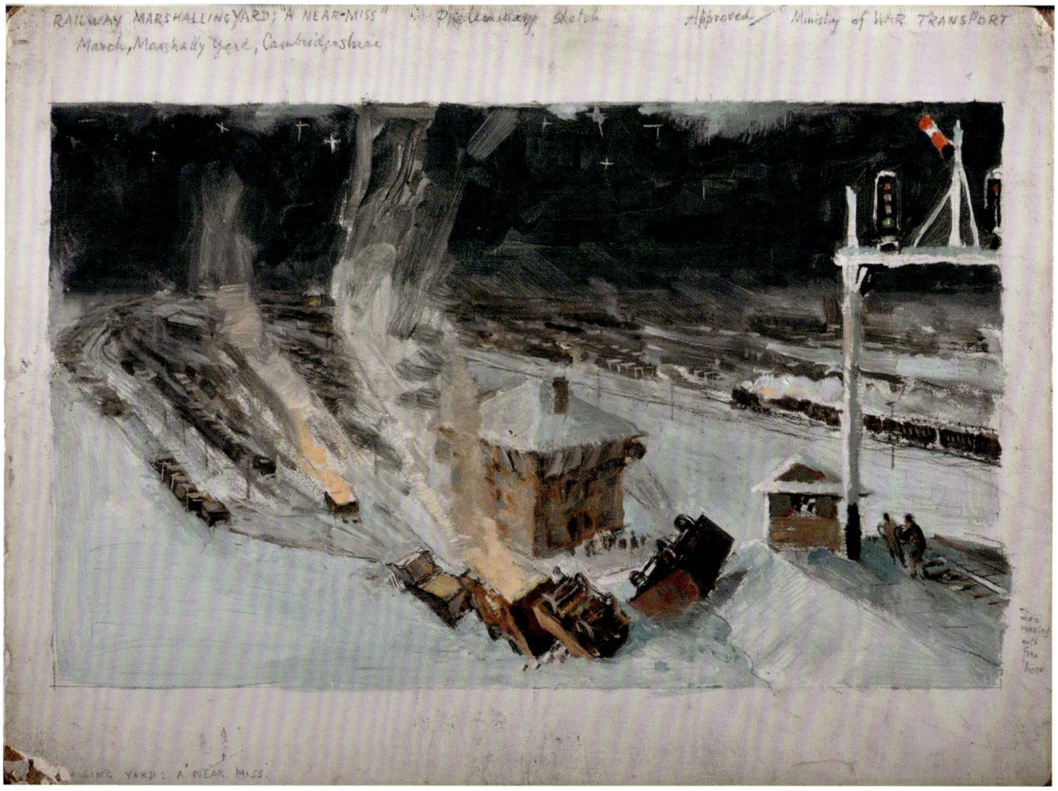

CAT. 158 – **John Edgar Platt** (1886-1967), *A Near Miss*, 1943, (preliminary sketch approved by Ministry War Transport),
oil on board, 6 ½ x 10 in. (16.5 x 25.4 cm).

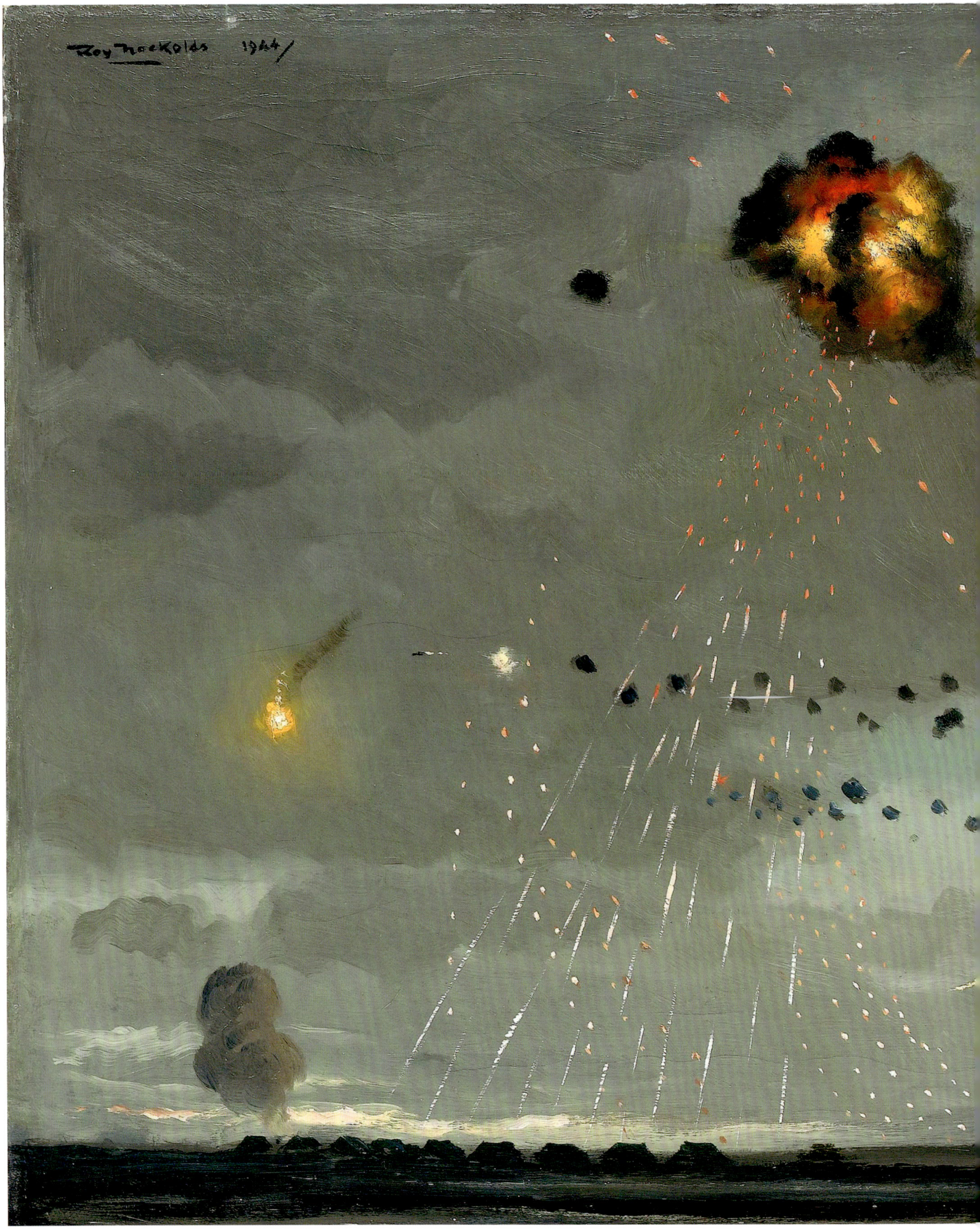
Roy Nockolds 1944

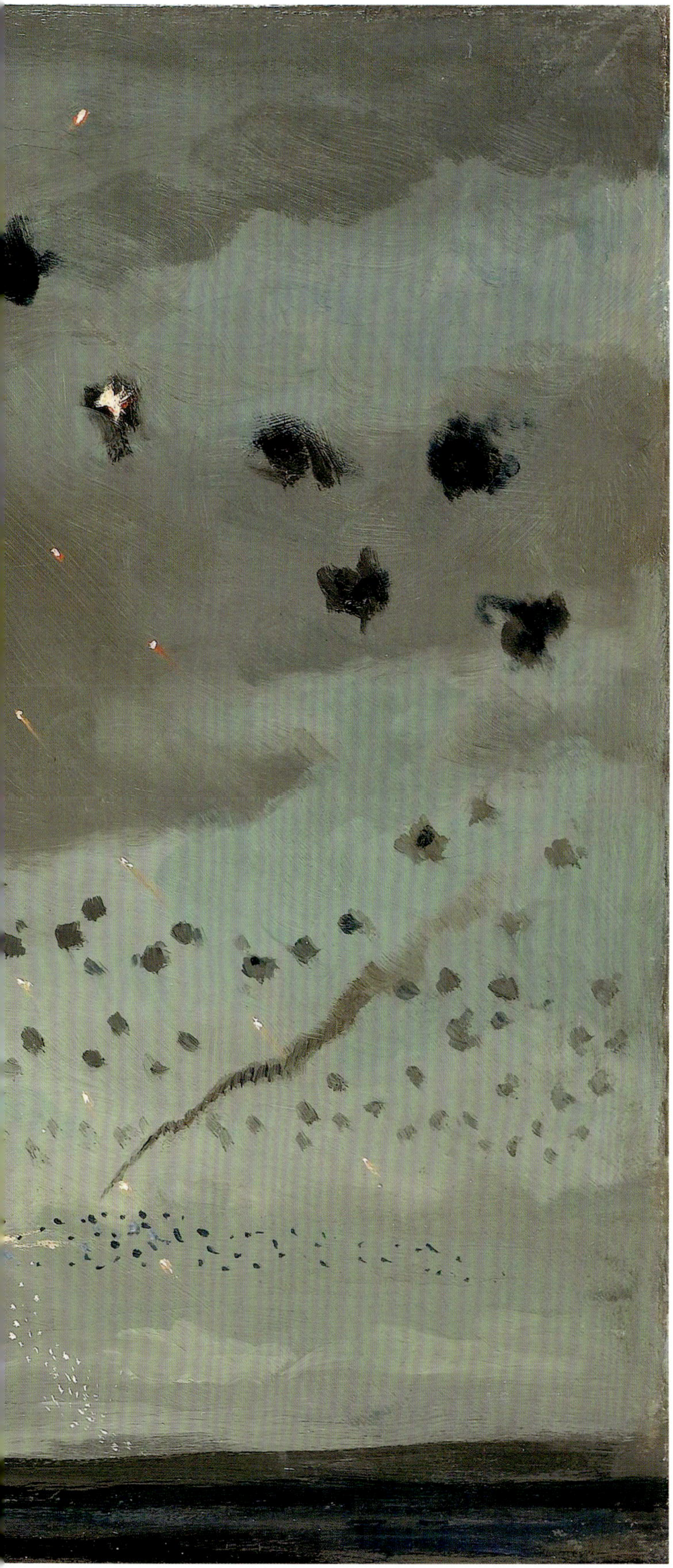

CAT. 159* –
Roy Nockolds (1911-1979), *Anti-aircraft batteries attack*, 1944, signed and dated,
oil on canvas, 28 x 36 in. (71.1 x 91.5 cm).
Provenance: Private collection.

In June 1944 the first flying bombs fell on London; they were usually called 'buzz-bombs' or 'doodle-bugs'. This historically important, dramatic skyscape, recording the arrival of buzz-bombs in Britain, depicts most probably the landscape of Kent – buzz-bombs were launched from Northern France. Propelled by pulse engines (indicated by the intermittent black puffs of smoke), buzz-bombs flew at 400 mph. This unprecedented speed rendered artillery fire largely ineffective so, rather than being directed, artillery was sent up as a wall of fire. Buzz-bombs announced the dawn of a new form of warfare. The most effective counter to the V-1 was to use the first British jet fighter – the Gloster Meteor – against them. Other – piston-engined – aircraft could catch up with them in a dive, but the Meteor matched their speed in level flight.

During the war Nockolds not only served in the RAF but developed for them a revolutionary camouflage for Mosquitoes. Whilst most artists chose as their subjects the almost picturesque aftermath of bomb damage, Nockolds engaged with the technology of war. *Stalking the Night Raider* and *Three Spitfires attacking a formation of Junkers* (Imperial War Museum) are among the most atmospheric paintings of aerial combat produced during the war.

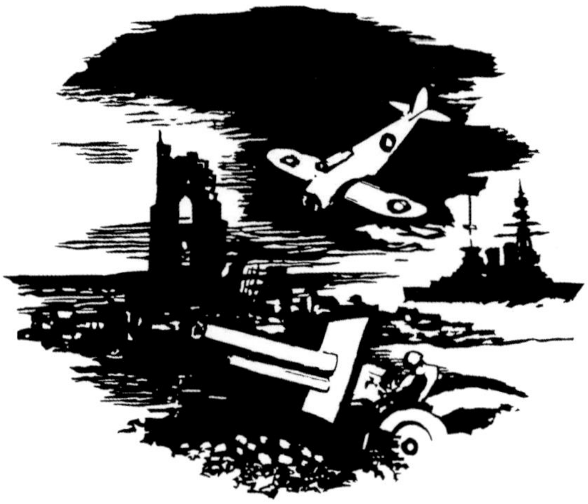

APPENDICES

Artists whose work appeared in the 8 *War Pictures by British Artists* books

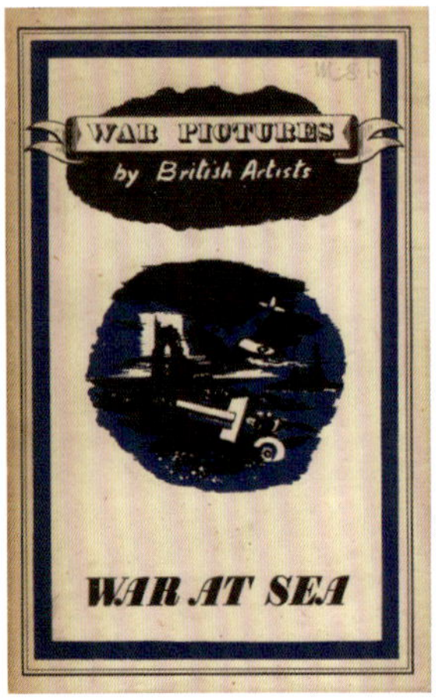

War at Sea N° 1

Muirhead Bone
Charles Cundall
Edward Eurich
Hubert A. Freeth
Eric Kennington
Henry Lamb
John Nash
Charles Pears
Eric Ravilious
C.W. Dyson-Smith
Stanley Spencer
J. Worsley

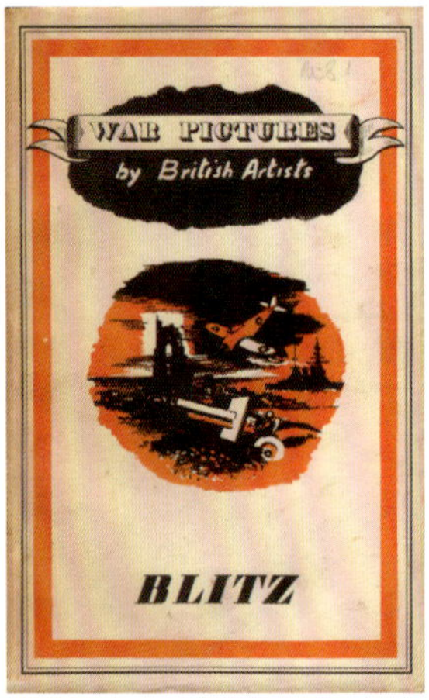

Blitz N° 2

Edward Ardizzone
John Armstrong
Muirhead Bone
William Conor
Frank Dobson
L. Duffy
Evelyn Dunbar
Ethel Gabain
Anthony Gross
B. Hailstone
Clifford Hall
Eric Kennnigton
Robert Medley
James Miller
Henry Moore
John Nash
John Piper
R.V. Pitchforth
R. Schwabe
Graham Sutherland
A.R. Thomson
Feliks Topolski

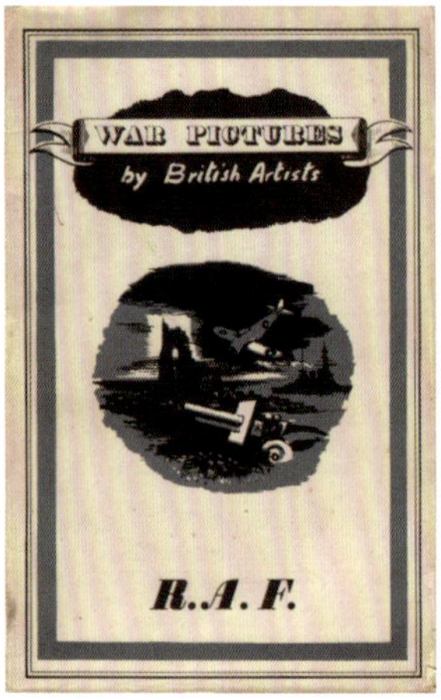

R.A.F. N° 3

Robert Austin
Robin Darwin
T.C. Dugdale
Richard Eurich
Keith Henderson
Eric Kennington
Laura Knight
J. Mansbridge
Raymond McGrath
Paul Nash
Roy Nockolds
Cuthbert Orde
Sir W. Rothenstein
Graham Sutherland

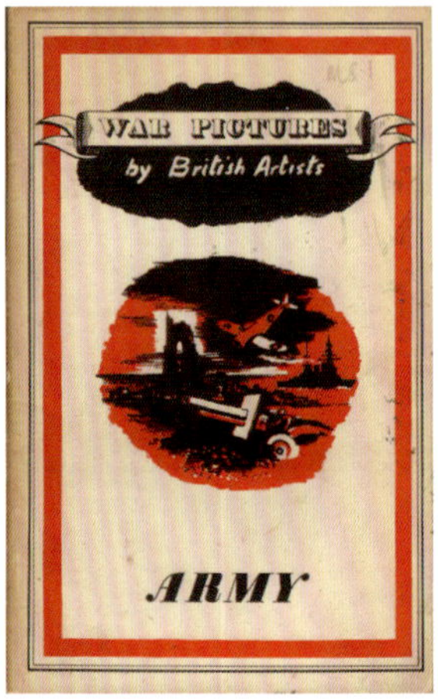

Army N° 4

Edward Ardizzone
Edward Bawden
Muirhead Bone
Dorothy Coke
W. Conor
R. Coxon
Charles Cundall
T.C. Dugdale
R.G. Eves
Barnett Freedman
Anthony Gross
Robin Guthrie
Henry Lamb
Harry Morley
C. Mozley
Feliks Topolsi

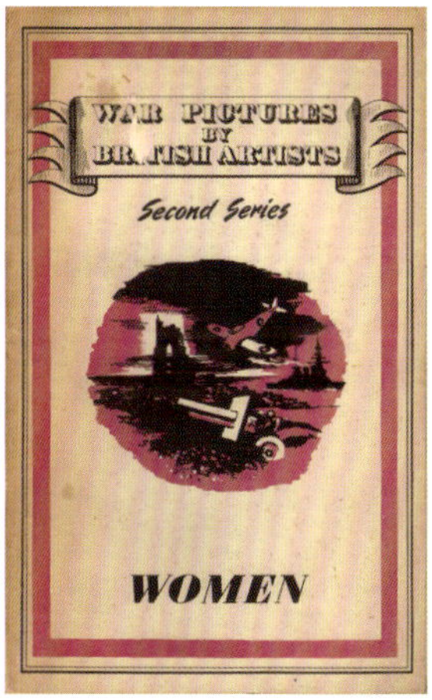

Women N° I

Dame Laura Knights, R.A.
Robert Austin, A.R.A
J. Bateman, R.A.
Ethel Gabain
Anthony Gross
Doris Zinkeisen
Gordon Smith
William Dring
Evelyn Dunbar
A.R. Thomson, A.R.A.
Francis Dodd, R.A.
Edward Ardizzone
Leslie Cole
R.V. Pitchforth, A.R.A.
A.S.Hartwick, R.W.S.
Mona Moore
Henry Rushbury, R.A.
Dorothy Coke
Anthony Devas

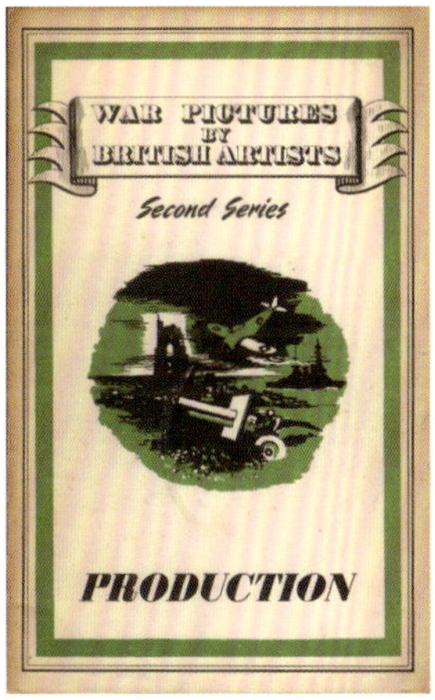

Production N° II

Henry Rushbury, R.A
R.V. Pitchforth, A.R.A.
Francis Dodd, R.A.
Ethel Gabain
Leslie Cole
Stanley Spencer
Vincent Lines
Thomas Hennell
Michael Ayrton
Ceri Richards
Graham Suherland
F.E. Jackson
Charles Murray
Harold Bubb
Charles Cundall, A.R.A.
Kenneth Rowntree
Henry Moore

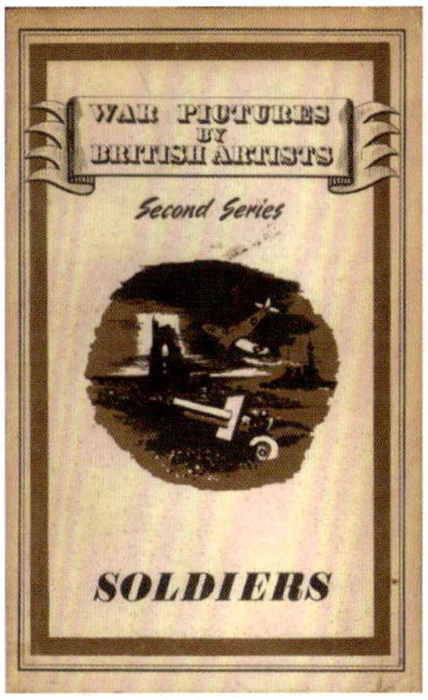

Soldiers N° III

Henry Lamb, A.R.A.
Anthony Gross
I.K. Sydee
Edward Bawden
Edward Ardizzone
C.A. Salisbury
Robert Scanlan
G. Lambourn
Eric Ravilious
Feliks Topolski
Rodrigo Moynihan
William Roberts
Christopher Perkins
Kenneth Rowntree
Hubert Freeth
E.R. Payne
J.E. Brown
Henry Carr

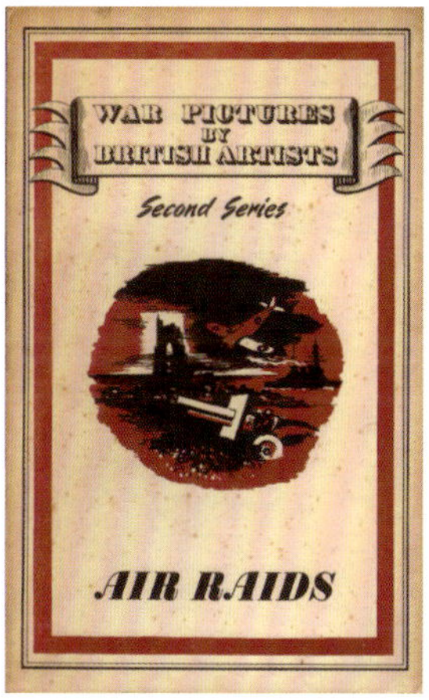

Air Raids N° IV

Duncan Grant
Leonard Rosoman
Paul Dessau
Graham Sutherland
John Piper
R. Murray
Henry Carr
Leonard Daniels
William Clause
E. Boyd Uden
Edward Ardizzone
Christopher Perkins
Gilbert Spencer
Alexander Macpherson
Eric Ravilious
Kenneth Holmes
George Quarmby
Louisa Puller
W. Douglas Macleod
R.V. Pitchford, A.R.A.
A.R. Thomson, A.R.A.
M.F. de Montmorency
Carel Weight
H.S. Merritt
Feliks Topolski
B. Howitt Lodge
Phyllis Ginger
Dennis Flanders
B. Hailstone
Henry Moore

The WAAC's Artists

By Brian Foss

This appendix first appeared in *War Paint: Art, War, State and Identity in Britain 1939-45* published by Yale University Press in 2007.

Thirty-six men and one woman were given full-time employment by the Committee, a hundred other artists were given short-term contracts and works by a further 264 artists, both professional and amateur, were purchased. Three artists donated works to the collection.

I) Full-time, salaried artists:

* Also worked on short-term contracts for the WAAC
** Also sold work to the WAAC
*** Also worked on short-term contracts and sold work to the WAAC
**** Also donated work to the WAAC

Edward Ardizzone (1900-79): War Office Artist, 1940-45.

In France and Belgium with the British Expeditionary Force (BEF), Ardizzone sketched the 300th Highland Artillery in such towns as Merris, Bailleul and Tournai, reaching Brussels and Louvain in May 1940 before retreating to Boulogne. He was evacuated back to Britain with the British Expeditionary Force. There he recorded troops in Salisbury and other Southern Command centres, shelter life in London, Home Guard and infantry training, and – in January 1942 – the arrival of American troops in Northern Ireland. Sent to North Africa in 1942 to replace Edward Bawden, he joined the British First Army on its march to Tunisia and followed the Eighth Army's successes in the Second Battle of El Alamein (October). Ardizzone arrived in northern France at the time of the D-Day invasion, and later travelled with the 50th Division to Sicily. During the invasion of Italy he witnessed the fall of Reggio and of Naples, worked his way north to Rome, and spent the winter of 1944-45 in such towns as Rimini, Cattolica, Ravenna and Forli. He concluded his travels in Germany, documenting the 8th Hussars and visiting Bremen and other cities.

Edward Bawden (1903-89): War Office Artist, 1940-43; Ministry of Information Artist, 1943-45

On the Continent before the German invasion, Bawden made records of defence preparations at Halluin, on the French-Belgian border, and witnessed both the bombing of Armentières and the evacuation from Dunkirk. He was subsequently posted to North Africa, where he painted panoramic landscapes from Libya to Ethiopia and made portraits and recorded troops, facilities and landscapes in Sudan, Cairo, Eritrea and Ethiopia. He reached Addis Ababa in May 1941 before going west to Egypt and Libya. Bawden travelled with Anthony Gross to Palestine and Lebanon at the beginning of 1942, and later that year made records of the Marsh Arabs of southern Iraq before being recalled to London in the late summer – a journey on which his ship was sunk and he was briefly a prisoner in Casablanca. Back home he drew military portraits in Colchester and Scotland, but returned to Iraq in September 1943 as a Ministry of Information artist. There he worked on portraits, landscapes and other subjects in Baghdad and Kurdistan before joining the Middle East Anti-locust Unit's trek across Saudi Arabia, bound for Jeddah. He returned briefly to southern Iraq and the Marsh Arabs before travelling into Iran, documenting supply shipments to the USSR. Recalled to England in the late summer of 1944, he worked briefly at the Southampton docks before leaving for Yugoslavia, via Rome. Unable to enter Yugoslavia, he moved on to Ravenna, to Greece and to the Austrian frontier before returning to Florence. Bawden travelled back to Britain in July 1945.

<u>Muirhead Bone</u> (1876-1953): Admiralty Artist, 1939-43

Bone worked throughout Britain, producing group portraits of officers, troops evacuated from Dunkirk, naval installations in Portsmouth, Rosyth, Clydebank, the West Highlands and elsewhere, London ruins, ceremonies at the Guildhall and at the Painted Hall, Greenwich, and numerous general views of ships and of minelaying. Following the death of his son Gavin in 1943 he took what was intended to be a temporary leave from his salaried war artist position, but did not return.

<u>Stephen Bone</u> (1904-58): Ministry of Information Artist, 1943-45 (specialisation: Admiralty subjects) ***

Appointed in June 1943 following his father's abandonment of his position with the Admiralty, Bone produced large numbers of works showing a wide variety of naval craft, as well as convoys, harbours, and shipboard life at locations throughout Britain; these included Stornoway, Loch Roag, Lismore, Belfast, Greenock, Campbeltown Loch, Plymouth, Loch Erriboll and Scapa Flow. He was present to record the 1944 Normandy invasion, including post-landing inland scenes in towns and cities such as Corseulles and Caen, as well as the assault on Walcheren Island (Netherlands). In late 1944 he joined an expedition to Norway, where he recorded the wreck of the Tirpitz.

<u>Henry Carr</u> (1894-1962): War Office Artist, 1943-44 ***

Soon after his appointment in early 1943 Carr – who was already well-represented by purchases and one-off commissions in the war art collection – voyaged to North Africa and Italy. There he painted army facilities, equipment and actions, portraits of British and allied service personnel and officers (including the Commander-in-Chief of Allied Forces in North Africa, General Dwight Eisenhower), ruins and portraits in Algiers (Constantine), Tunis (Carthage) and Italy (Sessa, Cassino), and the eruption of Mount Vesuvius in 1944. That same year, tired and ill, he successfully petitioned the WAAC for permission to leave Italy, and his place there was taken by William Coldstream.

<u>William Coldstream</u> (1908-87): War Office Artist, 1943-45

Appointed in 1943 to an Indian transit unit stationed near Cairo, Coldstream painted four portraits of Indian soldiers before travelling to Italy. From Capua he went to Rimini (December 1944) and Florence (May 1945), painting buildings and a bailey bridge on the Volturno River. His time-consuming painting process resulted in only nine pictures over the course of his full-time work as a war artist.

<u>Leslie Cole</u> (1910-72): Ministry of Information Artist, 1943 (specialisation: Malta; Royal Marine subjects); War Office Artist, 1944-46 ***

Sent to Malta in May 1943, shortly before the end of the German siege, Cole concentrated on civilian subjects and also participated in the successful mission to capture the island of

Pantelleria, between Sicily and North Africa. He returned to teaching art in Hull by November 1943, but – following his resignation from that job – was given his second commission and sent in July 1944 to France, where he worked with the Royal Marine Commandos in Normandy. Transferred to the War Office in mid-October, he was in Cairo at the end of the year and in Greece by the beginning of the next, recording the violence of the resistance group ELAS's attempt to seize control of the country following the German retreat. He later travelled to South East Asia Command, sketching troops in the Burmese jungle beginning in May 1945, and later progressing to Singapore and Borneo.

<u>Charles Cundall</u> (1890-1971): Admiralty Artist, 1940-41; Air Ministry Artist, 1941-45 ***

In July 1940 Cundall – with whose short-term contract work the WAAC was pleased – was given a salaried commission to record the work of the Merchant Navy, in fulfilment of which he worked on the Thames and the Medway, at Falmouth and St. Mawes, and in the West Country. Mistakenly believing his six-month commission was for a full year, he had several canvases still in progress when the contract ended at the beginning of 1941. He was assigned to the Air Ministry shortly thereafter, and was given permission to complete his Admiralty pictures while also producing Coastal Command, Bomber Command and other subjects for the Air Ministry. He was in Northern Ireland to paint American subjects in the spring and summer of 1942, and in Scotland (Orkney, Glasgow) in September-October. Along with painting several RAF subjects at various sites within Britain in 1943-44, he spent several months in the last quarter of 1943 on a major painting of the commemoration ceremony for the Battle of Britain (Imperial War Museum).

<u>William Dring</u> (1904-90): Ministry of Information Artist, 1942-44 (specialisation: Admiralty portraits); Air Ministry Artist, 1944-45 ***

The WAAC had previously commissioned and purchased several portraits from Dring when, beginning on June 1st 1942, he was awarded his first full-time contract, supplying the Committee with many more dozens of pastel portraits. Dring worked quickly (he usually completed a portrait in less than an hour), and during his time with the Admiralty his search for male and, occasionally, female sitters required extensive travel, including trips to Scotland, Portsmouth and the Western Approaches. He was briefly between full-time contracts in the late summer of 1943, but was soon given another, focused on general portraits but also allowing for some naval examples at the discretion of the Admiralty's representative on the WAAC. His final contract – this one with the Air Ministry – took effect in mid-1944 and resulted in another series of casual pastel likenesses of sitters from a variety of locations.

<u>Evelyn Dunbar</u> (1906-60): Ministry of Information Artist, 1943-44 (specialisation: agricultural and women's subjects) ***

One of the first three women to be appointed war artists in April 1940, Dunbar was initially contracted to record Women's Voluntary Service and Women's Institute activities. Her brief was extended to include the work of the Women's Land Army (WLA). In 1942, at the request of Lady Pamela Mountbatten, she was seconded to record nursing scenes, before resuming her WLA work in January 1943 at the Institute of Agriculture, Usk (Monmouthshire), in Kent and in the Borders. A contract to paint Women's Auxiliary Air Force subjects took her to RAF stations in Gloucestershire and Kent, while her later work for the WAAC included scenes from East Malling agricultural research station, Houndsditch in London (for women sewing army tents) and an unspecified location for her single ATS painting. From her appointment until the end of the war Dunbar was subject to an uninterrupted series of rolling contracts of irregular length, and in this sense she was the only female war artist to be salaried throughout the war.

Richard Eurich (1903-92): Admiralty Artist, 1941-45 *

Eurich worked for the WAAC on short-term contracts before becoming an official Admiralty artist in 1941; he replaced Charles Cundall, who had been transferred to the RAF. As an Admiralty artist he produced paintings of boats and ships (the latter both individually and in convoys), dramatic images of shipwreck survivors, and views of action on the south coast (Portsmouth), in British waters, in Italy (the Battle of Salerno), in Norway (including the wreck of the Tirpitz), and in France (the Bruneval and Dieppe Raids and the D-Day invasions). Some of these works relied upon his ability to build panoramic images of action-filled scenes that he had not actually witnessed.

Reginald Eves (1876-1941): War Office Artist, 1940 ****

Eves painted portraits of senior officers with the British Expeditionary Force in France in the first half of 1940, and returned home on April 18th, well before the Dunkirk evacuation. Back in Britain the WAAC had difficulty finding high-ranking officers with time to spare, and directed Eves toward other sitters. By August the Committee noted that he had been working industriously, but considered that his portraits were too much alike. It therefore decided not to renew his commission.

Barnett Freedman (1901-58): War Office Artist, 1940-41 ***

Arriving in northern France in April 1940, Freedman attempted to work in and around Arras, Amiens and Boulogne, but was frustrated by a lack of transport. At Thélus with the Air Component South, he documented runway construction; later he worked as a portraitist. After returning to Dover in May he was sent to Eastern Command, notably at Sheerness, where he worked from July to November. His persistent complaints about his working conditions irritated the WAAC, and his work after early 1941 (his commission ended in February of that year) was limited to sales and short-term contracts.

Anthony Gross (1905-84): War Office Artist, 1941-45 **

Gross was given a one-month assignment with the War Office in March 1940, working at the Caterham and Catterick barracks, but his salaried commission proper did not begin until the second half of 1941. He travelled to Cairo and then visited sites in Palestine, Lebanon, Syria, Persia, Iraq and Iran, the latter in a bid to reach the Caucasus. Frustrated in his attempt to get into Russia, he travelled with a hospital train to Cairo in the summer of 1942, recorded the 2nd Armoured Brigade's assault on the German front in July, reached El Alamein, and returned to Cairo. Sent at the behest of the India Office to record the work of the 4th Indian Division, he reached the front line in Arakan, and crossed into Burma in early 1943. During his six months with the British and Indian armies in eastern India and in Burma he approached the front line from the south, reached the heavily contested Chin Hills, and there documented the anti-Japanese work of the Chin levies. Gross afterwards drew troops from the 21st Army Group and the US 1st Infantry Division, landed in Normandy with the 50th Division during the June 1944 invasion, followed Free French forces to Paris, and documented the American-Russian meeting on the Elbe River on April 25th 1945.

Bernard Hailstone (1910-87): Ministry of Information Artist, 1940-41 (specialisation: Ministry of Supply portraits); Ministry of War Transport Artist, 1943-45; Ministry of Information Artist, 1945-46 (specialisation: South East Asia Command subjects) ***

After being released from his duties with the National Fire Service, Hailstone spent time painting portraits of inland transport (civil defence) workers at various locations. In 1943 he was named war artist to the Ministry of War Transport, worked at Hull, and then – in the autumn – became the only one of the Ministry's four artists to work outside Britain. In Algiers, Malta and southern Italy he documented the work and personalities of the Merchant Marine. His contract ended in April 1945. In June, after being transferred from War Transport to the MoI, he painted portraits in South-East Asia Command, including that of Lord Mountbatten, the Command's Supreme Allied Commander.

Keith Henderson (1883-1982): Air Ministry Artist, 1940

To his frustration, shortly after becoming the first full-time Air Ministry artist Henderson discovered that William Rothenstein – who was often but mistakenly assumed by aerodrome commanders to be an official war artist – had pre-empted him by making large numbers of portrait drawings of airmen in England. He therefore concentrated almost entirely on paintings of aircraft and hangars at Scottish aerodromes at Leuchars and elsewhere. Dissatisfied with both Henderson's speed of production (the artist incorrectly assumed that he had a one-year rather than a six-month contract) as well as with the quality of his work, the WAAC's Air Ministry representative terminated his appointment at the end of October.

Thomas Hennell (1903-45): Ministry of Information Artist, 1943-45 (specialisation: Iceland and Admiralty subjects, Far East airfields); Air Ministry Artist, 1945 ***

After the full-time war artist Eric Ravilious was killed in an aeroplane crash in September 1942, Hennell successfully proposed himself as Ravilious's replacement as the WAAC's full-time artist in Iceland. He departed for Iceland at the end of July 1943, worked at Reykjavik and elsewhere on the island until the end of November, and in January 1944 went to northeastern England to paint fishing and shipbuilding subjects. For his three-month commission (from April 1944) for Admiralty subjects he was intended to go to the Mediterranean, but administrative problems resulted in him travelling to Portsmouth instead (May) to document preparations for the June invasion of northern Europe. He subsequently accompanied invasion troops on D-Day and spent two months with the Canadian 1st Army in northern France (Dieppe, Rouen, Calais) before being transferred in October to a Royal Navy unit, which he accompanied into Belgium and Holland. Following surgery in Chatham, Hennell was assigned to the Air Ministry for six months in 1945. He reached Burma in June, at the time of the Japanese retreat, and was stationed at an airfield near Rangoon. He travelled from there to Calcutta and Colombo, witnessed the retaking of Penang (August-September), and moved on to Singapore (September) and Indonesia. He was in Surabaya, Java, when the Dutch East India Colonies declared independence. In the ensuing violence he was attacked by a mob and disappeared, becoming the third and final salaried artist to die while under contract.

Eric Kennington (1888-1960): Air Ministry Artist, 1940-42 ***

Having supplied the WAAC with pastel portraits produced in fulfilment of short-term contracts prior to his appointment as a full-time war artist, Kennington went on to complete many more following his appointment as Keith Henderson's replacement at the Air Ministry as of the end of 1940. The WAAC was only slightly successful in encouraging him to expand his scope beyond portraiture; Kennington was fervently devoted to the solidity and heroism of his sitters, producing dozens of pastels of bomber crewmen, Coastal Command figures, parachutists, and – in the spring and summer of 1942 – allied airmen from various countries. He resigned his commission in September 1942 because of his conviction that the WAAC was not making effective propaganda use of his art.

Henry Lamb (1883-1960): War Office Artist, 1940-44 ***

Lamb was appointed as of December 1st 1940, the successor to R.G. Eves when the latter's commission was not renewed. He drew and painted portraits (notably generals and allied servicemen), recorded Army-RAF co-operation at the Old Sarum aerodrome in early 1941, and beginning in July that year spent several weeks documenting tank training exercises in South-East Command. At the request of Vincent Massey (the Canadian High Commissioner) he was attached to the 12th Canadian Army Tank Battalion in southern England from the autumn of 1941 to February 1942, returning to doing British portraits – including those of ATS and Anti-Aircraft Command personnel – in the spring of 1942. Several ATS portraits date from the spring of 1943. Following the end of his full-time commission in May 1944 he returned to working on short-term contracts for the WAAC.

W.T. Monnington (1902-76): Ministry of Information Artist, 1943-45 (specialisation: Air Ministry subjects)

Monnington was employed at the Directorate of Camouflage (Leamington Spa) when he wrote to the WAAC to note his wartime experience in aerial observation and to complain that the war as seen from the air had not received the attention it deserved from the Committee. The WAAC agreed, and issued a three-month contract in November 1943. Aerial encounters, pencil portraits of RAF personnel, and painted views of facilities and bases, notably in England and Belgium, made up his work following this appointment. His contract was renewed from the first half of 1944 onward. Monnington's representations of flight and of battle as seen from within various aircraft comprise the largest and most important body of such images in the WAAC's collection.

James Morris (1908-?): Admiralty Artist, 1945 **

Morris was in the Royal Navy from before the war, selling the WAAC records of his experiences on arctic convoys and in Archangel and Murmansk. Remaining in the Royal Navy, when he was made a salaried war artist, he – along with Leonard Rosoman – was sent to record the British Pacific Fleet in the Far East. There he worked in liberated Burma (Rangoon), Hong Kong, Formosa, Shanghai, Tokyo and Yokohama, capturing subjects as diverse as shipboard activities, city views, damage to harbours and to the Yokohama cityscape, the interior of the Imperial Diet in Tokyo, and post-surrender celebrations in Shanghai.

Rodrigo Moynihan (1910-90): Ministry of Information Artist, 1943-44 (specialisation: War Office portraits) ***

Moynihan was invalided out of the Army in 1943. In September 1943, largely on the strength of The Medical Inspection (his second short-term contract submission to the WAAC), he began a full-time commission, replacing Edward Bawden, whose assignment to the War Office ended that year. In this capacity Moynihan supplied principally portraits of senior male officers and of ATS sitters. Following the end of his appointment in 1944 he returned to doing portraits on short-term contracts.

John Nash (1893-1977): Ministry of Information Artist, 1940 (specialisation: Admiralty subjects)

Appointed to a six-month contract in early 1940, Nash worked in Plymouth, Swansea and Bristol, portraying ships, submarines and smaller vessels at sea, in port and in drydock, as well as harbour activities and facilities, and gun emplacements. Nash was dissatisfied with life as a war artist, preferring a more active involvement in the War. He did not seek a renewal of his commission when it expired, and instead took an intelligence position with the Royal Marines.

Paul Nash (1889-1946): Air Ministry Artist, 1940 ***

Nash was little more popular with the Air Ministry than was Keith Henderson, the Ministry's other full-time artist in 1940. Fascinated by flight but unable to fly because of his poor health, he carried out his contract from his home in Oxford. As a salaried war artist he produced two important series of watercolours: Raiders (crashed German aircraft) and Aerial Creatures (anthropomorphic British aircraft); but the WAAC's Air Ministry representative was critical of the latter and – to Kenneth Clark's displeasure – Nash's full-time employment was ended in December 1940. In January 1941 the WAAC set aside £500 to purchase his upcoming RAF pictures, for which Nash gave the Committee first refusal rights. Of his major oils, only Totes meer (Dead sea) was begun while he was a salaried artist, although it was not completed and submitted until the next year.

Mervyn Peake (1911-68): Ministry of Information Artist, 1943 (specialisation: Ministry of Production subjects)

After repeatedly failing to interest the WAAC in his ideas for war pictures, Peake began 1943 with a short-term contract to make drawings and paintings of work in a glass-blowing factory. The results were so successful that he was issued a three-month, full-time commission to document factory subjects, including the making of cathode ray tubes needed for radio-location. The WAAC deemed the resulting paintings insufficient to meet the terms of the contract, so Peake subsequently submitted a large painting of RAF pilots being debriefed.

John Piper (1903-92): Ministry of War Transport Artist, 1944-45 ***

From 1940 to 1944 Piper fulfilled a series of short-term contracts for the WAAC: pictures of ARP control rooms in Bristol, bombed architecture in Coventry, London, Bristol and Bath, shelter experiments, and land reclamation work. (Although his 1943 and 1944 contracts were, in the manner of commissions for salaried war artists, associated with specific durations of time, they do not appear to have constituted salaried work per se. The timings between his contracts was intended to allow Piper time to work slowly without being called up for military service.) In July 1944, however, he replaced John Platt as a salaried artist to the Ministry of War Transport. As such he documented subjects that he had originally proposed to deal with in 1940: train and coastal transportation in Cardiff and Bristol, as well as in Southampton and elsewhere on the south coast.

Roland Vivian Pitchforth (1895-1982): Ministry of Information Artist, 1940-41, 1942-43 (specialisation: Ministries of Supply and Home Security subjects); Admiralty Artist, 1943-45 ***

On the strength of pictures of bomb damage produced in fulfilment of short-term contracts, in 1940 Pitchforth was appointed to a salaried position, for which he painted a large number of factory subjects. After a break of several months he renewed his commission in the spring of 1942, working on such themes as WAAFs in underground operations control rooms. Beginning in the spring of 1943 he was assigned to the Admiralty, but painted tanks and related subjects before turning to Admiralty themes proper. For his second Admiralty commission, issued in October 1943, Pitchforth recorded a variety of vessels and subjects in locations ranging from the west coast of Scotland to London, Horsham and Portland, before leaving for the Western Approaches in the spring of 1944. He was subsequently sent to South-East Asia Command, touring Ceylon and ultimately reaching Rangoon at the time of the battle for control of Burma.

John Platt (1886-1967): Ministry of War Transport Artist, 1943-44 ***

Platt was given his contract in the spring of 1943, and was charged with documenting maritime traffic, having previously supplied the WAAC with comparable subjects. Over the next year he worked principally on the Thames as well as in Liverpool and Cornwall. His favoured subjects included ocean transport, wartime river traffic, and marshalling yards. The WAAC, discouraged by Platt's slowness in delivering paintings, declined to renew his commission.

Eric Ravilious (1903-42): Ministry of Information Artist, 1940, 1941-42 (specialisation: Admiralty subjects) **

Appointed in February 1940, Ravilious was posted to Nore Command, working at Chatham, Sheerness and Grimsby before sailing to Norway in April to document the attack on Narvik. In July-August, after leaving Nore Command, he drew submarine interiors at Gosport and coastal defences at Newhaven (September-October). From July 1941 he worked at Dover (making watercolours of coastal defences), then in the Dunfermline area (concentrating on convoy subjects), and at the end of the year at a Fleet Air Arm station at Dundee, where he enjoyed painting the slow-flying Walrus flying boats. When his contract was renewed in February 1942 Ravilious was assigned to the RAF bases at Clifton, Debden and Sawbridgeworth, before being sent to Iceland in August. On September 2nd he became the first salaried war artist to die while under contract; he was a passenger in a rescue plane when it crashed into the sea.

Albert Richards (1919-45): War Office Artist, 1944-45 **

Richards – with experience as a sapper in the Royal Engineers (1940-43) and also with the 591st (Antrim) Parachute Squadron – accepted a six-month contract in December 1943. (Three months earlier he had declined a three-month contract because of his commitment to his squadron.) He parachuted into Normandy with the invasion forces in June 1944, and documented the progress of Airborne and ordinary infantry forces through France and Holland on their way to Germany. Richards died while planning a painting of Allied troops near the Maas River, having accidentally driven his jeep into a minefield.

Leonard Rosoman (b.1913): Ministry of Information Artist, 1945 (specialisation: Admiralty and other subjects) **

Rosoman was one of two salaried war artists to document the British Pacific Fleet, the other being James Morris. In April 1945 he replaced Thomas Hennell as an MoI artist working under the protection of the Admiralty. He reached Sydney in May and sailed out with the *HMS Formidable*, on board which he sketched RADAR indicators, and storage facilities for on-board aircraft. Rosoman returned to Sydney three months later to work his shipboard studies into larger paintings (August-September) before travelling to Hong Kong (September-October), where he recorded war damage. He reached the Japanese coast – although he did not land there – in July.

Rupert Shephard (1909-92): Ministry of War Transport Artist, 1945 ***

Having earlier (1940-44) contributed several views of home front industrial production to the war art collection, Shephard was named war artist to the Ministry of Transport in the spring of 1945; he was Bernard Hailstone's replacement when the latter was appointed a salaried war artist to the MoI. In this capacity he focused on war transport in London.

Graham Sutherland (1903-80): Ministry of Information Artist, 1940-45 (specialisation: Ministries of Supply, Home Security and Production subjects) ***

After fulfilling a short-term contract to record rural and urban bomb damage in Wales during the latter third of 1940, Sutherland embarked on five years of almost continuous work as a salaried war artist beginning on January 1st, 1941. After documenting bomb damage in London (the City and the East End) he returned to South Wales in September-October to begin a series of paintings of blast furnaces (1941-42), and then travelled to Cornwall (from June 1942) to record tin mining subjects, to Derbyshire to cover limestone quarrying (1942-43), and back to Wales in the summer of 1943 to start work on pictures of opencast coal mining and production. While posted to northern France in December 1944 he painted damaged railway yards at Trappes and flying bomb depots at St-Leu-d'Esserent.

A.R. Thomson (1894-1970): Air Ministry Artist, 1942-44

Thomson replaced Eric Kennington as the salaried portraitist to the Air Ministry following Kennington's resignation in September 1942. In addition to painted and drawn portraits, including those of several members of bomber crews, he also supplied a small number of related 'subject' pictures. These included documentation of medical procedures, an air raid in London, and a view of a grounded aeroplane.

Carel Weight (1908-97): War Office Artist, 1945-46 **

Having discharged several short-term contracts for the WAAC, Weight was made a salaried war artist in the spring of 1945, filling the position opened by Albert Richards's death. Sent to Italy, where he replaced Ardizzone after the latter had moved on to Germany, he landed in Naples in March and, from there, travelled to Rome, Perugia, Verona, Florence and Ravenna (March-October). By November he was in Vienna, returned to Rome and Florence in December 1945 and January 1946, and arrived in Athens in February 1946.

Charles Wheeler (1892-1974): Ministry of Information Artist, 1942-43 (specialisation: Admiralty portrait busts) *

The recipient of two (1941 and 1942) commissions for Admiralty portrait busts, Wheeler subsequently became only the sculptor to be given a full-time WAAC contract. He was able to execute only three bronze busts before the end of the contract: one captain and one lieutenant commander (awarded the George Cross and the Victoria Cross, respectively, in 1942), and one rear admiral (Sir Philip Vian). However, these were deemed to be "3 very good portraits which represent good value for £325" (May 1943 note by MoI administrator F.H. Dowden; IWM: GP/55/170).

John Worsley (1919-2000): Admiralty Artist, 1943-44 ***

As a midshipman in the Royal Naval Reserve Worsley sold the WAAC sketches of life aboard an armed patrol ship on the North Sea in 1940. Removed from active naval duty and given a commission as a full-time war artist, he was assigned in July 1943 to record Mediterranean activities and personalities, including the Commander-in-Chief of the Mediterranean Fleet. During the invasion of Italy he was present at the landings in Salerno. The WAAC then planned to send him to southeast Asia, but this ambition was frustrated when Worsley was reported missing in November 1943. The committee subsequently purchased the visual records he submitted of life in a prisoner of war camp in Germany.

II) Artists Given Short-term Contracts:

* Also sold work to the WAAC
** Also presented work to the WAAC
*** Also sold and presented work to the WAAC

Rosemary Allan
Leonard Appelbee
John Armstrong *
Robert Austin *
Edward Baird *
Malcolm Baker-Smith *
James Bateman
Walter Bayes
Frank Beresford
Oswald Birley *
David Bomberg
Rodney Burn
Thomas Carr *
Bernard Casson *
Evan Charlton
Derek Chittock
Dora Clarke
William Clause *
Dorothy Coke
Robert Colquhoun
Philip Connard
William Conor *
James Cowie
Raymond Coxon *
Barry Craig *
Hugh Crawford
Terence Cuneo
Robin Darwin
Anthony Devas *
Frank Dobson *
Francis Dodd *
Paul Drury *
T.C. Dugdale *
C.W. Dyson-Smith
Ian Eadie *
John Ensor *
Jacob Epstein *
Vincent Evans *
Hubert Freeth ***
Ethel Gabain *
Evelyn Gibbs *
Charles Ginner
Duncan Grant
James Grant
Kenneth Green
James Gunn
Robin Guthrie
Alan Gwynne-Jones *
Patrick Hall
A.S. Hartrick
Norman Hepple *
C. Eliot Hodgkin
Percy Horton
Ray Howard-Jones ***
Blair Hughes-Stanton *
F. Ernest Jackson
Edmond Kapp *
Mary Kessell *
Laura Knight
Wyndham Lewis
L.S. Lowry *
Lowes Luard *
Neville Lytton
Frances MacDonald *
Alexander Macpherson *
Raymond McGrath
Robert Medley
Bernard Meninsky
Paul Methuen *
James Miller *
Henry Moore *
Mona Moore *
Harry Morley *
W.P. Moss *
Cuthbert Orde *
Charles Pears *
Patrick E. Phillips
Elizabeth Polunin
Patricia Preece
William Roberts
Claude Rogers
Kenneth Rowntree *
Henry Rushbury *
Walter Russell
Randolph Schwabe *
Peter Markham Scott
Robert Sivell
John Skeaping
Alan Sorrell *
Ruskin Spear *
Gilbert Spencer
Stanley Spencer *
Steven Spurrier
David M. Sutherland
E. Heber Thompson **
A.R. Thomson
A.R. Middleton Todd
Feliks Topolski *
John Wheatley *
Harold S. Williamson
W. Matvyn Wright *

III) Artists Who Sold Work to the WAAC:

* Also donated work to the WAAC

Enid Abrahams
L. Abrahams
G. Worsley Adamson
Mary Adshead
Edgar Ainsworth
Griselda Allan
Kathleen Saywell Allen
Adrian Allinson
Joshua Armitage
Michael Ayrton
Denis Barnham
Joseph Bato
Ivor Beddoes
Bernard Beekes
John Berry
D.S. Bertram
Paul Bird
B.V. Bishop
Douglas Bissett
George Bissill
Sam Black
Doris Blair
R. Henderson Blyth
A. Boothroyd
James Boswell
A.C. Bown
Oliver Brabbins
William Brealey
J. Brooks
John Brown
Kenneth G. Browne
Maurice Brownfoot
Harold Bubb
Norma Bull
William Burwell
Robert Butler
Robert Campbell
Patrick Carpenter
Jack Chaddock
D. Champion
Miles Chance
Charles Chaplin
Daphne Chart
Malvina Cheek
George Claessen
Joy Collier
A.C. Collins
Joan Connew
Frederick Cook
Hubert Cook
J. Kingsley Cook
Frederick Coventry
E. Bainbridge-Copnall
Raymond Cowern
H.R. Cox
B.J. Cumming
Peter Curl
J.S. Dalison
A.D. Daniels
Leonard Daniels
W.D. Brokman Davis
Miles de Montmorency
Paul Dessau
John Dixon
Louis Duffy
F. Dunbar-Marshall
Charles Dunn
Pamela Dunton
Alan Durst
Gil Dyer
Eric Earnshaw
G.O. Eldridge
Clifford Ellis
F. Elwell
Simon Elwes
L. Faithfull
John Farleigh
David Feilding
V. Ferguson
Frank Field
D. Flanders
F.M.R. Flint
Victorine Foot
Michael Ford
Mollie Forestier-Walker
Meredith Frampton
Thomas Freeth
Roger Furse
Abram Games
G.R. Geary
A.H. Gerrard
Mrs. K. Gerrard
Patrick Gierth
Paul Gillett
Grace Golden
W. Goodin
Thomas Gourdie
Frank Graves
A.A. Gregson
Julius Griffith
Kathleen Guthrie
Karl Hagedorn
Harold Hailstone
W.S. Haines
Clifford. Hall
Eric L. Hall
Thomas Halliday
H.L. Harcourt
Hilda Harrisson
Carl Haworth
Rudolf Haybrook
Colin Hayes
J.C. Heath
Francis Helps
Rose Henriques
Elsie Hewland
L. Hinshelwood
Francis Hodge
Kenneth Holmes
Francis Holtermann
Stanley Houghton
Blair Howitt-Lodge
Eleanor Erlund Hudson
Ruth Hurle
Mabel Hutchinson
Philip Hutton
Alex Ingram
Edward James
Norman Janes
H. Johns
Barbara Jones
G.W. Kairigo
Katongale
Pegaret Keeling
L.E.D. Keene
Cedric J. Kennedy
James Kenward
B. Ley Kenyon
M. Kestelman
C. Kestin
S. Kioni

Eve Kirk
T.E. La Dell
G. Lambourn
Akinola Lasekan
Nora Lavrin
Lawrence S. Lee
V.J. Lee
Olga Lehmann
Vincent Lines
A.K. Lugolobi
Richard Macdonald
W. Douglas Macleod
P.W.G. Maloba
John Mansbridge
Norman A. Mansbridge
E. Mansfield
Charles Marsden
Frank H. Mason
Denis Mathews
J. McCulloch
Herbert Mcwilliams
G. Melhuish
H.S. Merritt
Robert Miller
Reginald Mills
V. Baber Mimpriss
Louis Mitelle
Colin Moss
C. Mozley
Brian Mullen
John Munday
Charles Murray
Richard Murry
E.B. Musman
John Napper
Edmund Nelson
C.R.W. Nevinson
Roger Nicholson
Roy Nockolds
L. Noke
Frank Norton
G. Obath
S. Okello
G.W. Lennox Paterson
T.W. Pattison
Edward Payne
R.H. Payne
C.J. Pearce
Ivan Peries
Christopher Perkins
Roger Pettiward
George Plante
Louisa Puller
George Quarmby
F. Quinton
W.T. Rawlinson
Frances Reed
Retziba
Ceri Richards
Leonard Richmond
S. Robertson-Rodgers
Alan Ronald
Michael Rothenstein
William Rothenstein
C.A. Russell
J.A. Russell
C.A. Salisbury
Noel Sampson
Robert Scanlan
Stella Schmolle
Edward Seago
Richard Seddon
E. Shepherd
B. Gordon Smith
David T. Smith
Sidney Smith
Alexander Sonnis
J.M. Spence
John Staerck
Julius Stafford-Baker
P.T. Stainforth
John Stephenson
Juan Stoll
Ian Strang
Felicity Sutton
I.K. Sydee
Eric W. Taylor
Richard Taylor
Patrick Thompson
N.B. Town
Julian Trevelyan
E. Trimnell-Richard
Henry Trivick
G.A. Tuckwell
C.C. Turner
E. Boye Uden
Clive Uptton
Keith Vaughan
Paule Vezelay
S. Curnow Vosper
F.C. Ward
John Ward
William Ware
William Washington
Aubrey Waterfield
Barbara Watson
G.P.H. Watson
A.M. Weston
Garth Weston
Peter Whalley
Tom White
G.W. Whittam
Kaete Wilczynski
Norman Wilkinson *
Anne F. Wilson
J. Wood
Frank Wootton
E.J. Worrall
H.W. Yates
J. Yunge-Bateman
A. Zabalam
Anna Zinkeisen
Doris Zinkeisen

IV) Other:

Phyllis Ginger (work presented by the Court of the Worshipful Company of Goldsmiths)
Martin Hardie (gift)
Herbert A. Olivier (gift)

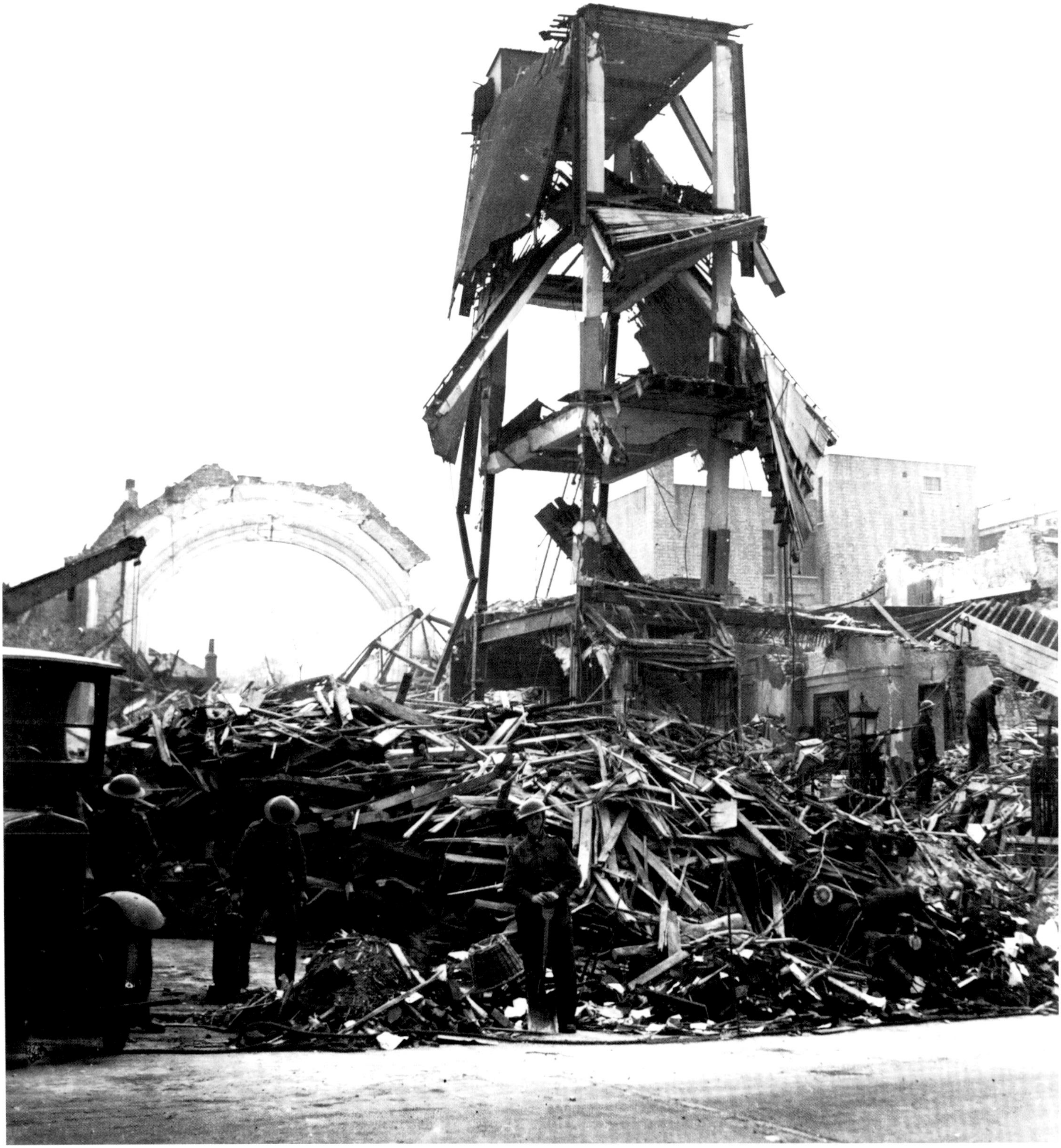

Morley College during the war

By Elaine Andrews

Volunteers Needed.

The London County Council is asking for volunteers for work in war time in connection with the evacuation of mothers and of children under five years of age. A large number is required as the Council hopes to arrange for one adult to look after every ten children, and it is known that with children under five the proportion of adults may have to be even greater. The services required are of three alternative kinds: (a) to accompany children to London stations when a state of emergency is declared; (b) to go with the children for the first week; (c) to remain with them for a considerable period.

Those students who wish to have their names added to the list of volunteers should apply at the College office, where they will be given the necessary form for completion.

EVA M. HUBBACK.

Fig. 2 – Notice from March/April 1939 issue of *Morley magazine.*

In the summer of 1939 Morley College was all set for another successful year. The prospectus was finalised, the students were enjoying the new extension, finished in 1937, which had given them eight fine classrooms, a small concert hall and a purpose-built library. But the possibility of war was known and a notice about the evacuation of children appeared in the March/April 1939 issue of *Morley Magazine*. (Fig. 2)

September 1939 marked the Golden Jubilee of the College, but with the outbreak of war, there was a closure of four weeks for the installation of blackout and other precautions. Twenty tonnes of earth was supplied from Hyde Park for filling flour sacks (sandbags being at a premium), which was done by staff and students. It had been necessary to convert the gymnasium and refreshment room into air raid shelters.

By the end of November, just over half the planned 150 classes were running, and 1,400 students had enrolled, half the peace-time number. At the Emergency meeting of the Morley College Council on September 26th 1939, it was mentioned that last year's students had been contacted with a view to discovering how many might attend and what subjects they would like to study. Sir Ronald Davison from the College Council suggested that Morley should protest strongly about the severity of the black-out conditions in London. A resolution was to be sent to the Ministry for Home Security, "That the Minister for Home Security be invited to reconsider the policy of the Blackout on the ground of its very serious effect on social and cultural life and its depressing effect on the morale of the population."

Fig. 1 – Morley College after being bombed, October 1940, © London Borough of Lambeth

The next meeting was not till November 27th 1939, and it was noted that there was evidence of a strong revival of club life in the College. Also that it had been decided to bring out a duplicated magazine of four or five foolscap pages of the *Morley Magazine* before Christmas, and to open the College on Sunday evenings. In the event a magazine did appear in January 1940 and it was to be the last until the autumn of 1945, although at least two student-compiled magazines are known to have been produced, 'Hyphen' and 'Interrogation Point' (Fig. 3).

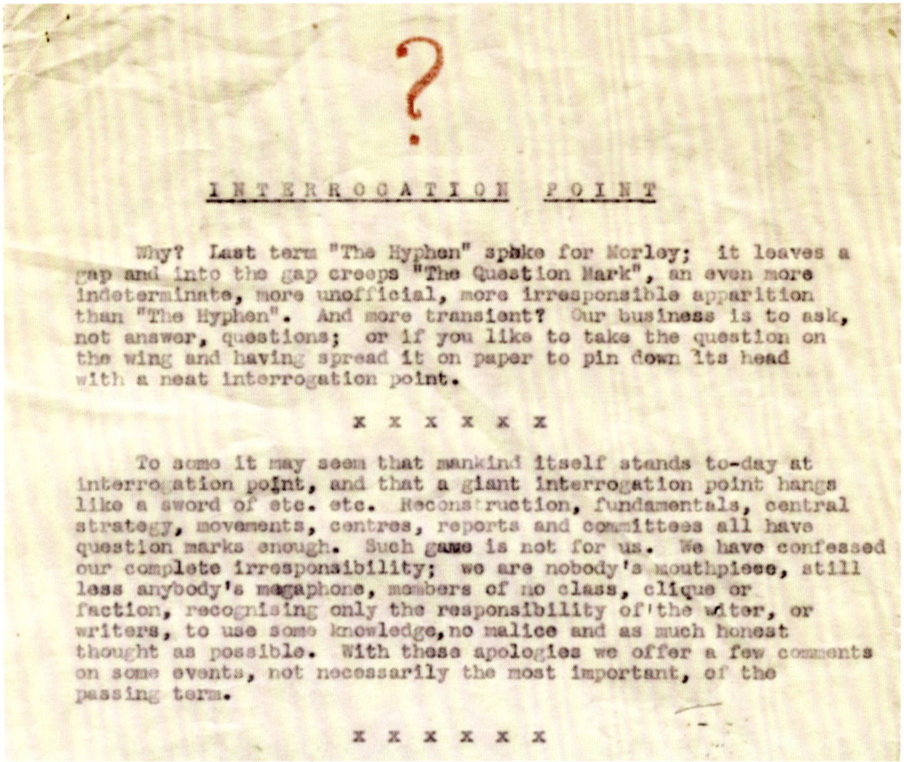

?

INTERROGATION POINT

Why? Last term "The Hyphen" spoke for Morley; it leaves a gap and into the gap creeps "The Question Mark", an even more indeterminate, more unofficial, more irresponsible apparition than "The Hyphen". And more transient? Our business is to ask, not answer, questions; or if you like to take the question on the wing and having spread it on paper to pin down its head with a neat interrogation point.

x x x x x x

To some it may seem that mankind itself stands to-day at interrogation point, and that a giant interrogation point hangs like a sword of etc. etc. Reconstruction, fundamentals, central strategy, movements, centres, reports and committees all have question marks enough. Such game is not for us. We have confessed our complete irresponsibility; we are nobody's mouthpiece, still less anybody's megaphone, members of no class, clique or faction, recognising only the responsibility of the writer, or writers, to use some knowledge, no malice and as much honest thought as possible. With these apologies we offer a few comments on some events, not necessarily the most important, of the passing term.

x x x x x x

Fig. 3 – Excerpt from student magazine 'Interrogation Point', 1942.

The year 1939 started with a bold new venture – a Theatre School, led by former ballet dancer Rupert Doone, supported by an impressive list of tutors and patrons. After the destruction of the main building, the Theatre School moved its activities to the Mary Ward Settlement, putting on plays in the Holst Room and elsewhere, and once the debris was cleared, created an open-air theatre on the bomb site. Winifred Leigh, a founder member, left her archive to Morley, and this gives us a unique picture of the Theatre School, chronicling Morley in wartime, and includes photographs, programmes, posters and reviews. Winifred writes, "On that first day in the Great Hall of Morley College (before it was blitzed), there we were – Rupert Doone, Francis James, Geoffrey Dunn, Miss Mary Skeaping, Miss Gunde von Dechend, about one hundred expectant students and me. The tutors sat in an awe-inspiring row, while one by one the students filed up on the platform, each reading a few lines of prose or verse of their own choosing. Long before it was my turn to go up, the session was over, which was as well as my knees were trembling at the prospect. This did not mean that we were not to be accepted, no one was turned away and the outline of the classes was explained to us." The first production was *The Importance of Being Earnest* in 1941 (Fig. 4) at the Tavistock Little Theatre, followed by *Dido and Aeneas* at the Arts Theatre in 1942.

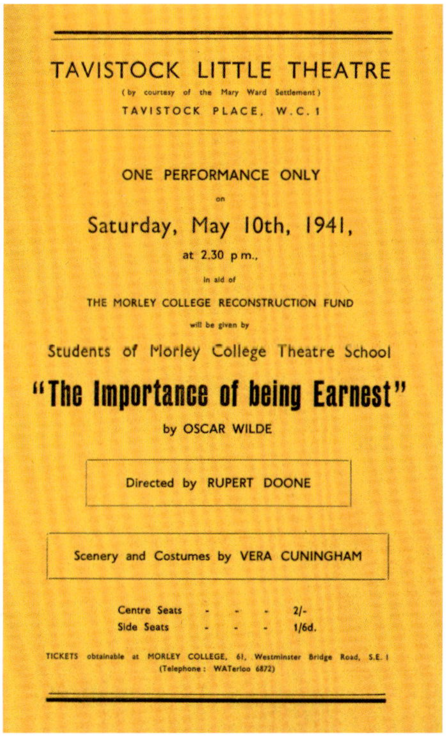

Fig. 4 – *The Importance of Being Ernest*, 1941.

A new series of public lectures were planned, 'The war and the peace' in Spring 1940 was led by 'Strategicus' (H C O'Neill) on 'The War' and a variety of speakers on 'The Peace' which proved very popular. The Arts were not neglected with six lectures on 'Art To-day' in the summer of 1940, with John Piper speaking on Cubism, and Paul Nash on Surrealism.

The Principal reported that attendances in general throughout the session had been excellent in spite of the difficulties of the severe winter, the black-out and the war situation. (College Council Minutes, 28th May 1940)

Enrolment week opened as planned in September 1940, but this coincided with the bombing raids on London. On September 11th the London County Council (L.C.C.) decreed that all evening classes should cease until further notice. Two weeks passed with bombing continuing night after night, and it became plain that holding evening classes was impossible. Eva Hubback devised a still further reduced programme, in which all classes would be held during the daytime and at weekends. These classes were advertised to start on Saturday, October 19th, 1940.

The College had been designated as an emergency rest and feeding centre, and when three blocks of Council flats – Lidford House, York House and Colwyn House had been hit in early October, many families moved into the College. They were cared for by workers from the Lady Margaret Hall Settlement, who supplied them with three meals a day. A few days later a further group from Mountain House joined them. This made around 250 men, women and children being housed in the College. At night about a third of them went across the road to Lambeth North Underground station; the remainder slept in the gymnasium and refreshment-room, which had been protected with sandbags

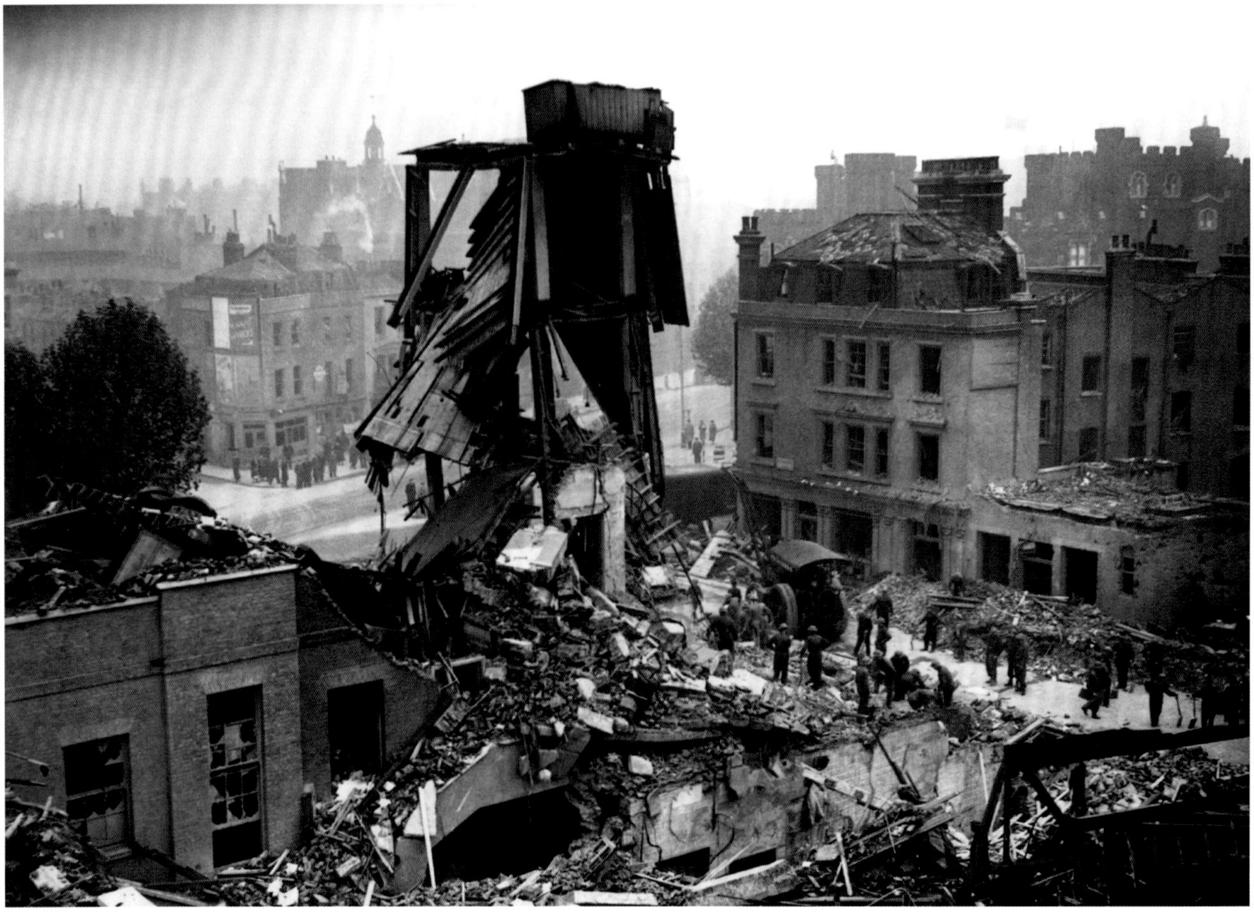

Fig. 5 – Morley College after being bombed, October 1940, © London Borough of Lambeth

On Tuesday evening, October 15th, the alert sounded as usual. Most of the families had gathered in the two protected rooms, but many others continued to chat and play elsewhere in the building. At 7.45 p.m., a 1,000 kilogram high explosive bomb seared through the roof of the Prince of Wales Hall and exploded. The entire block collapsed like a pack of cards. Debris from the blast obliterated many of the houses opposite, leaving an immense cloud of thick dust. With the help of Mr. Dovey, the College school keeper, the rescuers were able to reach most of the trapped families fairly soon; but it was twenty days before the last two bodies were recovered. In all, it was found that 195 people had been on the premises. Eighty-four people escaped unhurt but fifty-four were injured and fifty-seven were killed outright or died later in hospital. The dead included the assistant schoolkeeper, Rosser, and three of his family – the only casualties connected with the College. Lost were the beautiful murals, souvenirs of the days at the Old Vic, and virtually every record except the Council minutes and Cash Books, which had been placed in a small safe, discovered undamaged under piles of debris. The structure of the steel-framed Extension appeared sound, and the Library and Holst Room were undamaged except for broken windows and skylights. A volunteer party armed with picks, shovels and sledge-hammers established a path to it through the debris (Figs. 1 and 5).

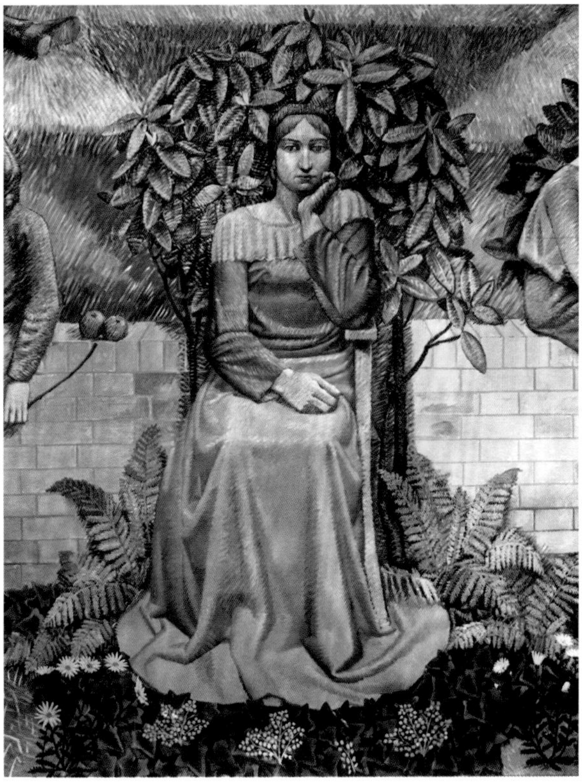
Fig. 6 – Melpomene, from the *Pleasures of life* by Charles Mahoney

Eva Hubback made no fuss about the loss of the building, but deplored only the loss of life. Morley, she declared, would get a much better building when peace returned. By January 1941 she had written her vision for the new Morley. Sadly she never saw it as she died in 1949. She wrote letters of sympathy to the four artists responsible for the mural decorations in the old building: Eric Ravilious, Edward Bawden, Charles Mahoney (Fig. 6) and John Anthony Greene.

It was suggested that the College close for the duration of the war, but that was found unacceptable, so the L.C.C. offered to lend a school, if the College could find one. The College Secretary and Assistant Secretary set off on a search of the neighbourhood, and found Johanna Street School. By the Saturday after the bombing, 21 classes had been scheduled and 164 students had enrolled. An emergency canteen (Fig. 7) was set up in a corridor at the College and the administration functioned from a corner of the Library. By Saturday 21st December, a tea was held in the Holst Room with entertainment from the Theatre School and Orchestra. The following day a discussion was held about the Future of Morley and a Carol Service was held in Christ Church. By the middle of 1941, the bombing raids had lessened and classes began to pick up.

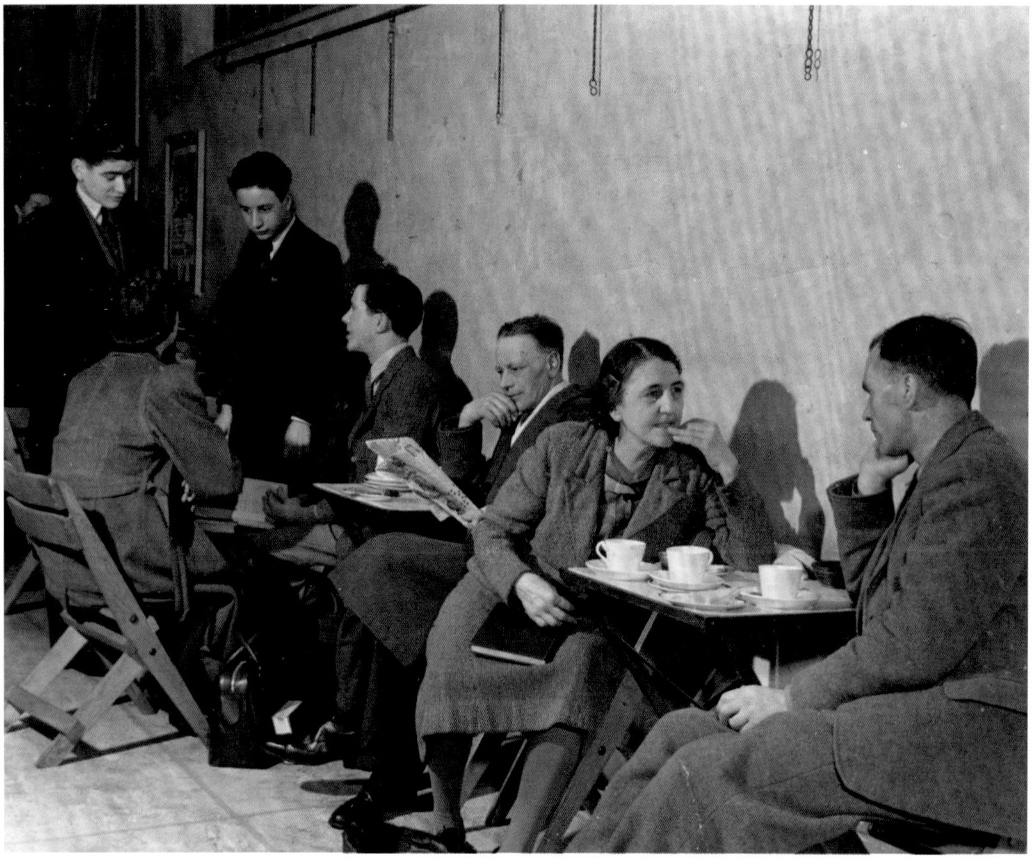

Fig. 7 – Canteen in the corridor of Morley College.

With the loss of the Prince of Wales Hall, the scope for lectures was reduced as the maximum number allowed in the Holst Room was 100. Nevertheless an ambitious programme was organised, with a series called 'From Now On" featuring George Orwell and Stephen Spender. Two sets of lectures on 'Ballet' in 1942 and 1943 proved to be really popular with people having to be turned away. Ninette de Valois lectured twice, and on the second occasion refused to take a fee. Lydia Sokolova, a former dancer with Diaghilev talked first on The Diaghilev Russian Ballet, and came again to talk on Nijinsky, Karsavina and Pavlova. A letter survives in the archive from Tamara Karsavina herself, who was too busy to talk and another former Diaghilev dancer, Lydia Lopokova sent two charming postcards declaring 'Giving a lecture is not my cup of tea' (Fig. 8).

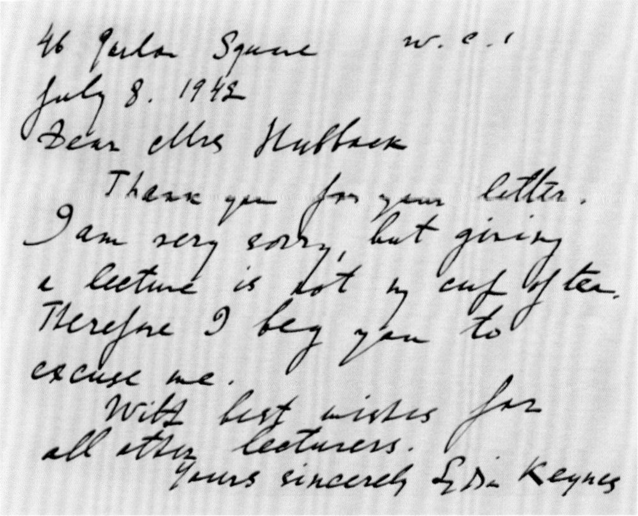

46 Gordon Square W.C.1
July 8. 1942
Dear Mrs Hubback
Thank you for your letter.
I am very sorry, but giving
a lecture is not my cup of tea.
Therefore I beg you to
excuse me.
With best wishes for
all other lecturers.
Yours sincerely Lydia Keynes

Fig. 8 – Postcard to Morley College from Lydia Lopokva.

In its December 1939 issue, *Music in Schools* had reported on Morley's musical life: "The madrigalists meet on Mondays at 6.30 (about thirty turned up for the start), and from 7.30 to 9 (the hour when the law now decrees such institutions must close their doors) the choir of about sixty meets. Morley College is full of that friendly spirit, under the Principalship of Mrs. E. M. Hubback. Here democracy, musicianship, good cheer still flows as, a generation ago, they flowed under Holst's direction: the spirit that makes plain people do things they never thought they could, losing shyness and forgetting their troubles as they work. That is the spirit, above all, in which to meet and beat these gruelling times." The Choir at one point had shrunk to only eight members, and the Orchestra just nine, but both were back to full strength by 1944-45.

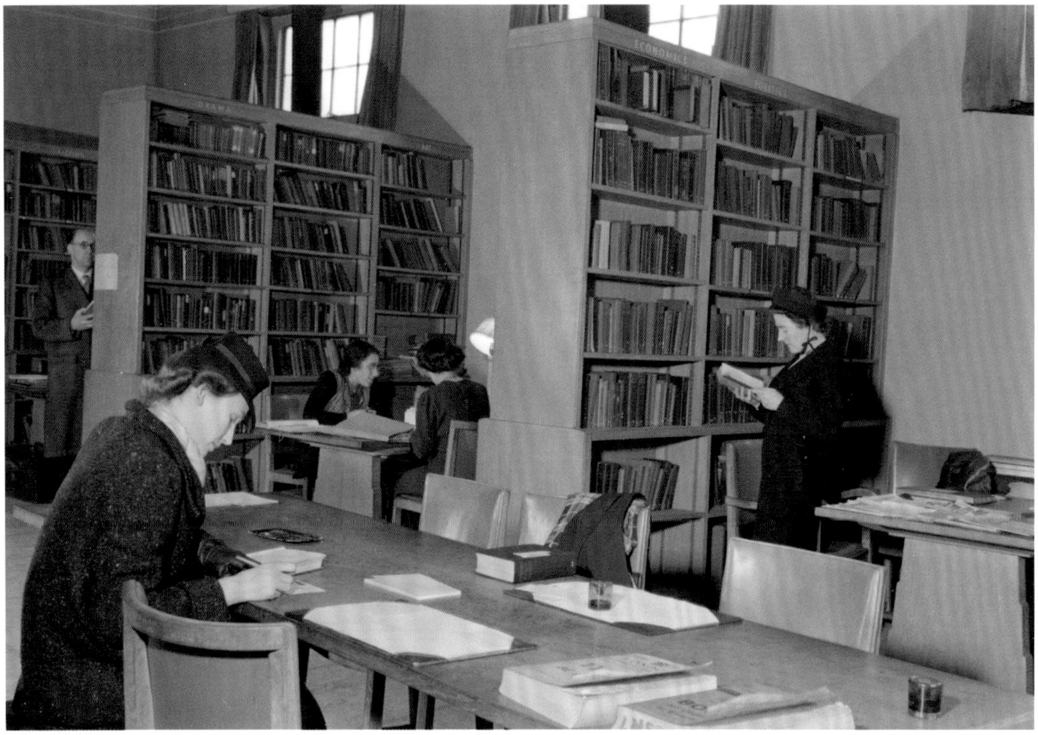

Fig. 9 – Morley College library during the war.

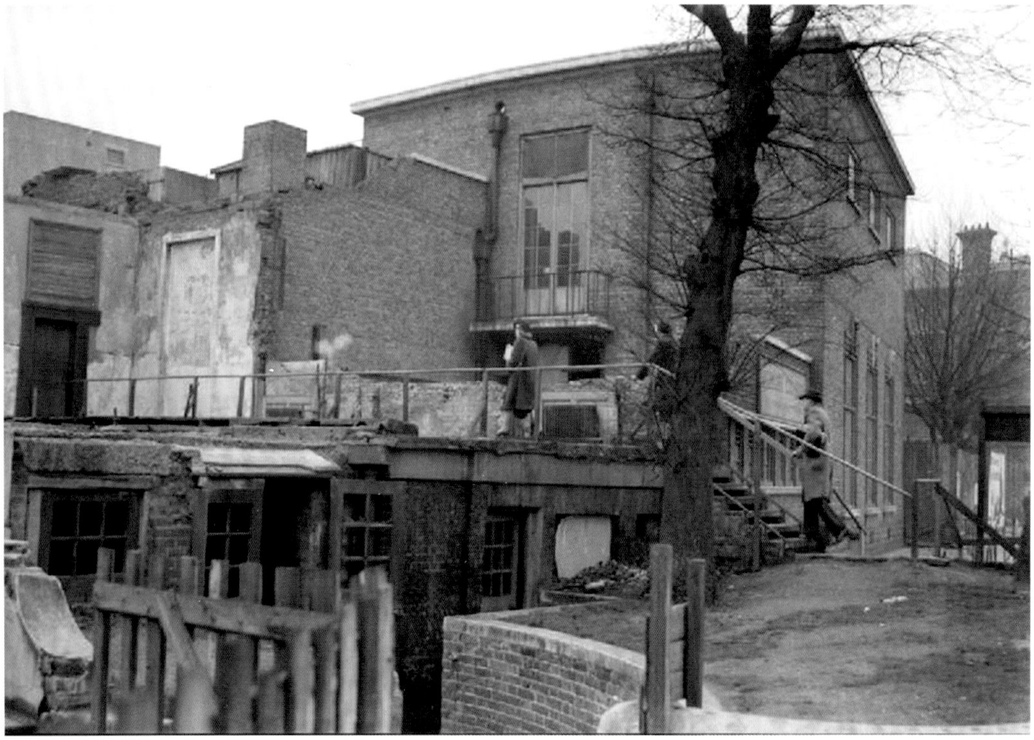

Fig. 10 – Morley College.after the bombing.

The Director of Music, Arnold Foster, left London in 1941 and his place was taken by Michael Tippett, who had been running an orchestra for unemployed musicians at the College since 1933. The College Council Minutes of 26th February 1943 reported, "the College Choir, under Michael Tippett, had recently fulfilled two public engagements, each at short notice and in place of known choral societies. The first was a concert of Christmas music at the Orpheum, Golders Green, with the London Philharmonic Orchestra, the College Choir in this instance taking the place of the Bach Choir; and the second a programme of French songs by Ravel and Debussy at the Wigmore Hall, in place of the Fleet Street Choir. Both concerts were highly successful. The Council agreed that Michael Tippett was to be congratulated upon his initiative and enthusiasm in undertaking this work and the choir upon their wholehearted and enthusiastic support of their tutor. But that enthusiastic work faced an interruption in 1943, when he was sentenced to three months imprisonment for refusing to comply with an order of the Ministry of Labour and National Service to undertake agricultural work. Both Eva Hubback and Ralph Vaughan Williams were called as witnesses when the case was brought up. In the end, Tippett spent only two months in Wormwood Scrubs where he worked with the prison orchestra, and managed (against normal prison rules) to act as page turner for a concert given by Benjamin Britten and Peter Pears. Later that year, Matyas Seiber took the College Choir to the BBC's Maida Vale Studios to record a programme of Yugo-Slav folk songs, which was broadcast in September. New tutors taken on during war-time included Walter Bergmann, who introduced the Recorder to the music students, Matyas Seiber, Antony Hopkins, and Walter Goehr. The Morley Choir took part in the first performance of Tippett's oratorio 'A Child of Our Time' in 1944, and this sealed Tippett's reputation as a leading figure in English music.

The end of the war brought large numbers of students back to Morley and they soon overfilled the depleted accommodation, classes took place in various local schools for many years until the new building was completed in 1958. The battle to get Morley rebuilt was faithfully recorded by Denis Richards (Principal 1950-65) in his history of the College, *Offspring of the Vic*, and later in his memoirs, *It might have been worse: recollections 1941-1966*.

Sources: *Offspring of the Vic: a history of Morley College*, Denis Richards, Routledge, 1958.
Morley Magazine, College Council Minutes, ARP Report.
'October Incident' by George Cottrell, *Morley Magazine,* 60th anniversary issue, 1952.

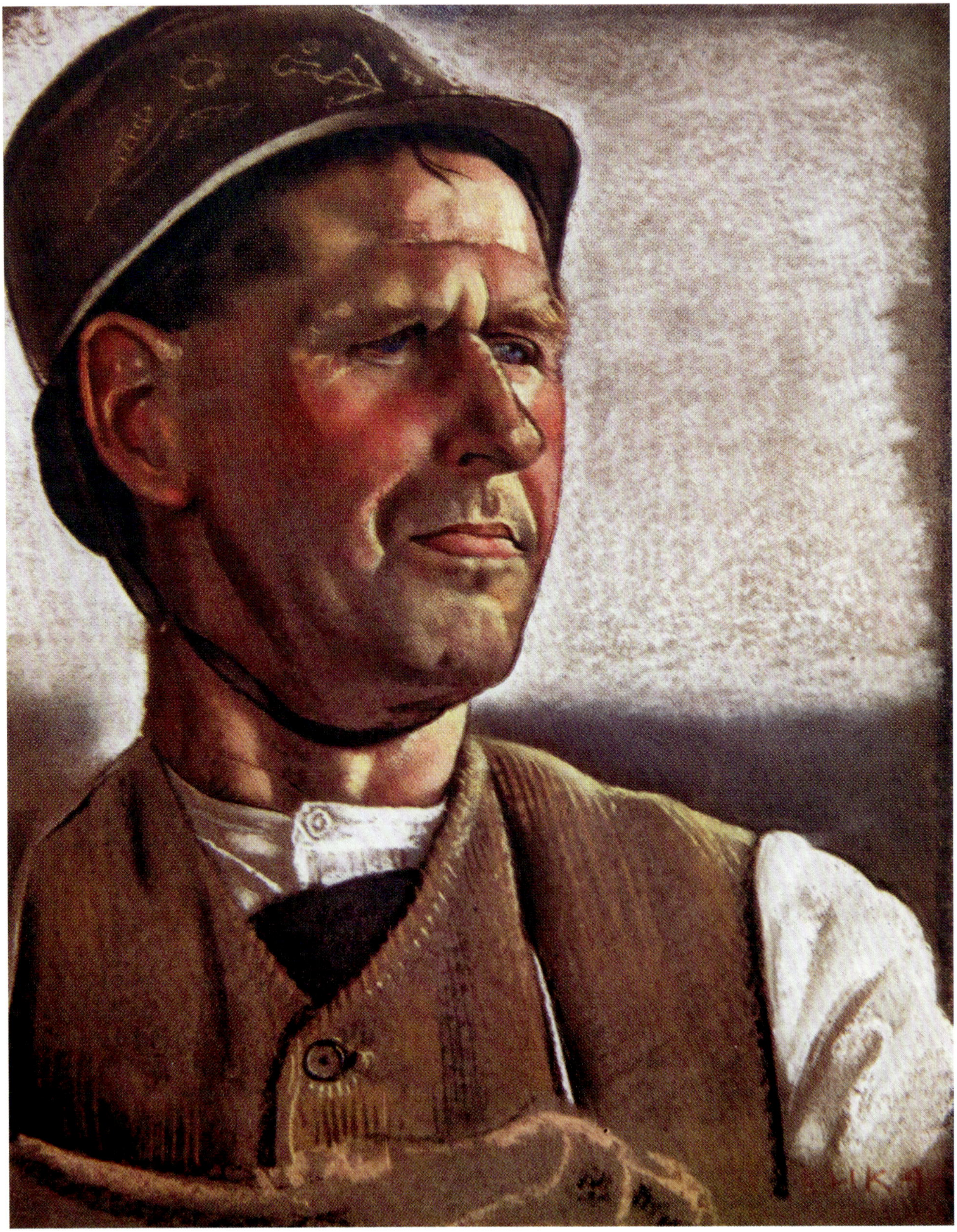

William Henry Pickford by Eric H. Kennington.
The sitter was employed in quarrying limestone in Derbyshire.

ICI: PORTRAITS OF AN INDUSTRY PRESTIGE ADVERTISEMENTS

By Margaret Bear

> *Within these covers there are brought together, for the first time so far as I know, the portraits of a representative selection of the people on whom one of the basic industries of Britain depends for the efficiency of its production and for the research which is necessary to enable it to keep at least abreast, and often ahead of the best that our overseas competitors can achieve.*[1]

Imperial Chemical Industries made advertising history during WW2 by conveying its message not only on its own behalf but also on behalf of British artists. In an endeavour to raise the prestige of British research and the British chemical industry throughout the world, their public relations controller, Sidney Rogerson, obtained permission to adopt a different approach to advertising.[2] To this end, fifty-six portraits of ICI employees were commissioned by ICI from leading British artists between 1942-1944, for use in a nationwide newspaper advertising campaign.

It was Rogerson's contention that, as commercial advertising was unnecessary during the war, it was important to develop a strategy to keep ICI's profile high. Having been the largest advertiser in the British trade press, rather than withdraw all advertising, he would use the space to inform the public about the chemical industry itself. He would choose topics of interest not commonly known, in order to communicate the uses of chemicals for processing primary commodities. To achieve this goal, he devised a unique approach – deliberately designed to escape convention – which he called 'Prestige Advertising.'[3]

The first in the series of three was *Aspects of an Industry* which appeared in the national press July 1941- June 1942. This was immediately followed by *Services of an Industry*, July 1942 - August 1944, and finally the third, *Portraits of an Industry*, September 1944 - March 1946. Each had a different theme, but collectively served a similar purpose specific to the war years. Between 1946 and 1950 there were three further series of prestige advertisements, *Equipment, Ancestors and Elements of an Industry*; however this essay is confined to *Portraits of an Industry*.

There were several layers of intent in the *Portraits* series. Lord McGowan stated that one of the objects of these advertisements was 'to show one half of the ICI family what the other half looked like, what it did, and how its work affected the life of the community'.[4] More broadly, it was aimed at informing the public of the sort of men and women employed by the company and how their work 'benefited the nation in health or wealth, in peace as in war'.[5] To achieve this, the plan was to adorn the page on which the advertisement appeared – not merely inform. Crucially, the commissions provided badly needed employment for British artists. But the key objective was propaganda. It was a means to counter Germany's dominance in the field, pursuant to its military and scientific successes. Disseminating information would help regain the prestige of British trade in overseas markets.[6]

As well-painted portraits were critical to the success of the advertisements, Rogerson wanted 'men who were doing serious work without being fashionable' to paint them.[7] To this end he sought advice from Sir Kenneth Clark – Provisional Chairman of The Central Institute of Art and Design (CIAD)[8], who provided a list of willing and available artists.[9] These included such distinguished artists as Charles Cundall; William Dring; Eric Kennington; B. Fleetwood-Walker; F. Ernest Jackson and Rupert Shephard, among the nineteen artists.

For each portrait, the artists were given a choice from six to ten people selected by different ICI divisions, from which they were at liberty to chose their subject.[10] Most of the artists did several portraits, involving much travel around England, Scotland and Wales, as the portraits were done on site. The media used included oil, watercolour, pastel drawings and gouache. The artists were paid fifty pounds per portrait upon completion, plus expenses. Not only did the artists benefit from the commissions, but the public was afforded fresh and extensive contact with the arts.

Rogerson wanted portraits of typical men and women from the factories, workshops and research laboratories around the country, illustrating ICI's great diversity of products. It was intended to heap praise and publicity on the unsung heroes of the war effort, who received none of the plaudits given for instance to government workers filling the bombs. The ICI workers performed the essential work without which there would be no explosives to fit into shell cases or bombs.

The sitters, of whom eleven were women, varied in age from a war disabled man in his twenties to some over seventy and everything between. Several due for retirement had volunteered to stay on because their expertise was required during the war. Many had started work as early as eleven years old and put in over fifty years on the job. In many instances, a specific trade had been in a particular family for three or more generations, with all members of the family on the job. One worker had a record of seven sons, one daughter, two grandsons, and eleven nephews and nieces employed at the same time!

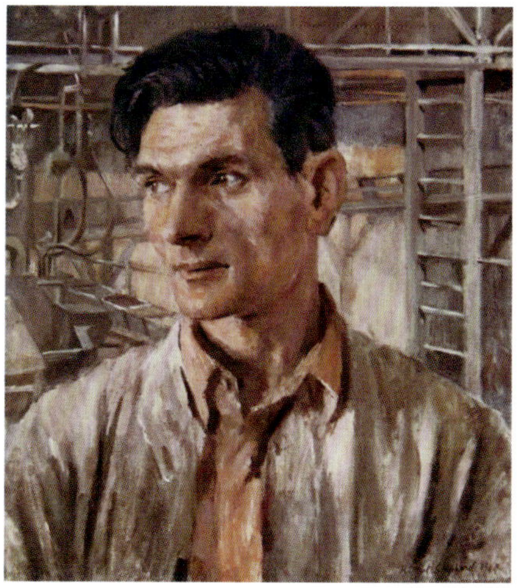

Henry Jack Bowmer
by Rupert Shephard

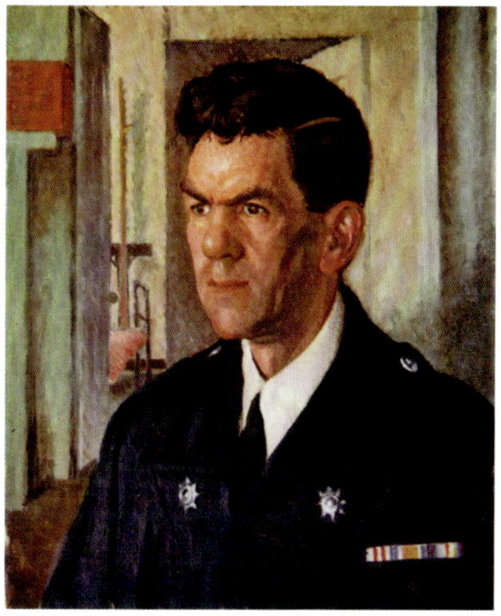

William Tyler
by F. Ernest Jackson

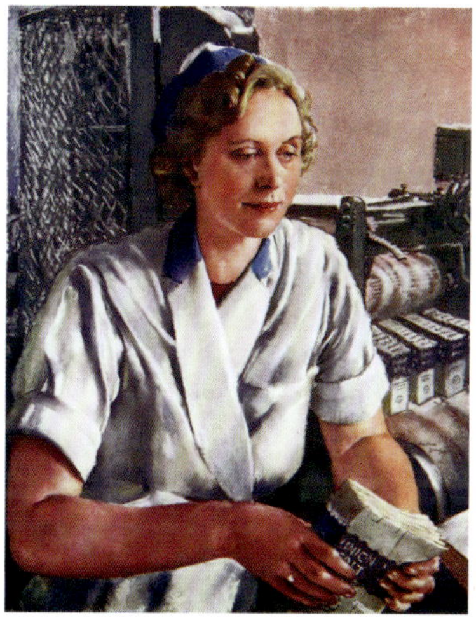

Lily Brookes
by William Dring

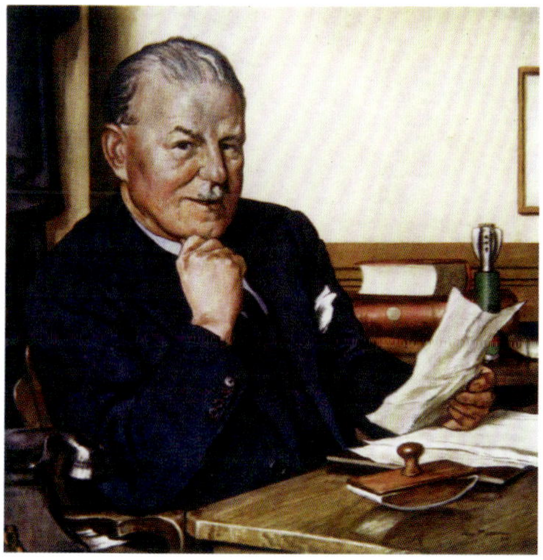

Adam Wilson
by Alex Macpherson

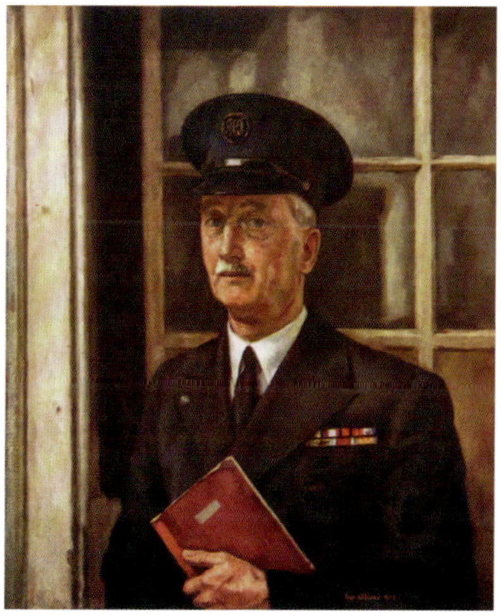

John A. Carleton
by Ivor Williams

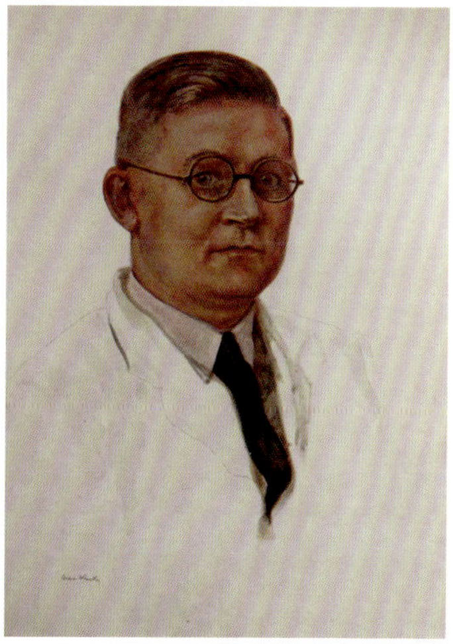

Arthur George Fishburn
by Grace Wheatley

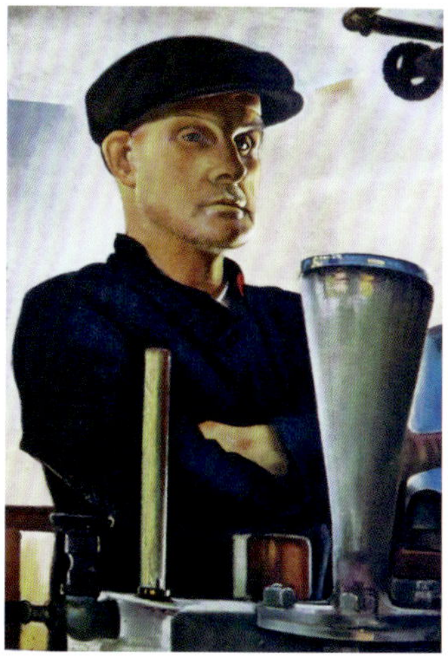

William Farrell
by Eric H. Kennington

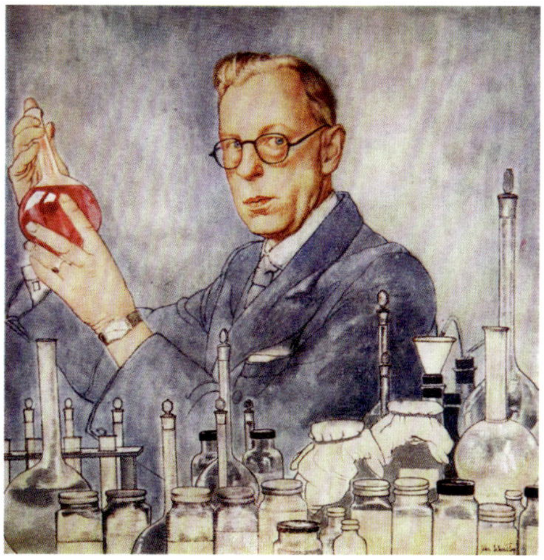

George Oswald Mitchell
by John Wheatley

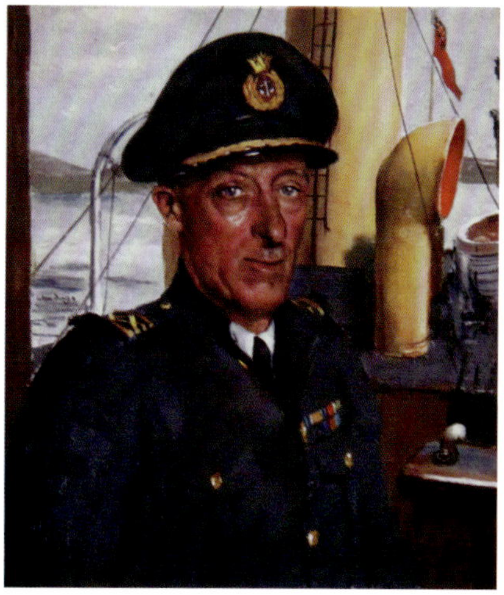

Robert Bond
by William Dring

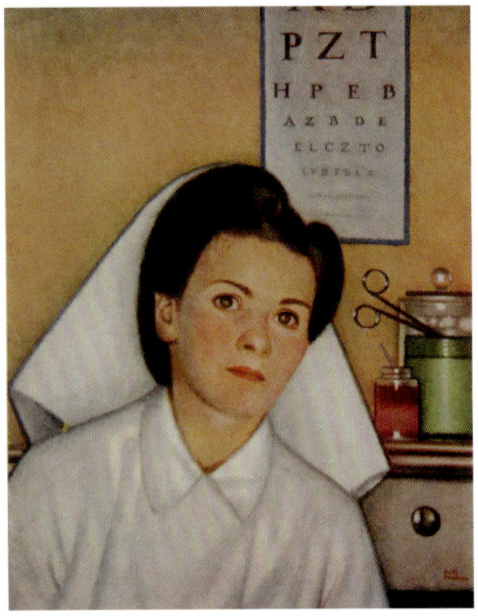

Sister Childes
by Keith Henderson

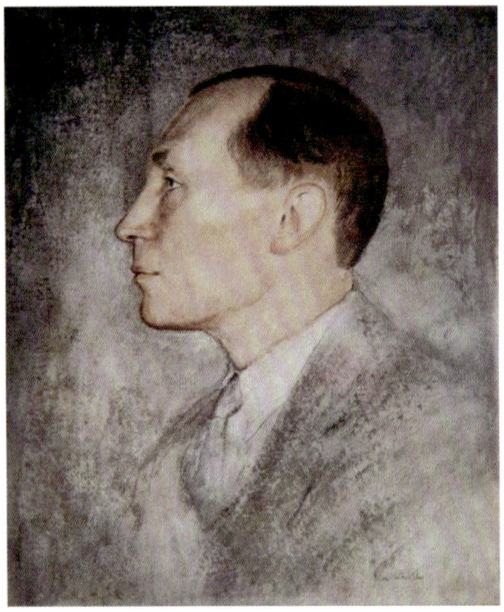

W.S. Bristowe
by John Wheatley

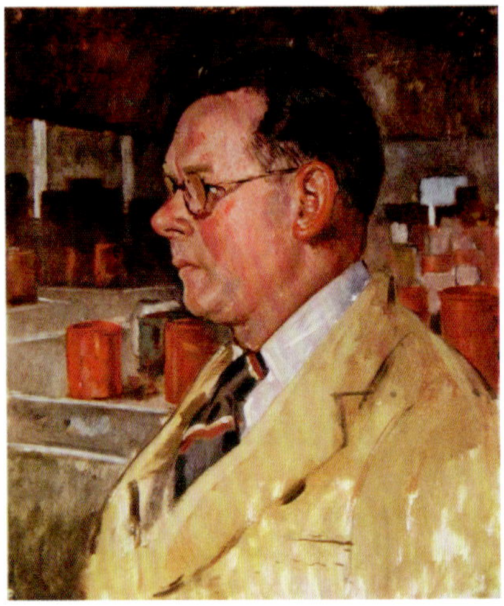

John Francis O'Malley
by F. Ernest Jackson

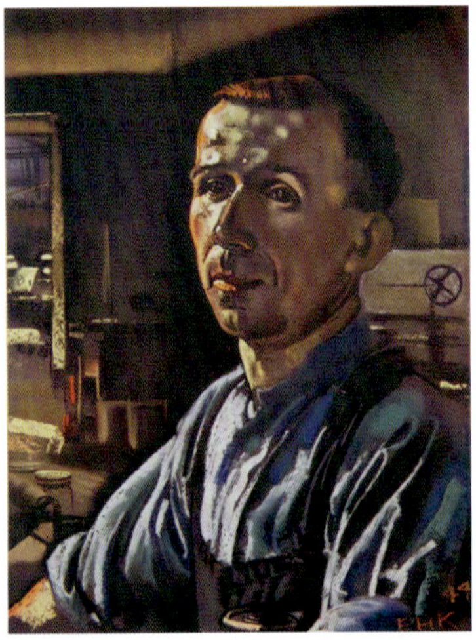

George Robinson
by Eric H. Kennington

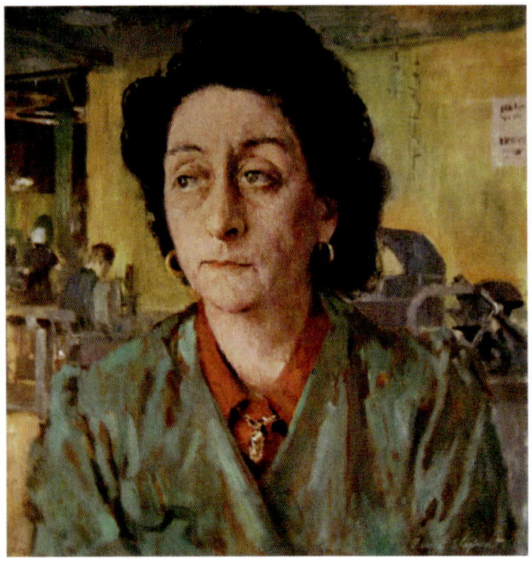

Olive Herman
by Rupert Shephard

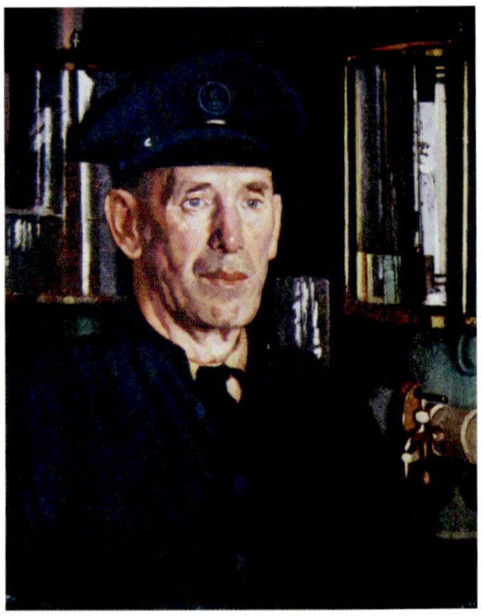

William Ritchie
by Miles de Montmorency

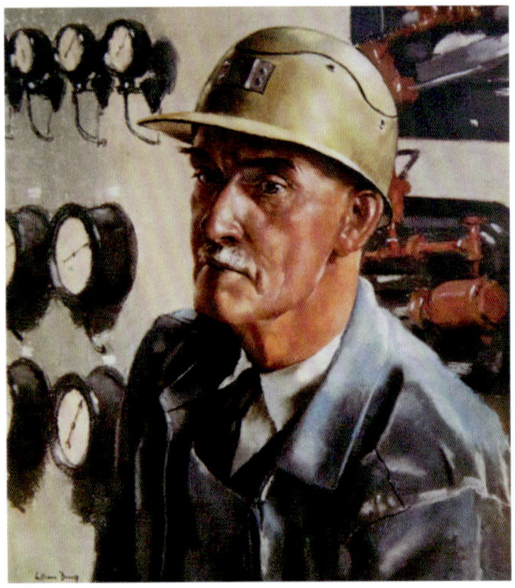

Thomas Merrill
by William Dring

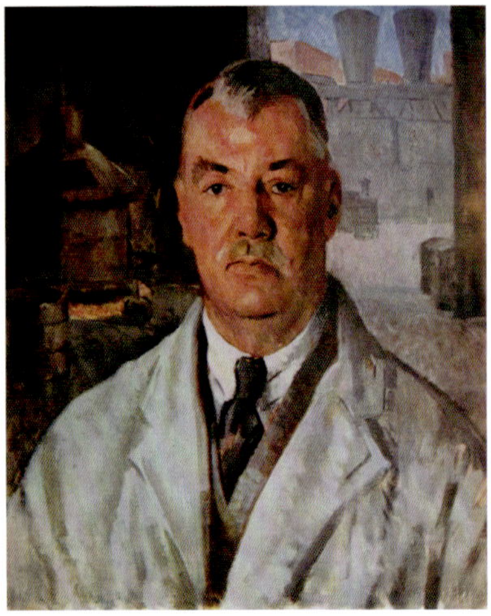

Albert Roberts
by F. Ernest Jackson

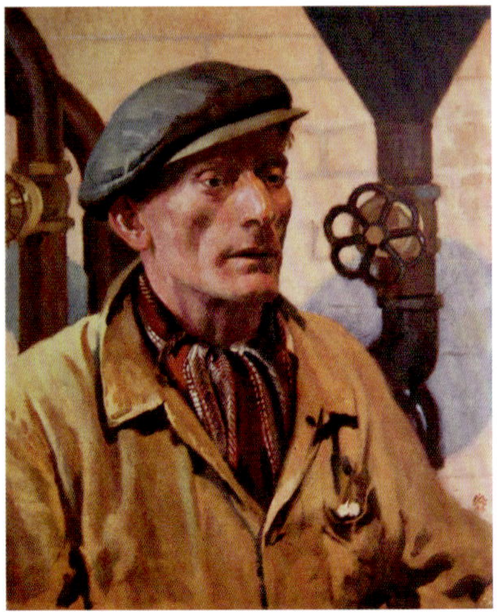

James Cunningham
by Miles de Montmorency

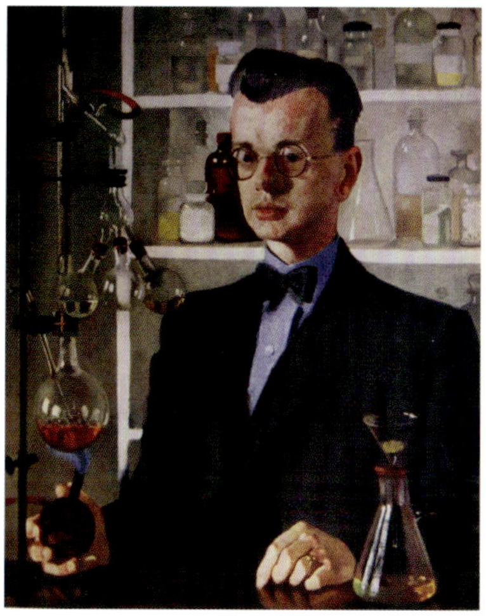

Norman Haddock
by Doris Zinkeisen

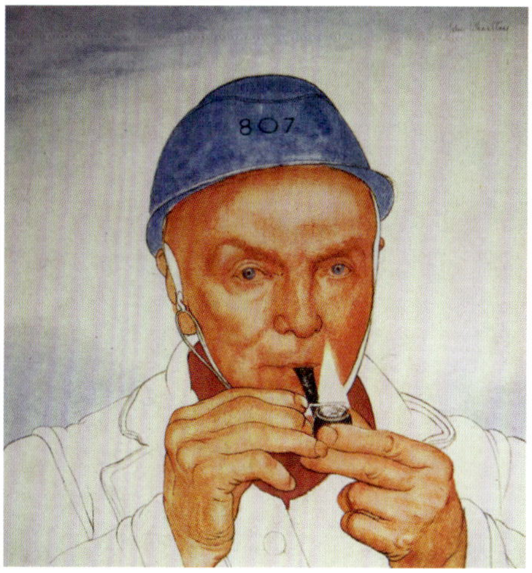

James Spencer
by John Wheatley,

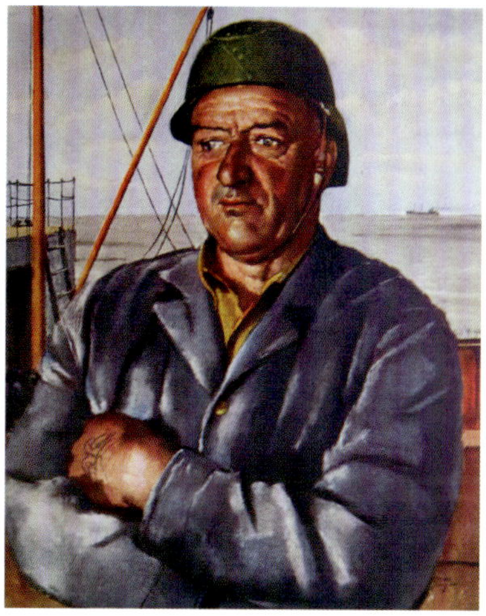

Edward Jones
by William Dring

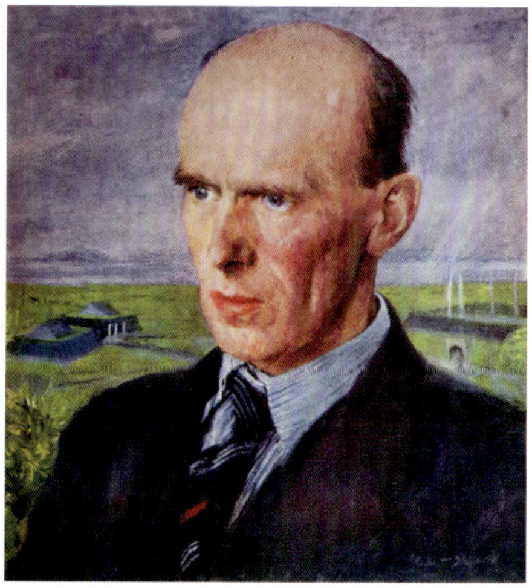

John Robert Douglas
by Rupert Shephard

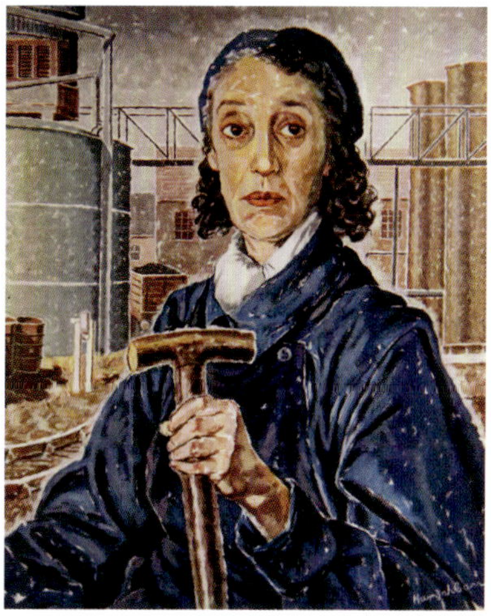

Sarah Ann Brown
by Hamzah Carr

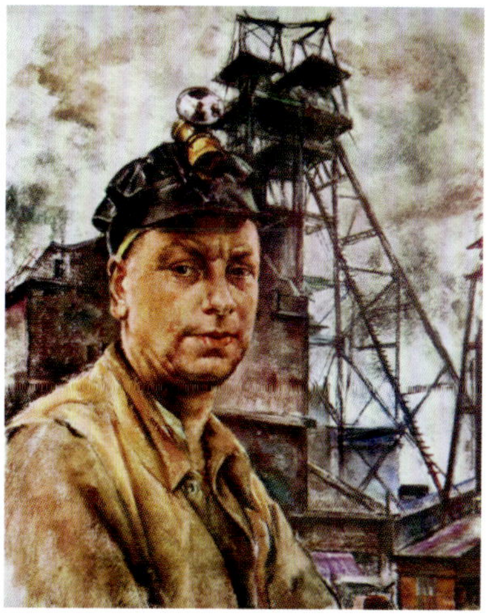

John Whitehead
by J.A. Grant

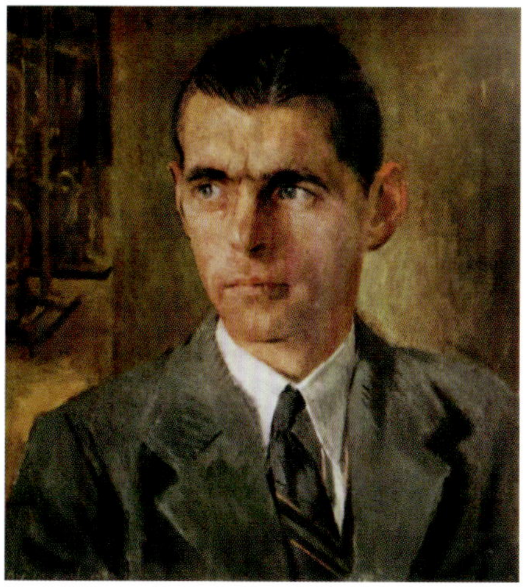

Peter Andrew Gardiner
by Rupert Shephard

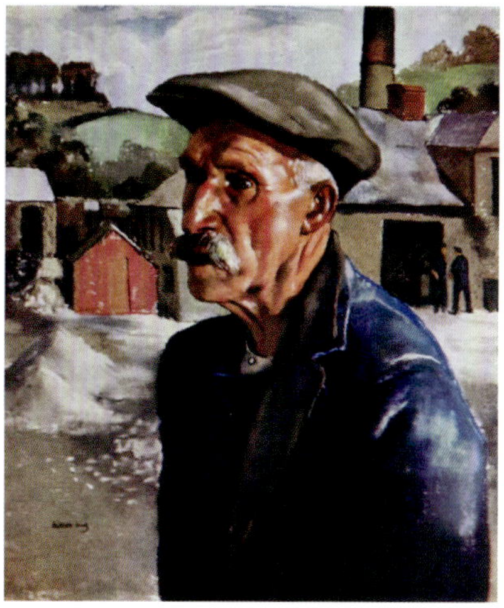

Alan Lobb
by William Dring

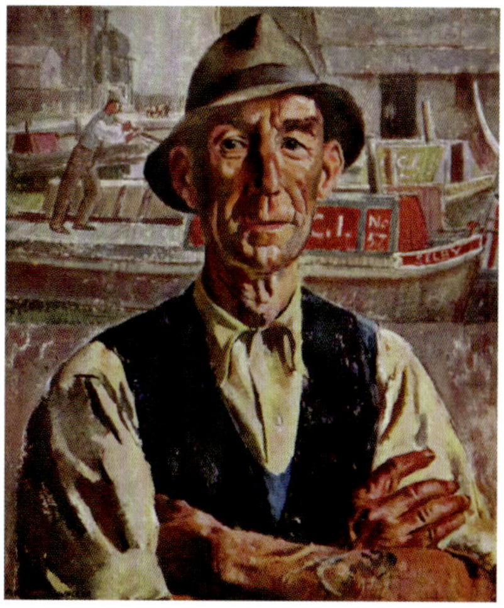

George Henry Garner
by B. Fleetwood-Walker

The resultant advertisements were intentionally not commercial in appearance, with only the ICI rondel inserted in a corner. Besides the reproduction of the portrait, they included some text with background information about each individual, plus a description of their occupation at ICI. Collectively, they illustrate a wide range of workers representing a huge diversity of labour, which involved salt, coal, limestone, plastics, varnish, dyestuffs, paints, brass, leathercloth, industrial explosives, synthetic drugs, to name but a few products. Management is represented along with research chemists, medical staff and safety officers, but the majority of the portraits represent those doing the essential labour, often very specialised craftsmen. Depicting what each individual was doing was a means of showing appreciation, as well as conveying the importance of their role and that of ICI. What particularly appealed to the public was best expressed by Henry Rushbury, who, in his praise of the Portraits, remarked that 'nobody before had ever thought of drawing the common man in industry'. [11]

No longer confined to the trade press, the advertisements appeared in a wide variety of newspapers and publications throughout Great Britain, including *The Times*, *The Scotsman*, *The Glasgow Herald*, *The Studio*, *Art and Industry* and *War Illustrated*, among many others. In fact, for five or more years, 'pictures commissioned by ICI from painters of good standing have appeared in the magazines of Britain and the Commonwealth, of Western Europe, the Middle East and South America'. [12]

Because of the interest these portraits generated within and outside ICI, an exhibition was held in London at the RBA Suffolk Street Galleries from 18th October to 9th November, 1946. It was organised with help from the CIAD and the New English Art Club. An illustrated catalogue was published in association with the Arts Council of Great Britain – *Portraits of an Industry: An Exhibition of Paintings depicting the Personnel, Aspects, and Services of the British Chemical Industry.* Sir Charles Tennyson stated that these advertisements had made advertising history by carrying a message overseas, 'not only on behalf of the British chemical industry, but all British Art'. [13] So successful was the exhibition that it subsequently travelled around England and Scotland over a period of two years, 1947-1948.

A glowing review in a Scottish newspaper described the exhibition as 'most out of ordinary' largely because of the subjects being 'ordinary working people ... some of whom have the sweat of the day's toil on their brows and grime on their hands ... which tells the story of the British man-in-the-street's inherent capacity for hard work.' It went on to say, 'It tells one aspect of our rough island story, and it leaves a message of rehability and sound craftsmanship'. [14]

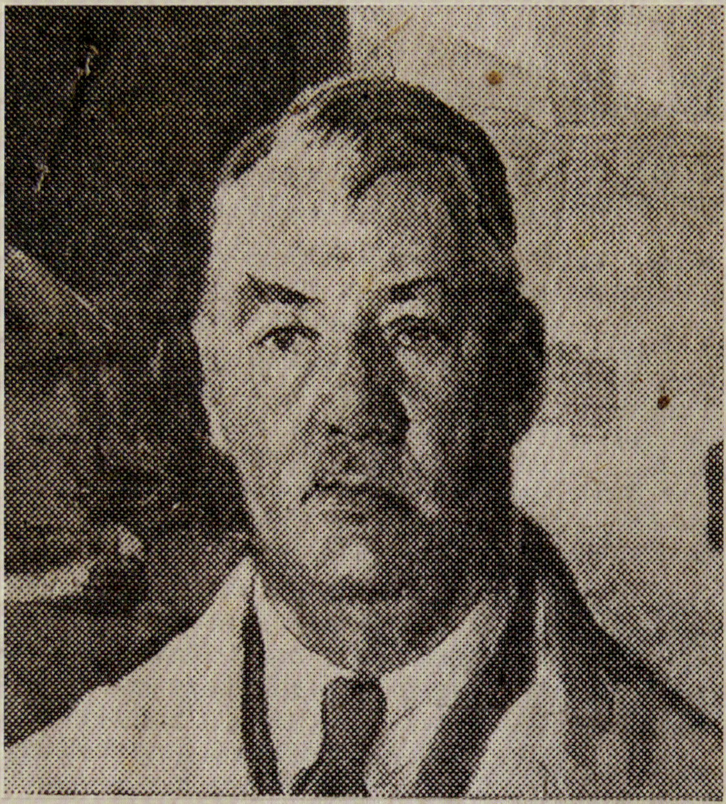

Painted by F. Ernest Jackson, A.R.A.

ALBERT ROBERTS is a Londoner born at Silvertown 65 years ago. For half a century he has been a varnish maker, as were his father and his grandfather before him. For six years he learned his craft as his father's apprentice, and next spent three years with a French paint-mixer near Paris. He was then qualified to follow his calling and entered the chemical industry in 1904. In those days varnishes were made entirely from natural products, from vegetable oils and from gums gathered in the forests of the Congo and East Africa, Batavia, Brazil and New Zealand. These raw materials varied from parcel to parcel and only long experience and expert skill could teach a man how to treat each consignment by sorting and heating and blending, to give a product of uniform quality. Since then the chemist has evolved in the laboratory resins made from chemicals whose purity is known, and the chemical engineer has devised plant in which the commercial manufacture of these can be controlled to one degree of temperature. The art of the varnish-maker as represented by Mr. Roberts has thus been combined with chemical precision to produce paints, varnishes and lacquers far in advance of the products of earlier days. Whereas in peacetime those made by Mr. Roberts were used for industrial and domestic purposes, today they go to protect the gun, the ship and the plane, and range from gas-resistant paints to matt paint for camouflaging ships and buildings. Were it not that his expert services are needed in the national effort, Mr. Roberts would before this have been enjoying a well-earned retirement. When he is at last able to leave his post he will take with him the satisfaction that he has handed on his experience to others who will make the still better paints and varnishes of Tomorrow.

ICI

An example of a typical advertisement incorporating both portrait and biographical text with the ICI rondel.

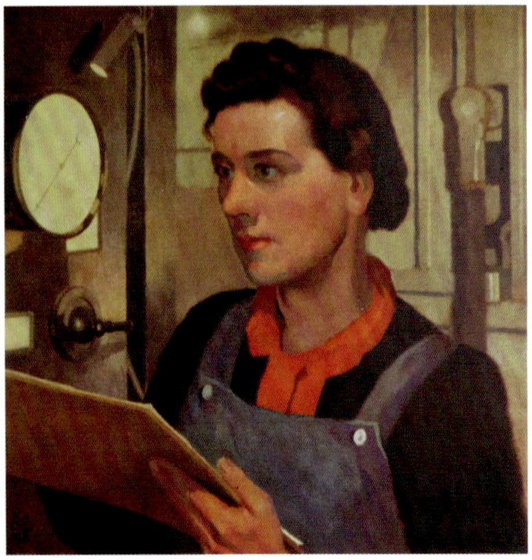

Ellen McCoy
by Miles de Montmorency

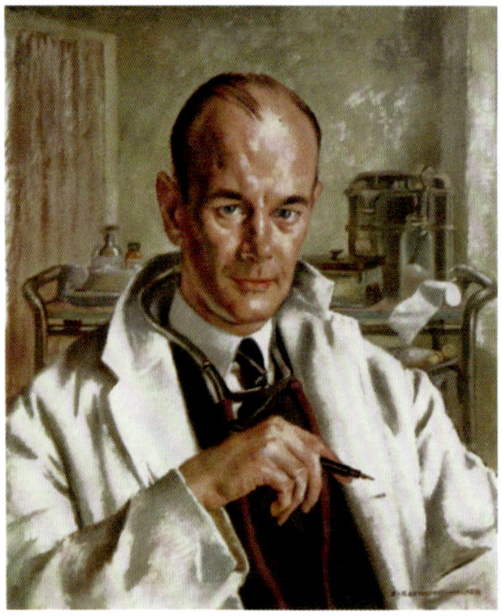

Neil G. Marr
by B. Fleetwood-Walker

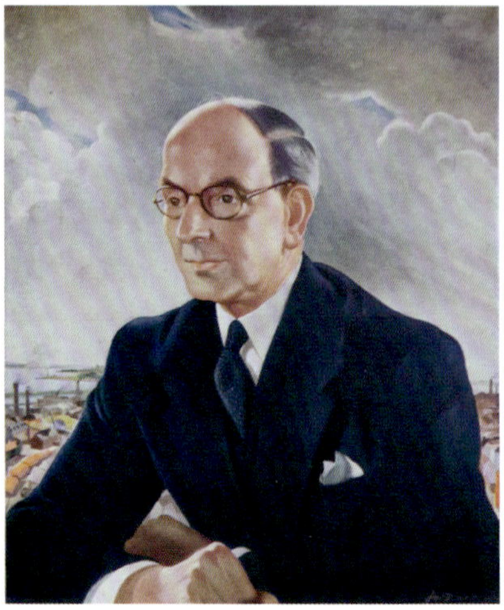

John Williams
by Anna K. Zinkeisen

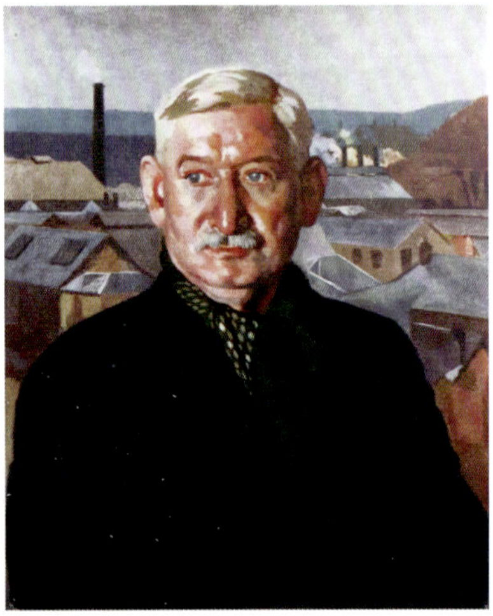

Tom Davies
by Miles de Montmorency

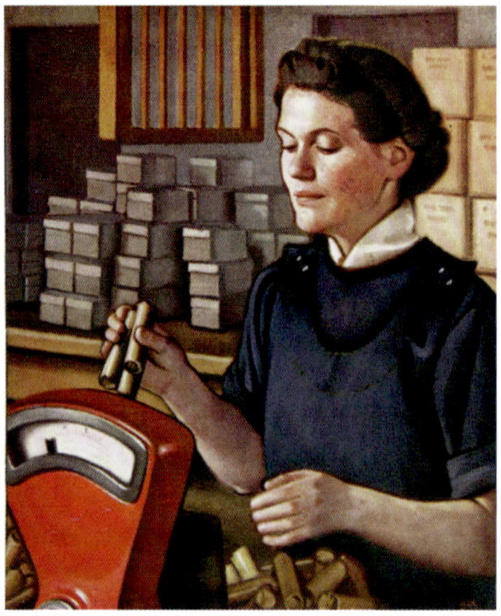

Agnes Hamilton
by Keith Henderson

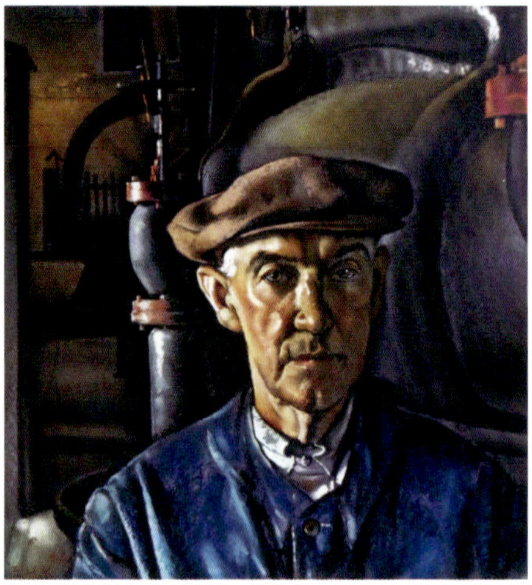

Oswald Carter
by Eric H. Kennington

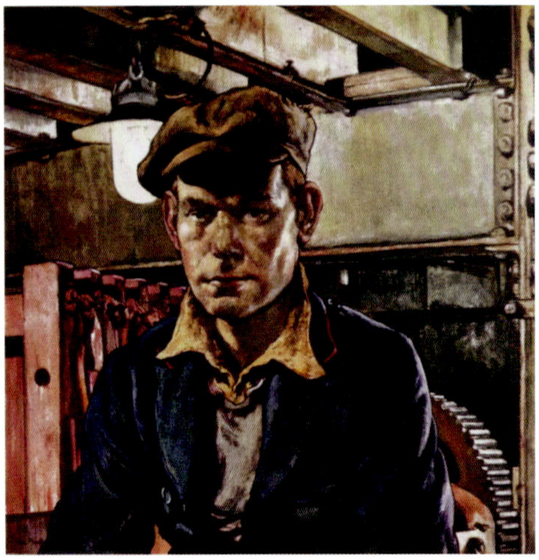

Thomas Sneddon
by Alex Macpherson

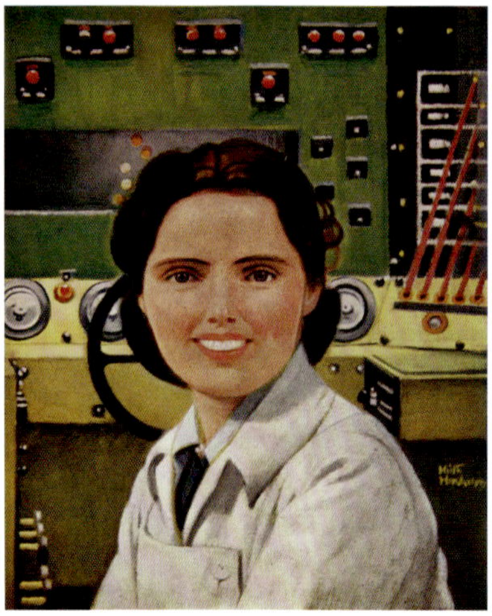

Winifred Burgess
by Keith Henderson

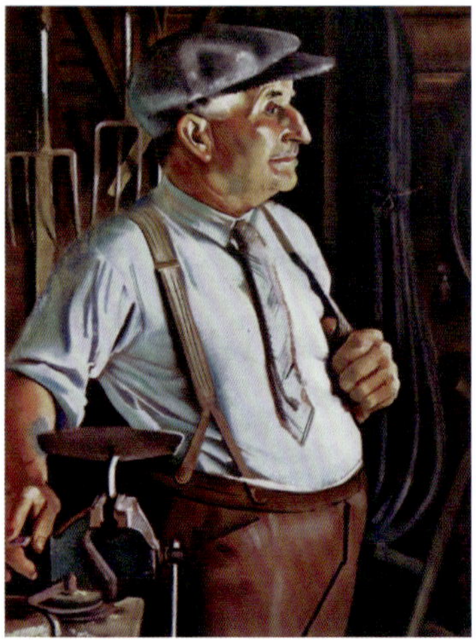

John Lugg
by Eric H. Kennington

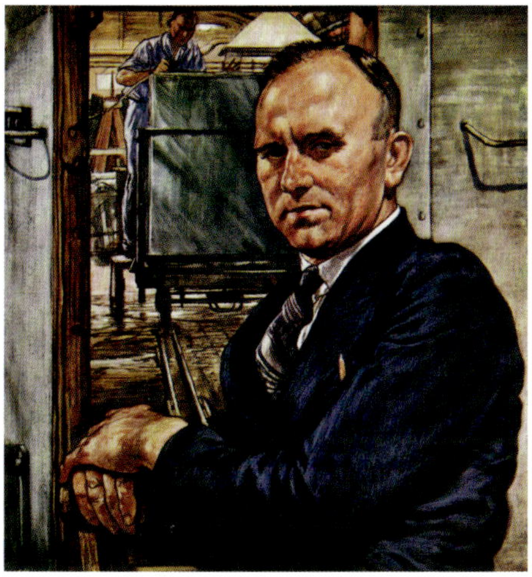

James Jackson
by Alex Macpherson

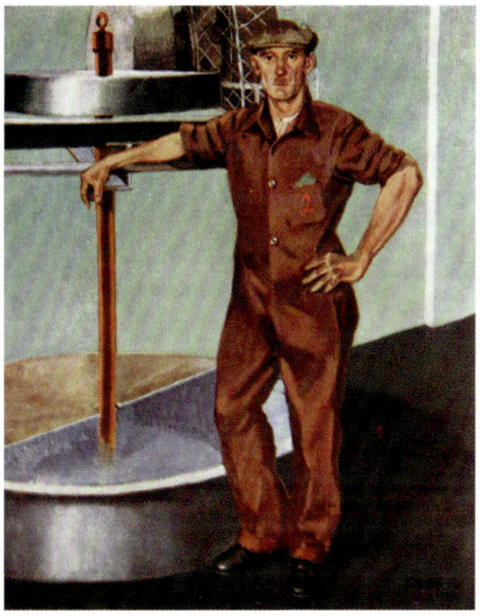

Alfred Berry
by J. Kinnersley Kirby

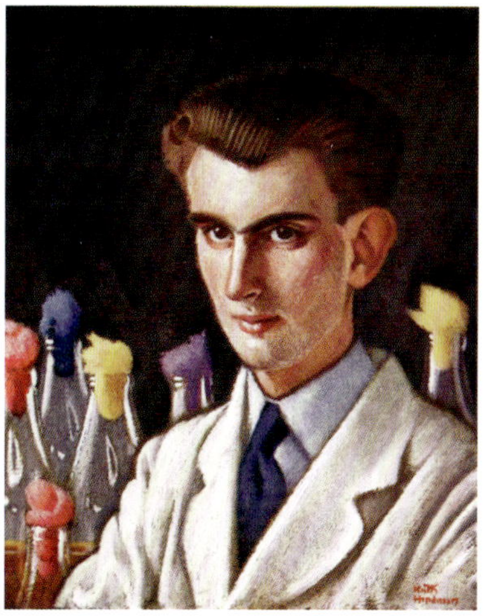

Frank Albert Kendrick
by Keith Henderson

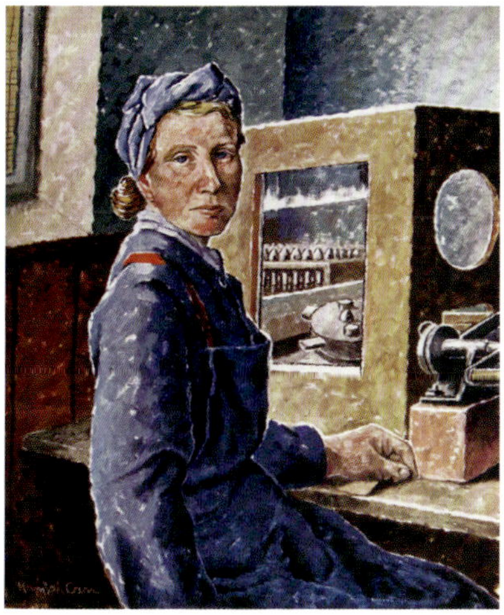

Agnes Wilson
by Hamzah Carr

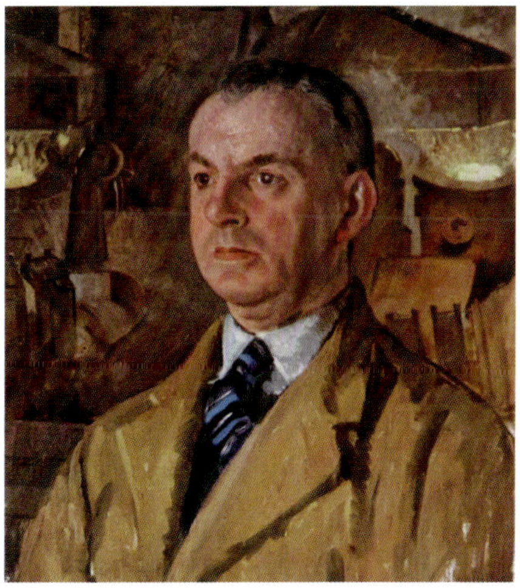

Joseph Russell
by F. Ernest Jackson

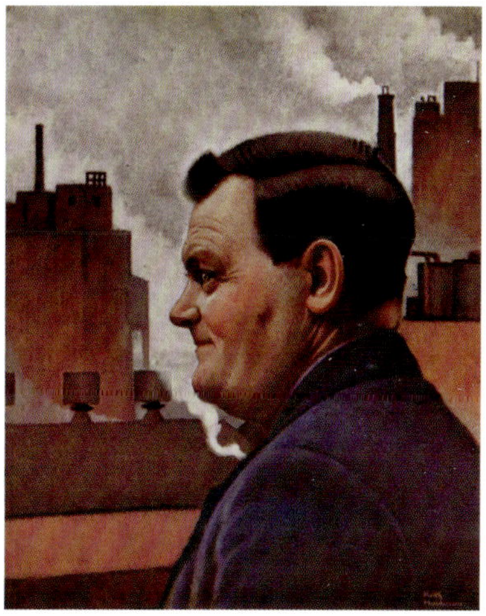

Thomas Hunt
by Keith Henderson

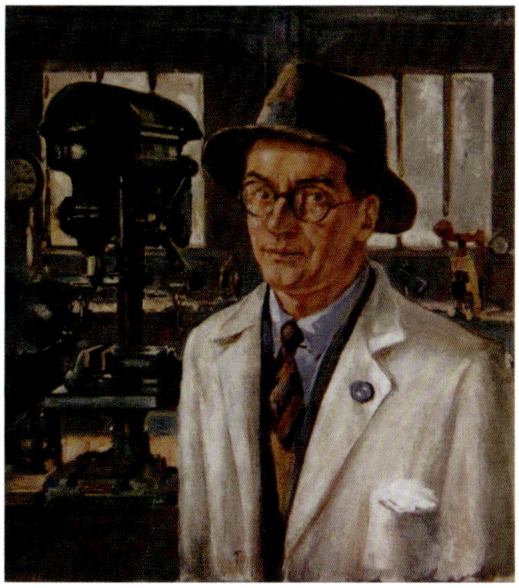

John Hedley Roberts
by Charles Cundall

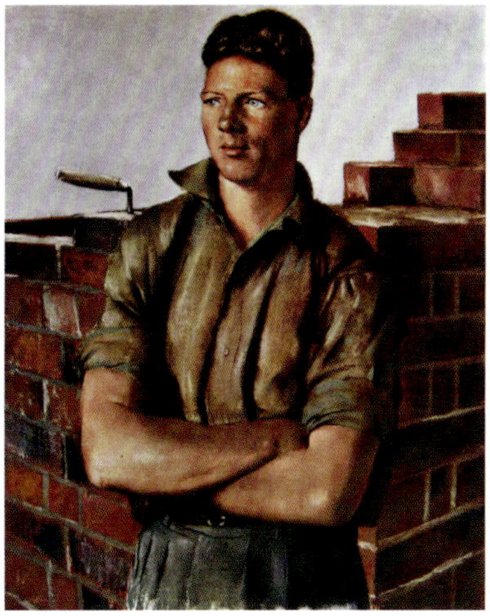

Edwin Maiden
by William Dring

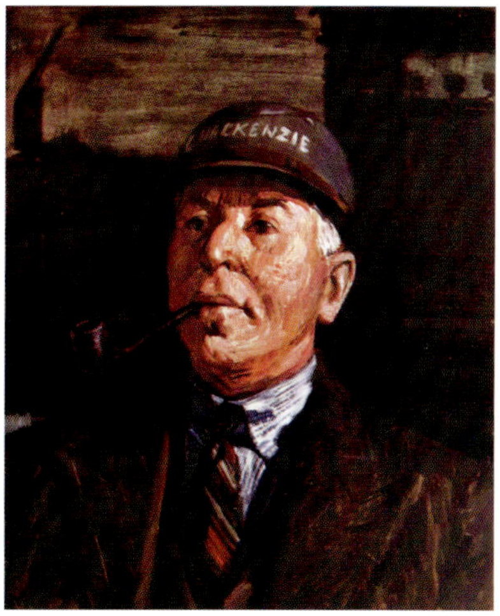

Gustav Mackenzie
by Ruskin Spear

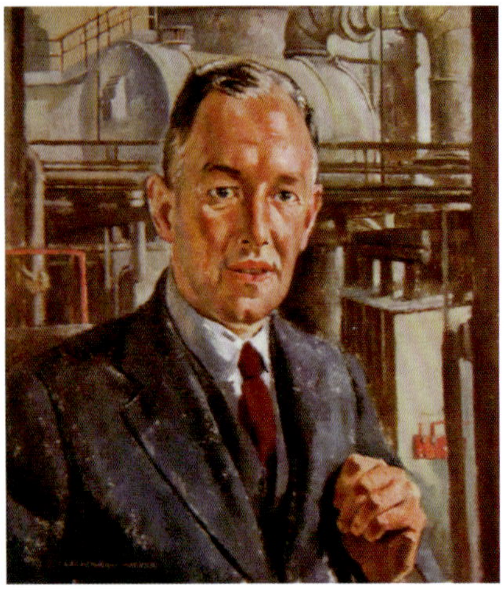
E.B. Wright
by Fleetwood-Walker

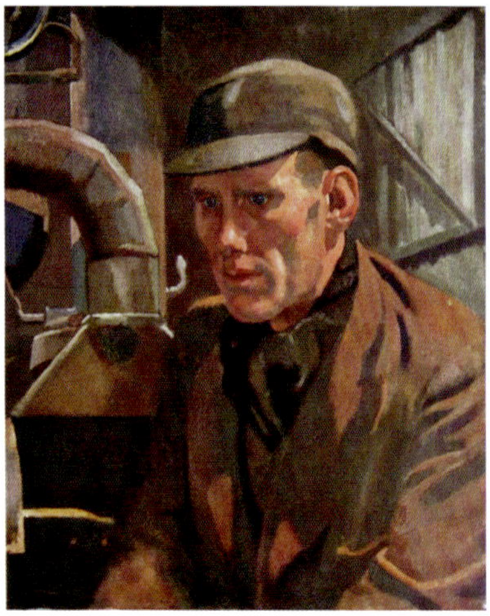
Frank Beckenham
by Miles de Montmorency

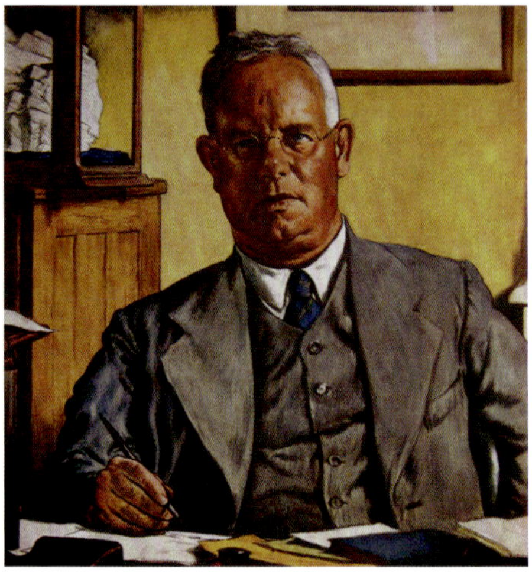
William Lye Pattison
by Alex Macpherson

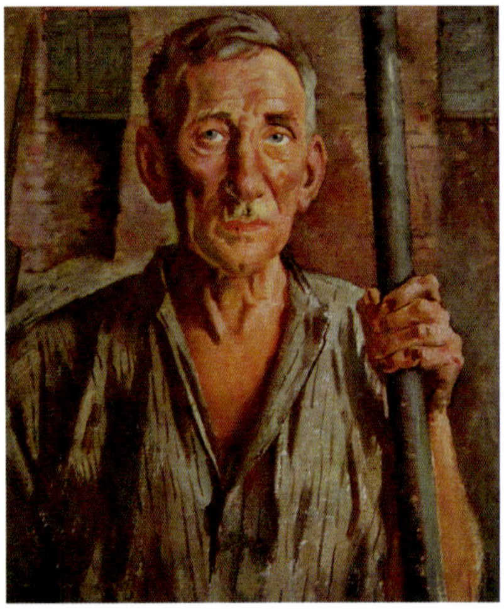
John Thomas Hawker
by B. Fleetwod-Walker

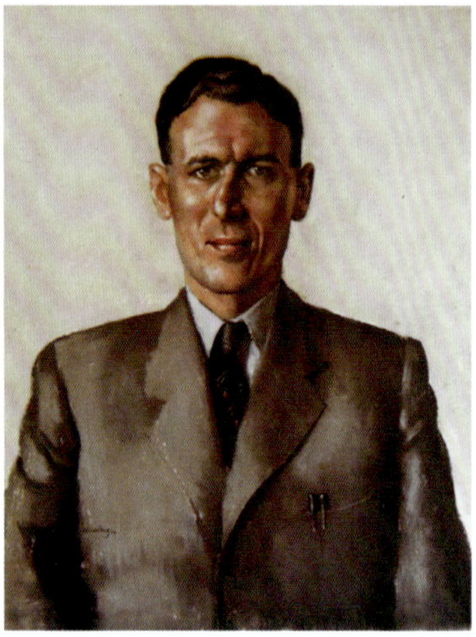
Donald Summers
by William Dring

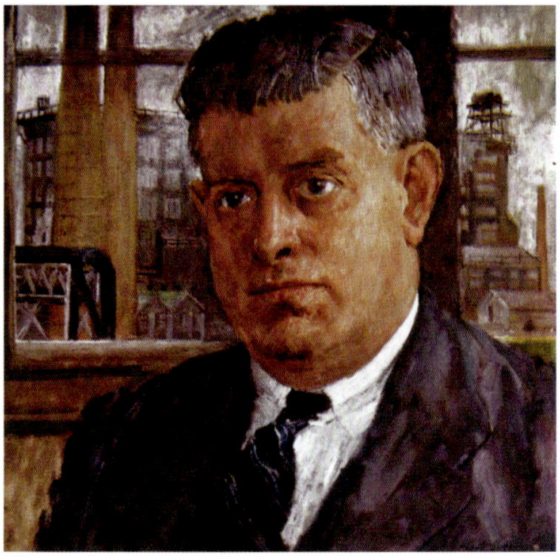
Albert Phillips
by Rupert Shephard

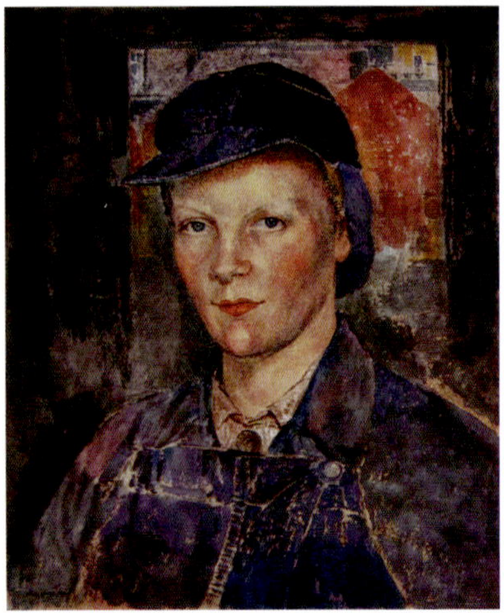
Florence Smith
by John Wheatley

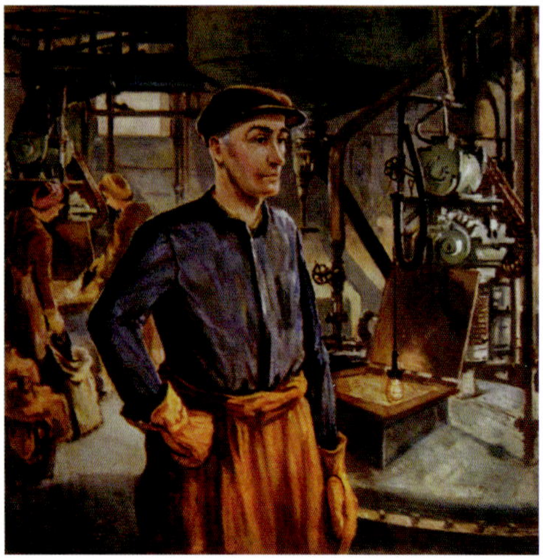
Samuel Wilson
by Charles Cundall

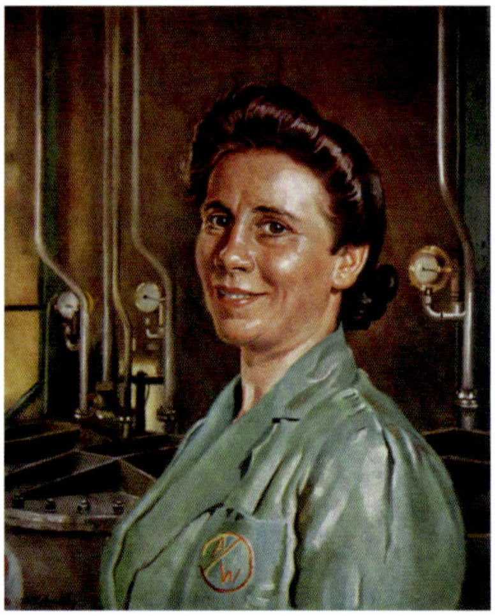
Alice Wright
by W.R. Brealey

Not all the press was as enthusiastic and the exhibition came under some criticism. Kennington wrote that some questioned the employment of artistic power for and by a large organisation and likened it to 'half-way to State Patronage; and was that not the tomb of aesthetics and freedom and the individuality of the soul?' However, it is clear he was quite dismissive of these criticisms, and elaborated on the many advantages the unusual employment had provided, not least of all a sense of 'worthwhileness'.[15]

This 'worthwhileness' is best expressed in Jonathan Black's book, *The Face of Courage: Eric Kennington, Portraiture and the Second World War,* in which he records Kennington's response to his involvement in the ICI project. In a letter to his daughter, Kennington wrote, 'I love people, and people and more people, ... it's all fascinating .... The salt works had been going on ever since the Romans were here and perhaps before .... You see, I'm really learning something about my own country and my own race.' His portrait of Oswald Carter was done deep inside a salt mine.[16]

In other correspondence concerning an artist, we read of Jackson's enjoyment in doing four ICI portraits at different factories which Pamela Ovens considered 'superb',[17] but also how angered he was over those badly reproduced.[18]

As a token of appreciation, all the subjects were presented with their portraits in 1949. Rogerson hoped the beneficiaries would appreciate good art, but, always with an eye to publicity, he saw the benefits of permanent publicity for ICI. The sitters were also each given a copy of the book produced by Clifford Martin in 1947, containing colour reproductions of all 56 portraits with their accompanying text. Due to paper shortage, this volume was produced in limited edition – enough only for each subject and artist to receive a copy.[19]

In 1949 ICI gave a dinner at the Dorchester Hotel to pay tribute to all those artists – over thirty in number – who contributed to all the Prestige Advertisements during the war. In response, both the President of the RA, Sir Alfred Munnings, and Henry Rushbury paid tribute to the lead given by ICI in supporting British artists and allowing them freedom of choice in the matter of their subjects. Rushbury further noted that it was unique in the annals of art patronage for so many portraits to be commissioned at one time, and likened ICI's policy to that of the Medicis of old.[20]

As Sir Charles Tennyson wrote in the foreword to the exhibition catalogue for *Portraits of an Industry*, '*the application of art to advertisement by this company ranks high among the many notable developments in the relation of the arts to the public that have taken place during recent years.*'

ENDNOTES

1 Lord McGowan, in his foreword to the book, *ICI: Portraits of an Industry*, Lund Humphries & Co.Ltd., London, 1947. McGowan was Chairman of ICI from 1930-1950.
2 Sidney Rogerson joined ICI in 1930; promoted to Publicity Controller 1932-1952.
3 Rogerson papers, Imperial War Museum archive.
4 McGowan, op. cit.
5 McGowan, op. cit.
6 Among Rogerson's books published was *Propaganda in the Next War*, 1938. It was a matter on which he placed much importance post WW1 and which greatly influenced his decisions.
7 Rogerson papers, IWM archives.
8 The CIAD was initiated in 1939 in order to form a central, representative body to meet the serious economic position with which artists, craftsmen and designers were faced at the outbreak of the war. The provisional committee included Sir Kenneth Clark, Sir Charles Tennyson (who succeeded Clark as Chair) and Thomas A. Fennemore (Honorary Secretary) who all assisted and supported the ICI Portraits project.
9 Letters from Rogerson to Clark, 16 November, 1943, and 15 March 1944, Kenneth Clark archives – Tate.
10 Rogerson papers, IWM archives.
11 *The ICI Magazine*, July 1949 p.155. Henry Rushbury was an eminent artist who was elected Keeper of the Royal Academy and Head of the Royal Academy Schools in 1949.
12 *The Manchester Guardian*, 16 October 1946 – which described ICI's unique approach to advertising starting in 1941.
13 *The I.C.I. Magazine*, January 1947 p 23.
14 *Arbroath Herald and Advertiser*, 16 July 1948.
15 Eric Kennington, 'Portrait of an Industry', *Art and Industry*, March 1947, pp. 76-79.
16 Jonathan Black, *The Face of Courage: Eric Kennington, Portraiture and the Second World War*, Philip Wilson Publishers Ltd, London, UK. 2011. p 133-137.
17 Letters from Pamela Ovens to Patrick Phillips, August 1944 and March 1945, private collection. Ovens was Jackson's secretary at the Byam Shaw School of Art. Phillips had been both a student and teacher there.
18 Jackson was angry about the poor reproduction of his work and complained to Clark that his portrait of Albert Roberts had been cropped in *The Times* without his knowledge or permission. (See illustration p 233 versus the uncropped original on p 230) In a letter to Rogerson 6 March 1945, Clark wrote; "It is worth remembering that every time these things happen, it will become more difficult to get first rate artists to work for you". Clark archive – Tate.
19 *Aberdeen Journal*, 13 May 1947.
20 Henry Rushbury, 'Industry as patron of the Arts', *The I.C.I. Magazine*, July 1949, pp 170-175.

Margaret Bear has been researching her grandfather's (F. Ernest Jackson) life and works for some years now. Intent on finding the four portraits he painted for the ICI Portraits series, she was led to examine the nature of the ICI project itself. This obscure piece of art history is documented for the first time in this publication.
There is currently an ongoing search for these portraits which is difficult as they are largely in private ownership. To date seven have been located, two of which are in public collections. One of these is the portrait of William Tyler by F. Ernest Jackson at the Catalyst – Science Discovery Centre in Cheshire. The other is the portrait of Lily Brookes by William Dring at the Weaver Hall Museum in Northwick.

For further information please contact: mrbear@uniserve.com.

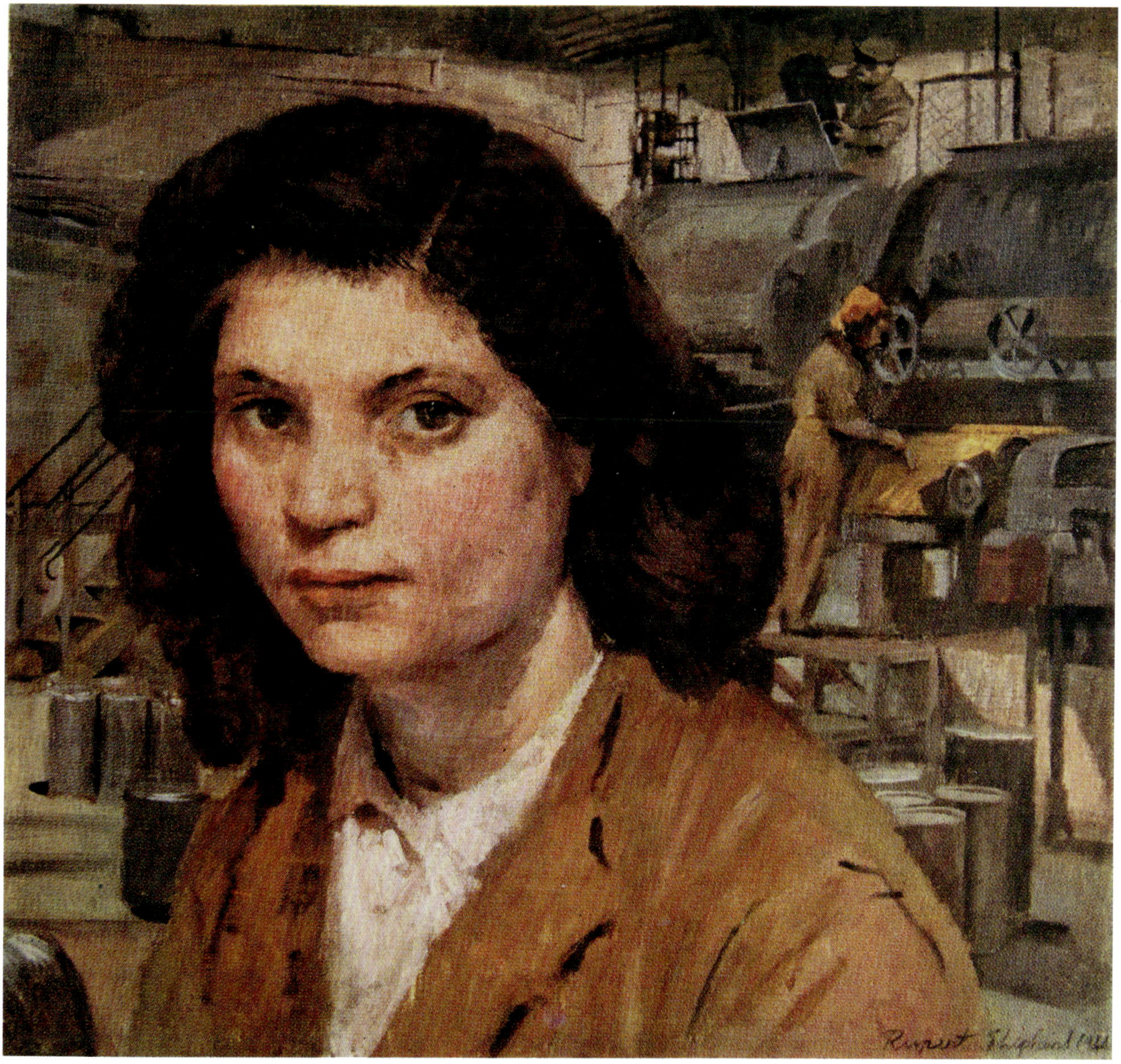

Ada Crawley by Rupert Shephard
The sitter operated a triple roller mill at the Paints Division factory, Slough, Berks.

LISS
LLEWELLYN
FINE ART
ESTABLISHED 1991

paul@llfa.gallery sacha@llfa.gallery

Founded in 1991 by Paul Liss and Sacha Llewellyn, Liss Llewellyn Fine Art specialises in the unsung heroes and heroines of British art from 1880 to 1980. For 25 years Liss Llewellyn Fine Art has worked in association with museums to develop a series of in-depth exhibitions to encourage the reappraisal of some of the lesser known figures of 20th century British Art.

www.llfa.gallery